Max Wertheimer
& Gestalt Theory

Max Wertheimer 1880-1943

D. Brett King
Michael Wertheimer

Max Wertheimer & Gestalt Theory

Transaction Publishers
New Brunswick (U.S.A.) and London (U.K.)

Second paperback printing 2008

This book is printed on acid-free paper that meets the American National Standard for Permanence of Paper for Printed Library Materials.

Library of Congress Catalog Number: 2004058038
ISBN: 978-1-4128-0718-0
Printed in the United States of America

Library of Congress Cataloging-in-Publication Data

King, D. Brett.
   Max Wertheimer and Gestalt theory / D. Brett King and Michael Wertheimer.
      p. cm.
   Includes bibliographical references and index.
   ISBN 0-7658-0258-9 (alk. paper)
   1. Wertheimer, Max, 1880-1943. 2. Psychologists—United States—Biography. 3. Psychologists—Germany—Biography. 4. Gestalt psychology—History. I. Wertheimer, Michael. II. Title.

BF109.W47K56   2004
150.19'82'092—dc22   2004058038
[B]

Contents

Illustrations follow page 184

Preface

This essay in intellectual biography evolved for a long time before it was finally published. It was first conceived in the spring of 1943, when Michael Wertheimer, then a teenager, consulted his father Max about how to spend the coming summer. He had an offer to be a junior counselor at a summer camp on Lake Otsego in upstate New York, where he had already spent several happy summers as a camper, but was also strongly tempted to spend the summer doing intensive interviews of his father, to begin preparing a biography of him. He had only recently become aware that his father was an illustrious intellectual, revered by many people Michael had met. Max Wertheimer clearly was deeply touched that his young son wanted to understand him and his work better, but gently and firmly advised him to go to camp that summer. Several months later Max Wertheimer was dead.

The project remained a distant hope thereafter for decades. During the late 1960s, Michael interrogated his mother at length about her reminiscences of Max Wertheimer and recorded the discussions on audio tape, and by 1970 he had generated rough drafts of the first five chapters of a then-projected nine-chapter biography of Max Wertheimer. A graduate seminar he taught the next year, focused on providing feedback on the manuscript, made it clear that the draft was indeed very rough and preliminary; it was essentially an unorganized compendium of everything that he had found out about Max Wertheimer by that time, with little perspective and no balance. The project was laid aside.

In 1978, a rich cache of papers, correspondence, and manuscripts was discovered in the basement of Michael's older brother Val's summer home in northwestern Connecticut, and Michael's interest was rekindled. Michael made an extended visit to the New York Public Library, which held the papers that happened to be in Max Wertheimer's office at the New School for Social Research, where Max had taught during his last years, when Max died; that collection (MW-NY) dovetailed in intriguing ways with the collection from Connecticut (MW-CU), which consisted of Max Wertheimer's papers at home when he died, and which Michael brought to the University of Colorado at Boulder, where Michael was employed. These collections (and many other sources) were used productively by Mitchell G. Ash for his doctoral dissertation on the evolution of the Gestalt school of psychology, in the department of history at Harvard University, and for his later book, *Gestalt Psychology in German Culture 1890-1967: Holism and the Quest for Objectivity* (Cambridge, England: Cambridge University Press, 1995). The present work contains many citations of Ash's dissertation, but the interested reader is referred to his 1995 book, which is more readily available, and much of which is a revised version of the dissertation.

During the 1970s and 1980s Michael visited all the places where Max Wertheimer was known to have lived and worked in Europe and the United States, and various archival collections on both continents known (or surmised) to hold materials related to Max Wertheimer. In 1990, after completing his doctoral degree in experimental psychology with Wayne Viney at Colorado State University, D. Brett King joined Michael at the University of Colorado at Boulder as a post-doctoral research associate (and as an instructor, and, later, senior instructor, in psychology) to resume work on the biography of Max Wertheimer. Together he and Michael went through the collection of materials gathered on Max Wertheimer, and during the limited time when King was not consumed by his teaching duties and other obligations, King drafted a new set of chapters for the biography. Those drafts were shared with a combined undergraduate general honors seminar and graduate seminar in cognitive psychology during the spring of 1995; the many constructive suggestions that emerged from that seminar were used to modify the draft during the next summer. In the following years, Michael Wertheimer further revised the manuscript, which was then reviewed by several knowledgeable consultants. We are most grateful to all of them. Any remaining errors, problems of balance, or other shortcomings of the book are not their responsibility, but ours.

Countless people in Germany, the former Czechoslovakia, and the United States have contributed to the final product. Ideally, they would all be credited here by name. But there are so many (including not only original sources, archivists who provided information in ways that went far beyond their regular duties, innumerable correspondents, and thoughtful students, but also the critical readers of the penultimate draft who provided especially useful advice which, for various reasons, we did not always follow) that it is difficult to give credit to every one of them. They know who they are, and they have our heartfelt gratitude. We hope that they will find the final product reasonably satisfying.

We would also like to thank Agnes Conley, Mary Ann Tucker, and Donna Huckaby for their extensive patient labors in translating Michael Wertheimer's scribbled pencil drafts and changes in successive hardcopy versions of the chapters of this volume into a much more legible form. Additional assistance came from Michael's daughter, K. W. Watkins, who would gladly have provided it silently had she not been instructed to compose an insertion acknowledging her activities, such as providing many stylistic improvements as well as much enthusiasm, and preparing the final manuscript and index in camera-ready form.

DBK   Boulder, Colorado
MW   April 15, 2004

1

Introduction

Most impressive of all was [Wertheimer's] personal example, the combination of passionate concern and of a passionate demand for strictness in thinking. The orientation he sketched remains as fresh and challenging today as in the past, as capable of stirring the imagination. We will not find in him answers to all our questions; what one is likely to find is more valuable—an appreciation of what matters in the human sphere, and an art of thinking about human nature.
—Solomon E. Asch (1980)

Abraham H. Maslow during the 1940s identified a few people as "fully functioning," "living up to their full potential," and "self-actualized."[1] These rare individuals are "radiantly alive," consumed by their creative projects, keenly but realistically aware of the beauty of their world, and they display a genuine acceptance of themselves as well as others, exuding a refreshing sense of spontaneity and simplicity. They have a remarkable capacity to transcend petty bodily, egoistic, and status needs, and are able to devote themselves totally to worthwhile endeavors that use their capacities effectively. Maslow's list of such people included historical figures such as the U.S. Civil War president Abraham Lincoln, but also several of Maslow's contemporaries, such as cultural anthropologist Ruth Benedict, physicist Albert Einstein, First Lady Eleanor Roosevelt—and Gestalt psychologist Max Wertheimer.

Who was this Max Wertheimer? He lived from 1880 to 1943. People who knew this short, slight man described him as a visionary, passionately dedicated to the quest for truth, for dispassionate objectivity, and for beauty—and all of these concepts were for him fundamentally the same. Wertheimer's lifestyle was that of the competent intellectual, the responsible scholar, the human being genuinely living life to its fullest, striving incessantly to do justice to the situations, problems, and issues encountered

1

throughout life whatever the nature of these challenges: scientific, political, ethical, interpersonal. Artificial boundaries between different phases of a human life, rigid barriers between work and play or between one intellectual field or discipline and another, he believed, serve only to interfere with the human striving to meet each situation, each problem, directly—and to do it justice. A broad, open-minded overview of any problem "from above," as it were, is more likely than piecemeal analysis "from below" to reveal the core features of the problem as it is embedded in its total context, to help strip away superficial considerations and to generate an understanding of the problem that is true to its actual nature, and thus to deal with it adequately, fully, and without excessive attention to inappropriate, irrelevant features.

Wertheimer's charge when he was a member of the faculty at the University of Frankfurt from 1929 to 1933 was to fill a professorial chair dedicated to "philosophy, with specialization in psychology." Psychology was for Wertheimer a part of philosophy; there is an intimate affinity between the two disciplines—and neither psychology nor philosophy should be artificially severed from other great fields of intellectual endeavor, be they "scientific" such as physics or economics or physiology, or "humanistic" such as linguistics or music or fine arts. Everything must be viewed in terms of its place, role, and function within the whole of which it is a part—and this principle applies with equal force in natural science, social science and humanistic endeavors as well as in everyday life. Do justice to every situation, every problem, every human being; be unswerving in your devotion to truth, justice, beauty, and parsimonious elegance; get to the heart of every issue and don't let yourself be fooled by artificial, superficial features.

Wertheimer's intellectual integrity; his unswerving devotion to honesty, justice, and truth; his impassioned quest for the best solution to every problem; and his impatience with stupidity, with pomposity, with piecemeal and unthinking "thinking," and with blindness or prejudice in human affairs were displayed in all aspects of his life and lifestyle. These themes colored everything he did, whether it was a formal lecture on a problem in logic, his correspondence with a colleague, playing with his children, or engaging in a heated political discussion. He did his utmost to determine what would be best to do in every situation, and then, without compromise, to devote himself to doing what he had decided was humanly, ethically, and esthetically right. Work, science, politics, ethics, play, music, art are all inextricably interrelated, and typically blend into one another in specific situations.

Understand the structure of a problem situation completely, and you can deal fully and adequately with the problem. Approach a new problem blindly or in a mechanical, habitual way that does not do justice to the problem's inherent and crucial component parts, or does not place the problem adequately into its current relevant context, and you won't be able to deal with the problem creatively and constructively. Insight, wisdom, and careful attention to the structure of a problem situation and to its essential features and internal dynamics are far more likely to lead to productive, constructive problem resolution than is a blind, automatic, and habitual approach.

This philosophy or world-view, while fundamentally optimistic about human nature and the human capacity to solve problems and to engage in constructive and productive conduct, was also fiercely dedicated to realism: if a situation remains problematic, that fact itself must be recognized and dealt with. Seeing the world through rose-colored glasses does not change the actual color of the world. Human conflict, wars, misery, meanness, ugliness, and destitution must be recognized for what they are; tragedies are not averted or resolved or overcome by wishing them away or ignoring them. The admonition inherent in Wertheimer's philosophy of everyday life was to do justice unflinchingly to *every* aspect of the essential features of a problem or situation.

Wertheimer has often been credited as the first to propose a Gestalt theory in psychology.[2] How does the Gestalt orientation fit with his world view? It ties in intimately. Gestalt theory, evolving further in the hands of Wertheimer's colleagues Wolfgang Köhler and Kurt Koffka, successfully combined two major themes that were salient among the European intelligentsia during the late nineteenth and early twentieth centuries— holistic thought, and total allegiance to scientific rigor and objectivity. Gestalt theory soon received recognition worldwide and became an influential school of psychology during the first half of the twentieth century. What made it, rather than other holisms that were more vague and elusive, successful at the time was its consistent use of scientific methods of research for generating convincing evidence in support of its principles and laws. Gestalt theory was scientifically rigorous without being atomistic or reductionistic, and was thoroughly holistic without being mystical or vague. Hence it developed a strong worldwide appeal, particularly suited to a time when both natural science and responsible holism were major ideals among many members of the intelligentsia.

Wertheimer and his colleagues were, of course, deeply immersed in the intellectual climate that revered the two themes of holism and rigorous scientific precision. All three, Wertheimer, Köhler, and Koffka, studied at various times with Carl Stumpf, a versatile general psychologist at the University of Berlin who championed objectivity and experimental rigor in psychological research, and who in his holistic perspective severely criticized the then-prevailing elementistic, piecemeal character of both psychological theory and psychological research. Stumpf also advocated the "phenomenological method" in psychology: the unbiased description of experience as it comes, without preconception and without predetermined categories. This method, which the Gestalt theorists later used extensively, became a viable alternative to the atomistic effort to analyze the content of the human mind into its constituent elemental components, which characterized much of experimental psychology at the beginning of the twentieth century. The three Gestalt psychologists-to-be absorbed Stumpf's ideal of rigorous objective scientific research, his view of the promise of the phenomenological approach, and his endorsement of a theory of mind that goes beyond inert associations among discrete mental elements—a perspective that permits holism as long as that holism does not spill over into vague, unscientific mysticism. Out of these leitmotifs, all clearly discernible in the spirit of German academia in the first decade of the twentieth century, Stumpf's three students constructed the influential new school of Gestalt psychology.[3]

Gestalt theory and Max Wertheimer's Weltanschauung are not identical, but they are closely related to each other. While Köhler brought a strict natural-science perspective to the development of the new theory and Koffka contributed a large number of experiments, prodigious energy, and a mammoth integrative effort in the form of his 1935 book, *Principles of Gestalt psychology*,[4] Wertheimer provided the initial formulations and a broad humanistically—and logically—oriented perspective. His version of Gestalt theory matched his philosophy and his personal style, and his scholarly contributions to the Gestalt literature were also consistent with them. His publications were few, sparse, revised many times, tightly written, and typically published years after they were first conceived. But almost all of them turned out to be articles to which the Gestalt theorists and their students—and critics—referred repeatedly for decades.

Max Wertheimer has on various occasions been characterized as a charismatic individual, an inspiring teacher, a warm parent, an original philosopher, and a fiercely passionate seeker after truth. Quite aside from his profound personal effect on many people during his lifetime, Gestalt theory and other aspects of Max Wertheimer's thought and work were once again being recognized late in the twentieth century as potentially relevant to a wide array of contemporary research endeavors, in such fields as visual neuroscience, cognitive psychology, social psychology, perception, and personality. A number of recent scholars interested in these fields have found in the thought of Max Wertheimer inspiration for a constructive, fruitful perspective, a new twist on their own thinking that could lead to productive new directions in their own research.

Several of Max Wertheimer's colleagues have expressed their esteem for him in print. Among them were Rudolf Arnheim, whose distinguished career included the world's first professorship in the psychology of art, at Harvard University, and the late Solomon E. Asch, who brought the Gestalt perspective to his influential writings on social psychology. Their homages differ from the usual descriptions of Max Wertheimer and his work found in most textbooks on the history of psychology, which generally emphasize

Wertheimer's contributions in perception and the psychology of thinking. But they provide vivid images of Wertheimer the man, his intellectual strategies, and his lifestyle.

Consider first Arnheim's tribute, which he presented orally on November 10, 1943 at a memorial meeting for Wertheimer at the New School for Social Research in New York, where Wertheimer taught during the last ten years of his life. Arnheim's remarks were published in 1989 in *Psychological Research*, in a special issue of that journal dedicated to Wertheimer.[5] They are reproduced here with minor editorial changes and several omissions.

> Max Wertheimer's work and life were one and the same thing. His insight into the functioning of the human mind inspired the games he played with his children, and the thoughts and fancies of the children often illustrated his lectures and writings. This unity of life and scientific reasoning exercised the strongest influence on those who studied with him. Whoever saw only his theory, a new scientific method of describing and explaining the things of nature, probably did not even grasp his theory because those who grasped it could not help finding their entire outlook changing. It meant becoming a different person, centering on what is natural, harmonious, good, and young in this world.
>
> Take his optimism, his belligerent and sometimes almost reckless optimism! Was it an accidental personal trait—an emotional attitude apt to disturb the objectivity of his scientific judgment? Those of us who have worked and lived with him—and nobody ever worked with him without living with him to some extent—know that this optimism sprang from the very basis of his scientific conception; namely from his belief that order, harmony, and lawfulness are the fundamental facts of nature and that all deviations from them are secondary. To be good meant for Max Wertheimer: to live in conformity with natural law. That is why he objected so passionately whenever what is wrong, evil, or deformed was presented as the rule, as the main object of the scientist's attention. His use of the word 'ugly' had the same metallic precision and objectivity that a low correlation has for the statistician.
>
> Such teaching was a tonic for his pupils and directly affected their attitude towards life. Perhaps it tended to make us into dreamers with regard to the imperfections of reality. But the world in which he asked us to live with him was certainly not cloudy. Work with Max Wertheimer was hard. He never proposed or accepted a subject for a thesis unless he felt that it led into the very frontline of scientific attack, and then he would go about it with the implacable rigor of his logic. It happened to all of us: we would send him a paper that we thought was sound, and he would return it, the margins of our pages covered with his neat, microscopic shorthand notes that were so beautiful to look at, but meant so many blows against what we had considered a shockproof piece of argumentation. One never felt that one was doing academic homework for the purpose of getting a degree, nor did he feel that way. Rather it was like going in search of exciting adventures with an experienced fellow-explorer. Once on the trail, he would spare neither himself nor his followers. With some distress we watched him heading straight towards the more inhospitable spots of the jungle,

which we had hoped to bypass with a few non-committal sentences. Work was hard, but invariably he did most of it. Often, after a week of ardent labor, the student would appear at the next meeting, only to find that Wertheimer had himself covered dozens of sheets with tabulations, drafts for new experiments, and theoretical formulations which pushed the project ahead beyond expectations and opened disquieting new perspectives.

At such a conference in his study at his home in New Rochelle, closely surrounded by piles of dusty papers, he frantically continued the discussion for hours until his children insisted that supper was getting cold. After the meal he started again, finally interrupted himself, and said: 'Now let's have a good fire.' And the children made a fire in the living-room fireplace. Sometimes their father opened the piano and played some of the little pieces by Bach that we knew so well from his demonstrations in class, or old German folk tunes in the minor key. Or, in his armchair, he looked into the fire and, with a smile in his voice, told the curiously meaningful fables that life staged for him wherever he went. After the day's work, his attentive eyes seemed more deeply embedded in his tired, soft face, and with the little knitted cap he used to wear he would look like one of the old rabbis in the mysterious city of Prague, where he was born.

Max Wertheimer created through personal contact. In discussion, he produced a startling wealth of ideas, suggestions, theories, plans for experiments to be made, results of experiments he had performed 20 years before, but had never published. All over this war-torn world, there are people who have carried away a spark of this wealth and who are trying to materialize in extensive studies what he may have suggested to them in a few discussions a long time ago. They had come to him from South America; they are now in the United States and in Europe; they are busy in Japan.

Now that he is gone, we wish we had written down the many things he told us and which now will have to wait until somebody rediscovers them while traveling on one of the many roads indicated by Max Wertheimer. Too much is lost, but there is one thing that we hope to save: his way of looking at the world with open eyes, in a friendly, understanding way; his manner of catching the things of nature alive with concepts clean and clear, yet not apt to destroy what they were meant to describe. This we hope to keep.

Solomon Asch prepared a contribution for a symposium at the 1980 convention of the American Psychological Association celebrating the centenary of Wertheimer's birth. Entitled "Max Wertheimer: Memories and Reflections,"[6] his paper has never been published. While the essay concentrates on Wertheimer's contributions to social psychology, which are not as widely known as his other work, Asch could not avoid going far beyond the borders of that major subfield of psychology. Just as Arnheim's comments above have been slightly modified, so too the paragraphs which follow are a slightly edited and abbreviated version of the remarks that Asch delivered at that symposium in August, 1980.

The ideas and discoveries of Max Wertheimer have transformed the situation of psychology in this century, yet he is only incompletely understood. Most psychologists are familiar mainly with his contributions in perception and thinking. The fuller scope of his views—in particular those concerning humans' social nature, including their ethical and esthetic powers—are less widely known, although they are at least as significant and challenging as those with which his name is now most connected. The task here is to say something about Wertheimer's treatment of humans as social beings.

A number of circumstances—the historical convulsions in Germany before World War II, as well as others—prevented the wider spread of these latter ideas. Wertheimer left no published record in this area comparable to his works in perception and thinking. During the years that remained to him in the U.S., he concentrated, at times against waning energies, on completing the manuscript of *Productive Thinking* (which he succeeded in doing shortly before he died in 1943).[7] If one adds to this the painfully scrupulous care Wertheimer took to express his thoughts in the most precise way, the sparsity of his writing in this area is not surprising.

Nevertheless, we do possess several significant sources of evidence concerning Wertheimer's social thought. Wertheimer migrated to the U.S. in 1933, where he joined the Graduate Faculty of the New School for Social Research in New York City, composed of refugees like himself from Nazi Germany and neighboring countries. At this school (then also known as the University in Exile) his lectures included topics in social psychology. The audiences at these lectures were heterogeneous and, aside from a few past students of his from Germany and occasional visitors, included few who were or eventually became psychologists. I was among those who attended his lectures whenever I could. I occasionally jotted down a few notes, but kept no systematic record. In addition, Wertheimer published in this country several papers of a social-psychological character; these were reprinted in 1961 in a volume edited by Mary Henle *(Documents of Gestalt Psychology*, University of California Press).[8] During part of this period I assisted Wertheimer—if that is the right expression—when he was working on the manuscript of his book *Productive Thinking*.

What follows are some of my memories and reflections on Wertheimer's thought on social psychology. They are certainly incomplete, but I believe they contain no serious distortions.

First a word about the setting of Wertheimer's lectures. They cover the very brief span of ten years between his arrival in the U.S. in 1933 and his death in 1943. There were then the beginnings of an empirical social psychology in this country, limited in size, somewhat on the order of a corner grocery compared to a present-day supermarket. The main direction was behavioristic, best exemplified by Floyd H. Allport's *Social Psychology;*[9] often it came with an admixture of psychoanalysis. On the behavioristic side this psychology rested on conditioning and association. Psychoanalysis figured largely as an account of how persons deceive themselves and cling to infantile impulses they rarely outgrow. This theme merged with a major concern of academic social psychology: its specialty was how persons and groups are deceived by propaganda and advertising. These intellectual currents, abetted by the confusion of the times, affected psychologists themselves and contributed a further ingredient. In retrospect the period preceding World War II, fueled first by the Depression and then by growing threats of war, was one of pervasive distrust of social ideas and forces among academic circles. This outlook affected the most concerned and the most idealistic. Its manifestations could be extreme and extremely different. At times the distrust verged on cynicism, in the form of a psychology of debunking; at other times one observed the feverish adoption of political convictions, not rarely self-sacrificing, but not well thought out. It was not unusual to find these extremes in the same person. In either case propaganda and its illusions figured as *the* social forces. Interestingly, the objectivism of conditioning and association fitted neatly into a subjectivistic conception of humans as social beings. Under the circumstances it seemed to many that the best one could do was not to be fooled, not to be taken in.

The gathering war clouds in Europe provided a portentous backdrop to this way of thinking in psychology. Having only recently fled Hitler Germany, Wertheimer and his fellow refugees were in a better position than many Americans to realize the dangers that loomed. One of the most peaceful of men, Wertheimer saw that the Nazi menace would be immeasurably enhanced by lack of firmness in the West. This sketch is highly incomplete, but it is not difficult to gauge how Wertheimer responded to the psychological situation here. First, what a poor, miserable picture of human beings did the psychology he found portray. Second, and more immediately urgent, how senseless and dangerous was this psychology in the face of the actual problems that were confronting the world.

Turn now to the psychological substance of Wertheimer's lectures, usually announced under the modest title 'Basic problems in social psychology.' Let me try first to convey in a personal fashion some of their spirit.

1. The exposition of the human as a social being was profoundly different in spirit and content from anything I heard or read before or since. First, Wertheimer came out of a tradition that was at home with much of the thought of the last 2,500 years about human character. The roots of this thought were embedded in classical problems of philosophy, of political theory, of history, literature, art, of the humanities generally. That tradition had been visibly eroded, in the name of science, among the students who were drawn to social psychology (not to mention general psychology) in this country, and equally so among their mentors. Those concerns were largely abandoned and replaced either by indifference or by a distaste often amounting to antipathy. Under these circumstances Wertheimer became for his students a bridge to a rich cultural past. He did not often refer to it specifically, but it was an ever-present background to his thought. This was one unusual feature of Wertheimer's lectures.

2. Wertheimer's students could not help but realize that the discussion was about some of the most serious issues of human existence. He conveyed this by the manner of his presentation. The topic, people as social beings, matters scientifically *and* humanly, in equal measure. Social psychology is not a specialty, a chapter tacked on to others. The human dimension was for Wertheimer the starting point, the center from which all else in human psychology proceeds.

This concern, as readers of Wertheimer know, pervaded all his efforts. His

Productive Thinking [10] is as much about education as about thinking; it is a study of processes of thinking and a treatise on the improvement of thinking. Similarly, Wertheimer's studies of perception, with all their exactitude, were far from having the impersonal connotation that the term has come to acquire. Social psychology too was not a preserve of its own for sterile discussions unconnected with urgent human problems.

Impersonality was thus the last characterization that one could apply to Wertheimer. Nor did he believe in being impersonal in science. When he discussed doctrines of human nature, it became evident to his students that it is no light matter what one thinks and believes about human beings, that we are not talking just about anonymous others, but also about our own character and strivings, about our own fate and that of those near to us.

3. Most central in Wertheimer was his vision of what it is to be human. It was a dramatic vision that colored all he had to say, but it is not easy to describe, even if space permitted, for it cannot be summed up in a formula or a set of rules. Let me try to state a few points briefly.

Wertheimer sought always to find the constructive side of psychological processes, that which enables human beings to become productive. This aim alone separates him from the social psychology of his day and of nearly the entire present period. What is more productive than thinking? Wertheimer's starting point was accordingly a human being capable of understanding the difference between true and false, and of discovering some truths about the world. Coming from the author of *Productive Thinking*, this formulation held untold implications for nearly every human activity. Historically the contrary emphasis has been and continues to be the leading theme in social psychology: the failures of thought, its fragility and vulnerability to distortion. Thinking and understanding have been, historically, the casualties of social psychology. Virtually alone among psychologists of his day and the present, Wertheimer took seriously the possibilities of a life of reason for ordinary men and women. Present-day cognitive psychology has improved somewhat in this respect; nevertheless, it has little in common with Wertheimer's account of thinking and understanding.

This position of Wertheimer would have incurred, had it been known, the scornful charge of being rationalistic. Are we really to conduct a social psychology without giving the central place to prejudices, preconceptions, biases, illusions, errors—the lifeblood of our dear discipline? Wertheimer did not deny or minimize these unpleasant yet fascinating phenomena; he did want to understand them, and he raised a deep question. Briefly, he asked about the relation between thinking and affective processes. Thinking was not for Wertheimer what it generally was (and is) for psychologists, philosophers and logicians—a bloodless process. First, he questioned the divorce between thinking and emotion, and the assumption of their necessary antagonism. For him thinking was inseparable from striving and feeling. With the capacity to perceive and think goes the need to perceive clearly and the need to understand. Trying to become clear about one's situation is essential to being human. (Here incidentally is the significant source of Wertheimer's principle of *Prägnanz*.[11]) True, emotions and thinking can and often do conflict, with substantial consequence. At the same time, the most serious achievements of thinking could not occur in the absence of appropriate feeling and striving.

Underlying this basic orientation of Wertheimer's was a vivid sense of what it is to be an organism sensitive to the forces of its environment. He thought of the relation as one that strives toward harmony, and of an organism's activities as directed toward this end. Thinking and feeling are basically ways of establishing harmony with the world. In their developed human form, they come to expression in work, in esthetic activity, and in striving to establish a more just social order. He repudiated the reductionistic views that thinking is merely a weapon of survival, that reasoning is a prostitute of the emotions, or that esthetic sensitivity has the sole function of promoting reproduction.

As a most instructive introduction to Wertheimer's social psychology, consider what many may believe is an unlikely and unpromising example—his 1912 study of number concepts among primitive peoples,[12] perhaps his first serious effort of that magnitude. This work contains in pristine form some of the essentials of Gestalt theory, and provides an important illustration of his approach to human inquiry.

The specific question was about the thought processes of aboriginal peoples when they engage in counting. (Wertheimer spoke in this connection of *Naturvölker*, or nature peoples, an expression that has unfortunately not taken root in the English language.) Immediately one comes across a formulation striking for that time. What, Wertheimer asked, are the categories that *they*, the preliterates, employ, not how far do they fall short of the standards *we* employ. His first point was that 'to consider primitive thinking a mere preliminary stage, a vague, rudimentary, and perhaps relatively incomplete form of our own thinking, is sure to do little more than obstruct genuine inquiry.' Specifically, the Western ideal of abstractness and universality in counting is not theirs. The main reason is that primitive groups do not abstract from natural contexts and natural relationships; thus counting is not for them the repeated addition of units.

There were several strands to this opening theme. (1) First was the insistence on starting with the concrete conditions rooted in the life-situation of a group, not with standards imposed from without. In this manner Wertheimer at the outset placed the thinking operations of civilized and preliterate groups on the same level. Not that they are identical—indeed he stressed the differences; however, they are of equal interest and importance. Wertheimer realized the enormous technical advantages of Western counting, but he admired primitive systems for their naturalness and aptness. He stressed particularly their reliance on natural grouping and on qualitative concepts— such as many, few, a herd, a flock, a troop, a good weight, a round dozen. (2) Second, Wertheimer was emphatic that it is in no way helpful to label certain 'primitive solutions' as indicative of 'inferior mental ability'—this at a time when ideas about racial inferiority were beginning to acquire significant scientific standing on both sides of the Atlantic.

This procedure contrasts interestingly with that of Lucien Lévy-Bruhl, then at a heyday of its popularity. Lévy-Bruhl postulated a 'prelogical mentality' to account for the peculiarities of primitive thinking and its conclusions. Wertheimer would have none of this. Unlike Lévy-Bruhl, Wertheimer was engaging in concrete psychological analysis and demonstrating for the first time the power of Gestalt ideas. He eschewed the mystifications of 'collective representations' and the assumption of stages, although he was as insistent as Lévy-Bruhl about the reality of the differences between the thinking operations in question. (To the credit of Lévy-Bruhl it should be mentioned that he withdrew his interpretation in his later years, and that his early account at no point contained any implications of racial inferiority.)

Wertheimer turned to aboriginal groups (and also to children) not in order to discover the rawest, most inchoate origins of thinking. To the contrary, he was seeking the most natural (a term significant in his perspective) and most vital operations of thinking. These valuable operations he hoped to find at early points, before certain disfiguring cultural influences had their influence.

What is the relevance of this work to social psychology? First, it provides a model of how to think about culturally determined differences, about questions of cultural relativism. It also illustrates Wertheimer's concern to do justice to achievements that Western scholars had been likely to denigrate. Subsequently, Wertheimer and his pupil Karl Duncker developed the point further in the concept of requiredness. Shortly I will try to show that the implications for social psychology generally are much more far-reaching.

To complete this introductory account, consider a later study on a very different topic by H. Schulte, a student of Wertheimer: an approach to a Gestalt theory of paranoiac conditions.[13] The voice of Wertheimer is unmistakable in the pages of this study. It is primarily about an affective problem, the situation of a naive Russian prisoner of war in a German hospital during World War I, who when isolated from familiar persons and in the midst of an incomprehensible language developed paranoid symptoms.

This effort is an early example of a field-theoretical account that concentrates on interrelated events in an individual, on their coherence and dynamics, one that can be extended to group conditions. At its center was the concept of tension produced in the Russian patient by an endangered 'we' relation with other persons. The unlivable character of this tension fostered preoccupation with the difficulty, increasing self-reference, and a compulsion to transform the trouble into a bearable condition. The consequence was a set of delusional reinterpretations and elaborations that served to abolish the insufferable isolation.

This work bristles with concepts that, though uncrystallized, were highly significant—from the crucial 'we' relation, to the narrowing and wrong centering of the mental field, to the resulting mental blindness, to the precariousness of the quasi-equilibrium that the patient established, and to the possibilities of changing the field in a healthier direction. Reading the work today, many decades later, one is impressed with its freshness and the questions that still cry for solution; one wonders why psychology has turned this engaging way of thinking into a lost art.

These old, seemingly out-of-the-way studies contain, as suggested earlier, a most significant foundation for social psychology. First came the faithful, unprejudiced description of experience and action, qualitative where necessary. Here Wertheimer's procedure was near in spirit to that of novelists who live themselves into the situation of another, with the aim of asking: what is the sense, the meaning of this action, in these circumstances, for this person? How do the forces acting upon the person determine this person's decisions?

This cognitive psychology of Wertheimer—so unlike what passes currently as cognitive psychology—held, as mentioned, untold implications for nearly every phenomenon and topic in social psychology: from the ways one comprehends the actions and characters of persons and of groups, the ways they exert effects upon each other, to the meaning of rules and the workings of education and propaganda. In each case Wertheimer put an astonishingly simple question: what might be the sensible, understandable basis of this phenomenon, however odd it might appear at first glance? Wertheimer presented countless illustrations of this approach in his lectures. Two provisos are in order. First, to be fruitful this way of proceeding requires a foundation in Gestalt ideas. Second, it represents, as Wertheimer well knew, the beginning, not the end, of investigation.

In this brief account, it was necessary to omit much: how Wertheimer took issue with the age-old premise that the social human is basically egoistic and egotistic; in what sense he held to an optimistic view of humanity; and not least, the contrast between his vision of what it is to be human and the visionlessness of so much contemporary social psychology. Wertheimer had much to say on these and other matters; most impressive of all was his personal example, the combination of passionate concern and of a passionate demand for strictness in thinking. The orientation he sketched remains as fresh and challenging today as in the past, as capable of stirring the imagination. We will not find in him answers to all our questions; what one is likely to find is more valuable—an appreciation of what matters in the human sphere, and an art of thinking about human nature. It is important to clarify the sources of inspiration of this remarkable man. This one can do best by turning to Wertheimer's writing, regardless of the issue he happens to discuss.[14] I cannot think of a worthier inquiry if it is conducted in the right spirit.

Notes

1. See, for example, Abraham H. Maslow (1950). Self-actualizing people: A study of psychological health. In Werner Wolff (ed.), *Values in personality research*, Personality-Symposium No. 1, Personality Symposia on Topical Issues. New York: Grune and Stratton, pp. 11-34, or Abraham H. Maslow (1955). Deficiency motivation and growth motivation. In Marshall R. Jones (ed.), *Nebraska Symposium on Motivation*. Lincoln: University of Nebraska Press, pp. 1-39.
2. For example, Mitchell G. Ash (1995). *Gestalt psychology in German culture, 1890-1967: Holism and the quest for objectivity*. Cambridge, England: Cambridge University Press; see also Martin Leichtman (1979). Gestalt psychology and the revolt against positivism. In Allen Buss (ed.), *Psychology in social context*. New York: Irvington, pp. 47-75.
3. See, e.g., Helga Sprung and Lothar Sprung (1995). Carl Stumpf (1848-1936) und die Anfänge der Gestaltpsychologie an der Berliner Universität [Carl Stumpf (1848-1936) and the beginnings of Gestalt psychology at the University of Berlin]. In S. Jaeger, I. Staeuble, L. Sprung, and H.-P. Brauns (eds.), *Psychologie im soziokulturellen Wandel: Kontinuitäten und Diskontinuitäten [Psychology in*

sociocultural change: Continuities and discontinuities]. Frankfurt am Main: Lang, pp. 259-268.

4. Kurt Koffka (1935/1963). *Principles of Gestalt psychology.* New York: Harcourt, Brace & World.

5. Rudolf Arnheim (1989). Max Wertheimer. *Psychological Research,* 51, 45-46.

6. Solomon E. Asch (1980). Max Wertheimer: Memories and reflections. Unpublished contribution to a symposium on Max Wertheimer delivered at the annual convention of the American Psychological Association.

7. Max Wertheimer (1945). *Productive thinking.* New York: Harper. Enlarged edition 1959; Harper Torchbook 1971; University of Chicago Press 1982.

8. Mary Henle (ed.) (1961). *Documents of Gestalt psychology.* Berkeley, CA: University of California Press.

9. Floyd H. Allport (1924). *Social psychology.* Boston: Houghton Mifflin.

10. See note 7.

11. Roughly, the principle of *Prägnanz* (or "pregnance") asserts that the organization of any whole will be as "good," clear, simple, and elegant as all relevant prevailing conditions allow. Chapter 7 discusses the emergence of this principle in Wertheimer's thinking.

12. Max Wertheimer (1912). Über das Denken der Naturvölker I: Zahlen und Zahlgebilde [On the thinking of aboriginal peoples I: Numbers and numerical structures]. *Zeitschrift für Psychologie,* 60, 321-378.

13. Heinrich Schulte (1924). Versuch einer Theorie der paranoischen Eigenbeziehung und Wahnbildung [Attempt at a theory of paranoid ideas of reference and of psychotic etiology]. *Psychologische Forschung,* 5, 1-23. Translated by Erwin Levy (1986) into English as A Gestalt theory of paranoia. *Gestalt Theory,* 8, 230-255.

14. The interested reader is encouraged to follow Asch's advice. Perhaps the most rewarding place to begin reading Max Wertheimer's rather sparse set of publications is his final major work, *Productive thinking,* cited in note 7 above. Chapter 14 in the present essay is devoted to this book. In further recognition of the wisdom of Asch's suggestion, a few of Wertheimer's papers are also discussed, excerpted, or summarized in various places here, and a translation or précis of a few papers has been added to some of the chapters as appendices. A few have not been translated before; in all cases, the translations in this book are by Michael Wertheimer (with assistance from K Watkins in the case of the songs in Chapter 9).

2

Ancestry, Family, and Childhood

*I could still assert categorically that Max will
some day become someone significant, someone
famous. In what, in which area, I don't have the
faintest idea, because he seems to me to be great
and mighty in each and every thing.*
—Walter Wertheimer (1895)

Max Wertheimer's father, grandfather and great-grandfather were all born in Kamenitz, a small town in east central Europe. The ancestral village was a modest old resort hamlet some sixty miles south-southeast of Prague. The town nestled among rolling hills, one of the partly Czech- and partly German-speaking communities of northwestern Bohemian Austria-Hungary that would later become part of western Czechoslovakia. Kamenitz had remained largely unchanged over the preceding two or three centuries. The modest shops and stucco buildings that constituted the community during Max's childhood were roughly the same as during his great-grandfather's lifetime. One of several Czech towns with the same name, the Kamenitz of Wertheimer's ancestry was distinguished at one end of its village center by a magnificent old linden tree. Indeed, the formal name of the village, *Kamenitz an der Linde* (or *Kamenice nad Lipou* in Czech), acknowledged the venerable tree; a large three-story boys' school was built so as partially to surround the impressive landmark. The Wertheimer generations apparently flourished in this community, whose environs consisted of deep forests of evergreens and hardwood deciduous trees with dense undergrowth, fields of clover and mustard, and dozens of small dairies and family farms.

Although the countryside was untouched by major urban development, Kamenitz had survived significant political upheavals. The region was primarily Catholic and prosperous by the seventeenth century, but prosperity was threatened following the "Defenestration of Prague," when the Regents Jaroslav von Martinitz and William Slawata were thrown by Protestant rebels from a window of Prague's Hradcany Castle in 1618. By the end of the ensuing Thirty Years War, the most devastating war that had plagued Europe until that time, the Bohemian people lost their political independence, and their fate continued to be affected by European wars during the next few centuries.

The Wertheimer Ancestry

In the context of the volatile political history of the region, Max Wertheimer's ancestry was largely a product of wealth and privilege. Born into affluence as the son of a Baron von Wertheim in 1765, Max's great-grandfather Moises Wertheimer was a respected figure in the community of Kamenitz. Like many other Jews born into the nobility, he abandoned his father's title and changed his surname to Wertheimer. With his wife, Susanna, Moises had a son who, like his parents, spent his years primarily in the humble village of his ancestors. Born in 1792 and supported in part by family resources, Alexander Wertheimer engaged in a lifetime of variegated activities in military service, as a business entrepreneur, and as an administrative official in the community.[1] While still a young man, he enlisted as a soldier and received official recognition for his skill as a grenadier. After his two-decade military career, he established a successful business merchandising wines and spirits near the triangular village green of Kamenitz. But then his livelihood was severely threatened a few years later when the actions of a business associate resulted in the loss of all of Wertheimer's property. This devastating financial event came in addition to tragic developments in his personal life: his first two marriages were with wives who died young and did not bear children.

Over the course of several years, however, Alexander Wertheimer succeeded in overcoming his fiscal crisis and regained financial independence and authority in the Bohemian community. He attained the political office of rector of the district of Kamenitz despite widespread anti-Semitism in central Europe. Then, although sixty years old, Alexander married Franziska Pollak, the young daughter of Rabbi Markus Pollak, a venerable figure in the Jewish community in Kamenitz, on January 19, 1853, in her father's synagogue. Alexander's third marriage resulted in the birth of two sons and two daughters, all born in Kamenitz. The first child, Wilhelm, was born on November 6, 1853. A second son, Moritz, on March 11, 1855, was followed by Anna on July 21, 1858, and Wilhelmine on July 1, 1862.

While Alexander became a father late in life and reportedly relished his interactions with his children, in his determination to avert another financial disaster he was often consumed by his work. Religion was a significant part of the Wertheimer household and Alexander and Franziska saw to it that their children received a proper Jewish education. In later years, he remained an active participant in family and community affairs until he died of natural causes, just two years short of completing his ninth decade as a citizen of

Kamenitz. That Alexander Wertheimer had become a significant figure in his nation was indicated by his obituary in German in July, 1880, in the prominent Prague newspaper, the *Prager Tagblatt*, a clipping of which has been retained for generations in the family's archives. It says, in part:

> In Kamenitz an der Linde, on the 9th of this month, died the rector of the district, Herr Alexander Wertheimer, an old man whose life was certainly among the more interesting.... Until debility forced him to his couch shortly before his death, Herr Wertheimer marched with straight, erect bearing, unbent and in military step, could read even the finest print without glasses, and enjoyed a complete, healthy set of teeth.... The conduct of his life was honorable; gentle and peaceful his departure.[2]

Three of Franziska and Alexander Wertheimer's four children matured to adulthood. The fates of Anna and Wilhelmine are unknown, although they may well have spent all their lives within the communal boundaries of Kamenitz. Moritz became infatuated with a young woman who apparently did not share his passionate yearnings, and killed himself on December 31, 1873. But Alexander and Franziska's first-born child, Wilhelm, had a happier and more illustrious fate.

Wilhelm demonstrated a fascination for numbers coupled with impressive mathematical ability. By the early age of ten, he moved east from Kamenitz to become an apprentice in an agricultural accounting firm in the town of Znojemo, some fifty miles north of Vienna.[3] Although he had had only a grammar-school education, Wilhelm was a diligent worker who rapidly advanced in the company. By the time he was fifteen, following several promotions, he was a full-fledged accountant in the firm. Shortly thereafter, Wilhelm became an accountant for a local brewery, and later traveled throughout Europe selling agricultural commodities.

Wilhelm developed a successful career in the financial aspects of agriculture. The heart of eastern Europe was one of the wealthiest sections in the continent as a result of its extensive agriculture, especially its abundant crops of sugar and hops. The prosperity was also due in part to a move from absolutism to constitutionalism in a governmental system begun in 1848 which included Austria-Hungary's encouragement of industrialization in Bohemia. Wilhelm's experience and understanding of agricultural commodities promoted his professional career. In 1875, while he was still in his early twenties, he was offered the vice presidency of the commercial department of a Prague bank. The appointment offered prestige and greater financial security, but it meant separation from his fiancée, Rosalia ("Rosa") Zwicker.

Born December 15, 1855, Rosa was the daughter of Helene and Jacob Zwicker, a male nurse and hospital administrator. Rosa's parents provided her with a rich classical education. She met Wilhelm during their mutual participation in an amateur dramatics troupe. The two became engaged on December 6, 1870, when he was seventeen and she not quite fifteen years old. They shared interests in politics and the arts, especially music and drama. Although they had been apart frequently during Wilhelm's business trips throughout Europe, his appointment in Prague meant still greater periods of separation from her. Nevertheless, Wilhelm decided to accept the vice presidential position offered by the bank in Prague.

Set between the Carpathian Mountains to the northeast and the Danube River to the south, the industrialized but picturesque old city of Prague provided not only a dramatic change from Wilhelm's rural past but also the opportunity for greater future prosperity. Prague was the jewel of central Bohemia and had evolved into the capital, the largest city, and the cultural and economic center of the area. But the turbulent political difficulties of the time may have posed a threat to Wertheimer's professional security. The late nineteenth century was a volatile time in central Europe, characterized by dramatic changes in national borders and mounting tensions not only between but also within nations. Within the Austro-Hungarian empire itself, there was strife among language groups (principally among the speakers of Hungarian, Czech, and German)[4] and anti-Semitism was rampant in Prague, where many Bohemians had become Protestant during the late sixteenth century. Nonetheless, Wilhelm was able to succeed in a career that combined finance and education. Shortly after his arrival in Prague, he began teaching bookkeeping and business management privately. Soon he completed the requirements for a teaching certificate, after which he obtained a position as a lecturer in accounting and business correspondence at the Prague Gremial Specialized Business School, later renamed the Business Academy.

His occupational success apparently sufficed for Wilhelm to bring his fiancée to Prague. On November 11, 1877, Rosa and Wilhelm were married, some seven years after their engagement. The wedding was celebrated with grand festivities including a formal dinner and dance in the apartment where the couple would live during the first years of their marriage. This second-floor apartment, in a modest two-story house, was located in the heart of the Jewish ghetto, Rabinergasse 16, in Prague's Fifth District, some two blocks south of the flourishing "Old-New Synagogue" and an old Jewish cemetery.

In addition to continuing his teaching activities, Wertheimer published works on a number of different economic issues and was encouraged by the faculty of the Gremial School to write up his course on the *Theory of Practical Accounting and Business Correspondence* into a textbook. The book, published in 1880, was widely adopted and became a significant source of revenue for the Wertheimer family; by 1918 the text had appeared in a sixteenth edition with a print run of 31,000 copies and had been translated into several foreign languages.

Wilhelm also became a recognized expert on the problems of warehouse systems. According to his obituary,

> the Austrian government asked him in 1885 to draft a warehouse and inventory statute, which later was passed into law by the legislature. The breadth and depth of his knowledge as a self-taught expert are underscored by the trust that the conservative Roman Catholic Austrian government showed in Wertheimer, a Jew without academic credentials. For his eminence and his knowledge in his field, the Domestic Criminal Court and Business Court honored him by certifying him as an expert in business accounting. A local bank also made him an inspector.

Although devoted to scholarly and business activities, Wilhelm Wertheimer also was a philanthropist and a leader in a benevolent association. In 1879, shortly after the International Order of Oddfellows crossed the English Channel from Great Britain to continental Europe, Wilhelm became a member at age twenty-six of the IOOF Mozart Lodge in Berlin. Soon after his induction, he assembled the Prague members of the Grand Lodge of the German Empire and encouraged the founding of a Prague branch of the Oddfellows; in his obituary, Wilhelm Wertheimer was called the "Founder of the Prague Lodge of the Order" for his efforts. The obituary also reported that he was instrumental in the founding of several other IOOF lodges. During many years of participation in the IOOF, Wertheimer made significant financial contributions and held many offices including Grand Master of the Prague branch, Representative of the District Grand Lodge of Saxony, and delegate to the Congress for the German Empire, where he later was elected to the post of Grand Secretary of the Grand Lodge. Wertheimer also became the Grand Master of the Grand Lodge of the Czechoslovakian Republic, and was elected Grand Patriarch in 1924.

Thus Wilhelm Wertheimer carried on the tradition of worldly success established by his father, Alexander. Apparently endowed with an unusual amount of energy, he was a contributor to national legislation in Austria, a practical businessman, an investor, and a philanthropist. In addition to his scholarly, patriotic, social, and vocational successes, Wilhelm was also described as a devoted husband and father, married to a woman who remained active in artistic and intellectual pursuits as an accomplished violinist and as an enthusiast for German literature.

Max Wertheimer's Childhood

Rosa's and Wilhelm's first son, Walter, was born at their Prague home on December 6, 1878. From the beginning of his life, the child's health was precarious; among other illnesses, Walter contracted pulmonary edema, an abnormal accumulation of fluid in the lungs, at less than two years of age.

After numerous consultations, several physicians offered little hope for the child's survival. But Wilhelm was able to write in his journal (in MW-CU) that Walter had been "rescued, with God's help, by Dr. H. Drumel on April 8, 1880." Walter slowly regained his health, but had a bout with scarlet fever the next month which persisted until June of the following year. This history of illness continued, and Walter was plagued by physical infirmity into his adult years.

Despite Walter's varied and continuing health problems, Rosa became pregnant with a second child in 1879. Wilhelm recorded in his journal (MW-CU) that "Max Wertheimer was born in Prague, Rabinergasse No. 16, second story, on Thursday, 15 April 1880, at 6:00 in the morning." Listed in the journal as attending the birth were a man identified only as "Carl Drener," Marie Zwicker (presumably Rosa's sister or aunt) and a rabbi, named in Wilhelm's journal as "M. Hirsch." Rosa's delivery of Max was lengthy and arduous. Max's generally robust good health contrasted with his brother's delicate physical constitution. However, given the difficulty of Max's birth and the trauma of Walter's medical problems, Wilhelm and Rosa decided not to have any more children. The illness of their first son was not the only source of distress for Wilhelm and Rosa in 1880: less than three months after Max's birth, word came from Kamenitz about the death of Wilhelm's father, Alexander Wertheimer.

Following the birth of his children, Wilhelm continued to be occupied with his teaching and was also deeply immersed in responsibilities related to the IOOF and to the drafting of the Austro-Hungarian warehousing law. Wertheimer lectured at the Prague Business Academy for the next eighteen years, and also soon managed to accumulate sufficient financial resources to found and direct his own business school ("Handelsschule Wertheimer") in the fashionable commercial district of downtown Prague. The school occupied part of a massive four-story building at Poříč number 6. Wilhelm used the spaces between the eleven windows on the second floor facing the street to display the successive letters, large enough to be clearly visible from a distance, of the founder's surname; the word WERTHEIMER prominently decorated the façade (as can be seen in a photograph in MW-CU; see following p. 184). In addition to the business school, the building contained a number of diverse stores on the ground floor and several residential apartments, all surrounding a tranquil central courtyard.

The Handelsschule Wertheimer appears to have been successful from the start and, according to school records, attracted students from all regions of the Austro-Hungarian empire as well as from Bulgaria, Denmark, Germany, Holland, Italy, Serbia, Sweden, Switzerland, Romania, Russia, and even Asia, North America, and Brazil. Wilhelm Wertheimer developed a reputation as a gifted and innovative teacher and administrator. He became known for pioneering a unique method of teaching business procedures in typing, accounting, shorthand, and related skills based on a novel, individualized system of pedagogy. He rejected the traditional lecture style on the grounds that it induced mediocrity in students and instead used more personal methods of instruction. The author of his obituary claimed in 1930 that Wertheimer

> was the first to institute the individual method of learning, individualized instruction. With admirable originality, Wertheimer went far beyond even the teaching and learning techniques used today.... But it was not only Wertheimer's original ideas about education that made his school so popular and eminent; also significant were his unselfish character, his self-discipline, and his practical knowledge.

The business school was so successful that Wertheimer amassed a fairly substantial fortune from its operation. Wilhelm's financial success allowed him to purchase the entire building and, during the summer of 1895, the family moved from the second-floor flat in the Jewish ghetto (where both boys had lived since they were born) to a substantial residential apartment in the building that housed Wilhelm's school.

Wilhelm and Rosa regularly attended the synagogue and the family took an active part in the Jewish community in which they lived; the Jewish holy days were occasions for celebration and recommitment to the Mosaic heritage. German was the language spoken at home, as was the custom among the "gebildet" or cultured homes of the period, both Jewish and non-Jewish, in the major western cities of Austria-Hungary during the latter part of the nineteenth century and the early part of the twentieth; most of the more affluent residents saw themselves as part of the culture of Germany and especially of Austria. They spoke Czech language only when shopping, with service people, and in the street. Wilhelm, who himself had acquired a modest capacity with Hebrew, also saw to it that his sons were educated in that language.

Walter and Max were, then, part of a close-knit family that actively socialized with other members of the community. They also had frequent interactions with members of both parents' extended families. Family vacations offered numerous educational and cultural experiences; the Wertheimers traveled extensively throughout central Europe to such destinations as Bodenbach, Franzensbad, Gablonz, Kamenitz, Karlsbad, Marienbad, Reichenberg, and Zittau, as well as in Germany to Berlin and the Baltic resort town of Heringsdorf an der Ostsee, on the Isle of Usedom, a few miles northwest of the harbor city of Swinemünde. Evenings at the Wertheimer home typically brought spirited intellectual discussions about the political, social, and cultural events of the day. As was the custom in other "gebildet" households in Europe during the same period, live chamber music was also an everyday occurrence in the house; evenings, weekends, and holidays were the occasions for cooperative efforts at making amateur music in the home. Walter in particular recorded in his diary his admiration for the remarkable vigor and intense character of his younger brother's musical renditions on the violin and the piano.

Walter and Max enjoyed a warm brotherly friendship founded on mutual interests. The boys regularly attended the royal German national theater, as well as live performances of operas and symphonies that were frequently available in the rich urban cultural life of Prague; and they traveled together by rail to neighboring towns. The two celebrated New Year's Eve together in 1894 with Walter, Max, and a friend playing chess and cards, drinking, eating, and smoking cigarettes while their parents were away. Despite their close relationship, there were some contrasting personality characteristics between the two brothers. Walter seemed to be sensitive, reserved, and moody while Max tended to be spontaneous, lively, and occasionally brash.

With their parents' emphasis on education, Max and Walter were encouraged to read widely both in religious and in secular literature. As one historian (Mitchell G. Ash) noted,

> The picture we have of the Wertheimers' family life and of Max Wertheimer's education corresponds to that of many German-speaking Jewish families in Prague at that time—a combination of successful assimilation in the larger society with attempts to maintain Jewish identity at home.[5]

Thus, reading of religious texts was complemented by exposure to German classics and also to the extensive Czech literature of the late nineteenth century which, because of the Czechs' strong cultural traditions and historical circumstances, was often suffused with intense patriotic sentiment. Although the Czechs lost their political independence after the Thirty Years War in the middle of the seventeenth century, the people never lost their ideal of regaining independence. By the 1870s, Czech literature had fully established itself in poetry and the novel, although not yet in drama. During Max Wertheimer's childhood, two local Prague magazines were popular: *Lumir*, which argued the need to Europeanize Czech literature, and *Stir*, the editors and writers of which emphasized strong native traditions and themes. Toward the end of the nineteenth century, the historical novels of Alois Jirásek claimed a wide readership and several Prague writers during the first part of the twentieth century achieved international recognition, among them Franz Kafka, Rainer Maria Rilke, Franz Werfel and Max Brod. The Wertheimers probably also appreciated the work of the German cartoonist Wilhelm Busch, who became the first professional and popular comic-strip artist, first in periodicals and later in separately published albums, at the end of the nineteenth century. With their child pranksters "Max and Moritz," Busch's stories provided social satire, including spoofs depicting the vulnerability of human dignity.[6]

Max Wertheimer's Early Education

Five-year-old Max was enrolled on August 2, 1885, at a private elementary school maintained by the Piarist order of Roman Catholics in the New City section of Prague. The Piarists were established about 1600 in Rome as a special teaching congregation with the aim of founding schools throughout much of Poland and Austria for the education of the poor; however, by the late nineteenth century, the Piarist school in Prague had already earned an excellent reputation for a rigorous academic program, taught in German rather than Czech.

It was not unusual for a Jewish child to attend a Catholic school in central Europe at the end of the nineteenth century. Albert Einstein, for example, had an elementary and secondary education quite similar to that of Wertheimer. According to Ronald Clark, one of Einstein's biographers,

> From the age of five until the age of ten [Einstein] attended a Catholic school near his home, and at ten was transferred to the Luitpold Gymnasium [in Munich], where the children of the middle classes had drummed into them the rudiments of Latin and Greek, of history and geography, as well as of simple mathematics. The choice of a Catholic school was not as curious as it seems. Elementary education…was run on a denominational basis. The nearest Jewish school was some distance from the Einstein home and its fees were high…. The dangers of Catholic orientation were outweighed by the sound general instruction which the school gave.[7]

Similar comments could probably be made about Max and his education at the Piarist Grammar School. Doubtless Max was fully aware of the differences between Jewish and Catholic mores, and he could not have avoided awareness of the smoldering anti-Semitism of the predominantly Christian community.

At the time of Wertheimer's early education, the four quarters of the school year ended in December, February, April, and July. Although Max did miss school occasionally because of illness, especially during the first two years, he had no unexcused absences during his entire elementary schooling. Records preserved in the family archives (MW-CU) show that he studied the traditional academic fare of reading, writing, arithmetic, religion, drawing, singing, history, geography, and science; by the third grade he also had classes in the Bohemian or Czech language. His exemplary record of the first two years (including high grades in effort and comportment) slipped a bit in the later years, especially in Bohemian language and physical education; as in his later life, Wertheimer was more interested in scholarship than in athletic competition. Throughout the time of his schooling, he earned mostly the equivalent of A's, some B's, and an occasional C.

On July 15, 1890, Wertheimer, now ten years old, graduated from the

Piarist Grammar School with high grades in effort, comportment, German, and religion, and an above-average grade in arithmetic. Following his graduation, Max attended the Royal Imperial New City German State High School (K. K. Neustädter Deutsche Staats-Obergymnasium) located on the ancient hollow known as the Graben near his home, in which the language of instruction was German, and from which he could expect to receive a diploma that would permit him to go to a university thereafter. As in elementary school, he maintained a record of not a single unexcused absence. Still, there were a few excused absences, presumably because of illness, especially during the 1890-to-1892 school years.

The program at the Neustädter Gymnasium was structured around a semester rather than quarter schedule. Wertheimer took a typical classical set of courses in natural science, religion, Latin, Greek, mathematics, history, and geography, as well as some work in penmanship, stenography, art, choir, and philosophy. His grades declined slightly from his first year at the Gymnasium to his last, but he maintained a respectable overall record, with religious studies emerging among his strongest subjects. Wertheimer graduated from the Gymnasium on July 7, 1898. His graduation qualified Max to enter any German university without further tests except for the comprehensive "matura" exam, which he took and passed one week after his graduation, on July 14.

When Max became aware of the diversity of courses in a university curriculum and contemplated his future, he may already have realized how deeply fascinated he was with philosophy. Perhaps one can see his interest in philosophical subjects showing as early as his high marks in religion in grammar school and gymnasium. In addition, his enthusiasm for philosophical thinking had been encouraged and fostered years earlier by his maternal grandfather, Jacob Zwicker. As a child, Max was often invited to sit with the old man and wonder about the complex beauty and mysteries of nature. One such discussion, initiated by Max when he was four or five, focused on the visual similarities between salt and sugar and their difference of taste. [8] How could two substances, so similar in apparent outward physical properties, be perceived so differently by the tongue? Such encounters doubtless stimulated and encouraged Jacob Zwicker's grandson's intellectual curiosity.

On Max's tenth birthday, Jacob presented him with a German edition of the complete works of the rationalist Jewish philosopher Baruch Spinoza. When they found out about the gift, Max's parents objected to the book and forbade him to read it. Perhaps the Wertheimers considered such fare too advanced for their young son. Their prohibition may also have been rooted in the condemnation of Spinoza's radical philosophy by Jewish officials. Whatever the source of their objection, Rosa and Wilhelm removed the book from Max's room and placed it elsewhere in the house. But reportedly, an obliging and sympathetic maid realized Max's dismay at losing the gift, stole the book back for him, and hid it in a wicker trunk with her laundry so the boy could peruse it at leisure.

The Boyhood Diaries of Walter and Max

As was typical of well-to-do adolescents in that time and social setting, both Walter and Max kept journals (with Walter's far lengthier and more detailed than Max's). Walter's impressions of himself, his family and his world are documented in two successive diaries that span the period from December 6, 1892, to November 2, 1897. He pasted tickets and programs from musical and theatrical performances into the pages of his journal, as well as newspaper clippings and occasional pen or pencil sketches interspersed with personal narrative. Several of Walter's diary entries relate directly to his younger brother and cast further light on the activities, familial relationships, and general characteristics of Max Wertheimer's life during his early years. Max's entries in his own diary are much less informative than those in Walter's. But the cultural setting in which Max grew up is also described in much of what Walter wrote that is not explicitly about his brother. The diaries, preserved in family records (MW-CU), provide a rich account of life in an affluent Jewish family in Prague during the last decade of the nineteenth century, as seen through the eyes of a youth coping with the problems of becoming an adult.

Many of Walter's journal entries suggest an adolescent identity crisis, deep depressions, and self-doubt. The first entry, dated December 6, 1892, is a record of Walter's fourteenth birthday. In detail he listed his gifts, including a cake with "Congratulations" inscribed in icing, a silver chain from his mother, a little savings bank and a white tie from Max, and a diary, a purse, and a small memo booklet from various friends and relatives. Many later entries concern Walter's work experiences at his father's school and his trials and tribulations with young women whom he idolized and idealized.

The influence of Walter's parents permeates nearly every page of his diary. Wilhelm guided his older son's vocational plans as well as the outcome of his romantic life. Walter was fascinated by a young woman identified in his journal only as "Fräulein Kauders," perhaps the sister of Walter's childhood friend Hans Kauders. Indeed, an early entry details his efforts to follow the young woman at a distance as she traveled the streets of downtown Prague on various errands. Walter was concerned about the impression he made on her, and his journal is filled with such wistful queries as "Is she thinking of me?" But Walter was also uneasy about his parents' obvious disapproval of his idol. In an entry early in January, 1893, Walter, then a student at his father's school, realized that he had to keep his admiration for Miss Kauders secret from Wilhelm: "Papa must have noticed that I am pursuing her, since he asked me what I'm doing when I always disappear from the school at ten o'clock. If she only loved me, I would be the happiest man on earth."

Walter was shattered on February 16, 1893: although Miss Kauders had given him a pink rose, which had made him jubilant, he later found out that she had given another young man a *red* one. Solemnly he wrote: "Praise not the day before evening has come." Hoping to find support and comfort, he approached his mother for advice, but she called Miss Kauders "common" and admonished her son to forget her. His mother's words had a strong, but not long-term, effect on Walter. He immediately vowed to forget Miss Kauders, arguing to himself that their love was not founded on mutual regard and was, therefore, not genuine.

February 20 found him in a better mood, thinking about God and his parents, and happier that he had forsworn his forbidden love. But less than a month later he was again brooding about Miss Kauders. He had danced almost all evening with her on March 11, from 8:30 p.m. until four the next morning, in spite of his parents' warning that the relationship could only lead to grief for Walter. That fall, several other young ladies received Walter's attention, but Miss Kauders clearly remained his favorite. He recorded at length his dreams about her and his yearnings for her. In his journal, Walter scolded his parents for stifling his freedom, especially for their wish that he stop seeing Miss Kauders. He yearned to understand her completely and learn everything about her, to discover both her negative and her positive qualities. He was not satisfied to regard her only as an unrealistic ideal from afar. Perhaps he may even have thought of how unrequited love had led his uncle Moritz to commit suicide.

Walter's infatuation with Miss Kauders may have been related to his obsession with the image and fate of the character Gretchen in Johann Wolfgang von Goethe's 1808 play *Faust, Der Tragödie erster Teil* (*Faust, The First Part of the Tragedy*). Together with Max, Walter attended a performance of the play on May 10, 1895, and he reviewed it in detail in the pages of his journal the following day. Although impressed by the grand theme of the play, Walter recounted at length how deeply moved he was by the portrayal of Gretchen, the young and innocent girl whom Faust seduces with the aid of Mephistopheles's sorcery. His diary entry ended by recounting: "Her image was constantly in my mind. I walked home in a dream, stumbled often, sobbed I know not why. At home I left my evening meal untouched, and just wanted to go quickly to bed. My loyal brother wished me a friendly good night but I hardly heard him." Four days later, still obsessed by thoughts of Gretchen, he got up at 5 a.m. and wandered through the streets of Prague. He returned by streetcar more than two hours later and was astonished to find his family still in bed. "They hadn't even noticed that I'd been away. Only Max."

The image of Gretchen haunted him for months thereafter, well into the summer of 1896, when he attended a performance of Charles François Gounod's 1859 dramatic opera *Faust and Margarethe*. On May 6, 1897, he recorded with enthusiasm that he would join his family at successive performances of Part I and of the longer, more allegorical Part II of Goethe's *Faust*. The similarity between Gretchen's simple, lower-class status and the "common" status that his mother ascribed to Miss Kauders appears to have appealed to Walter's romantic nature. Although it is not stated explicitly in the diary, he may have seen the resemblance between his admiration of the literary character, doubtless condoned by his parents, and his unfulfilled and forbidden yearning for Miss Kauders. However, he remained dutifully obedient to his parents' wishes, and their command ultimately prevailed over his own desires; he finally stopped writing, and perhaps thinking, about Miss Kauders.

Back in February 1893, when Walter was still only fourteen years old, Wilhelm had arranged a job for his son at the business school to assist in the teaching of business correspondence, accounting, and Czech. Walter spent many hours at the school, working under the supervision of one of Wilhelm's employees, Eduard Lustig, the bursar of the school, who also set the level of Walter's salary "according to his accomplishments." On March 1, Walter received his first paycheck and exulted in the amount of his first wages. His advancement at the school was steady but not rapid. More than a year and a half after his initial employment, Walter recorded in his journal in mid-September, 1894, that he had now begun teaching stenography. An entry in March, 1895, records that for slightly more than half a year he had been a student at the Prague Business Academy, a member of the beginning class, whose students "until hardly a month ago I had seen as far below me. I had always thought, according to what I'd heard from others, that Prague Business Academy was a place for laggards, for guys who couldn't make it in the Gymnasium." This prejudice seems to have been quickly dispelled.

Walter, working for his father, was apparently being groomed gradually to assume Wilhelm's position and responsibilities at the school upon his father's retirement. But Walter lacked his father's enthusiasm for the business school and struggled to maintain interest in his work, an orientation that was noticed early by his supervisor, the bursar Eduard Lustig. In a January 31, 1894, note to Wilhelm, Lustig shared his unflattering opinion of Walter's performance at the business school:

> Honored Director, if I should lie, I would say that I am satisfied with Walter; but I really am not. That he was eager at first, I attributed to his youth; but now that he has been with us a year, it's going badly. Please be so kind as to admonish him to be more attentive at work;…I am very dissatisfied. Very truly yours, Lustig.

Walter pasted the letter into his diary and on February 1 penned a lengthy outpouring of melancholy thoughts, among them:

> I have no hope for the future, I don't enjoy the present, and I don't think of the past. Life flows on monotonously, and I am constantly aware that I am already 16 years old, without supporting myself or being able to support myself.

Walter's lament was that he had little hope of earning a significant salary that would offer him financial independence from his parents. Another sheet pasted into the diary shows that Walter's salary at the time was 15 gulden, a rather modest sum when compared with the salaries of regular instructors at the school, who were earning 70 to 250 gulden. Reflecting upon his anemic wages, Walter concluded that

> I hardly could live from my 15 gulden, and gloomy thoughts enter my mind without the hope that things might be better some day. I live, simply because I live—or rather, because I have to live, and life brings no joy.... So I have to continue living this way, without hope for the future, supported by my parents....

In an April 1895 entry, Walter mused that his survival was exclusively due to his parents' generosity, a situation that increased his insecurity and obliged his undying obedience to them:

> [A]bove all, I must thank God for having given me such parents. Slowly I raise my hands and fold them, in order to thank Thee, All-bountiful, Sublime One. How have I earned the grace which Thou pourest over me, over this sinful human, over the wretched creature that I am?

Walter ended that diary entry with a sketch in blue of a heart pierced by a dagger, accompanied by the word "Thanks" in stylized, formal letters. A loose slip of paper inserted at this page contains, in both Hebrew and German, the prayer "Forsake me not when I am in need, and no help is in sight." Walter's orientation toward his work is also documented in a journal entry from May 1895: "This morning, instead of working, I went with a fellow student and Max to the pub 'City of Prague' at the Belvedere. Drank, and smoked 13 cigarettes."

Eventually, Walter was able to satisfy the requirements for graduation from the Business Academy. In his diary, Walter pasted ephemera from the celebration of this event on July 10, 1897, including the menu for the banquet held in the Eagle Suite of the Prague Grand-Hôtel, the booklet of official songs for the occasion (in German and in Latin—including phrases such as "Vivat, academia! Vivant, professores!") and a newspaper clipping dated July 12 from *Deutsches Abendblatt*, with a by-line showing that it had been written by Walter himself, reporting the events of the ceremony. The article included some of his own whimsical public remarks on that occasion:

> Most honored ones! I have the honorable duty of enlightening you by reading to you what will appear in tomorrow's paper. Since I wrote the article, I can assure you that it is most interesting indeed, and not so long that you will get thoroughly bored. So for just a few moments, be so kind as to lend me your ear, or, better yet, both ears; and rest assured that I won't abuse the ears you have so kindly lent me. On the contrary, I intend to leave a large part, indeed most of the article, unread, so that you will retain something you can read to yourselves—when you want to go to sleep.

His article recorded in detail the illustrious guests, the music of the evening, a toast to Kaiser Franz Josef, the principal speakers with the topics of their respective addresses, and other details of the festivities that lasted well past midnight. The article also described the yearbook produced for the graduation, and named the committee responsible for it, a group of twelve graduates (including Walter) who "undertook the arduous task of editing the volume, and accomplished it efficiently and with skill." Walter pasted a similar clipping from the newspaper *Bohemia* into his journal along with letters of congratulation, and also several mementos from a short graduation trip to Carlsbad.

Walter had obediently acquiesced to his father's wish that he graduate from the business school, but, at a few months short of nineteen years old, was still uncertain about his future. He had evidently agreed to consider succeeding his father as director of the business school, but remained haunted by a general disinterest in the position and concerns about assuming such responsibility.

By contrast, Max apparently did not yield so easily to parental rule. On June 15, 1895, Walter used his stenographic skills to record an event that reveals the character of his fifteen-year-old brother and the sometimes volatile goings-on in the Wertheimer home. "Today at dinner, as usual," wrote Walter, "there was again a terrible row, so drastic that I wrote the whole conversation down right afterwards, reconstructing it from stenographic notes." As if writing a play, he provided a dramatis personae consisting of the following characters:

Papa = P.
Mama = M.
Max = Mx.
Walter = W.
Uncle = U.

Walter's narrative records the conversation while the Wertheimer family was dining.

P: "Children, what's the Sidrah this week?" [The Sidrah is the portion of Hebrew Scripture read or chanted each particular week, to assure that the entire scripture is read each year.]

W: (is silent)

Mx: "I don't know."

M: "But you learn this from Herr Wiesner."

Mx: "Yes, well…"

M: "Well!? You really should know it. You'll learn it tomorrow."

Mx: "We already learned it last Saturday. But why should I memorize what the Sidrah happens to be?"

M: "Do you know its meaning then?"

Mx: "No, what for? It is not at all essential for religion to know what the Sidrah is."

P: "Do you know, Max, what we had done to us when we were children, if we were asked what the Sidrah was and didn't know? We were slapped a couple of times. Isn't that how it was, Jacob?"

U: "We even had to be able to recite them by heart. And if we made a mistake…—Lord!"

Mx: "It is completely unnecessary for religion or for knowledge of the Bible to know what the Sidrah happens to be today. Demanding that would be nonsense."

M: (excited, wants to rebut)

U: (shouts louder than she) "And what…"

P: (starts screaming, to drown him out) "Don't argue about it. A person who firmly takes a stand, who refuses to let himself be convinced, can't be convinced."

M: (wants to scream)

P: (gets up and goes to his room)

M: "Now that's the limit, talking like that; how dare you attack what's said by someone older than you!? Knowledge of the Torah is nonsense, what, *that's* what you're saying—you…."

Mx: "Mama, you're lying—excuse me for accusing you of lying. But lying is unfair. I didn't say that knowledge of the Torah is nonsense, only such an application of it, this having to know just what particular Sidrah it is."

M: "What, you dare to say to me, dare to say to your mother, to say to her face, that she's lying!"

P: (sticks his head in the door) "Rosa, I implore you, don't argue." (Leaves)

M: "That was very wicked of you!"

Mx: (excited—says nothing)

U: (tries to make a scornful face, but looks so stupid that—in spite of the seriousness of the occasion—I laugh out loud)

All: (turn to look at me with astonishment)

Mx: (leaves)

The curtain falls.

"That's how it goes in our house," Walter concluded. "Something like this every other day." Although Wilhelm may have had some concerns about rote memorization in business training, apparently he still believed in the utility of the practice for religious teaching. But Max clearly found little value in memorization regardless of the content or context. The scene prophetically illustrates the striving for independence of thought and the impatience with blind rote memorization that were to be central in Max Wertheimer's later life, not only in adolescent rebellion against his parents' orthodoxy.

This exchange in the Wertheimer household also reveals the contrast between Max's fiery self-assurance, even in the face of three respected elders, and his brother's relative passivity. But Rosa and Wilhelm were probably accustomed to their son's occasional passionate outbursts; by the next day, all was forgiven and, according to Walter's entry for that day: "Naturally everything is reconciled again. It is Sunday afternoon. Papa is at the school. Mama and Max are playing music again. I again don't feel like working, and here I sit at my desk, my diary open before me."

Walter spent many evenings writing in his journal, frequently while listening to his mother and brother play music. Such moments may have appealed to his romantic nature, and Walter occasionally chose them to comment on his respect for his younger brother:

> Daily life masks the lustre of glory; daily contact with significant men makes them appear less illustrious in the eye of the beholder. Nevertheless, I could still assert categorically that Max will some day become someone significant, someone famous. In what, in which area, I don't have the faintest idea, because he seems to me to be great and mighty in each and every thing. Last night I was groveling in despondency about death again, when he brought me back to my senses with such imploring words that at the moment I would have given him *anything*. His conversation was intended to drag me away from my thoughts. He began arguing with me about his vital question "What is the purpose of life?" He gave me clear proofs for everything, so that I was filled with admiration for him.

This extravagant entry, written on August 17, 1895, when Max was only fifteen years old, concludes with an appreciation of Max's musical ability and commanding character:

> But what enchants me most is his piano playing. He never took piano lessons; he learned to read notes only through his violin playing. He has a unique finger dexterity that is truly astonishing. His improvisations have something daemonic about them, a wonderful strength which erases all other thoughts; you are swept along by the melodies, which are now wild and mighty, now gentle and quiet, as though sounding from far, far away, wonderfully mild. When I hear him play, I can't tear myself away until he stops. Not long ago, in the evening, when we were still in the old apartment, I sat in the dark in the rocking chair in the next room and I don't remember what had happened to me that day, but I was in a very sad state of mind. Then suddenly he started improvising next door, and my mood became so wonderfully gentle and quiet, as though the tones were leading me into a realm of dreams, into a peaceful, sweet land which

knows no calamity, no tears. And I became more and more melancholy, my head sank lower toward my knees, my rocking became gentler, and finally I didn't know any more where I was, I wasn't asleep or dozing, but I could do nothing other than soak up the marvelous tones with all my senses, with all my strength. When Papa came into the room I didn't even hear him. Max had stopped playing long before, a deep darkness already filled the room, and when I went to bed I told myself, perhaps for the first time in my life: that was a heavenly evening.

The family occasionally shared their more formal writings with one another; the parents encouraged their sons to do so. One day in May, 1896, Walter wrote: "One should always be practical in this rough world. I used yesterday's foul mood to write a feuilleton [a brief thematic essay]. After I read it out loud, Mama cried, Papa gave me a kiss without saying anything, and Max called me a colleague." It is striking that Max, younger than Walter by more than a year, should think to honor his older brother with the title "colleague," and even more striking that the older brother apparently felt honored by his younger brother's use of that term.

Max kept his diary much more sporadically than Walter did. Max's entries tended to be briefer, and more often in poetic form, than Walter's. They are also (with the exception of the first entry) less revealing about events in everyday life. In general, the entries in Max's diary are more abstract, and far less graphic, concrete, and personal. Hence they are described here in less detail, and quoted from more sparsely, than has seemed fitting for Walter's diary.

In 1891, Wilhelm presented Max with an elaborate book of blank shiny paper in celebration of the boy's eleventh birthday. The volume had a green leather cover with brass hasps and an impressive black velvet spine. On the cover was an inlaid gold metal cutout surrounding the word "Poesy," while garlands of leaves and flowers and an intricate gold leaf design trimmed the outside edges of the pages.[9] In delicate and careful handwriting, Max entered the words "Birthday gift from Papa" above his own flourished signature on the first page, and, at the bottom of that page, printed his name in purple ink from a rubber stamp, surrounded by a colored laurel wreath. Over the course of two years, Max filled nearly half the pages of the book, always carefully with precise and steady penmanship. His neat penmanship doubtless reflected his father's strict methods at the business school, but may also have been an early sign of his life-long concern with precision. Max's self-critical editorial style, characteristic of his later professional life, was already hinted at in this early writing. Occasional ink entries contain pencil corrections that clearly were added later; some pages have been crudely torn from the diary while still others are completely crossed out—but usually with a single straight, neat, diagonal line. All this suggests Max Wertheimer's painstaking attention to detail at an early age.

Max's first entry, not written until two-thirds of a year after he received the book, dated December 12, 1891, and boldly labeled with the roman numeral I, was entitled "The first Bar Mitzvah—a sketch" and recounts the eleven-year-old boy's impression of his older brother's ritual passage into Jewish manhood. Illness prevented Max from attending the actual ceremony of Walter's Bar Mitzvah, but he was able, from a distance, to record an impression of the guests prior to his brother's arrival. Max's entry shows feelings of brotherly pride as well as pangs of insecurity and envy:

I was only allowed to look [at the guests] through a glass door, the curtain of which was pushed aside just a little, into the living room. When I first looked in among the people and heard them telling each other how beautiful my brother's speech was, a feeling of pride, of joy, came over me. Now I can be proud of my brother, for he is a man, a finished man, a third adult member of our family, a man who is being praised by the words of such a large collection of people. And my own life appears in such harsh contrast in comparison with his. What am I, after all? A child who has hardly managed to escape from sickness, who still has a long time to go before he can carry the name "man."

I stood at the door window and looked into the happy throng. Suddenly the aunts and the uncles, cousins and distant relatives arrived. Then finally, greeted with loud calls, came the honoree, and after him our parents. The crowd grew larger and more dense. Finally I make my presence known by knocking loudly on the door. And finally the aunts come to greet me, but it's always the same: "How are you?" This constant questioning was a pain to me, and if a few hundred years ago I had been the Grand Inquisitor[10], I would, as a kind of torture, have placed the prisoner in a chair, and would have let an endless series of aunts, constantly asking, "How are you?" pass in front of him…. After the series had finally run out, they all sat down, waited, ate, and drank. Suddenly absolute silence. My brother had gone to the lectern, and started. I saw and heard his inspiration, and all the guests paid attention and listened closely to his speech. When he finished, the men discussed his theme and the impression the talk had made on them, the women wept, and the children nibbled at the dainties. Only I couldn't. —And again! I have to use the expression "child" for myself. —Many a German poet says: "How beautiful is the time of youth!" I would like to, but I can't, rebut them with: "How beautiful is the time of manhood!" But since I don't know the troubles of adulthood, only those of youth, I'm really not qualified to judge…. I glance at the table which bears a great heap of gifts. A melancholy feeling comes over me. I thought, this is how all joys on earth end. One could use here the saying, "Dust thou art, and to dust thou shalt return." But the Bar Mitzvah celebration has made a very good impression on me. And since today, because of it, I realized how transitory everything is, I call out to you, "Enjoy yourselves, enjoy yourselves as long as you can, for life too is transitory."

Despite this record of Walter's Bar Mitzvah, Max did not mention this religious ceremony when he himself turned thirteen in 1893.

Max's later entries reveal more concern with philosophical themes than purely emotional ones. For instance, one five-stanza poem in strict meter, titled "Luck" and written in large and flowing ornate script, notes that "Fortune" may hold out her hand to you, but soon passes you by and is smiling at someone else. In another poem simply entitled "Life," the first sentence stands apart from the rest of the entry: "Human life runs on and on; like the seasons it goes from spring to winter." Then there are two solid pages of carefully written script, without breaks to indicate stanzas; but each page has a single line drawn through it from upper left to lower right in apparent dissatisfaction. The poem lays out the venerable analogy of human life to the four seasons, with a few idiosyncratic fresh thoughts. Max also authored an ode to youth in strict ABBA rhyming pattern, a conventional poem in praise of friendship, and a tribute to a dead friend of the family, Otto Waldstein.

His reverence for his maternal grandmother, Helene Zwicker, is evident in a February 17, 1893, tribute entitled "Grandmama! On the day of her death." In his musings about the meaning of death, Max created a gentle poem, expressing disbelief in his grandmother's death, and conjuring up an image of her standing in the twilight, as well as participating in the family's dilemmas and successes. He envisioned Helene standing before him, providing him—at his request—with wise counsel. The tribute ends with his incredulity at "being left behind," and wistfully asks, "Grandmama, can you hear me?"

Max, like his brother Walter, exhibited in his journal his sensitive and brooding side, and may have found some satisfaction in capturing wistful meditations in its pages. But Max was far less inclined than Walter to write about infatuations with the young women in his community. By 1895, one year after the last entry in his journal, Max had grown into a rather handsome young man with thick, wavy black hair, sideburns, and mustache. But his interests in romantic relationships were seldom mentioned in the pages of his journal. In one passage that is somewhat reminiscent of his brother's romanticism, Max did pen a sentimental farewell to a girl, Clara Mende, in AA, BCCB rhyme. He asserts matter-of-factly that perhaps their paths will never cross again. If the days are now bringing her joy, it is all right if she has forgotten him. But if tears are moistening her cheeks, she could think of him, who would never forget her.

But even though he may occasionally have been tempted to record an impassioned relationship, most passages in Max's journal suggest a fascination with the complexities of ideas, of nature, justice, and truth, rather than an attempt to generate an introspective record of events in his daily life. His entries also include some poems on religion. The last section of a sixteen-stanza elaboration of his earlier work on the four seasons, "The Winter's Joys and Sorrows," is divided into two parts, one bemoaning winter's cold and drabness and the second expressing admiration for Christmas, with the typical Christian child's prayer to the Christ Child to bring presents as a reward for good behavior. Like many urban Jews in Europe at the time, the

Wertheimers apparently experienced no conflict in celebrating both Jewish and Christian holidays. Yet on Christmas Day, 1892, Max saw fit to write a poem that had nothing to do with Christmas, a diatribe against obsession with wealth entitled simply "Money." It asserts that everyone is evaluated in terms of how much money they have, rather than in terms of what they can do. Consequently people knock each other down in the quest for wealth; the greatest evil in the world is "ugly, cursed money." The sentiment expressed in this poem was in some ways to characterize Wertheimer for the rest of his life. As an adult, he lived frugally, in almost ascetic surroundings, and was disdainful of materialistic showiness and of wealth for its own sake.

In February, 1893, Max wrote a poem extolling the virtues of elderly women, and containing a fervent promise to help and protect them, as well as an elaborate description of a Sabbath ritual. The same month he wrote a poetic appreciation of his mother, and then did not write in the journal again for almost a year. In December 1893, he wrote a seven-page sentimental fantasy in verse about a mother with two children whose husband dies, who has nowhere to turn, and who, at dusk, lies down to die at her husband's grave.

Other poems, such as "The Jewish Religion" (originally entitled "The Messiah") in 1893, were written in a handwriting style that is somewhat less ornate than his earlier calligraphy, and noticeably more similar to the rather austere style Wertheimer was to use in his adult years. One somewhat obscure section of the poem recommends taking the "middle road" and hints at Wertheimer's already polemical opposition to memorizing and blind extremism, and his striving for the ideal and for truth—themes that would dominate his later psychology.

The quest for truth and for the ideal balanced life may reflect how Max then viewed the Jewish religion and his own mission in the world. The poem displays less formalism, a looser form, and a more individualistic and adult handwriting than earlier entries. His thoughts, while still far from clear or mature, seemed to be evolving in new directions.

He also devoted some poems to music. One, entitled "Music: Sorrow and Joy," dated February 17, 1894, is an appreciative account of a recital by his violin teacher, Herr Markus. The last entry in Wertheimer's journal is a poem entitled "Music: Scorn," dated March 22, 1894. It begins with a lyrical description of hearing some beautiful, sad music at dusk; the music then becomes harsh. Later, "A dreadful, ugly claw-like hand grabs my heart and twists and turns it scornfully"; he plunges "out into grass and forest," dashing outside to "gulp fresh air," but the relentless tune continues to call "sneeringly" after him.

There are, then, hints in Max's youthful journal of the passions that were to remain features of his interests and personality throughout his life. As an early adolescent, Max Wertheimer apparently preferred to concentrate on ideas more than on personal events, an orientation that in some ways also characterized his adult life.

Notes

1. Much of the information on Max Wertheimer's heritage comes from a family tree in his handwriting that was found among his unpublished papers. Other documentation (in MW-CU) includes a sheet providing "birth, wedding, and death data for the family of Alexander Wertheimer, purveyor of wines and spirits in Kamenitz a/L," signed by Isaak Kopperl, director of the Israelitic Register, and dated at Kamenitz on November 26, 1872, with an official documentary stamp and seal.
2. Obituary of Alexander Wertheimer, *Prager Tagblatt*, July 1880, MW-NY.
3. Gustav Reimann, Wilhelm Wertheimer obituary, based on a September 11, 1930, oration, *Czechoslovakian Newsletter of the Independent Order of Oddfellows in the Czechoslovakian Republic* 3 (1930, September 25): 1-4. In Czech (MW - CU); English translation by Gustav Svehla. Most of the material on Wilhelm in these and the next few pages comes from this funeral oration.
4. While all Slavic peoples at an early time had a common tongue, the Czechs gradually evolved a separate language that absorbed many German, English, and Latin words. The spoken language varied in dialect in Bohemia, Moravia, Silesia, and Slovakia.
5. Mitchell G. Ash, *The emergence of Gestalt theory: Experimental psychology in Germany, 1890-1920* (Unpublished Doctoral Dissertation at the Department of History, Cambridge, MA: Harvard University, 1982), p. 246. All the documentation from Ash's work in this book is in the form of citations from Ash's dissertation rather than from the later book, based in part on that dissertation: M.G. Ash's *Gestalt psychology in German culture, 1890-1967: Holism and the quest for objectivity.* Cambridge, England: Cambridge University Press, 1995.
6. In 1897, Rudolph Dirks created a comic strip in the United States, for the newspapers of William Randolph Hearst, based on "Max und Moritz" and called the "Katzenjammer Kids" (literally the "cat-yowling kids"), which became the first fully developed cartoon strip in the United States, featuring speech balloons and a continuous cast of characters, with the action divided into small, regular panels. After establishing residence in the United States in 1933, Wertheimer and his family enjoyed reading about the exploits of the "Katzenjammer Kids."
7. Ronald W. Clark (1971). *Einstein: The life and times.* New York: New World Publishing, p. 28.
8. Interview with Anni Hornbostel, July 15, 1974, MW-CU.
9. It is notable that Max, although younger than his brother, received his journal (MW-CU) more than a year before Walter was given a diary; Max's parents might have noticed his penchant for writing before Walter's. Further, the title "Poesy" may help explain why more of Max's than Walter's diary entries were in the form of poems.
10. The reference may well be to the Grand Inquisitor in Dostoyevsky's *The Brothers Karamazov.* Eleven-year-old Max may already have read the massive novel or, perhaps more likely, heard it discussed by others.

3

Formal Education, 1898-1904

I really believe there are very few who have been
so little harmed by learning as yourself.
—Albert Einstein to Max Wertheimer
(quoted by Fritz Stern, 1987)

In accord with his father's wish to have him eventually assume the directorship of the business school, Walter Wertheimer pursued an education in business practice rather than the liberal arts. Max, instead, embarked upon a classical education that would prepare him for university studies and a career in a profession. Although he was already drawn to music and philosophy, he began to study law after graduation from the Prague Gymnasium. From an early age, Max had shown evidence of a strong sense of morality and an idealistic belief in justice. Yet Max's legal studies may have been as pragmatic as Walter's business training; whether his reading for the law was his own decision or was due to the urging of his parents is not known. Wilhelm may not only have been instrumental in persuading his younger son to study law—perhaps a profession of use to the Wertheimer business school—but may also have urged Max to stay in Prague.

During the time that he was a student in Prague, Max taught for a year at his father's business school, perhaps employing Wilhelm's method of personalized instruction and possibly also applying knowledge he was gaining at the university.[1] While he was working for his father during this period, one of Max's later students reported, Max and a friend developed a calculating machine to automate painstaking computations efficiently and accurately; Max soon realized that the success of this machine might mean unemployment for many workers such as accountants, so he abandoned plans for marketing the device.[2]

Law and Philosophy at the University of Prague

Following his satisfactory completion of the comprehensive "matura" exams at the Prague Gymnasium, then, Max matriculated at the Faculty of

Law of the Royal Imperial German Karl Ferdinand University of Prague (K. K. Deutsche Karl-Ferdinand-Universität zu Prag, or Universita Karlova) in October, 1898. The University of Prague was the earliest university established in central Europe, having been founded in 1348 by Emperor Charles IV; in 1882 it was divided into two separate institutions, one Czech and one German, each called Charles-Ferdinand or Charles University.

The central European university system in which Wertheimer was educated, and in which he was to spend most of the rest of his years, was intended to promote learning in the broadest sense. Specialized preparation for academic and professional careers was complemented by and based on a foundation of classic liberal education. This philosophy of learning focused on "Wissenschaft," a concept roughly equivalent to the English "science" or, more literally, "knowledge." Indeed the neo-Kantian philosopher Wilhelm Windelband observed that the classic Greek word "philosophia" means the same as the German word "Wissenschaft"; and the term "philosophy," in turn, is derived from Greek roots that mean "love of wisdom." [3] Students had substantial discretion in decisions about what to study. They could attend lectures on a wide array of subjects by many different professors—whose status was, in that system, exalted. Students could also work with *Dozents* (roughly equivalent to the American rank of "instructor"), who gave lectures or tutorials. Social life among students was lively, libatious, and often irreverent. Current political and social issues were often the focus of heated, emotional discussions. In the intelligentsia of that time, a quarrel was "supposed to be only about some matter of scholarship. In a learned dispute one may become very angry indeed without violating decorum. [One] may even in an extremely heated argument grow so angry that [one] foams at the mouth." [4] The student group considered itself an elite (indeed, only a very small proportion of the college-age population actually attended a university), and was viewed by the wider community with a combination of admiration, contempt, and a slight dash of fear.

In this volatile academic system, a prominent historian has observed, German intellectuals were attacking their own era, dominated by professors and specialists, as an age of decline. [5] A reverence for Rembrandt and Goethe was complemented by a mistrust of natural science and its "false objectivity." Cultural creativity was considered to occur more at the periphery than at the center of academia, and many scholars were demanding a departure from traditional "objectivity" to a more "subjective" quality in scholarly and artistic enterprises.

The intellectual foundation of late nineteenth-century German academia was largely the legacy of Immanuel Kant, the Königsberg philosopher who had developed a critical philosophy that attempted to determine the nature and limits of human knowledge as well as the inherent categories of consciousness and their ethical and esthetic consequences. According to one historian of psychology, Kant's philosophy had significant implications for the study of natural and social sciences in German academia:

> The gulf between [humans] and nature created by Kant's critical idealism...induced Kant's disciples to distinguish between cultural or historical sciences (*Kultur-* or *Geisteswissenschaften*) on one hand, and natural sciences (*Naturwissenschaften*) on the other. Accordingly, natural sciences seek general laws; they are *nomothetic.* The historical or cultural sciences, however, are concerned with the individual case, for every human action is an unrepeatable and unique phenomenon. Cultural sciences study these unique idiophenomena; thus they are *idiographic.*[6]

This distinction between the nomothetic and the idiographic orientation was not made by Kant, but later by Wilhelm Windelband. However, Kant himself had distinguished between "natural" sciences (which concern laws) and "historical" sciences (which cannot develop laws in the same way as natural sciences). At any rate, the nomothetic-idiographic contrast remained salient in intellectual circles for more than a century. At the time that Wertheimer began his university studies, the nomothetic approach was being questioned, even derided, and the idiographic one idealized. In this intellectual climate in academia, then, Wertheimer began his studies of law.

Max enrolled in traditional courses on the classic canons of Roman, German, and Austrian law. He took classes that explored the history and philosophy of law, the requirements of due process, as well as contracts and the history of civil rights. But like his fellow students, Wertheimer did not limit his studies to a single field; rather, he enrolled in a rich array of elective courses on art, history, and music. Among the courses he took early in his college career were ones in philosophy and the relatively new discipline of psychology. These courses apparently exerted a more profound impact on his evolving thought than did his work in law or his teaching duties at his father's academy. The ideas raised in his psychology and philosophy classes may well have been more stimulating to Wertheimer than the relatively static information on precedents in his classes on Austrian law. At any rate, he increasingly devoted his studies to philosophy, the broadest and most general of all the disciplines.

German philosophy at the turn of the century was, as mentioned earlier, engaged in controversy about the alleged narrowness and limitations of the methods of the natural sciences. Calling a scholarly work "wissenschaftlich" simply implied praise for its sound scholarship. But characterizing a work as "naturwissenschaftlich" (akin to the natural sciences) or, worse yet, "positivistisch" (positivistic), was typically a deprecating remark. "German academics," noted Fritz Ringer, a distinguished European historian, "preferred to find in learning itself a dimension of philosophical contemplation and wisdom," a "dimension" which was cut short if the scholar remained limited to the methods of the natural sciences. "There was universal agreement among German scholars after 1898 that the modern German idea of the university and of learning was irrevocably tied to its intellectual origins in German Idealism and neohumanism."[7] The German ideal of higher education, as embodied in the pre-eminent German institution of higher learning, the University of Berlin, was tied to the neo-Kantian thought of such intellectual giants as the philologist Karl Wilhelm von Humboldt, the theologian Friedrich Ernst Daniel Schleiermacher, and the philosopher Johann Gottlieb Fichte, and was dedicated to learning for its own sake. Practicality was not only a secondary consideration, but was even disdained as superficial and not really scholarly.

Philosophy was the overarching, all-encompassing discipline. But a subpart of it was beginning to develop a new identity of its own. At the time of Wertheimer's birth, psychology was gradually becoming a distinguishable branch of the *Geisteswissenschaften* or humanistic disciplines in the German university system. Perhaps more than any other scholar, Wilhelm Wundt helped usher in this identity and the institutionalization of psychology; following appointments at the University of Heidelberg and the University of Zürich, Wundt directed the influential psychological institute at the University of Leipzig, then the largest German-language university. Wundt was politically astute; he realized that

> present holders of academic chairs in philosophy did not welcome psychologists as competitors for their professorships.... Wundt urged the establishment of special chairs in philosophy for psychologists beside the existing professorships of philosophy. He did not support those of his fellow psychologists who sought refuge in separate chairs and examinations for their discipline. He tried to overcome the philosophers' objections to his own proposals, because he wished to preserve the working connection between philosophy and psychology. He was certainly not inclined to exaggerate the similarities between psychology and the natural sciences.[8]

When Wundt founded the journal *Philosophische Studien* in 1881, he intended it as an outlet for work in experimental psychology. However, as noted in Mitchell Ash's doctoral dissertation at Harvard University on the history of science, Wundt's journal

> also contained numerous essays in the theory of knowledge, philosophy of science and other philosophical fields, mostly by Wundt himself. He later remarked that the title [of the *Philosophische Studien*] was meant to be "a call to battle," but the aim of this struggle was to show only "that this new psychology had the claim to be a subdiscipline (*Teilgebiet*) of philosophy."[9]

In his voluminous books and journal articles, Wundt challenged the humanistic disciplines with his new empirical approach to the cognitive processes in his research on reaction time, psychophysics and the physiology of the sense organs.

Wertheimer apparently immersed himself in the full breadth of philosophical studies implied by *Wissenschaft*. He extensively studied the neo-Kantian idealism of the time as well as ethics, epistemology, logic, and metaphysics. He also became acquainted with Wundt's experimental psychology as well as Wundt's enormous work on *Völkerpsychologie* (sociocultural psychology).

After five semesters of law school, he apparently could not tear himself away from psychology and philosophy. While maintaining an abiding interest in law and the concept of justice until the end of his life, Wertheimer seems to have been repelled by the idea that the mechanics of litigation bind the duty of the attorney to the client, rather than to the unconditional pursuit of truth and justice. In the summer semester of 1901, Max formally left the Faculty of Law for the Philosophical Faculty at Charles University in Prague. Even though he was close to completing studies for a law degree, he abandoned his legal coursework and concentrated on the study of philosophy, with an emphasis on psychology. For the rest of Wertheimer's life, the important questions were those asked in philosophy—and repeatedly his answers to such questions had a significant holistic component.

The Tradition of Holism and the Uneasiness about Reductionism

The "geisteswissenschaftliche" perspective of the philosophy of the time frequently had a holistic tinge. But the holistic theme was not limited to formal academic philosophical writings. Holism was a major focus for every kind of intellectual endeavor in the decades just before and after 1900, and had been a significant part of the culture of even the smaller Jewish towns (the "*shtetlach*") of eastern Europe, from which Wertheimer's earlier ancestors had come. This holistic heritage doubtless also colored everyday life in the home and subculture in which Max grew up.

The European *shtetl* of the nineteenth and early twentieth centuries, indeed the fabric of Wertheimer's Jewish social and cultural heritage, was dedicated not only to learning and understanding for their own sake, but also to the idea of the "organic whole." An analysis of this heritage argues that the Jewish intelligentsia were devoted to "Penetration, scholarship, imagination, memory, logic, wit, subtlety—all [were] called into play for solving a [problem]. The ideal solution [was]...an original synthesis that has never before been offered."[10] According to this orientation, the universe

> is a complex whole, but basically it is characterized by order, reason and purpose. Everything has its place, its cause, its functions. Apparent contradictions, inconsistencies and irregularities fall into place as complements

rather than incongruities. It is not a static universe, for all its parts are interdependent and interacting. The dynamic whole extends in time as well as in space, so that the apparent inconsistencies of the present may be interpreted as parts of a long-term process building toward ultimate integration. In such a universe, behavior—human or divine—must also be rooted in reason, order and purpose. Any act must be rational, motivated and directed toward some goal.... The basic assumptions of order, reason and purpose are apparent in any area and at any level of *shtetl* life, as are the principles and mechanisms which express them: the complementary character, the interdependence, the interaction of the parts which make up any whole. Each element is seen always as a part of the whole to which it belongs, yet each is able to retain a vivid and functioning individuality. Any element is incomplete in isolation, and though some parts are considered superior to others, each is regarded as equally indispensable. The separate parts in turn are not unbroken unities. Each element contains components which interact.... The structure and process [of the community and its functions] can best be described by borrowing from physics the concept of a "field of forces." The relationships between the parts—their contrast, interdependence and interaction—create a field of reciprocally functioning forces resulting in a dynamic equilibrium.[11]

This passage has remarkable similarities with the kinds of principles and concerns that characterized the later, mature versions of Gestalt theory. There can be no doubt that this heritage must have contributed to the eventual emergence of formal Gestalt theory.

To the *shtetl*'s way of thinking, the role of an individual in a group is governed by "the structure and mechanism of complementary parts, interdependent, interacting, equally indispensable.... Like the family, the community is a close-knit unit, made up of interacting parts."[12] Wertheimer's cultural heritage, then, included a *Weltanschauung* in which the idea of a dynamic whole, with interdependent, interacting parts, characterized everything from the family to the community to ethics to the structure of the universe itself. Combined with a belief in the rationality of humanity, these convictions are at the core of what was to become Wertheimer's later Gestalt theory.

While he was still a child, Wertheimer's reading of Spinoza probably also offered a glimpse of the power of holism as a theme in philosophy. In Spinoza's view, holism unites nature and the universe. Spinoza viewed even the mind and the body not as separate constituents of the human being, but rather as distinct *aspects* of nature.

Beginning with his first semester at the University, even while he was concentrating on law, Max heard lectures by one of the greatest champions of holism of the time, and one of Charles University's most distinguished faculty members, Christian von Ehrenfels. Born in the town of Rodaun near Vienna on June 20, 1859, Ehrenfels had earned his doctoral degree in philosophy under the radical philosopher Franz Brentano at the University of

Vienna in 1885. Ehrenfels taught at the University of Graz from 1885 to 1888 and then returned to the University of Vienna as Brentano's colleague in 1889. He became a faculty member at the University of Prague in 1896, only two years before Wertheimer's enrollment.

During the fall semester of 1898, Max heard lectures from Ehrenfels on psychology and esthetics, and was apparently sufficiently captivated to enroll in more of Ehrenfels's courses in subsequent semesters. Ehrenfels drew on Franz Brentano's philosophy as support for his own thought concerning the necessity of holism in psychology. In his 1874 book, *Psychology from an Empirical Standpoint* (*Psychologie vom empirischen Standpunkt*), Brentano argued against the assumptions of scientific reductionism found in Wilhelm Wundt's book *Physiologische Psychologie,* published the previous year. Although he acknowledged that Wundt's work in the study of mental events was a pioneering effort, Brentano objected to Wundt's construction of consciousness following a Newtonian model of elements held together by mechanical processes. Wundt taught that any psychic whole is composed of associated elements, and that the task of psychology is to analyze any mental whole into its constituent parts and to study how these parts are connected. True, Wundt claimed that the mind is capable of performing a "creative synthesis" on any psychic whole, which may transform that whole in such a way that its constituent elements are hardly recognizable in the whole. Yet the basic orientation still was that the whole is fundamentally nothing more than the sum of its parts; the elements are contained within the whole.[13] Neither Brentano nor Ehrenfels could accept this view. Like Brentano, Ehrenfels offered an approach that radically revised the Wundtian model of consciousness.

In 1890, Ehrenfels published a significant and influential paper, "On Gestalt Qualities," that challenged the mechanism and elementism which characterized the philosophy and psychology of his time. He observed that an esthetic appreciation of a melody is *not* derived from hearing single isolated tones, but rather from hearing a succession of tones combined in a meaningful way.[14] Ehrenfels recognized that, for many wholes, the whole is somehow *more* than the sum of its parts; furthermore, a melody can be transposed into a different scale and thus contain an entirely different set of notes as elements, yet be easily recognizable as still the same melody. Comparably, a square will be recognized as a square even if its size or its color is changed completely, and there is no commonality among the "elements" of different instances of squares. He argued that the melody as a whole possesses a quality or *Gestaltqualität* independent of the qualities of the separate notes; and a square has the quality of "squareness" over and above the particular "elements" of which it happens to be composed. Hence Ehrenfels proposed that many wholes possess an element over and above the elements present in a strictly Wundtian sense: a Gestalt or form quality such as squareness or a particular melodic character.

Ehrenfels's position was one among several holistic European philosophies near the turn of the century that exemplified a marked discontent with a simplistic, reductionistic, mechanical scientism. Ehrenfels's lectures on holism introduced Wertheimer to fascinating questions, but Wertheimer was later to come up with radically different answers to them.

During that first semester Max also heard lectures on philosophy from another younger philosopher, Anton Marty, who probably also had a lasting influence on Wertheimer's intellectual development. Like Ehrenfels, Marty joined the philosophical faculty at Charles University in 1896, and he too, like Ehrenfels, appreciated Brentano. Before arriving in Prague, Marty had published on the psychology and philosophy of language and logic. [15] He may well have helped Wertheimer become more steeped in concerns about logic and holism, and in psycholinguistic issues, that were salient in late nineteenth-century German intellectual circles.

Documents preserved in the family archives (MW-CU) show that following his inaugural semester, Wertheimer took additional philosophy courses, including one on metaphysics with Marty and both a seminar on philosophy and a course on the theory of evolution with Ehrenfels. During the next three semesters, Max continued to study law, but also took further philosophy courses not only with Marty and Ehrenfels but with two other philosophers as well: Emil Arleth (who was at the time working on the writings of Plato and Aristotle) and Julius Schultz (who had just published a book on the psychology of axioms). He also attended courses by an educator, Otto Philipp Gustav Willmann (a prolific devotee of the renowned psychologist and educational theorist Johann Friedrich Herbart), and by two physiologists, Johannes Gad (a researcher in the mainstream of medical physiology at the time) and Arnold Pick (a pioneer in neuropathology).

After his switch to philosophy, Max maintained ties with a friend in the law school, Julius Klein, who apparently shared Wertheimer's fascination with criminology. While at Charles University, Wertheimer and Klein performed some groundbreaking experimental work on lie detection with the consultation of the distinguished criminologist Hans Gustav Adolf Gross.

Tatbestandsdiagnostik:
The Psychological Diagnosis of Criminal Guilt

Hans Gross published a major work, *Criminal Psychology*, in 1898 and an encyclopedia of criminology in 1901, and was editor of the *Archiv für Kriminalanthropologie und Kriminalistik* (the *Archives of Criminal Anthropology and Criminology*). In his *Criminal Psychology*, Gross systematically examined how experimental psychology could be applied to the determination of the facts in criminal cases. With Gross's encouragement, Julius Klein began an experiment at the Prague Physiological Institute in the spring of 1902, with Wertheimer initially a participant and later the lead author in its publication.[16] Wertheimer and Klein studied *Tatbestandsdiagnostik*, the diagnosis of a person's knowledge about a particular event, set of facts, or special circumstances. The two applied this diagnostic process to criminology, focusing on the determination of guilt using a controlled word-association technique. The *Tatbestandsdiagnostik* method was part of a general interest in testimony that was prevalent in both jurisprudence and experimental psychology at the turn of the century. William Stern had studied this area in his seminal book *On the Psychology of Testimony*, and a new journal had recently been founded on the same topic. Any "lie detecting" technique that could help determine whether a suspect had participated in a crime was of substantial interest and had significant potential applied value.

In a typical Wertheimer-Klein *Tatbestandsdiagnostik* experiment, a participant was given a series of specific details about a criminal case. In one scenario, the crime involved the theft of a golden chalice engraved with the ornate monogram "MR" from the third shelf of a large, heavy cabinet of oak and glass in the dining room of a "Mr. Q." The "evidence" included the fact that a crowbar had been used to shatter the lock on the cabinet door.

Wertheimer and Klein proposed that the methods of experimental psychology could pinpoint the culprit. The logic of this exercise was that only the true thief is privy to specific details, while other suspects are aware that they have been arrested in connection with a robbery, but have little detailed knowledge about the case. Presumably, the true thief should react differently from an innocent suspect when presented with such details as the specific letters "MR," a chalice made of gold, the facts that it sat on the third shelf and that the cabinet it came from was in Mr. Q's dining room, and so on. Even if the culprit tried to conceal any trace of guilt during interrogation, that person's behavior should be incriminating if the interrogation is conducted appropriately. The researchers methodically attempted to evoke expressions of guilt that would be unmistakable even if the participant attempted to obstruct the results. According to Wertheimer and Klein,

> The concrete combination of objects, persons, etc. which occur together in a particular set of events evokes a particular combination of mental phenomena (through perception and inner experience). The coexistence in space and time, the common external characteristic of belonging to a particular event, connects the individual elemental contents, and brings with it certain judgments and feelings.

This conception was quite consistent with the prevailing Wundtian analysis of mental contents into elements, judgments, and feelings.

Wertheimer and Klein contrasted their proposed methods with typical courtroom procedures for ascertaining the facts. Most reliance was placed upon sworn testimony of witnesses and experts; if there were contradictions, attempts were made to assess the credibility of the mutually inconsistent witnesses. Wertheimer and Klein argued that

> Sometimes attention is also paid to psychophysiological phenomena, such as becoming pale, shuddering, or explosions of affect. There is no scientific basis for such interpretations, no basis founded in methodological observations. There are only occasional striking individual cases of this kind and several sources of error must be considered.

The authors outlined the dangers of excessive reliance on testimony and emotional reactions, and expressed their intent to replace this content-based method with an empirical psychological one based on "diagnosis of the psychological consequences of the facts of a case in a person, by use of experimental methods." In keeping with Wertheimer's later uncompromising advocacy of natural science, the authors explicitly proclaimed their support for objective scientific methods rather than "apriori assumptions or unmethodological experience." Wertheimer and Klein warned against testimonial methods that unduly bias or influence the will of the witnesses, and claimed that their methods provide a solution:

> Experimental results cannot be influenced by the will in the same way as the content of testimony in the conventional mode of interrogation. With some methods it will probably be possible to exclude the disturbing influences of the will completely; with others, the possibility of influence is minimal. Many methods can be expected to yield results which will be particularly characteristic of attempts to deceive, and therefore especially useful.

A significant portion of the Wertheimer and Klein paper is devoted to a series of association methods designed to discriminate among the cases of a confessing guilty suspect (Type "A"), an innocent suspect (Type "B"), and a lying guilty suspect (Type "L"), with primary attention to the last category. The authors proposed presenting to the suspect a set of several kinds of "contents": a) irrelevant contents with no relation whatever to the experimental "complex"; b) contents more or less related to the experimental complex; and c) contents central to the experimental complex. The reactions of the truthful, innocent person should be quite different from the reactions of the lying, guilty person, since the former has no way of associating critical items with the complex, while the latter does.

They recommended that the suspect be given as "contents" a series of stimulus words successively, on each occasion measuring reaction time with a telegraph key, and recording repetitions of the stimulus word as well as checking whether the first word that comes to mind makes sense or not. Types of association and reaction times could then be compared across the several kinds of stimulus words.

In their discussion of this procedure, Wertheimer and Klein predicted the likely results with all three kinds of individuals. "B" (or innocent) people are unlikely to give reactions that relate to the experimental complex, since they have not experienced it, but "A" and "L" people (guilty suspects who confess and lie respectively) can be expected to give such associations, and also to react differently to the three types of stimuli, which are presented in a mixed order. "L" individuals should have a hard time avoiding some betrayal of their knowledge of the experimental complex, irrespective of their intentions. The authors, anticipating such betrayal, indicated various strategies that an "L" person might use to avoid detection. Variations in the stimulus series were also proposed, such as longer or shorter exposure times, calling out certain items more loudly than others, or use of new stimulus words derived from the suspect's responses when they are clearly associated with the experimental complex.

Wertheimer and Klein suggested numerous variations and procedures such as reproduction of appropriate drawings or projected visual patterns and measurement of attention and physiological reactions. The authors argued that many standard laboratory techniques in experimental psychology at the time were potentially applicable to the problems of discriminating the "L" type from the "B" type, and suggested a variety of both laboratory and "practical" studies to assess the feasibility of these methods.

The published article concluded with reports of a few informal preliminary experiments, the results of which were intended only as illustrations of the methods. Detailed accounts of different crimes were presented to several participants; the experimenter, who did not know whether a given participant was an "A" type, a "B" type, or an "L" type with respect to a given account, had the task of deciding which participant was privy to which of the accounts. The experimenter succeeded in identifying the participants correctly using the technique of controlled association (participants were instructed to respond with the first word that came to mind when a stimulus word was presented, such as "table–chair," "green–leaf"). "B" and "L" reactions were more frequently irrelevant to the experimental complex than were "A" reactions; and the frequency of associations relevant to the complex was greatest in "A" and lowest in "L" participants. Additionally, "L" participants gave the most nonsensical associations to stimuli related to the complex. Reproduction experiments were comparably promising, with "L" participants frequently recounting details that gave away their status without their awareness.

The forty-one page article was published in Gross's journal in 1904 with the long title, "Psychologische *Tatbestandsdiagnostik*: Ideen zu psychologisch-experimentellen Methoden zum Zwecke der Feststellung der Anteilnahme eines Menschen an einem Tatbestande" ("Psychological Diagnosis of Specific Knowledge: Ideas about Psychological Experimental

Methods for the Purpose of Determining the Participation of a Person in a Set of Events").

Philosophy and Psychology at the University of Berlin

By 1902, Max Wertheimer had received a thorough elementary education and a classical secondary education in Prague, and had attended the university in his home town for eight semesters, five in law and three in philosophy. He had lived comfortably at home with his family for all of his twenty-two years. But now, a year and a half after he abandoned preparation for the legal profession, he also left his native city. It was common at that time for students to study successively at several different universities, and Max was no exception. On October 27, 1902, he matriculated as a student of philosophy at the Friedrich-Wilhelms University of Berlin, then the most prestigious university in the German-speaking world. Why Wertheimer chose that university at that particular stage in his studies is no longer explicitly known, but the reputation of its philosophical—and psychological—faculty may well have played a role.

At the time, the German academic elite were located both in small university towns (such as Heidelberg, Göttingen, Würzburg, and Bonn) and in the larger cities (Hamburg, Berlin, Munich, and others). Yet, according to the intellectual historian H. Stuart Hughes, "the greatest intellectual center was undoubtedly Berlin, both as the national capital and as the seat of the university which, although less than a century old, was usually conceded to rank first in cultural eminence."[17] Formally the capital of the kingdom of Prussia, Berlin was the capital of the German Empire from 1871 to 1918 and, although the city's universities, schools, art galleries, orchestras, and theatres were newer than those in Munich, Dresden, and Leipzig, they were challenging their older rivals for preeminence. The university was founded in 1810 under the reign of Frederick William III of Prussia, and was christened the Royal Frederick William University of Berlin as a tribute.

This institution, and indeed the city of Berlin, provided a heady setting for Wertheimer. There was constant intellectual, artistic, and political ferment; new things were being tried out in the theater, in architecture, in literature and in patterns of social interaction. Berlin held a leading place in sculpture and painting. The Royal Library, one of the largest in the world, was affiliated with the university, and the royal museums and the national gallery were filled with art treasures from throughout the world. Berlin's musical conservatory and philharmonic orchestra were very popular, and beginning to rival those of Leipzig. Berlin dominated German theater in the production of both modern German drama and German translations of plays by Molière, Shakespeare, Ibsen, and George Bernard Shaw. The Berlin of the first decades of the twentieth century was the birthplace of beautiful and grotesque new ideas, as well as both short-lived and long-lasting intellectual movements. In music, art, literature, journalism, science, philosophy—in every aspect of cultural endeavor, the old was being questioned and the new was being vigorously explored there. True, this orientation carried with it an inherent cultural instability—but the instability itself contributed to the conviction that, once freed from the restrictions of arbitrary tradition, the potentials of the human spirit were almost without limit. For Max the benefits of this fascinating environment included not only his academic experiences, but also a network of like-minded friends and colleagues.

Early during his stay in Berlin, Wertheimer became acquainted with Lisbeth Stern. Married to a successful Berlin industrialist, Georg Stern, Lisbeth enjoyed a lively social circle of young intellectuals; she developed a coterie of university students whom she invited to liven up the evenings in her home. Max Wertheimer was soon brought into this vivacious enclave, and eventually even moved into the Stern household. Lisbeth was highly talented in the arts, a skill shared with her sister Käthe Kollwitz, who was to become a world-renowned graphic artist and sculptor. Wertheimer's evenings at the Stern house were filled with music, parlor games, and lively discussions of art, theater, music, education, philosophy, and politics. Some of Wertheimer's late afternoons or evenings were also spent at the theater, at a concert, or at a lecture. On warm summer days the Sterns often hosted picnics and outings in the copious parklands of Berlin.

The four Stern daughters, born between 1896 and 1906, grew to regard Max warmly and matter-of-factly as a member of the family. When not studying or conversing with the adults, Wertheimer would design imaginative thought games that entertained and stimulated the girls. They in turn gave Max the nickname of "Maggusch," which in time became "Maggi"; by association with the brand name of a dehydrated soup concentrate, the family sometimes also fondly called him *Suppenwürfel* ("Bouillon Cube"). He found a second home with the Stern family, a large, warm, and close-knit household.

How significant a role Wertheimer played in the Stern household is indicated by the fact that the diary of Lisbeth's sister, Käthe Kollwitz, contains 74 citations to Wertheimer in its index.[18] She wrote admiringly of his contributions to the family's musical events; she liked his piano and violin playing, and his singing voice, especially when rendering Christmas songs, often in duet with Georg. He was a masterful player at charades, and thought up endless activities to amuse the Stern daughters. Kollwitz also wrote about Wertheimer's concerns about other members of the extended family and the impact of everyday problems (as well as political catastrophes such as the first World War) on their lives. One entry, from May, 1917, is about an exhibit that Kollwitz had prepared, and documents Kollwitz's pride in Wertheimer's reaction to it. Apparently Wertheimer had sketched out some informal notes about it that Kollwitz found sufficiently moving to enter in her diary—even though they were so cryptic as to be almost incoherent. The entry[19] in the diary reads:

> Haven't written anything for more than a month. Had lots to do with the exhibition and was somewhat exhausted.... After Easter I worked concentratedly on the exhibition. On Sunday the 15th with [my husband] Karl I had the house opened in the afternoon by the doorkeeper and showed Karl the exhibition.
> Monday the 16th it opened.
> The success of the exhibition was huge. I heard from many sides that it makes a unified and strong impression. The review by Stahl, the introduction by Deri, Lise's [Lisbeth's] review in the *Monatsheften* [*Monthly Review*], the written comment by Wertheimer. The way they expressed themselves almost made me think that the last two would not have let themselves be so affected by it if it had been a totally unfamiliar artist. Combined with it is their love for me. Because I can hardly believe that I should have been *so* capable of communicating myself or—more than that—of having been the direct mediator between people and anything of which they were unaware, transcendental, primal. Suggestion probably contributes. If my works *continue* to have this effect—even after decades—then I really have achieved a great deal. Then people will have been enriched through me. Then I have contributed to the rebuilding. Which of course everybody does, but it would have been my lot to a higher degree than for many others.
> Was there with my dear mother one afternoon. She looked at everything, rejoiced and admired how much I had done, and grasped very quickly the emotional content of an engraving. But she found the large self-portrait of 1916 bad: 'You shouldn't have exhibited that one....'
> I am copying here what Wertheimer wrote about my work.

Wertheimer used such terms as "powerful force," "innermost," "serious intimacy," "unutterably enhanced purity," "an essence that is imbued throughout with power," and "something that is most intimate about life" in his lavish praise of the works in the exhibition: nine short paragraphs that Kollwitz included verbatim in her diary.

The Sterns' youngest daughter, Maria, published an autobiography in 1994;[20] she became a professional dancer and film star in both Germany and the United States. Her book also contains many references to Wertheimer. An informative passage occurs on page 29:

> People have friends and they have relatives. I learned that early. But there are friends who are much more related to one than true relatives. Such a one was Max Wertheimer. He simply belonged to us. I will try to describe him completely objectively. He was Privatdozent, then Professor, of psychology at Berlin University. I don't know how he came to us. Maybe Mother got acquainted with him through the lectures she attended, and one day simply brought him home. He fell deeply in love with her. His love, which he showed

openly and never concealed, impressed my mother and doubtless troubled her as well. There were no secrets, no lies. Neither of them could have tolerated that. At some time there must have been a discussion with my father. Then Max avoided our house. But not for long. He came back, accepted by the knowing as a friend, and beloved by us sisters. I never visited him in his often-changing residences, which probably were furnished rooms or *pensions*. He always deposited his empty trunks in our attic. One day when he had to travel to his father in Prague, he asked our maid to bring them to him from the attic. In one of the trunks lay a tiny blue embroidered linen peasant shirt from the Engadine, and an envelope that contained a thin red-blond lock of hair. The peasant shirt had once been mine. And the lock of hair too came from me. After Max had gone away, I asked my mother whether Max might not perhaps be my father. 'No, that's impossible,' she said, amused. 'Go look in the mirror.' I did so. My mirror image corroborated her words. I look unmistakably like my father.

Max's days in Berlin were spent listening and talking, doing research and reading, immersed in music and in absorbing philosophical, political, and psychological issues. [21] At the University of Berlin, as in Prague, Wertheimer gave his intellectual interests wide rein. He enrolled in courses on musicology, economics, pedagogy, literature, and philosophy. He studied with the esteemed panpsychist Friedrich Paulsen, who lectured on Kant's philosophy and whose monumental book *Immanuel Kant: His Life and Doctrine* had been published in 1882. [22] Wertheimer also heard lectures on the history of philosophy by the philosopher Wilhelm Dilthey, who had received his doctorate at the University of Berlin in 1864 and had returned there in 1882, succeeding to the chair vacated by the death of the psychologist Rudolf Hermann Lotze. Dilthey was wrestling at the time with the idea of structure and especially holism in his epistemological analysis of the *Geisteswissenschaften* (the "mental" or "human studies") and in his attempt to develop a philosophy of history. In his lectures and writings, Dilthey argued that philosophers could address a "philosophy of life" in a meaningful way because life is not a conglomeration of disconnected facts, but is interpreted and organized through cognitive categories. The holistic spirit that Wertheimer had encountered at Prague was not foreign to the faculty at the University of Berlin.

Like Dilthey, a number of scholars at Berlin rejected atomistic models of psychology. According to the intellectual historian Fritz Ringer,

> In psychology as in every other discipline, many German scholars of the 1890s…assumed the role of revolutionary innovators; intent upon the much-discussed need for an intellectual and spiritual renaissance, they found it hard to be fair to their predecessors. They chose to make war upon associationist and positivist tendencies in psychology and they began by exaggerating the importance—and the intellectual simplicity—of these tendencies in the "old psychology"…. They described the period between 1850 and 1890 as one of decadence and sterility. Experimental psychology, the argument ran, was born

in the shadow of the natural sciences. It was therefore infected with "naturalistic" errors from the very beginning. It took physiology as its model; it made the associationist scheme an epitome of all mental processes; it adopted the theory of parallelism. It tried to "dissolve" the notion of an integral soul, and it favored an atomistic and mechanistic analysis of consciousness in terms of primitive and logically isolated units of sensation. It was Lockean, simple-mindedly empirical and positivistic.[23]

This criticism of the Wundtian model was shared by the founder and director of the Psychological Institute at the University of Berlin, Carl Stumpf, a disciple of Lotze and Brentano. Stumpf's interests ranged from space and auditory perception, phenomenology, and psychophysics to the emerging discipline of musicology. Under Stumpf's direction, Wertheimer studied psychophysics, experimental psychology, logic, and philosophy, and Max was again exposed to the deficiencies of the elementarism advocated by Wundt at Leipzig. Ash described the situation:

> Wertheimer must have admired Stumpf's protest against the rigid and artificial reductionism that survived from the previous century. Stumpf's work was an appealing blend of philosophy and psychology, without neglecting the value of holism. Like Ehrenfels, Stumpf shared Brentano's zeal to engage in the study of mental events with something other than piecemeal reductionism, and to scrutinize psychology from an empirical standpoint—but one that takes into account the rich, dynamic and holistic quality of human nature. Although he was more than a decade younger than Wundt, Stumpf had managed to establish Berlin as a dominant competitor to Leipzig as the leader in European psychology. By the time of Wertheimer's arrival in Berlin, Wundt and Stumpf had already engaged in a bitter clash in print over the perception of musical tones. Stumpf argued that a trained musician could make more valid judgments about tone than a trained but non-musical introspectionist [a Wundtian analyst of consciousness]. Like Ehrenfels, Stumpf used music to demonstrate the need to study the holistic quality of mental phenomena. In particular, Stumpf was interested in the impressions of consonance and dissonance which are generated by different pitch combinations. He also remarked upon the fact that these impressions are not ordinary summations of the sensations caused by different notes. Rather, the quality of dissonance appears to be attached to a given note constellation as a whole.[24]

Music was consistently central in Stumpf's psychology: he had written a two-volume work (1883, 1890) on *Tonpsychologie* (*Tone Psychology*) and founded in 1898 a journal devoted to musicology, *Beiträge zur Akustik und Musikwissenschaft* (*Contributions to Acoustics and Musicology*). He was also amassing what would become one of the world's leading ethnomusicological collections, the basis of the Phonogrammarchiv or Phonograph Archives at the Psychological Institute in Berlin. Founded in 1900, the Phonograph Archives consisted of a large assembly of wax Edison cylinders containing recordings of music from a wide variety of cultures throughout the world.

Although Stumpf initially absorbed the cost of the archives himself, in time this work was supported by several foundations:

> From 1904 to 1909 came regular grants from the Virchow Foundation of the Prussian Academy of Sciences and additional private gifts. The Ministry provided single appropriations of 3,600 marks in 1910..., and the newly-established Albert Samson Foundation of the Academy of Sciences guaranteed an annual grant of 5,000 marks in 1912, subsequently raised to 7,000 marks. The activity required to raise these sums and the amounts themselves—more than the institute's budget—testify effectively to the degree of Stumpf's commitment to this enterprise.[25]

Wertheimer regularly visited the Phonogram Archives, listening to recordings from the large collection of tribal music. The relatively new technology offered concrete data on foreign cultures captured in real time on hard wax cylinders. Wertheimer wondered about how to conceptualize this music and how to characterize its complex beauty. While spending time with this diverse accumulation of recordings, Max became close friends with Erich Moritz von Hornbostel, an assistant whom Stumpf had hand-picked to oversee the activities of the archives. Some three years Wertheimer's senior, von Hornbostel had successfully completed requirements for his doctorate in chemistry in 1900 and had been instrumental in the founding of the Phonograph Archives in the same year.

Wertheimer and von Hornbostel shared the prevalent ambivalence about analytical, reductionist methodology which on the one hand was producing impressive breakthroughs in science and technology, but on the other appeared to be inadequate for understanding life's richer experiences in areas such as art, religion, literature, and music. Frequently discussed at the time was the nature of a symphony orchestra. It appeared to be inconsistent with the atomistic, mechanistic assumptions in so much of contemporary science and philosophy. A symphony is obviously something more than—and fundamentally different from—the sum of the sounds produced independently by the individual players. In fact, it is the hallmark of a good conductor to blend the parts played by the individual instruments into a totality that transcends the sounds made by the individual players. Such observations, and the work of Ehrenfels, Stumpf, Dilthey, and others, doubtless contributed to Wertheimer's growing if still inchoate sense of a need for a robust new system of psychology that does justice to the rich holistic aspects of experience that seemed to be lost in the then-current atomistic ways of thought.

Wertheimer was intrigued by the scientific method and by the psychological knowledge it had been able to generate. He concentrated intensely on experimental psychology and reportedly read through all twenty-five then-extant volumes of the *Zeitschrift für Psychologie*, the principal

German journal of psychology. He enrolled in experimental psychology work with Friedrich Schumann, an assistant of Stumpf's, who supervised Wertheimer on studies of visual space perception in the laboratory. Having received his doctorate in physics in 1885, Schumann had studied and collaborated with Georg Elias Müller, who worked chiefly in psychophysics, verbal learning, and memory, at the University of Göttingen. Shortly before Max's arrival in Berlin, Schumann had begun collecting empirical evidence on space perception which was inconsistent with the reductionism claiming that a whole is no more than the sum of its elements.[26] In a major article published in the *Zeitschrift für Psychologie*, Schumann reported a number of compelling findings about human perception, many of which could be viewed as anticipations of what was later to become Gestalt theory: attention may either join the parts of a figure into a whole or else emphasize a part so that the perception of the whole becomes secondary; incomplete figures tend to be perceived as complete; nearness among the components makes for the grouping of visual components into larger wholes; vertical symmetry also improves grouping; ambiguous figures tend to be seen as "good" or "interesting" figures; properties of figures, such as grouping and organization, have their origin in both central factors (how the brain works) and stimulus factors (the physical display being observed).[27] Although he made no attempt to derive a specific theoretical viewpoint from these findings, Schumann's studies demonstrated the possibility of opposing simple reductionism with solid, meaningful experimental data.

With his training in physics and his skill in experimentation, Schumann provided a model for Max in his campaign against reductionism. The holism offered by Ehrenfels and Stumpf, joined with the experimental rigor of Schumann, was a promising antidote for what Wertheimer by then doubtless considered the anemic account of human experience offered by reductionism.

Psychology at the University of Würzburg

Max's time in Berlin was filled with studies at Stumpf's Psychological Institute and with interactions in the Stern household. Stumpf was known, though, to permit only a few students from his seminars to obtain the doctorate.[28] According to one count, "Between 1900 and 1915 four theoretical and ten experimental dissertations on psychological topics were completed under Stumpf's direction; the total for Leipzig in the same period was fifty-nine."[29] Perhaps apprehension about his fate with Stumpf contributed to Wertheimer's decision to transfer to the University of Würzburg, where he began work on his doctoral degree in philosophy with Oswald Külpe. Max may also have concluded that his dissertation plans would be more compatible with research in Külpe's laboratory than with the primarily perceptual work then going on in Stumpf's Berlin Institute. Külpe and his students were doing exciting experimental studies of core phenomena in thinking and cognition, related to Wertheimer and Klein's early work on *Tatbestandsdiagnostik.*[30]

Max enrolled at Würzburg during the summer semester of 1904. He took a room next door to Karl Marbe, more than a decade older than Wertheimer, who was then on the faculty in Külpe's department as a *Privatdozent* (lecturer or instructor). As in his earlier studies, Wertheimer continued to pursue his broader liberal education with courses in the history of literature, the history of education, and ancient world views, as well as continuing his studies in philosophy and psychology. Max took a course on logic with Marbe, a seminar entitled "Philosophical Society," and a course on Talbot's law (a psychophysical principle concerning the brightness of a flickering light). Wertheimer also heard Oswald Külpe lecture on esthetics and on experimental psychology.

Külpe's laboratory at Würzburg did turn out to be an appropriate place for Max to continue the research he had begun with Julius Klein. Külpe had worked in history, philosophy, and experimental psychology at Leipzig, Berlin, Göttingen, and Dorpat. Before he went to Würzburg in 1894, Külpe had spent eight years at Leipzig, including five years of service as Wundt's assistant. Promoted to *ausserordentlicher* Professor (roughly comparable to the American "associate professor") at Leipzig after the publication in 1893 of a major general treatise on psychology, he was offered and accepted the full professorship at Würzburg the next year.[31] Külpe had already been at Würzburg for a decade by the time Max arrived there, and by 1904 the Würzburg school was widely recognized as a major research center in the psychology of thought. Although Külpe's interests were broad (he was also a fine musician, and devoted much attention during his career to esthetics and the psychology of music), most of his work and that of his students was concentrated on problems similar to those Wertheimer and Klein had started to work on at the Prague Physiological Institute in 1902.[32]

In 1901, A. Mayer and J. Orth at Würzburg published on the qualitative nature of associations, and Marbe, then a *Dozent* there, published a report of experimental work on judgment. These two papers, both strictly empirical and utilizing objective laboratory techniques, helped clarify the focus of the Würzburg school's position on thought: much of genuine thinking is "imageless," in that while the generation of judgments is a conscious task involving much conscious content,

> introspection reveals "no psychological conditions of the judgment." That is to say, the judgments come, they are usually right (in Marbe's task of judging which of two lifted weights is the heavier), and the [judges do] not know how they got into [their] mind.[33]

Külpe, Mayer, Orth, and Marbe suspected that the laws of logic may not be the laws of thought after all; the mind may be "an irrational associative train of mental contents that nevertheless reaches a rational conclusion."[34] In a 1903 paper, Orth suggested that the thinking mind may be occupied by "conscious attitudes, obscure, intangible, unanalyzable, indescribable contents that are neither sensations nor ideas."[35]

Another of Külpe's students, Henry Jackson Watt, also made a significant contribution with a study in which participants formed partially-constrained associations, such as producing a superordinate for a subordinate (a more inclusive category for a given term, such as "bird" for "robin" or "animal" for "bird") or a part for a whole. Watt used precise measurement of reaction times; asked the observer to report on only one of four periods in the judgment process (the preparatory period, the appearance of the stimulus word, the search for the reaction word, or the occurrence of the reaction word), thereby using the "method of fractionation"; and stressed the task itself, the *Aufgabe*.

This last emphasis was to persist in the experimental psychology of thinking: a proper orientation to the task, or "set" ("*Einstellung*") is sufficient to produce a thought process which runs along smoothly—and in a sense unconsciously—once the stimulus is presented, until a proper response is found; acceptance of the task results in an automatic sequence of thinking that leads to the solution with very little introspective content. The *Aufgabe* or task establishes in the participant "an Einstellung or 'set'; and the participant, in accepting an *Aufgabe*," becomes "eingestellt."[36]

During the same year, Narziss Kaspar Ach was doing further research along the same lines at Würzburg, work he had previously started with Müller at Göttingen. He preferred the term "determining tendency" (*determinierende Tendenz* or *Bewusstseinslage*) to Watt's *Aufgabe* or "task." The determining tendency—essentially the same thing as the *Einstellung*—strengthens certain associative linkages over others:

> Thus, given a 5 with a 2 below it, printed on paper, the most usual associates would be 7, 3 and 10. If, however, the [participant] has been instructed to add, one association will be strengthened so that 7 will almost invariably occur; or if the task has been to subtract, then another association is reinforced and becomes the strongest.[37]

It was clear from the work of the Würzburg psychologists by early 1904 that not all thought is sensory or in images, and that one of thinking's most salient characteristics is its directedness.

Külpe and his students were devoting their energies to experimental studies of what Wundt had called the higher mental processes—a field that Wundt did not consider appropriate for study by experimental means. But Külpe and his "Würzburg school" were nevertheless deeply and successfully immersed in unraveling the nature of genuine thought processes, particularly the directedness of thought. In describing Külpe's approach, the intellectual historian Ringer observed:

He and his followers were less interested in sensation and memory than in active problem solving. They felt the difficulty of describing this process in terms of elementary association, and they stressed the importance of volitional and attitudinal states in the achievement of intellectual tasks. While Wundt, Ebbinghaus, Stumpf, and Müller represented the status quo in German psychology around 1890, Külpe's thought psychology could be chronologically and logically grouped with the new movements of the period between 1890 and 1932, which were generally described as reactions against the condition of German psychology before 1890.[38]

Thus, under Külpe's guidance, Orth, Marbe, Watt, and Ach were doing research at Würzburg on problems that were similar to the ones Max Wertheimer and Julius Klein proposed for study in their 1904 paper. And Watt was studying associations using almost exactly the same kinds of procedures—albeit for somewhat different goals—that Wertheimer and Klein had explored as techniques for diagnosis of guilt, or *Tatbestandsdiagnostik*. So Külpe's Würzburg laboratory was indeed congenial to the kind of work Max wanted to do for his doctoral dissertation, and he doubtless found colleagues there with whom he could talk about his area of interest and who shared his excitement about this work.

Tatbestandsdiagnostik Revisited: Wertheimer's Doctoral Research

Max continued attending classes at the University of Würzburg for several months after he completed his Ph.D. dissertation. But the culmination of his formal education was the preparation and defense of that dissertation,[39] a direct outgrowth of the work he had begun several years earlier with Klein at the University of Prague. In his doctoral thesis, Wertheimer reported findings from a combination of introspective and objective techniques, providing introspective protocols (participants' personal reports of their thought processes) and statistical analyses of the objective results from an extensive series of related experiments. As in his 1904 article with Klein, the basic strategy was to induce an experimental "complex" by providing certain participants with a detailed account of the facts of a case. He then used various "diagnostic" techniques to discern if a given participant had been privy to the details of a particular case.

Wertheimer began his dissertation with the distinction between what he and Klein had called "B" and "L" cases, witnesses who knew little, if anything, about the facts of a case as contrasted with those who were trying to conceal their intimate knowledge about the crime. Wertheimer wondered, "Isn't it possible to find experimental methods which determine whether or not someone knows about a particular *Tatbestand*?" He generated, for example, the following scenario for use with such methods:

There has been a break-in at a lovely villa. The criminal is being sought. The police record provides the *Tatbestand*—the facts of the case, the specific details of the location and nature of the deed as far as they can be determined (items broken into or stolen, damaged locks, broken window panes, any objects that were left behind, etc.). Suspects, such as all vagabonds in the region, are arrested. All of them deny that they know anything about the crime. At the initial hearing they are not informed about the details of the deed; only general questions are posed to them. All of them claim never to have set foot in any villas of the region, or at least not in this particular villa. Now it becomes a matter of determining which (if any) of the vagabonds, in spite of his denials, happens to know details of the break-in: the inside of the villa, the particular circumstances of the deed that the police have been able to determine. Psychological experiments will be used in an effort to decide this question.

The spatio-temporal and other features of the real circumstances of the deed normally and necessarily produce a series of psychic consequences in the perpetrator: certain associations among individual mental images, and connections with feelings and judgments. If, for example, he uses a crowbar to open a cupboard with glass doors and steal a small silver bowl from it, this engenders in him a very specific set of associations.... Thus a series of psychic consequences is uniquely and saliently present in the perpetrator, but not in an innocent suspect, because he does not know the details of the deed. Are there methods for determining such differences *objectively*? And, considering especially that the perpetrator is strongly motivated to hide the fact, can use of such methods also reveal these differences against the will of the perpetrator?

The cited study [the Wertheimer-Klein 1904 paper] suggests a series of methods whose feasibility for these (and other) purposes is to be assessed here. One of the basic principles behind these methods is this: if one shows a critical object to the perpetrator, or if one names a critical circumstance, it should as a rule set up characteristic psychic consequences. It already happens occasionally that a perpetrator unintentionally reveals himself under such circumstances. It could also happen that an innocent suspect might react similarly; for him too, of course, presentation of a corpse, for example, or the naming of a standard tool for breaking and entering has particular psychic consequences. But it is possible to get around this difficulty. First of all, one can be careful not to use such generally critical objects, but rather to employ ones which do *not* appear critical to the innocent suspect. Further, an obvious technique is to show not only the relevant object, because the sheer fact of exhibiting it at the hearing makes the item "critical," but rather a series of objects, among which *only a few* are distinctive for the person who knows the concrete details of the deed, while the majority are irrelevant. In its simplest form, such a series might consist, for example, of valuable objects of all kinds that might be relevant, such as silver spoons, a gold watch, an iron strong-box, and a gold bracelet, with the addition of the critical silver bowl. It is still more useful to include a variety of critical items among a number of totally irrelevant ones....

Thus a methodical presentation of "stimuli" would in principle consist of a mixed series of irrelevant and critical contents...to determine whether the guilty party (or an individual who knows the detailed facts of the case) exhibits characteristic reactions to the critical stimuli. These reactions could be of several kinds.... The indicated methods are to be examined to determine whether one can ascertain the presence of such consequences objectively and with sufficient certainty.... Little systematic investigation has yet been made in this field.

He indicated that the present experiments used only one of the many suggestions made in the Wertheimer-Klein paper: "the participant is asked to react with any word at all to each of a series of stimuli: words either spoken out loud to, or shown to, the participant."

The seven participants in Wertheimer's study included Külpe and Henry Jackson Watt as well as various other members of the Würzburg school. Three different cases were used to induce the "complexes" intended to be diagnosed by the word-association method, each case containing much detail about the events in question, including a detailed floor plan of the location where the events supposedly transpired. Different participants were made familiar with one or another of the stories, so that each could serve as a control for other participants, since all of the stimuli (some relevant to one or another story, some entirely irrelevant) were presented to each participant. Chapter 3 (by far the longest in the dissertation) presents the results in full, classified as participants' introspective reports and general objective results, and provides a lengthy statistical evaluation. Wertheimer prepared twenty-five tables of results and five frequency distributions which revealed an almost complete lack of overlap in reaction times to the same stimulus as a function of whether the stimulus was presented as a "B" case (to a participant who had not been exposed to the story for which the stimulus was "critical") or an "L" case (to a participant who had been exposed to the relevant story, but was trying to hide the fact). "L" case reaction times were, almost without exception, longer. Likewise, for individual participants, reaction time to "critical" stimuli averaged much longer than that to neutral or irrelevant stimuli. Qualitative results were also most encouraging, in that "L" cases produced more bizarre responses, or, paradoxically, produced irrelevant associations which nevertheless could be shown to be clearly related to the story or *Tatbestand* in question. For good measure, a few "A" cases (knowing the relevant story, but not trying to hide that fact) were also run; results with them thoroughly fit with Wertheimer's expectations.

One among a series of variations on the basic experiment reflects the holistic concern of the intellectual ambience, and may foreshadow Wertheimer's later absorption in the nature and structure of genuine wholes:

A further task is dividing complexes into their components. Is the integral unity of a complex a necessary condition for the occurrence of the effects we have demonstrated? Integral unity coalesces and congeals a larger group of associations. In order to approach this question more closely, some preliminary experiments were also performed with word pairs and individual words.

The result of these additional experiments, involving only related pairs of words or a list of unrelated words, was painstakingly presented in further tables. The basic finding was unaffected: the participants' behavior (their reaction times and the qualitative characteristics of their associations) still revealed which set of words was familiar to them. So integration of the "elements" of the material on which word association tests are performed is not necessary for the success of the technique. Wertheimer concluded the dissertation with a thirteen-page theoretical summary, plus some hopeful notes concerning the potential practical use of these methods.

The Ph.D. degree was officially conferred on Max Wertheimer *summa cum laude* on December 21, 1904, for his dissertation, "Experimental Investigations of *Tatbestandsdiagnostik* [Diagnosis of the facts of a case]" and other work at the Philosophical Faculty of the Royal Bavarian University of Würzburg. His doctoral degree was granted "in the major field of the philosophical disciplines and in the minor fields of general pedagogy and *Germanistik* (German philology)." The title page of the dissertation announced, "Experimental investigations of *Tatbestandsdiagnostik*, submitted on November 30, 1904, to the high Faculty of Philosophy of the Royal Bavarian Julius Maximilian University of Würzburg in partial fulfillment of the requirements for the doctoral degree by Max Wertheimer of Prague, with 3 figures and 5 graphs in the text." On the obverse of the title page was a notice to the effect that a sequel to this work, "Tatbestandsdiagnostische Reproduktionsversuche" ("Reproduction Experiments on Diagnosis of Tatbestand") was to be published in the *Archives of Criminal Anthropology and Criminology*, which was edited by Wertheimer's mentor in criminology, Hans Gross. This sequel duly appeared, as discussed in Chapter 4.

Immediately after his stay at Würzburg from July 1904 to Easter 1905, Wertheimer continued to work on developing an academic reputation as an expert in legal psychology. This was a time when the application of techniques in experimental psychology to law—such as the psychology of testimony—was of major psychological concern. He had already published two articles on the determination of legal guilt, and had a third article in press on the same subject, to appear in 1906. Wertheimer's identification as an expert in this area was important enough to him that it soon led him to challenge another young scholar, Carl Gustav Jung, on the priority of the use of the word-association technique in legal psychology.

Notes

1. Wertheimer mentions this one-year teaching appointment at the business school, about which no other information has been located, in a curriculum vitae

prepared in 1919 or early 1920 (MW-CU). Although he remained in Prague, Max may have moved into one of the apartments in the same building that housed the Wertheimer Business School. See Abraham S. Luchins and Edith H. Luchins (1982). An introduction to the origins of Wertheimer's Gestalt Psychologie. *Gestalt Theory*, 4, 145-171, p. 152.

2. Erwin Levy, personal communication to Michael Wertheimer, 1991.

3. Another translation of *Wissenschaft* might be "discipline" (in the sense of an organized body of information), or even "scholarship" in general.

4. Fritz K. Ringer (1969). *The decline of the German mandarins: The German academic community, 1890-1933*. Cambridge, MA: Harvard University Press, pp. 102-103.

5. H. Stuart Hughes (1958). *Consciousness and society: The reorientation of European social thought 1890-1930*. New York: Knopf, pp. 44-45.

6. Benjamin B. Wolman (1968). Immanuel Kant and his impact on psychology. In B. B. Wolman (ed.), *Historical roots of contemporary psychology*, pp. 229-247. New York: Harper and Row, p. 242.

7. Ringer, p. 103.

8. Ringer, p. 315.

9. Mitchell G. Ash (1982). *The emergence of Gestalt theory: Experimental psychology in Germany, 1890-1920*. Unpublished doctoral dissertation at the Department of History, Cambridge, MA: Harvard University, p. 18.

10. Mark Zborowski and Elizabeth Herzog (1952). *Life is with people: The Jewish little-town of eastern Europe*. New York: International Universities Press, p. 409.

11. Zborowski and Herzog, pp. 409-412.

12. Zborowski and Herzog, p. 422.

13. One might argue that the "creative synthesis" performed by Wundt's process of "apperception" in effect specifies a major problem to which later Gestalt theory became the solution: how is it that we have organized, coherent experiences rather than mere awareness of unstructured sums of elementary impressions?

14. According to Ehrenfels's son, Christian von Ehrenfels may first have become aware of the meaning of structure when, as a youth, he studied counterpoint with the illustrious Austrian composer Josef Anton Bruckner. See Luchins and Luchins, 1982, pp. 153*f*.

15. Wilhelm Wundt had already devoted considerable attention to the psychology of language, and a journal on psycholinguistics, edited by Lazarus and Steinthal, was published in Berlin for a number of years, beginning as early as the 1860s.

16. Max Wertheimer and Julius Klein (1904). Psychologische *Tatbestandsdiagnostik* [Psychological diagnosis of specific knowledge]. *Archiv für Kriminalanthropologie und Kriminalistik*, 15, 72-113.

17. Hughes, p. 47.

18. Käthe Kollwitz (1989). *Die Tagebücher* [*The diaries*]. Edited by Käthe's granddaughter, Jutta Bohnke-Kollwitz. Berlin: Siedler Verlag.

19. Kollwitz, pp. 314-316.

20. Maria Matray (1994). *Die Jüngste von vier Schwestern: Mein Tanz durch das Jahrhundert* [*The youngest of four sisters: My dance through the century*]. Munich: Langen Müller. The authors thank Professor Viktor Sarris of the University of Frankfurt for bringing this work to their attention.

21. Wertheimer was also in Berlin at the time of the investigation of "Kluger Hans," the equine savant who purportedly could comprehend and compute mathematical values; one source suggests that Wertheimer may have participated in the examination of this case, although there is no compelling evidence to support this assertion. See Luchins and Luchins, 1982, p. 157; Ringer, 1969, pp. 313-314.

22. Wertheimer was well acquainted with Kantian teachings before the time of his Berlin education, but Friedrich Paulsen, given his extensive scholarly knowledge, doubtless encouraged Max to explore Kantian ideas further.

23. Ringer, pp. 313-314.

24. Ash, p. 44.

25. Ash, pp. 44-45.

26. Edwin G. Boring (1950). *A history of experimental psychology* (2nd ed.). New York: Appleton-Century-Crofts, pp. 401-407.

27. Wolfgang Metzger, Friedrich Schumann, ein Nachruf [Friedrich Schumann, an obituary]. *Zeitschrift für Psychologie* 148 (1940): 118.

28. Kurt Lewin, Carl Stumpf, *Psychological Review* 44 (1937): p. 189.

29. Ash, p. 60.

30. Stumpf had some training in law before shifting to philosophy and psychology (as was also true of Wertheimer's studies), and in 1903 and 1904 offered a seminar on "Legal Psychology" at the University of Berlin. See Ash, p. 57. Given Stumpf's interest in legal psychology, it seems reasonable to conclude that he might have approved of Wertheimer's *Tatbestandsdiagnostik* research. To some degree, however, personality differences may have disturbed their professional relationship. In a 1931 address to the Eastern Psychological Association, Kurt Koffka declared that a "difference of personalities" existed between Wertheimer and Stumpf. See Kurt Koffka, "Beginnings of Gestalt Theory" (1931, April 8). Unpublished manuscript, Archives of the History of American Psychology, University of Akron, Akron, OH.

31. Boring, pp. 401-407.

32. Indeed, one variation in the Wertheimer and Klein article that restricted the associations to subordinate, superordinate, or coordinate concepts was very similar to situations that were being intensively studied by Oswald Külpe and his students at Würzburg at the time. Although Wertheimer and Klein did refer to Preyer, Stern, Gross, Binet, Lehmann, Müller, Lombroso, and others in the published report of their studies, the authors somewhat surprisingly never explicitly cited the work of Külpe or his colleagues.

33. Boring, p. 403.

34. Boring, p. 403.

35. Boring, p. 403.

36. Boring, pp. 403-404.

37. Boring, p. 405.

38. Ringer, p. 314.

39. Max Wertheimer (1905). Experimentelle Untersuchungen zur *Tatbestandsdiagnostik* [Experimental investigations of diagnosis of the facts of a case]. *Archiv für die gesamte Psychologie*, 6, 59-131. Also published as a separate as an "Inaugural-Dissertation" by Engelmann in Leipzig, 1905, pp. 1-70.

4

Years of Incubation, 1905-1910

Max Wertheimer felt uneasy about a certain human barrenness in the scientific psychology of his time. The questions are empty, the answers are dead. The conceptual scheme, the logical tools do not fit, and thus violence is done to many marvels.
—Kurt Riezler (1944)

Max Wertheimer had achieved a fine educational record but, beyond the effort to develop his image as an expert on psychology and law, his professional life did not exhibit a clear trajectory during the period immediately following his dissertation work. He was doubtless fascinated by the philosophical and psychological issues raised by the European intelligentsia during the first decade of the twentieth century. Immersed in the general ambient dissatisfaction with the intellectual status quo, he was one of the intelligentsia arguing for change. Like several of his mentors, he was convinced that something essential was missing in contemporary philosophy and psychology.

Wertheimer spent much time with the Stern family and their artistic and cultured circle when he was in Berlin. He occasionally visited his parents in Prague, where little had changed. Wilhelm was still following his demanding schedule as teacher, school administrator, and leader of IOOF activities. Rosa continued to run the household and participate in amateur musical performances. Walter, still in poor health, was teaching at the Wertheimer Business School, and prepared and published several instructional textbooks for business education.

Max had successfully earned his Ph.D., but knew that he must come up with yet another dissertation if he were to have a chance for a career in academia. A doctoral degree was a necessary preliminary credential, but did not qualify one to teach at the university level without a second major scholarly work, the *Habilitationsschrift*, or habilitation thesis. One could achieve the right to lecture at a university or academy only after becoming "habilitiert" there, that is, producing an approved habilitation thesis and then delivering an acceptable public lecture. But even a lecturer could keep only a portion of the student fees; habilitation as a *Privatdozent* (roughly, a lecturer or instructor) did not assure an adequate income. For a fortunate few, the next step after *Dozent* was *ausserordentlicher* Professor, literally "extraordinary professor," approximately (but only approximately) corresponding to the American rank of assistant or associate professor. While it assured at least a modest salary, this rank did not carry tenure, and one served at the pleasure of the full professor and the university authorities. Only a very few became *ordentlicher Professor*, or *Ordinarius*, a position more powerful than that of the American full professor, indeed close to department chair. There was a single *ordentlicher Professor* in each department who essentially served as its head, making every departmental decision—typically in an autocratic rather than a democratic manner. This rank did carry lifetime tenure, a substantial salary, high social status, and many financial and social perquisites.

Further Publications on *Tatbestandsdiagnostik*

Perhaps in an attempt to find a promising topic for his habilitation thesis, Wertheimer continued to do research in the diagnosis of knowledge about the facts of a case, the area of both his first publication and his doctoral dissertation. Wertheimer reported in small print at the end of his dissertation that the *Tatbestandsdiagnostik* method had already generated further research:

> A second part of this work, reproduction experiments in the diagnosis of *Tatbestand*, reports on a number of experiments performed on B and L persons using the method of reproduction, which showed strong effects of knowledge of a complex.

Wertheimer did publish a paper on reproduction experiments in the *Archiv für Kriminalanthropologie und Kriminalistik* in 1906 with the title, "Über die Assoziationsmethoden (On the association methods)."[1] In this article Wertheimer did not employ the word-association test used for his dissertation, but instead required participants to retell a story after some of them had been given a *Tatbestand* to induce a "complex." Some details of the story to be retold had nothing whatever to do with the complex, some were vaguely similar, and some exactly reproduced certain elements in the complex. After the participants retold the story, they answered a thorough set of questions designed to address details in both the story and the complex. In responding to them, participants tried to conceal their knowledge of the complex. According to Wertheimer, in every case, the results made it clearly evident which people (L) knew the original complex and which (B) did not; this occurred primarily a.) through characteristic errors appropriate to the material in the original complex (falsifications, intrusions from the original complex), and b.) through the relationship of irrelevant errors to such "complex errors" (i.e., errors which can be seen as having been induced by the original complex). Errors occurred mostly with the complete conviction that they were not errors at all.

Thus, although not aware of it, participants were likely to add elements related to the complex to their retelling of the story. Wertheimer's results corroborated those of William Stern, a student of Hermann Ebbinghaus who in 1903 had published an article on *Aussage* or testimony. In a typical *Aussage* experiment, participants were presented with pictures and asked to recall their details under different forms of questioning and suggestive contexts, with the general finding that such conditions produce inaccurate recollection of details.[2]

Wertheimer also used association tests in conjunction with his reproduction experiments. In one of many variations, the original complex was not read by or told to, but actually experienced by, the participant in a real situation that was acted out. In every case, as in the previous studies, the objective data made it possible to identify the "culprit" by determining who did or did not have knowledge of the "complex": the facts of the case in question.

A fourth work came out in this series, coauthored by Wertheimer and Otto Lipmann, who had reviewed Wertheimer and Klein's 1904 article in the *Zeitschrift für Psychologie und Neurologie* (*Journal of Psychology and Neurology*). This 1907 article[3] was titled "Tatbestandsdiagnostische Kombinationsversuche" or "Combination experiments on the diagnosis of knowledge about the facts of a case" and was published in the first volume (pp. 119-128) of the new *Zeitschrift für angewandte Psychologie* (*Journal of Applied Psychology*). Wertheimer and Lipmann summarized the central issue:

> The problem of *Tatbestandsdiagnostik* is to find and try out methods under which someone for whom a set of facts of a case are lively (i.e., who has experienced it with affective emphasis or intense interest, or knows it well) will react in a measurably different way than someone who does not know it. The methods should be so constructed that they can lead to the desired result even if the participants try not to reveal the fact that they have knowledge of the event in question.

This article added still further techniques, beyond those contained in the 1906 paper on reproduction experiments and his collaborative paper with Klein. Wertheimer and Lipmann examined *Tatbestandsdiagnostik* by means of a "fill-in-the-blanks" method proposed by Ebbinghaus in 1897. As in the earlier reproduction experiments, the general design involved inducing a "complex" in some participants by describing the facts of a case in detail. Then another, similar story was told to each participant, who was then asked to fill in the blanks in a partially truncated version of the second story. As documented in detailed and lengthy tables, Wertheimer and Lipmann found that this method too was successful:

> "L" people make many intrusions from the original complex, and there are other signs that give their knowledge away even if they try to conceal it, and even without their being aware that they are inadvertently revealing their knowledge of the facts of the case.

By this time, three years after his doctorate, Wertheimer's career was thoroughly identified with his work on *Tatbestandsdiagnostik*. But he and his colleagues were by no means the only published authors in this area. Carl Gustav Jung had also gained recognition for his work on using the word-association technique in the psychological diagnosis of guilt. Only a few years older than Wertheimer, Jung was a rising young psychiatrist who was also exploring the method of association for detecting emotional complexes. Jung used the word-association technique in a 1904 habilitation thesis which he submitted to permit him to teach at Zürich.[4] His publications on the method for detecting complexes appeared in the *Zeitschrift für Psychologie und Neurologie* in 1904 and 1905 in a series of five articles, the first few of which were co-authored with Franz Riklin, a Swiss psychiatrist who had married Jung's cousin. The 1904 paper by Jung and Riklin reported studies, instigated by their mentor, the Swiss psychiatrist Eugen Bleuler, of the associations of control participants in order to provide a baseline for the study of pathological associations by psychiatric patients.[5] Jung's 1905 article on the reaction-time ratio in association experiments (the ratio of average reaction times to critical words compared with those to neutral words) was published both in the *Zeitschrift für Psychologie und Neurologie* and separately as his habilitation thesis.[6]

Thus both Jung and Wertheimer began publishing in the field in 1904. There was also some overlap in the journals where their articles appeared: both had papers on the method in the *Archiv für Kriminalanthropologie und Kriminalistik* and in the *Zeitschrift für angewandte Psychologie*. In a November 1905 article in the *Zentralblatt für Nervenheilkunde und Psychiatrie*, Jung accused Wertheimer and Klein of inexcusably failing to credit Jung and Riklin for preceding them in proposing the use of associative techniques for the diagnosis of complexes. Jung recognized that the eminent British scientist Francis Galton had pioneered the word-association test and that Wilhelm Wundt had used it in his laboratory at Leipzig.[7] But as for more recent publications, Jung claimed that Wertheimer and Klein should have displayed more respect "for the workers who had preceded them" and should have "cited the source out of which they created their seemingly original ideas."[8]

Wertheimer's rebuttal appeared in the 1906 volume of the *Archiv für die gesamte Psychologie* under the title, "Zur *Tatbestandsdiagnostik*: Eine Feststellung" ("On the diagnosis of the facts of a case: A confirmation"). At issue was credit for priority in the use of associative methods for the diagnosis of complexes—a set of techniques that have been linked primarily with the name of Jung ever since.[9] Wertheimer's note was far from conciliatory, and emphasized the dates of Jung's April 19 and his own April 7 publication in 1904 to establish his claim to priority. He also pointed out:

> The particular section of Jung and Riklin's studies (I.2) in which the authors begin discussing things that have to do [specifically] with *Tatbestandsdiagnostik* appeared in September 1904, thus more than a quarter of a year after our work. Jung's habilitation work came out more than a year later than our work, and moreover later than my further "Experimental investigations of *Tatbestandsdiagnostik*" (*Archiv für die gesamte Psychologie*, vol. VI), which was submitted as a dissertation in Würzburg on November 30, 1904.

To further strengthen his claim to priority, Wertheimer noted that he and Klein conducted research as early as May 1902:

> our work was already known in a number of places for a considerable period before the appearance of our article. From October 1903 on we carried out related experiments at various institutes, and indeed more than 3½ years ago J. Klein already performed (with me as a participant) individual experiments of this kind at the Prague Physiological Institute, including, at the time, correlated observation of concomitant physiological phenomena.

The young psychologist and the freshly habilitated psychiatrist did not mince words in their indignant claims to priority and equally indignant rebuttals. The vituperation of their exchanges in print may have been due to both men feeling attacked at the core of their professional identities: at stake was the foundation on which each of them was trying to build what was to become a successful career. This work was important to their respective self-images, and neither appeared able to tolerate having his efforts belittled. The time was apparently ripe for applying such associative techniques to the diagnosis of "complexes," whether induced by psychopathology or resulting from participation in or knowledge about a criminal act.

While Jung may have been the one who started the quarrel, he also tried to end it. A handwritten October 10, 1906, letter to Wertheimer (MW-NY), bearing the printed letterhead of "C. G. Jung M.D., Privatdozent in psychiatry at the University of Zurich," reads:

> Most honored doctor, please accept my best thanks for your kindness in sending me your reprints, which I had already read earlier with great interest. I

deeply regret that you do not have reprints of the reproduction experiments. I know about these experiments only from the reviews in Stern's journal. Unfortunately the (so far!) imperfect correspondence between us led to our using the same name for different methods. Perhaps a *modus vivendi* can be found in the future. Coming back to your last letter, I would like to remark that Prof. Gross did not express himself in a way that could be misunderstood; he wrote me the following, word for word, in response to my inquiry concerning priority: "I believe that this matter (Tatbestandsdiag.) is also of great significance for us,—if something comes of it, *Burghölzli* [where Jung had conducted his studies] will for all time be *the birthplace* of the important discovery." It really is impossible to misunderstand this, isn't it? I am still absolutely unable to explain how Prof. Gross came to write such a thing. I have no personal relationship with him whatsoever that could come into question here. He owes me no favors or anything of that kind. With this news I unfortunately fell into it, which could, of course, easily have happened to anyone else. With this clarification let us consider the matter closed. I hope that you will forgive the way I acted. May I ask you, at your convenience, to provide me with the title and exact bibliographic information for your reproduction experiments? With best regards, yours very faithfully, C. G. Jung.

So Jung in effect blamed Hans Gross for the misconception concerning priority—and at the same time declared that his and Wertheimer's methods were different, even though they used the same name. Gross sent Wertheimer an explicit if brief apology dated November 13, 1906 (MW-NY):

Honored Doctor, I am very pleased with the solution, and am very sorry if I am responsible for the misunderstanding. Best wishes for good luck in your further work, and hearty greetings! H. Gross.

Thus both Jung and Gross finally acknowledged the priority of Wertheimer and Klein's published work. It is doubtful whether Wertheimer was fully appeased by this. Nevertheless, Jung kept his word and continued to credit Wertheimer in his later writings; indeed, Jung's mentor Sigmund Freud mentioned the work of Wertheimer and Klein in a June 1906 lecture on "*Tatbestandsdiagnostik* und Psychoanalyse" delivered at a seminar on jurisprudence at the University of Vienna.[10]

During the next decade and a half, Jung engaged in extensive further use of the method, far more than did Wertheimer. The two scholars never did develop a close relationship; a collaborative effort might have been productive, since both Jung and Wertheimer, in their late twenties at the time, were deeply interested in the issue of holism in psychology, although they would pursue it in radically different ways in the course of their mature work. But the two young scholars, both barely launched on their careers, were unable to resolve their differences.[11]

Wertheimer, immersed in his research and writing in the area of *Tatbestandsdiagnostik*, may well have hoped that it might yield a habilitation thesis. But the work was interrupted by a family crisis. His brother Walter had recently married, and his wife was expecting a child. Before the child Waltera (later nicknamed "Walti") was born, her father contracted a severe cold. Walter's lungs, already weakened by the edema that had nearly proved fatal in early childhood, were unable to sustain him further. In 1908, Walter suddenly died. Max immediately traveled to his parents' home in Prague. A draft of a letter from this time to an unidentified friend named Hans was preserved in Wertheimer's papers:

> Dear Hans, this letter is to you and Klein; I have to ask the two of you for a number of favors. My brother is dead and buried. However things may develop here in the future, I am staying with my parents at least for the time being. I therefore sent you a telegram yesterday, asking you to notify relevant people for me about the harmonium [a pedal reed organ that Wertheimer had apparently rented]…and the apartment. I have already sent notice about the apartment, but it is probably necessary to repeat the notice, since it already happened at the end of last month, and the people may be counting on me. The harmonium (I don't even know whether it was ever delivered; it was to have been set up at R̶ü̶s̶t̶o̶w̶'s Ungerer Street 90 and, of course, either of you can use it in any way you like, since the dealer will probably not take it back right away). Perhaps you, Hans, could take it into your apartment for now, or you could let Paul Frankl take it, since I have to pay for the month in any case. And now third: Could you send my things here? This is a difficult chore. It would of course be possible to give the whole task to a mover; but nothing is packed. The books are strewn around open, and my trunk is not packed, but papers and clothes are mixed together loosely. And then there is still the bicycle and the violin and the rest. If you, Hans, or perhaps both of you, are willing to take on all this trouble, please write to me. I wouldn't saddle you with this unpleasant matter if I believed that I could travel away from here for a day.[12]

The handwriting in this letter is larger and more irregular than Wertheimer's mature style, which had evolved to its adult form by about 1900; perhaps his emotions were disturbing his penmanship. The letter makes clear that his apartment (presumably in Berlin) in 1908 was already the clutter of clothes, papers, and books that was to be typical of his home for the rest of his life. The reed organ was also already part of his world. He kept such a harmonium in his home for the remainder of his life in Europe.

Wertheimer's Research on Aphasia and Brain Injury

His skirmish with Jung may have made Wertheimer less eager to base his habilitation thesis on *Tatbestandsdiagnostik* research. Although this work had been productive, he was also developing ideas about a variety of other research topics. Fully subsidized by his father's resources, Wertheimer wandered both geographically and intellectually during the period following his doctoral research.[13] He returned to the Psychological Institutes at Berlin, Würzburg, and Prague as well as studying at Frankfurt and Vienna. During these excursions, he gained experience in psychological, physiological, neurological, and psychiatric settings. He studied at the physiological institute at Prague with Johannes Gad and spent time at neurological institutes and psychiatric clinics in Frankfurt with Ludwig Edinger. His work during this period ranged from psychological experiments, *Völkerpsychologie* (sociocultural psychology), pedagogy, epistemology, and psychopathology to logic, philosophy, and music. Wertheimer worked with Sigmund Exner in Vienna on the perception of apparent movement and became thoroughly familiar with Exner's apparatus and procedures for such experimental studies. By 1907, Wertheimer joined Vienna neurologist Wagner von Jauregg in detailed and extensive research on the psychopathology of language. His interest in this area was also sparked by his work with Arnold Pick, an expert in neuropathology who specialized in language pathology produced by brain injury.

During this time, Wertheimer spent many painstaking hours working with patients who had sustained a brain lesion resulting in aphasia, the partial or total loss of the ability to generate or comprehend words.[14] He developed hundreds of detailed protocols and tests of the linguistic, psychological, and neurological condition of individual aphasic patients. Wertheimer's procedures involved the same general strategy that he had developed for the study of *Tatbestandsdiagnostik*, in generating a specific series of stimuli and questions pertinent to the facts of a particular case. He constructed stimuli that were individually designed to fit the specific symptoms and problems of a particular patient. He adapted the methods of experimental psychology to diagnose precisely a given patient's deficits, occasionally conducting dozens of different experiments on a single person.

Wertheimer asked aphasic patients to identify stimulus materials that in some ways resembled various line figures that were to be used in the later Gestalt theory of his maturity. In a passage that foreshadows his later work, Wertheimer wrote in a marginal notation (MW-NY): "The parts are different: bd MW nu db qp"; he presented such diagrams to aphasic patients, trying to determine whether they could discriminate among the patterns that had the "same" parts but in different arrangements so that, functionally speaking, the parts were "different." Thus the lower-case letters d, b, q and p all consist of a straight vertical line tangent to a circle, but in different configurations. Some of the notes made use of hidden figures as well as letters; he apparently asked patients to try to trace simpler forms embedded in more complex ones—a procedure that Kurt Gottschaldt was to employ in his extensive Gestalt experiments during the 1920s. He also created panels of words and numbers painted in various colors, to determine whether particular patients could quickly and accurately identify the colors and read the words or numbers. One such panel, for example, contained such items as "Mann 692 Haus XII XII Ehe Himmel Morgen Meer," etc.: man, 692, house, the Roman numeral twelve with and without horizontal lines, marriage, heaven, morning, ocean—in red, green, blue, and yellow.

In the course of his studies of neurological patients, Wertheimer took detailed clinical notes on his cases in the form of hundreds of case reports with extensive observations. One of the more thorough is the following description of a male aphasic patient (MW-NY):

> The presenting symptom complex was typical of so-called pure alexia: inability to read; impossible to recognize words (even own name!), with simultaneous relatively intact (at least much better) recognition of individual letters (occasional difficulties and errors in recognition of letters). He can not generally read words that consist of letters which he was able to recognize well individually before or thereafter; what is lacking is not only the verbal image: he doesn't have the faintest idea of the meaning of the presented word; speech, spontaneous writing, understanding of speech intact; intelligence intact; orientation and recognition of persons intact.
>
> Right lateral hemianopsia [blindness]; otherwise, ocular findings good; no peripheral disturbance; occasionally a bit of exophthalamus [protrusion], only affecting the right eye.
>
> A case of stroke; steady course.
>
> Trouble with walking; headaches; occasional vertigo.
>
> General status somewhat vacillating: better, poorer days (often in connection with sleep, evacuation, etc.).
>
> If a word is presented to pat[ient]. for him to read, he clearly makes an effort to read it, but it is completely impossible for him; he sits working at it a long time (5 minutes and 10—more), exerting himself mightily, without succeeding with anything at all—except perhaps with the first letter; meantime he fixates well, and tries to spell it out (usually without success); he is aware of the length of the word, and of whether it is written or printed.
>
> He recognizes the relevant letters [in isolation] much more easily; often quite promptly; sometimes with difficulty and occasional misidentification.
>
> What is missing for him is clearly not only the spoken image; he has no idea whatever of the meaning of the presented word.
>
> The situation appears quite clear:
>
> He can see well (as demonstrated, e.g., by the positive results of the opthalm. investig.); only in reading is a gross disturbance demonstrable. Since only reading is disturbed—and since reading is distinguished from other optical recognition by the (learned) association between optical and acoust[ic].-mot[or]. speech images—it is a case of a disturbance of the associative pathways between the optical and the acoust. mot. centers.

Wertheimer surmised, though, that something more was involved since some recognition of letters was evident. He wondered whether experimental studies might help:

Might it be possible to penetrate further into the nature and operation of this particular disturbance with the help of ad hoc experimental procedures, designed expressly for this purpose? How does the process occur? What is it in the process of reading that is really disturbed? What can specific experimental qualitative analysis reveal about the presenting deficiencies? The process of reading certainly involves a variety of specific skills; where are there difficulties? What does the particular quality of the impossibilities, of the errors, indicate?

Wertheimer also generated methods to test for

the ability to develop visual images. "Imagine a large printed letter F, a capital letter; now add, at the bottom end of the long vertical stroke, a third horizontal line like the one at the top; what letter do you have then?" "M; no, an E; I had thought of the M as turned to the right."..."Imagine a Roman numeral 5; now stand it on its head, and add a small horizontal stroke in the middle." Promptly: "That is an A."

He considered other similar tests, yielding W and M from V, H and N from two parallel vertical lines, NIE ("never") from four vertical lines, and so on.

Wertheimer paid close attention to two specific patients and developed eighty-seven different tests for one of them. Drafts of his theoretical discussion focused on the association of optical with acoustic items, such as association of the appearance of the letter M with the M-sound. His notes contained diagrams such as o ⟶ ac.; o ⊣⊦⟶ ac. (presumably to designate an intact and a destroyed "optical-acoustic connection"), and the following diagram, with presumably intact connections between two optical and two acoustic items on the left, but a damaged system on the right (intact connection from 0_1 to ac_2, damaged between 0_1 and ac_1 and between 0_2 and ac_2, and destroyed or missing between 0_2 and ac_1):

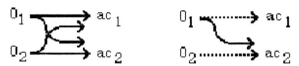

Wertheimer observed that

Both of the cases studied so far are characterized technically by difficulties in the automatic occurrence of acoustic or acoustic-motor content that is normally expected on the basis of customary associative connection.

He planned to test the capacity to determine whether two stimuli are identical or different, an ability he acknowledged was apparently impaired in at least one of the patients. He also examined the existing literature related to his topic and concluded that his ideas were indeed consistent with it, especially a 1907 paper by Giulio Bonvicini and Otto Pötzl "On 'pure word blindness.'"[15]

Wertheimer continued this work for several years, as indicated by records of studies with alexic patients dated as late as March 1912. But his extensive work on aphasic patients never did come fully to fruition. All it yielded by way of publications was a brief 1912 abstract and a short account in a weekly medical newspaper published the following year.[16] Wertheimer ultimately dropped his research on aphasia, like his work on *Tatbestandsdiagnostik*, despite its possibilities as a habilitation topic. In part, this decision may have been based on pragmatic career considerations; as Mitchell Ash pointed out:

> Although leading neurologists and physiologists were evidently willing to let Wertheimer do research in their institutions at his own expense, he lacked the medical degree he would have needed to establish himself in such a setting; and it is not immediately clear whether he would have been able to obtain a position in philosophy with work on such problems.[17]

Philosophical Preoccupations

Wertheimer's early research appears far removed from his later Gestalt theory, although there were already a few faint glimpses of ideas that were to emerge more fully in his later work. While he was working on aphasia, he also studied cultural anthropology, linguistics, musicology, and logic. He was continuing to think about the role of holistic issues in psychology. On page after page of scratch paper he scribbled ideas about holism in *Gabelsberger*, the stylized, personal shorthand that he developed in childhood and used throughout his life. He studied the work of the German philosopher and phenomenologist Edmund Husserl.[18] The holistic issue was a central focus of Husserl's work perhaps because he, like Ehrenfels, Stumpf, and Marty, had studied with Brentano. Husserl's philosophy fervently and vigorously opposed reductionism. In Husserl's phenomenology, a mental event can be understood only as a whole, intact, meaningful experience; it is destroyed when reduced to fragments of conscious experience such as isolated sensations.

Wertheimer did not accept Husserl's ideas unequivocally and uncritically. While living in Halle in 1905-1906, Wertheimer wrote a seven-page draft of a letter to "L. Kl." (probably "Lieber Klein," his friend Julius Klein[19]), part of which expresses his disillusionment with Husserl (MW-NY).

Wertheimer was apparently wrestling with the problem of the nature of the whole, and of the relation between part and whole. One passage in his draft includes several geometric sketches and the following comments:

⬜▷ ... ⬜▷   ╱╲ ... ⌃ First principle: if two objects combine in an ontologically real way, i.e., so that each object remains identical in the two [in the isolated and combined forms]...then a "Gesamtgebilde—a joint form" [also] emerges (the Gesamtgebilde is only tentatively named, in order to proceed precisely; [the new structure is seen] not as a sum but as a Gesamtgestalt—a total structure).... Second: in such a structuring of the [new] whole, something logically new occurs: the "whole" contains as genuine contents (1) a and b, c...and e, f...but also, in addition, (2) *new parts*.

Further on, he refers to "cases of Gestalten in the genuine sense." He further tells Klein, "I am trying to do a logical analysis of your principle of ontological connection via the 'same' part [before and after combination into a new whole], in terms of consequences." In still another place: "In general: If an object [a whole] is given, then *all* of the relations among its parts are really given.... It is only a matter of thinking about two parts of a 'whole' as genuinely parts."

In addition to his critique of Husserl, Wertheimer was contemplating the role of logic in human thinking, as evidenced in a somewhat obscure set of notes pinned to a March 1906 card (MW-NY):

It is believed that for the refutation of logical principles one must find cases that do not follow them. The principle of contradiction, for example, is supposed to be absolutely valid as long as it is impossible to find cases in which, e.g., A and not-A coincide or are not mutually exclusive, which has never occurred and could never happen. But the principle of contradiction requires a very specific categorical form for the structure of A as well as not-A. There are structures in which the principle of contradiction does not apply. Hegel has indicated some of them; they can be made to fit the principle of contradiction only by sheer distortion, can be changed into cases subsumed by that principle only if violence is done to them. In principle: the task of logic is not fulfilled by investigation of relations [among parts] that are valid if the basic structures [of the whole] are conceived dogmatically. Logic has the obligation of at least demonstrating the correctness of the structures, and it could not even begin to perform this task, because the unequivocal uniqueness of its structures is dogmatic. [Classical logic is based on a dogmatic conception of the nature of the whole and its parts, a conception which is invalid.] The categories (and categorical formations) [i.e., parts and their relations] can appear not further reducible, not further to be investigated, and not further testable only to the extent that they are treated as nothing more than signs or symbols. The study of their *functions*, their unique *roles in thinking*, of their relation to the *goals of thought*, and of them as elements, as *technical aids to thought*, makes it possible to reduce, investigate, and test them further.

Although sketchy and somewhat vague, these fragmentary notes carry a hint of the kind of deliberations that Wertheimer would later develop into a formal Gestalt theory. Another instance of such foreshadowing is a brief note attached to a form letter dated April 10, 1908, to Wertheimer at Niederschönhausen (presumably Georg Stern's house in Berlin, where he was living at the time), inviting him to attend a small informal dinner at the Fürstenhof Palast Hotel in conjunction with the Third Congress for Experimental Psychology, to be held April 22-25 in Frankfurt am Main. The note (MW-NY), in Wertheimer's handwriting, reads,

> In conceptual thinking, changes and differences in the characteristics of objects go completely parallel with changes in the concepts [as, for example, transposing a melody to a different key]. But for some kinds of conceptual analogues, in contrast, laws hold which are similar to those which Ehrenfels set up for Gestalt qualities [as, for example, creating a variation on a melody].

Among the threads leading to the later Gestalt theory, then, may have been Wertheimer's wrestling with Ehrenfels's thoughts on perceptual qualities from the point of view of logic.[20] Max's deep concern with logic must have led him to speculate about a wide array of questions in philosophy as well as in psychology.

The Music of the Veddas: A Rudimentary Gestalt Analysis

Perhaps the clearest anticipation of Wertheimer's later Gestalt work occurs in a 1910 paper on musicology published in the *Sammelbände der Internationalen Musikgesellschaft* (*Collected Papers of the International Music Society*). Wertheimer had been fascinated with music since his early childhood. He had also been involved for several years already at the Berlin Phonogram Archives (see note 25). In addition, he frequently used musical illustrations in later lectures and works, to demonstrate various Gestalt principles. Music is a fertile medium for examining structural features of artistic creations. This early article dealt with the music of the Veddas, considered to be among the most primitive tribes still extant at the time. By coincidence, another investigator, C. S. Myers, independently wrote an article on the same topic at about the same time. The contrast between the approaches of the two scholars hints at the Gestalt mode of thinking beginning to take shape in Wertheimer's mind.

Several years older than Wertheimer, Charles Samuel Myers was a respected British psychologist who earned his M.D. at Cambridge University in 1901 and was a member of the faculty at Cambridge when his chapter on the musicology of primitive people appeared in 1911. Myers engaged in studies of aboriginal people during an 1898 Cambridge University anthropological expedition to the Torres Strait northeast of Australia with two colleagues, William Halse Rivers and William McDougall. This venture yielded some of the first measurements of individual differences in nontechnical societies.[21] Wertheimer's paper is mentioned in a footnote to Myers' chapter on music in the 1911 book *The Veddas*, edited by C. G. Seligmann and Brenda Z. Seligmann:[22]

> We received the manuscript of this chapter by Dr. Myers in November 1909, but owing to our absence from England, publication was deferred for six months. Meanwhile, in the *Quarterly Magazine of the International Musical Society* (Year xi, Part 2, 1910) there appeared a short account of Vedda music by Herr Max Wertheimer, based on an examination of four phonographic records obtained by Frau M. Selenka. Dr. Myers has thus had no opportunity of alluding to Herr Wertheimer's observations in this chapter.

The Veddas were a small tribe that inhabited a section of Ceylon (now Sri Lanka). Myers based his studies on thirty-four Vedda songs while Wertheimer used recordings of four phonograph cylinders that contained about forty songs. Myers classified his songs, which he claimed "are probably simpler in structure than any other native songs hitherto studied," into three groups.[23] Group A consisted of "nine...tunes...composed of only two notes," as well as three more which consisted "also of two notes, but with the addition of one or more unimportant grace-notes." He included in Group B "twelve other songs [that] consist of three notes only." Group C contained nine songs of four notes, and one of five. "Of the songs in Group A, in no case is the range sensibly greater than our whole-tone interval," and the range in Groups B and C is no "greater than our minor third" and no "greater than a fourth," respectively. Myers observed that there "is evidence that the songs of Group A are more archaic than those in groups B and C."

In his analysis of Vedda music, Myers concluded that "in the absence of musical instruments, musical intervals are by no means fixed among the Veddas, and...this want of fixity becomes more striking, the greater the number of notes introduced into the song."[24] Intervals in Group A are relatively fixed; they are less so in Groups B and C. However, Myers mentioned that "from what we know of primitive music elsewhere, it was not to be expected that the Veddas would sing pure minor or major thirds. For a long time, even in European music, thirds were regarded as dissonant." According to Myers, the fifth is considered as more consonant than the fourth by Europeans:

> for [this] reason we might have expected to have found the fifth preferred to the fourth, but the fifth only occurs in one song, while the fourth is sung in several.... The intervals of the Veddas appear to have been developed...not by taking a harmonious interval and dividing it into smaller intervals, but by starting with small...intervals and adding further intervals to them. It is only in the more advanced songs (and there are very few in number) that relatively large intervals are sung.... Despite the fact that to our ears tonality is so well-worked throughout the Vedda songs, the approximate consonance of intervals is only reached when the two tones immediately succeed one another.
>
> As regards the rhythm of the Vedda songs, it is noteworthy that in Indian music Abraham and von Hornbostel found frequent instances of the interpolation of a 3- or a 5-pulse measure in music otherwise of common time. They note that change of rhythm is "so frequent that we are often unable to

detect any constant primacy of rhythm at all, but are compelled to imagine a continual modification of measure." [25]

Myers believed that "the observation of Abraham and von Hornbostel is applicable to much of Vedda music, while in other Indian and Vedda songs a definite rhythm can be readily comprehended. In many parts of the world primitive music is characterized by a delight in change and opposition of rhythm, and a demand that relatively long periods filled with measures of a diverse length be apprehended as an organic whole or 'phrase.' This is a characteristic of several of the Vedda songs."

The next to last sentence, incidentally, with its reference to an "organic whole," is quoted from a 1905 article by Myers in the *British Journal of Psychology*.

Myers' account is descriptive and dispassionate, but contains the implicit ethnocentric assumption that European music is the most developed in the world. He saw primitive music as an early version of such "higher level" music and assumes that primitive music gradually evolves so as to achieve a better approximation to European music. This orientation is not evident in Wertheimer's independent analysis of the music of the same people. Another major difference between the two is that while Myers chose to classify melodies based on their range of tones, Wertheimer concentrated on identifying the internal "laws" that govern their structure. This emphasis upon the inherent structure of a whole was to be a major hallmark of later Gestalt work. While Myers made scant reference to the holistic theme in his account (it occurs explicitly only in the penultimate sentence of his chapter, in which he quoted his earlier 1905 assertion), this theme is clearer in Wertheimer's article—although it is still by no means an unequivocal formulation of the Gestalt thesis.

Wertheimer's paper, entitled "Musik der Wedda" ("Music of the Veddas")[26], appeared in sufficiently small print that it is several pages shorter than Myer's chapter in the Seligmann book, despite containing approximately the same number of words. The title page of a reprint of the paper indicates that it is a contribution "from the Phonogram Archives of the Psychological Institute of the University of Berlin." Wertheimer based his analysis of Vedda music on a collection of recordings donated to the Phonogram Archives in March 1907 by Mrs. M. Selenka, the wife of a prominent zoologist. In addition to her work with the Vedda music, Mrs. Selenka also contributed recordings of Tamil, Singhalese, Japanese, and Balinese music to Stumpf's archives. Wertheimer also referred in his paper to articles on the music of Patagonia and of the Kubu in Sumatra, the latter published in 1908 by his friend and colleague Erich von Hornbostel.

According to Wertheimer, the Vedda songs "are certainly among the most primitive known musical expressions....Primitive above all," he continued, are the singers who, according to their physical and cultural characteristics, are generally considered among the most primitive still-extant tribes. Further, the conditions of their music making are primitive: they possess no musical instruments of any kind, not even percussion devices or noise-makers. Finally the extraordinarily restricted tonal range of their songs themselves seems primitive to start with.

In his analysis, Wertheimer quoted Mrs. Selenka's observations while recording the music of the Veddas:

> Here, as with all other stimulation, there was no curiosity at all, no spontaneous interest, as would have been the case with the Dajaks and without question with the Malays. Through Korali, the Singhalese village chief (a half-blood Vedda), I told them that a small bird, sitting in the box, wanted to hear the Veddas sing. He could only hear them, though, if they came very close to him. Thus with long pauses and much encouragement from Korali, I got three of them to the point of sitting down close enough to the gramophone horn. After the first two recordings I played back what had been recorded. I said, now the bird wants to sing. And now for the first time there was real joy and real astonishment in their faces (a European recording I had played for them earlier had resulted only in indifference and listlessness). They recognized their own words and also their voices, making this clear through their gestures: one pointed to another and stated his name when the relevant voice sounded in the instrument. This also happened where I had recorded the same song successively from several of them.—It was a group of six Veddas, among them an old one, whose age I judge to be about 50 (but this is a tentative estimate due to the difficulty of accurate age judgments for members of this tribe), one about 10 years younger, two about 30 years old, and one very young one; there were no women among them. I could only get them to sing together at first (the younger ones). Soon one of them was designated as the best singer by the group itself; I have several solos by him.—During singing they gently moved their upper bodies, rocking a bit; I had the impression that they to some extent followed the rhythm. In the old one I also observed a rhythmic beat with his big toe, which he seemed to be able to move quite independently. —I was also struck by the sure musical pitch of the people; I had the impression that they always started out their singing on the same pitch. I noticed no unmusical deviation upwards or downwards, nor any slurs.

Wertheimer matter-of-factly began his analysis as follows.

> The investigation of the phonograms yielded the following picture: The tonal raw material is limited to two, at most three, notes and the tonal range to a whole note or at most an augmented minor third; but the notes are precise and clear. As a number of frequency measurements demonstrated, the pitch is generally very constant, except for a few atypical cases of sharps or flats at the beginning of a recording cylinder.

Wertheimer's (and Mrs. Selenka's) description differs sharply from Myers's; but Wertheimer's last remark suggests that perhaps Myers's impression that pitch was variable in the Veddas' singing may have been due to technical problems in the recording, rather than to actual uncertainty in the singers' notes. "Particularly constant," continued Wertheimer,

> are the pitches of the two notes of the typical closing part.... The average size of their interval is...about between the tempered three-quarter tone and the whole tone....
>
> Almost everywhere the voice goes only from one tone to its direct neighbor; among all the songs there are only three cases of a third (and apparently only as a variation).
>
> The phonograms consist of serial lines of verses identifiable rhythmically and melodically as certain lawful little structures. In spite of the limited tonal range and the simple rhythm, they display a few characteristic differences—even if, without paying close attention, one at first believes one is hearing continual repetitions of a monotone melody.
>
> The phonograms include well over a hundred such motifs; several of the lines of verses recur frequently. In several cases we also have the same verse sung by different singers.
>
> The relationship between text and melody is very close; the rhythm is to a large extent subordinate to the number of syllables.

Myers did not comment on this connection among text, rhythm, and the internal articulated structure of the melodies. But this relation is fully consistent with a Gestalt analysis of the structure of musical compositions. Wertheimer continued,

> The same text is also always associated with a melody of the same type; the individual syllables have the same temporal values....
>
> Our conception of the musical measure is not absent, but it cannot be applied throughout because of the frequent temporally free structuring (*Gestaltung*) of the closing syllables. Nevertheless the value of a quarter or eighth note...corresponds regularly to every syllable except the last one; the last syllable always has a longer duration (usually a half note, but sometimes three, five, or more eighth notes)....
>
> In this analysis I am working forward from the end: almost all the motifs divide themselves unmistakably into two rhythmic-melodic parts, the second of which (penultimate structure plus ending) always has the same typical structuring (*Gestaltung*) in all the different melodies.
>
> The penultimate structure (*Schlussvorbau*)—mostly the two quarter notes before the ending—is also frequently clear in the text, in that the last word (usually of three or four syllables) includes both the penultimate structure and the ending....

Wertheimer discussed the typical forms of the penultimate structure in some detail melodically and rhythmically, and commented that

Quite aside from the ending portions, many structures exhibit a simple rhythmic-melodic articulation (*Gepräge*). Usually two quarter notes occur twice (occasionally three times); so the entire melody consists of the simple schema (in quarter notes) 2 2 2 2, occasionally 2 2 2 2 2.

He noted that "this schema holds for most of the song lines," and gave numerous detailed examples. He also commented that

Observation of the "motifs," of the penultimate structure and the ending, and of their variations shows that their essence does not lie in a particular sequence of intervals or rhythmic form; rather, intervals and rhythmic parts can vary within specified limits....

It can be asserted that a melody is not provided through individually determined intervals and rhythms, but is a structure (*Gestalt*) whose individual parts possess a free variability within characteristic limits. The structure of the melody (*Melodiegestalt*) is thereby precisely characterized by negative conditions (here, e.g., "no ascent"). Thus a limiting case can occur, in which the same rhythmic-melodic motif can be derived in various cases from two different "motif structures" (*Motivgestalten*).... This is decided by the other formations (variants) of the same song line....

Thus the rhythmic-melodic construction of most of the forms essentially follows the rule that a small motif (two quarter notes) initially occurs twice. Thereafter there are two quarter notes or a single one, with which the lowest note is regularly reached (penultimate structure), and then the ending. The ending is constituted of the second tone or the lowest, or an ascent from the first to the second. The phonograms contain more than 100 motifs of this fundamental type. Their structure exhibits a similarity to our strict classical eight-beat phrase, the more so as they regularly have a paired structure and the first ending sometimes gives the impression of a half-ending.... But the penultimate structure is characteristic.

Within this frame there occur different specific forms with specific structural laws; even if they are simple, they do not blindly follow a formula, and in their changes they result in certain characteristic structurings (*Gestaltungen*).

The other structures too—which deviate in their first part from the basic type—demonstrate firm rhythmic-melodic articulation.

Despite his evident attempt to remain objective, the account makes clear that Wertheimer admired the Veddas' music. The tones are precise and clean; a song makes use of no more than two, or at most three, tones; and tone length varies only minimally. The music has its own clear rules, such as the repetition of, and then variation on, a short motif. Within the limits of this medium, there are different specific forms with specific structural rules. Although simple, the music has a strict rhythmic and melodic character.

Thus this music is in principle different from what has so far typically been assumed to be true about the most primitive music: not unclear, unsteady execution of tones, but precise, clearly segregated notes; not irregular tonal movement, but patterns that are rhythmically and melodically strict.

This form need not be the only one out of which further musical developments originated. It appears quite possible that music developed here and there out of several quite different forms of primitive origins.

Wertheimer concluded his article with thanks to Mrs. Selenka, Stumpf, and von Hornbostel for their "friendly support of this work," and appended three pages of notes and lyrics for thirty-one different songs sampled from the Selenka collection.

What is most significant about this paper is not its conclusion about the clear structure and execution of very primitive music, nor its use of the word "Gestalt" (a word frequently used in German quite aside from its more technical meaning in the context of Gestalt theory), nor its difference from Myers' work on the same topic. What is striking about the article is the similarity between its mode of approach and the typical later Gestalt analytical procedures. Although the paper contains no mention of Gestalt theory, it focuses on Gestalt-related themes in Wertheimer's attempt to discover the internal laws and the particular characteristic articulation of a specific set of wholes—in this case, the songs of a primitive tribe. It is clear that he was functionally analyzing the specific, concrete parts of a Gestalt, its internal organization, and its meaningful structure. Wertheimer's 1910 article on the music of the Veddas might be considered the first published instance of the Gestalt approach to a problem.

Quite aside from hinting at an evolving Gestalt way of thinking about a problem, the article also ties in with Wertheimer's abiding interest in music and musicology. As mentioned earlier, Wertheimer often used music later in his career as a persuasive medium for concretely illustrating Gestalt principles. It is possible that some of his own insight into Gestalt theory derived from his immersion in music and its structures.

Yet another feature of the paper is its focus on the cultural artifacts of a primitive tribe. A respect for, and admiration of, non-European cultures and their creative products was, for that matter, characteristic of the ethos at the Berlin Phonogram Archive and of its main figures, Erich M. von Hornbostel and Carl Stumpf. Wertheimer was deeply interested in ethnopsychology or sociocultural psychology (*Völkerpsychologie*). He enjoyed the ingenuity of peoples who, from a European perspective, were "exotic" or "aboriginal," and whom he saw as frequently coming up with strikingly apt solutions to everyday problems, solutions which often are quite different from those considered natural by European adults. Any genuine, fresh, creative, or insightful artistic or thought process that does justice to its subject-matter was a source of enjoyment and satisfaction for Wertheimer.

Notes

1. Max Wertheimer (1906). Über die Assoziationsmethoden [On the association methods]. *Archiv für Kriminalanthropologie und Kriminalistik*, 22, 293-319.
2. Recognizing the difference between experiments in a psychological laboratory and legal activities in a courtroom, Stern in 1939 published reports of "Reality Experiments," more realistic simulations of crimes and courtroom events with the typical scenario being a theft in full view of witnesses. Stern then asked the witnesses to describe details of the crime and found poor recall for such specific information as conversation, weapons, etc. He also found even poorer recall over longer lapses of time following the initial observation and also after leading questions by an authority. During his career, Stern occasionally trained police officers and judicial officials about the fallibility of eyewitness testimony.
3. Max Wertheimer and Otto Lipmann (1907). Tatbestandsdiagnostische Kombinationsversuche [Combination experiments on the diagnosis of knowledge about the facts of a case]. *Zeitschrift für angewandte Psychologie*, 1, 119-128.
4. Jung edited the book in which his thesis and several other works appeared: Carl Gustav Jung, ed. (1906). *Diagnostische Assoziationsstudien: Beiträge zur experimentellen Psychopathologie* [*Diagnostic association studies: Contributions to experimental psychopathology*], Vol. 1. Leipzig: Barth.
5. Jung was perhaps first introduced to the word association method by Riklin, who had returned in 1904 from Germany to Switzerland, where he had worked on the association test with Gustav Aschaffenburg (see Barbara Hannah (1976). *Jung: His life and work*. New York: Putnam, p. 151). Shortly thereafter, Jung established a laboratory for experimental psychopathology at Burghölzli and enlisted the aid of Riklin, Ludwig Binswanger, and Alphons Maeder. Riklin went on to a distinguished career, serving as secretary for the International Psycho-Analytic Association in 1910, the same year that Jung served as president of that Association. In addition, he edited the *Correspondenzblatt der Internationalen Psychoanalytischen Vereinigung* (Correspondence forum of the International Psychoanalytic Association). Riklin was one of the few analysts who supported Jung following Jung's break with Freud.
6. Jung, *Experimental researches*. Vol. 2 of *The collected works of C. G. Jung*, 1957 on. New York: Pantheon Books and Princeton, NJ: Princeton University Press, 18 vols., p. 587.
7. In his 1883 book *Inquiries into human faculty and its development*, Francis Galton described a study in which he printed seventy-five words on separate cards and tested himself by spontaneously saying aloud the first idea that came to his mind when he exposed each card successively.
8. In his 1904 dissertation, Wertheimer had included a long footnote mentioning articles by recognized experts in legal psychology, including Vladimir Mikhaylovich Bechterev, Hugo Münsterberg—and Jung and Riklin. For a fuller account of the Jung and Wertheimer exchange, see Michael Wertheimer, D. Brett King, Mark A. Peckler, Scott Raney, and Roddy W. Schaef (1991). Carl Jung and Max Wertheimer on a priority issue. *Journal of the History of the Behavioral Sciences*, 28, 45-56.

9. Max Wertheimer (1906). Zur *Tatbestandsdiagnostik*: Eine Feststellung [On the diagnosis of the facts of a case: A confirmation]. *Archiv für die gesamte Psychologie*, 7, 39-40. Jung strongly identified with the word-association experiments and chose to lecture on that work at the September, 1909 vigentennial celebration of the founding of Clark University at Worcester, Massachusetts—the same ceremonies at which Freud delivered his famous lectures on psychoanalysis.

10. Hans Gross later published Freud's talk in the *Archiv für Kriminalanthropologie und Kriminalistik* (see Sigmund Freud, Psycho-analysis and the establishment of the facts in legal proceedings, Vol. 9 of *The standard edition of the complete psychological works of Sigmund Freud*, ed. and trans. James Strachey. London: Hogarth, 1962, p. 106).

11. Several scholars have speculated that Wertheimer may initially have been interested in the tenets of psychodynamic theory (see e.g. S. Bernfeld [1934]. Die Gestalttheorie, *Imago*, 20, 32-77; Bruno Waldvogel [1991]. Psychoanalyse und Gestaltpsychologie: Historische und theoretische Berührungspunkte, [Psychoanalysis and Gestalt psychology: Historical and theoretical points of contact]. *Gestalt Theory*, 13, 19-48), but he expressed unambiguous animosity toward psychoanalysis in his later career.

12. MW-NY. The letter may have been intended for Hans Kardos, a Prague friend of Max and Walter. The "Klein" referred to was doubtless Julius Klein, Wertheimer's former fellow law student at Prague. Rüstow was a student who was to become an historian, and Paul Frankl, a lifelong friend of Wertheimer's, was to have a distinguished career in art history. The name Rüstow is crossed out in the draft.

13. A curriculum vitae found among Wertheimer's papers (MW-CU), prepared (according to internal evidence) in 1919 or early 1920, provides a few details about the years 1905-1910, as well as indicating which professors Wertheimer considered particularly significant in his own development.

14. See Viktor Sarris and Michael Wertheimer (2000). Max Wertheimer's research on aphasia and brain disorders: A brief account. *Gestalt Theory*, 23, 267-277.

15. Bonvicini and Pötzl worked at the Neurological Institute (in the Institute for Anatomy and Physiology of the Central Nervous System) at the University of Vienna. They published their work in a *Festschrift* and also as a separate work, edited by Heinrich Obersteiner, in Leipzig and Vienna, issued by Franz Deuticke in 1907.

16. Wertheimer commented once again on the work he had done with brain-injured patients many years later, in a brief invited "Discussion" appended to Lauretta Bender's paper "Gestalt function in visual motor patterns in organic disease of the brain, including dementia paralytica, alcoholic psychoses, traumatic psychoses and acute confusional states," which appeared in 1935, pages 300 to 329 in volume 33 of the *Archives of Neurology and Psychiatry*. In agreement with Bender's use of what is now called the Bender-Gestalt test, Wertheimer reported (page 328): "Decided disturbances of figural patterns occur in cases of alexia, agraphia, aphasia [inability to read written language, to write in a language, and to understand spoken language, respectively], etc. In such cases there is often a great lability in the grasp of a figural pattern. The subject is

incapable of conceiving and holding fixed, clear, integrated figural patterns; there is a tendency toward simpler, less integrated, less secure *Gestalt* processes." But Wertheimer was critical of Bender's efforts to use the Bender-Gestalt test for individual differential diagnosis: "The method which Dr. Bender has chosen for practical reasons, the method of drawing a thing by sight, of slowly copying a given drawing which is continuously in view, is a somewhat dangerous method of solving the problem because it has, under certain circumstances, a slight tendency toward disintegrating figural patterns; it is also a complicated method, because it is not known in each case what is conditioned by the tendencies of the visual field and what by motor abilities and tendencies; the tendencies in both visual and motor patterns are mutually interwoven in the results. I agree that the two are closely connected, but the connection is not as simple as one may be tempted to infer."

17. Ash, 1982, p. 254.

18. Wertheimer's interest in Husserl's work was fostered at least in part by Carl Stumpf and Oswald Külpe. Husserl dedicated his 1900-1901 two-volume book on *Logische Untersuchungen* (*Logical investigations*) to Stumpf. Külpe and others in the Würzburg school, such as Bühler and Messer, looked favorably on Husserl's work. See Boring, 1950, p. 408.

19. Although Wertheimer was no longer living in Prague, he maintained close ties with Klein, as evidenced for example by a 1908 postcard that Klein sent from Vienna to Wertheimer in Frankfurt (MW-NY), forwarded on August 15 to Wertheimer's vacation address in Zabot near Danzig.

20. Wertheimer remained a loyal follower of Ehrenfels for some time, although there were many differences between the two men. In 1907, Ehrenfels wrote a series of essays on sexual ethics in which, according to Ash, 1982, p. 248, he advocated, among other things, the eugenic selection of superior individuals who would be permitted to engage in polygamy, while others would be forbidden to breed. Wertheimer carefully underlined the first of these essays, accompanying the key points of the argument with exclamation points in the margin, suggesting shock or indignation; he did not do the same with the others, and may not have read them at all.

21. Rivers also conducted studies on color vision, the perception of geometrical illusions and other visual phenomena among the Torres Strait aborigines in 1901. Later, Myers helped Rivers and James Ward found the *British Journal of Psychology*. He went on to become a leader in industrial psychology in Great Britain.

22. C. S. Myers (1911). Music. In C. G. Seligmann and Brenda Z. Seligmann (eds.), *The Veddas*. Cambridge: Cambridge University Press, pp. 341-365. The authors are grateful to Dr. Horst Gundlach of the University of Heidelberg for bringing this chapter to their attention.

23. Myers, p. 341.

24. Myers, pp. 364-365.

25. Myers, p. 365. The reference here is to Erich Moritz von Hornbostel, Wertheimer's friend and colleague at the Berlin Psychological Institute and the Phonogram Archive, and Otto Abraham, an obstetrician and gynecologist who as a hobby spent much time at the Berlin institute, and who also became a close

friend of Wertheimer. Wertheimer later asked Abraham to be in attendance when his first two children were born. Wertheimer apparently spent a significant amount of time at the Phonogram Archive during his Berlin years, and in fact contributed to its collection of recorded music. In June, 2000, the cylinder project manager of the Berlin Phonogram Archive, Dr. Susanne Ziegler, reported (personal communication to Michael Wertheimer) the discovery, among the 337 collections composed of more than 16,700 cylinders, of a collection of five wax cylinders entitled "Wertheimer Prag 1906," together with "documentation and a letter from Wertheimer to Hornbostel describing the informants, the text, and the context of the recordings." Dr. Ziegler wrote that this collection "is in fact one of the oldest (if not the oldest) recording of Hebrew liturgical chant."

26. Max Wertheimer (1910). Musik der Wedda [Music of the Veddas]. *Sammelbände der internationalen Musikgesellschaft* (*Collected Papers of the International Music Society*), 10, 300-309.

5

Emergence of Gestalt Theory, 1910-1913

Max Wertheimer, in 1910, was disturbed by the
narrowness of [psychology's] enterprises.... I
had a feeling that his work might transform
psychology, which was hardly a fascinating
affair at the time, into a most lively study of
basic human issues.
—Wolfgang Köhler (1967)

It is impossible to specify an exact date on which the Gestalt theory first became explicit and clear to Wertheimer; there were occasional foreshadowings in several of his early writings and projects. Extant scribbled notes, many of them without a precise date, contain suggestive hints regarding logic, epistemology, thinking, and other areas. Drafts of letters contain comments, phrases, or passages that can be seen as premonitions. Fragmentary notes about Husserl, Mach, and Ehrenfels refer to ideas that can be interpreted as preliminary versions of some aspects of the later Gestalt approach. Diagrams in discussions of logical thought or used in the testing of patients with aphasia occasionally contain the germ of later Gestalt thinking—or were used years later for quite different purposes, once Gestalt theory had been formulated. And the mode of approach with which Wertheimer analyzed the music of the Veddas appears to have been tinged with Gestalt theory.

During his early post-Ph.D. years, Wertheimer grappled with philosophical, ethical, and psychological issues. Immersed in the current questions of philosophy and psychology, he was trying to establish a career in an academic setting somewhat hostile to his ethnic background. This was a time of relative political stability in Europe, and the society was generally supportive of academic pursuits, but there was little direct economic support in the then-current institutions of higher learning for a young Ph.D., especially one with Jewish ancestry.

After completing the requirements for his doctoral degree, Wertheimer had devoted attention to further work in the same field, determination of guilt, primarily by variations on a word-association procedure, and to a new set of problems in the area of language deficits produced by neurological damage. Neither of these programs led to a major work sufficient to qualify as a *Habilitationsschrift*, and by 1910, six years past his doctorate, he still was not "habilitiert"; yet most intellectuals who aspired to an academic career took less than six years to complete their habilitation thesis. Whether his exercise in musicology that resulted in the 1910 paper on the Veddas had been another effort to develop expertise in a field that could lead to his habilitation is not known; at any rate, he did not pursue this area further directly, either. Nor did his next major publication, on ethnopsychology, lead to his habilitation—but it was replete with Gestalt thought.

Thinking and Ethnopsychology:
The Emergence of Gestalt Theory

Wertheimer's 1912 ethnopsychology article[1] offered an exploration of thinking in non-industrial societies, using examples from a wide range of anthropological sources. As was also true of Wertheimer's later Gestalt work, the discussion in the paper is very concrete, concentrating on specific cases, situations, and structures; from the beginning, he strove to stay close to the facts and remain undistracted by inconsequential tangents. The article makes a number of recommendations for how to investigate the modes of thinking of people who do not share Western European thought styles, and who do not take for granted the presumed adequacy—and superiority—of such styles. It should therefore be considered a contribution to sociocultural psychology, "Völkerpsychologie," or even cultural anthropology. Interest in ethnopsychology had already been strong in German intellectual circles since the middle of the nineteenth century; Lazarus and Steinthal in Berlin, and Wundt in Leipzig, had made substantial contributions to "Völkerpsychologie." In a similar vein, Wertheimer's paper was a study in the comparative psychology of cognition. Its title and subtitle, "On the thinking of aboriginal peoples: I. Numbers and numerical structures," left no doubt that it was intended to be the first in a series of contributions about the thinking of aboriginal peoples, although no additional papers appeared in this series.

The article provides a wide variety of examples of how various tribes deal, often ingeniously, with quantities. Wertheimer's admiration for the modes of thought he describes is evident throughout the paper. Many of the numerical ideas used in aboriginal societies are clearly suitable in their context, constructively serving the cultural, cognitive, and social purpose for which they are needed. They are sensible, often creative, and highly functional. The examples include special numerical structures associated with children's thought, and with European trades such as baking (for example, the "baker's dozen"). They include very simple instances, such as one horse plus one horse equals two horses, and one person plus one person equals two persons, but one person plus one horse may equal a rider; and quite intricate ones, such as a builder's conception of how many pieces of what kind of wood of what size will be needed to frame a hut.

Wertheimer argues that, in order to determine the characteristics of aboriginal thought processes, it is not enough to ask which numbers and operations of our own mathematical system they happen to use. That is much too ethnocentric, even though it had often been standard practice among European anthropologists. Rather, the question should be, what thought systems do they use in this or that field? What does their thought achieve, what capacities does it demonstrate? The aim should be to discover the typical characteristics of their thinking in the quantitative area.

The introduction to the article engages in some gentle scolding about the ethnocentrism of earlier workers, and argues for the necessity of introducing some new theoretical concepts—concepts which turn out to be prototypic of later Gestalt thinking. "What we have available so far about the thinking of aboriginal people in reports from research expeditions is for the most part insufficient for a genuine psychological understanding. The following remarks are intended to make a first attempt at pointing to the real issues."

There follow nineteen different numbered sections of varying length, each containing a title and a variety of examples from a broad selection of cultures around the world. The first, examples of group structures, includes the posts or beams needed to construct a house, selected on the basis of the conception of the house frame one has in one's head (rather than specifically counting the number of logs required), and a mast held up by stays (the shipwright is aware of the arrangement or form of the entire structure rather than specifically of the number three), as well as other instances in which the Gestalt or structure is "characteristically decisive."

The second section concerns transposition; the "five" of the fingers of one hand can be transposed to groups of five in the natural world, as in a blossom which has five petals. But it is not the number as such which is transposed; rather it is the specific structure. One can, for instance, readily recognize a rectangle without necessarily being aware of, or counting, the "fourness" of the corners or of the sides.

The next part of the paper, entitled "natural groups," discusses different structures for the same number. Here essential characteristics determine whether a number structure applies; for example, eyes are two, a pair, but plate and table are not, nor are stem and blossom. Two trees close together and one far away, or two oaks and a maple, are not immediately three, but more precisely two and another one. A footnote elaborates on an "intuitive numerical conception of several in one": A school teacher explained the Christian concept of the Holy Trinity to children in the classroom, and then asked during the next hour whether the pupils could say what trinity means; one child responded, "Oh, that's like a braid." The child had invented an example of a number pattern, a three-in-one.

The fourth subdivision concerns non-transposability. A house, for instance, involves different structures (such as the main beam) than a collection of fruit or grains of rice. Numbers as such are inherently transposable, but structures or natural groups are not: for the latter, the arrangement, the natural relations of the parts to each other and to the whole, and even the material, may be essential. Two eyes, two beams, two fighters are different kinds of two-patterns. And three of our boats and two of the visitors' are only five under special circumstances, such as when all are combined in a warring expedition.

The next section is devoted to "sensible operations," operations which are reasonable in the real world. A Native American who was asked by a linguist to provide a translation of the sentence "Today the white man shot six bears" could not be persuaded to do so, because it was not possible for anyone to kill that many bears in one day. And if you have eaten your fill of dumplings, and you eat one, two, or three more, what do you have then? Answer: too many— or a stomach ache. Reasonable thought does not engage in piecemeal arbitrary operations, but takes into account the concrete, realistic relationships and possibilities in the problem domain.

Section six discusses the variability of arrangements. Some arrangements are inherently arbitrary and therefore variable (such as the pattern in which one could place five apples), but others are not. Even the class "rectangle" has prototypes; it may be a shock to realize that one which is two meters long and one centimeter high is still a rectangle. A "fivesome" is destroyed if I place four in my pocket and you put the fifth in yours; and one can speak of "a so many of" certain objects, such as the French "une trentaine de," a thirty of, or a thousand-man troop, when what is intended is not "so and so many objects," but roughly "a so many of these objects."

Part seven deals with structures of large numbers, which may be significant in natural life but play no role in mathematics: a flock, a handful, a camel load, a pinch (of salt). Typically the arrangement is irrelevant; what is crucial is the amount relative to other amounts.

The next section explicitly concerns structures the numerical quantity of which is approximate. A person's age may be in the forties, or one may have been born in the thirties. A dozen people means something like eleven to fourteen; a bunch of radishes or of parsley is not numerically precise. It is inappropriate to view such approximate structures as deficient, imprecise or wrong because of their numerical variability. Certain thinking tasks require numerical precision because of the structure of the tasks. For others, a limited degree of numerical precision makes more sense. Some, a few, many, and very many are numerical concepts that can work better in many tasks than specific integers.

Section nine goes into more detail on the ideas of much and many. Often it is too much trouble, and unnecessary, to specify the exact number; it may even be irrelevant, and make no sense, to determine the particular number; there may be more than it makes sense to count or than one could imagine. We also use particular numbers (or their plurals), usually salient or round numbers, such as in dozens or hundreds or thousands of people. Expressions such as "he has lots of money in his pocket" do not signify a completely indeterminate quantity; an amount within particular limits is intended. Expressions conveying approximate quantities are typically used with materials that are never thought of in terms of individual counting, such as with grain; somewhat more definite are "a day's ration," or "a camel load."

The next part concerns distinctive numbers, which also occur in European thinking as "round numbers." Consider a base five or base ten arithmetic, which is found in many parts of the world (the fingers on one or two hands). Numbers close to distinctive ones may be indirectly expressed in relation to them, such as conveying nine as ten minus one, or five as four plus a friend, seven as two threes plus one. In the Czech language, when you buy a certain number of something, you typically get "nádavek," or one or two more: you pay for five bread rolls but get six, for twenty link sausages but get twenty-one or twenty-two—and in English there is the "baker's dozen." Nobody seems to buy precisely eleven of something.

At this point in the discussion a section is devoted to a brief summary statement: comprehensive sets of numerical structures that occur throughout the world reflect the rich variety of natural conceptions, groups, and arrangements rather than arbitrarily assigning the same fixed, rigid system of counting in integers to all quantities. The Western system of counting uses a single additive unit and is abstracted from reality; other systems permit a wealth of differentiated conceptions of groups and quantities that are true to the material being represented, and in that sense truer to reality.

The next subdivision considers the factor of counting as such, which does achieve a new kind of generality; but then the number structures are no longer as tightly rooted in naturally given groups. Yet natural group conceptions still play a direct role in counting itself, as in systems based on the five fingers of the hand, or ten in both hands, or five times four if toes are included. Some Oriental cultures base their counting on three times four (the finger bones of one hand, excluding the thumb). Sometimes there are special sets of numbers for calculations involving money.

Section thirteen is devoted to the structure of the number series, to series determined by the material, and to money. Such systems need not be based on a single additive unit, but may contain such structures as groups of five, which may in turn be arranged not into fives but into four groups of five (such as the anatomical digits). Some systems have different distinct numerals from one to nine for coconuts, for animals and people, for trees or canoes, for houses, and for plantings. Some forms of money can be used only for the purchase of certain commodities, while other forms are used to buy other goods. The two kinds of money may not be interchangeable.

The following section is devoted to examples of complicated series and of scales of value. In one culture (the Bangala) the number one is the raised index finger, two the same plus the middle finger, three the last three fingers (middle, ring, and little), four is all four fingers raised (but in pairs divided by the thumb inserted at the roots of the fingers), five is all of one hand, six is three in each hand, and so on, with ten symbolized by clapping both open hands together and twenty by two claps. Among the Yap islanders a "basket of taro" may contain as few as thirty larger or as many as sixty smaller roots (much like a bushel of apples in the United States). According to some anthropologists, for barter within a Native American nation in Missouri, two knives equal one pair of trousers, two knives plus a pair of trousers are worth one blanket, two knives plus one pair of trousers plus one blanket equal one rifle, and so on.

The next section considers various arithmetic operations in some detail, particularly division. Operations are typically not abstract or oblivious to the arrangement or organization of the material, or to the material itself, and are only performed in places and manners that are consistent with natural properties and realistic requirements. Thus certain arrangements, by virtue of their form, predetermine particular divisions along certain natural lines of cleavage and in ways such that the division results in natural unitary wholes or Gestalten. Natural structures imply particular divisions; while it may be possible to perform other divisions, arbitrary divisions appear abstracted from, or contrary to, reality. Even pies are typically cut along a diameter and then at angles to the first cut.

If I break a stick in two, the Western approach says that I now literally have "two." Two what? It doesn't matter: two—new—units. But the more realistic approach takes a different perspective which may become even clearer if it is not a stick but a spear: the result is not two units, but a piece of a spear (with the tip) and a small piece of wood (part of the shaft). Clearly, the units have changed; the division in a sense results in two new units: the part with the tip and the piece of shaft, or even in one plus zero, the reusable tip and a useless piece of wood—or in a kind of zero, a useless broken spear.

Perhaps even more striking is successive division of a chain of eight rings. The Western conception, in principle applicable to all cases, is that the first division results in eight divided by two, four rings, one half; then eight divided by four, two rings, one quarter; then eight divided by eight, one ring, one eighth. The natural conception, though, recognizes the structural changes: you start with a chain of eight rings; the first division results in half a chain; the second—a quarter chain? Do two rings qualify as a chain? The third division generates a discontinuity: one ring clearly is no longer a chain.

And if the division were to continue farther, the Western conception blindly talks of half a ring, then a quarter of a ring, but the other conception recognizes the discontinuities for what they are: one ring is no longer a chain, and half or quarter of a ring is no longer a ring. Similarly, you can't break down a melody into individual notes (or parts of notes!) and half a pot isn't a pot but a shard. Parts, to be real parts, must be possible meaningful parts of a whole.

Section sixteen considers the upper limit of the number series and related concepts. The limits of conceptions of true individual numbers are relatively low; number analogies do not, like the series of integers, in principle continue on indefinitely. The upper levels of psychological series consist of approximate conceptions of quantity, such as more, or much more, than can be conceived of as a specific realistic amount; "incredibly many" signifies a quantity that exceeds the meaningful domain of numbers. One South Sea islander, for whom an attempt was made to make the number one hundred meaningful by reference to pigs, retorted "But there aren't that many pigs in the whole world." A story about Frederick the Great had him visiting a school and asking, "Where are you?" followed by "Where is Berlin?" and then "Where is Germany?" and getting the reply to his final question of "Where is the world?": "In God's hands." "I am in Berlin" is inherently different from "Germany is in Europe"; inclusion is a different idea in reference to a room in a house, a house in a city, or Europe on earth. Realistic thinking will not arbitrarily repeat an operation that is inherently meaningful in certain situations in other situations where it has no concrete meaning. Such refusal is in no sense a reflection of a "lower level of thinking," but exhibits a determination to understand every object in terms of its actuality, its genuine nature, and its specific relevant relationships.

The next subdivision of the article considers "quasi-localized" or "predetermined" divisions, ones related to natural, spatial, or logical quantities. One more or less than a distinctive number specifically means "close to that number," so that 101 is "right next to 100," "the next one," and 299 is "next to 300," not really "1 plus 1 plus 1 plus 1" and so on. 50 is the middle of 100, 51 just past the middle, and 75 is three of the quarters of 100. Furthermore, a times b is not the same as b times a; something substantial repeated a few times is not the same as something small repeated many times: the two conceptions have inherently different structures. It can be a matter of genuine discovery to realize that 3 plus 3 is really equivalent to 1 plus 1 plus 1 plus 1 plus 1, to 5 plus 1, to 3 times 2, and so on, each of which have their own quite different inherent structure.

Not every meaningful form of counting consists only of the addition of one more. You might be able to count very far using this principle, but not have the slightest idea of the range of numbers within which you happen to be counting; you may have little or no idea of the true quantity. You need to know about how many "plus ones" have already occurred. Without a structural understanding of the quantity, an understanding of its location relative to other known quantities (even if this location is only approximate), you really don't have a meaningful concept of that quantity. A good arithmetic teacher emphasizes understanding a problem and getting an overview of it, so that, for example, an error in setting the decimal point does not lead to acceptance of senseless results.

The genesis of numbers probably does not lie in the process of counting, but in natural groupings and articulated quantities. The primary basis is probably not concepts like "one" and a repeated "plus one," but particular structures that are analogous to concepts, to articulated wholes.

Examples used in this section come from many cultures throughout the world, including Europe, as in the system for specifying time. If it is eleven o'clock now, what time will it be in five hours? Easy: four o'clock. But consider how the equation for this problem looks: eleven plus five equals four. Since twelve is a distinctive number in the European system of telling time, we automatically divide the five added hours into the one required to get to twelve, plus the four hours beyond twelve.

The next-to-last section concerns the parallel of numbers to value and to effectiveness, with the observation that numbers or amount and value or effectiveness are by no means always fully parallel. If there already is a substantial amount (grains of rice, or drops of water) present, small changes are inconsequential. Half a pot, 1/26 of a penny, and so on, are mathematically permissible divisions which are not realistically sensible. I can divide four arrows into four arrowheads and four shafts, but not into three plus five. Increase in quantity does not guarantee an increase in value. In economics, there is a law of diminishing returns: equal increments may consistently produce smaller increases in value. One plus one hundred is different from one hundred plus one. And one plus two is different from one hundred plus two—in the first case, the added two is very substantial, but in the second it is an almost inconsequential change.

The final, nineteenth, part of the article considers the category "large," and makes clear that "large" and "small" are relative concepts, and work only within certain ranges. A child might argue that no flea can be large, and may answer a question about what cannot be small with "the world." Thinking is directed at each object in its setting, in its natural environment and natural relationships. Cases like a large head, a large man, a small arrow quiver, or a dwarf tree do not permit arbitrary relativity; their sizes are determined by their natural domains of comparison. The distance to a particular village is not reduced for a person walking there by thinking of the earth as "a grain of sand" in comparison with the size of the sun. As these examples demonstrate, the categorical abstract relativity of absolute measurement is absent even in much Western thinking, for closely related to size are other structural properties to which such relativity is hardly relevant. High or low are determined structurally no less than are tiny or huge. The abstract measuring rod can, it is true, be applied to almost anything, but it is an arbitrary measure isolated from reality; most structures specify natural units that are not arbitrary and abstract.

Distances are reckoned in "about so many steps" or minutes, not in specific numbers of specific units. Precise measurement makes sense only in a few conditions. There are also parallels to such modes of thought in the domains of movement, warmth, and weight: heaviness characterizes a rock, or lead, while lightness is inherent in a mosquito or a butterfly. Categories for warmth include hot, tepid, cool, cold, icy, and so forth.

Wertheimer concludes with the admonition that various types of cognition that differ from our own are not therefore necessarily inferior. The researcher should try to become immersed in the kind of thinking in question, and in the problem situations which give rise to that kind of thinking. Indeed, the article continues for twelve pages with questions for researchers studying thinking among primitive peoples, including many suggestions for how to conduct such studies without falling into the mistake of assuming that anything different from what we are used to is necessarily inferior or less well developed. "The central question is, what structures, operations (and capacities) exist in the realm of the categorical 'how many'?," especially if these conceptions are based on ways of thinking different from the foundations of our own mathematics.

Wertheimer's study is a testament to human diversity, human worth, and the ingenuity of human thought. It is an homage to the insightful, witty, and sensible in human nature. In summarizing the contributions of this article, Daniel Robinson observed that Wertheimer

> successfully escaped from the *Enlightenment* and nineteenth-century myths of the "noble savage" and the even more offensive application of evolutionary principles to the description of primitive peoples. Wertheimer recognizes his subjects for what they are: men, women, and children reared under unique cultural and environmental conditions, which have inevitably altered their cognitive styles, their perceptual tendencies, their daily "logic." To understand the cognitive psychology of such people—or of any people—it is necessary to understand their language, and to understand it as they do. And to understand their language is to comprehend more than grammar and myth. It is to observe them at play; to record the manner in which they settle disputes; to penetrate their rules of conduct and their justifications. Wertheimer recognizes this, and recognizes also that such inquires are especially appropriate to psychology. Indeed, it is in this article that he most fully reveals that most summoning of *Gestalt* injunctions: that a developed psychology is, at once, a social psychology, a developmental psychology, an experimental psychology, a psychology of perception, and a linguistic psychology.[2]

The entire article is imbued with the Gestalt mode. It appears to be the first extensive instance of this kind of approach, and is unmistakably a product of Gestalt-theoretical thinking, a way of thinking that was clearly hinted at in the 1910 paper on the music of the Veddas. But, while the basic Gestalt orientation is clearly evident, there is as yet no self-conscious, self-styled Gestalt theory. Nevertheless, the paper makes clear that the early Gestalt mode of approaching issues occurred in cognition, the psychology of thinking, and "Völkerpsychologie." It is difficult to assign much importance to the absence of explicit mention of a "Gestalt theory" as such, given that Gestalt principles are implied and implicitly used throughout the paper. There is also little explicit mention of Gestalt theory in the later 1912 paper on apparent motion,[3] the paper around which the Gestalt theorists later rallied, and which they considered the paper that founded the Gestalt school. Indeed, there is much less evidence of a Gestalt-theoretical approach in the paper on apparent motion than in the paper on the thinking of aboriginal people.

The article on numerical concepts was a sufficiently major contribution that one might think that Wertheimer would have tried to use it as his habilitation thesis, but apparently he did not. Perhaps the approach and the mode of thinking were too radically different for any psychological or philosophical faculty to consider it acceptable as a habilitation work. Perhaps the fact that it contained no formal experimental studies, measurements, or empirical findings made it insufficient. Perhaps, in spite of its broad range and the variety of examples it contains, it was not considered long enough or substantial enough. At any rate, neither this nor the alexia studies resulted in Wertheimer's habilitation. It was the 1912 paper on apparent movement that finally made him a *Privatdozent* at the Frankfurt Academy.

Apparent Motion and Gestalt Theory:
Research on the Phi Phenomenon

Wertheimer had by now spent years seeking a new theoretical system for analyzing psychological phenomena that would be adequate to their inherent nature and complexity. Although he drew upon many resources in the development of his perspective, a major one was Ehrenfels's 1890 paper, "On Gestalt Qualities." Indeed, Ehrenfels's thought can be viewed as part of the bridge that connected the philosophical and psychological beliefs and approaches prevailing in the late nineteenth century with the new departures that emerged in Gestalt theory early in the twentieth century. To oversimplify, the sequence from classic associationism to Ehrenfels to Wertheimer went like this: First, the associationist notion was that the whole is *equal* to the sum of its parts. With Ehrenfels's formulation, it was believed that the whole is *more* than the sum of its parts—the whole equals the sum of its parts *plus* another element, the Gestalt quality. But for Wertheimer, the new Gestalt theory was founded upon the position that the whole is entirely *different* from a sum of the parts, indeed is *prior to* the parts; wholes are integrated, segregated systems that have an inherent structure of their own, and the structure of the whole in fact determines the nature of the parts. With his research on apparent motion, Wertheimer succeeded in demonstrating the Gestalt viewpoint experimentally and convincingly with perceptual phenomena.

Wertheimer's interest in apparent motion may have been, in part, a product of the popular fascination with this technical phenomenon. The persistence of vision, the neurological retention of images on the retina following the disappearance of the stimulus from the visual field, has been known since antiquity.

The mystique of seen movement attracted scores of investigators prior to Wertheimer's work. Previous scholars, including Jan Purkinje, Hermann von Helmholtz, Joseph Antoine Plateau, William James, Henry P. Bowditch, G. Stanley Hall, Ernst Mach, and Wilhelm Wundt, wondered and wrote about the phenomenon of apparent motion during the nineteenth century. Wertheimer's curiosity about this phenomenon was probably fostered during his student years by lectures on apparent movement by Karl Marbe at Prague and Friedrich Schumann at Berlin. He doubtless was introduced to the sophisticated technical apparatus available for its study in the period shortly after he completed his dissertation during his training with Sigmund Exner. Born in 1846, Exner had spent the majority of his life and academic career in Vienna, where he produced important research on the physiology of the senses, brain localization, color contrast, hue adaptation, and reaction time, and where he edited the prestigious *Zeitschrift für Psychologie*. In 1875, Exner published studies of apparent motion that were described as follows by E.G. Boring, the distinguished historian of experimental psychology:

> He had presented [participants] with two spatially separated, successive, electrical sparks and had found that the time-order of the sparks can be correctly perceived (on the average) when the interval between them is not less than 0.045 seconds. Then he put the sparks closer together in space and got, not succession, but the stroboscopic appearance of the movement of a single spot from the earlier position to the later. The threshold for the correct perception of the direction of this moving spark was only 0.014 seconds.... Movement must, therefore, involve a special process, and Exner argued that it is thus a sensation and not a complex-like perception.[4]

Interactions with Marbe, Schumann, and Exner all must have played a role in Wertheimer's decision to undertake studies on the perception of motion, and in how he chose to study it. But there is no evidence that he expressly chose this area because of its potential implications for the new Gestalt theory.

During 1910, the year in which he turned thirty, Wertheimer managed with his research on apparent motion to demonstrate certain fundamental aspects of Gestalt theory in precise experimental work. This research turned out to become some of the most influential work of his career. As with the popular accounts of Isaac Newton's insight about gravity after being struck by a falling apple, and James Watt's understanding of the inherent power of steam after watching his mother's teakettle react to boiling water, the anecdote of the "founding" of Gestalt psychology[5] cannot be definitively verified, and no extant documentation exists that guarantees it other than an apocryphal status, but it may very well be at least roughly true. In the summer of 1910, Wertheimer was reportedly traveling by rail from Vienna to the Rhineland, probably on vacation with funds supplied by his father. While contemplating popular explanations of apparent motion, including Wundt's idea that such perception can be accounted for by eye movements, he had a significant insight into the phenomenon. He disembarked from the train at Frankfurt am Main, purchased a zoetrope, and tested his ideas in a hotel room (and, presumably, aborted his plans for the Rhineland). The zoetrope, a nineteenth-century optical toy, consisted of images printed on vertical strips inside a rotating cardboard cylinder; when examined from outside through vertical slits in the circumference of the revolving drum, the images appeared to move. The effect was so convincing that the zoetrope was popularly known as the "wheel of life," which is actually a translation of the Greek roots. This toy would have been a suitable instrument for a crude study of apparent movement. If the legend is accurate, Wertheimer recognized the implications of the perception of motion in rapidly altered, successively presented stationary figures as a convincing demonstration of the validity of some Gestalt ideas.

At the time of his insight about apparent motion, Wertheimer did not hold a major university position. Perhaps because of his uncommitted circumstances, Wertheimer saw no need to return to Vienna or Berlin and instead decided to try to work in Frankfurt. At the *Akademie für Socialwissenschaften* (Social Science Academy) in Frankfurt was his former teacher Friedrich Schumann, who had left Berlin and had been appointed only a few months earlier in 1910 to the psychology chair at the Frankfurt Academy, where he had already established an experimental psychology laboratory. Wertheimer approached Schumann, who agreed to let him use laboratory space in the Psychological Institute of the Academy. While at the Academy, Wertheimer was introduced to one of Schumann's brightest laboratory associates, Wolfgang Köhler.

Born on January 21, 1887, in Reval, Estonia, Köhler was a handsome man whose polished formal manner suggested nobility. Like Wertheimer, he was dedicated to rigorous experimentation. Köhler attended universities in Tübingen, Bonn, and Berlin and was trained in the natural sciences, particularly physics, under the eminent physicists Max Planck and Ernst Mach. For his dissertation, Köhler conducted acoustic experiments for which he affixed a tiny mirror to his own eardrum, so that a light beam directed at it could, by reflection, record its movements when stimulated by a sound.[6] Köhler received his Ph.D. in 1909 from Carl Stumpf at the University of Berlin.

Shortly after his arrival in Frankfurt, Köhler was joined by another student from the Berlin Institute, Kurt Koffka. Koffka, born in Berlin in 1886, also developed an avid interest in experimental psychology and holistic theory. Koffka earned his doctorate in 1908, one year before Köhler, also under the supervision of Stumpf, based on a dissertation on imagery and thought. Koffka served as an assistant at Würzburg before taking on a research position at Frankfurt.

In 1910, Köhler was promoted to second assistant at the Psychological Institute in Frankfurt am Main where Koffka was now also an assistant. Köhler remembered:

> The winter term had barely begun when Max Wertheimer appeared with a primitive stroboscope in his suitcase and with many ideas in his head. At the time, none of us knew much about the two others; but Wertheimer stayed, and working together we became the first three Gestalt psychologists.[7]

As was typical in experimental psychology early in the twentieth century, Wertheimer's research did not feature a large sample size, nor did he study naive participants; instead he used trained psychologists. Unlike Wundt's research participants, however, they were not trained introspectionists. Ash observed that although this research

> required precision instruments and carefully controlled conditions, the chief instrument was the observer; hence Wertheimer's confidence in the validity of his results despite the use of only three subjects. "It proved to be unnecessary to obtain a large number of subjects," he said, "since the characteristic phenomena appeared in every case unequivocally, spontaneously and compellingly."[8]

Perhaps at the suggestion of Schumann, Wertheimer invited Köhler, Koffka and Koffka's wife, Mira Klein,[9] to participate in his experiments late in 1910.

When they were both in Berlin, Wertheimer and Schumann may possibly have discussed future plans for investigating apparent motion—long prior to Wertheimer's fateful train trip. At any rate, Schumann put a tachistoscope at Wertheimer's disposal for perceptual research on motion. This instrument could project a beam of light and then interrupt it at measured fractions of a second; it was more versatile than a stroboscope or kinetoscope, which presented continuously occurring discrete displacements.[10] During the experiment, Wertheimer used the tachistoscope to vary the temporal presentation of lights and thereby present discrete displacements of simple geometrical figures, usually a line or a curve. One figure, *a*, was presented to the observer followed by a second, *b*. In this way, he could study stroboscopic motion, the perception of motion in actually stationary, but temporally and spatially displaced, objects.

Wertheimer's general finding was that if the interval between the disappearance of one figure and the flashing on of the next one was brief (about 30 milliseconds or less), both *a* and *b* appeared to be simultaneously present. Conversely, if the time between the presentation of the figures was long (about 200 milliseconds or more), the observer perceived two figures flashing on and off in clear succession. However, if the interval between flashes was about 60 milliseconds, somewhere between simultaneity and succession, it appeared that *one figure* was moving from one position to the other. Thus, when two stationary figures were alternately presented, at an angle or parallel, with proper exposure durations and an appropriate distance between them and brief intervals between the removal of one figure and presentation of the other, a single figure was perceived to be moving back and forth.

At certain relatively brief intervals, Wertheimer observed the curiosity of "pure movement" that connects the figures, but is not in itself an object. His observers reported that they perceived motion without seeing anything that moved. He called this phenomenon by the Greek letter phi, ϕ, for "phenomenon," and designated the perception of motion without perception of a moving object "pure phi." According to Boring:

> Wertheimer pointed out—essentially—that this finding shows that movement is movement. The succession *a–b* is not essential to it. It can occur as ϕ without being an object. For optimal movement one sees a single object moving, not *a* turning into a *b*. In this contention Wertheimer was following out the tradition of Mach and Exner, but he went further. He insisted on the validity of movement as an immediate experience without reference to basic constituents, on the "givenness" of ϕ and its irreducibility to terms of space and time. Out of such an intransigent phenomenology arose Gestalt psychology.[11]

Wertheimer wanted to understand the basic mechanism of phi-movement and, consistent with his early training in physiology, speculated about the physiological foundation of stroboscopic motion; his paper contained a significant, though somewhat undeveloped, reference to a "short circuit" explanation of this phenomenon. An elegant experiment demonstrated conclusively that eye movements cannot explain the perceived motion: stimulus patterns above and below the fixation point in which the apparent motion is simultaneously in opposite directions (for example, from right to left in the upper pattern while simultaneously the apparent motion in the lower pattern is from left to right). Obviously the eyes cannot be moving in two opposite directions at the same time. After rejecting eye-movement explanations of apparent movement, Wertheimer concluded that the perception of movement in these experiments may be a consequence of a physiological "short circuit" or functional pattern in the visual cortex of the brain that is correlated with the perception of motion. According to Wertheimer:

> Recent research in brain physiology has made probable the supposition that when a central spot, a, is stimulated, a certain area surrounding it is physiologically affected. If two places, a and b, are stimulated, the area around both would be so affected.... Were a stimulated and then, after a given, short time, the closely related place b, a kind of physiological short circuit from a to b would appear. In the space between the two places there would be a specific transfer of stimulation.... The closer the two places a and b are, the more favorable are the conditions for the occurrence of the phi process.[12]

Apparently Wertheimer took his time before sharing his findings and their implications with the scientific community, and even with his closest colleagues. Wertheimer's general results were not novel; the revolutionary feature of his work was his innovative analysis of apparent motion. The perception of motion of a single line, rather than the piecemeal discernment of two stationary alternately presented vertical lines, presented a dynamic model of perception. Koffka remembered that in "one of the crucial moments of my life," Wertheimer decided to reveal his interpretation of apparent movement:

> It happened at Frankfurt on the Main early in 1911. Wertheimer had just completed his experiments on the perception of motion in which Köhler and I had served as chief observers. Now he proposed to tell me the purpose of his experiments, of which, as a good subject, I had been entirely ignorant. Of course I had had many discussions with those two men before. One could not live in constant contact with Wertheimer without learning some aspects of Gestalt theory, even in those old times. But on that afternoon he said something that impressed me more than anything else, and that was his idea about the function of a physiological theory in psychology, the relation between consciousness and physiological processes, or in our new terminology, between the behavioural and the physiological field. To state it in these new terms, however, is not quite fair, because this very statement was only made possible by Wertheimer's idea; before, nobody thought of a physiological or, for that matter, of a behavioural *field*.[13]

Like Wertheimer, both Köhler and Koffka were disenchanted with the static tone of psychology in the first decade of the twentieth century, and were captivated by Wertheimer's Gestalt interpretation of apparent motion. According to Köhler,

> Wertheimer's was a masterpiece of experimental investigation in the field of perception. It was also the beginning of extremely fruitful studies in general Gestalt psychology. Much thinking and many discussions followed. The number of basic questions which Wertheimer now began to consider increased rapidly. At the time, he did not publish what he found; rather, he told Koffka about his questions and his tentative answers, and Koffka in turn began to tell his students what he had learned from Wertheimer and about further ideas that he himself had developed in the same productive spirit. These students investigated one interesting possibility after another in the new field. For a brief time, I was able to take part in this development.... I was aware of what Wertheimer was trying to do and found it not only objectively interesting but also most refreshing as a human endeavor. He observed important phenomena regardless of the fashions of the day and tried to discover what they meant. I had a feeling that his work might transform psychology, which was hardly a fascinating affair at the time, into a most lively study of basic human issues.[14]

Wertheimer, Köhler, and Koffka doubtless had many long, exciting discussions in the fall, winter, and spring of 1910 to 1911. These discussions among the three cemented their resolve to promote Gestalt theory.

The choice of Koffka and Köhler as participants in Wertheimer's experiments profoundly affected the future of the Gestalt movement. By the time Koffka left in 1911 to take a post in Giessen, some forty miles from Frankfurt, both he and Köhler were convinced of the promise of the Gestalt theoretical perspective.

But despite the proto-Gestaltists' enthusiasm, Schumann did not accept the new Gestalt theory in general or the short-circuit explanation in particular. In an address at the 1912 Congress of the Society for Experimental Psychology, Schumann did mention Wertheimer's results on phi-movement; while responding to a discussant, Schumann commented that

> the "sensory something" (*sinnliche Etwas*) that Wertheimer had found was "not merely postulated," but "directly observed under various conditions." He [Schumann] did not yet admit theoretical defeat, however, but claimed that attempts to explain this and other phenomena in terms of illusions of judgment "cannot be regarded as hopeless."[15]

Edwin B. Newman, one of Wertheimer's later students, claimed that some tension did exist after the 1912 publication of Wertheimer's paper:

> Schumann had set [his student Wilhelm] Fuchs the task of developing certain observations of Schumann's about the phenomenon of transparency [the perception of looking through one transparent object at another object]. It soon appeared to Fuchs that only by following Wertheimer's new principles could the results be understood, a view not at all to Schumann's liking. As a result, a coolness developed between these two older men, a break which was never really healed. Fuchs unhappily could not get Schumann to agree to publication of his work until more than ten years had passed.[16]

Despite Schumann's reservations, Wertheimer's work on apparent motion was sufficient finally to satisfy the requirements for his habilitation. Thus in 1912 Wertheimer formally became a *Privatdozent* at the Frankfurt Academy.

About the same time that Wertheimer earned his habilitation degree, he resurrected his earlier research on aphasia. Although he had collected a massive amount of data on the psychopathology of language in the period following his dissertation, he had not published any of his findings. Indeed, the only reports to emerge from this large body of work were a lecture at the 1912 International Congress and a short 1913 account in a medical periodical.

An abstract of the lecture, so brief that it provides little useful information, is part of the official proceedings of the Fifth Congress for Experimental Psychology, held in 1912.[17] Titled "On experimental-psychological analysis of certain symptoms of brain pathology," it reads as follows:

> The lecture reports special experimental formulations of questions, and their results, devoted to detailed study of the nature of certain pathological symptoms; the work is among the investigations performed by the lecturer in collaboration with O. Pötzl (Vienna) on so-called "pure" cases of aphasia.

The program refers the reader to a forthcoming publication in the *Zeitschrift für Psychologie*, "Experimental-psychological investigations of cases of pure alexia," by O. Pötzl and M. Wertheimer. What happened to this promised paper is unknown; attempts to locate it (in the *Zeitschrift* and in other journals of the time) have remained unsuccessful.

The 1913 account is part of the official protocol of a meeting of the Frankfurt Medical Society (*Aerztlicher Verein in Frankfurt a.M.*), held on October 20, 1913, at the Society's meeting room.[18] The amanuensis, a Mr. Benario, recorded that Wertheimer lectured on "pathological brain phenomena and their psychological analysis."

> In studies designed to enhance our understanding of phenomena associated with brain pathology, there emerge problem areas in which clinical interests and those of experimental psychology come in close contact.
>
> The theory of phenomena associated with brain pathology has reached a critical stage in recent years. Several authorities have urged a fundamental revision of the theory of aphasia and related syndromes. Several have demanded a return to a more psychologically sound basis (as in the fundamental statement in Külpe's book, *Psychology and Medicine*, published in Leipzig in 1912).
>
> Required in the first place is detailed qualitative and experimental analysis, free of dogmatic adherence to the (ingenious) traditional schemata; a series of examples shows how such procedures can yield precise and essential theoretical decisions. [And here Benario too referred to the forthcoming publication, jointly with C. Pötzl of Vienna, on alexia, agnosia, agraphia, etc., which has proved impossible to locate.]

> Instead of making hypothetical assumptions, it is often possible to draw conclusions based on appropriately designed experiments.
>
> Take, e.g., the question of whether the presenting symptom of a reading deficiency is due to disturbance in the connection between the optic and the acoustic-motoric field. An answer can be provided by the formulation of three auxiliary questions: analysis of the quality of erroneous designations, thorough testing of the recognition of identity and differences, and testing with appropriately designed non-acoustic associations.

There continues a list of several additional clinical and theoretical questions, and how each can be answered, or at least clarified, by apt use of techniques from experimental psychology. These notes obviously pursue the same kinds of ideas about "acoustic and optic motoric connections" that emerged in Wertheimer's aphasia research several years earlier, discussed in the preceding chapter.

The last paragraph of Benario's notes on Wertheimer's presentation includes the lecturer's recommendation that "psychologists thoroughly versed in the experimental method be included in the investigation of theoretically important cases."

Following Wertheimer's talk, Köhler presented his own research on the testing of functions in aphasics, specifically on examinations of hearing. At the conclusion of Wertheimer's and Köhler's papers, several members of the medical society participated in a lively discussion, mostly related to Köhler's comments on the auditory frequencies necessary for the clear understanding of spoken language.

Köhler and Wertheimer were hard at work at this time on studies pertaining to Gestalt theory. Wertheimer had an active teaching schedule at Frankfurt, and in his lectures used illustrations of thinking and perception that fit his theory. He continued to devote his efforts to the essential features of Gestalt psychology and was working on a series of experiments that were inspired by the theoretical formulations. However, he did not formally publish his ideas. Wertheimer's mind was, as his wife was later to describe it,

> constantly bubbling, brimming, seething…. His thought was not linear, nor circular, nor even in the form of an ascending spiral. Rather, it went simultaneously in many directions at once, always keeping the whole, its constituent parts, and its context in mind. If he began writing a sentence, his thought was already so far ahead by the time he got to the middle of the sentence that the first part was already no longer correct or apt. As a consequence, he published relatively little after the Gestalt school was launched…. Doubtless his frustration with the sequential, largely piecemeal nature of written text was responsible at least in part for the relatively small volume of his published work.[19]

Although the general approach of Gestalt theory had been outlined in the 1912 publications on thinking in aboriginal people and on apparent motion, there was no formal statement of the general theory outside Wertheimer's lectures. His failure to generate an explicit précis of his doctrine was no doubt troubling for him; it also was frustrating for his colleagues. In particular, Koffka "became somewhat impatient with the lack of a formal statement of Gestalt principles and included in his discussion a good deal of what Wertheimer had been saying in his lectures in Frankfurt."[20]

Köhler was the first to respond to the need to publish the ideas of Gestalt theory as an alternative to the older reductionist psychologies. He did so in a 1913 attack on the "constancy hypothesis," as he called the nineteenth-century assumption that a strict point-for-point relationship exists between physical stimuli and sensations. As Gestalt theorist Solomon E. Asch put it, Köhler argued that

> sensory organization is a basic, underived function. He was critical of the belief in a one-to-one correspondence between local stimulation [such as a small gray circle] and local sensation [such as how light or dark the circle looks]. Identical local stimulation does not produce identical local effects. [The same circle looks lighter against a dark background than a white one.] Past experience and hypothetical higher mental processes will not explain deviations from the constancy hypothesis.[21]

Köhler's paper was a tightly-reasoned challenge to the older traditions of psychology; but it did not explicitly refer to Gestalt theory. Indeed, the first explicit allusion to Gestalt psychology in print appears to have come not from Wertheimer, Koffka, or Köhler, but from one of the students at Frankfurt, Dr. Gabriele Gräfin (Countess) von Wartensleben.

Wartensleben published a paper in the 1910 *Zeitschrift für Psychologie* on the psychology of translation.[22] In 1913, still a student at Frankfurt, she published another article, presenting the results of a study of the influence of a delay on the reproduction of a set of tachistoscopically exposed letters; for her experiments, designed for a dissertation, Wartensleben recruited several of the Academy's psychologists as participants, including Wertheimer, Köhler, Fuchs, and, for a few experiments, Schumann.[23] In that same year, she received her Ph.D. from Schumann at Frankfurt and began teaching there.[24]

In 1914, Wartensleben published a 71-page monograph entitled *Die christliche Persönlichkeit im Idealbild: Eine Beschreibung sub specie psychologica [The ideal Christian personality: A description from the perspective of psychology]*.[25] In the opening sentence of the monograph, she wrote: "The word *personality*, one of the weightiest, most problematic words in the language, means—from a psychological point of view—neither more nor less than a *'Gestalt'* of a particular kind, in the proper and absolute sense of the word." Attached to the word "*Gestalt*" is a superscript number 1. Lengthy footnote number 1 fills most of the next few pages. In it

Wartensleben discussed Ehrenfels's 1890 article on Gestalt qualities and a work by Hans Cornelius, a Neo-Kantian philosopher who advanced an empirical theory of perception and was a professor at Frankfurt from 1910 on. In 1903, Cornelius published a paper on Gestalt quality. But the primary focus of the footnote concerned

> M. Wertheimer's *Gestalt theory* (which has not yet appeared in print, but about which I learned in a lecture on epistemological problems which he gave at the Frankfurt Academy in the summer semester of 1913, and in many private conversations) [, which] contains the following basic thoughts, presented here freely and in a fragmentary way:
>
> 1. Aside from chaotic impressions (which cannot really be, or cannot yet really be, apprehended in a genuine sense), the contents of our consciousness are mostly not summative, but constitute a particular *characteristic "togetherness,"* that is, a segregated structure, often "comprehended from an inner center" (which, depending upon the nature of the conscious context, can be quite different: e.g., perhaps an optical or acoustic center or, according to the prevailing relationships, a dynamic or an intensity center, etc.), to which the other parts of the structure are related in a hierarchical system.
>
> Such structures are to be designated as "Gestalten" in a precise sense.
>
> 2. Almost all impressions are grasped either as chaotic masses (a relatively rare extreme case) or else rather "poorly structured" on the one hand, or as Gestalten on the other—or as chaotic masses on the way to becoming more sharply structured. What is finally grasped are "structured impressions" (including "objects" in a broad sense of the word, and also "contextual relationships"). They specifically are something *different from...*the summative totality of the individual components. Often the "whole" is grasped even before the individual parts enter into consciousness.
>
> 3. The epistemological process...is very often a process of "centering," that is, of "structuring" or of grasping that particular aspect which provides the key to an orderly whole, of "unifying" the particular individual parts that happen to be present; what results is that a structured unit emerges as a whole due to, and through, the power of this centering. The specific result of the epistemological process is the "springing forth" of the Gestalt from the "not yet structured." The parts acquire particular characteristics from the one specific total conception; parts and their particular attributes can now be understood on this basis.
>
> The structure that results from the epistemological process depends to some extent not only on the object, but also on the observer. Thus many givens can be comprehended in several different ways, but usually only *one* is correct: namely the one which makes all the attributes understandable, and derivable in a simple way from the central idea, and thus provides meaning to the entire given.
>
> 4. The same attributes, as parts of different wholes, can have quite different meanings, depending upon how they fit into the structure, that is, e.g., depending on whether they are closer to or farther from the center. Thus in, for example, "the wall is red," the "red" is different from the red in "blood is red" (in which case, of course, the idea becomes logically more complicated)...

—For knowledge of these facts we are obligated to Wertheimer's Gestalt theory, as well as to a series of useful detailed suggestions, which indeed made possible our attempt to sketch the conception of the ideal Christian personality in the way we have done it, since other theories would not, in our opinion, have sufficed at all for such a simple overview and presentation of most of the relevant matters.

Here the footnote ends. There are problems with the relatively abstruse prose and with the elaboration of Gestalt theory in terms of "centering"; several principles also remain rather obscure in this account. Furthermore, the idea of an "inner center" to which other parts of a whole are hierarchically related does not fully capture the intricate articulation characteristic of many Gestalten, as already detailed in countless examples in Wertheimer's paper on number concepts. And the extension of the Gestalt concept to the "ideal personality," while clearly of heuristic value, does not appear to fit with the precision of thought to which Wertheimer, Köhler and Koffka always aspired in their writings. How much the "fuzziness" of this summary actually characterized Wertheimer's Gestalt thought at this time, and how much it may have been due to Wartensleben's difficulty in trying to formulate the theory in specific yet general terms, can not be determined. But at any rate, this account, a long footnote to the first sentence in a relatively esoteric monograph, appears to be the first explicit published reference to the new Gestalt theory. As documented in the footnote, "Wertheimer's Gestalt theory" appears to have become an identifiable system of thought by the summer of 1913.

Notes

1. Max Wertheimer (1912). Über das Denken der Naturvölker: I. Zahlen und Zahlgebilde [On the thinking of aboriginal peoples: I. Numbers and numerical structures]. *Zeitschrift für Psychologie, 60,* 321-378.
2. Daniel N. Robinson (1978). *The mind unfolded: Essays on psychology's historic texts.* Washington, D.C.: University Publications of America, pp. 200-201.
3. Max Wertheimer (1912). Experimentelle Studien über das Sehen von Bewegung [Experimental studies of the seeing of motion]. *Zeitschrift für Psychologie, 61,* 161-265.
4. E. G. Boring (1942). *Sensation and perception in the history of experimental psychology.* New York: Appleton-Century-Crofts, p. 594.
5. Edwin B. Newman (1944). Max Wertheimer. *American Journal of Psychology, 57,* 428-435, p. 431.
6. Siegfried Jaeger (ed.) (1988). *Briefe von Wolfgang Köhler an Hans Geitel 1907-1920, mit zwei Arbeiten Köhlers, "Über elektromagnetische Erregung des Trommelfelles" und "Intelligenzprüfungen am Orang" im Anhang [Letters of Wolfgang Köhler to Hans Geitel 1917-1920, with two works of Köhler, "On electromagnetic stimulation of the eardrum" and "Intelligence tests on the orang" as appendices].* Passau, West Germany: Passavia Universitätsverlag.

7. Wolfgang Köhler (1942). Kurt Koffka: 1886-1941. *Psychological Review*, 49, p. 97.
8. Ash, *The emergence of Gestalt theory: Experimental psychology in Germany, 1890-1920*, pp. 297-298.
9. Mira Klein Koffka, daughter of a publisher, was also a subject in Koffka's dissertation research on rhythm (as was Erich von Hornbostel). Kurt Koffka (1909). Experimental-Untersuchungen zur Lehre vom Rhythmus [Experimental studies on the theory of rhythm], *Zeitschrift für Psychologie*, 52, 1-109, esp. p. 16.
10. Boring, p. 595.
11. Boring, pp. 595-596.
12. Quoted in Richard J. Herrnstein and Edwin G. Boring (eds.) (1965). *A source book in the history of psychology*. Cambridge, MA: Harvard University Press, p. 260.
13. Kurt Koffka (1935, 1963). *Principles of Gestalt psychology*. New York: Harcourt, Brace, pp. 53-54.
14. Wolfgang Köhler, Gestalt psychology. In Mary Henle (ed.) (1971), *The selected papers of Wolfgang Köhler*. New York: Liveright, pp. 108-122, pp. 110-111.
15. Ash, *The emergence of Gestalt theory: Experimental psychology in Germany, 1890-1920*, p. 303.
16. Newman, p. 433. Fuchs' article on transparency was published in the 1923 volume of the *Zeitschrift für Psychologie*.
17. Max Wertheimer (1912). Über experimentalpsychologische Analyse bestimmter hirnpathologischen Erscheinungen [On experimental-psychological analysis of certain symptoms of brain pathology]. In F. Schumann (ed.), *Bericht über den V. Kongress für experimentelle Psychologie in Berlin vom 16. bis 20, April 1912 (Report on the fifth congress for experimental psychology in Berlin from April 16 to 20, 1912)*, p. 188. Leipzig: Johann Ambrosius Barth.
18. The report was published in the November 25, 1913 issue of the *Münchener medizinische Wochenschrift [Munich medical weekly]*.
19. Michael Wertheimer (1980). Max Wertheimer, Gestalt prophet. *Gestalt Theory*, 2, 3-17, p. 14.
20. Newman, p. 433.
21. Solomon E. Asch (1968). Wolfgang Köhler: 1887-1967. *American Journal of Psychology*, 81, p. 113. Wolfgang Köhler (1913). Über unbemerkte Empfindungen und Urteilstäuschungen [On unnoticed sensations and errors of judgment]. *Zeitschrift für Psychologie*, 66, 51-80.
22. Gabriele Gräfin v. Wartensleben (1910). Beiträge zur Psychologie des Übersetzens [Contributions to the psychology of translation]. *Zeitschrift für Psychologie*, 57, 89-115.
23. Wartensleben (1913). Über den Einfluss der Zwischenzeit auf die Reproduction gelesener Buchstaben [On the influence of the time interval on the reproduction of alphabetical letters that have been read]. *Zeitschrift für Psychologie*, 64, 321-385, p. 327. In her paper, von Wartensleben included a description of each participant's imagery type and attitude toward the experiment. The authors are grateful to the late Professor Edwin B. Newman of Harvard University for bringing this article to their attention.

24. Ash, *The emergence of Gestalt theory: Experimental psychology in Germany, 1890-1920*, p. 300.

25. Gabriele Gräfin v. Wartensleben (1914). *Die christliche Persönlichkeit im Idealbild: Eine Beschreibung sub specie psychologica* [*The ideal Christian personality: A description from the perspective of psychology*]. Kempten and Munich: Kögel. The authors are indebted to the late Professor Fritz Heider of Kansas University for directing them to this reference.

6

The World War One Period, 1914-1921

*Gestalten are in no way less immediate than
their parts; indeed one often apprehends a whole
before anything regarding its parts is
apprehended.*
—Kurt Koffka (1915)

By the early months of 1914, Gestalt theory was taking shape as a fairly radical movement that posed a significant challenge to the largely elementaristic orientation of traditional European experimental psychology. Wertheimer was already deeply immersed in studies of the organization of perception, focused on what made parts of the perceptual field coalesce into integrated units. This work did not reach fruition as a publication until 1923, although he wrestled with the formulation of the article for at least a decade before that. Wertheimer's dedication was persistent and tireless; in one practical human concern after another, he brought the Gestalt orientation to shed new light and replace what he called "out-worn" modes of thinking, to try to get at the heart or the "radix" (Latin for "root") of the matter. As the theory blossomed, Wertheimer's professional career also advanced, although not at the rate he might have preferred.

Wertheimer taught philosophy and psychology as soon as he was appointed Dozent at the Frankfurt Academy in the spring of 1912. This lowest academic rank did not, of course, provide him with financial independence; his family continued to subsidize his career, as was the case for most Dozents. Following further work on acoustics, Köhler earned his habilitation late in 1911 and was also Dozent at the Academy. Ash[1] wrote that Wertheimer and Köhler "were among the first to habilitate in Frankfurt, and thus part of the growing tendency of the school to take on the lineaments of a full-fledged university."

As Dozent, Wertheimer acquired teaching responsibilities in philosophy and psychology which, from 1912 to 1914, included courses on "Sociocultural Psychology" (*Völkerpsychologie*), "Theory of Knowledge," "Psychology of Memory," and "The Origins of Philosophy." He also offered courses on "History of Nineteenth Century Philosophy," "The Physical Basis of Consciousness," and the thought of the French vitalist philosopher Henri-Louis Bergson.[2]

Further Research on Motion
and Early Criticisms of the Gestalt School

Wertheimer's research and animated teaching style inspired several young psychologists, such as Gabriele Gräfin von Wartensleben, to pay serious attention to Gestalt theory. The publication on apparent movement not only earned him his habilitation, but also served as an impetus for extensive further work on motion within the Gestalt framework. In particular, Koffka became a vigorous advocate of Wertheimer's theory at his new position in Giessen. Robert Sommer, a psychiatrist at Giessen, not only granted Koffka permission to use laboratory space at the university clinic but also purchased a Schumann tachistoscope for Koffka's perception studies. As early as 1912, Koffka introduced his students to Wertheimer's ideas, although he was not yet formally permitted to supervise doctoral dissertations.[3] Shortly after Wertheimer's 1912 paper on perceived movement, Koffka directed the research of a student at Giessen, Friedrich Kenkel, who studied illusory figures and identified three separate types of apparent movement.[4] Koffka also advised Adolph Korte, a Gymnasium (high school) instructor, in a 1915 study of the effects of stimulus intensity on apparent motion. This analysis led to the characterization of "delta" movement, a reverse apparent motion that takes place when a first stimulus is much brighter than the second. Movement is then perceived to take place in the direction opposite to the order of presentation. Based on this research, Korte developed "laws" of optimal movement that were purely empirical generalizations. Later research largely supported Korte's observations.

By 1914, Gestalt theory had emerged as an identifiable entity in European psychology. This was evident in, for instance, the published critique of the theory by the Italian-Austrian psychologist Vittorio Benussi. In 1900, Benussi earned his Ph.D. from Austrian philosopher Alexius Meinong, an ardent pupil of Brentano,[5] at the University of Graz; some 15 years earlier, in 1885, Ehrenfels had also received his Ph.D. from Meinong. Meinong's student Fritz Heider wrote years later that his mentor had recognized an important feature of Ehrenfels's formulation of Gestalt qualities:

> Ehrenfels had tried to show that there are two kinds of [mental] elements: sensations and Gestalt qualities. Meinong, in his passion for clearly articulated theories, developed the idea of his friend and former student and said that there is a two-step process. The first step leads from stimuli to the sensations, and the second from sensations to Gestalt. The first step is mainly determined by external factors—that is, by the stimuli—while the second goes on by virtue of

an internal factor, an act of the subject, which he called the act of production.... Ehrenfels seems to have accepted this idea for the most part, in spite of the statement in his paper that the Gestalt qualities require no special activity and that they can appear simultaneously with the sensations.

In the period following his degree, Benussi became a prolific researcher on perception as well as a major figure, like Ehrenfels and Meinong, in the Austrian school of form quality. Heider remembered Benussi as "an elegant-looking, lean person with a finely chiseled, melancholy face and a dry skeptical smile. He went around in a black laboratory smock and when he took a walk he put on a black hat with a wide brim and puffed on a long black cigar."[6] He was a tireless worker, often known to spend the night sleeping in his laboratory, who wanted to provide experimental evidence for Meinong's "second step." Following his mentor, Benussi advocated the importance of the "productive process" in perception: a mental agency combines sensory elements into wholes.

Benussi's orientation was a source of tension with the Gestalt psychologists at Frankfurt, Giessen, and later Berlin:

> During the years from 1902 to about 1912, Benussi must have felt that he was in the position of a pioneer battling with the old-fashioned view that perception begins and ends with the study of sensation elements. But in the years immediately preceding World War I, his experiments were suddenly and unexpectedly attacked from another side, the new Berlin [Gestalt] group. He found himself forced out of the role of the progressive rebel into that of defender of the established view.[7]

At the 1914 congress of the Society for Experimental Psychology, a talk by Benussi on his research on motion phenomena drew a response from Wertheimer during the discussion of Benussi's paper. According to Heider, though, Benussi was not offended by Wertheimer's remarks:

> He once visited a German congress at which he met the three Berlin psychologists, and apparently they had a very good time together. He talked in a rather wistful way about these youngsters who were newcomers in the field of Gestalt psychology but had very interesting ideas.... When I went to Berlin in 1921, Benussi sent me letters of introduction and told me to be sure to look up Wertheimer who, he said, was a remarkable man.[8]

Although Wertheimer's comments at the congress apparently were not a direct attack on Benussi's theory, theoretical differences were beginning to emerge between the new Gestalt school and the older orientation of "form quality."

In 1914, the same year as his talk at the congress of the Society for Experimental Psychology, Benussi published an article criticizing Gestalt theory in general and the interpretation of apparent motion by Koffka's student Kenkel in particular.[9] The following year, in the *Zeitschrift für Psychologie*, Koffka wrote a 79-page reply to Benussi's paper which included the comment: "In criticizing Kenkel's studies Benussi maintains that apparent differences between his own theory and ours are merely the result of misinterpretations of his doctrine."[10] But Koffka did not agree. He was interested in providing more than a defense of Kenkel's research. Heider remembered that "Meinong's theory and Benussi's experiments...served as a foil to set off the new theory. Koffka explicitly rejected the two-step process and, with it, the concept of sensations as basic elements in perception."[11] After addressing Benussi's arguments in painstaking detail and offering his own criticism of the "production theory," Koffka boldly described the Gestalt position as "an opposing theory." The

> principle of a fixed relationship between stimulus and sensation...has been discarded in favor of a biological point of view: the organism in its environment.... *Descriptively* this theory holds that objects of experience (both simultaneous and successive) are not typically summative, composed of and decomposable into elements.... *Functionally* the theory rejects sensations...as the typical connection between stimulation and experience.... Attempts to derive the whole from its parts or to erect it upon them are very often futile, wholes not being direct experience-correlates of the stimuli.... *Physiologically* the theory will treat the brain process correlated with an experience not as the individual excitation of one brain area plus association, but as a whole-process with its whole-properties.[12]

However important the physiological model was to Gestalt theory, Koffka denied that it was the quintessential feature of the new school:

> The essential aspect of Wertheimer's theory is not, as Benussi claims, "a physico-physiological short-circuit analogy," but a recentering of the entire question. Whoever is not interested in the physiological aspects of the theory may leave this part out of consideration; for even without it the new apprehension of the functional relation between stimulus and experience is still possible.[13]

In his reply to Benussi, Koffka demonstrated that he was not only an astute theoretician but also an ardent advocate of the Gestalt school. As Heider wrote, he may be viewed as having produced the "first more thorough presentation of the new theory."[14]

During his efforts on behalf of Gestalt psychology at Giessen, Koffka maintained his professional and personal interest in what was going on at Schumann's Psychological Institute at Frankfurt. Regardless of Schumann's apparent ambivalence about Gestalt theory, several of his assistants at the Psychological Institute were actively working under the assumptions of the Gestalt orientation. Wertheimer and Köhler were lecturing on the new psychology and investigating a variety of perceptual phenomena, as were others who had not yet explicitly joined the Gestalt camp, among them Adhémar Gelb. Born in Moscow, Russia, Gelb had earned his Ph.D., based on a dissertation on Gestalt qualities, with Stumpf at Berlin in 1910. He arrived in Frankfurt in 1912 as Koffka's replacement in the Psychological Institute and immediately began producing work that had implications for Wertheimer's theory. Gelb collected experimental data on the perception of space and time, and concluded that the general result of his work "lies essentially in the direction of the 'Gestalt laws'"—which he learned about only at the conclusion of his research.[15] Wertheimer had not produced a major publication since his 1912 habilitation thesis. Because of his lack of a clear statement on Gestalt theory, Gelb, Koffka, and Köhler were forced to rely on Wertheimer's lectures and conversations in presenting the Gestalt thesis. Indeed, when responding to Benussi in 1915, Koffka drew upon an unpublished quote that he attributed to Wertheimer, implying that it was essentially an "official" statement of the Gestalt position on perception:

> [E]xperiences are usually organized wholes whose parts are co-ordinated in a hierarchical system around a central point. Such structures [Gestalten] are in no way less immediate than their parts; indeed one often apprehends a whole before anything regarding its parts is apprehended.[16]

Wertheimer's Research During the First World War

In 1914, the Frankfurt Academy was formally granted the status of a university, and the University of Frankfurt was officially founded. Dramatic events occurred in the same year southeast of Frankfurt that would culminate in the First World War. During a June 28, 1914, military inspection of Sarajevo, the capital city of the province of Bosnia, Austrian archduke Francis Ferdinand and his wife, Sophie, duchess of Hohenberg, were murdered by the Serbian nationalist assassin Gavrilo Princip. This episode, and the consequent July 28 declaration of war by Austria-Hungary on Serbia, impacted the lives of countless millions. Without question, Wertheimer's life and career, like almost everyone else's in Europe—and elsewhere—at the time, were deeply affected by these events. As a participant in the German academic system, he found the course of his life changed by Germany's declaration of war on Russia on August 1, 1914. Like many Czechs and Slovaks, he may have felt greater sympathy for the cause of the Triple Entente of England, France and Russia than for that of the Triple Alliance of Germany, Austria-Hungary, and later Italy. But the realities of his circumstances, and those of his comrades in Austria-Hungary, offered little promise for any significant opposition to the Germanic powers. Thus, following the outbreak of World War I, Czech citizens were compelled to forge an alliance with a country from which they had tried to free themselves;

and, by the system of conscription, all Czechs and Slovaks of military age were taken into the Austro-Hungarian army. As the war progressed, thousands either deserted individually or surrendered en masse to the Allied armies, particularly those of Russia. Already an ardent advocate of peace at almost any price, Wertheimer doubtless followed every new episode in the war with intense interest.

In the early months of the war, several intellectuals of the "Prague Circle" met repeatedly in the Café Arco to discuss their opposition to the war. During one such session, the Austrian writer Max Brod, author of novels, plays, and poems as well as political treatises on pacifism and Zionism, and a close friend of Franz Kafka, together with a fellow dramatist and poet, Franz Werfel, developed some specific ideas about bringing a peaceful end to the war. Brod and Werfel agreed that a plea for peace published in a foreign, neutral newspaper might help resolve national differences. They hoped that the support of Czech statesman and philosopher Tomás Garrigue Masaryk, a vigorous critic of German encroachment on the Austrian government, might add significant weight to their appeal for peace. At the time, Masaryk was a professor of philosophy and sociology at the University of Prague, a member of the Austrian Reichsrat (Parliament), and the chief figure in the Realist or Progressive Party. The Prague Circle regarded him as "realistic" and "humanistic," and as a "liberal" who was not bound by nationalism. In an attempt to add credibility to their petition, Brod and Werfel asked Wertheimer, an old friend and an occasional participant in the Prague Circle discussions, to join them in meeting with Masaryk, in the hope that he might be swayed by his "rising young colleague" from Frankfurt.[17]

Despite the clamorous parade of a military regiment that was going on at the time, Brod, Werfel, and Wertheimer made their way to the nerve center for Masaryk's political newspaper, a cramped office on Wenceslas Square in Prague. Over the loud sounds of the military demonstrations outside, Wertheimer presented the logic behind his friends' arguments while Masaryk quietly listened. In time, however, Masaryk interrupted with a story about a Jew who had earlier in the day told the authorities about a Czech woman who had made a disparaging remark about the military parade, resulting in her arrest. He then admonished his Jewish visitors: "You should rather see to it that your fellow citizens cease their provocations." The young intellectuals were stunned by the remark. Brod later reminisced that Masaryk "had spoken as a Czech nationalist." For Masaryk, the ruin of the alliance between Germany and Austria-Hungary stood as the best hope for the Czech dream of independence, but the situation seemed bleak and, in 1914, he fled from Austria to seek asylum in Switzerland. According to one source, Wertheimer was extensively interrogated by authorities following Masaryk's exile, largely because their meeting took place shortly before the Czech iconoclast left the country.[18]

Although Wertheimer's career was not yet directly affected by the war, the same was not true of his friend and colleague Wolfgang Köhler. In 1913, Köhler had accepted a formal invitation from the Prussian Academy of Sciences to direct an anthropoid station in Tenerife, one of the Canary Islands off the west coast of Spanish Africa. A year after Köhler's arrival in Tenerife, the advent of the war, particularly a blockade of the region by the British, made it impossible to leave the island. Köhler, his wife Thekla, and their children were effectively detained there for seven years. Köhler was remarkably productive during this period, both in the application of Gestalt theory to the problem-solving skills of animals and in the general theoretical development of Gestalt psychology as a prominent theory of natural science. Animal research was of interest to all three Gestalt psychologists, particularly because of the international attention paid to the American psychologist Edward Lee Thorndike, who had argued at the end of the preceding century that animal learning proceeds in an automatic, gradual manner. Such conclusions did not fit with the orientation of the Gestaltists.

Köhler was a rather young, yet not inappropriate, candidate for the directorship of the anthropoid station. In 1913 at Frankfurt he taught a course on animal psychology, and was presumably well-versed in the literature on animal behavior.[19] Köhler quickly adapted to conditions far more crude than at his laboratory in Germany and conducted several experiments demonstrating that chickens visually distinguish and transfer stimulus relationships (such as choosing the lighter of two gray patches) rather than responding to absolute stimulus values (such as medium gray no matter what shade the other patches are).

Köhler studied learning and transposition of such relationships in children and chickens, but his research on problem solving by primates generated the most fame. Köhler performed many experiments such as one in which a banana was placed outside the cage bars, beyond reach, prompting a chimpanzee to use a stick to rake in the banana or even to join two short hollow bamboo rods together to make a stick long enough to retrieve the fruit. Based on his observations, Köhler claimed that the chimpanzees did not try to solve the problem by blind trial and error or by random efforts to get the banana. They seemed to realize that the banana was out of their reach, and that they had to devise some way to bring it within reach. The chimpanzees appeared to demonstrate a genuine understanding of the problem, discovering its critical components. A meaningful solution was attained when the primate "reorganized" or "restructured" the various parts of the problem. Many of them displayed what he called insight into the situation.

In another problem, a banana was suspended by a string several feet above the head of a chimpanzee, high enough so that the lure could not be reached by jumping. The chimpanzees typically found a solution if boxes were lying on the ground in the vicinity of the suspended fruit. The problem could be "restructured" (and solved) by dragging a wooden crate directly beneath the banana, so that the chimpanzee could climb up on it and reach or jump successfully for the fruit. If a single box was not sufficient in helping the chimpanzee to jump and reach the banana, one insightful solution was to stack several crates to construct a higher tower from which the animal could seize the objective. While the towers were often irregular, they were sufficiently stable to permit attaining the objective before the tower collapsed. Several of Köhler's chimpanzee subjects used other tools, such as a stick, in conjunction with stacked boxes.

Between 1916 and 1920, Köhler also undertook extensive studies of problem solving by a young female orangutan, who demonstrated intelligence not only in the ability to use tools but also in tool *making*. However, he did not publish his findings on this research because he was uneasy about publishing studies performed only on a single exemplar of a species, particularly in light of numerous individual differences among his chimpanzee subjects.[20]

Unlike Thorndike and the behaviorists, Köhler, like his colleagues Wertheimer and Koffka, believed that learning is not governed by blind trial and error or by mechanical associations in which every correct response is followed by a reward. Given an open field and the ability to see the relevant parts of the situation, the chimpanzees demonstrated an ability to restructure and solve problems with inventive and insightful methods. A traditional behaviorist experiment, such as a rat blindly finding its way through an arbitrarily constructed maze, seldom if ever allows such solutions. Consequently he argued that insightful learning is more likely to take place in a natural field setting, in which there are numerous opportunities to demonstrate lucid understanding, than in an artificial laboratory setting. His observations were published in the influential 1917 book *Intelligenzprüfungen an Anthropoiden,* later translated into English and published as *The Mentality of Apes*[21] (although *Intelligence Tests on Anthropoid Apes* would have been a more literal translation of the original title).

While on Tenerife, Köhler also undertook extensive analytical work on the natural sciences from the perspective of Gestalt theory. He had admired the precision of the physical sciences since his youth. During his years at the Gymnasium, Köhler studied with Hans Friedrich Geitel, a physicist, mathematician, and inventor who published over one hundred research articles and who, with his colleague Julius Elster, was credited with the construction of the first practical photoelectric cell and first photoelectric photometer. In his youth, Köhler spent a summer working in Geitel's research laboratory, which helped him develop a sophisticated facility for experimentation. Köhler's proficiency and ingenuity were evident not only in his dissertation on recording the movement of the eardrum, but also in daring experiments, conducted soon after arriving at Tenerife, on the stimulation of the eardrum. He compensated for the impoverished technology at the island in very resourceful ways, including gluing tiny iron filings to his own eardrum so as to permit electromagnetic (rather than acoustic) stimulation of the auditory apparatus. Köhler described his findings in a contribution to a 1915 *Festschrift* for Geitel and Elster.[22]

From his early mature years on, Köhler did his utmost to be a rigorous natural scientist. Indeed he was, in effect, a physicist who devoted his expertise to psychological phenomena. He managed to fuse his appreciation of physical science with Gestalt theory. In a 1915 letter, Köhler thanked Geitel for earlier advising him that the only hope to achieve anything in philosophy was to ground it in a thorough study of mathematics and the natural sciences.[23] In this spirit, Köhler reacquainted himself with the natural sciences of his early training by a careful and exhaustive study of a limited set of books on biology, chemistry, physics, and physiology that he had brought with him to Tenerife. His formal education and thorough grounding in the natural sciences were put to good use in his major work on the ubiquity of Gestalten in the physical and chemical world of natural science. Köhler

> saw that perceptually organized experiences have characteristics in common with certain well-known phenomena of field physics, first described by Faraday and Maxwell. There are physical systems; in fact, all natural closed systems are functional wholes in the sense that there are properties of the system which are dependent upon the relations among local conditions and cannot be compounded from the actions of their parts separately. Such systems also tend to develop toward an equilibrium, in the direction of maximum regularity and simplicity. They are, in short, physical *Gestalten*.[24]

Geitel helped make arrangements to have Köhler's influential work, *Die physischen Gestalten in Ruhe und im stationären Zustand (The Physical Gestalten at Rest and in a Stationary State)*, published in 1920 by Friedrich Vieweg in Braunschweig.

Despite the difficulty and isolation of his situation, Köhler managed to remain highly productive in advancing Gestalt theory. Koffka was elated with the work on physical Gestalten, and in a 1921 review of the book for the periodical *Die Naturwissenschaften [The Natural Sciences]*, declared that Köhler had produced "a wonderful unification of two areas of knowledge.... The future will show what this means for science and—let this be expressly emphasized—also for philosophy."[25] Wertheimer too was deeply pleased with Köhler's efforts. He, like Koffka, was actively teaching and doing research on Gestalt theory, although the events of the war were doubtless never far from his mind.

The Triple Alliance collapsed when Italy declared war on Austria-Hungary in 1915 and on Germany in 1916, and joined the Entente Allies. The new Allied Powers, composed of England, France, Russia, and Italy, became increasingly resolute in their campaign against the Central Powers of Germany and Austria-Hungary.[26]

By 1915, the promise of armistice appeared more remote than ever and, for the first time, the war directly impacted Wertheimer's career as several university researchers were commissioned as civilian scientific experts by the Austro-Hungarian army. In the summer of 1915, Wertheimer joined Erich von Hornbostel, Kurt Koffka, and Hans Rupp, as well as two physicists (Max Born, who had arrived at Berlin the same year, and Carl Stumpf's son Felix), in work directly related to the war effort.[27] Wertheimer and von Hornbostel joined Born's department in the Prussian army's "Artillerie-Prüfungs-Kommission," the commission for testing artillery. Wertheimer was required to shave off his thick black beard in accordance with military protocol. At the age of 35, he was assigned an officer's rank and, despite their difference in training and thinking, made a significant impression on Born, who reported:

> Wertheimer became a great friend of ours. He was a deep thinker, but of a different type from any I had known before: skeptical in the extreme, inclined to take nothing for granted and to regard any observations as a deception of the senses or the mind, until its truth was shown by correct psychological experiment. We spoke a rather different language; when I said "space" I meant the geometric space of the physicist, while he understood the spatial order of sensory impressions. It was most instructive for me to see the other side of the picture, to learn something about the psychological phenomena, the "Gestalten" which are the raw material of all observation. On one point we could never agree. He did not even accept logic and arithmetic, and he tried to construct a meta-logic and meta-arithmetic, based on different axioms. He said, "Look at primitive people, savages, who cannot count past five; they have a different arithmetic." But that did not convince me. I think today that to some extent he was right although the material available at that time was insufficient to show the fertility of such ideas.[28]

Psychologists proved useful to the military in several ways. Abraham S. Luchins's and Edith H. Luchins's correspondence with several acquaintances suggests that Wertheimer may have helped with selection and training methods and the recruitment of soldiers who could adapt to the non-pressurized cabin of an airplane.[29] Wertheimer and von Hornbostel worked together on several projects, including one that involved two Swedish

> inventors who had claimed to have an apparatus that could detect ammunition from great distances. In order to test the apparatus, Wertheimer and von Hornbostel filled 98 of 100 identical boxes with sand and only two with ammunition. All the boxes were arranged in a circle, and the two inventors and their instruments were placed in the center of the circle. On the inventors' first trial, the instrument selected a box with ammunition. The representatives of the army, who had reluctantly agreed to the test, were satisfied with the instruments

and wanted the testing to stop. But after much pleading [from Wertheimer and von Hornbostel], they allowed the testing to go on. In all the remaining trials, the instrument selected the boxes that were full of sand.[30]

However, Wertheimer and von Hornbostel made their greatest contribution to the Artillery Testing Commission with their development of an acoustic device for detecting ships. Wertheimer and von Hornbostel set themselves the task of designing a device that would locate a sound such as a submarine engine or cannon fire with a degree of precision that would suffice for defensive counter-measures. They used binaural directional horns to detect and locate the precise direction of sound. The apparatus greatly increased the functional distance between an operator's two ears, thus enhancing substantially the precision of determining the angle of a sound's orientation. According to Born, Wertheimer and von Hornbostel

> had discovered the ability to estimate the direction from which a sound comes, based on the time difference with which the wave front reaches the two ears. The accuracy is limited by the base (distance between the two ears) but accuracy can be increased by mounting two microphones at a greater distance and by listening with earphones. With such an instrument the direction of a firing gun can be determined to a fraction of a degree, and it has been used successfully at the front.[31]

Wertheimer and von Hornbostel later patented their binaural listening device and lightheartedly dubbed it the "Wertbostel" (a partial combination of their names). Wertheimer and von Hornbostel also published on this work in a 1920 article, "Über die Wahrnehmung der Schallrichtung" ("On the perception of the direction of a sound").[32] The Wertbostel proved so successful that Wertheimer and von Hornbostel were still discussing licensing fees with manufacturers as late as 1934.[33]

Following his military assignment, Wertheimer returned to the University of Berlin, now as Dozent, in 1916. Berlin's imposing buildings, beautiful parks, and splendid avenues must have provided a welcome contrast with the military settings. At the eastern end of Unter den Linden, a street renowned for its equestrian statue of Frederick the Great, stood the palace formerly occupied by Emperor Wilhelm II. Between the palace and the Brandenburg Gate, a distance of less than a mile, was the University of Berlin, in addition to an opera house, fine hotels and elegant shops, and the palaces of emperors Wilhelm I and Frederick III. Although only a little over a century old at the time, having been founded in 1810, the University of Berlin ranked first among German universities in number of students prior to the First World War. The University of Berlin turns out to have played a central role in Wertheimer's entire academic and professional life: he spent nearly half the years between 1902 and 1933 in Berlin, and much of his most influential work occurred while he was associated with that university.

Aside from his research and teaching activities, Berlin offered Wertheimer the opportunity to renew old friendships, such as his warm relation with the Stern household, and to foster new ones. Among the luminaries at Berlin was the physicist Albert Einstein, already a significant figure in science. Born on March 14, 1879, some thirteen months before Wertheimer, Einstein had already published many highly influential articles on molecular dimensions, motion, light, electrodynamics, and inertia—as well as his general theory of relativity—in the prestigious *Annalen der Physik*, and had taught at several European institutions by the time of Wertheimer's return to Berlin. Married to his university sweetheart, Mileva Marič, in 1903, Einstein was the father of two children when he accepted a position with the Prussian Academy of Sciences in Berlin in April 1914. Wertheimer probably met Einstein about the time of his divorce from Mileva in 1916. Wertheimer and Einstein became close friends after Wertheimer's arrival in Berlin that year.

Einstein enjoyed intellectual discourse with scholars from other disciplines, including the Bengali poet and mystic Rabindranath Tagore on the nature of truth, and Sigmund Freud on the necessity of war, as well as with the physicists Max Born, Paul Ehrenfest, and Hendrik Antoon Lorentz. He seemed also to relish his intellectual and social exchanges with Wertheimer. Wertheimer was once amused when he and Einstein consecutively covered their right and left eyes with their hands to test the effects of retinal disparity (the slightly different images of the same object on the two retinas because of the spatial separation of the eyes) as they stared at a church steeple. Watching these figures on the street corner, a crowd soon gathered and the two were surprised to see that the onlookers were also engaging in this curious behavior, shifting their hands back and forth over their eyes.[34]

Their common interests included playing chamber music and sailing, with many shared hours spent sitting in Einstein's study or on a boat on a lake talking physics and psychology. Wertheimer was fascinated by Einstein's revolutionary thinking that had led to the development of the theory of relativity. "Those were wonderful days," Wertheimer later recalled, "beginning in 1916 when for hours and hours I was fortunate enough to sit with Einstein alone in his [Berlin] study, and hear from him the dramatic developments which culminated in the theory of relativity."[35]

In 1919 Einstein's general theory of relativity was confirmed following a scientific expedition by the Royal Society of London to Principe Island, in the Gulf of Guinea, to photograph the solar eclipse of May 29, 1919. The results from the expedition brought Einstein international recognition, and he was awarded the Nobel Prize in 1921.

In addition to admiring his friend's professional accomplishments, Wertheimer found much in Einstein's scientific philosophy that resonated with Gestalt psychology. The relationship between the two scientific theories did not go unnoticed. George Humphrey, Director of the Institute of

Experimental Psychology at Oxford University, wrote a 1924 article on "The Theory of Einstein and the Gestalt-Psychologie: A Parallel." Although Humphrey believed that "psychology lags infinitely behind the exact and powerful mathematical technique of the physical sciences," he was struck by the historical and theoretical parallels between the two approaches:

> In the fields of physical and psychological science there have lately appeared, under the names of the Einstein and the *Gestalt* theories, innovations which, unnoticed, at least in print, by both sets of workers, appear to lead by fundamentally similar methods of attack to fundamentally similar conclusions. In each case the attack is headed against an older theory whose postulate is discreteness of data, and in each case there is substituted a postulate of the primary interdependence of data, implying the necessity of a relative rather than an absolute treatment. This common point of departure results in parallelisms of which examples are the non-additiveness of data and the insistence upon whole processes rather than parts.[36]

Einstein and Wertheimer clearly shared similar scientific assumptions; they both also had a strong common commitment to humanitarian affairs and causes. Einstein, fond of the writings of the French pacifist and author Romain Rolland, was outraged over the senselessness and brutality of the war. Indeed, unlike his friends Born and Wertheimer, he adamantly refused to participate in the war effort.

Like Born, Einstein marveled at the fresh character of Wertheimer's thinking and his spirited belief in the search for truth. This is evident in a letter of recommendation which Einstein wrote in 1939:

> Because of common interests in scientific problems and common human concerns, Professor Max Wertheimer and myself have been in contact with each other for many years. I know few people who seek truth and understanding as passionately as he does. This explains his ability to arouse enthusiasm in young people for scientific work.... Not only in the field of psychology, but also in the field of philosophy in general, he is original and exceedingly stimulating. He is not a man of dusty erudition but of independent lively thinking.[37]

The relationship among Born, Einstein, and Wertheimer became closer through the years. Born, for instance, sent Einstein a postcard in July 1918 bearing a photomontage of portraits of Born, Einstein, and Wertheimer in partly overlapping ovals; Einstein received the postcard with delight and declared it a "cloverleaf."[38]

Thinking and Gestalt Logic

Near the end of the war, Wertheimer had the opportunity to pay a whimsical tribute to Carl Stumpf at an April 21, 1918 celebration of his mentor's seventieth birthday.[39] Together with Erich von Hornbostel and several other former students, Wertheimer saluted Stumpf's contributions to psychology and philosophy. In a talk on that occasion, Wertheimer apologized for Köhler's absence as he "marches along the Gulf of Tenerife" and characterized Koffka, also unable to attend, as "standing on the bridge of a torpedo boat." He acknowledged the influence of Stumpf's ideas on his own work and pointed out that "Stumpf's students have called to Wundt to turn again to the importance of metaphysics, law and freedom, mind and body, life and death." Wertheimer was particularly flattering when comparing Stumpf's work to that of his contemporaries, who treated the study of natural phenomena "as an enemy; they set up traps and try to defeat [Nature], or they are like sportsmen who want to show off their own skill and strength." Wertheimer then addressed Stumpf, "How different are you!" And in describing Stumpf's method he used an illustration: "With one African tribe there exists the...custom: When they want to show a guest that they trust him, a mother puts a baby into his arms and says, 'Hold the child.' That is how you hold the facts in your hands, and what you have taught us: reverence for reality." The celebration included musical tributes, the presentation of a *Festschrift*, and several humorous skits, one of which was entitled "Mind and Body: A Dialogue" where Wertheimer assumed the role of the mind and Otto Abraham acted as the body, and another of which was a conversation among the five vowels (Wertheimer was "A," von Hornbostel "I," and other former students took the roles of the remaining three vowels).

During the same evening, Wertheimer presented a paper on productive thinking. His fascination with cognitive processes was already evident in his 1912 paper on the thinking of aboriginal peoples. In the time after that paper, he used Gestalt theory to develop a more meaningful explanation of thinking in his lectures and in his discussions with Einstein. Despite the attention that Wertheimer devoted to cognition in his lectures, he still had not published a thorough statement on productive thinking (or anything else) based on Gestalt theory.

Wertheimer's presentation at the Stumpf celebration was "On reasoning processes in productive thinking" ("Über Schlussprozesse im produktiven Denken").[40] The arguments in it were succinct, sometimes almost opaque in their brevity. In it, he attacked the sterile conclusions of Aristotelian logic as an artificial exercise in that it provides little insight into meaningful thinking: "The assumption that nature operates according to arbitrary, piecemeal, mutually indifferent elements pervades traditional logic as much as it pervaded the psychology of a half-century ago."[41] Drawing a formal conclusion by argument from humdrum premises, as in a logical syllogism (the familiar "*modus barbara*"), is arid and lifeless:

All animals with four legs are quadrupeds.

The horse has four legs.

Therefore, the horse is a quadruped.

Wertheimer argued that if the syllogism is to mirror actual human thinking adequately, the conclusion should produce a "new" proposition that follows from its major and minor premises, with the requirement "that the conclusion must not appear as a premise." This requirement is fundamental because

> if the conclusion merely repeats in a new way (i.e., as a kind of recapitulation) what was already known in the premises, the result is "meaningless." But what are the conditions imposed by [this] requirement?
>
> In its essentials the situation before the process is this: I possess, somewhere in my knowledge, the judgments that are to be used as premises; I do not yet possess the judgment which will appear as conclusion. Later [after the process] I do possess this [conclusion].[42]

As part of his challenge to traditional logic, Wertheimer hoped ultimately to construct a Gestalt logic that would offer a more meaningful account of productive thinking. The history of science, he argued, is replete with achievements that were *not* born from Aristotelian logic, including

> the comprehension of the nature of stellar movements ("falling" toward one another); the theory of the screw (seeing the screw as a wedge); the history of the conception of inertia. Until recently such accomplishments were thought of as essentially the results of "imagination," or "chance," or "the intuition of genius." But it is not these alone. *Formal* determinations, expressible in definite laws, are also involved.... In still other cases the essential process may be one of *centering*, where the important point is: *from the point of view of which part shall the remaining parts be seen?* Thus centering leads to a penetration into the essential content and hence to an apprehension of the concrete inner structure and inner necessity of the whole with which one is dealing.[43]

Although Wertheimer presented this talk earlier, he did not publish it until 1920. (A translation of that publication is appended to this chapter. The paper essentially states most of the points and several examples published in expanded form more than two decades later as Wertheimer's posthumous book, *Productive Thinking*.) Shortly thereafter, another psychologist interested in similar problems, Otto Selz, published extensively on productive thinking. He had studied cognition since 1913 and detailed his ideas about productive thinking in two books: *Zur Psychologie des produktiven Denkens und des Irrtums: Eine experimentelle Untersuchung* (*The Psychology of Productive Thought and of Error: An Experimental Investigation*), published in 1922, and *Die Gesetze der Produktiven und Reproduktiven Geistestätigkeit* (*The Laws of Productive and Reproductive Mental Capacity*), published in 1924. Like Wertheimer, Selz had worked at the Würzburg laboratory, where Külpe and Bühler had participated in his experiments. He opposed associationism in his analysis of thinking. An experimental psychologist, George Humphrey, reported that, drawing upon the research of the Würzburg school, Selz argued that thinking is governed by Watt's principle of *Aufgabe,* or task.

> *Aufgabe,* with the determination (determining tendencies) which it contains, initiates certain special mental operations, already in the repertoire, which lead to the solution of the problem...[called] Means (i.e., means to the end of the solution), and an important part of the process of solution is accordingly that of the Finding of Means.[44]

According to Selz, the "Finding of Means" represents the fundamental method by which the problem solver moves from an aim to a solution:

> The final solution is, of course, not given explicitly in the data, or there would be no problem.... [T]he problem is a set of data with a gap; and the effect of the determination is to initiate previously applied methods to fill the gap. So that the newness of productive thinking consists essentially in the application of such previously applied means to new material.[45]

Like Wertheimer before him, Selz employed his own approach to the psychology of productive thinking to examine the accomplishments of eminent scientists, including Faraday's discovery of the induction current, Darwin's development of the theory of evolution by natural selection, and Franklin's "bringing down the lightning from the clouds." Selz also claimed that Köhler's research with primates fit his theory.[46]

Although they shared a similarity in their terminology and non-associationist approaches, Wertheimer and Selz differed radically in their interpretations of productive thinking. For Selz, successful mental operations are achieved by selection of appropriate strategies from past experience; "the mental operation is reproduced, while the material on which it works is novel."[47] For Wertheimer, reproduction of a previous solution process does not constitute a productive solution. Rather, the recentering of the task in a manner that fits the material in the problem is crucial. On another issue, Selz suggested in his 1924 book that some process of "reflexoidal coordination" is central in thinking:

> We shall understand by reflexoidal co-ordination every co-ordination between a stimulus (that is to say, any occasion for reaction) and a motor or intellectual operation, which has for its result that the stimulus effects the release of the operation.[48]

Although Wertheimer speculated about a physiological mechanism in explanation of apparent movement, he did not invoke any such process in his analysis of productive thinking. This kind of reductionism may have appeared irrelevant to him. George Humphrey in his 1951 book on thinking declared that Selz was "the first psychologist to incorporate an explicitly non-associational doctrine into an experimentally induced psychology of thinking."[49] Selz was indeed the first to publish an "explicitly non-associational doctrine" on the psychology of thinking specifically backed by experimentation. It may well be due to the relative obscurity of the outlet in which Wertheimer published his own significant, though not specifically experimental, "explicitly non-associational" work on productive thinking that Selz (and Humphrey) happened to overlook it.

Germany Following the First World War

Wertheimer's native country underwent substantial upheaval in the period following the First World War. Indeed, the new Czechoslovak Republic was built on the ruins of the defeated and disintegrated Austro-Hungarian monarchy. On October 28, 1918, a declaration of independence by the National Committee in Prague established a provisional government. Czechoslovakia was born. The First National Assembly met on November 14, and Tomás Masaryk was elected the new country's first president; by February 29, 1920, a permanent constitution was adopted.

In the midst of such change, Wertheimer was persuaded to join Max Brod and other members of the "Prague Circle" in contributing to a 1918 book, *Das jüdische Prag (Jewish Prague)*. Wertheimer's contribution, "Vom Geistesleben des Prager Judentums" ("On the Mental Life of Prague Jewry"), was, characteristically, brief: only a paragraph. But it unmistakably conveyed his optimistic belief in the potential of youth, in this case, students from Prague:

> In recent years signs of strong spiritual life have come again and again from the youth of Prague. As often as I now think of Prague, I remember the report about the Prague School for Refugees—a joyful sign of active, heart-felt work—in ancient words, of work "for the sake of God" ["*zu Gott zu*"]. These are also my wishes and hopes for the youth of Prague; as it was expressed long ago in the Jewish will, that God should live in every daily deed, in the powerful present [*im kräftigem Diesseits*]. That seems to be coming again often; and much from Prague: heartfelt work in the midst of reality, toward life [*mitten im Wirklichen, dem Leben zu*].[50]

Wertheimer was also affected by the radical developments in Germany. Berlin entered a period of turmoil with the signing of the Treaty of Versailles on June 28, 1919, and the subsequent change in government from the German Empire to the German Republic. Following a meeting of the new National Assembly at Weimar from February 6 to August 11, 1919, the Weimar Republic was established and Friedrich Ebert was named president of the Reich. Although doubtless pleased that the First World War had ended, Wertheimer must have been troubled by the severe social upheavals that followed the radical changes in government. Throughout the period, strikes and food riots became commonplace and resistance to new governmental change was frequent—among students at the University of Berlin as well as in other groups of citizens.

During this time, a crowd of students from the University of Berlin seized control of the administrative building and locked up the rector (or provost). Doubtless because of his preeminence and credibility in the intellectual community, and also because of his open, liberal ideology, Albert Einstein was called to speak to the mob and, it was hoped, appease them. Before leaving for the occasion, Einstein called Max Born and Wertheimer and asked if they would join him in addressing the student council. The three men hurried by rail to the Reichstag, where the students were meeting. A large number of people had gathered, making entrance difficult. Einstein was recognized and the three professors were given permission to speak to the council. When it became apparent that the student council had little authority in the matter, Born and Wertheimer accompanied Einstein in defeat to the Reich Chancellor's Palace and were received by President Ebert. "How naïve we were, even as men forty years old," Einstein later wrote Born. "I can only laugh when I think about it. Neither of us realized how much more powerful is instinct compared to intelligence."[51]

Wertheimer was deeply engaged in his work, but the war and the turbulent changes in the German governmental structure must have exacted a toll on him. His mother's health was also failing. In 1919, Rosa Wertheimer died in Prague. Max's father was devastated. While he had been immersed in his vigorous professional and philanthropic activities, Wilhelm had relied heavily on Rosa. Her belief in orthodox Judaism had always apparently been deeper than his and had probably been a source of comfort for him. Wilhelm was crushed by her death, as he had been by Walter's. He became increasingly isolated, almost reclusive, and stopped following his rigorous, consuming schedule. Max, too, was deeply saddened by Rosa's death. At the same time, he was already encountering health problems of his own: although always more robust than Walter, Max had suffered from chronic spastic constipation since 1910, and by 1920 this condition had apparently become quite serious.[52]

Despite these challenges, Wertheimer continued to advance Gestalt theory in his classroom, study, and laboratory, and the prolific efforts of Köhler and Koffka were bearing fruit. Indeed, by 1920, there was sufficient interest in the theory that it was decided to undertake negotiations to establish a journal to be edited from the Berlin Institute.

Psychologische Forschung: The Gestalt Flagship

In May, 1921, Wertheimer, Koffka, Köhler, Kurt Goldstein (a professor of neurology in Frankfurt), and Hans Gruhle (a philosopher and psychiatrist in

Heidelberg) signed a contract with Julius Springer Verlag for the publication of a new psychology journal, *Psychologische Forschung: Zeitschrift für Psychologie und ihre Grenzgebiete* (*Psychological Research: Journal of Psychology and its Neighboring Fields*). At the time of the journal's founding, Springer Verlag, founded in 1842, was widely respected as a scholarly medical and scientific publishing house in Berlin. In spite of Springer's prominence, a new psychology journal may have been something of a risk; there were already a number of competing periodicals. A survey of the history of the journal contains the following observation:

> German psychology was already served by a sizeable number of professional journals, with the *Zeitschrift für Psychologie* [Journal of Psychology] and the *Archiv für die gesamte Psychologie* [Archives of General Psychology] dedicated to basic research and various journals to the applied fields of psychology. Although World War I had brought reductions in the size of the older journals, none of them had ceased to exist and in 1921/1922 all of them were doing quite well, despite the catastrophic economical conditions prevailing at that time.[53]

From its inception, the editors of *Psychologische Forschung* insisted that the new journal should be an outlet for the full range of psychology and related fields—a point that was made clear in an unsigned editorial in the first volume of *Psychologische Forschung*:

> This journal is intended to serve psychology in its entire extent, including the working relations that psychology has, or ought to have, to other sciences. Among the neighboring disciplines, particular attention will be given to psychopathology. Papers will be accepted on the basis of achievement rather than school affiliation. In addition to original papers, the journal will carry reviews on important new works. It is planned to publish, from time to time, surveys of the state of the problems in certain areas. The times require that the writing be as tight and the reasoning as stringent as possible.[54]

Although Wertheimer, Koffka, and Köhler of course intended to promote Gestalt theory, their interest in a pluralistic journal is evident in their editorial alliance with Goldstein and Gruhle. Kurt Goldstein received his M.D. from the University of Breslau in 1903 and, at the time of the journal's founding, was professor of neurology and Director of the Institute for Research into the Consequences of Brain Damage at the University of Frankfurt. Although not a disciple of Gestalt theory, Goldstein found value in a holistic orientation to neurology; his research on brain injury, published as *Die Behandlung, Fürsorge und Begutachtung hirnverletzter Soldaten* (*The Treatment, Care, and Certification of Brain-Injured Soldiers*) in 1919, revealed a deep respect for holistic-organismic theory. Hans Walther Gruhle received his M.D. from the University of Heidelberg in 1905 and wrote numerous articles and books on psychopathology during his career. He worked at a psychiatric hospital in

Heidelberg during the establishment of *Psychologische Forschung*. The selection of a psychiatrist and a neurologist as co-editors may have been a pragmatic choice because

> though Goldstein and Gruhle certainly were not inimical to Gestalt ideas, their inclusion in the editorial board was probably equally due to their professional background in neurology and psychiatry, which was consistent with the desire of the psychologist editors (and perhaps of the publishing house) to stress the working relations between psychology and psychopathology.[55]

The inaugural volume of *Psychologische Forschung* appeared in 1922. As promised in the introductory editorial, the journal explicitly endeavored to maintain an interdisciplinary and theoretically neutral perspective. Yet its Gestalt orientation was unmistakable from the start. Koffka served as managing editor in the early years of the journal (and later Köhler took on this chore) while Wertheimer edited manuscripts and occasionally contributed publications and book reviews. Through the editorial labors of Koffka, Köhler, and Wertheimer, the journal did become the central publication organ of the Gestalt movement. By the middle 1920s, *Psychologische Forschung* had become closely identified with the Berlin school of Gestalt psychology, and served as the primary publication outlet for the explosion of research activity generated by the robust new theory.

Wertheimer's Perspective on Aptitude Testing

One little-known feature of Wertheimer's concern with the potential utility of psychological knowledge, quite different from the Wertbostel sound-direction device and its military application, or, earlier, *Tatbestandsdiagnostik* and its role in legal proceedings, is his perspective on the practice of aptitude testing, which was beginning to be widely used primarily in the United States early in the twentieth century and expanded world-wide thereafter. As revealed in a letter to the editor of the *Sozialistische Monatshefte* (Socialist Monthly) in 1920, he expressed strong skepticism about the use of aptitude tests. Such tests, he wrote, are "growing in number, their use is expanding incredibly and mostly in the worst way." For their purposes of helping people make vocational decisions, Wertheimer considered the "qualitative" more important than the "quantitative," which can actually be destructive. He also deplored the whole medium of "testing" as such, in which "test-wiseness" (test-taking skills) may play a larger role than aptitudes themselves. Further, tests provide information usually about peripheral dimensions, rather than about central ones such as patience and persistence. Rather than taking on the role of an examiner, a psychologist should serve as a consultant for someone seeking vocational guidance. He proposed an alternative system in his letter, in which youngsters during their last school year, or even earlier, would be given an opportunity to spend two or three weeks in an actual or simulated work environment typical for a profession in which the youngster is potentially interested, to obtain a first-hand impression of what the work setting, and its demands, would actually entail, and to discover whether the youngster really would be able to handle the everyday details of the job and find it fulfilling.[56] No documentation has been found that Wertheimer ever pursued this idea further.

Appendix
On Reasoning Processes in Productive Thinking

The article translated in full in this appendix contains many ideas and examples that were to become central in Wertheimer's posthumous book, *Productive Thinking*, published by Harper and Brothers in 1945. It demonstrates that much of this material was clearly part of Wertheimer's thought by 1920, a full quarter-century before its more mature presentation in 1945. He doubtless had included many of these ideas and examples even earlier in his lectures. Much of the argument, and several of the examples, in the article are so condensed that the paper was difficult to translate in a coherent and easily comprehensible form; the reader may find some of this appendix hard to follow. Nevertheless, the article makes clear that theories, formulations, and ideas, as well as detailed analyses of concrete examples, of productive thinking that were not published in full until 1945 were evolving in Wertheimer's thought, and had been passed on to his students, for decades before their final publication. The paper also contains some (occasionally somewhat obscure) hints of what Wertheimer may have meant by a "Gestalt logic" that he tried to develop during his academic career, but which never did come to full fruition (see especially the paragraphs numbered 1-4 and 10, but elsewhere as well).

Über Schlussprozesse im produktiven Denken
On reasoning processes in productive thinking, by Max Wertheimer
Berlin and Leipzig 1920
Consortium of Scholarly Publishers Walter de Gruyter & Co.
Formerly G. J. Göschen's Publishing Firm • J. Guttentag, Book Publishing Firm • Georg Reimer • Karl J. Trübner • Veit & Co.

This treatise—comments on the *modus barbara* [all A is B; X is A; therefore X is B]—constitutes a part of the Festschrift that was delivered to **Carl Stumpf** on his seventieth birthday by his students as an expression of their respect and gratitude. Because of unfavorable circumstances in the bookselling trade, the Festschrift could not be issued as an assembled work.

Printed by Metzger & Wittig in Leipzig

How thinking really works; what happens when thinking sometimes really progresses; what are the decisive features and steps in this process: these are questions that have seriously engaged inquiry since antiquity.

Often what has been proposed has been an extension or a twist on the problem, but typically one that retains little direct relation any longer to what really may go on in lively forward-penetrating processes.

Here we would like to approach the problem in a sense more directly; and to do so even though we begin with an old problem in logic: the problem of the *petitio* or tautology in the syllogism—and reflect on which formal conditions such a conclusion [i.e., X is B] must fulfill in order to be able pregnantly[57] to yield an advance in thinking.

The *modus barbara* has a prominent place in traditional logic; for many logicians, it is the fundamental form, the epitome, of all reasoning. Discussions about the most basic logical questions have often been undertaken simply as discussions of the *modus barbara* syllogism. Highly contradictory theories exist; consider, for example, in contrast with the old Aristotelian doctrine, John Stuart Mill's perspective, which—with substantial consequences for the fundamental character of logical endeavor—really sees in the major premise a disguised induction. The situation has by no means been fully resolved to date; several not unessential features in the process have not yet been subjected to a thorough analysis.

If one has frequently consciously drawn the conclusion about good old Caius [all men are mortal; Caius is a man; therefore Caius is mortal], under various circumstances, in a vivid process, with attention; perhaps also in the midst of thought transactions of daily life and even in the course of processes that really generated further knowledge, there easily arises a curious discrepancy:

Usually it appears astonishingly paltry; quite inconsequential; indeed empty and insignificant; with the pale coloring that is so typically characteristic of the examples in traditional textbooks. In such cases one finds it easy to understand how it was possible to have apprehended it as a tautology, or as only a classificatory identification. It often then appears to be among the kinds of events that, day in day out, characterize the work of a clerk in a records office or the work of a person who earlier may well have achieved a good deal but now bustles about formally, empty and with dead knowledge.

But this is not always the case. Processes following the *modus barbara* sometimes appear quite clever; one senses that one really has made some progress; there is something of the beauty of penetration, of enhanced knowledge.

What really happens in such processes? Why is it that the same reasoning on different occasions can appear so different?

In what follows, several instances which, for clarification of this matter, appear not to be unimportant will be selected from more extensive studies.

The attempt will be to focus on real processes that, fortunately, actually occur in life, and not to restrict ourselves to the traditional orientation that is concerned merely with logical validity.

1. The syllogism should—there is no disagreement about this—lead in its conclusion to a "new" proposition. (This requirement is transparently clear in the extreme case: the conclusion cannot already be a premise.)

    Impurity with respect to this requirement is often an inherent factor of "meaninglessness": the conclusion then appears simply as a kind of recapitulation, the sheer saying of something that was basically already known, perhaps only in a superficially new form.

    What conditions are placed on the process by this requirement?

    In the most pregnant case, the situation before the process occurs could be like this: I *have* (somewhere in my knowledge, somehow available) the judgments that later appear as premises; but *don't* yet have the judgment that later appears as the conclusion (or don't yet realize that it is valid or that it follows validly from the two premises). Afterwards I do have it.

    (One should not be distracted by the temporal circumstance. Two different situations can be distinguished even from the viewpoint of the most formal logic; at the least: one, corresponding to the current one, in which there is a difference among the three assertions with respect to their type of "reliability"; another, in which that is not the case.)

2. How would that work with Caius? What would the situation have to be, if he were to suffice for this pregnant requirement? Thus:

    First of all—before the resolving syllogism is executed—I don't know whether this Caius is mortal or not. I don't know that, can't decide it.

    I write S ? P [does predicate P apply to subject S?]. But somewhere in my knowledge—I realize it well—there lies hidden that all humans are mortal; and somewhere that Caius is human. Both of these, *without* my knowing whether Caius is mortal... How could that be?! Is something like that possible? Are there such cases?!

3. The requirement contains in the pregnant case: neither SM (minor premise) nor MP (major premise) may—individually, in itself—already include knowledge of SP (the conclusion); SP also should not follow as a simple consequence of one of the premises; nor should I be able to know simply on the basis of Caius's mortality that he is human, nor that "all" humans are mortal because of the way they—including Caius himself—are constituted.

    The first is easy to fulfill: that Caius is human, I could perhaps know on the basis of immediate live observation; or on the basis of his particular bipedal nature; or from the tax rolls; for none of that has anything to do with his mortality. I only am not permitted to know it specifically because of his mortality. (Or: I might know it on the basis of his similarity to God; but then he certainly would not necessarily be mortal.)

But: now I am also supposed to know that all humans are mortal, without knowing it specifically about Caius.

(And one draws the consequence: that doesn't work; it is not at all true that I know it about "all humans"; I only know it about many: the major premise is basically not general at all, but includes a hidden induction.)

4. Let us replace the example; let us take one which fulfills both requirements well.

Caius goes to pay his taxes. He asks the receptionist at the central tax building to which office he should go, whereupon the receptionist inquires, in which tax district are you? And Caius shrugs. "But sir! You just ambled in here; don't you know to which tax district you belong?" — No, he doesn't know that; he has not yet received a tax bill, nobody told him anything about it; how, after all, should he know that? —"Now, we'll find that out right away—: you *do* know your street address, I trust?!" — "Fine; so you live on X Street—(SM) [minor premise]—; and X Street is part of tax district 426.—(MP) [major premise]—. Therefore—."

That *would* be such a process, even if it is not very impressive; but it does meet the requirements; that Caius happens to live on X Street entails nothing (without a classification scheme) about the tax district to which he belongs; Caius is totally innocent about this fact that X Street happens to be part of tax district 426; and the receptionist would know it even if there happened to be no Caius or if he happened to live the Lord knows where.

(The case[58] has, though, for good reasons been selected to be more general than the *modus barbara*: at the beginning the situation here is not S ? P but more general, in that what is asked for is Px [what predicate applies here?]. In cases of the simple S ? P form, the initial question would not be in which tax district Caius belongs, but rather perhaps "Am I in the right place here or not?" and other similar formulations.)

5. It is easy to realize why the requirements are fully satisfied in this kind of case. The major premise was constructed by humans; a decision has been made (here technically by law); this decision, not "knowledge," is contained in the major premise. The major premise asserts: in all cases that ever happen to have the characteristic *a*, the characteristic *b* shall "prevail"; and this ruling reigns supreme. For such a "determination" one surely need not know anything about particular characteristics specifically of Caius himself; he himself is entirely irrelevant for the determination.

This is generally true; thus also of cases in which the major premise is a nominal definition; or a proposition which is somehow—at least tentatively—decided by human decree; also, for example, a "tentatively formulated hypothesis in natural science." That is how, for example, Mill also saw it.

6. Everything seems to depend on the possibility of the major premise being general, without SP [the subject-predicate relation] necessarily having

been established beforehand by it. Then the decision would culminate purely in the old and beautiful problem of whether—and how—general knowledge is possible in the first place, without being based on confirmation of all individual cases. Doubtless this is one of the most important questions; but perhaps we can ignore it here. If I assume that [predicate or property] P *has* actually been confirmed in all individual cases; that the major premise is a general proposition which is actually based on investigation of all special cases; is every syllogism then a *petitio*, a sheer recapitulation of the already known? Are the above requirements then unfulfillable?

7. Let us go one step further in the formal analysis. How was the minor premise related to the fulfillment of the requirement?

Before the syllogism, I have SaM [the subject has attribute M]; but I should not thereby already have SaP [the subject has the attribute of the predicate]; SaM should not already entail SaP; for the statement of SaM, the characteristic that occurs in P must be irrelevant.

Therefore: neither S nor M are permitted to contain the characteristic P already.

That was quite simple in the tax example. I could know a great deal about S or, more strictly, some things about S could be specified; for instance, that Caius is tall and thin; that he looks similar to Cornelius, etc.; I could know all that; or even only that this creature who stands before me bears the name Caius; and I also could know—and this is provided in the minor premise, which adds this information to the rest— that this Caius has rented himself a place to live at number 34 on X Street. Only: nothing in S indicated anything about "an individual who belongs to tax district 426"; I could know nothing about that; that was not specified in S.

Formally: Any characteristics you wish can be specified in S and can be asserted in the minor premise, except that the characteristic that appears as predicate in the major premise may not already be specified [in S or in the minor premise].

It does make good sense to ask, pregnantly, how did Caius get into the syllogism? And it is good to distinguish sharply here: do I mean by "Caius" the "object" designated by the name, which necessarily includes all his (known and unknown) properties, which validly belong to him— aside from all nonessential fortuitous knowledge (also that which someone might spoofingly call "purely psychological")? (This is a conception which is closest to logical description—.) Or do I mean precisely Caius with his known properties and perhaps with his directly decisive characteristics—that which is actually specified?[59]

The same is true of M.

In the simplest case: S is introduced as having a particular attribute; S is defined by a1. A further attribute, a2, is added to Sa1, which was defined by (and only by) a1; this addition is the significance of the minor premise. Neither a1 nor a2 may contain a3, the attribute that appears in the predicate of the major premise.

I write: a2 is combined with Sa1; Sa1 + a2. Or, broadly, Sa1 is a member of the group that is characterized by a2.

8. Now: how about the major premise?

According to the requirement in Section 6, the major premise asserts that all cases which have attribute a2 also have a3; and asserts it on the basis of its confirmation in all cases; therefore also in S; therefore—

And nevertheless it's possible; one must take into consideration only that which has been asserted specifically with respect to Sa1; one must not think of characteristics that have and have not been assumed about S (including those which cannot be known before the process has taken place).

That really sounds self-evident—; nevertheless this is precisely the reason why from the start it appears to be so conclusive that our case would have to be a *petitio*. Especially in a broader perspective, it is close to thinking of S as being defined by its classificatory location, by its belonging in a particular domain, so that thus naturally everything substantive about S, including the unknown, the not-yet clarified, is necessarily also asserted, also localized; but when S already "contains" everything which could validly be asserted about it, then naturally no progress to "new" knowledge in the pregnant sense of the word is possible. This is no logically impossible form; quite the contrary; it has its good roots in the traditional treatment of logic: The object is specified by the asserted attribute; its characteristics are valid, whether or not one knows them. And for a logic that is oriented purely toward issues of validity, this timeless validity—with its total indifference to all validity with respect to fortuitous knowledge—is what is essential.

However, with respect to the problem we have addressed, this is a logic for a God; or—better: for a scholar who basically already knows everything and has examined everything, and is only engaged in further arranging and polishing the form of the assertion—

But for real progress in knowledge, this kind of perspective is really oblique. One may, when considering the other perspective systematically in terms of its consequences, call it a logical-genetic treatment; and such a treatment leads to a variety of consequences that are not unimportant; —including, just as a brief comment here, for the pure logic of validity.—

But if one does take account of it, then it is easily possible; what does it really mean when I say that S has already been examined with respect to P? The object is S; but must it already be Sa1? Must I already know, must it already have been asserted, that the examined object—which is one of those that have attribute a2—also has the attribute a1? Would it be identical to the S that has attribute a1?

Once again: S as an object has necessarily been examined; is necessarily one that has attribute a2; but there is no necessity that during this examination I have had, recognized, asserted it as Sa1.

There is no necessity that the proposition Sa1 a P is a basis for the major premise.

And thus: that Sa1 emerges—newly, indeed surprisingly—as one of the members of the group that has been searched thoroughly one by one for attribute a3, is often the genuine progress in the process.

Two things are now confirmed:

On the one hand (I) it is confirmed that all cases characterized by attribute a2 (the group of a2s) also have attribute a3; on the other (II) Sa1 is demonstrated to be a member of the group characterized by a2.

If I now set the condition that confirmation I occurs in circumstances in which there is no reference to a1 or there can be no reference to a1— and likewise that in confirmation II, a3 is not considered or cannot be considered—then I have a pure case of the desired kind.

9. Just a small alteration in the tax example basically suffices here: in place of what was specified by human regulation, one need only insert an unknown such as: Is Caius already recorded as "taxes paid"?—but the records are not by name but by the number of the tax bill.—The two confirmations have nothing to do with each other; the fact that all the numbers from, say, 1 to 1000 are already recorded as "taxes paid" has nothing to do with Caius happening to have the number 43; and this in turn has nothing to do with whether or not a record has been entered yet.

[This relationship of facts also plays a role in the natural sciences: but completely pure examples are not so easy to find there, because mostly there are no pure confirmations, but immediately deductive laws and inductive generalizations necessarily play a role. Perhaps a pure case might be: I investigate a body whose constitution is unknown to me. I expose it to increasing temperature; successive vapors emanate from it, until everything is turned to vapor. I am interested in the relation: is the substance with the lowest vaporizing temperature also the lightest of them? These would be the gas that first develops, and the gas that always ends up on top. Now in no way can I determine the relationship directly, until I notice the color of the gases; then I see that a yellowish gas develops first, then a bluish one, and then a gray one; at the end the yellowish one is consistently on top. It turns out:

The gas that develops first is yellowish.

The yellowish gas floats highest at the end.

The gas that develops first floats highest at the end. (Or: the substance with the lowest vaporizing temperature is also the lightest.)

In general: a certain number of objects are to be investigated. These actually have the attributes

$$
\begin{array}{cccc}
a\,1 & b\,1 & c\,1 & d\,1 \\
a\,1 & b\,1 & c\,1 & d\,2 \\
a\,2 & b\,1 & c\,1 & d\,3 \\
a\,2 & b\,2 & c\,2 & d\,4
\end{array}
$$

I am interested in the relation a–c; but the circumstance of the investigation is such that when I investigate a, it is impossible to determine c; similarly, when I investigate c, a cannot be determined. One might perhaps imagine it intuitively as follows:

$$
\text{I.}\quad
\begin{array}{cccc}
a\,1 & b\,1 & - & - \\
a\,1 & b\,1 & - & - \\
a\,2 & b\,1 & - & - \\
a\,2 & b\,2 & - & -
\end{array}
\qquad
\text{II.}\quad
\begin{array}{cccc}
- & b\,1 & c\,1 & - \\
- & b\,1 & c\,1 & - \\
- & b\,1 & c\,1 & - \\
- & b\,2 & c\,2 & -
\end{array}
$$

In one situation all attributes except a and b are "masked," in the other all except b and c. But at any given time, ab and bc can be determined simultaneously.

(And of course, science does often in fact deal with such masked or hidden characteristics…)]

10. But let us consider still other examples.

A very busy lawyer, because of the restricted space in his office, has the habit of burning superannuated files; thus he recently burned all files relating to Case A. One day he is searching for a receipt concerning currently pending Case B, which at the moment is of extraordinary importance to him. He searches, no luck; stops to think. What did this receipt in Case B concern? And then it occurs to him: this receipt from B was also relevant to Case A (and before the last conference he duly moved everything related to A to the A files)—Oh, Lord—!

In the construction of the major premise, the files were dealt with exclusively as related to A; thus not as related to S, nor Sa1, but Sa2. But in Sa1 lies a receipt related to B.

—True, in such cases the time between asserting the premises and reaching the new conclusion is often very brief, but that makes no difference; one can clearly observe what—surprisingly—is going on here. Just to hint at it here, one can clearly see how the mere simultaneous "having" of the two premises in itself by no means yields the conclusion; how a remarkable "snapping in," a "tipping over into one another," occurs—.

But further:

—For a long time Caius together with his best friend Xavier have been among the directors of a firm; for quite some time both of them have not been enjoying the direction the firm has been taking, and have not taken part in the meetings of the board of directors, except in the regular annual meeting that deals with their departments' statement of accounts. —One day Caius returns from a trip and finds a message informing him of a unanimous decision by the board of directors to handle business item Y in such and such a way. Caius vehemently declares that this is atrocious; this is too much; I'm ready to resign. I must phone Xavier immediately! And reads further: In connection with business item Y, the statement of accounts concerning…, which had to be decided before its regular place in the agenda, was approved after a lengthy speech by Mr. Xavier…"—

—Here at first something may become distinct that is of great importance in such processes: the "turning upside down" of S—. For a moment both premises are there next to each other, then suddenly what a process of "snapping"! (What?! Xavier was there?! So even Xavier is—). What a step from Sa1 via the in-itself unimportant a2 to a3!, which now is seen as an attribute of S and revolutionizes the old concept of S.

Such a phenomenon, among others, is often of great significance in the writing of history; not infrequently radical changes occurred in how an historical character was viewed because facts which previously had never been properly confronted in that light produced by their very confrontation a totally new centering of the historical character.

11. Now we can still simplify the formal state of affairs.

In the formulation above, S was "a member of the investigated a2-group." But how? This group consists of only *one* member: let the major premise be "S a P";[60]—nevertheless it isn't necessarily a *petitio*.

That is easily evident: the fact that other objects in addition to S may occur in the major premise is fundamentally irrelevant for our problem; it is essential only that Sa1 not be asserted in the major premise.

I write $\underline{Sa1\ ?\ P}$
$\underline{Sa1\ is\ Sa2}$
$\underline{Sa2\ a\ P}$
$Sa1\ a\ P.$

12. Here again, we really need only a small change in our examples; in the tax example, that only one person has been recorded so far as "taxes paid"; in the lawyer example, that not several A files, but only a single A file, the receipt, is relevant; in the business firm example, instead of a unanimous decision of the board of directors, that the decision was based on a motion by the leading member of the board of directors (that this happened to be Xavier himself is first revealed in the minor premise); and in the chemical example, there basically was already only one member in the major premise.

13. Something else should be briefly added here. The tax example and the business firm example could suggest: now this is simply a matter of the same object occurring with two names; thus I only determine that—aside from the one real confirmation 1—the other name—Sa1—also designates

the same object. Then what has been shown is to be sure not false, but rather of no consequence.

But one need only consider the lawyer example to see that this misses the point; there it is not that the same object simply occurs under two names, but logically two very different objects are specified: a file concerning A is logically something entirely different from a file concerning B[61]; and when I write, with logical precision: $Sa1 = a1 + x$ (with x indicating the unknown attributes, that which is unspecified in S) and $Sa2 = a2 + y$, these are logically two very different objects; even if in the outcome it turns out that a2 occurs in x, and a1 in y.

(Consider the role of x in mathematics; if I have the task of finding a number that satisfies this and that condition, I call it "x," about which nothing is specified to begin with, other than the attributes specified in the condition—a1.)

How relevant this difference is in its consequences may already have become clear in the business firm example: what a chasm between the Xavier before and after the syllogism—(actually: the concept I have of an object is often not only enriched in such a process, but changed, improved, deepened).

14. Some of what is essential in "recentering" may, though, become clear in other—modest—examples, in which the restriction to pure substantiation may now be left out.

I choose mathematical tasks that because of their simple structure may make several features important for the process thoroughly clear to the reader.

1. Given is a square with a band–parallelogram lying on top of it as shown below:

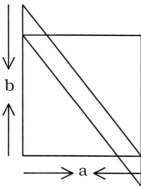

Given are the lengths a and b.

Question: What is the sum of the areas of both surfaces?

Now it is possible to calculate: the area of the square is a^2; and the area of the parallelogram is....

This approach, because it is too laborious, is not permitted.

Then one gets the idea that with respect to the area:

[Sa1 =] (square + band) = (2 triangles, base a, height b) ! [= Sa2]

[Sa2 =] = $\left(2 \frac{bh}{2}\right)$ = ab [= P]

and has solved the task, so to speak, in one stroke.

(The reader can follow the solution in the figure.)

2. The following, simpler, task is similar:

Given is an isosceles triangle with the equal sides of length s and the angle at the tip 90°. What is the area?

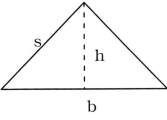

Now one could, in order to reach $\frac{bh}{2}$, calculate the base b and the height h; or instead one could proceed as follows: this isosceles triangle is a (tipped) right triangle with the base and height s—! And its area = $\frac{s^2}{2}$.

3. Question: Is 1,000,000,000,000,000,000,008 divisible by 9 without remainder? (The method of summing the digits of a number is not permitted, or is unknown.) The solution:

$$(10000...+8) = (10000...- 1) + (8 + 1)$$
$$.... = 9999... + 9.$$

4. Or similarly: Is a^2 + ac + ba + bc divisible by (a + b)? The solution:

$$a^2 + ac + ba + bc = \overbrace{a \cdot a + a \cdot b} + \overbrace{a \cdot c + b \cdot c}$$
$$= a (a + b) + c (a + b).$$

5. What is $\sqrt{a^2 + \dfrac{b^2}{4} + ab}$?

The solution:

$$\sqrt{a^2 + \frac{b^2}{4} + ab} = \sqrt{a^2 + \left(\frac{b}{2}\right)^2 + 2 \cdot a \cdot \frac{b}{2}}$$
$$= \pm \left(a + \frac{b}{2}\right)$$

6. If one is asked, what is one third of 10, times six?, one may, following the problem, proceed by first dividing ten by three, getting to

3.33333333..., and get stuck—. Only to realize:—6 is, of course, a good multiple of 3—:

$$6 \cdot \frac{\frac{10}{3}}{3} = \frac{6}{3} \cdot 10$$
$$.... \quad = 20.$$

7. As a simple example, consider here too a beautiful achievement of young Gauss in elementary school. According to reports, the incident may have occurred roughly like this: the teacher asked the boys, which one of you can write down most quickly the total sum of $1 + 2 + 3 + 4 + 5 + 6 + 7 + 8$ added together? The young boy very soon raises his hand, saying "Ligget se!" ("There it is!" in his peasant dialect). Asked how he could find it so quickly, he said, to the astonishment of the teacher, "Yes, Teacher, if I had added them one after the other, as you said, 'one and two,' and then 'and three,' and then 'and four'..., it would have taken a long time. But one and eight are nine, and two and seven are also nine, and three and six again have to be nine...and so,..."

$$1 + 2 + 3 + 4 + 5 + 6 + ... + n \quad = \overbrace{1 + 2 + 3 + ... + (n-2) + (n-1) + n}^{n+1}$$
$$\text{or} \quad = (1+n) + (2+[n-1]) + (3+[n-2])...$$
$$= (n+1) \cdot \frac{n}{2}.$$

Whereby the kid had discovered an important proposition (at least for whole numbers).

8. The task is to calculate the sum of the external angles of a planar polygon. (The roundabout way of dividing it by triangles from a midpoint is not permitted or is viewed as inelegant.) One tries to see the state of affairs in principle, and now thinks:

The polygon must be considered as a closed figure; for this closure the surrounding line must be broken several times; not everything at a resulting external angle is equally relevant for the closure of the circumference:

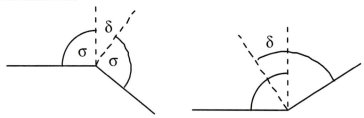

The external angle is equal to the two "side angles" (σ), which are constructed as two right angles, plus or minus a "genuine rotation angle" δ. But closure requires a complete rotation (= 360°): for closure the external angles must comprise a positive complete angle (the internal angles a negative one).

$$\Sigma\,(\alpha+\beta+\gamma+\ldots)=\Sigma\delta+\Sigma\sigma$$
$$=4R+n\cdot 2R.$$

(The sum of the external angles = the sum of the rotation angles + the sum of the side angles.)

Suddenly the state of affairs is transparently clear. The insight is applicable even to curvilinearly circumscribed figures; also to three- and n-dimensional bodies: the insight of the interdependency of the closure of a planar figure with the Gestalt of the sum of its angles.[62]

15. In S?P the object is given, known, specified as Sa1. There is no direct route from Sa1 to P; logically, in the most pregnant case, in sRp, the R [that is, the relation] is indeterminate—I cannot answer the question ?P (or ?Px). But: the object proves to be "recenterable" into Sa2, and from Sa2, aP is determined or, better, determinable.

This kind of relationship is of the greatest significance for progress in science (aside from the sheer collecting and arranging of facts)— especially mathematics. Often I can confirm a3 (that is, aP) only when Sa1 is restructured, comprehended differently, recentered in some particular way; often only if I penetrate more deeply into the intrinsic nature, the structure, of S.

Geometry, for example, contains a myriad of such steps of recognition. But this "recentering" is not restricted only to the spatial and mathematical; this is something far more general. Something similar to what happens to parts of spatial figures and mathematical structures occurs with attributes in the attribute hierarchy of a concept; here too there are certain structures, certain structural principles (and something similar happens also when concepts are combined); here too "recenterings" and, in general, structural operations are of the greatest significance.—

In the history of science one could refer briefly to the conception of stellar motion ("falling"), to making possible the theory of the screw (the screw conceived as a wedge); to the history of coming up with the idea of inertia.—

As a simple example of a purposeful activity, consider also determining the area of a circle by conceiving of it as a polygon.

—So far such achievements have been attributed essentially to "fantasy," to "luck," or to "ingenious intuition"; a matter of chance recognition or something "merely psychological"; but formal properties also play a role, and they can be comprehended in certain laws.

16. Consider the examples from this point of view: the recentering, the transition from Sa1 to Sa2 contains certain formal properties. However, here we can indicate only a few—relatively obvious—ones in brief.

In some cases, the decisive step often occurs directly in an (appropriate) *extraction*: certain properties of S are pulled out, into the foreground. In others, the decisive step is executed in a particular *combination* of elements (particularly clear in example 7; in general, with concepts as well, "sums of attributes" can be viewed one time as a + b + c + d..., another time as [a+b] + [c+d]..., yet another as a + [b+c] + d...). In still others one can speak pregnantly of *centering*, when it is a matter of the part with respect to which the other parts are set in order (as in the "base" of the isosceles triangle in example 2, or, in the example of the area of the circle, when the circle is meaningfully viewed not as a surface limited by the line of points that are equidistant from the center, nor as the rotation surface of the rotating radius, etc., but as the surface of a polygon with an infinite number of sides). —And the centering leads to penetration into the state of affairs, to the grasping of a certain inner structural coherence of the whole, to the recognition of inner necessities.

(—One can see that fortunately we have other cognitive operations than just those of the knife [division or subtractive abstraction] and the sack [addition or the concept of classes]—.)

17. The established Sa2 or the established step Sa1:Sa2 is in our conception *not arbitrary*. It is not formally equivocal which one of the different possible restructurings is employed: the assertion stands in a good recognition process in the context of P, in the context of the question ?P.

From the beginning here I don't have to do with S and P in a purely disparate "next-to-each-other"; rather, a "together" is there with specific formal properties.

Several of the examples may have generated a recourse to what accidentally was already familiar to the reader (for instance, in example 5, the form $a^2 + 2ab + b^2$); but one might just ponder, in the circle example, how the linearly determined conceptions do not "belong," but the question about the area *requires* recourse to a conception that emerges from the enclosed space. And the same holds for the problem of the sum of the external angles.

18. In the simple case:

S?P is presented; there is no evident direct way to determine aP or eP and so on.

From the combination of S and ?P the question arises: what in Sa1, what in the known, specified, recognizable in S, has anything to do with ?P? To *what* in S must I pay attention? Or: In the context of the task, *how* must I view, conceive of, S? How perhaps must I change or reorganize my present concept of S, from the point of view of ?P? Formally: not everything in S, not every conception or reorganization of S, is equally disparate with ?P; there are stipulations for the solution.

(With well formed "concepts"—which are not perhaps constructed on the basis of the mere coexistence of disparate attributes—this is ideal: from the inner structure, from a few central features, emerge stipulations for all other attributes.)

—One should by no means interpret what has been said as expressing a rationalistic orientation! No: thinking about a concept and structural operations must be well rooted in experience; and actually the most beautiful processes (how clear that is, for instance, in Einstein's discoveries!) are specifically distinguished by their purifying the situation from false rationalistic ingredients, by seeking to depict the state of affairs in total purity. But: here too one cannot achieve or even approach such clarity by merely setting attributes together in total disparity! Rather everything is devoted to achieving more adequate concepts, such structures, such centerings as are required by the facts, conceptions in which a few central features make all the rest determinable, comprehensible.

Comment. What has been said generally plays an important role in "comprehending," in the pregnant sense of the word; but similar events are also inherently evident in processes of perception and imagination. Basic here are certain laws about which I hope to be able to report in print soon.

19. Even if a state of affairs is not always provided in such purity as in the form that has been sketched out, the sketched-out properties often do have the greatest significance. To repeat the crudest ones:

In the circle task it is "senseless" to think of the circle as *red*, or as essentially *linearly* determined; and comparably to think of old Caius, about whose *immortality* I am inquiring, as clean-shaven or as having a mole—; him too I must view directly in the context of the mortality issue in a rather particular manner.

And as for the circle: doesn't the S?P already contain the relation to the quadrilateral figure and from there the way to the "polygon" or to other corresponding conceptions?

20. Here we have now arrived at the most essential property of the question: when the process appears sensible, when senseless.

Now we can formulate the state of affairs for the *modus barbara* in general as follows:

The state of affairs S?P stands in relation to the state of affairs

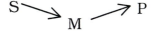

The bridge between S and P is provided in M (the old middle term).

Then there are two extreme forms:

One in which the M in the syllogism has *no other formal relation* than to mediate between S and P via the two mere coexistence relations (to S on the one hand, to P on the other): these are two relations that specify merely a "chance occurrence."

The other:

The bridge in M is *sensibly required* by the question, by the being together of S and P. M—and Sa2 as well—stands in the context of S?P[63]; M has *specific* formal relations in the entire process, in the whole state of affairs, perhaps *in addition to* its empty bridge function.[64]

Two forms, then: in the first, M is in principle *arbitrary*, when it only fulfills the empty bridge function. One could, in order to satisfy this requirement, select the most senseless examples; they correspond to the requirements of syllogistics, when only the "chance occurrence" of both the propositions is given; thus for instance the mortality of good old Caius could be immaculately derived from the "ai" in his name, if it only happened to be the case that mortals do, but immortals do not, have an "ai" in their names. But no sensible person would see the "humanity" in the syllogism about Caius's mortality in this way.

In the second form, in addition to the mere bridging achievement (that is, in addition to the coexistence of features and the relation to the environment), there are other formal properties; and while the first form achieves nothing, brings nothing other than the empty confirmation of the coexistence of S and P (that is, a1 and a3) or the localization of S in a classificatory drawer—the second brings genuine progress in knowledge: a grasping of a coherent connection, a penetration into a state of affairs.

Notes

1.   Ash, *The emergence of Gestalt theory: Experimental psychology in Germany, 1890-1920*, pp. 299-300.

2.   Ash, *The emergence of Gestalt theory: Experimental psychology in Germany, 1890-1920*, p. 300. The course titles are translated from the Frankfurt Academy course bulletin for the years 1912-1914.

3.   Ash, *The emergence of Gestalt theory: Experimental psychology in Germany, 1890-1920*, p. 330.

4.   Friedrich Kenkel (1919). Untersuchungen über den Zusammenhang zwischen Erscheinungsgrösse und Erscheinungsbewegung bei einigen sogenannten optischen Täuschungen [Investigations of the relationship between apparent size and apparent motion in some so-called optical illusions]. *Zeitschrift für Psychologie*, 61, 358-449.

5.   In later years, Meinong became disenchanted with Brentano and another of Brentano's disciples, Husserl. See Fritz Heider (1973). Gestalt theory: Early history and reminiscences. In Mary Henle, Julian Jaynes, and John J. Sullivan (eds.), *Historical conceptions of psychology*, New York: Springer, p. 64.

6.   Fritz Heider, Gestalt theory: Early history and reminiscences, p. 66.

7.   Heider, p. 67.

8.   Heider, p. 69.

9.   Vittorio Benussi (1914). Referat über: Koffka-Kenkel, 'Beiträge zur Psychologie der Gestalt- und Bewegungserlebnisse' [Review of Koffka-Kenkel,

'Contributions to the psychology of Gestalt and motion experiences']. *Archiv für die gesamte Psychologie*, 32, 41-56.

10. Kurt Koffka (1915). Zur Grundlegung der Wahrnehmungspsychologie. Eine Auseinandersetzung mit V. Benussi. *Zeitschrift für Psychologie*, 73, 11-90. Condensed and translated as Reply to Benussi, in Willis D. Ellis (ed.) (1938, 1967). *A source book of Gestalt psychology*. New York: Harcourt, Brace; Humanities Press, 371-388, p. 371.

11. Heider, Gestalt theory: Early history and reminiscences, p. 68.

12. Koffka, Reply to Benussi, pp. 377-378.

13. Koffka, Reply to Benussi, p. 378.

14. Heider, p. 68. Professor Lothar Sprung, of Humboldt University in Berlin, made a comment on an earlier draft of this chapter for which the authors are grateful: A recent book on Benussi contains a lengthy, detailed discussion of the Benussi-Koffka controversy. It is by Mauro Antonelli (1994): *Die experimentelle Analyse des Bewusstseins bei Vittorio Benussi* [*The experimental analysis of consciousness in Vittorio Benussi*]. Studien zur Oesterreichischen Philosophie [Studies on Austrian philosophy] (Ed. Rudolf Haller), vol. 21. Amsterdam and Atlanta, GA: Rodipi.

15. Ash, p. 305.

16. Koffka, Reply to Benussi, p. 377.

17. Max Brod (1969). *Streitbares Leben* [*Belligerent life*], rev. ed. Munich: F. A. Herbig, pp. 136ff., especially 142-143.

18. Valentin Wertheimer, as quoted in Luchins and Luchins (1985). Max Wertheimer: His life and work during 1912-1919. *Gestalt Theory*, 7, 3-28, p. 10.

19. Abraham S. Luchins and Edith H. Luchins (1985). Max Wertheimer: His life and work during 1912-1919. *Gestalt Theory*, 7, 3-28, p. 6. The Luchins also suggest, based on comments by Wertheimer's student A. B. Wood, that Wertheimer, rather than Köhler, was scheduled to direct the research station at Tenerife, but became ill and could not make the trip. No further evidence has been located to support or refute this assertion.

20. Siegfried Jaeger (ed.), *Briefe von Wolfgang Köhler an Hans Geitel 1907-1920, mit zwei Arbeiten Köhlers, "Über elektromagnetische Erregung des Trommelfelles" und "Intelligenzprüfungen am Orang" im Anhang* [*Letters of Wolfgang Köhler to Hans Geitel 1907-1920, with two works of Köhler, "On electromagnetic stimulation of the eardrum" and "Intelligence tests on the orangutan" as appendices*] (Passau, West Germany: Passavia Universitätsverlag, 1988), second supplement.

21. Wolfgang Köhler (1925). *The mentality of apes*. (Ella Winter, translator). New York: Liveright.

22. Jaeger, *Briefe von Wolfgang Köhler an Hans Geitel*.

23. Jaeger, *Briefe von Wolfgang Köhler an Hans Geitel*.

24. Solomon Asch, Wolfgang Köhler: 1887-1967, p. 115.

25. Quoted in Ash, *The emergence of Gestalt theory: Experimental psychology in Germany, 1890-1920*, p. 488.

26. The United States joined the Allied Powers following a declaration of war against Germany on April 6, 1917 and against Austria-Hungary on December 7, 1917.

27. Ash, *The emergence of Gestalt theory: Experimental psychology in Germany, 1890-1920*, p. 490.

28. Max Born (1978). *My life: Recollections of a Nobel laureate.* New York: Scribner, p. 173.

29. Luchins and Luchins, Max Wertheimer: His life and work during 1912-1919, p. 10.

30. Born, *My life: Recollections of a Nobel laureate*, p. 173.

31. Born, *My life: Recollections of a Nobel laureate*, p. 174.

32. Max Wertheimer and Erich von Hornbostel (1920). Über die Wahrnehmung der Schallrichtung [On the perception of the direction of a sound]. *Sitzungsberichte der preussischen Akademic der Wissenschaften*, 20, 388-396.

33. Max Wertheimer to Atlas Company, July 17, 1934, MW-CU. Atlas Company to Max Wertheimer, February 12, 1935, MW-CU. Wertheimer and von Hornbostel discontinued their patent around 1935.

34. Michael Wertheimer (1965). Relativity and Gestalt: A note on Albert Einstein and Max Wertheimer, *Journal of the History of the Behavioral Sciences*, 1, 86-87.

35. Max Wertheimer, *Productive thinking*, p. 213.

36. George Humphrey (1924). The theory of Einstein and the Gestalt-Psychologie: A parallel. *American Journal of Psychology*, 35, p. 358.

37. Quoted in Luchins and Luchins, Max Wertheimer: His life and work, p. 19.

38. Banesh Hoffman (with the collaboration of Helen Dukas) (1972). *Albert Einstein: Creator and rebel.* New York: Viking, p. 13.

39. The program and text of the Stumpf tribute are preserved in MW-NY.

40. *Über Schlussprozesse im produktiven Denken.[On reasoning processes in productive thinking].* Berlin: De Gruyter, 1920 (22 pages).

41. Michael Wertheimer (1989). Max Wertheimer's challenging legacy. *Psychological Research*, 51, 69-74, p. 70.

42. Max Wertheimer, The syllogism and productive thinking. In Willis D. Ellis (ed.) (1938, 1967). *A source book of Gestalt psychology.* New York: Humanities Press, p. 274.

43. Wertheimer, The syllogism and productive thinking, p. 281.

44. George Humphrey (1951). *Thinking: An introduction to its experimental psychology.* London: Methuen, p. 139.

45. Humphrey, p. 140.

46. Humphrey, pp. 140-142.

47. Humphrey, p. 143.

48. Humphrey, p. 146.

49. Humphrey, p. 149.

50. Quoted from and translated in Ash, *The emergence of Gestalt theory: Experimental psychology in Germany, 1890-1920*, pp. 504-505.

51. Quoted in Ronald W. Clark (1971). *Einstein: The life and times.* New York: World, p. 198.

52. Abraham S. Luchins and Edith H. Luchins (1986). Max Wertheimer: 1919-1929. *Gestalt Theory*, 8, p. 24.

53. Eckart Scheerer (1988). Fifty volumes of *Psychological Research/ Psychologische Forschung*: The history and present status of the journal. *Psychological Research*, 50, 71-82, pp. 71-72.

54. Quoted in Scheerer, p. 71.
55. Scheerer, p. 72.
56. Letter from Max Wertheimer quoted in part on page 1103 of *Sozialistische Monatshefte* [*Socialist Monthly*], 1920, volume 55, 26th year, with approval by the (unidentified) editor. The authors are grateful to Helmut E. Lück of the Fern Universität in Hagen, Germany, for bringing this item to their attention and providing a photocopy of the relevant pages.
57. See Chapter 7 for a discussion of the concept of "pregnance" in Wertheimer's thought.
58. It would suffice if the receptionist had moved, and then wondered, to which tax district do I now belong?
59. Suffice it to refer here only briefly to the relationship of this distinction to recent research on "meaning."
60. Which may serve to clarify formally a decisive change relative to traditional logic.
61. (Important roots for the problem of the concept of "thing" already lie in this.)
62. As a further formal example of a somewhat different form, the essential point of this essay itself might be considered.
63. (In this S?P, in the posing of clever, fruitful questions, there often already lies what is most essential in the achievement—.)
64. For this, pregnantly, it also does not at all suffice for M to represent the "real cause"; there are—despite all validity—causalities that are quite empty of sense, that are not understood—. What is necessary is inner requiredness, a required coherent connection from the essence of the structure; —which, to be sure, is remote from common usage in logic or from Hume's theory of knowledge and psychology.

7

The Gestalt Movement Matures, 1922-1929

When we [students] did catch on [to Gestalt theory], we were delighted! Our whole lives changed, our whole outlook on life changed. All of a sudden, everything became colorful and lively and had meaning.
—Anni Hornbostel (1972)

The end of the First World War placed a great fiscal hardship on Germany and profoundly changed the political, social, and economic circumstances in the country. These radically altered conditions, though, led to the blossoming of the Weimar period. Berlin, which had earlier been the intellectual center of Germany and the home of Goethe and Schiller, once again began to thrive as a center for artistic and intellectual innovation. The Weimar period is sometimes called a "golden age" in German cultural history. As the historian Peter Gay put it, this was a time

> of modernity in art, literature and thought; we think of the rebellion of sons against fathers, Dadaists against art, Berliners against beefy philistinism, libertines against old-fashioned moralists; we think of *The Threepenny Opera*, *The Cabinet of Dr. Caligari*, and *The Magic Mountain*, Marlene Dietrich.[1]

Gestalt psychology shared in the widespread excitement of this age. If the previous decade brought growth and expansion of the theory, then the 1920s were its time of maturity. Gestalt psychology became one of the dominant schools of German, of European, indeed of world-wide psychology. One feature that helped elevate the status of Gestalt psychology was the extensive research conducted by its adherents, which was widely viewed as productive. Another was a transition of power at the Institute that placed Gestalt psychologists in positions of authority at the University of Berlin.

Establishment of Gestalt Psychology at Berlin's Psychological Institute

During the Weimar period, Wertheimer began to be recognized for his role in the formulation of Gestalt theory. But despite his reputation as a dynamic teacher and as the founder of Gestalt psychology, he was still *Privatdozent* at the Institute, an unsalaried instructor. He may have become guardedly hopeful when in 1920 Carl Stumpf announced that he would retire in the next year, after more than a quarter of a century at the university. In August, Stumpf claimed that weakening eyesight was largely responsible for his decision to step down from the directorship of the Institute, but, as Mitchell Ash points out, another concern may also have motivated his resignation:

> Though he submitted a physician's letter to attest his disability, he had another motive for proceeding as he did. The new education minister in Prussia, Carl Heinrich Becker, had proposed to introduce mandatory retirement at age sixty-eight for professors…as part of a comprehensive university reform plan. At seventy-three, Stumpf was already well past that limit.[2]

The opportunity to head the Institute would have been a major professional victory for Wertheimer; as Hughes observes, "The call to a chair in Berlin was something that was nearly impossible for any German scholar to resist."[3] But Wertheimer knew that his prospects for winning the chair were poor, especially since his colleague Wolfgang Köhler was under serious consideration for the position. Stumpf had in fact written to a Ministry official recommending that Köhler be selected as the new chair and director. Köhler, though only thirty-four years old, had already gained some experience as a chair, having been appointed in August 1921 to succeed G. E. Müller at the University of Göttingen. Müller, like Stumpf, was a victim of the by-then enacted retirement provision. Other candidates considered along with Köhler for the Berlin chair were Karl Bühler, William Stern, and Munich professor Erich Becher.

Although Wertheimer was probably never seriously considered as a candidate for the appointment, it could be argued that his qualifications would have satisfied the Philosophical Faculty's requirements for a candidate who had a strong interest in philosophical issues. He also had more teaching experience than Köhler. But Wertheimer had not published at the prolific rate of his younger colleague—who had amassed a rich and impressive body of publications. Furthermore, Wertheimer's meager articles had not received the widespread, almost universally positive, scholarly recognition that hailed Köhler's rigorous monograph on physical Gestalten. Although Wertheimer was not a practicing Jew, his Jewish heritage probably also worked against him. Indeed William Stern later reported that he had been invited to negotiate for the chair at Berlin and was offered the position if he would renounce his Judaism, but refused to do so.[4]

If Wertheimer had any hope of being appointed to Stumpf's prestigious professorship, this hope was not long lived. By February 1922, it was clear that Köhler would become the next director at Berlin. Although the younger "apostle" rather than the older Gestalt "prophet" was appointed to the position, this seems not to have harmed their relationship. Indeed, on several occasions when Köhler was called away from Berlin for extended periods of time, he asked Wertheimer to fill in for him as Acting Director of the Institute. Köhler also proposed a promotion for Wertheimer, resulting in his appointment in 1924 as *ausserordentlicher* Professor. (Erich von Hornbostel was promoted to *ausserordentlicher* Professor at Berlin in 1925, and Kurt Lewin in 1927.) The central core of scholars at the Institute was steeped in Carl Stumpf's holistic legacy, but under Köhler's leadership at the Psychological Institute the direction shifted explicitly toward Gestalt theory. Koffka also performed impressive and prolific studies at Giessen from 1920 to 1928 (during which time he supervised 12 dissertations) and was a staunch promoter of Gestalt psychology, but the far better known, more prestigious, and much larger University of Berlin soon became identified as the major center of Gestalt theory.

Koffka's Article in the Psychological Bulletin

Articles on a wide variety of themes in Gestalt psychology in *Psychologische Forschung* disseminated extensive information about Gestalt theory to German-speaking audiences. But little had as yet been published in English about the school. By the early 1920s, Kurt Koffka, who early in his life had become fluent in English, was persuaded to try to acquaint American audiences with the principal themes of the school. On January 19, 1922 the American psychologist Robert Morris Ogden wrote Koffka an invitation to publish a review of perception in English:

> I wonder if you would not find it somehow to your interest to help me out with a general critical review (*Sammelreferat*) on Perception for publication in the *Psychological Bulletin*? I have been one of the cooperating editors of the *Bulletin* for a good many years…. I have accepted editorial responsibility for the topic Sensation and Perception…. There has been nothing published on the recent work in perception, the bulk of which has been done in Germany.[5]

The opportunity to describe perception from the Gestalt perspective was tempting; although occasional references to the new theory had appeared in American journals, none had been written yet by any of the school's founders. Koffka accepted Ogden's offer under the condition that the review article could present a formal statement of the Gestalt position. Ogden gladly agreed and Koffka's fifty-five page article, "Perception: An Introduction to the Gestalt-Theorie," appeared in the October, 1922 volume of the *Psychological Bulletin*.[6] Although the article concentrated on summarizing and integrating a large number of papers on perception, Koffka made it quite clear that the Gestalt school covered far more than this area alone:

> The *Gestalt-Theorie* is more than a theory of perception: it is even more than a mere psychological theory. Yet it originated in a study of perception, and the investigation of this topic has furnished the better part of the experimental work which has been done. Consequently, an introduction to this new theory can best be gained, perhaps, by a consideration of the facts of perception.[7]

Despite Koffka's cautionary words, many psychologists, especially those in the United States, came to identify Gestalt psychology almost exclusively with the study of perception. Several of Wertheimer's articles during the 1920s may inadvertently also have reinforced this misconception.

Principles of Organization and Grouping

Wertheimer's experiments in perception that demonstrated various principles of Gestalt theory consisted of both formal and informal studies at the Berlin Institute, most of which he had already begun in Frankfurt many years earlier. In 1925, a Munich colleague, Annelies Argeländer, contacted Wertheimer about his research on synesthesia, or the evocation of images in other sensory modalities by a sensation in one modality (for example, perceiving red as a warm color and blue as a cool one, or judging high notes to be light in color while low ones are dark).[8] Wertheimer admitted that he had been performing research on this area as early as 1910 and had large amounts of data that should have been published long ago,[9] but he never did formally publish any of this work.

Wertheimer did manage to complete a few projects and write them up for publication. Some of his best-known works appeared in print during the 1920s. In the same year in which Koffka's article appeared in English, Wertheimer published a paper entitled "Untersuchungen zur Lehre von der Gestalt: I. Prinzipielle Bemerkungen" ("Investigations in Gestalt Theory: I. Comments on Principles") that presented some of the fundamental tenets of Gestalt theory.[10] His most celebrated article from this period, though, was the second part of his "Investigations in Gestalt theory" ("Untersuchungen zur Lehre von der Gestalt: II").[11] Based on his own laboratory and classroom demonstrations, many of which dated back to more than a decade before in Frankfurt, and on an earlier paper by Schumann, Wertheimer addressed the basic organizational principles in perception. In contrast to structuralists like Edward Bradford Titchener who studied perception as a synthesis "from below up," Wertheimer declared that perception is a transsummative process that proceeds "from above downward" or from the whole to the parts.[12] He satirized the structuralist procedure of categorization of hues and brightnesses of visual images. "I stand at the window and see a house, trees, sky," Wertheimer stated.

Theoretically I might say there were 327 brightnesses and nuances of color. Do I *have* "327"? No. I have sky, house, and trees. It is impossible to achieve "327" as such. And yet even though such droll calculation were possible—and implied, say, for the house 120, the trees 90, the sky 117—I should at least have this arrangement and division of the total, and not, say, 127 and 100 and 100; or 150 and 177.

The concrete division which I *see* is not determined by some arbitrary mode of organization lying solely within my own pleasure; instead I see the arrangement and division which is given there before me.[13]

He asserted that percepts are organized into meaningful configurations that are generated by the inherent structure of the stimulus array; perception is not just a result of experience and context. Form perception is not driven by associative factors but by a dynamic process of organization that entails the active recognition of meaningful patterns and whole-relations in the stimulus array. Assemblages of lines and dots are not perceived as unrelated, piecemeal units, as a mere sum-total, or as a chaotic mass, but are instead grouped into meaningful configurations or Gestalten. According to Wertheimer, Gestalten are integrated, articulated structures or systems within which the constituent parts are in dynamic interrelation with each other and with the whole.

Wertheimer sought to demonstrate phenomenologically the principles of organization "with a few simple characteristic cases" to illustrate those principles.

- The law of "proximity or nearness" is the perceptual tendency to group items together as Gestalten according to their nearness or proximity to one another.
- The law of "similarity" describes the perceptual tendency to group together items into Gestalten if they are similar in respect to some feature such as shape, color or texture. Wertheimer provided auditory as well as visual examples of this phenomenon and pitted proximity against similarity in further examples.
- He pointed out that the "common fate" of objects that are undergoing the same motion or change may also result in their being perceived as constituting a whole.
- The law of "good continuation" notes that items are grouped together on bases such as their continuity in following a consistent, lawful direction; items that are natural successors in a series will be seen as belonging to that series.
- The law of "closure" identifies the tendency to perceive a complete or incomplete part or whole so as to attain maximum stability, balance, or symmetry in the entire configuration.

Wertheimer argued that all of these laws reflect a "tendency to the good whole configuration" or the principle of *Prägnanz*—a tendency for the organization of any whole or Gestalt to be as good as the prevailing conditions allow.[14]

All of these factors and principles make clear that the way in which parts are seen, in which subwholes emerge in a perceptual field, in which grouping occurs, is not via an arbitrary, piecemeal and-summation of elements or by sheer associations based on past experience, but by a process in which characteristics of the whole play a major determining role. Wertheimer did not provide detailed reports of experimental results in this 1923 paper but instead used numerous illustrations to induce the reader to experience the perceptual phenomena directly and unequivocally. The methodology of the report was what might be called experimental phenomenology rather than the rigorous systematic experimental design that characterized most of the other empirically based publications of the Gestalt psychologists.

The general themes of this seminal 1923 paper had occupied Wertheimer since long before the article was published. As early as 1910-1911, when he was working on apparent motion, he was already concerned with the related issue of how parts of the perceptual field coalesce into integrated units or figures, that is, what later were called the principles of perceptual organization. At the 1914 congress of the Society for Experimental Psychology (after Adhémar Gelb had presented some findings on the perception of space and time and Vittorio Benussi had discussed his research on the perception of motion phenomena), Wertheimer mentioned that he had recently discovered,

> among several Gestalt laws of a general kind, a law of the tendency toward simple formation (law of the *Prägnanz* of the Gestalt), according to which visible connection of the position, size, brightness, and other qualities of components appears as a result of…Gestalt apprehensions.[15]

Thus the basic idea of *Prägnanz* was already beginning to become clear to Wertheimer a decade or so before he first published formally about it. In his influential 1920 work on physical Gestalten, Köhler too referred to the law of *Prägnanz* and noted that the identification of these dynamic processes

> comes from Wertheimer, not as a description of inorganic physical behavior, but of phenomenal and therefore also of physiological process-structures. Nevertheless it is possible to apply the terms to physical phenomena also, for the general tendency and line of development observed by Wertheimer in psychology and designated by him as the law of *Prägnanz* is obviously the same as we have here been discussing.[16]

As in both earlier and later intellectual endeavors, Wertheimer conceived of and developed his ideas many years before he was ready to commit them to print.

During the decade of the 1920s, Wertheimer was devoting substantial amounts of time to editorial work on the *Psychologische Forschung* and prepared numerous book reviews for the journal. Some of his commentaries, such as his 1923 "Bemerkungen zu Hillebrands Theorie der stroboskopischen Bewegungen" ("Remarks on Hillebrand's theory of stroboscopic motion"),[17] in which he defended his earlier work on apparent motion, were lengthy essays in their own right. These activities, and his lecturing and supervision of student research, may have limited the amount of time he felt he could devote to writing up more of his own empirical and theoretical studies.

Wertheimer's major 1923 article soon became recognized as an important document in the literature of Gestalt psychology; indeed Wertheimer's principles of perceptual organization soon became a standard topic in introductory textbooks of psychology. Scholars outside of the field of psychology also took note of this paper, as well as of Gestalt theory. These scholars included a coterie of artists loosely associated with the Bauhaus school.

One of the more significant institutions during the Weimar period, the Bauhaus (literally "Construction House" or "House of Architecture") tried to unite functionally the creative arts with the technology of twentieth-century mass production. Founded in Weimar, Germany, in early 1919 by the illustrious architect Walter Adolf Gropius, the Bauhaus began as a combination of two older institutions, an academy of art and a school of applied arts. Under his direction the Bauhaus flourished in the 1920s as a mecca for artisans and students interested in a broad range of visual arts, including architecture, handicrafts, industrial design, painting, sculpture, theater, and typography.[18] In addition to his trail-breaking products as an architect, Gropius was an inspiring visionary, theoretician and educator, and under his tenure the Bauhaus became a significant force in the visual arts:

> The Bauhaus persuaded designers to adopt a new, clean vocabulary in lamps, in chairs, in typography; it changed the face of modern architecture;...it propagated its views with enthusiastic shows and striking pamphlets; it earned the gratitude of modern art by appointing artists like Vasily Kandinsky, Paul Klee, Lyonel Feininger, Josef Albers, László Moholy-Nagy, and others to its staff; it undertook an experiment in esthetic education unprecedented in its imaginative sense for the whole person.[19]

In 1925 the school moved to an innovative complex designed by Gropius in Dessau and still later to Berlin in 1932 under the direction of Mies van der Rohe.

From the beginning, Gropius believed that the Bauhaus should be founded on a set of assumptions that was not

> simply a "functional" philosophy limited to the practical or to industry; it was explicitly an esthetic philosophy resting on psychological investigations.

"Architects, painters, and sculptors," he wrote in his opening manifesto of April 1919, "must once again recognize and grasp the multiform shape—*vielgliedrige Gestalt*—of the building in its totality and its parts."[20]

With a determination that in some ways paralleled the vigorous enterprise of the Berlin Psychological Institute during the same period, the

atmosphere at the Bauhaus was curious, exhilarating: the Bauhaus was a family, a school, a cooperative business, a missionary society. Neither Gropius nor the other masters believed in disciples; it was not an academy where the great teacher reproduces little editions of himself, but "a laboratory," where "students stimulated teachers" and teachers, students.[21]

Like members of the Berlin school of Gestalt psychology, the Bauhaus artists reveled in radical new ideas that challenged the more conventional perspectives of their discipline and that also aroused the curiosity of their students. At certain periods, activities of the two schools even overlapped to some degree during the course of their separate projects. This is perhaps most evident in the work of the Swiss artist Paul Klee, who came to the Bauhaus in 1921. Klee's teaching and art had long been informed by psychological research on sensation and perception, especially through the writings of Theodor Lipps, Friedrich Schumann, and Ernst Mach.[22] During the Dessau Bauhaus period, Klee drew upon the Berlin school for inspiration in his lectures at the Bauhaus, most notably Wertheimer's 1923 paper as well as a 1923 article by Wilhelm Fuchs on transparency. He described the effect of the "law of grouping" in checkerboard patterns he used in classroom demonstrations and in his seminal book *The Thinking Eye*.[23] In 1929, Karl Duncker, one of Wertheimer's and Köhler's brightest students, was invited to lecture at the Bauhaus school and Klee attended this talk. During the 1930-1931 winter term Vasily Kandinsky and Josef Albers frequently attended a Bauhaus course on Gestalt psychology taught by Count Karlfried von Dürckheim from the University of Leipzig.[24]

By the late 1920s, Klee began to incorporate a number of themes, principles and figures from the Gestalt literature explicitly into his paintings. In 1935 Klee was afflicted with scleroderm, a neurological disease that would claim his life in 1940. Following his frustrating debilitation, he took to his easel and "painted in a new style: his forms had become terse; his lines heavy, black, and signlike; his colored surfaces brilliant."[25] Klee's use of Wertheimer's patterns emerged especially clearly and directly in a series of pastels during the 1930s; it was perhaps most notable in Klee's celebrated 1937 painting, *Blue Night*.

Further Elaborations of Gestalt Theory

As mentioned above, Wertheimer commented on work by Hillebrand on stroboscopic movement.[26] According to Hillebrand in two articles in the *Zeitschrift für Psychologie* (vols. 89 and 90), stroboscopic motion is produced by a displacement of the visual field that is determined by the field's borders; the "locus of maximal clarity" in effect drags the visual field along with itself. The displacement of the visual field can occur either as a result of actual eye movements or as a consequence of a shift in attention even with the eyes fixated.

Wertheimer presented Hillebrand's arguments in support of this theory in some detail, but then asserted point blank that "the theory...is untenable."[27] It is "in principle contradicted by clear and well-known facts." Any theory of stroboscopic motion that depends upon eye movements (or upon displacement of the visual field), he argued, is categorically disproved by the fact that it is easy to demonstrate simultaneous perception of apparent motion in two opposite directions within the same visual field, as when a dot above a fixation point appears to move to the right while simultaneously a dot below the fixation point appears to move to the left. Wertheimer referred to several such findings reported in his 1912 paper on apparent motion. He also argued that, for the same reason, Hillebrand's theory cannot account for the perception of cinematic or even actual movement, since in the cinema, for example, several objects can be seen to move in different directions at the same time.

In addition to his rebuttal of several of Hillebrand's arguments by reference to various findings in the 1912 paper, Wertheimer also presented a detailed critique of some of the conditions used in Hillebrand's own experiments. In particular, Hillebrand exposed small circles—rather than the lines or dots used in most of Wertheimer's experiments—that generated apparent motion *within* the circles that sometimes was consistent with and sometimes inconsistent with the major apparent motion of the object from the location of one circle to the location of a second circle. He further argued that the distance between the circles in some of Hillebrand's experiments was so great that the display was inherently unlikely to generate the perception of apparent motion. According to Wertheimer, Hillebrand's experiments in no way confirmed his theory but merely corroborated what was already known about how stroboscopic motion can capture attention and focus it on a subpart of the visual field.

Another section of the paper concerned apparent motion in a well-articulated space filled with objects rather than in a dark or a totally undifferentiated visual field. Such perception of motion was also well known, as was the apparent stability of objects in the visual field even when the eyes (or the foci of attention) are moving. All these facts, Wertheimer argued, are entirely contradictory to Hillebrand's basic assumptions. Hence, his basic assumptions, with their "oversimplified generality," are "no longer tenable today."[28]

As for the "short circuit" theory of stroboscopic motion in Wertheimer's 1912 article, Hillebrand had claimed that it cannot be derived from other regularities that have already been established about the spatial sense. Wertheimer vehemently agreed, and asserted that therefore it must lead to entirely different experimental studies; "how must physiological processes be envisaged, if they are actually to correspond with the psychological findings?"[29] For Wertheimer, this research direction had to be pursued if there were to be genuine progress in the scientific understanding of the perception of apparent movement.

After a few additional critical comments about Hillebrand's theoretical orientation and research methodology, Wertheimer concluded:

> It would have been gratifying if, as a result of Hillebrand's investigations, we had a new, improved theory of stroboscopic apparent motion. Nothing brings science forward better than objective experimental investigation in the confrontation between perspectives that differ in principle.
>
> But as we have seen, Hillebrand's experiments are defective in essential ways, the theoretical assumptions are so oversimplified and general that they are no longer tenable today, and his theory is simply inconsistent with the facts.[30]

In this paper, as in the printed exchange with Carl Jung almost two decades earlier, Wertheimer did not hesitate to be acerbic in attacking his opponent; the tone of the article is sharply critical of Hillebrand and of his work.

On December 17, 1924, Wertheimer presented a lecture "Über Gestalttheorie" ("On Gestalt Theory") to the Kant Society; the lecture was published during the following year. This was perhaps the first time—more than a decade after the "founding" of the school—that he put into print a formal statement of Gestalt theory and its place in psychology, science, and epistemology. "Gestalt theory has to do with concrete research," he observed in response to criticisms that the school lacked experimental rigor;

> it is not only an *outcome* but a *device*: not only a theory *about* results but a means toward further discoveries. This is not merely the proposal of one or more problems but an attempt to *see* what is really taking place in science.... Gestalt theory is not something suddenly and unexpectedly dropped upon us from above; it is, rather, a palpable convergence of problems ranging throughout the sciences and the various philosophic standpoints of modern times.[31]

While several of his publications were theoretical or concerned perception, Wertheimer nevertheless remained primarily interested in the psychology of thinking. In response to a request from the publisher—and possibly at the suggestion of his colleagues who were concerned about Wertheimer's sparse publication rate—he published a slim book in 1925 reprinting several of his earlier publications under the title *Three Contributions to Gestalt Theory*. In an unpublished draft of a preface for this volume (MW-CU), he made clear that

> the widespread misunderstanding that Gestalt theory is an extension of perception is objectively and historically false. The first major Gestalt theoretical work was the 1912 one, "On the Thinking of Aboriginal People."

This fragment unequivocally establishes that Wertheimer himself was convinced that this paper was the first Gestalt publication. The Gestalt analysis of thinking was Wertheimer's primary interest from the beginning and remained the main focus of his entire professional career.

Wertheimer's 184-page book *Drei Abhandlungen zur Gestalttheorie* (*Three Contributions to Gestalt Theory*) was published in 1925 by the Verlag der Philosophischen Akademie (the Publisher of the Philosophical Academy). An advertisement for it in a reprint of Wertheimer's 1924 lecture to the Berlin Kant Society indicates that the book was a new edition containing "Experimentelle Studien über das Sehen von Bewegung" ("Experimental Studies on the Seeing of Motion"), "Über das Denken der Naturvölker: Zahlen und Zahlgebilde" ("On the thinking of aboriginal peoples: Numbers and numerical structures"), and "Über Schlussprozesse im produktiven Denken" ("On reasoning processes in productive thinking"), papers that Wertheimer had originally published in 1912, 1912, and 1920, respectively. Wertheimer had presumably abandoned initial plans to publish further articles on the thinking of aboriginal people, for he removed the Roman numeral I from the title of this reprinting of the second paper (which was chronologically actually the first of the three to have been published). The text of the advertisement states, "The essays in this collection were all out of print; because of their far-reaching significance, it was necessary to make them accessible once again to philosophically and psychologically interested readers. The three essays have achieved a prominent position in the theoretical situation of our time. A thorough knowledge of them is indispensable for the modern psychologist."

In the published preface to his *Three Contributions to Gestalt Theory*, Wertheimer wrote:

> The three essays which, at the request of the publisher, are united in this volume in a new release, were duly selected for publication from among more extensive studies. In combination, they can provide for the researcher and the student a picture of how, in concrete studies simultaneously in the most diverse research fields, Gestalt theory began and evolved. They concern problems in three essentially very different fields of research: psychological optics, sociocultural psychology, [and] logic; everywhere the objective procedure itself unmistakably pointed toward a central problem that fundamentally was always the same, the problem of Gestalt theory.

It is precisely this placement next to each other that may make clearer to the reader that it is not merely a matter of an abstract general problem that has been raised for science [nor] a matter of pale generalities, but that it concerns something central, that has its roots and its life in the concrete.

A large number of Gestalt-psychological investigations has appeared since then; in principle I refer here primarily to the studies of W. Köhler. —In the three essays presented here, essentially only a bit of the third work has been altered to make it easier to understand.

Entirely different problem areas that are much closer to everyday concerns should really also have been included here [Wertheimer mentions in a footnote his article "On Gestalt Theory"]; for publication, the "Gestalt theorists" have so far favored problem areas that make decisive progress possible in a strictly scientific manner.

In 1926, Wertheimer presented a paper "On the Problem of the Threshold" at the International Congress of Psychology. A somewhat cryptic abstract of this talk was published the next year:

When examined carefully, the usual conception of the nature of the threshold involves certain basic fundamental assumptions. A Gestalt-theoretical conception leads to the formulation of experimental questions in which these fundamental assumptions become testable.

Is the threshold in fact based on piecemeal sensation and a piecemeal association of stimulus and sensation? Or, in principle, do primary characteristics of the whole come into question here, the resulting sensations as parts of their whole, the processes as parts of the integration of environment and organism?

That the purely piecemeal interpretation, without ad hoc assumptions of another character, does not suffice, follows already from well-known older findings from typical experimental designs; but these experimental designs themselves appear, from the point of view of Gestalt theory, as mere special cases, and there arises the task of experimenting with entirely different, more extensive, research designs (that are also more biological and more human).

The experiments demonstrate whole-laws that are not mere combinations of piecemeal determined sensations, but on the contrary are relevant to the emergence of "sensations" (etc.) *as* parts.

This also deepens the concept of "sensation" (and of "the stimulus"); the pure sensory threshold emerges within threshold events as a late special part of a very different, far more biological and more human character.[32]

The abstract does not succeed in conveying fully how Wertheimer believed Gestalt theory could contribute to a fuller or richer understanding of the sensory threshold or of sensation as such, nor what specific experimental studies could be generated by such an orientation. Altogether, Wertheimer's contributions to the published Gestalt literature were relatively sparse and sporadic. But the prestige of the Berlin school was greatly enhanced meanwhile by Köhler's publication of more than twenty articles, books, and reviews during the 1920s, culminating in his book *Gestalt Psychology* in 1929. During this period Koffka, Hornbostel, and Lewin also produced important works that strengthened the position of Gestalt psychology at Berlin. While Wertheimer, Köhler, Koffka, Lewin, and Hornbostel, as faculty members, were the driving inspiration behind this productivity at Berlin, the energetic labors of their students and laboratory workers provided momentum to the 1920s Gestalt program of research on sensation and perception, memory, learning, thinking, personality, social psychology, and psychopathology. The published output of the students of the Gestalt theorists during the 1920s became enormous.

The Second Generation of Gestalt Psychologists

The positive impact that Gestalt psychologists had on students may have been due in part to the general fascination with holism that characterized young people during the Weimar period. According to Gay,

> The hunger for wholeness found its most poignant expression in the youth. After the war, German youth, restless, bewildered, often incurably estranged from the Republic, sought salvation in poets, but it also found other, more prosaic if not less strenuous, guides. The youth movement, which had its modest beginnings at the turn of the century and flourished mightily through the twenties, collected among its ranks and preserved among its graduates many would-be thinkers hunting for an organic philosophy of life.[33]

While many of these idealistic but disaffected youth explored the political theories of communism and socialism for answers, Gestalt theory became the banner for at least a small cluster of students.

By the early 1920s, Köhler, Wertheimer, and Koffka had succeeded in constructing a significant new school of psychology that increasingly attracted the notice of European and American psychologists and students. Soon the laboratories in the Psychological Institute were buzzing with research, most of it grounded in Gestalt theory. One student remembered that the Institute

> was splendidly located in the Imperial Castle, which had been vacated by Wilhelm II during the German Revolution in 1918. Those two floors gave us plenty of space for the experiments that continue to figure in the text books of psychology. Under the daily supervision of Wertheimer, Wolfgang Köhler and Kurt Lewin, we served as each others' subjects for our dissertations on perception and motivation. Closeted in the former living quarters of the courtladies, we neglected the lecture halls of the university, except for the courses of our own teachers.[34]

Like many members of the *Wandervogel*, the youth hiking movement, the majority of the doctoral students at the Psychological Institute were from affluent backgrounds with fathers who were professionals. Beyond that, however, the composition of the graduate student body in the Institute was different from that of the rest of the university: Almost half (48%) of the students were women and 29% were from foreign countries.[35] During Köhler's directorship, 33 doctoral dissertations were completed at the Institute, nearly double the number of dissertations during Stumpf's tenure.[36] And, although initially claiming no affiliation with any school or ideology, *Psychologische Forschung* was becoming clearly identified as the major publication outlet for the Berlin school of Gestalt psychology.

The number of major articles on Gestalt psychology published during the 1920s made this decade the most prolific in the history of the school.[37] In the pages of *Psychologische Forschung*, Kurt Gottschaldt published on the role of Gestalt factors in the detection of simple figures embedded in more complex ones, Joseph Ternus reported extensive experiments on phenomenal identity, Friedrich Wulf wrote about his studies of changes in memory over time for line figures, Wilhelm Benary examined configurational determinants of brightness contrast, and M. von Frey reported experimental studies of tactile impressions. In the first significant Gestalt research on comparative psychology since Köhler's work on Tenerife, Mathilde Hertz reported her studies of pattern discrimination and escape learning by a raven and a jackdaw as well as the results of influential experiments on figural perception in bees and jaybirds. This is just a small sample. Many other students in the Berlin school furthered the cause of Gestalt theory with their research. Gestalt theory also found fertile ground in Japan during this decade, where it was promulgated by, among others, Sadaji Takagi, Kanae Sakuma, Usao Onojima, Ryuen Iinuma, Taro Obonai, and Shiro Morinaga, several of whom later received appointments to major professorships at Japanese universities.

Outstanding among the students was Karl Duncker, considered the most promising by both Wertheimer and Köhler.[38] Born February 2, 1903 in Leipzig, Germany, Duncker was raised in a liberal family that was responsible for producing an underground socialist paper. When Köhler traveled to the United States in 1925, he was given the opportunity to award a Clark University fellowship to someone of his choice; he selected Duncker. Duncker completed the requirements for a master's degree from Clark University in 1926. His thesis, "An experimental and theoretical study of productive thinking," was signed by John Paul Nafe, a doctoral student of Edward B. Titchener. But with his structuralist orientation, it is doubtful that Nafe made a major contribution to the thesis. Indeed, Köhler—and Wertheimer—were probably far more responsible for directing it than Nafe.

In 1926, Duncker returned to the Psychological Institute at Berlin. Under the supervision of Wertheimer and Köhler, Duncker received his Ph.D. from the University of Berlin in 1929. His dissertation on induced motion was published in 1929; it soon was considered one of the most significant Gestalt contributions and a brilliant complement to Wertheimer's 1912 paper on the phi phenomenon. In this work, his participants reported perceived personal movement if their body was stationary but another encompassing object in their perceptual field was in motion. For example, standing at the middle of a bridge looking down at a passing stream may give the distinct impression that the perceiver, rather than the water, is in motion. In his dissertation, Duncker acknowledged his debt to Wertheimer in a footnote, did not explicitly mention Köhler's name, but did express gratitude for use of laboratory space at the Psychological Institute.

Duncker served as laboratory assistant for Köhler at the Berlin Psychological Institute from 1929 to 1935. Under Wertheimer's direction, Duncker also conducted an ingenious series of experiments on problem solving. Originally published in German in 1935, Duncker's monograph was translated a decade later into English ("On problem-solving," *Psychological Monographs*, 1945, 58, 5; it has been widely cited, including in the recent literature of cognitive psychology). After conducting numerous experiments in which participants were requested to "think aloud," i.e., to generate what now are called "verbal protocols," Duncker demonstrated that many of them exhibited a "functional fixedness," an inability to find productive solutions to new problems once they had "fixed" upon a particular way to structure or view the problem domain.

Two other assistants also generated significant contributions to the Gestalt literature: Otto von Lauenstein and Hedwig von Restorff. Von Restorff's work on memory in particular turned out to lead to extensive further studies. Born in 1903, she received her Ph.D. in 1933 before becoming a research assistant at the Psychological Institute in 1934. In a 1935 *Psychologische Forschung* publication, Köhler and von Restorff reported experiments demonstrating that isolated or distinctive items are recalled better than a series of homogenous items.[39] Participants in one of their experiments learned nonsense syllables composed of consonant-vowel-consonant combinations (CVCs). However, when an individual three-digit item was inserted into the list of CVC triads, participants showed superior recall for the three-digit number over that for a CVC in the same location in the list. According to Köhler and von Restorff, the numbers acted as a figure in contrast with the relatively homogeneous ground of undifferentiated syllables. The same result was obtained when the nature of the material to be memorized was reversed: a single CVC syllable embedded in a list of three-digit numbers was better recalled than a three-digit number at the same location in the list. This phenomenon is widely referred to in the psychological literature as the "Köhler-von Restorff effect" or, occasionally, as just the "von Restorff effect."[40]

Lewin's students too were breaking new ground with their contributions to the Gestalt literature. Among them Blyuma Vulfovna Zeigarnik, for example, born in Lithuania in 1900, earned her doctoral degree from the University of

Berlin in 1927. Working primarily with Lewin on her dissertation (although officially supervised by Köhler), Zeigarnik found that participants in her experiments recalled tasks that were interrupted or incomplete better than they remembered completed tasks. According to Zeigarnik (and Lewin), the incomplete task produces a state of tension or "quasi-need" because of a lack of closure; completion brings the tension to an end and therefore makes the task less salient in memory. Other students of Lewin, such as Maria Ovsiankina and Anitra Karsten, followed up on Zeigarnik's findings in their 1928 dissertations, the results of which were also published in *Psychologische Forschung*.

> Wertheimer supervised the 1926 dissertations of Kurt Gottschaldt and Wolfgang Metzger and was a second reader on Joseph Ternus's dissertation the year before. He joined Köhler in the supervision of Duncker's work, and took an active role in research conducted by Rudolph Arnheim that culminated in his 1928 dissertation on judgments of posed facial expression and handwriting that appeared in *Psychologische Forschung* during the same year. Although Köhler was officially listed as Arnheim's supervisor, the inspiration for Arnheim's dissertation was largely Wertheimer's course on "Knowledge of People" or what is now called person perception or social cognition (*Menschenkenntnis*), and early experiments that Wertheimer had undertaken during the First World War.[41]

Arnheim shared Wertheimer's interest in the arts and recognized that Gestalt theory could be fruitfully and widely applied in architecture, music, painting, film, poetry, sculpture, radio performance, and theater. Like Wertheimer, Arnheim realized that the principles of Gestalt theory are productive not only in the natural world, not only in the rigorous constraints of the laboratory, but also in all realms of artistic endeavor. The principles are especially applicable to the visual medium of cinema. Arnheim undertook extensive analyses of the implicit use of Gestalt principles in the successful films of the time.[42] By the first decade of the twentieth century, European and American audiences had been captivated by German cinema. But in Germany at that time the majority of films were imported from other countries, many of them from Denmark. The few German films that were produced early were relatively inexpensively and crudely made. The audiences were typically members of the working class and poorly educated. In time, master directors such as Ernst Lubitsch, Fritz Lang, and Friedrich Wilhelm Murnau, together with cinematographers like Karl Freund and Fritz Arno Wagner, ushered in radical changes in cinema that helped bring the intelligentsia into the theater.[43] In films of fantasy and horror, the new school of German Expressionism introduced distorted sets and dramatic lighting effects. Drawing upon nineteenth century *Schauerromane* (literally "shudder novels" or horror stories) of Teutonic ghost stories and folk tales, the expressionist cinema of the Weimar period created a surrealistic world which was intended to inspire terror in the audiences.

Robert Wiene's remarkable film *Das Kabinett des Dr. Caligari* (*The Cabinet of Dr. Caligari*), released in Berlin in February 1920, was one of the first products of the new German Expressionism of the Weimar period.[44] Set in the fictitious North German town Olstenwall, the film recounts a series of brutal murders attributed to a traveling mountebank who believed himself to be the reincarnation of the eighteenth century hypnotist Dr. Caligari and his terrifying somnambulist assistant, Cesare, who could predict the time of any person's death.[45] Wiene hired three prominent Expressionist artists, Hermann Warm, Walter Röhrig, and Walter Reimann, to design sets with exaggerated dimensions and deformity in spatial relationships; to economize on electricity (rationed in postwar Germany), bizarre patterns of light and shadow were painted directly onto the scenery and even into the characters' makeup.

Basic Gestalt principles were at least implicitly utilized in Soviet film-making during the same period as that of the rise of German Expressionist cinema. During his lectures at the Vsesoyuznyi Gosudarstvenyi Institut Kinematografii (VGIK or "All-Union State Institute of Cinematography") in the 1920s, Soviet director Lev Kuleshov used sequences of montage that were dramatic examples of the kind of contextual effects that could be expected on the basis of Gestalt theory.[46] In what became known as the "Kuleshov effect," he would edit two consecutive shots in a combined manner so as to generate a new meaning. An example would be the presentation of a close-up shot of the famous Soviet actor Ivan Mozzhukhin

> acting out amorous passion in an old film, juxtaposed with a close-up of a bowl of soup. The message of the sequence came out to be pangs of hunger, not pangs of love. Edited with a scene showing a coffin with a body of a child, the same close-up of Mozzhukhin conveyed the father's inconsolable grief, and so on. Thus a frame as such carries no independent meaning of its own: it is but a letter in the word, a brick in the edifice of film.[47]

Although Kuleshov's work was influenced by Soviet constructivism, it was also informed by Kandinsky's efforts at the Bauhaus "to establish a science of artistic effects. Kandinsky used his students as subjects in laboratory-like research on the impact of color, shape and the like—a procedure that anticipated Kuleshov's editing exercises."[48] Like the abstract sketches and paintings of Klee and Kandinsky, German Expressionist and Soviet cinema during the 1920s at least implicitly reflected the Gestalt understanding of meaningful relationships within and among diverse patterns.

A Gestalt Model of Psychopathology

Although most of the work published from the Berlin school of Gestalt psychology was firmly based in experimental psychology, occasional articles also appeared on clinical topics. In 1923, Heinrich Schulte published an article in *Psychologische Forschung* entitled "Versuch einer Theorie der paranoischen Eigenbeziehung und Wahnbildung" ("Attempt at a Theory of Paranoid Ideas of Reference and Delusion Formation").[49] At the time, Schulte was on the psychiatric staff of the University Clinic in Berlin. He worked with Wertheimer on a Gestalt theory of paranoia that differed radically from the then-dominant Freudian model. According to the Gestalt perspective, a human is seen not only as an individual but also as a "we-being"; people are considered to be "essentially both a whole in [their] own right and part of encompassing groups."[50] Although Schulte is listed as the sole author of the publication, Erwin Levy states that Schulte approached Wertheimer at a psychology conference in Leipzig and asked his mentor for help, whereupon Wertheimer dictated the paper to Schulte.[51] According to Levy, such episodes were not unusual: "much of the work out of the Berlin and Frankfurt psychological institutes was inspired and closely supervised by [Wertheimer] but published under his students' names. As long as the work was done, recorded authorship was of secondary importance."[52]

In addition to the German doctoral students at Berlin, the Psychological Institute attracted a large number of foreign students and psychologists. Kanae Sakuma from Japan and G. Usnadze from the Soviet Union visited the Institute, as did Usnadze's compatriot Alexander Luria, who was to become a world-renowned expert on the psychological sequelae of brain injury. Several scholars from the United States also came to work at the Institute: Donald K. Adams, John F. Brown, Jerome Frank, Donald McKinnon, and Karl Zener.[53] Many visiting students attended Wertheimer's classes and seminars, as well as those offered by Köhler and Lewin.

Wertheimer's Teaching Activities

During his appointment at Berlin, Wertheimer taught a wide variety of courses on philosophy and psychology, and students flocked to hear his lectures. He was developing a reputation as one of the most dynamic professors at the university. The courses and exercises he taught most frequently were on experimental psychology, logic, epistemology, and the psychology of thinking, but they ranged even more broadly than that. Among the courses he taught there were, for example, "Psychology of Law," "Psychology of Scientific Thought," "History of Modern Philosophy," "Experimental Exercises in the Psychology of Recognition and Understanding," "Experimental Psychological Exercises on Mental Achievements," "Psychology of Good and Poor Instruction," "Exercises in Sociocultural Psychology [*Völkerpsychologie*]," and "Experimental Psychological Exercises in Sensory Psychology."[54]

On occasion, Wertheimer would co-teach a course or seminar with his colleagues. In 1925, for example, he was listed together with Kurt Lewin for

"Directing of Scientific Works," and he offered a number of seminars and courses with Köhler. Wolfgang Metzger remembered a distinct contrast in the teaching styles of Wertheimer and Köhler:

> One [Köhler] was younger, blond, tall, straight, and with a cutting sharpness of thinking; the other [Wertheimer] somewhat smaller and older, with long hair and deep, kind eyes, with an astounding boldness and wealth of theoretical and experimental ideas. He always made new objections to his own suggestions and required us, his listeners, to consider again and again what one could do to examine these objections and support or refute them. Again and again he also proposed new experimental variations and encouraged us to make predictions about the results.[55]

Although Wertheimer's primary purpose was to inform students about Gestalt theory and to get them to think in a manner that was consistent with the theory, he was not above allowing personal biases to creep into his lectures. Fritz Heider remembered that Wertheimer attacked one of his chief opponents in psychology in a subtle but devastating way in a Berlin exercise on "expression and physiognomic characters":

> One of the main points was that each person has a certain quality that Wertheimer called his radix—the Latin word for root. This quality will express itself in different ways: in his physiognomy; in his handwriting; in the way he dresses, moves about, talks, and acts; and also in the way he thinks, what kind of outlook he has, and if he is a scholar, in the kind of theory he builds or adopts.... Wertheimer demonstrated what he meant by projecting pictures and handwriting of two people on a screen and asking the audience to match the samples of handwriting with the faces of the writers. Then he gave other items to be matched. He described the one as broad-minded, generous, open, attractive, and inclined to think in holistic terms; the other, as more restricted, petty, a person who thought in terms of parts and pieces, altogether not very likable. I am not sure that many in the audience recognized that the second picture was of G. E. Müller.[56]

Teaching was doubtless a fulfilling but challenging process for Wertheimer, one that allowed him to articulate Gestalt psychology further and helped him generate fresh ways to apply the basic tenets of the theory to an ever-expanding array of specific concrete problems. In addition to the intellectual rewards, Wertheimer's career as a professor at Berlin also brought him into contact with the woman whom he would marry.

Marriage to Anni Caro

The publication of his article on the principles of organization in 1923 was a significant milestone in Wertheimer's professional life. That year also brought a significant milestone in his personal life: in July of that year he married Anna (nicknamed "Anni") Caro, born June 16, 1901, the daughter of a physician in Landsberg an der Warte in eastern Prussia, now part of Poland. Her paternal grandfather was also a physician; he died in a plague in the nineteenth century. Anni's father, Rudolf Caro, practiced medicine for many years before he too perished as a result of disease; already a diabetic, he contracted tuberculosis from Russian soldiers whom he was treating during the First World War and died shortly thereafter in 1915. Following her husband's death, Margarethe Pick Caro raised her three daughters alone. She encouraged her youngest daughter, Anni, to become a teacher like her oldest sister.

In a transcribed tape-recorded interview (MW-CU),[57] Anni reported that because Rudolf's death left the family impoverished, Anni lived with her mother's younger sister, Emilie Pick, who agreed to help pay for her niece's education, when Anni matriculated at the University of Berlin. Emilie, or "Tante [Aunt] Miele" as Anni called her, was married to Fritz Rosenberg, whom Anni described as an affable and wealthy curator at a prominent Berlin art gallery that specialized in old copper engravings. During her childhood, Anni occasionally visited the Rosenbergs, and she felt grateful for the later opportunity to live in their house and study at the university.[58] While living with her aunt and uncle, Anni began dating Richard Hamburger, an engineering student more than a decade her senior who was fascinated by philosophy, particularly by Nietzsche. Although she considered herself rather naive and shy, Anni felt a spirited curiosity about philosophy and psychology and deeply enjoyed discussing such matters with Hamburger.

During a conversation early in 1919, Hamburger convinced her to accompany him to a lecture by one of his favorite professors, Max Wertheimer. As Anni remembered the occasion, she was captivated by Wertheimer's appearance when he entered the lecture room at the Institute. Although well dressed in a spotless black suit and white shirt, he had apparently misplaced his necktie and had instead tied a black shoestring around his collar as a last-minute substitute. In addition, his small, slight build struck her as contrasting with his long hair, large eyes, thick eyebrows, and prominent walrus moustache. Before beginning the lecture, she remembered, he quietly reached into his black vest, retrieved a large gold pocket watch, and placed it on the table in front of him. Wertheimer then launched into what Anni called an impassioned, animated discourse on Gestalt theory. Anni initially had no idea what he was talking about so intensely, but was impressed by his fiery conviction and his zeal for his own ideas. Following his lecturing, Wertheimer would often continue enthusiastic discussions with a band of disciples who followed him to the train station from which he rode by rail back to his room in the Sterns' house. On some occasions, before boarding the train, he would eat dinner with a few students at the Aschinger restaurant, a modest site often frequented by truck drivers.[59]

At the conclusion of the first lecture that Anni attended, Anni and Hamburger joined several other students who walked with Wertheimer to the restaurant and discussed philosophy, psychology, and Gestalt theory as he ate what Anni called his usual meal of pea soup, pork cutlets in gelé, and beer. Anni recalled that she sat quietly in awe, feeling privileged to sit at a table with a professor of the University of Berlin, watching this remarkable man with his warm, penetrating eyes and vigorous gestures, hoping to make sense out of at least some of the conversation. She reported that Wertheimer was so consumed with Gestalt theory throughout the entire meal that he never acknowledged her presence at the table. Nonetheless, she was so fascinated with his acumen and intensity that she decided to enroll as a student in a class with him.

In 1921 Anni formally enrolled in Wertheimer's course on "Logic and Epistemology" and again found, as did several other members of the class, that she was having difficulty understanding the content of his animated lectures. She also enrolled in a seminar conducted jointly by Wertheimer and Köhler on visual contrast and the blind spot in vision. Although both men of course employed Gestalt theory to describe the visual phenomena studied in the laboratory demonstrations, Anni noticed a substantial difference in their presentation styles. Her description of their teaching styles is consistent with Metzger's (p. 169). Köhler would approach a problem in a precise, concrete manner as a natural scientist. Although Wertheimer did not contradict Köhler, he would consider the problem in a more complex way as his insatiable curiosity circled each issue, analyzing and revisiting every alternative. After several courses on logic, epistemology, and psychology, Anni developed a deeper appreciation of the messages in what she called Wertheimer's "temperamental and lively" lectures:

> I…had the impression when I was his student that most of us had no idea what he was talking about. It took me, particularly, about half a year going to his lectures two or three times a week until I caught on. When we did catch on, we were delighted! Our whole lives changed, our whole outlook on life changed. All of a sudden, everything became colorful and lively and had meaning.[60]

Max was in his early forties when, according to Anni, he first appeared to notice the intense yet reserved slight young woman who regularly attended his lectures. Anni was flattered when this popular university professor first invited her for a social occasion; he may have been pleased to interact with an intelligent and attractive person who seemed to share his passion for Gestalt psychology. Indeed, when asked about their early courtship, Anni was fond of saying that she "fell in love with Gestalt theory."

The inspiration of the Gestalt message combined with the charisma of its messenger, Anni recalled, helped give some meaning to her previously rather sheltered life. In the spring of 1922, Anni suffered what she later called "a nervous attack" and became profoundly depressed. She described a visit from Wertheimer to her at the Rosenberg house, where he met Emilie and Fritz Rosenberg and was ushered into the parlor where Anni was lying on a couch. Max asked her relatives to leave the room. Without speaking, he walked to a nearby piano and began playing while Anni quietly listened. Dramatically, she began to feel better than she had in months. Her breathing became less labored and she wanted to cry. Wertheimer would occasionally look over at her as he played until, after some time, he stopped, looked at her intently, and then left the parlor as quietly as he had come. Anni's condition slowly improved, and she continued to convalesce at the Rosenbergs', where, she reported, Max visited her every week. Wertheimer had been troubled by pain in his knee and would occasionally arrive at the house with a walking stick; she was always elated to hear the sound of his cane echoing down the hallway as he would come to visit her.

During one visit, she told Max about a vision that she had about the meaning of Gestalt theory, about its truth and its impact in helping her to understand the world. She said Max began to weep as she described the way that Gestalt theory and Wertheimer had touched her life. Anni expressly began to consider the possibility of marriage, but Max was initially reluctant. She reported many years later that he warned her about his obsession with his work: "You must always remember, I will always be at my desk. I will always work. I must create Gestalt theory." She had already noticed that he was constantly deep in thought about Gestalt psychology. During later walks with her, Max would often interrupt their conversation to scribble on a slip of paper some new insight about the theory that had occurred to him. Nonetheless, Anni's conviction that she should marry him deepened, and finally he did propose to her.

As Anni described the events, Max traveled to Landsberg and, while Anni waited in her room, formally asked Margarethe Caro for her daughter's hand in marriage. Despite any reservation that Anni's mother may have had about their ages—Max was close to twice as old as Anni—she gave her blessings to the marriage. Having obtained Anni's mother's consent, they traveled to Prague and Max introduced Anni to his father as, Anni recalled, his "best logic student." Although Wilhelm was polite to the couple, Anni said, he pulled his son aside and expressed some concern about their significant age difference; born in 1901, Anni was twenty-one years Wertheimer's junior. Anni apparently was impressed with and warmly amused by Wilhelm, whom she described as a slightly vain, aristocratic "Bohemian gentleman" who had two large mirrors in his office that allowed him to check that his appearance was proper. Although she was barely acquainted with Wilhelm or Rosa, Max appeared to her to be qualitatively different from his parents. Many years later, she commented that Max seemed to her to be like "a huge blossom in a desolate cactus."

Some time after having her meet his parents, Max took his fiancée to play string quartet with Albert Einstein. She felt that the occasion was a kind of test. Perhaps because of the eminence of Einstein's reputation, Anni was amazed at her observation that he played the violin poorly. But she was impressed with his warm and gentle nature, a temperament that reminded her of Max's.[61] She recalled that, like Wilhelm, Einstein was pleased that Wertheimer was engaged, but felt compelled to ask Max how he could marry such a young, inexperienced woman.

Like Max, Anni was of Jewish descent, but her family did not observe the religion strictly. Because several of her close friends had been confirmed in the Christian faith at age fourteen or fifteen, Anni had also decided as a teenager to undergo the rituals required for her to join the Protestant religion. Although this apparently did not concern Max, he knew that Wilhelm could be disturbed by her non-Jewish affiliation on the wedding certificate. To be sure, Wilhelm was never as devout as Rosa, but after Rosa's death he occasionally reminded Max of his mother's identification with Judaism. When Max asked Anni to repudiate her Protestant affiliation, she requested as much from the church in Landsberg—only to learn that she had never officially been recognized as Protestant because of some overlooked minor paperwork requirement in her confirmation.

With Wilhelm Wertheimer and Margarethe Caro acting as witnesses, Max and Anni were married in a Berlin municipal office on July 6, 1923. Following a celebration and dinner with Anni's family, they traveled to Korsero, a small coastal town where Anni was able to see the ocean—for the first time in her life. Their honeymoon was brief; Wertheimer had to return to the Institute to teach summer classes—with a bad case of sunburn.

During his courtship of Anni, Wertheimer left the Stern house and began living at the home of Erich von Hornbostel, his wife Susi, and their son Johannes. After their honeymoon, Fritz Rosenberg agreed to let Anni and Max move into a small furnished apartment that he owned in the middle of Berlin.

Family

Gestalt psychology always occupied much of Wertheimer's waking moments. He was constantly seeking new problems and situations to which he could apply fundamental aspects of the theory, and striving to attain an ever clearer way to explicate its role in human cognition, perception, and logic. Anni eagerly strove to help Max in these efforts. She attended most of his lectures and took dictation from him as he paced the floor of his study. What she said was hardest on her was his occasional frustration and even rage as he struggled to find appropriate expression for his ideas.

One day while she was at home and Max was lecturing at the university, Anni experienced a sudden spasm of pain as she was carrying a heavy bucket of coal to heat the stove in their small apartment. She consulted her gynecologist, Otto Abraham, Max's friend and colleague at the Psychological Institute, who informed her that she was pregnant, and forbade her to lift heavy objects. Although the Wertheimers were both apparently pleased at the prospect of being parents, Anni felt that Max seemed worried that he might be too old to be an effective father, but Anni tried to convince him otherwise. They decided to leave her uncle's small apartment for a larger house. In the early spring of 1924, they moved into a suburban home in Karlshorst near the residence of Lisbeth and Georg Stern. Max renewed his close relationship with his old friends, and the Wertheimers spent nearly every evening at the Stern house discussing art, psychology, and politics, singing, and playing chamber music. Although he seldom engaged in formal practice, Wertheimer continued to be proficient at playing the piano, organ, violin, and viola.

Several months after their move, Anni gave birth to a baby boy on her own birthday, June 16, 1924. The infant was named Rudolf Wilhelm Walter Georg Wertheimer after his maternal and paternal grandfathers, his paternal uncle, and Georg Stern. But Max and Anni's happiness was short-lived: Rudolf contracted diphtheria, and died only weeks after his birth, on July 10.[62] The Wertheimers were devastated—Anni so much so that she did not even attend her baby's funeral. Two months later, in an effort to bolster Anni's spirits, Max arranged for a vacation with the Sterns in Austria.

Otto Abraham too, Anni claimed, was deeply affected by Rudolf's death and felt indirectly responsible for the tragedy. He appeared to be elated when he was able to help deliver the Wertheimers' second child, a healthy baby boy, on May 12, 1925, in Abraham's clinic. Valentin Jacob Thomas Wertheimer was named after San Valentino (Saint Valentine), a small Italian mountain town where he was presumably conceived. This village had also been a favorite vacation spot of Max's grandfather, Jacob Zwicker; he was the source of the name Jacob. The name Thomas had no special significance, but was simply one of Anni's favorite names.

Max's concern about being a father appears to have dissipated quickly. He spent much time, often in his nightshirt, by the crib, singing and rocking his son to sleep. Because of what had happened to Rudolph, Anni and Max were greatly concerned about Val's health. Their caution was so extreme, Anni recalled, that they decided to move when they suspected that a faulty heating system might be causing poisonous gas to leak into the home.

Late in January 1927, then, with generous financial support from Wilhelm, the Wertheimers bought another house in Karlshorst, again close to the Stern residence. Max hired a maid to help with the housework, apparently hoping that this would free Anni to spend more time with him in his work on Gestalt theory. At the time, Wertheimer was struggling to develop a mathematical system for Gestalt theory that would be precise and objective without doing violence to his ideas. He spent numerous hours discussing this matter with mathematicians and physicists at the university, but was constantly frustrated in his efforts to generate a satisfactory Gestalt mathematics.

When not assisting her husband, Anni occasionally wrote poetry. She showed some of it to Max who, she remembered, did not offer her his impression of the work but instead encouraged her to write a paper on the "poetic image," in particular on the Gestalt qualities of a simile. Still unconvinced of her own intellectual prowess, Anni did not pursue the suggestion.

The years after their move brought the birth of two other children in rapid succession, both in good health: Michael Matthias was born March 20, 1927, in the new house and Lisbeth Rosa (named in honor of Lisbeth Stern and Max's mother) October 12, 1928. Max spent much time interacting with Val, Michael, and Lise and seemed to be captivated by their fresh young perspective and humor, but Anni had the impression that he acted more like a grandfather than a father with his children. He tended to engage in roles that were physically not very active, such as playing games and telling stories. In particular, he delighted the children with tales about on-going gentle adventures of two characters, Stefan and Anton Poniz, who during the story-telling were acted out by the thumbs, respectively, of his left and right hands, bowing and speaking to each other, and engaging in other interesting movements such as hiding in their respective clenched fists. He also shared with them various words and names that he either made up or had learned about during his own childhood from his parents. A "Laban" was any long, fairly thin object such as a slice of cheese; a spot of light reflected from a mirror or through a glass prism, dancing on a wall or ceiling, was a "Puripu." A bit of dust or a small light mass of dirt was a "Fusel." A small, cheerful, rather stout lady about whom stories were told was called "Gelchen-ku," a transformation of "Kugelchen," literally a diminutive of "sphere." Puns and word play were admired and encouraged; one sentence that all the children learned early used the two syllables "laden" six times in succession, with the meaning exquisitely determined by context in a Gestalt-like manner: Kaufmänner, die vor einem Schokoladen Laden Laden laden, laden Ladenmädchen zum Tanze ein [shopmen, who are loading shutters in front of a chocolate store, invite shopgirls to dance]. There was a ritual performed on the birthday of every member of the family, a dance in honor of the "birthday child"—that was the term used, even if the person whose birthday was being celebrated was an adult. The rest of the family (and other members of the household, or guests, if there happened to be any) formed a ring, facing inward and holding hands, around the "birthday child." Then, in rhythm to a nonsense song ("A la bumsta bumsta bi, a la bumsta bumsta bi, a la bumsta bumsta billi bi, di bumsta bumsta bi"), the circle rotated slowly clockwise while the "birthday child" inside the circle turned counterclockwise. All in the ring then repeated the song, this time rotating counterclockwise while the "birthday child" turned clockwise. Thereafter all members of the circle knelt down and simultaneously embraced the "birthday child."

The children brought Wertheimer a minor fiscal benefit: the university gave him a modest raise in his annual salary for each child. But Wertheimer—48 years old at the time of his daughter's birth—had still not received a call to a full professorship; and his father continued to contribute to covering the expenses of Max's household.

Professional Recognition: The Call to the University of Frankfurt

Max Wertheimer was deeply immersed in the lively, exhilarating, and influential work going on at the Psychological Institute at the University of Berlin during the 1920s. But as the end of the decade approached, he may have become somewhat frustrated about his academic status. Would he never become a full professor?

During the 1920s, Koffka and Köhler vigorously promoted Gestalt psychology in America. In 1925, Köhler accepted an invitation to lecture at Clark University in Worcester, Massachusetts. Before leaving Germany, Köhler recommended to the authorities at the University of Berlin that Wertheimer be appointed temporary Director of the Psychological Laboratory during Köhler's absence from the post; they acceded to his request. As acting Director, Wertheimer now had to balance his teaching and research responsibilities with some administrative duties.[63]

Koffka arrived in the United States in 1924, two years after his introduction of Gestalt theory to American psychologists with his article in the *Psychological Bulletin*. Following brief appointments at Cornell and the University of Wisconsin, Koffka chose to immigrate permanently in 1927 in response to an offer from Seth Wakeman, a former student of Ogden, to a named chair, the William Allan Nielson professorship, at Smith College in Northampton, Massachusetts.[64]

Before making this move, Koffka had achieved an impressive and conspicuous record of research and publication and had succeeded in his efforts to strengthen psychology as a natural science at Giessen.[65] The Giessen faculty solicited the opinions of thirteen psychologists and physiologists about an appropriate successor to the ausserordentliche professorship Koffka had vacated. According to Ash, ten of the respondents rated Wertheimer as their first choice:

> David Katz, for example, called Wertheimer "one of the researchers who are determining the development of modern psychology." William Stern of Hamburg wrote that by appointing him "your university would compensate for an injustice done him by the German universities." Even Erich Jaensch of

Marburg, a well-known critic of Gestalt theory, expressed the opinion that although Wertheimer was not the sort of all-round talent one might wish, "as a mind," he clearly outranked all other candidates.... [And] Koffka acknowledged, "I myself owe him the best in my development."[66]

Köhler was also petitioned and, not surprisingly, praised Wertheimer as a researcher and teacher. In addition to laudatory comments on the quality of Wertheimer's scholarship, Köhler pointed out the important political and fiscal reasons for the appointment by noting that in earlier years,

> Wertheimer placed no value in a university position, since he wanted to be independent and had independent means. His property has disappeared in the inflation[;] he has since married, has two children, and [has] no proper income besides a stipend of not even 2,000 Marks. When he becomes ill, the income from lecture fees is gone.... Of course his race is involved. But I should think that every German who is proud of Lessing and "Nathan the Wise" should disregard this viewpoint in cases of outstanding giftedness. We count Einstein and James Franck as Nobel prize-winners, but we do everything to make it difficult for outstanding Jewish colleagues.[67]

In June 1928, the Ministry offered Wertheimer the position of Department Head for experimental psychology and pedagogy at Giessen with a base salary of 8,600 Marks (1,200 Marks more than Koffka's Giessen salary had been) and, as Ash reports, "a guarantee that the state would make up any difference between his total income, including lecture and examination fees from students, and 12,000 Marks—a reasonable amount at the time, even for a full professor."[68] The Ministry at Giessen had, unfortunately, decided earlier in the year that it could only promise to try to upgrade the position to a full professorship, with no guarantee that this would occur. Confronted with only a possibility of an upgrade in the appointment, Wertheimer decided in July 1928 to decline the offer and stay in Berlin.

The American psychologist Edwin G. Boring, like his mentor E. B. Titchener, followed the development of Gestalt psychology with strong interest, but also some trepidation. Boring had been at Harvard University since early 1922 and was determined to bring a Gestalt psychologist to the faculty. He had been instrumental in making several attempts to bring Köhler to Harvard in the 1920s.[69] When these efforts proved unsuccessful, Boring approached Wertheimer about an appointment at Harvard. Boring had heard positive reviews of Wertheimer from Robert M. Ogden of Cornell University, who had met the Gestalt psychologist in 1927 and described him as "very likeable and very stimulating."[70] On April 3, 1929, Boring wrote to Wertheimer with an invitation to teach at Harvard University during either the October 1929 to January 1930 term or the February to May 1930 term.[71] Although Wertheimer's response has not been found, it is obvious in two letters from Boring that the invitation was declined.[72] Boring was skeptical about a later invitation for Wertheimer, since the resources that were to have been allocated for the temporary position were designated for Harvard's newest faculty member, Gordon Allport.[73] In a September 9, 1929 letter to Wertheimer, Koffka expressed disappointment that Wertheimer had to decline the appointment since "psychology is not in a good state" at Harvard.[74]

Although tempted by the prospect of lecturing in the United States, Wertheimer had become interested in a regular full professorship: the chair vacated by his old mentor, Friedrich Schumann, at the University of Frankfurt. Indeed, Wertheimer wrote to his father that the Frankfurt opening was a major factor in his decision to decline the Harvard appointment.[75] It was late in Wertheimer's career for a call to a full professorship, but it became clear that Wertheimer was indeed under serious consideration for the post at Frankfurt.

Although it would mean a significant improvement in Wertheimer's academic status, the call to Frankfurt would dramatically threaten his family's lifestyle in Berlin. In particular, their cherished friendship with the Sterns would at best be reduced to occasional visits. Following their marriage, Anni felt that her shyness had been abating in their comfortable, informal interactions with the Sterns. Georg's gentle warmth and humor made her feel like a welcome and competent participant in conversations about art, music, and politics—and far less like an awkward and immature school girl. Georg even invited Anni to be the librettist for an opera that he was composing about the tribulations of the Biblical figure Job. Anni agreed, and did produce a libretto, but the project was hardly begun before it was ended by Georg's death.

Because Berlin was closer to Prague than Frankfurt was, the new appointment would also further increase Max's distance from his father and thus make it less convenient to visit him. In the years following his wife's death, Wilhelm Wertheimer frequently became sick and depressed; by 1929 he had become somewhat reclusive, relying almost exclusively on the care of his friend and long-term maid Karolin, and seldom venturing out of his apartment.

Aside from personal considerations, the new appointment for Max would also require a significant change in geographical and cultural conditions. Frankfurt could not compare to Berlin in terms of raw size and scope: according to a 1925 census, Berlin, occupied by over four million citizens, was then the fourth largest city in the world (after London, New York, and Tokyo), while Frankfurt's population was only 540,115 people in the same year. And while he was usually totally absorbed in his work, Wertheimer had managed to enjoy Berlin's cultural riches; by 1929, the city's conservatory and philharmonic orchestra enjoyed wide renown. The former royal museums and the national gallery were full of masterpieces of art from around the world. Berlin theatre offered imaginative productions of both modern German drama and translations of the works of Molière, Shakespeare, Ibsen, and George Bernard Shaw. Frankfurt was not without its cultural attractions, but they were somewhat pale in comparison with those in Berlin. Yet Frankfurt could boast of a strong intellectual heritage. It was famed as the birthplace of Goethe, the jurist Paul Johann Anselm von Feuerbach, and the historian Friedrich Christoph Schlosser, and was widely noted for its Städel Art Institute and its Rothschild Library. Its cultural pride was reflected in the city's most prestigious academic institution; in 1932 the University of Frankfurt was renamed the Johann Wolfgang Goethe University in honor of the nation's most distinguished poet. One commentator (Colin Loader) observed:

> Frankfurt, like Budapest and unlike Heidelberg, was a large cosmopolitan city with a sizeable cultivated Jewish community. The university itself was relatively new and, being a city university, was less susceptible to the forces of traditionalism present in the older state universities and the bureaucracies that ran them.[76]

This greater freedom may have appealed to Wertheimer. At any rate, in due time an official offer was made to Wertheimer. Probably with some ambivalence because his years in Berlin had been so rewarding, Wertheimer did accept the call to succeed Schumann as full professor and Director of the Psychological Institute at the University of Frankfurt in 1929.

Notes

1. Peter Gay (1980). *Weimar culture: The outsider as insider.* New York: Harper & Row, p. xiii.
2. Mitchell G. Ash, *Holism and the quest for objectivity*, p. 305.
3. Hughes, 1958, p. 47.
4. Ash, p. 307. Drs. Lothar and Helga Sprung located a document that is of interest in this connection and made a photocopy of it; the authors are most grateful to the Sprungs for giving them this copy. It is a hand-written letter from Carl Stumpf to Georg Misch, dated 7.5.1922, document Cod. Ms. G, Misch, 263, in the Handschriftenabteilung der Niedersächsischen Staats- und Universitätsbibliothek in Göttingen. Misch, a professor of philosophy at Göttingen, was a son-in-law of Wilhelm Dilthey, and Stumpf succeeded Dilthey in his Berlin chair. The letter concerns a Göttingen vacancy. Clearly Misch had asked for Stumpf's opinion, but Stumpf cautioned confidentiality. "I can only answer your question under the condition that my name in no way is mentioned as the source," wrote Stumpf, and later in the letter he wrote, "All this is only for your orientation about my impression. But keep it between us, and destroy this letter." Clearly Misch did not honor Stumpf's request. In the body of the letter, Stumpf wrote, among other things, "W. has been so friendly and grateful to me

personally that he would be most deeply hurt if he were to discover that in this case I spoke against him.... With a clear conscience I proposed him here for a non-tenured post ('Extr.'), and he has been named to it. But he has a characteristic which, in such a prestigious position as the one there, could become damaging: a kind of party fanaticism for the school—some call it the clique of the Gestalt theorists, who again value him as leader and authority.... I'm not really against the theory itself, except for the exaggerations, from which...it will gradually free itself. But the manner in which W. holds the group together and strengthens their faith—a second St. Paul—gives me a no longer purely scientific impression. Köhler too is not free from this school-consciousness, but with him I hope it is much more likely that with time it will weaken." Thus Stumpf clearly had his misgivings about Wertheimer's fervor, and may well have played a role in Köhler being appointed to the chair and Wertheimer being only an "extraordinary" (roughly, associate) professor at Berlin.

5. Quoted in Mary Henle (1986), Robert M. Ogden and Gestalt psychology. In M. Henle, *1879 and all that: Essays in the theory and history of psychology*. New York: Columbia University Press, p. 256. Henle provides a rich and detailed account of the relationship between Ogden and Koffka.

6. Kurt Koffka (1922). Perception: An introduction to the Gestalt-Theorie. *Psychological Bulletin*, 19, 531-585.

7. Koffka, Perception, p. 531.

8. Annelies Argeländer to Max Wertheimer, January 11, 1925, MW-CU. Annelies Argeländer to Max Wertheimer, February 8, 1925, MW-CU.

9. Max Wertheimer to Annelies Argeländer [undated; probably January or February, 1925], MW-CU.

10. Max Wertheimer (1922). Untersuchungen zur Lehre von der Gestalt: I. Prinzipielle Bemerkungen [Investigations in Gestalt theory: I. Comments on principles]. *Psychologische Forschung*, 1, 47-58.

11. Max Wertheimer (1923). Untersuchungen zur Lehre von der Gestalt: II [Investigations in Gestalt theory: II]. *Psychologische Forschung*, 4, 301-350.

12. Edward Bradford Titchener, the chief advocate of structuralism, made a distantly related point in describing the "mistake" of the Gestalt school. In a July 8, 1925 letter to Harry Helson, Titchener wrote:

> The more I consider the general standpoint of the Gestalt people, the less tenable their position seems. They are making precisely the same mistake as the Freudians, erecting a whole system of psychology on a single dictum in the form of an inverted pyramid.

Quoted in Henle, Robert M. Ogden and Gestalt psychology, p. 262. Presumably the "single dictum" in the Freudian system concerned the power of unconscious sexual drives, while in the Gestalt case it was that the whole is different from a mere sum of its parts.

13. Max Wertheimer (1923). Untersuchungen zur Lehre von Gestalt: II., *Psychologische Forschung*, 4, 301-350. Condensed and translated as Laws of organization in perceptual forms, in W. D. Ellis (ed.) (1938, 1967). *A source book of Gestalt psychology*. New York: Harcourt, Brace; Humanities Press, 71-88, p. 71.

14. According to Rudolf Arnheim, members of the Psychological Institute often referred to Wertheimer's 1923 paper as the *Punktarbeit* or "dot essay" because many of the figures, demonstrations, and examples of Gestalten in it are composed of patterns made up of dots. Marianne L. Teuber (1976). *Blue Night* by Paul Klee, in M. Henle (ed.), *Vision and artifact: Essays in honor of Rudolf Arnheim*, pp. 131-151. New York: Springer, p. 149.

15. Ash, *The emergence of Gestalt theory*, p. 306.

16. Wolfgang Köhler, Physical Gestalten, in W. D. Ellis, p. 54.

17. Max Wertheimer (1923). Bemerkungen zu Hillebrands Theorie der stroboskopischen Bewegungen [Remarks on Hillebrand's theory of stroboscopic motion]. *Psychologische Forschung*, 3, 106-123.

18. Gropius's earliest architectural achievement was the Fagus Shoe-Tree factory, designed with his close collaborator Adolf Meyer in 1911. Following this success and the First World War, he began undertaking specific actions to establish the Bauhaus school. Among the colleagues whom he consulted about his plans was Wilhelm Köhler, director of a Weimar museum and brother of Wolfgang Köhler. Walter Scheidig (1967). *Weimar crafts of the Bauhaus, 1919-1924: An early experiment in industrial design*. New York: Reinhold.

19. Peter Gay (1976). *Art and act: On causes in history—Manet, Gropius, Mondrian*. New York: Harper & Row, pp. 123-124.

20. Gay, *Weimar culture*, p. 98.

21. Gay, *Weimar culture*, p. 99.

22. Klee read Mach's classic 1886 book *The analysis of sensations* when he was twenty-five and wrote of its powerful effect on his work in his diary. Klee's friend and colleague Vasily Kandinsky was also influenced by the precursors to Gestalt psychology as reflected in both of their Bauhaus lecture notes during the 1921 to 1924 period. See Teuber, *Blue Night* by Paul Klee, pp. 142-143.

23. Marianne L. Teuber (1973). New aspects of Paul Klee's Bauhaus style. In Marianne L. Teuber (ed.), *Paul Klee: Paintings and watercolors from the Bauhaus years, 1921-1931*, pp. 6-17. Des Moines, IA: Des Moines Art Center, p. 14.

24. Teuber, *Blue Night* by Paul Klee, p. 144.

25. Teuber, *Blue Night* by Paul Klee, p. 131.

26. Max Wertheimer, Bemerkungen, pp. 106-123.

27. Wertheimer, Bemerkungen, p. 108.

28. Wertheimer, Bemerkungen, p. 121.

29. Wertheimer, Bemerkungen, p. 122.

30. Wertheimer, Bemerkungen, p. 123.

31. Max Wertheimer, Gestalt theory, in W. D. Ellis, p. 3.

32. Max Wertheimer (1927). Zum Problem der Schwelle [On the problem of the threshold]. *Bericht über den VIII. internationalen Kongress für Psychologie, 1926 [Report on the 8th international congress for psychology, 1926]*. Groningen, The Netherlands: P. Noordhoff, p. 447.

33. Gay, *Weimar culture*, p. 77. Gay further notes (p. 78) that many members of this youth movement often sought escape from commercialism and fragmentation in the holistic symbolism of music:

   Hans Breuer, who compiled the songbook of the youth movement ["*Der Zupfgeigenhansl*"]—one of the biggest sellers of twentieth-century Germany—

insisted in his prefaces that he had gathered his folk songs for "disinherited" youth, a youth "sensing in its incompleteness—Halbheit—the good and longing for a whole, harmonious humanity." What, he asks, "What is the old, classical folk song? It is the song of the whole man, complete unto himself—*in sich geschlossen.*"

34. Rudolf Arnheim (1984). Remembering Max Wertheimer. *History of Psychology Newsletter*, 16, 7-9, p. 8.
35. Ash, *Holism and the quest for objectivity*, p. 308.
36. Ash, *Holism and the quest for objectivity*, p. 308.
37. The majority of articles selected by American psychologist Willis D. Ellis for condensation and translation in his 1938 anthology on Gestalt psychology were papers from *Psychologische Forschung* during the 1920s.
38. According to Mandler and Mandler (1969). The diaspora of experimental psychology: The Gestaltists and others. In D. Fleming and B. Bailyn (eds.). *The intellectual migration: Europe and America, 1930-1960.* Cambridge, MA: Harvard University Press, p. 393, "there is reason to believe that [Duncker] was the most brilliant of the Gestalt group.... His main contribution has made a continuing impact on the psychology of thinking, both in the United States and elsewhere." For a brief biography of Duncker, see D. Brett King, Michaela Cox, and Michael Wertheimer (1998). Karl Duncker: Productive problems with beautiful solutions. In Gregory A. Kimble and Michael Wertheimer (eds.). *Portraits of Pioneers in Psychology*, vol. 3. Washington, DC: American Psychological Association and Mahwah, NJ: Erlbaum, pp. 162-178.
39. According to Henle, the work of Köhler and von Restorff provided an important test of the contrast between Sigmund Freud's concept of isolated ("unique impressions") and crowded items ("analogous impressions"). See Mary Henle, Freud's secret cognitive theories. In M. Henle, *1879 and all that: Essays in the theory and history of psychology.* New York: Columbia University Press, p. 73.
40. Wolfgang Köhler & Hedwig von Restorff (1935). Analyse von Vorgängen im Spurenfeld. II. Zur Theorie der Reproduktion [Analysis of events in the trace field. II. On the theory of reproduction]. *Psychologische Forschung*, 21, 56-112. This research produced practical applications as well. The Applied Psychology Unit at Cambridge employed the research of Köhler and von Restorff for the British Post Office in the design of their postcode. See R. Conrad (1960). Very brief delay of immediate recall. *Quarterly Journal of Experimental Psychology*, 12, 45-47.
41. Ash, *Holism and the quest for objectivity*, pp. 437-438.
42. See, e.g., Rudolf Arnheim (1974). *Film als Kunst [Film as art].* Munich: Hauser.
43. Siegfried Kracauer (1947). *From Caligari to Hitler: A psychological history of the German film.* Princeton, NJ: Princeton University Press. Bruce Murray (1990). *Film and the German left in the Weimar period: From Caligari to Kule Wampe.* Austin, TX: University of Texas Press.
44. Gay comments that "Next to the Bauhaus, probably the most celebrated artifact of the Weimar Republic was...The Cabinet of Dr. Caligari." Gay, *Weimar culture*, p. 102.
45. Following the release of *Caligari* a number of German films echoed similar morbid themes. In the 1920 film *Der Golem*, director Carl Boese filmed the Jewish legend of a gigantic clay statue without a soul that becomes a raging

monster; Friedrich Wilhelm Murnau resurrected the vampire mythos in his 1922 film *Nosferatu—eine Symphonie des Grauens* (*Nosferatu, a symphony of horror*); and Henrik Galeen combined Faustian legend with the motif of a *Doppelgänger*, seeing one's double before a fearful death, in the 1926 film *Der Student von Prag* (*The Student from Prague*).

46. Two of Kuleshov's greatest students, Sergei Eisenstein and Vsevolod Illarionovich Pudovkin, made numerous Soviet films that attracted the attention and appreciation of Rudolf Arnheim.

47. Neya Zorkaya (1989). *The illustrated history of the Soviet cinema*. New York: Hippocrene, p. 49.

48. Vance Kepley, Jr. (1992). Mr. Kuleshov in the Land of the Modernists. In Anna Lawton (ed.), *The red screen: Politics, society, art in Soviet cinema*. London: Routledge, p. 136.

49. Heinrich Schulte (1923). Versuch einer Theorie der paranoischen Eigenbeziehung und Wahnbildung [Attempt at a theory of paranoid ideas of reference and delusion formation]. *Psychologische Forschung*, 5, 1-23.

50. Erwin Levy (1986). A Gestalt theory of paranoia. *Gestalt Theory*, 8, 230-255, p. 248. Levy provides a complete translation of the Schulte paper as well as a critical commentary on the themes of the article and how they compare and contrast with classic psychoanalysis.

51. Levy, p. 230.

52. Levy, p. 230.

53. Ash, *Holism and the quest for objectivity*, p. 311.

54. Siegfried Jaeger, personal communication to Michael Wertheimer, 1993.

55. Quoted in Ash, *Holism and the quest for objectivity*, p. 310.

56. Heider, *The life of a psychologist*, pp. 45-46.

57. The account of the relationship between Wertheimer and his future wife is based on the transcripts of extensive tape-recorded interviews with her in 1968 and 1972 (MW-CU) that have been deposited in the Archives of the History of American Psychology at the University of Akron in Akron, Ohio.

58. The Rosenbergs did not survive past the end of the Second World War. Fritz had an operation for a stomach cancer near the end of his life and Emilie was able to visit the United States in 1938 but was forced by the authorities to return to Germany. Both Emilie and Fritz committed suicide a year or two later. One of Anni's paternal aunts, Lotte Caro, died in a Nazi concentration camp sometime between 1936 and 1945.

59. Like Wertheimer, Lewin often invited students to his home for dinner and conversation or would continue student meetings and seminars at a Berlin restaurant. See Alfred J. Marrow (1984). *The practical theorist: The life and work of Kurt Lewin*. New York: Columbia University Teachers College Press, p. 25.

60. Anni Hornbostel, *Synergist* (1972), p. 76.

61. Anni was also fond of Einstein's second wife, although one of their earliest encounters was awkward. She reported that she and Max were invited to a party at the Einstein house and were greeted by Mrs. Einstein, who was wearing a wide ribbon tied around her head and across her nose. Anni was mystified by such fashion, but because of her shyness waited until after the event to inquire about

the apparel. Max informed her that Mrs. Einstein had a mosquito bite on her nose and that she was wearing the ribbon to cover it.

62. Penicillin and its antibacterial action were not discovered until late in 1928.
63. Max Wertheimer to Annelies Argeländer [January or February, 1925], MW-CU
64. Ash, *Holism and the quest for objectivity*, p. 314. Koffka also received an offer from the University of Wisconsin, but agreed to go to Smith because, in part, his position at the New England women's college allowed him five years free of teaching, the construction of a new laboratory with a budget of $6,000, and two laboratory assistants. Ash notes that Koffka acknowledged in a letter that his $9,000 salary made him "one of the highest paid professors in America."
65. Ash, *Holism and the quest for objectivity*, p. 313.
66. Ash, *Holism and the quest for objectivity*, pp. 314-315.
67. Quoted in Ash, *Holism and the quest for objectivity*, p. 315.
68. Ash, *Holism and the quest for objectivity*, p. 315.
69. Michael Sokal (1984). The Gestalt psychologists in behaviorist America. *American Historical Review*, 89, 1240-1263.
70. Henle, M. (1986). Robert M. Ogden and Gestalt psychology in America. In M. Henle, *1879 and all that: Essays in the theory and history of psychology*, pp. 254-267. New York: Columbia University Press, p. 264.
71. Edwin G. Boring to Max Wertheimer, April 3, 1929, MW-CU.
72. Edwin G. Boring to Max Wertheimer, April 25, 1929, MW-CU. Edwin G. Boring to Max Wertheimer, August 27, 1929, MW-CU.
73. Edwin G. Boring to Max Wertheimer, August 27, 1929, MW-CU.
74. Kurt Koffka to Max Wertheimer, September 9, 1929. MW-CU.
75. Max Wertheimer to Wilhelm Wertheimer, 1929. MW-CU.
76. Colin Loader (1985). *The intellectual development of Karl Mannheim: Culture, politics, and planning*. Cambridge: Cambridge University Press, p. 125.

Wilhelm and Rosa Wertheimer, 1877

Handelsschule Wertheimer, Prague, about 1920

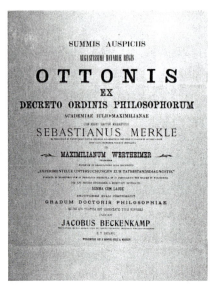

Max Wertheimer's doctoral diploma, 1904

Max Wertheimer with apparatus for studying apparent movement, 1913

Max Wertheimer, May 1917

Anni and Max Wertheimer, August 1923

university administrators. He was an aggressive diplomat whose "great negotiating skill was coupled with his high standing as a scholar and as an honorary professor, which made his judgment on appointment matters highly valued by the faculty."[3] Under Riezler's direction, Frankfurt recruited many distinguished scholars, including the sociologists Karl Mannheim and Max Horkheimer, historian Ernst Kantorowicz, economist Adolf Lowe, and theologian Paul Tillich, as well as Wertheimer.

Wertheimer's call to Frankfurt was not free of complications. There had been some initial opposition to his appointment. Riezler fought to bring Wertheimer to Frankfurt following the retirements of the neo-Kantian scholar Hans Cornelius in philosophy and Friedrich Schumann in psychology. The Philosophical Faculty supported Wertheimer's appointment, arguing that his "investigations [on Gestalt theory] are of fundamental importance for the clarification of epistemological issues," and ranked him with Martin Heidegger, the prestigious existential philosopher at Freiburg, and psychiatrist and philosopher Karl Jaspers as the leading candidates.[4] Although Heidegger and Jaspers had published far more, Wertheimer's reputation in experimental psychology may have been an important consideration in attempts to fill the vacancy caused by Schumann's retirement from the Psychological Institute.

However, the Natural Sciences Faculty recommended instead Adhémar Gelb, already established at Frankfurt, and Erich Jaensch at Marburg. David Katz at the University of Rostock was listed as a third possibility after Gelb and Jaensch. All three were considered competent to fulfill the requirement of "psychologically and philosophically a fully educated person, capable of thinking biologically and [with] thorough training in the design and execution of exact experiments."[5] Although the Natural Sciences Faculty recognized Wertheimer's contribution to psychology, they argued that he would be more appropriate for a chair in philosophy than in psychology. Indeed, the faculty members wondered if Wertheimer, "in spite of all his significance for experimental research, [was] a suitable head of a large institute; neither his interests nor his capabilities seem to lie in this direction."[6] Gelb wrote Wertheimer that "The Ministry was afraid that by giving philosophy to you and psychology to me Frankfurt would be without 'proper' philosophy, a fear surely nourished by Jaspers, but also by others."[7] With his position of authority in hiring new faculty, Riezler was influential in arriving at a suitable, if atypical, settlement: Wertheimer was appointed with Gelb as co-director of the Psychological Institute, and also became co-director with Paul Tillich of the Philosophical Seminar. Wertheimer's appointment included a significant increase in fiscal support; the Psychology Institute's budget increased by 40% and substantial additional funds were provided for the purchase of books.[8]

Wertheimer's Professional Relationships at Frankfurt

Despite his reluctance to leave Berlin, Wertheimer soon adjusted to Frankfurt, a new academic community that functioned, as one commentator (Lewis Coser) has written, as "a harbor of liberal and even radical thought in the twenties and early thirties."[9] In addition to his contacts with Gelb, Kurt Goldstein, and Riezler, Wertheimer also established relations with other colleagues on the faculty. One of his earliest and closest acquaintances was the co-director of the Philosophical Seminar, Paul Tillich, who had resigned from the Dresden Institute of Technology in March 1929 to accept Frankfurt's offer of a position as Professor of Philosophy and Sociology.[10] In June of that year, Tillich delivered his inaugural lecture on "Philosophy and Destiny." In addition to general philosophy, Tillich was immersed in ethics, history, personality, and theology. According to his biographers Wilhelm and Marion Pauck,

> Tillich's formal task at the University of Frankfurt was in fact to teach social education, and in his lectures and seminars between the years 1929 and 1933 he thus emphasized the aspects of social ethics, historical action, and political direction rather than the speculative or metaphysical interests of the thinkers with whom he dealt in the classroom.... As the leader of a seminar or wherever he gathered and interpreted answers to questions, he inevitably went beyond the questions asked and by his enthusiastic introductory response, "Oh, that's an interesting point!" made the most foolish student sound far more intelligent than he often was.... An even more potent factor was his ability to listen to the other person and take him seriously. His lack of bigotry rested on a much greater quality, the gift of openness. It lured his hearers to say things, utter ideas, they had not sensed were in them—ideas which until that moment had lain silent and dormant.[11]

In her tape-recorded interviews with Michael Wertheimer, Anni reported that during the summer of 1929 Wertheimer and Tillich developed a close relationship, and would often stay up until one or two in the morning discussing philosophy and psychology.

Wertheimer and Tillich shared similar teaching styles and both taught large classes to enthusiastic students.[12] Gabrielle Oppenheim, a wealthy patron who hosted numerous dinners for university intellectuals, interacted with Tillich and Wertheimer in both social and academic settings. In contrasting their methods of teaching, she recalled that Tillich

> was a clearer, much better lecturer. Wertheimer was not always organized in his lecturing but he was always interesting. Tillich played with something in his hands, he always found something to play with, but more or less stayed in one place. Wertheimer was very agitated. He walked up and down the large flight of stairs (of the lecture hall), pacing it. He would stop and talk to students[;]...he would go back up and down the stairs.[13]

Gabrielle's husband, Paul Oppenheim, also attended Wertheimer's seminars and was inspired to co-author with Kurt Grelling a manuscript on "The Gestalt Concept in the Light of the New Logic."[14]

As in Berlin, Wertheimer's enthusiastic, vivid, humorous, serious, and stimulating yet erratic teaching style won disciples as well as detractors. One student, Erika Oppenheimer, observed:

> There were a number of my co-students who found him difficult to understand both in what he wrote and when he lectured. Actually the student group was split down the middle: those who considered him to be an absolutely fabulous teacher and those who just couldn't understand him. I belonged to the group who [considered] him a fabulous teacher and we called the others the Philistines. He was difficult for them to understand because Wertheimer never spun out a thought totally; he gave you his thoughts in jumps and he expected the student to bridge the gaps, which some of us found great fun and very interesting as a teaching method and the others found too difficult.[15]

Tillich and Wertheimer also became involved in the progress of each other's students. For example, Theodor Wiesengrund-Adorno, one of Tillich's assistants and doctoral students, was a gifted musician whose interests resonated with Wertheimer's; and one of Wertheimer's doctoral students, Gertie Siemsen, became interested in Tillich and his work.[16]

The close relationship between Wertheimer and Tillich was doubtless encouraged by the proximity of their respective offices, which were located at opposite ends of the philosophy library. Erika Oppenheimer was taken aback by the unorthodox appearance of Wertheimer's workspace. According to her report:

> His office in the university was painted a rather bright red, really for walls a very bright red; a color somewhere between strawberry and salmon. It was painted that way intentionally. Wertheimer felt that one is stimulated by colors and that if the walls of a room are gray or light green or some kind of dull color, one does not work as well as if they are painted in an exciting color such as red.[17]

Another close associate of Wertheimer's during this period was the religious existentialist Martin Buber. As a student, Buber had attended lectures by Mach, Stumpf, and Wundt. In particular, Buber was impressed with Wundt's work on ethnopsychology and later was a laboratory assistant at Wundt's institute at the University of Leipzig.[18] Before arriving in Frankfurt, he edited the Zionist journal *Die Welt* [The World], had founded the German Jewish monthly periodical *Der Jude* [The Jew], and later helped to establish the *Freie Jüdische Lehrhaus* [Free Jewish School]. He joined the faculty at Frankfurt as Professor of Jewish Religion and Ethics, the only chair of Jewish religion at any major German university at that time.

Wertheimer might have resonated somewhat to Buber's emphasis on holistic themes in his analysis of humanity, nature, and God. Buber had developed an early interest in psychotherapy following several years of working at various German psychiatric clinics, one under the direction of the eminent Zurich psychiatrist Eugen Bleuler. In an essay written in 1919 on "The Body and Spirit of the Hasidic Movement," Buber argued for a more holistic "psychosynthesis" over orthodox Freudian psychoanalysis. According to Buber's biographer, Maurice Friedman,

> Taking as his problem the understanding of the healing practiced by the *Zaddik* on the Hasidim who came to him with their diseases, Buber suggested that one could best do justice to its deeper dimension if one bore in mind "that the relation of the soul to its organic life depends on the degree of its wholeness and unity."[19]

The radical nature of Tillich's and Buber's work fit well with Frankfurt's innovative program of social research, even if it was only distantly, if at all, related to Wertheimer's thought.

Shortly before and during Wertheimer's appointment at Frankfurt, the former academy evolved into a major university and, in particular, the social sciences prospered and challenged traditional, established academic programs. Frankfurt's *Institut für Sozialforschung* (Institute for Social Research) was founded in 1923 and, under the direction of Austrian Marxist scholar and editor Carl Grünberg, its program was largely devoted to a Marxist history of the labor movement and closely tied to the Marx-Engels Institute in Moscow.[20] Indeed, initial plans were made to call it the *Institut für Marxismus* (Institute for Marxism) but these plans were abandoned for a more moderate emphasis, on social research; nonetheless students in the 1920s nicknamed it the "Café Marx."[21] In 1930, Grünberg was succeeded by Max Horkheimer who, as a student at Berlin, had become acquainted with Wertheimer and had initially come to Frankfurt in 1918 to study with Gelb. In time, Horkheimer switched to philosophy and worked with Hans Cornelius on a dissertation on Kant which earned him a doctorate *summa cum laude* in 1922. In his inaugural address, Horkheimer stressed the importance of an interdisciplinary approach for the development of a comprehensive social philosophy.[22] Unlike Grünberg, Horkheimer was more interested in esthetics, psychoanalysis, and theoretical revisions of Marxism than in economics.[23] His appointment was a victory for the younger staff of the Institute and provided a new direction in the evolution of the program. The members of the Institute outlined their philosophy and agenda for the new social research program:

> As social and economic crises recur and become more gripping, the social sciences are assuming greater importance for the reorganization of modern

society in the sense of an adaptation of the social processes to the growing needs of humanity.... The economic and technical factors of social processes interact inextricably with cultural and psychological factors.... It is, therefore, necessary to combine economics, sociology, philosophy and psychology for a fruitful approach to the problems of the social sciences.[24]

Under Horkheimer's tenure as director, the Institute attracted many prominent scholars to the faculty, including Leo Lowenthal and Friedrich Pollock, and later Erich Fromm, Herbert Marcuse, and Theodor Adorno.[25]

The goals of the Frankfurt Institute for Social Research appeared to be consistent at least with Wertheimer's beliefs about the advantages of an interdisciplinary approach to science and humanism. The principal figures in the Institute were determined to employ some form of Marxism for the reorganization of modern society. However, several of the faculty at the Institute tried to combine its neo-Marxist approach with Freudian psychodynamic theory, and some wished to reduce emphasis on traditional Marxist thought. Despite, for example, Max Horkheimer's respect for Gestalt theory as a prominent system of psychology, Wertheimer doubtless had a difficult time endorsing the Institute's support of psychoanalysis.

Indeed Wertheimer's vehement rejection of the Freudian approach often found its way into his lectures and his conversations with colleagues and students. According to Erika Oppenheimer, Wertheimer believed that

psychoanalysis belonged to those parts of psychology which approached the human being in a piecemeal fashion, not as a whole, and the reason for that was that psychoanalysis works on the basis of free association.... I often talked to Wertheimer about psychoanalysis which as a younger student I was interested in too, but to no avail. He just wouldn't hear of it. Even when I tried to point out to him that there were really great parallels between Gestalt theory and psychoanalysis, he just would not hear of it.[26]

Considering his earlier exposure to the Social Democrat philosophy of Georg and Lisbeth Stern and their circle, Wertheimer probably was more appreciative of the Marxist aspect of the Institute than of its psychoanalytic one.

Outside of psychology and philosophy, Wertheimer made contact with colleagues at the Frankfurt Mathematics Institute, among them Max Dehn and Ernst Hellinger. Based on their common interest in logic, Wertheimer and Dehn co-taught a seminar on the law of contradiction at Frankfurt. Edwin Rausch, a mathematics student under Dehn, took Wertheimer's course on productive thinking and was so impressed that he changed to psychology, formerly his minor, as his major focus of study.[27] Wertheimer also consulted his colleagues in mathematics as he continued to try to develop a Gestalt mathematics.[28]

Wertheimer's Teaching and Research at Frankfurt

By the time he arrived in Frankfurt, Wertheimer had been teaching for well over a decade, and had evolved his lecture style in many Berlin classrooms and laboratories. Several of his Frankfurt courses closely resembled those offered at the University of Berlin, although he was continually altering the content, examples, and ideas. Along with courses on productive thinking, philosophy, and logic, Wertheimer also offered courses on sound detection and on social psychology.[29] Max took advantage of the ample facilities at Frankfurt and prepared impressive and sophisticated devices for demonstrations in perception for his courses and for use in his laboratories. He also collaborated with Gelb, Tillich, and Riezler in several colloquia and seminars. For a time, he tried to develop a collection of recordings at Frankfurt modeled on the phonographic archive that Carl Stumpf and Erich von Hornbostel had established at Berlin. He consulted von Hornbostel about phonographic technology (the original Edison phonograph was recommended).[30] Hornbostel also made some copies of exotic music and sent them on cylinders to Wertheimer's musicology collection.[31]

Wertheimer attracted the interest of a number of loyal graduate students such as Erwin Levy and Erika Oppenheimer, who attended many of his courses. According to one student, Wertheimer was always interested in the scientific background and training of his students because he found it "appropriate for the study of psychology and philosophy, when someone had intensive contact with another science—if possible a science with a methodologically good structure."[32]

Wertheimer participated in the interdisciplinary activities at Frankfurt. He became a frequent and vigorous contributor to the university's *Weisheitsseminar* or "wisdom seminar" that attracted a large and diverse group of scholars who would debate a variety of critical social, political, and philosophical issues.[33] During such sessions, he typically was part of a prominent and erudite panel of scholars including Tillich, Riezler, Horkheimer, Gelb, and Adorno as well as the Greek philologists Karl Reinhardt and Walter Otto, the physicist Madelung, and the jurist Hermann Heller.[34] According to one student, the evening symposia would usually commence at seven and by "10:00 the institute certainly had to be closed and then most of the people, professors and students alike, would track to a coffee house, where the debate would go on till the wee hours of the morning."[35] Gestalt theory was often discussed at these seminars and Wertheimer quickly earned a reputation as a fierce and vigorous discussant, on occasion shouting at his colleagues as he challenged some polemic. He occasionally wrote letters of apology on the following day to those whom he believed he might have offended during the previous evening.

By the time of his call to Frankfurt, Wertheimer had, despite his meager publication record, managed to achieve an international reputation as the founder of Gestalt psychology, and students came from Germany, Finland, Japan, and elsewhere to study with him. Many students also came from the United States. At the University of California at Berkeley, Edward Chace Tolman promoted Gestalt theory after he studied with Koffka at Giessen. With Tolman's encouragement, Berkeley student Willis D. Ellis went to Frankfurt in 1930 and soon began a project to translate into English and condense significant contributions to the Gestalt literature from 1915 to 1929. Another American student, Edwin B. Newman, gave this account of his first encounter with Wertheimer:

> In late October of 1931 a tall young man in a brown leather jacket knocked on the large oak door just to the right as one entered the *Philosophische Seminar* in the *Universität* at Frankfurt/Main. A small sign just to the left of the door said *"Dr. Max Wertheimer, Professor der Psychologie, Besprechung: Dienstag 13-14, Donnerstag 10-11"* [Dr. Max Wertheimer, Professor of Psychology, Office Hours: Tuesday 1:00 - 2:00 p.m., Thursday 10:00 - 11:00 a.m.]. The door was opened by a short man, slightly bald with graying curly hair drooping over his collar, a large walrus moustache, and a twinkle in his eye. He greeted me with a hearty *"Guten Tag! Was möchten Sie?"* [Hello! What can I do for you?].... I told him that I had come to Frankfurt as an exchange student from the University of Kansas where my professor had been Raymond Wheeler. Wheeler had embraced Gestalt psychology as a way of escaping the apparent narrowness of Titchener's structuralism on the one hand and what Wheeler saw as Watson's hopeless [behavioristic] oversimplification on the other. I explained that we had read all that we could find, especially in English, written by Koffka and Köhler, but that he, Wertheimer, seemed something of a mystery to us. He laughed, commented that writing was something he did not find easy, that I was more than welcome to join the group there and to take part in all that was going on.... I told him that we were really looking forward to an occasion when he might come to America. That would not be soon, he replied—his English was not fluent. To which I could only reply that my German was pitiful.[36]

After his move to Frankfurt, Wertheimer maintained his strong relationship with Köhler and with his former students at the University of Berlin. In 1929, when Christian von Ehrenfels told Wertheimer that he wanted to learn more about Gestalt theory, Wertheimer recommended Karl Duncker and Wolfgang Metzger, both still assisting Köhler at Berlin, to serve as consultants to Ehrenfels. Unfortunately, the contact never occurred; Duncker and Metzger were both married and did not have the financial resources that would have been required to bring their wives with them for extended visits to von Ehrenfels. In 1932, Ehrenfels died and the opportunity was lost.

In 1931, when Gelb left Frankfurt for the University of Halle, Wertheimer invited Duncker to come to Frankfurt as an assistant at the Institute. Duncker declined, choosing to stay with Köhler at Berlin. After Duncker declined, Wertheimer asked Metzger, another of Köhler's assistants, who accepted the opportunity to work with Wertheimer at Frankfurt. Metzger began work on his *Habilitationsschrift* on phenomenal identity with Wertheimer in 1931 and became a core figure at the Institute, conducting research, teaching laboratory courses and later directing the doctoral work of several of Wertheimer's students.

Wertheimer formally supervised four dissertations at Frankfurt and was on the committee for the doctoral work of several additional students, including Herta Kopfermann, who earned a Ph.D. in 1930, and Ellis Freeman, who earned his in 1931. As was true for Duncker and Ternus at Berlin, Wertheimer's continued interest in the study of perception was reflected in the graduate research that he supervised. Wolfgang Metzger, Walter Krolik, and Erika Oppenheimer all performed studies on motion perception.[37]

Although the majority of his doctoral students performed experimental research, Wertheimer also supervised work on philosophical topics. Edwin Rausch, initially a student of mathematics, chose Wertheimer as examiner for the philosophy portion of his *Staatsexamen*, a state oral examination for high-school teachers. As Rausch recalled, Wertheimer drew upon his long-standing interest in Spinoza's writings to question Rausch:

> From the oral exam I recall Wertheimer's method of questioning that now seems very appropriate to me: From the collection of letters of and to Spinoza. In it the philosopher is asked for his opinion concerning the existence of ghosts. Wertheimer asked me how Spinoza could possibly have answered this letter. By the way, I was no Spinoza specialist; moreover, I did not know about this correspondence. Nevertheless, I knew enough about Spinoza to indicate to Wertheimer's delight that philosopher's reaction and reasoning.[38]

Wertheimer accepted Rausch as a doctoral student in philosophy after he successfully passed the *Staatsexamen* and encouraged him to study epistemology (*Erkenntnistheorie*). Rausch agreed, and prepared a dissertation entitled, "On Summativity and Non-summativity."

Although directly involved in the design, execution, and writing up of the projects, Wertheimer did not include himself as an author on the publications of his doctoral students (Rausch, Metzger, Krolik, and Oppenheimer), all of whom were the sole authors of the papers reporting their doctoral research, and all of which were published in *Psychologische Forschung*. Probably in part because of teaching and administrative duties, editorial responsibilities for *Psychologische Forschung*, and poor health, Wertheimer published only one article during his years at Frankfurt. As he mentioned to Newman, writing was a chore that he did not find easy. Published in the 1933 volume of the *Zeitschrift für Psychologie* was a brief but profound article in which he addressed the problem of the distinction between an arbitrary component (*Einzelinhalt*) and a necessary part (*Teil*).[39]

Wertheimer's Life, Work, and Home in Frankfurt

For their residence in Frankfurt, Max and Anni purchased a roomy stucco house on Klaus-Groth Street in a relatively quiet setting in the northern part of the city. Located in a community largely populated by upper-middle class neighbors, their new residence was warm and comfortable, graced by a small rose garden in front and trees in the back yard. The Wertheimers hired two maids, Paula Schläger and Kätti Moser, to help with the household chores and with the children.

Max set up a study in the attic above the second floor of the house. He placed a substantial oak table under a large window that provided ample light. Before long, Wertheimer resumed his life-long pattern of covering his desk with stacks of lecture notes, reprints, and correspondence, as well as scraps of paper containing idiosyncratic abbreviations to remind him of his latest ideas for lectures, thoughts about research projects, correspondence obligations, etc. One guest remembered that

> In the corner there was a very simple camp bed on which Wertheimer would [take naps]. He wanted to be close to his work day and night. There were, of course, lots of bookcases in the room and there was a photograph of one of the many sculptures on the outside wall of the Cathedral of Chartres.... It was called something like The Diligent One and shows a scribe or other kind of worker. I think it is a scribe who diligently works. To us it seemed an apt description of Wertheimer. He was (not only) an expert in Gestalt theory but it had become to him and all his disciples a philosophy of life, a *Weltanschauung*. Wertheimer lived for his work, in his work, and with his work.[40]

Max would rise early, usually around 6:00 a.m., and begin work immediately following a hasty breakfast of two hard boiled eggs, strong black coffee, and zwieback that Anni would bring up to his study. Because Wertheimer preferred to work while standing, two piles of wooden crates stacked atop each other had a large board placed across them on which he would spread his notes and papers, creating a standing desk. He typically worked without interruption all morning. He would often pace back and forth in his study and occasionally rush back to his standing desk to get his thoughts down on paper, then resume his pacing. On rare occasions, he might turn to the reed organ in his study and either improvise a melody or play a selection by a favorite composer such as Max Reger.[41] He usually spent his time this way from early morning until about one o'clock in the afternoon, when he would venture down the stairs to join his family for food and conversation. Max would then return to his study for a daily nap of an hour or so. Thereafter he typically arose for further thought, pacing, preparation of notes, and other work activities until dinner time.

Sometimes, after having spent part of the morning to compose his thoughts, he would ring a bell to summon Anni to join him in the study. Given his difficulty in writing, Max found it easier to dictate his thoughts. Anni recalled that "he had to have an audience and was really more of a teacher than a scientist. He had to stand and teach it to make it clear. He couldn't sit alone writing in a corner." Her primary responsibility was to take dictation, and occasionally act as a kind of sounding board on which Max could try out his latest thoughts. Probably he was unhappy with his anemic publication rate; Wertheimer once asked a student to take verbatim notes of his Berlin lectures, hoping that this might yield a possible publication. Unfortunately, his thoughts changed after delivering the lectures, so when he saw the notes he found them useless for generating possible publications.

Anni envisioned herself as a "helpmate" to Max in his efforts to advance Gestalt theory, but this often proved to be a difficult role. Wertheimer's inability to articulate his thoughts in a manner that satisfied him often consumed him until he lost his temper and shouted in frustrated rage. Anni tried her best to tolerate such eruptions quietly until Max composed himself, reconsidered the obstacle, and tried to tackle the problem from a new perspective. At first, she found such outbursts very difficult to endure. In Prague, about a month after their marriage, Anni remembered, she was helping Wertheimer prepare a critique of G. E. Müller, when he stopped and asked her to repeat something from her notes. After she confessed that she had not recorded all of his comments verbatim, Wertheimer angrily yelled at her, and she felt devastated. A close friend whom she consulted pointed out that Wertheimer was "engrossed and nervous," and counseled her not to take personal offense at his harsh actions.[42] Still, as a gentle and sensitive young woman, Anni felt reluctant to interrupt Max's tempestuous streams of ideas to ask him to repeat a previous thought. He often could not. In time, she learned to interrupt at suitable pauses in his thinking, but was often frustrated by her own inability to be more efficient in helping him find the right words to express his ideas. On some days she would take little more than one page of notes while on others Max would dictate as many as ten pages. She also played a role in helping him maintain some semblance of order in the endless task of trying to organize his profuse collection of papers and notes. Sometimes they would spend hours looking through stack after stack for a single sheet of paper that contained some idea that he considered central to his thinking at the time.

Two deaths made 1930 a sad year for the Wertheimers. Anni's mother, Margarethe Pick Caro, passed away in June, and Max's father died late that summer. Wilhelm was memorialized in the September issue of the

Czechoslovakian Newsletter of the Independent Order of Oddfellows in the Czechoslovakian Republic, in a September 11 funeral oration by Gustav Reimann, at the Friendship Lodge which Wilhelm Wertheimer had helped found:

> Wilhelm Wertheimer is an outstanding example of the self-educated man, a man who could not be without books, and who pursued knowledge during his entire long lifetime.... Wertheimer, accustomed to a high level of energetic activity in his professional work as an educator,...constantly strove to follow the ideas of our Order, and it was due to his efforts that Local Number Eight of Saxony of the Order of Oddfellows was formally founded in Prague in 1906. In 1909 Wertheimer became Grand Master of this branch, and donated one thousand crowns—a sum that was very substantial in those days.... His initiative and his diligence were evident in all of the many offices held by Wertheimer.... Wertheimer's striking head with his long, full, white beard will always remain in our memories.[43]

The Wertheimer Handelsschule had continued to flourish after its founder had retired. It had made Wilhelm a wealthy man and his fortune carried him through the remaining eleven years of his life. He died in the belief that his son and his grandchildren would be able to live from the proceeds of his estate for the foreseeable future. But Margarethe's and Wilhelm's deaths meant the loss of the last of Max and Anni's parents.

Max's health during adulthood had never been robust. Rosa and Wilhelm's concern about health and disease, and about the proper function of bodily processes, as well as Walter's delicate medical history and early death, affected Max's attitude toward his own health; he suffered, for example, from a lifelong concern about his digestion. Any sign that something in his body was not functioning properly could become a cause for alarm. Further, as a young adolescent, he had become addicted to smoking cigarettes, which doubtless added to his health problems. In 1930, Max suffered a heart attack that, according to an entry in his personal health record, forced him "to lie two weeks motionless in bed. Then about half of a year recovering. For one quarter year no cigarettes, had to take them up again due to irritability, etc."[44] In February 1932 another heart attack seriously interfered with his work, prevented him from lecturing for a time, and forced him to rest after the periods of excitement and exertion produced during his lectures. Anni reported a significant change in his personality following the heart attacks: he became "harder, less flexible in body, soul, spirit, and ideas." A physician told him that he should walk more, which made Wertheimer laugh: he was not accustomed to excusing himself from work for exercise. Nevertheless he did try to take up skiing at that time—but right after he had for the first time strapped on the rigid bindings that were in vogue then, he accidentally slipped on a patch of ice, fell, and broke his leg.

Wertheimer did make a few minor concessions to his poor health by engaging somewhat more systematically in recreation and relaxation. In 1931 the Wertheimers purchased their first automobile (which they nicknamed "Nepomuk" after a Czech hero, Johann von Nepomuk) with funds from an inheritance of 10,000 Marks from Anni's uncle who had died during the First World War. Anni believed that the car changed their lives somewhat by allowing them to take brief trips that may have helped Wertheimer relax. Anni described Max's driving style as aggressive and hard rather than smooth or elegant. He never did fully master the automobile; Anni did the majority of the driving for the family.

In the summer of 1932, the Wertheimers vacationed in Ascona, a mountain haven in the Swiss Alps, hoping to find some quiet rehabilitation for Wertheimer after his heart attack earlier that year. While there he did some sailing, rowing, and hiking. Once while he was rowing, Anni was struck by the power of his rough, coarse hands; she thought that his hands resembled those of an unskilled worker more than those she expected in "a scientist or prophet." Despite some efforts at exercise and recuperation, his time was still primarily devoted to his work; a trunk containing his most important books and papers always accompanied the family on its vacations. The Sterns sometimes vacationed with the Wertheimers, and visited them while they were in Ascona. Karl Duncker, a frequent visitor at the Wertheimers' Frankfurt home, also came to Ascona to visit with them there.

Refuge in Czechoslovakia

Meantime, Germany's political climate was undergoing major changes. Germany had been struggling to finance its war debt in the midst of a severe economic depression when Field Marshall Paul von Hindenburg succeeded Friedrich Ebert, the first president of the German Republic, in 1925.[45] The July 1932 elections surrendered 230 seats in the Reichstag to the National Socialist party, and on January 30, 1933 Hindenburg accepted Adolf Hitler as Chancellor—and the National German Socialist Workers became the ruling party in Germany.

With his avid interest in national and international politics, Max was aware of the ominously growing fascist crisis and had kept track of the rise of the National Socialist movement. He had encouraged Metzger in 1930 to work swiftly on his habilitation research because Wertheimer was not certain how long the university would continue to employ a professor with a Jewish background. Indeed, much to Metzger's frustration, Wertheimer would call him almost daily and ask, "How many pages [of your thesis] did you complete today?"[46]

Several of Wertheimer's colleagues thought he was overreacting to the Nazi movement. When the Tillichs hosted a costume party at their Frankfurt home, Adorno attended as Napoleon but Riezler arrived dressed as a fascist in a brown shirt.[47] Wertheimer was not convinced when Riezler reassured him that the Nazi movement would quickly pass over.[48]

Wertheimer was sensitive to the hostility of some of his students and of other young people with whom he interacted in Frankfurt, and occasionally questioned them at length about their political convictions. In 1931, while on vacation, Max and Anni were invited to spend an afternoon sailing on the Ammersee with a Fräulein Flechtner, a woman in her early twenties whose father owned the house in which the Wertheimers were staying. Miss Flechtner was already a confirmed Nazi and energetically preached Hitler's doctrine during much of the day on the small boat. In time, a tumultuous rainstorm arose and made further sailing impossible. Wertheimer left his place at the tiller, lowered the sail, took the oars and quietly and skillfully began rowing. Anni remembered that Miss Flechtner groveled on the floor of the boat and wept with fear. Throughout the tempest, Max said nothing but competently kept the boat from swamping until the crew of an approaching motorboat cast a line and hauled the small boat to shore, where a crowd of onlookers, including Kätti and the Wertheimer children, were anxiously waiting. Grateful to be alive, Miss Flechtner assured the Wertheimers that they were exceptions to the Nazi stereotype of Jews.

The children were not shielded from the political scene; students and other guests would discuss Nazi politics around the dinner table, where the children, especially the oldest, Val, were regular and active participants in the vigorous debates.

With his deep concern about the rising Nazi tide, Wertheimer became anxious to hear one of Hitler's speeches. The Wertheimers did not own a radio, so the first time that the Wertheimers heard Hitler speak was during a January 1933 radio broadcast to which Max and Anni listened in the home of the Ginsbergs, neighbors several houses away. It was rumored that Hitler had a cold at this time and would not hold forth in his usual intense manner. But even with its somewhat diminished passion, Hitler's address greatly disturbed Max and Anni. On their short walk back home, the Wertheimers decided to leave Frankfurt, at least temporarily, the next day.

The Wertheimers moved with Paula to Marienbad, in Czechoslovakia, to wait out the Nazi menace (Kätti came later). Marienbad was a reasonable choice because it was not far from Prague, where Wertheimer had access to money from his father's estate. They stayed in the Hotel Marienbad for about a week and then took up more permanent residence in a large apartment at the Inn of the Golden Harp.

From Marienbad, Wertheimer as best he could stayed abreast of activities at the Frankfurt Psychological Institute. Erika Oppenheimer, Walter Krolik, Kurt Madlung, Joseph Becker, Mümtaz Turhan, Erich Goldmeier, and Edwin Rausch had all begun doctoral research with Wertheimer, but it turned out that he was unable to see them through to completion of their dissertations. Wolfgang Metzger assumed responsibility for their supervision, and all of these students did complete their doctoral degrees with Metzger between 1934 and 1937.

A number of friends and colleagues, many of them threatened with adversity from fascism, visited the Wertheimers in Marienbad. The Prague poet Johannes Urzidil visited, and Georg and Lisbeth Stern stayed for an extended period, as did their daughter, Hanna Kortner, and her family. Georg was very ill with heart disease and was unable to participate in many of the social events, including the frequent musical activities engaged in by the Wertheimers and the Sterns.

Lisbeth's older sister, the renowned artist Käthe Kollwitz, and her husband, the physician Karl Kollwitz, also came to Marienbad, and lived for a time in the same building as the Wertheimers. Even more than Lisbeth, who at one time had contributed to the *Sozialistische Monatshefte (Socialist Monthly)*, Käthe was an active proponent of socialism, especially that of the German Social Democratic Party (*Sozialdemokratische Partei Deutschlands* or SPD). Indeed, their maternal grandfather, Julius Rupp, had been disciplined for his radical political and religious views in the mid-nineteenth century, and their father, Carl Schmidt, was described by Käthe as the person "who led the transition to socialism."[49] Konrad Schmidt, Lisbeth and Käthe's brother, was a professor of political economy at the Berlin Polytechnic Institute and a frequent correspondent with the renowned German socialist Friedrich Engels. As an internationally prominent graphic artist, Käthe had publicly supported socialist politics in her art and writings for decades. She wrote in a November 22, 1922, diary entry: "I have come to terms with the fact that my art serves *causes. I intend to have an effect* on these times in which human beings are so distraught and helpless."[50] In 1920 she created a series of posters depicting postwar suffering in Germany and Austria, and four years later produced drawings and prints for the Social Democrats and the Communist Party. In 1932, she joined Albert Einstein, Heinrich Mann, and others in signing a petition supporting Communist and Social-Democrat candidates in the upcoming Reichstag election. In the year in which she came to Marienbad, her outspoken political activities contributed to her membership in the Prussian Academy of Arts being revoked, and she was dismissed as director of the Academy's master classes for graphic art.[51] This action, largely initiated by the Reich Propaganda Ministry, was explicitly in response to her support of an appeal for a united workers' front against fascism; Karl Kollwitz was also a supporter and hence he was temporarily prohibited from practicing medicine.

The Nazi movement did not, of course, diminish but grew and flourished. As for the University of Frankfurt as such, the party proclaimed that the Jewish faculty of Frankfurt had persuaded innocent German students into accepting a kind of "cultural bolshevism" over Nazi dogma. According to Tillich's biographers,

> On 18 and 25 March the *Frankfurter Zeitung* published two articles in which the writer viciously attacked the Johann Wolfgang Goethe University.... Tillich was specifically referred to as the "embodiment of the enemy," and his defense of left-wing students, as well as his pro-Jewish and prosocialist utterances and writings, were cited as proof of his "unreliability."...Horkheimer and his assistants at the Institute for Social Research were considered equally dangerous and destructive. The most vicious attack of all was made on Kurt Riezler, who was scorned for having participated as a member of...a diplomatic mission to Russia. It was insinuated, not subtly, that Riezler was a communist. The newspaper urged in nearly hysterical tones that the university be purged of elements that endangered German youth and society, to return it to its rightful place in the city where German emperors had once been crowned![52]

During an April 1, 1933 raid, Riezler,

> who was delivering a lecture at the time of the occupation, was driven from the podium by uniformed troops. The only audible protest against this act of violence was that of Dr. Kövendi, a Hungarian who had come to Frankfurt to study classical philology. Karl Reinhardt reported that Kövendi screamed: "How is such a thing possible in the land of Schiller and Goethe!" Reinhardt noted that "as a stupid foreigner, one let him [Kövendi] go."[53]

Riezler was formally arrested later that day and his courses were suspended for the remainder of the summer.

On April 7, 1933, Wertheimer wrote to the administration at Frankfurt requesting a leave of absence—for reasons of health. On April 8, however, just before his letter arrived, the Dean of Natural Sciences wrote Wertheimer a note indicating that he was "among a group of teachers who can expect disturbances in their lectures in the coming semesters" and concluding with the advice to "make use of your right to take a leave of absence." And also on April 7, the Nazi party authorized the "Law for the Re-establishment of the Professional Civil Service," a bill that summarily forced employees of "non-Aryan status" into retirement. "Non-Aryan status" was defined as having at least one parent or grandparent who was not "Aryan"; faculty would even be dismissed pending a future marriage to an individual of "non-Aryan" descent.[54] On April 13, German newspapers listed the names of academicians who were designated as party adversaries. Tillich's biographers observed that:

> Enemies of the state fell into two categories: first, left-wing intellectuals, members of the Communist or Socialist parties, the politically suspect; second, the "racially" suspect, or Jews.... Within the next year 313 full professors, 300 associate professors, and 322 *Privatdozenten*—a total of 1,684 scholars—were removed from German university circles.[55]

Perhaps in deference to President Hindenburg, the Nazi government had exempted from this edict individuals employed continuously by universities since August 1914, participants in World War I, and those who had had a father or son killed in the war. Because he had served as a civilian research officer for the Austro-German army in the First World War, and had worked in the German university system since before 1914, Wertheimer at least loosely fit two of these criteria, yet he was not exempted from the punishing effects of the law; he was officially retired on April 24, 1933, one of the first victims of this Nazi ruling. Two days later, a leading German newspaper, the *Vossische Zeitung*, openly protested the dismissal of Wertheimer, who "with his economical and content-rich investigations founded one of the most fruitful schools of current psychology."[56] Altogether, the Nazi legislation resulted in the forced retirement of six of 15 full professors of psychology and 20 of 28 associate professors of psychology throughout Germany. In addition to Wertheimer and Gelb at Frankfurt, other prominent psychology professors terminated from academic institutions included David Katz in Rostock, William Stern in Hamburg, Wilhelm Peters in Jena and Otto Selz in Mannheim.[57]

Despite the devastating consequences of the Nazi civil service law, academicians made little opposition to this discriminatory legislation. As one historian describes the situation,

> The language of German nationalism, already so much at home in academia, was inspiring and overpowering. The goals of the government—honor to the Fatherland, restoration of Germanic lands to the Reich, revitalization of the German spirit—called forth loyalty and unity. The laws passed to effect that unity in 1933 met with little or no resistance from the university community.[58]

Indeed, even before the formal passage of the civil service ruling, few scholars had raised objections to German fascism in print.[59] A 1925 paper by Rudolf Heberle, published under the pseudonym "Jarno," criticized Nazism, and by 1930 several concerns had been raised about the National Socialist party in Social Democratic journals. Some social scientists friendly to the Social Democratic cause wrote critically on fascism—including Paul Tillich who, as an editor for the *Neue Blätter für den Sozialismus* (New Pages for Socialism) briefly referred to the Nazis at the end of a lengthy paper on the problem of domination. According to Tillich, the Nazi party "overlooks the most significant feature of domination: that domination without broad acceptance and without demands that derive from this acceptance is not domination but highway robbery and rape."[60]

Despite the general reluctance of many academicians to criticize Nazi politics publicly, Wolfgang Köhler took a strong stand against the National Socialists in an April 28, 1933, article titled "Conversations in Germany" in the *Deutsche Allgemeine Zeitung* [*German General Newspaper*].[61] Protesting the forced resignation of Nobel laureate physicist James Franck, Köhler began with an appeasing statement about Nazi racist policy: "None of the Germans to whom I refer denies the existence of a Jewish problem in Germany. Most of them believe that the Germans have the right to control the composition of their population and to reduce the proportion of Jews in the leadership of all the essential affairs of the people, which has become too large." However, he encouraged only political actions "which do not damage Germany indirectly, which do not sorely injure the significant, superior human beings among the German Jews. For my friends do not want to agree to the thesis that every Jew, as a Jew, represents a lower, inferior form of humanity."[62] Köhler went on to outline the many significant contributions that Jews had made to German science and culture.

On the evening of the letter's publication, Köhler played chamber music late into the evening with his Berlin Institute assistants, fully expecting to be served an arrest warrant that never did get issued. Köhler sent a copy of his article to Wertheimer with a letter (MW-CU) explaining that "It was simply that one could no longer do anything with oneself or do any work until that was written." Köhler did add that "nothing has happened to me, although care was taken that the issue came into every hand that it was intended for. In any case, everyone today reads this journal. As for the issue itself, naturally nothing has been achieved by it."

Meantime, Wertheimer was continuing to suffer problems with his health. He wrote in a May 1933 letter to Einstein (MW-CU) that "I have been in Marienbad for some time (my heart condition troubles me somewhat,—I am taking treatment, hope to be well soon)." Although prospects for resuming his career at Frankfurt—or any other German institution—were becoming dim, Wertheimer was not without other professional opportunities. In 1933 several English academicians began an emergency program to bring German professors to British universities.[63] While he was in Marienbad, Wertheimer was contacted by Cambridge University and Oxford University; his colleague Karl Mannheim, too, was approached about possibly teaching in Great Britain.[64] Martin Buber wrote (MW-CU) on August 24, 1933, that Judah L. Magnes, chancellor of the University of Jerusalem, had expressed interest in appointing Wertheimer to a newly created chair there in psychology. Although Buber hinted that the position could become permanent, it was only authorized for two years, with a modest annual salary. Buber mentioned that he too was under consideration for a position at the University of Jerusalem and added that "It is beautiful to think about the possibility that we might see each other again."[65]

Wertheimer also received an offer from an American institution, the New School for Social Research in New York City, from the New School's enterprising president, Alvin Johnson. Even though the New School was operating on a rather shaky fiscal basis, Johnson was assembling a faculty that included some of the most illustrious members of the European academic community. In time, the Graduate Faculty of Political and Social Science at the New School became known as the "University in Exile." Having been editor of the *Encyclopedia of the Social Sciences*, Johnson had examined German academia for the most promising contributors to the *Encyclopedia*, and was clearly impressed with the Gestalt psychologists. In his autobiography, he remembered that "In psychology we rated highest Max Wertheimer and his associates in the Gestalt school, Wolfgang Köhler and Kurt Koffka."[66] Indeed, Johnson believed that Wertheimer was "the greatest of the psychologists."[67] Max wrote to officials at the University of Frankfurt, diplomatically describing the New School position as a "guest professorship"; he received word that University administrators had "no objection" to his request for a leave to accept that position. But on September 25 he was informed that his status as a "non-Aryan" meant that he was officially retired.

Wertheimer was, of course, by no means the only prominent member of the intelligentsia whose life was radically altered by the Nazi policies. Bertolt Brecht, Ernst Cassirer, George Grosz, Thomas Mann, Max Reinhardt, Paul Tillich, and Bruno Walter all chose to emigrate. Gelb emigrated to Holland, where he died of tuberculosis in 1935. Shortly before leaving for the United States, Wertheimer received a letter at the Golden Harp from Lewin, who wrote that he was "glad that you are departing. I wish I could go on the same ship."[68] Lewin was returning to Germany from a guest professorship at Stanford University when the Nazi civil service legislation was put into effect. Although Lewin was presumably exempt from the law because of his distinguished service in the First World War, Köhler, writing to the Prussian education minister to extend Lewin's leave, noted that "the race aspect could lead to problems, if Herr Lewin...deals with students who know nothing about his participation in the war." Köhler told the minister that, given an extension of Lewin's leave, students would learn of his distinguished status as a decorated war veteran and would come to accept him. The Ministry granted an extension of Lewin's leave until July 31, 1934,[69] but Lewin emigrated to the United States, accepting an offer of a position at Cornell University. Einstein, who went to America for a lecture tour in 1921, renounced his German citizenship after Hitler's rise to power in 1933 and later the same year was appointed to a specially created position at the newly established Institute for Advanced Study at Princeton University. To the surprise of his pacifist friends, Einstein urged free Europe to arm and prepare for defense against fascism. The Frankfurt Institute for Social Research was robust enough to found the new *Zeitschrift für Sozialforschung* (*Journal of Social Research*) in 1932, but the Institute as a whole was devastated under Nazi doctrine, with Horkheimer and many of the other principals forced to direct its affairs from exile. In 1933 the institute established headquarters in

Geneva and late the next year moved to the United States to become part of Columbia University.[70]

Wertheimer and his family prepared to emigrate to the United States late in the summer of 1933. Max went to the American consulate at Prague to arrange for the family's passports, but was unable to secure permission for the immigration of their servants Kätti and Paula. Erich's wife, Susanne Hornbostel, asked the Wertheimers if they would allow Reiner Schickele, a young agronomist, to travel with them; Max and Anni agreed to help him leave Germany by taking him along as a "children's maid" on the ship.[71] After he had accepted the appointment at the New School, Wertheimer asked Johnson to consider Erich von Hornbostel for a faculty position there; Johnson agreed and the von Hornbostels immigrated to New York a short time after the Wertheimers.

The urgency of their emigration was intensified when on the night before the Wertheimers' departure one of Max's colleagues, a Jewish philosopher named Theodor Lessing, was assassinated in his Marienbad home not far from the Golden Harp. Lessing had corresponded with Wertheimer and Einstein and was well known for his critical attacks on Nazi politics. Intimations that the Gestapo was responsible for his death rapidly spread through the Marienbad refugee community. Anni heard about Lessing's murder just before leaving and, fearing that the news would disturb her husband, decided not to tell him about it until they had crossed the border. Traveling by rail, the family left Marienbad for Prague, carefully circumventing Germany through Austria, northern Italy, and Switzerland, and then on to Paris where they were met by Erwin Levy, the young psychiatrist who had worked with Wertheimer at Frankfurt.[72] After a brief tour of Paris, they went on to the northwest French port of Cherbourg, where they boarded the *S. S. Majestic*, bound for New York.

Originally called the *Bismarck* by her German shipbuilders, the *Majestic* was acquired by the British Cunard White Star Line as part of the reparation payments of the First World War; she was the largest Atlantic ocean liner during the 1920s.[73] Following the Depression, White Star had pressed the *Majestic, the Olympic*, and the *Homeric* into service transporting passengers from Europe to New York on a weekly basis. The Wertheimers joined many other European refugees on what turned out to be the last voyage of the *Majestic*. Reiner Schickele was assigned one cabin with Max and Val while Anni, Michael, and Lise stayed in another. Reiner and Anni took care of the children and occasionally went dancing in the evening, but Max, who was recovering from a bout of influenza, spent most of his waking hours on board sitting in a deck chair and working.

Because of the haste with which they had left for Marienbad, most of the Wertheimers' family possessions were still back in Frankfurt. After his arrival in America, Wertheimer contacted a Frankfurt student in an effort to retrieve some of his belongings, mostly books, from his former residence. Erika Oppenheimer Fromm remembered:

> While we were packing the Nazis did indeed march into the house and try to search it. I had just come across a copy of Marx's *Das Kapital*. To own that at that time was enough to be put into a concentration camp and all your belongings confiscated. I managed to throw it in a burning fireplace behind me as the Nazis marched in and fortunately they did not see it.[74]

The majority of the Wertheimer possessions, including a fine piano, Max's reed organ, and much furniture, bedding, and clothing were all left behind, with no further opportunity to retrieve them.

In 1933, as the liberal and refreshing spirit of the Weimar Republic came to an end, Wertheimer, at the age of 53 and in fragile health, faced the challenge of adjusting to a foreign culture, an unfamiliar language, and a large number of psychologists whom he did not know, most of whom were far from appreciative of Gestalt theory

Notes

1. Wayne C. Thompson (1980). *In the eye of the storm: Kurt Riezler and the crises of modern Germany*. Iowa City, IA: University of Iowa Press, p. 211.
2. Thompson, p. 212.
3. Thompson, p. 213.
4. Ash, p. 317.
5. Quoted in Ash, p. 318.
6. Quoted in Ash, p. 318.
7. Quoted in Ash, p. 318.
8. Ash, p. 319.
9. Lewis Coser (1971). *Masters of sociological thought: Ideas in historical and social context*. New York: Harcourt Brace Jovanovich, p. 446.
10. Wilhelm Pauck and Marion Pauck (1976). *Paul Tillich: His life and thought, Volume 1: Life*. New York: Harper & Row, pp. 112-113. According to Pauck and Pauck, pp. 117-118, Tillich also became close friends with Kurt Goldstein and Adhémar Gelb; Tillich said that he was first introduced to the "meaning of existential psychiatry" by Gelb.
11. Pauck and Pauck, pp. 113-114.
12. Gabrielle Oppenheim said that "about 120 students attended Wertheimer's lectures." Quoted in A. S. Luchins and E. H. Luchins (1986). Wertheimer in Frankfurt: 1929-1933. *Gestalt Theory*, 8, 204-224, p. 211.
13. Oppenheim, quoted in Luchins and Luchins, pp. 211-212.
14. Kurt Grelling and Paul Oppenheim (1937, 1938). Der Gestaltbegriff im Lichte der neuen Logik [The Gestalt concept in the light of the new logic]. *Erkenntnis*, 7, 211-225.
15. Erika Oppenheimer Fromm, quoted in Luchins and Luchins, p. 213.

16. Pauck and Pauck, pp. 116-117. Pauck and Pauck report that Siemsen later became the head of a women's prison in Berlin.

17. Fromm, quoted in Luchins and Luchins, p. 213. If her recollection is correct, then Wertheimer's color preference for his office was not reflected in the rather severe black suits that he wore to lecture and in the generally drab, dark decor of his residences.

18. Maurice Friedman (1981). *Martin Buber's life and work: The early years 1878-1923.* New York: Dutton, p. 22.

19. Friedman, p. 352.

20. Martin Jay (1985). *Permanent exiles: Essays on the intellectual migration from Germany to America.* New York: Columbia University Press, p. 30.

21. Martin Jay (1973). *The dialectical imagination: A history of the Frankfurt School and the Institute for Social Research, 1923-1950.* Boston, MA: Little, Brown, pp. 8, 12.

22. Loader, *The intellectual development of Karl Mannheim: Culture, politics, and planning,* p. 230.

23. Jay, *Permanent exiles,* p. 30.

24. *International Institute of Social Research: A short description of its history and aims* (New York, 1934), p. 3.

25. Like Horkheimer, Adorno had worked with both Gelb and Cornelius.

26. Quoted in Luchins and Luchins, Wertheimer in Frankfurt, p. 215.

27. Luchins and Luchins, Wertheimer in Frankfurt, p. 209.

28. At the time that Wertheimer was moving to Frankfurt, Kurt Lewin wrote Wertheimer that he was "furiously learning mathematics," especially topology. Kurt Lewin to Max Wertheimer, May 29, 1929, MW-UC.

29. Wertheimer's interest in teaching social psychology might, in part, have been inspired by the Frankfurt milieu, particularly the activities of the Institute for Social Research. According to Jay, Horkheimer "stressed the role of social psychology in bridging the gap between society and individual." In addition, Lewin was also strongly interested in social psychology and had contributed to the Institute's *Zeitschrift für Sozialforschung [Journal for Social Research].* But the approach to social psychology of Wertheimer and Lewin differed radically from the perspectives of their colleagues in the Institute for Social Research. Jay, *The dialectical imagination,* p. 27.

30. Erich von Hornbostel to Max Wertheimer, January 4, 1930, MW-CU.

31. Erich von Hornbostel to Max Wertheimer, March 2, 1930, MW-CU.

32. Edwin Rausch, quoted in Luchins and Luchins, Wertheimer in Frankfurt, p. 211.

33. Thompson, *In the eye of the storm,* p. 214. This seminar, sometimes also called the "Wahrheitsseminar," or seminar on truth, became the model for the later "General Seminar" in which Wertheimer participated after he joined the faculty of the New School for Social Research in New York.

34. Pauck and Pauck, p. 119.

35. Fromm, quoted in Luchins and Luchins, p. 215.

36. Edwin B. Newman (1989). Remembering Max Wertheimer: 1931-1943. *Psychological Research,* 51, 47-51, p. 47.

37. Viktor Sarris (1989). Max Wertheimer on seen motion: Theory and evidence. *Psychological Research,* 51, 58-68, pp. 62-63.

38. Edwin Rausch, quoted in Luchins and Luchins, p. 211.

39. Max Wertheimer (1933). Zu dem Problem der Unterscheidung von Einzelinhalt und Teil [On the distinction between arbitrary component and necessary part]. *Zeitschrift für Psychologie*, 129, 353-357. A translation of this article into English is part of the appendix to the enlarged editions of Max Wertheimer's book, *Productive thinking*.

40. Fromm, quoted in Luchins and Luchins, Wertheimer in Frankfurt: 1929-1933, p. 214.

41. Johann Baptist Joseph Maximilian Reger (1873-1916) was Professor of Composition at Leipzig Conservatory from 1907 until his death. He was especially accomplished in contrapuntal organ works, but also composed orchestral works, violin and piano concertos, chamber music, choral works, and sacred music.

42. Interview with Anni Hornbostel, 29 November 1968.

43. Gustav Reimann (1930). "Wilhelm Wertheimer obituary based on a September 11, 1930 oration." *Czechoslovakian Newsletter of the Independent Order of Oddfellows in the Czechoslovakian Republic*, 3, No. 1 (September 25), 1-4.

44. Quoted in Luchins and Luchins, p. 206. Much of the material in the next few pages is based on recorded interviews with Anni Hornbostel in 1968 (MW-CU and Akron Archives of the History of American Psychology).

45. Several programs, such as the Dawes Plan and the Young Plan, had been proposed that would allow Germany to make annual reparation payments. In 1932, Great Britain, France, Italy, Belgium, and Japan reached a new agreement that practically ended further reparations by Germany.

46. Interview with Wolfgang and Juliane Metzger, June 8, 1978 (MW-CU).

47. Pauck and Pauck, p. 122.

48. Interview with Anni Hornbostel, 29 November 1968.

49. Werner Timm (1980). *Käthe Kollwitz*. Berlin: Kunst und Gesellschaft, p. 15.

50. Quoted in Tom Fecht (ed.) (1988). *Käthe Kollwitz: Works in color*. New York: Schocken, p. 105.

51. Fecht, p. 105.

52. Pauck and Pauck, p. 129.

53. Thompson, p. 215.

54. Alice Gallin (1986). *Midwives to Nazism: University professors in Weimar Germany 1925-1933*. Macon, GA: Mercer University Press, p. 91.

55. Pauck and Pauck, p. 130.

56. Quoted in Mitchell G. Ash (1984). Max Wertheimer: In memoriam. *History of Psychology Newsletter*, 16, 3.

57. Ash, *Holism and the quest for objectivity*, p. 476.

58. Gallin, p. 87.

59. For a critical overview of the scholarly social-science literature on fascism, see Dirk Käsler and Thomas Steiner (1992). Academic discussion or political guidance? Social-scientific analyses of Fascism and National Socialism before 1933. In Stephen P. Turner and Dirk Käsler (eds.), *Sociology responds to fascism*. New York: Routledge, pp. 88-126. For a critical review of the response to German fascism and Nazism by social scientists after 1933, see H. Stuart Hughes (1975). *The sea change: The migration of social thought, 1930-1965*.

New York: McGraw-Hill; Jay, *The dialectical imagination*, especially pp. 113-172.

60. Käsler and Steiner, p. 114.

61. For a critical review of Köhler's article see Ash, *Holism and the quest for objectivity*, pp. 479-483. For a more personal account of Köhler during this period see Mary Henle (1978). One man against the Nazis—Wolfgang Köhler. *American Psychologist*, 33, 939-944 and Clarke W. Crannell (1970). Wolfgang Köhler. *Journal of the History of the Behavioral Sciences*, 6, 267-268.

62. Quoted in Ash, *Holism and the quest for objectivity*, p. 481.

63. Norman Bentwich (1953). *The rescue and achievement of refugee scholars*. The Hague: M. Nïjhoff, pp. 4-40.

64. Mannheim was, in part, persuaded to accept a temporary position at the London School of Economics because of the opportunity to serve "a pioneering role in the establishment of sociology in England." Loader, *The intellectual development of Karl Mannheim: Culture, politics, and planning*, p. 125. Like Wertheimer, Mannheim experienced difficulty with the English language, which initially hampered Wertheimer's ability to communicate effectively in New School classes after he came to New York in September 1933. Mannheim was very interested in collaborating with Wertheimer in America but this plan was never realized. Karl Mannheim to Max Wertheimer, June 9, 1933 (MW-CU).

65. Like Wertheimer, Buber had been warned about disruptions during his lectures, particularly seminars planned for the summer 1933 semester. Despite his optimism that the Nazi government would falter, Buber resigned from Frankfurt in October 1933. In 1938, Buber did emigrate to Palestine to become a professor at the University of Jerusalem, by then renamed Hebrew University. Maurice Friedman (1981). *Martin Buber's life and work: The middle years 1923-1945*. New York: Dutton, pp. 158-159.

66. Alvin Johnson (1960). *Pioneer's progress*. Lincoln, NE: University of Nebraska Press, p. 336.

67. Johnson, p. 343.

68. Kurt Lewin to Max Wertheimer, August 21, 1933, MW-CU.

69. Ash, *Holism and the quest for objectivity*, p. 478.

70. Jay, *Permanent exiles: Essays on the intellectual migration from Germany to America*, p. 30. In the 1940s, Horkheimer, Adorno, Pollock, and Marcuse relocated to the American west coast, producing, as Jay notes (p. 31), "a loss of the Institut's cohesion." In 1950, Horkheimer agreed to return and reestablish the Institute in Germany.

71. Reiner Schickele's son, the musical satirist Peter Schickele, later enjoyed wide success in America under the pseudonym of P. D. Q. Bach, a mythical son of Johann Sebastian Bach.

72. Max Wertheimer to Erwin Levy, August 18, 1933, MW-CU. Levy reserved rooms for the Wertheimers in a Paris hotel; he had been asked to find one with an elevator so that Wertheimer would not have to climb stairs. Erwin Levy to Max Wertheimer, August 24, 1933, MW-CU.

73. William H. Miller, Jr. (1981). *The great luxury liners, 1927-1954: A photographic record*. New York: Dover, p. 10. The *Majestic* weighed 56,551 gross tons, was 956 feet long and 100 feet wide, cruised at a speed of 24 knots,

and had luxurious interiors designed for 2,145 passengers. The crew affectionately called her the "Magic Stick."

74. Fromm, quoted in Luchins and Luchins, Wertheimer in Frankfurt: 1929-1933, pp. 215-216. Martin Buber's residence too was searched by the Nazis. During an uneventful March 1933 search Buber's library of 20,000 books was not damaged but a 1938 inspection resulted in the destruction of his furniture and of the remaining 3,000 books—after which the Nazis sent him a bill for 27,000 marks. Friedman, *Martin Buber's life and work: The middle years, 1923-1945*, pp. 160-161.

9

Wertheimer's Everyday Life
in the United States, 1933-1943

*What matters is not a rash and elegant
definition, but really facing the issues.*
—Max Wertheimer (1940)

Max Wertheimer had attained a professorship at a major German university fairly late in his life—and he was soon deprived of this post by the Nazis. Interrupted by health problems and then terminated by the advent of the Nazi government, Wertheimer's stay in Frankfurt lasted only four short years..

As Wertheimer crossed the Atlantic on the *Majestic*, many of his fellow passengers became seasick, but he did not, so he seized the opportunity to continue his work while on his way to a new continent.

His friend Tillich would write that "Emigration... means that one belongs to two worlds: to the Old as well as to the New into which one has been fully received."[1]

On September 13, 1933, the Wertheimers arrived in New York City. The weather was still hot in New York, and the air was humid and sticky. Although his family had left many possessions behind, Wertheimer saw to it that his lecture outlines, papers, and some books and notes, stored in dozens of wooden crates, crossed the Atlantic with him. Standing on the dock surrounded by Wertheimer's boxes, the family had to wait for hours with hundreds of other immigrants while the *Majestic*'s American passengers, who had been assigned a higher priority, made their way through customs past the others. Wertheimer may have been somewhat surprised when a *New York Times* "World Wide" photographer arrived to take the family's picture on their first day in the new country. The photo was published in the "Rotogravure Picture Section" of the Sunday *Times* September 24 edition. In the picture, a smiling Anni stood next to Max who, with papers firmly tucked under his left arm, had his right hand on the shoulder of his younger son. Lise was between Val and Michael, both of whom were dressed in traditional

German leather shorts, Lederhosen. The Wertheimer family photograph was next to snapshots of author James Barrie, Britain's Princess Elizabeth and Princess Margaret on a tour of Scotland, and advertisements proclaiming the virtues of products of New York shoe stores and hairstyling salons. The caption just below the photograph declared:

> A TEACHER EXILED FROM A GERMAN UNIVERSITY ARRIVES IN THE UNITED STATES: PROFESSOR MAX WERTHEIMER. Former Professor of Psychology at the University of Frankfort, and Founder of the Gestalt School of Thought Comes to New York City With His Wife and Children to Join the Exiles' University.

The day after his arrival, on September 14, the *Times* carried a brief article based on an interview with Wertheimer:

> Professor Wertheimer said he would deliver lectures upon his system, which includes not only psychology but also physics, philosophy and the natural sciences. He added that his system looks to a new system of thought for the entire universe. The professor ridiculed the report that very few scientists could understand his system. "Many scientists are capable of understanding my system," he declared. "Some aspects such as productive thinking can be understood by the ordinary intelligent lay[person]. Productive thinking substitutes inventive thinking for the leaving to chance of important inventions."[2]

The *Times* reporter added that "Professor Wertheimer said his theories of psychology were closer to behaviorism than to Freud's theories." The article also mentioned the arrival of Erich von Hornbostel (misidentified as "Ernest von Hornboste") and his son Johannes.

The family was met at the dock by Clara W. Mayer, an emissary from the New School (and soon to become its Dean), and, some four hours after the *Majestic* had docked, the Wertheimers registered at the Hotel Holley in Greenwich Village close to the New School for Social Research. It was Sunday and nothing was available for the family to eat until later in the evening when the hotel's restaurant opened. Dressed in his pajamas, Val awakened that evening from a nap and wandered to the elevator looking for his family, which had descended to the dining room. Although Val had not yet mastered English, a kindly elevator operator could comprehend enough to direct him to the family in the dining room. The Wertheimers stayed at the hotel for a week, and later at the Hotel Devon in Larchmont, New York, while they searched for a more permanent residence.

With the help of a physician, Dr. Gustav Bucky, the Wertheimers found a furnished house which Bucky had rented during the summer of 1933. The rental property was located in a quiet residential area of suburban New Rochelle. When he was later asked for the address of his new home, Wertheimer would typically respond: "Twelve, The Circle—the perfect

Gestalt!"[3] Although not extravagant, the house was comfortable with a generous yard, and faced a large park. A number of other refugee scholars moved to New Rochelle as well, and the Wertheimers became acquainted with, among others, the family of Richard Courant, a mathematician who left his post at the University of Göttingen in 1934 to accept a position at New York University, where he soon achieved international renown.[4] As he had done in Frankfurt, Wertheimer rode a commuter train to work, in this case one which took him to Union Square on Fourteenth Street and within walking distance of his office at the New School.

A New Life at a New School

When Wertheimer arrived in the United States, the universities, like the rest of the country, were staggering under the greatest economic depression in American history. The Great Depression stifled the direction of academia by threatening plans for faculty hiring, the development of innovative research and curricula, and the construction of additional campus facilities:

> As gifts fell off, interest from investments shriveled and tax support declined, capital expenditures dropped.... Appropriations for libraries and laboratories had to be reduced, salaries pared, and though the number of professors remained virtually unchanged, instructors' ranks were thinned. Numerous young M.A.'s and Ph.D.'s,...hatched by alma mater in expectancy of limitless demand, now joined the unemployed, which by 1933 included some two hundred thousand certified teachers.[5]

Despite the catastrophic fiscal conditions of the time, Wertheimer had joined an institution that managed to survive, albeit with difficulty and on a small scale, with a handful of faculty.

Although far less prestigious than many other academic institutions in the United States, the New School for Social Research had managed to achieve a reputation as a cultured, cosmopolitan center for academic freedom, social research and artistic expression. The New School was conceived in 1918, when a coalition of academicians, philanthropists, and other professionals created "A Proposal for an Independent School of Social Science for Men and Women" that called for the formation of a "New School" where "well qualified investigators and thinkers can enjoy the advantage of one another's thought and discoveries, and where they can talk freely upon any theme they judge fit to such grown up and responsible men and women as may wish to seek their instruction." The intended audience for the school, clearly, was not only typical college-age students, but mature men and women from all walks of life. The authors of the proposal envisioned an institution of research and education that "would become the center of the best thought in America, would lead in emancipating learning from the narrow trammels of lay boards of trustees, and would be a spiritual adventure of the utmost significance." They claimed that "Nothing like it has ever been attempted" and asserted that "This is the hour for the experiment; and New York is the place, because it is the greatest social science laboratory in the world and of its own force attracts scholars and leaders in educational work." [6]

Drawing upon the educational philosophies of John Dewey and Thorstein Veblen, the New School, upon its opening in February 1919 in the Chelsea neighborhood of Manhattan, stressed intellectual growth more than vocational training. By October the New School instituted a three-term schedule and in 1923 converted to a traditional fall, winter, and summer academic year, with each course meeting once a week for a ninety-minute lecture either in the late afternoon at 5:30 or in the evening at 8:30, so as to permit students to attend while working full time. The New School quickly proved appealing to local and visiting scholars. Lectures and classes were offered by such luminaries in the scientific and artistic world as poet Robert Frost, composer Aaron Copland, author Thomas Mann, painter Thomas Hart Benton, anthropologists Franz Boas and Margaret Mead, and philosophers John Dewey, Bertrand Russell, and Sidney Hook. The faculty and curriculum succeeded in attracting a diverse group of students including educators, social workers, office workers, business executives, and traditional college-aged people; the evening schedule also managed to attract both professional women and housewives, resulting in an atypically high proportion of female students. [7]

Despite early fiscal and popular success, several faculty and board members expressed concern that the institution had not succeeded in the ambitious task of establishing the school as an agent of social reconstruction. And although the adult education courses were well received, the grand design of social research suggested in the school's name had become anemic. In 1922, Herbert D. Croly, founder and editor of the liberal journal *The New Republic*, recommended that one of the original board members, Alvin Saunders Johnson, be assigned to reconsider the direction of the school. His recommendation prevailed, and Johnson was appointed president. Trained as an economist, Johnson had taught at several academic institutions, including Bryn Mawr, Columbia, Nebraska (his native state), Stanford, and Cornell, before becoming associate editor of *The New Republic*. With his midwestern charisma and economic knowledge, Johnson also had administrative skills that he managed to use constructively in his new role:

> As president of the New School, Johnson exhibited three invaluable traits—a remarkable capacity to attract creative individuals, a profound respect for talent, and an uncanny ability to accomplish ambitious projects with little or no money. He not only identified enthusiastically with other people's ambitions, but could communicate their ambitions to wealthy benefactors and board members. [8]

In an address to the board of directors, Johnson proposed some significant reforms that were consistent with the New School's mission. The adult lecture program should prosper—but not at the neglect of social research. Johnson understood the fiscal challenge in realizing this goal and immediately began to solicit aid from wealthy benefactors. One student from an affluent New York family, Clara W. Mayer, organized a committee of students to raise funds for the school. Johnson was so pleased with her efforts that he appointed Mayer to the board of directors and hired her as a secretary before promoting her to assistant director and later dean of adult education. Mayer assumed her professional responsibilities with zest and, according to Rutkoff and Scott, "Over the next fifty years only Alvin Johnson played a more important part in the life of the New School."[9] Although progress continued with the adult education program, Johnson's goal of reviving the social research program was not substantially realized until the mass emigration of European academicians in the 1930s.

The success of the school's lecture series permitted the New School for Social Research to relocate from the dilapidated and relatively inaccessible Chelsea neighborhood to a modern new building at 66 West Twelfth Street in the bohemian community of Greenwich Village. Johnson wanted the architecture of the new facilities to reflect a sophisticated sense of culture as well as "democratic liberalism." His hopes were fulfilled by the hiring of Joseph Urban, an Austrian architect who had immigrated to the United States in 1911 and had gained fame as the set designer for the Metropolitan Opera. Urban's sleek, modernist design boldly contrasted with most other buildings in the neighborhood and, from its opening day on January 2, 1931, helped establish the New School as a respected newcomer to the Greenwich community. A complementary relationship quickly developed between the unconventional school and its avant-garde setting:

> The presence in the neighborhood of numerous new and used bookstores, artists' lofts and studios, and small, inexpensive restaurants, cafés, and bars provided a perfect ambience for the New School's low-key academic innovation. Assuming some of the "arty" and exotic quality of its surroundings, the New School for thousands of New Yorkers became the academic heart of the Village.[10]

The New School's programs in visual arts, dance, music, and theater thrived. American artist Thomas Hart Benton was commissioned to paint murals inside the New School, German dramatist Erwin Piscator established a challenging, politically inspired Dramatic Workshop, and exhibitions were staged featuring the work of Kandinsky, Klee, Man Ray, and Mondrian.

In addition to the arts, the previously neglected social research program of the New School began to thrive after the move to West Twelfth Street, largely due to Johnson's aggressive hiring of twelve European scholars who became known as the "Mayflower Group."[11] As a founder of Gestalt theory, Wertheimer was also identified at the New School as one of the original emigré scholars in Johnson's ambitious plan for a "University in Exile":

> These were the individuals, out of hundreds of candidates, whom Johnson and the Rockefeller Foundation had agreed to rescue. Despite great diversity in perspective, discipline, and personality, these twelve represented a reasonably coherent intellectual position. They were nearly all social democrats; their scholarship was empirically oriented. In part, their affinities were a consequence of the purge itself. As "enemies of the state," they were fervently antifascist and almost all were Jewish.[12]

Among the initial refugee appointments, Emil Lederer was elected Dean of the University in Exile; Karl Brandt, Gerhard Colm, and Eduard Heimann were recruited to teach economics; Karl Mayer, Karl Salomon, and Hans Speier specialized in sociology; and Arnold Brecht and Frieda Wunderlich worked in political science. Johnson continued to add foreign scholars to the faculty and in 1934 formally assimilated the University in Exile into the rest of the New School and christened it the "Graduate Faculty for Social and Political Science of the New School for Social Research."[13] Together with Erich von Hornbostel, Wertheimer had been hired for the program in psychology and philosophy.

Prior to Wertheimer's arrival, Horace Kallen, one of the New School's original faculty, was responsible for much of the course curriculum in philosophy and psychology. Inspired by William James, Kallen was an advocate of pragmatism and pluralism, and his classes on the history of philosophy, psychology, and esthetic theory were well attended. As psychology gained popularity (five classes were already offered in the area during the late 1920s), other scholars were hired to deliver lectures. The Viennese psychiatrist and Freudian disciple Sandor Ferenczi offered a course on psychoanalysis. In 1923 John B. Watson, recently dismissed from the faculty at The Johns Hopkins University, joined the New School faculty and lectured on his system of behaviorism.[14] However, despite Kallen's regular courses, and occasional lectures by other instructors, psychology at the New School was not identified with a laboratory or a permanent faculty person with international recognition; Johnson hoped to correct this situation with the appointments of Wertheimer and Hornbostel.

Erich von Hornbostel taught briefly at the New School, but his health soon deteriorated. In 1934 he spent three months in Bermuda, hoping that the climate there would improve his health. That summer he and Susi went to England so that he could obtain special medical treatment there. After two months in a nursing home, he felt sufficiently better that he rented an apartment in London, hoping to return to New York that fall. But his physicians recommended that he stay in England. He moved to Cambridge, where he managed to obtain a teaching position in June 1935, but he died there on November 28, 1935. As a result, only Wertheimer and Horace Kallen remained to create the graduate program in psychology and philosophy at the New School.

Wertheimer's teaching responsibilities began as soon as he arrived in America. In the fall of 1933, he was permitted to teach in German: a lecture course on "The Psychology of Logic" and a seminar on "Psychological Problems." The following spring, he taught, again in German, a lecture course on "Gestaltpsychologie: Einführung in die Gestalttheorie, mit Demonstrationen und Experimenten aus den verschiedenen Gebieten der Psychologie" (Gestalt psychology: Introduction to Gestalt theory, with demonstrations and experiments from the various fields of psychology), but also a seminar, in broken English, on "Productive Research in Psychology."

Thereafter, Wertheimer had to do all of his teaching in English, and continued to do so for the remainder of his career. He never did achieve comfortable fluency in English, and frequently encountered difficulties expressing himself in the new language. One of his students, George Katona, remembered that

> The first two years in the U.S. may be characterized for [Wertheimer] as a constant struggle with the English language…. [H]e believed in expressing himself exactly all the time, and this he found very difficult (in English) for quite a while…. One English word of importance for Gestalt theory made for particular problems. Every time he used [the word whole] he turned to the blackboard and wrote "whole" because the word "hole" also played a role in explaining some of his problem solving experiments.[15]

Wertheimer also experienced some problems with the pronunciation of mathematical terms. For instance, his students were occasionally baffled until they realized that his references to obtuse and acute "angels" had to do not with heavenly beings but with trigonometric angles.

In later years, Wertheimer offered courses on "Gestalt Psychology," "Consequences of the Gestalt Theory of Psychology for Education and Teaching," "Current Problems in Psychology," and "Introduction to the Psychology of Music and Art." As it had been at Berlin and Frankfurt, Wertheimer's lecture style was vivacious and intense. He continued his practice of sometimes playing music on a piano during his lectures, to illustrate Gestalt principles such as "perceptual requiredness": the early part of a melody clearly sets constraints upon how the melody can be completed. Occasionally, at parties as well as in lectures, he would improvise musical caricatures of famous people (or of people who were listening) on the piano, caricatures which apparently were so transparent that his audience almost always recognized immediately whom he was caricaturing. Unfortunately, the facilities at the New School paled in comparison with those at Berlin and

Frankfurt, and Wertheimer was forced to lecture mostly without the use of the sophisticated perceptual demonstrations to which he had become accustomed in Frankfurt.

One student, Alex Sweet, M.D., Ph.D., who later became a psychoanalyst in southern California, remembered some comments about dream analysis in a course on thinking that Sweet attended in 1941 or 1942.[16] Wertheimer recommended against analyzing specific isolated elements in a dream (which was a standard procedure in traditional psychoanalytic practice). Instead, Wertheimer suggested that one should try to understand the general gist of the dream first, and then try to see how the various elements fit into the dream as a whole. Sweet reported that his later work as a psychoanalyst for many decades corroborated the wisdom of this advice.

Everyday Life at Home in New Rochelle

The house at 12 The Circle, New Rochelle, in which Wertheimer was to live during the last ten years of his life, was appropriate to his and his family's needs. In a relatively quiet residential district several blocks from a major thoroughfare and shopping area, it was less than half a mile from the railroad station of the New York, New Haven and Hartford line that Wertheimer used to commute to his work at the New School for Social Research in New York. Across the street from the house was a large open city park ("The Circle") with several mature trees, formal gardens, and extensive lawn areas that his children used for playing, running, flying home-made kites, and other activities. Wertheimer had exclusive use of two large rooms connected by an archway on the second story, with windows overlooking the park. The copious house had a full basement and a third story (part of which was attic, for storage, and part of which was two finished servants' rooms). In addition to Wertheimer's front rooms, the second story had two more bedrooms off the same large hall that had doors into Wertheimer's rooms, occupied respectively by his daughter Lise and by Anni at various times (or, later, by Peter; see p. 320). Another narrow hall went past a well-appointed bathroom (the "white" bathroom, because of the color of its trim) to a back hall with a smaller bathroom (the "brown" bathroom, because its wood trim was painted brown) and a back bedroom shared by Valentin and Michael. A massive, wide, formal staircase with several landings, stained-glass windows, dark wood paneling and an ornate dark wooden rail led from the entry vestibule to the large front hall upstairs. There were three narrow staircases in the house: from the upstairs front hall up to the attic level, from the kitchen down to the full basement, and, at the back of the house, from the upstairs hall down to the pantry. Ample storage space was available in a number of closets throughout the house and underneath the staircases.

The ground floor of the house contained several spacious rooms, and several functional fireplaces. The formal front entry hall had a fireplace and walls of dark stained wood. It gave access to the main staircase, and had doors to a study, the large living room, and the dining room. Each of these three rooms also had a fireplace. The living room had built-in bookcases, with glass doors, along one wall, and a piano as well as couches, tables, and easy chairs. It could be connected with the formal dining room by sliding two heavy wood doors, suspended from above, into the walls; the children occasionally used this arrangement for presenting skits and other performances, with the sliding doors serving as a curtain. A massive round Tiffany stained-glass lamp with a light metal chain fringe hung over the heavy, dark wood dining table, around which were eight large, upholstered wood dining chairs with carved backs and legs. A massive sideboard and a couch were also part of the dining room decor. A swinging door connected the back of the dining room with the main pantry, with two sinks and copious storage space and cabinets for dishes, pots and pans, and silverware; the pantry in turn led to the bright and airy kitchen. The kitchen was large enough to contain a big work table in its center, in addition to extensive counter space, sink, two stoves, and cabinets. Off the kitchen was a smaller pantry for food storage, as well as a back entry hall that contained a refrigerator and gave access to steps leading down to the back yard.

The rectangular lot on which the house stood was oversized. The house was set back some distance from the street and sidewalk, and there was ample clearance to the edges of the lot—enough so that there was room for a wide balcony off the dining room without restricting the side clearance. The back yard extended far behind the house, with lawn and several trees; at the back end of the lot was a mature stand of bamboo on one side and space for a vegetable garden during the warmer times of the year. An apple tree near the vegetable patch provided extensive crops of apples during Wertheimer's first few years in the house, but the tree came down by itself several years before Wertheimer died. An open porch wrapped around most of the front and part of one side of the house.

Wertheimer's duties at the New School could typically be accomplished by his going into the city for only one or a few evenings a week to lecture, hold office hours, and attend meetings; the rest of his working time was spent at home. On a typical day, he would wake up early (about 6 a.m.) and rise from the huge bed with massive dark wooden headboard and footboard in his workroom, and work for an hour or more before partaking of his morning meal. This meal usually was a cup of strong, unsweetened black coffee (he called it his "kabapsen") and several dry zwiebacks; as in Frankfurt, sometimes he also would consume a hard-boiled egg. Work would then continue until lunch time, after which he normally took a nap for an hour or more. There followed another stint of several hours of intense work, usually alone, in his two workrooms, and then dinner. After dinner was usually a time for leisure and family activities, except on the few evenings that he had to go to the New School in New York for lectures or other obligations.

Typical fare at the Wertheimer dinner table varied only a little as the individuals who worked in the kitchen and pantry changed; during most of the decade, Rosa Mae Dixon (later Anderson) presided over the kitchen, preparing hearty northeast-U.S. dishes, with only a few concessions to Wertheimer's longtime central European habits. Meat and potatoes were staples, but so were vegetables (carrots, onions, peas, beans, cabbage, beets, spinach) and salads as well as pasta (flat noodles and spaghetti were favorites) and fish. Fresh or stewed fruit was a frequent dessert, but Rosa was also an accomplished baker, producing a variety of cakes and pies and, on rather rare occasions, bread. Clabbered milk, gelatin desserts, occasional soups, poultry, egg dishes, and special holiday meals (such as for Christmas, birthdays, Easter, or Thanksgiving) rounded out the menu.

Dinner guests were not unusual. Many were refugees, most of them scholars or members of the intelligentsia in their country of origin, and many with strong foreign accents in English. Initially German was the house language among members of the family, but soon English became the more frequently used tongue; the language spoken at the dinner table was varied as necessary between English and German to suit the comfort and competence of any guests who happened to be present. Conversation during dinner was typically lively, even passionate, usually on topics of current political concern. The children were strongly encouraged to participate in these discussions, whether or not there were guests; the children's positions were respected as much as were those of adults—but they were expected to present cogent and articulate arguments for their perspectives if someone challenged them. Sometimes Wertheimer would pose thought problems to the other diners at the table, both adult and child, and would gently guide the problem solvers to the solution with a succession of hints if they were unable to solve the problems on their own. The usual result, when one of the participants caught on, was a radiant exuberance—on Wertheimer's part as well as the participant's.

Among puzzles shared with the children and occasionally with guests were stories about desert wise men from the Middle East, mullahs who solved problems for their fellow human beings. One brain-teaser went this way: A mullah was strolling in a tent city (in which the residences were of canvas held aloft by a single central pole) when he heard a cry of frustration from one of the tents. Through the open tent-flap, he saw a woman preparing dough for bread. She was standing in front of a tiny table next to the pole, upon which was the dough; she had reached across the table and around the pole to pick up exactly the required amount of flour in her cupped hands from a sack that was on the opposite side of the pole from the little kneading table.

But the pole prevented her from getting the flour onto the dough without separating her hands and spilling much of it. The mullah might have offered to have her dump the flour into his cupped hands, and then he could have placed it on the dough, but his hands were grimy and covered with desert sand. There were no bowls or other suitable receptacles available in the tent. What did the mullah recommend to her? Answer: while keeping her hands cupped, the woman should scoot halfway around the pole, so that she was standing at the bag of flour, and her hands containing the flour were directly above the dough; she could then release the flour directly onto the dough on the kneading table.

Another story concerned a mullah who was walking, bringing up the rear of a caravan belonging to a rich man. The caravan had crossed miles of hot desert sand, and was finally approaching an oasis. The rich man and his two lieutenants were riding on horses. All were tired, hot, and thirsty, and the rich man made an offer to his lieutenants: "To that one of you whose horse gets to the oasis *last*," he said to them, "I will give this donkey and its load of gold." They all continued toward the oasis, with the two lieutenants gradually slowing down, each waiting for the other to get ahead of him. Finally they both stopped, and the rest of the caravan passed by them. When the mullah, who was straggling at the end of the caravan, came upon them, they had both dismounted, and were sitting in the sand each waiting for the other to become so hot and tired that he would have to head for the oasis. "Why are you sitting in the sand here when the oasis is so close?," he asked them. They told him about the rich man's offer, and continued to sit unhappily on the hot sand. But then the mullah said two words to them, whereupon they jumped onto the horses and raced for the oasis. Problem: What did the mullah say to them? The situation seems incomprehensible to most people who hear this puzzle for the first time, but becomes transparent and elegant once the solution is found. The mullah's sage advice to the lieutenants was, "Trade horses."

Fictitious jokes were also popular in the Wertheimer household. Some were specifically related to the family's immigrant status. One, for example, went like this: A recent immigrant was hired by the Wertheimer household, and learned to answer the telephone. One day the phone rang, and the new servant answered it. "Yes," she said. Then "Yes," again, and finally, "It sure is," and hung up. Soon the phone rang once more, and again, after a pause, she said, "Yes," then after another pause, "Yes," and after another one, "It sure is," and hung up. When this same sequence was repeated a third time, she was asked what the caller had said. She reported that he first asked whether this was the Wertheimer residence, so she said "Yes"; then the caller inquired whether Dr. Wertheimer was at home and, since he was, she said, "Yes" again; and when the caller then asserted, "Long distance from Washington," she said, "It sure is."

Another story concerned a formal dinner party at which Anni was seated next to a distinguished gentleman who suddenly, to her astonishment, picked up some creamed spinach in his hand from his plate and rubbed it into his hair. When she falteringly inquired why he was rubbing the spinach into his hair, he apologetically answered, "Oh dear! Sorry! I thought it was the mashed potatoes."

Yet another joke referred back to poverty-stricken small-town central Europe. One youngster proudly told his schoolmates that his family was so rich that his father put on a clean white shirt every other day when going to work. Thereupon a second said, "That's nothing. *My* father puts on a clean white shirt *every day* when he goes to work." Then a third pooh-poohed them both, and reported, "*My* father is so rich that as soon as he puts on a clean white shirt he takes it off right away again and puts on another one."

At 12 The Circle, in New Rochelle, evenings after dinner were often the occasion for musical events. Sometimes there would be a "family orchestra," with every member of the family playing a different instrument: Max on piano, violin, recorder, or flageolet, Anni usually singing and also playing guitar, and each of the children with some device such as a clarinet or recorder for Val, a drum or ocarina for Mike, and bells (a metal xylophone) or kazoo for Lise. The pieces that the ensemble played were typically German folk songs that everyone in the family knew well by heart.

Often on cold evenings there would be an open wood fire in the living-room fireplace, with everyone singing to Anni's guitar accompaniment. Favorite songs included ones from Max's and Anni's childhoods; many were from a popular German songbook, the "*Zupfgeigenhansl*" or "*Fiddle-plucking Jack*," several copies of which were kept in the room in case one of the ensemble forgot some of the lyrics. Some were raucous love songs or drinking songs, and there were also sentimental songs about unrequited love as well as rollicking hiking songs. Christmas carols were also sung at the appropriate time of year, with the German version of "Silent Night" a particular favorite.

Rounds were especially popular. The internationally favorite "Frère Jacques" was memorized by all the children long before any of them had the faintest idea of what its French lyrics meant, and the American "Row, Row, Row Your Boat" became part of the repertoire as well. Among German-language favorites were the humorous "Was müssen das für Bäume sein" and "Heut kommt der Hans zu mir"; a variant of the more serious "Himmel und Erde, die müssen vergeh'n"; and the lugubrious melody "Käs und Brot" in German dialect, doubtless from Max's childhood, perhaps the best-loved one. The lyrics of the German rounds were, respectively:

> Was müssen das für Bäume sein
> Wo die grossen

E-LEF-anten spazieren geh'n
Ohne sich zu stossen?
   What mighty trees the forest holds,
   One supposes,
   Where huge e-LEPH-ants walk around
   And never bump their noses!

"Heut kommt der Hans zu mir,"
Freut sich die Lies'.
Ob er aber über Oberammergau
Oder ob er über Unterammergau
Oder ob er überhaupt nicht kommt
Ist nicht gewiss.
   "Today Hans is coming to me,"
   Liese is pleased.
   But whether via Oberammergau
   Or whether via Unterammergau
   Or whether he's not coming at all
   —That no one knows.

Himmel und Erde, die müssen vergeh'n
Aber die Musici, aber die Musici, aber die Musici
Bleiben besteh'n.
   Heaven and earth, they must decay
   Ah, but the Musici [musicians?], ah, but the Musici, ah, but the Musici
   Endure and will stay.

Käs und Brot, Käs und Brot,
Und ein Schlückche' Schnapps datu: dat schmet goot.
   Cheese and bread, cheese and bread,
   And a sip of schnapps with that: that tastes great.

There were patriotic songs, such as one about the Bohemian national hero Johann von Nepomuk, and various joking or spoofing songs. One of the latter had lyrics that consisted solely of the Italian name Piccolomini for five stanzas, each time with different syllables receiving emphasis because the rhythm of the melody does not quite match the five syllables of the name:

   *Pi*ccolo*mi*ni, Pic*co*lom*i*ni, *Pi*ccolom*i*ni, Pic*co,*
  *Lo*mini, *Pi*ccolo*mi*ni, Pic*co*lom*i*ni, Piccolom*i*ni, *Pi.*
   *Co*lom*i*ni, Piccolo*mi*ni, Pi, *Co*lom*i*ni, Picco*lo,*
   *Mi*ni, Pic*co*lom*i*ni, Piccolo*mi*ni, *Pi*ccolom*i*ni, Picco.
   *Lo*mini, *Pi*ccolo*mi*ni, Pic*co,*....

A spoof of tailors contained lilting nonsense material; it was among the songs sung most often at the 12-The-Circle evenings. The English translation would be:

In Regensburg, at the church spire tip, the tailors came together.
And then the ninety-nine of them, yes nine times ninety-nine of them
Went riding on a rooster.
Chorus:

> One more stitch for the billy goat; baa, baa, baa for the tailor (Repeat.)
> Hurrah! Hooray! Hurrah! Hooray! Thread out!
> (*Spoken:* Who's there?)
> (*Sung:*) Tailor baa, baa, baa, tailor baa, baa, baa, tailor baa, baa, baa,
> hurrah, hooray! Let the needle zoom now!

And when the tailors' birthdays came, they all were very happy.
So then the ninety-nine of them, yes nine times ninety-nine of them
Dined on a roasted flea.
(*Chorus.*)

And when they all had feasted well, they felt all full of courage.
So then the ninety-nine of them, yes nine times ninety-nine of them
Drank toasts out of a thimble.
(*Chorus.*)

And when they all had had their drinks, they all got very hot.
But still the ninety-nine of them, yes nine times ninety-nine of them
Danced on a needle tip.
(*Chorus.*)

And when they all had danced their fill, they vanished out of sight.
For then the ninety-nine of them, yes nine times ninety-nine of them
Curled up in a candle snuffer.
(*Chorus.*)

But once they all were fast asleep, a mouse came rustling by.
So then the ninety-nine of them, yes nine times ninety-nine of them
Went sneaking out the keyhole.
(*Chorus.*)

Now any proper tailor in the world weighs seven pounds.
And if he drops below that weight, yes any bit below that weight,
Be sure he is not well.
(*Chorus.*)

There were several upbeat and cheerful lilting songs, such as the well-known "Die Gedanken sind frei." Two songs with serious melodies but with an optimistic message were also popular in the family. One had the following refrain:

> Enjoy life because the little lamp still glows.
> Pluck the rose before its bloom is past.

The other, a drinking song, was repeated with pairs of glasses clinking on each beat between successive singers in a circle, with the last recipient of a clink eliminated (and required to empty the glass) at the end of each round—until there were only two left to clink for the last time, and drain their glasses with linked arms at the end of the game.

> Live and love and drink; be merry
> Wear a leafy crown with me
> Come, be sad when I'm unhappy
> When I'm glad, be glad with me

Another song, originally Dutch, reinforced popular cultural stereotypes. The theme concerns a horse-drawn carriage:

> I've loaded my wagon full of old women.
> As we came into town, they started to scold.
> So all my life long, I'll never invite old women into my wagon.
> Giddap, Dobbin, giddap!

> I've loaded my wagon full of old men.
> As we came into town, they grumbled and were noisy.
> So all my life long, I'll never invite old men into my wagon.
> Giddap, Dobbin, giddap!

> I've loaded my wagon full of young girls.
> As we came to the gate, they sang throughout the town.
> So all my life long, I'll invite young girls into my wagon.
> Giddap, Dobbin, giddap!

A German variant of an international circular song that had a stereotypic sexist theme went as follows:

> If the pot has a hole in it, dear Henry, dear Henry?
> Stuff it up, dear, dear Lise; dear Lise, stuff it up.
> With what should I stuff it closed, dear Henry, dear Henry?
> With straw, dear, dear Lise; dear Lise, with straw.
> What if the straw's too long, dear Henry, dear Henry?
> Cut it short, dear, dear Lise; dear Lise, cut it short.
> With what should I cut it short, dear Henry, dear Henry?
> With a knife, dear, dear Lise; dear Lise, with a knife.
> What if the knife's too dull, dear Henry, dear Henry?
> Sharpen it, dear, dear Lise; dear Lise, sharpen it.
> With what should I sharpen it, dear Henry, dear Henry?
> With a stone, dear, dear Lise; dear Lise, with a stone.
> What if the stone's too dry, dear Henry, dear Henry?
> Make it wet, dear, dear Lise; dear Lise, make it wet.
> With what should I wet it, dear Henry, dear Henry?

With water, dear, dear Lise; dear Lise, with water.
In what should I get the water, dear Henry, dear Henry?
In the pot, dear, dear Lise; dear Lise, in the pot.
But if the pot has a hole in it, dear Henry, dear Henry?
Throw it out, dear, dear Lise; dear Lise, throw it out.

Similarly sexist, and clearly raucously irreverent, was another song in dialect:

One time I went a-walkin', well well, well well, well well!
One time I went a-walkin', well well, well well, well well!
One time I went a-walkin', whoop la di da!
A gal and I got talkin', ha, ha ha, ha ha, ha ha, [laughter]
Ha, ha ha, ha ha!

She said that she was loaded,...
Big bucks were what she ow-ed,...

She said she was an heiress,...
'Twas air she would inherit,...

She said her folks were bluebloods,...
Her father stitches new duds [i.e., is a tailor],...

She said we should share kisses,...
No one is going to miss us,...

She said I should make free with her,...
I get on easily with her,...

The summertime has come now,...
I never got with her, somehow,...

Another one, in dialect, had a raucous meaning that was not understood by the children—and was never explained to them:

That you're my most beloved, I'm sure you know.
Come in the night, come in the night; say, what's your name? (Repeat.)
Come at midnight, come at one o'clock!
Father sleeps, mother sleeps; I sleep alone. (Repeat.)
Knock at the chamber door, grab the handle!
Father'll think, mother'll think that it's the wind. (Repeat.)

Another love song had a joyous melody but bitter-sweet lyrics:

Well, I have been deciding
It's time to saddle up my horse

The creature needs some riding
It's for me to stay the course
    Feedee roolla, roolla, roolla, roolla, roollalalala,
    Feedee roolla, roolla, roolla, la;
        The creature needs some riding
        It's for me to stay the course

In the garden that my parents keep
There many flowers bloom, aye, bloom
For three years still the time must creep
Three years I'll wait out soon
    Feedee roolla,…

You think that you're the prettiest
Who ever walked the land, aye, land
And also quite the wittiest
But I don't know how you can
    Feedee roolla,…

As long as I am still alive
Some tramping for you I can find
And then when past me you survive
You'll tramp along behind
    Feedee roolla,…

Similarly, another song had a cheerful melody, but a sentimental theme of unrequited youthful love.

Hark! What's out there coming in (hollahee, hollaho)?
That must be my own darlin' (hollaheeya, ho).
Goes on by not looking in (hollahee, hollaho).
Guess it wasn't really him (hollaheeya, ho).

Folks are saying it a lot (hollahee, hollaho):
That I've got me a sweetheart (hollaheeya, ho).
Let them talk; I need say naught (hollahee, hollaho).
I can love as I choose, that's what (hollaheeya, ho).

Tell me, people, help me see (hollahee, hollaho),
What kind of loving that must be (hollaheeya, ho):
The one I love won't come to me (hollahee, hollaho),
I want no other's company (hollaheeya, ho).

The day his wedding-feast is thrown (hollahee, hollaho)
Will be my day to grieve and moan (hollaheeya, ho).
The little room that's just my own (hollahee, hollaho)
Is where I'll bear my pain alone (hollaheeya, ho).

> Then when I have come to die (hollahee, hollaho)
> To the grave where I must lie (hollaheeya, ho).
> Set no stone beneath the sky (hollahee, hollaho)
> Plant no forget-me-nots thereby (hollaheeya, ho).

Often sung was a macabre song in a minor key that family lore held to be a favorite of Käthe Kollwitz's.

> Now love is a thing one should never give in to;
> It's ended some young men and all they have been through.
> She said we would wed, now says I was on trial;
> My complaint is on file. Tü terütütü tü; tü terütü tü tü
>
> That happens if you let girls go out to dances;
> Your grief is begun and goodbye to your chances.
> They'll fall for new guys and forget what you had;
> Such people are ba-ad. Tü terütütü tü; tü terütü tü tü
>
> And when I have died, let me buried be.
> And let them cut six wooden boards out for me.
> Paint two fiery hearts on the sides of the boards flat;
> My estate can afford that. Tü terütütü tü; tü terütü tü tü.
>
> And let them sing dirges—I know they have practice:
> Stretched out in that coffin there lies one more jackass.
> In life he went through some affairs of the heart;
> From this world he must part. Tü terütütü tü; tü terütü tü tü.

Max and Anni encouraged the children in many creative efforts. They patiently served as audiences for skits the children performed, admired their efforts at art work, read the stories the children wrote, and supported their musical training; Val became quite proficient at piano and clarinet.

Michael, when he was ten years old, was given a "hectograph" set, a device consisting of a film of reusable gelatin in an 8 1/2 by 11 inch tray that could be used to make about 40 copies of a master sheet; this generated a modest house "newspaper," the *Wertheimer Times*, that was "published" sporadically for several years, starting in January 1937. The almost-monthly edition ran between two and six pages per issue; it was used, for example (see Chapter 12), to report such events as the Wertheimers becoming U.S. citizens. There were reports about Max's lectures and family activities, as well as contests, crossword puzzles, poetry, and articles on the results of gubernatorial elections, Hollywood productions, various marriages, and the citizenship of Wertheimer's students. Val served as the editor for two issues until Michael assumed responsibility as the new editor, and Lise acted as chief reporter. Wolfgang Köhler's daughter, Karin, contributed a column from Swarthmore. By 1939 the *Wertheimer Times* boasted thirty subscribers in the New York and Pennsylvania areas.

One report, in its entirety, from the May 1939 issue (MW-CU), was headlined "PROF. WERTHEIMER TAKES ANOTHER TRIP." It read:

> Prof. Max Wertheimer left Thursday, April 13, 1939 for Brinmore [Bryn Mawr]. At the station he met Barbara Burks, a good friend. They were both going to the same destination, so Mr. Wertheimer had the trip with her. On the way they had many interesting discussions. At about 9 p.m. they arrived in Brinmore, and went to the headquarters of the A.P.A. meeting [presumably a meeting of a committee that was chaired by Burks; see Chapter 12]. Then they got their assigned rooms for the night in the dormitory. (Turn to page 2, please.) PROF. WERTHEIMER's TRIP (FRM PGE 1). The next day, filled with various scientific questions, Prof. Wertheimer had discussions with many psychologists. He was also busy with refugee questions.
>
> On Saturday morning there were speeches from Mr. [Edwin B.] Newman and Mr. [George] Katona. After the end of the meeting, at 5 p.m., he was driven to Swarthmore College by Mr. and Mrs. Newman. Mr. Wertheimer was together with Prof. [Karl] Duncker and his mother. He spent the evening in [Wolfgang] Koehler's house, where he met for a short time our Swarthmore reporter, Karin Koehler. He spent the night in a college apartment.
>
> The next day he worked in the home of Mr. and Mrs. Newman, and had dinner with them and Mr. [Hans] Wallach. (Continued on page 3) PROF. WERTHEIMER's TRIP (CONT. FRM PGE 2) That afternoon Prof. Koehler drove him to Princeton.
>
> Mr. Wertheimer stayed at the Princeton Tavern through 'till Tuesday. There he had many scientific meetings.
>
> Dr. Wertheimer returned on Tuesday evening with [Kurt] Koffka, who stayed at Dr. Wertheimer's house a while.

Another story from the same issue was headlined "MICHAEL WERTHEIMER CONTESTANT IN COUNTY MUSIC CONTEST." Its text read:

> Michael Wertheimer, the editor of this paper, played the drum and the (continued on page 2) MICHAEL WERTHEIMER (CONT. FRM PGE 1) 'cello in the band and orchestra of the Albert Leonard Junior High School at the music contest at Port Chester. The band and orchestra left in four busses at 9 AM o'clock on Saturday, April 21, 1939. The (Continued in next column) ORCHESTRA PLAYED (CONT FRM LAST CLM) orchestra played first, at 10:30, and, having no competition, won. The band played at 11:20, and won over its one competitor. Then the other (continued on page 3) COUNTY MUSIC CONTEST (CONT. FRM PGE 2) bands played, and Michael and the other band and orchestra members had lunch.
>
> The whole contest was very interesting, there being about twenty bands and orchestras competing in different classes.
>
> Since the band and orchestra won, they are going to Amsterdam, near Albany, for the state finals. The details will be told in the next issue.

The last item in that five-page issue was headlined "NEW GELATINE FOR PAPER's PRINTING." The two-sentence item read,

> Since the gelatine on the Wertheimer Times' printing apparatus had worn out, the editor bought some new gelatine from the store here in New Rochelle. The money was taken from the budget.

The subscription rate for the newspaper was listed at four cents per copy, and a table presented the rates for advertisements (though the issue contained no ads) as ranging from 25 cents for a full page through six cents for 1/4 column down to 5 cents for 1/10 page and 4 cents for "any less." The font of the typewriter used to prepare the master was the same as that of the Monarch typewriter on which many drafts of Max Wertheimer's papers were typed in the United States; clearly he allowed his son to use his machine to produce the "newspaper."

The role that the New School's dean played in the family's life is illustrated in a brief item from the "June - July 1939" issue. The item was simply entitled "PINOCCHIO."

> On June 28th Miss [Clara W.] Mayer invited us to see a play called 'Pinocchio.'
> We all enjoyed the play immensely. After it Miss Mayer gave each of us a big ball and an ice cream cone.
> Then, the wonderful play still in our minds, we happily went home.

Everyday life in the Wertheimer home was not without its emergencies. On one occasion, Max managed to avert what might have been a major catastrophe. Michael woke up from a nightmare in the wee hours one morning, turned on the electric light on the night table next to his bed and, looking around to check that the shadows in his bedroom were not threatening him, inadvertently let the lamp, with its bare bulb, fall over onto the quilt covering his bed. When he picked up the lamp again, he saw a small glowing circle on the quilt where the bulb had ignited the fabric. Having seen his father frequently blow out matches he used to light his cigarettes, Michael blew on the glowing fabric, hoping to extinguish it. Instead, it broke into flame. Michael dashed down the hall to his father's bedroom, shouting "Feuer, Feuer!" ["Fire! Fire!"]. Max slowly awakened, pulled on his long wool socks and his slippers, and sleepily followed his son back to his son's bedroom. By the time they got there, the entire quilt covering the bed was in flames. Max quickly folded over the quilt from its narrow ends, largely smothering the flames, and carried the quilt across the hall into the "brown bathroom," dumping it into the bathtub. With the faucets turned on full force, the fire was quickly doused. All that had been damaged was the quilt itself (which, as it happens, has been preserved in Michael Wertheimer's mountain cabin in Colorado with a large patch covering the burned area, but still with a noticeable hole in its stuffing).

As mentioned earlier, birthdays and Christmas were regular annual celebrations at 12 The Circle. Lise retained a cover note for a 1942 Christmas gift, in her father's clear handwriting: "Dear Lise: I should like to think that this little booklet may accompany you through the years. It may carry all the wishes of my heart for you. When you make notes in it I should wish they may signify good things to you; whenever troublesome things be noted may it be the turning point to the good. I wish you, from all my heart, a good life. I give this little booklet to you at Christmas 1942. I give the same to Val and Michael. Your father."   Christmas 1942 was the last Christmas that Max would experience.

Notes

1. Paul Tillich (1970). (Jerald C. Brauer, ed.) *My travel diary, 1936: Between two worlds.* New York: Harper & Row, p. 11.
2. "Three Professors Here For Exile College: Wertheimer To Lecture On His Thought System—Hornboste [sic] And Son Arrive," *New York Times*, September 14, 1933.
3. Rudolf Arnheim (1984). Remembering Max Wertheimer. *History of Psychology Newsletter*, 16, p. 7.
4. Courant later founded and directed the Courant Institute of Mathematical Sciences at NYU.
5. Dixon Wecter (1948). *The age of the Great Depression, 1929-1941.* New York: Macmillan, p. 190.
6. Peter M. Rutkoff and William B. Scott (1986). *New School: A history of the New School for Social Research.* New York: Free Press, p. 12.
7. Rutkoff and Scott, p. 26. Although women then accounted for only about 40 percent of the student body in American colleges, approximately two-thirds of the New School's students were female.
8. Rutkoff and Scott, p. 31.
9. Rutkoff and Scott, p. 34.
10. Rutkoff and Scott, p. 23.
11. Claus-Dieter Krohn (Rita Kimber and Richard Kimber, Trans.) (1993). *Intellectuals in exile: Refugee scholars and the New School for Social Research.* Amherst, MA: University of Massachusetts Press.
12. Rutkoff and Scott, p. 86.
13. Rutkoff and Scott, p. 102.
14. Rutkoff and Scott, p. 47.
15. From Abraham S. Luchins and Edith H. Luchins (1987). Max Wertheimer in America: 1933-1943, Part I. *Gestalt Theory*, 9, p. 73.
16. Alex Sweet, personal communication to Michael Wertheimer, August 18, 1994.

10

Early Reception of Gestalt Psychology in the United States

> *There can be no question that [the Gestalt] movement is the prevailing influence in contemporary German psychological thinking.*
> —Gordon Allport (1923)

By the early 1930s, Kurt Koffka and Wolfgang Köhler were primarily responsible for the American perception of Gestalt psychology. As early as 1926, Margaret Floy Washburn wrote, "Most American psychologists feel, I think, a cordial gratitude towards Gestalt psychology, particularly to the two missionaries, Professors Koffka and Köhler, who have expounded it so delightfully in this country."[1] Koffka wrote the first formal exposition of Gestalt theory for American psychologists in 1922, lectured in the United States in 1924, joined the faculty at Smith College in Northampton, Massachusetts, in 1927, and gave lectures at several American universities— including the New School—throughout the 1920s and 1930s.

A prominent historian of psychology, Michael Sokal, wrote in the 1980s that "To many people in the United States,...Gestalt psychology in the 1920s and early 1930s meant primarily the work of Wolfgang Köhler, and the history of his interaction with American psychologists through the mid-1930s reveals much about the way Gestalt ideas and Gestalt psychology were received."[2] In 1925, American psychology was introduced to Köhler through his invited lectures at Clark University. These lectures offered him an opportunity to present Gestalt psychology to an audience outside the German-speaking world and, as the fact that he prepared his 1929 book *Gestalt Psychology* in English demonstrates, Köhler was very interested in informing American psychologists about Gestalt theory.[3] During his 1925-1926 stay at Clark, he taught courses on animal psychology and on Gestalt theory and methods.[4] While in America, Köhler gave lectures at several other universities and colleges (but was not invited to lecture in Tennessee and other regions of the South, presumably because his early research on problem solving in primates was too controversial for a region dealing with the Scopes "monkey trial," the notorious case of a high-school teacher convicted of teaching evolution; concerns were raised that Köhler's research would "arouse a storm of indignation all over the state").[5] In addition to his lecturing, he oversaw the final draft of Ella Winter's 1925 English translation of his classic 1917 book, *The Mentality of Apes*,[6] and contributed chapters to the volume *Psychologies of 1925*, edited by Carl Murchison, director of the psychology laboratories at Clark. Murchison had persuaded his wealthy father-in-law, Elmer Ellsworth Powell, to finance the "Powell Lectures in Psychological Theory." Murchison hoped that the lectures would counteract the tendency to indoctrinate psychologists in only one school of psychology so that "students are born structuralists or behaviorists just as one may be born a democrat or Presbyterian."[7] The volume contained papers by John B. Watson, Robert Sessions Woodworth, William McDougall, and many others; Koffka wrote an essay for it on "Mental Development" and Köhler ones on the "Intelligence of Apes" and "An Aspect of Gestalt Psychology."[8]

Köhler arranged to bring Karl Duncker with him to Clark University,[9] where Duncker completed requirements for a master's degree.[10] Köhler's appointment and Duncker's master's project occurred during a productive time in the history of psychology at Clark University.[11] Although the atmosphere at Clark was eclectic, the department was largely ruled by Walter Hunter's behaviorism and the structuralism of Nafe. However, Duncker was not favorably impressed by the dominant systems of American psychology. Following his return to Germany, Duncker wrote a general article on American psychology in which he observed that behaviorism, in all of its piecemeal glory, was a typically American venture nurtured by the industrial revolution.[12] Duncker's critical reaction to behaviorism was also evident in his 1932 review of a book by Rudolf Carnap.[13]

In part, Duncker's negative reaction may have been fueled by Köhler, who was very critical of American psychologists, and of behaviorism in particular.[14] In an August 4, 1929, letter to Wertheimer, Köhler described the difficulty he was having in preparing his book *Gestalt Psychology,* and added that "the book is primitive, but the Americans will even find this too difficult."[15] He encouraged Wertheimer to travel to the United States, but cautioned him that American psychologists were "good but terribly lazy-thinking people."

The Ninth International Congress of Psychology

In 1929, Wertheimer was invited to present a talk at the Ninth International Congress of Psychology held at Yale University that year, but the imminence of his new appointment at Frankfurt forced him to cancel his travel plans.[16] The International Congress was hosted by James Rowland

Angell, vice-president of the Congress, who had established the Institute of Psychology at Yale in 1924 and had just founded the Institute of Human Relations in 1929.[17] James McKeen Cattell, a major pioneer in American psychology, served as the president of the Congress and devoted much of his presidential address to tracing the development of psychology in the United States.[18]

Despite the self-affirming nature of the proceedings for American psychologists, a significant effort was made to entice European scholars to the Congress. More than a thousand people registered for that International Congress, and the program did reflect the strong presence of foreign scholars: 104 foreign visitors attended, with twenty-six presentations by German psychologists, seventeen by British scholars, and thirteen by Russian researchers, including the illustrious physiologist Ivan Pavlov, who presented "A Brief Sketch of the Highest Nervous Activity."[19]

Gestalt psychology was represented by Koffka, Köhler, and Lewin, as well as David Katz from Rostock, William Stern from Hamburg, and Edgar Rubin from Copenhagen, all of whom were somewhat sympathetic to the Gestalt school. According to Sokal, "The theoretical perspective that attracted the most attention at the congress was that of Gestalt psychology.... Of course, most of the American papers at the congress reflected the 'normal science' of a middle-of-the-road applied, behavioristically oriented functionalism. But many of those papers which explicitly took—or challenged—a systematic point of view concerned themselves with Gestalt psychology."[20] Sokal's assertion is corroborated in a 1930 article by Katherine Adams Williams of Radcliffe College, who summarized the major themes and content of the International Congress but concluded that her descriptions

> do not give an entirely satisfactory picture of the trend of psychology in its theoretical and systematic aspects, even as they were exhibited at the Congress. The most serious distortion occurs in the case of *Gestalt* psychology. There is, to be sure, only one report (by Köhler) which is explicitly of that school. Even this one is not polemical. There are, however, numerous references to the school. There are also, no doubt, a considerable number of problems undertaken under its influence, but, since the writers of the abstracts make no such admissions, the number cannot even be estimated.[21]

The prevalence of Gestalt psychology at the Ninth International Congress was consistent with the interest that the theory had generated some six years earlier at the eighth biennial congress of the Gesellschaft für experimentelle Psychologie [Society for experimental psychology] held at the University of Leipzig in 1923. Gordon Allport, who had received his Ph.D. from Harvard the year before, attended the *Gesellschaft* Congress and noted the prevalence of Gestalt theory:

There can be no question that this energetic movement is the prevailing influence in contemporary German psychological thinking. The majority of the papers before the Congress assumed the axioms of *Gestalt*-psychology as their point of departure.... Among the remaining papers of the Congress were reports by psychologists whose general lines of research are fairly well known in America. Many of these papers contained a reshaping of old concepts to the prevalent *Gestalt*-psychology. Very little of the classical German psychology remains in active use. It was characteristic of the Congress that in none of the lectures or discussions was reference made to the name or teachings of Wundt.[22]

Although Wertheimer was unable to attend the Ninth International Congress, Koffka and Lewin wrote him at length in October with their respective impressions of the proceedings. Koffka reported that the Congress was pleasant but not very scientific—with some exceptions. Koffka was impressed with an address by Karl S. Lashley, who had studied with the eminent zoologists Herbert Spencer Jennings and S. O. Mast and received his Ph.D. in 1914 from John B. Watson at Johns Hopkins. Lashley worked with Watson in replicating some findings of Russian reflex physiology, most notably by Vladimir Bekhterev, on conditioned auditory responses and became interested in tracing the conditioned reflex paths through the central nervous system. In 1929, the year of the congress, Lashley had just moved from the University of Minnesota to the University of Chicago and, in the same year, was elected president of the American Psychological Association, which held its annual convention together with the International Congress. Some of Lashley's research with white rats led him to appreciate aspects of the field theory of Gestalt psychology, and he expressly rejected the conditioned reflex in favor of Gestalt theory in his presidential address on "Basic Neural Mechanisms in Behavior."[23] Koffka reported that Lashley's address, attacking much of the then-current work on brain physiology, left the Americans in the audience "shuddering," but Koffka was encouraged that "his theme went into what we want." Lewin agreed and called Lashley "the best head in America."[24]

Koffka also found some value in a presentation by Edward Lee Thorndike from Columbia University, who had developed his "connectionist" learning theory near the end of the nineteenth century founded upon a thoroughgoing associationism. Köhler had strongly criticized Thorndike in his writings on insight in animal problem solving. Koffka was especially critical of the ideas in Thorndike's three-volume work on *Educational Psychology* published between 1913 and 1914; in his 1925 book *The Growth of the Mind: An Introduction to Child Psychology*, Koffka forcefully presented many objections to Thorndike's work. Wertheimer might have been surprised, then, to read that Koffka was pleased by the words of Thorndike, who had reconsidered principal constructs in his work and "has done as much as he can to rescue his theory...—some nice work that also fits into what we want. Thorndike has given up sheer contiguity and come over to belongingness." Lewin mentioned that he thought Thorndike was "narrow" but was surprised when Thorndike said "'I am going to say something at this Congress which no one else has said...I was wrong.' Thorndike came to me and gave great praise for Zeigarnik's work. This work is extraordinarily well known because of Koffka." Lewin also reported that both the French genetic epistemologist Jean Piaget and the Swiss psychologist Edouard Claparède, the latter secretary of the International Congress, were interested in Gestalt theory.

Despite some favorable reactions, Koffka noted that the "influence of Gestalt was felt, but only in a superficial way. Young people who are drawn to Gestalt theory didn't have the courage to stand up. Köhler and I did all the talking."[25] Lewin reported that he was impressed with the younger generation of American psychologists: "Köhler is tired of the primitive and atheoretical approach of most psychologists, especially the older ones, but it is not as bad as Köhler thinks. Among the younger people there is a better theoretical set [*Einstellung*]." Lewin added that, despite the protests of William Stern, "Americans now identify Germany with Gestalt psychology."[26]

At the Congress, although he was white-bearded and frail at age eighty, Pavlov's presence was striking and, with his speech translated by G. V. Anrep, his vigorous gestures and animated voice punctuated his message in the first of the invited addresses at the Congress. Edna Heidbreder, a professor of psychology at Wellesley College, recalled that at one point

> Pavlov seemed to be speaking with great enthusiasm, and the empathizing audience broke into enthusiastic applause without waiting for the translation. When the translation came, the applauded passage proved to be a description of some apparatus used in Pavlov's laboratory![27]

Immediately following Pavlov's presentation on September 2, 1929, Köhler took the platform and delivered a lecture "Über einige Gestaltprobleme" (On some Gestalt problems), in which he summarized several problems and findings generated by the Gestalt approach. In describing Köhler's talk, Herbert S. Langfeld of Princeton noted, "His clear exposition of this latest tendency in psychology will undoubtedly be of considerable assistance to the members in understanding Dr. Köhler's recent book on the subject."[28] During the Congress proceedings, Lewin had a private meeting with Pavlov and observed that it was "a pleasure" to see Köhler and Pavlov discussing psychology, although Köhler turned to Pavlov and said "I don't know whether to include you with the Gestalt psychologists or not." Lewin did not record Pavlov's response, but in the years following the 1929 Congress, Pavlov became increasingly critical of Gestalt theory in general and Köhler in particular. During a January 1935 lecture to his staff and colleagues, Pavlov declared,

> Now gentlemen, we shall pass from peaceful affairs, if we may say so, to matters of war, to Mr. Köhler. We are at war with him. This is a serious struggle against psychologists. Köhler is a professor of psychology at Berlin University. A scientist of minor authority would hardly be elected to a chair in Berlin University; they respect hierarchy there.[29]

Indeed, during the last three years of his life, Pavlov supervised research at the Koltushi Biological Station on problem solving by two primates, "Raphael" and "Rosa," attempting to explain Köhler's notion of insight as a combination of classical conditioning and Thorndikian trial-and-error learning.[30]

Early Discussions of Gestalt Theory in America

The reports about the American psychological establishment by Köhler, Koffka, Duncker and Lewin helped give Wertheimer an impression of Gestalt psychology's reception in the United States. Before Wertheimer's arrival, it was already popular to categorize salient research efforts in psychology as clustered around schools or systems, coalitions of scholars who loosely—or vehemently—clung to a common theme. In the late 1920s, Edward Bradford Titchener's school of structuralism had long since given way to functionalism, which in turn had been largely replaced by the behaviorism of John B. Watson. American psychologists were interested in the development of their discipline since its inception, and several books on the systems or schools of psychology became influential during the 1920s and early 1930s, which became a period of "systematic psychology."

Edwin G. Boring's classic book, *A History of Experimental Psychology,* appeared in 1929; Gestalt theory was deemed sufficiently experimental that it could share a chapter with behaviorism in the section on "Modern Experimental Psychology." In the same year, Walter B. Pillsbury from the University of Michigan wrote in his *History of Psychology,* "Possibly the most thriving [system], and certainly the one which has added the most to our experimental and factual knowledge, is known as the Gestalt psychology."[31] The second edition of Gardner Murphy's *An Historical Introduction to Modern Psychology* did not include a chapter on Gestalt psychology but did briefly mention it in an appendix on "Contemporary German Psychology" by Heinrich Klüver.[32]

The trend to discuss Gestalt theory in treatments of the history of psychology soon surged. The prominent Robert Sessions Woodworth assembled the lectures from his Columbia University course on "A Survey of Contemporary Psychology" and published them in 1931; his book[33] did contain a full chapter on Gestalt psychology. In 1933, Edna Heidbreder included Gestalt psychology as one of *Seven Psychologies* in her widely-used systems book.[34] In the same year, J. C. Flugel at University College, London, discussed Gestalt psychology in a separate chapter, using Titchener's awkward translation of the school as "Configurationism," in his *A Hundred Years of Psychology*.[35] By the early 1930s, it was clear that Gestalt psychology had become one of the principal systems of psychology at a time when other schools such as Margaret Floy Washburn's "Motor Theory of Consciousness," William McDougall's "Hormic Psychology," and Robert Sessions Woodworth's "Dynamic Psychology" were beginning to disappear from books and courses on systematic psychology.

Despite the enthusiasm for writings on systematic psychology, some scholars objected to such "system-making." Edwin R. Guthrie, often loosely identified as a neobehaviorist, struggled with the need to impose "systems" on psychological work:

> Classifying psychologists has become a major interest for the increasing number of persons who find it desirable to be able to talk about psychologists and psychology without attempting the more exacting task of talking psychology. "Behaviorism," "Gestalt," and "psychoanalysis" are words that can now be used in current magazines without footnotes. Psychologists themselves often find it necessary to choose their party label, and strangely enough, become occasionally absorbed in partisan denunciations of rival schools instead of working at their science.[36]

In his 1933 attempt to provide "formal criteria of a systematic psychology," John A. McGeoch, a prominent researcher at the University of Missouri, observed,

> By explicit avowal most psychologists are experimentalists and their official attitude toward system-making is apt to be one of scorn. But systems continue to be constructed and debated and even those who scoff may be found among the debaters. Behaviorism and *Gestalt-psychologie* have been, for example, far more widely discussed at the level of general theory than at that of experimental fact.[37]

In a review of a book on *Theoretical Psychology*, McGeoch also noted, "Contemporary American writing upon the more general theoretical problems of psychology has, if one excepts the attention given to *[G]estalt-psychology*, been little concerned with theorizing."[38] Indeed, Gestalt psychology was not only mentioned in lectures on systematic psychology but was considered significant enough to merit an entire class on the topic at some American universities. One such course, offered at the University of Colorado at Boulder, was inspired by a college sophomore who requested information about the new school; the 1927 course resulted in the preparation of a 40-page unpublished manuscript.[39] Clearly Gestalt psychology was not being ignored in the United States. But, as in Germany, the response to the theory in the research literature of American journals was mixed.

Objections to Gestalt Theory
in the American Psychological Literature

Wertheimer's emigration came at a time when Americans were assuming dominance in international psychology. The proportion of psychological publications in German and English had shifted from the time of Wertheimer's paper on the music of the Vedda to the time of his emigration to America. In 1910, 52% of the publications abstracted in the *Psychological Index* were by German scholars compared with 30% by Americans; by 1933, 52% were written by Americans and only 14% by Germans.[40] Gestalt psychology had become a fairly popular topic for American and European articles by the time of Wertheimer's arrival. The first volume of the *Psychological Abstracts* in 1927 listed the term "Gestalt Psychology" (or "Configurationism") as a heading for 17 articles in psychology journals; in 1929, the year of the International Congress, 39 articles were referenced on Gestalt theory, and in 1933, 25 articles were devoted to the school.[41] In addition, 21 of 43 articles in the 1933 volume of the *Psychological Review* were either devoted to Gestalt psychology or at least mentioned it in the course of the paper. As at the International Congress at New Haven in 1929, the American psychological literature of the 1920s and early 1930s reflected the polarization of American psychologists concerning Gestalt psychology: although there were some ardent disciples and lukewarm supporters, there were also many critics who voiced a variety of objections to Gestalt theory, especially as presented in Köhler's book *Gestalt Psychology*.[42] Köhler and his colleagues only rarely bothered to reply in print to the objections, most of which they considered naive, misinformed, trivial, or simply wrong.

Philosophical and Theoretical Objections

In 1935, George W. Hartmann cited several barriers to the reception of Gestalt theory by American audiences:

> First of all, as a product of German thought, it was couched in an alien tongue with all the difficulties of translation and interpretation which that implies, particularly in a highly technical field. Second, the war and its consequences interposed a brief but huge obstacle to professional contacts. Third, Gestalt psychology is pitched in a rather high intellectual key and consequently offers more resistance to popularization than behaviorism, whose positivistic and materialistic features represent an extension of a familiar tradition to all phases of mental life.[43]

Hartmann also believed that, despite Köhler's *Gestalt Psychology*, an "adequate synthetic treatment" of the theory had not emerged because "the leaders of the movement have been so busy pursuing an ambitious research program, proselytizing, and engaging in polemics."[44] Hartmann's first two reasons were doubtless correct. But the third obstacle, the theoretical foundation and assumptions of Gestalt psychology that contrasted so fundamentally with the implicit associationistic orientation of most American psychologists, probably was the most significant barrier.

A number of critics were disturbed by the "ambiguity" of the Gestalt psychologists on theoretical and philosophical issues, such as their supposed dualistic stand on the perennial mind-body problem.[45] Some took issue with the meaning of the name itself and the vagueness of its central concept, "Gestalten." Walter B. Pillsbury at the University of Michigan was troubled that "Exactly what a Gestalt is has never been clearly stated."[46] Another critic, F. M. Gregg at Nebraska Wesleyan University, was less friendly in his effort at "Materializing the Ghost of Köhler's Gestalt Psychology":

> As one reads the literature of the Gestalters, one is impressed with the possible reality of an elusive "something" which they call a *Gestalt*. But no one seems to have defined the term clearly and about it everyone grows vague and mystic when urged to explain it. If in doubt about this statement, ask almost any psychologist the simple question, What is a *Gestalt*? and try to follow [the] attempt to reply.[47]

Frederick Lund at Bucknell University argued that the "phantom" concept of Gestalten was not empirically derived and was "of the same abstract and phantom-like nature attributable to the Hegelian universals and Platonic Forms."[48] Another writer critical of the Gestalt psychologists' inability to answer basic questions about the theory dismissed the school as the "*Gestalt* enigma."[49]

The "Gestalt Movement"

Aside from questions about the philosophical foundation of the theory, one concern about Gestalt psychology was the caustic style of several adherents of the Gestalt school. Indeed, it seemed to some American psychologists that the Gestalt theorists were bent more on "evangelical conversion" than on scientific illumination. In a satirical article for the *New Republic* entitled "A Little German Band: The Solemnities of Gestalt Psychology," Edward S. Robinson, a psychologist at Yale University and editor of the *Psychological Bulletin*, likened the "Gestaltists" to religious zealots:

> Perhaps the expositors of the Gestaltian propaganda feel that Providence fashioned them for a moral role.... The Gestaltists would say that there has been a desertion of the staid monogamy of the whole in favor of a dissolute promiscuity of the parts. It is doubtful, however, whether the evil is such a grand one.[50]

Robinson was not alone in comparing Gestalt psychology with a religious movement; Karl Lashley once confronted Köhler with the question, "Excellent work—but don't you have religion up your sleeve?"[51]

Among the more fervent critics was E. G. Boring, who in 1928 characterized Gestalt theory not just as a new school of psychology, but as a reckless and rebellious movement that was not always clear about its origins or focus:

> Who began *Gestalt* psychology? Just at present in America the names of Köhler and Koffka are on everyone's lips. Both of these men refer the origination of *Gestalt* psychology to Wertheimer. Wertheimer modestly finds the roots in the school of *Gestaltqualität* and points to Von Ehrenfels. He in turn certainly owed something to Mach. But what is the cardinal principle of *Gestalt* psychology that is so all-important?[52]

In a 1930 review of Köhler's book, Boring made a distinction between "the *Gestalt* psychology" and "the *Gestalt* movement"; although he called the former "the most valuable movement in psychology during the present century," he clearly disapproved of much of the hostile and negative tone of the "Gestalt movement."[53] Boring argued that Gestalt psychology was "a movement in a more extreme sense than behaviorism" and added that it seemed to have "a mind, and sometimes even a voice, of its own." He quipped that "we suspect telepathy when Gestalt psychology has an idea and ventriloquism when it speaks."[54] Stanford psychologist Lewis M. Terman expressed similar concerns in a letter to Boring: "Koffka I should want to watch for about five years yet and see whether he goes in for scientific psychology or Gestalt propaganda."[55]

Boring accused the Gestalt psychologists of being insufficiently aware of antecedent influences, with the possible exception of an occasional mention of Ehrenfels's work. A number of other psychologists joined this protest and blamed Gestalt psychologists for conveniently ignoring a long history of holistic thought by such European and American scholars as Johann Friedrich Herbart, John Stuart Mill, Wilhelm Wundt, William James, and John Dewey.[56]

Boring may, in part, have been trying to defend his mentor Titchener's structuralism against the attack on it by Gestalt psychologists. Boring downplayed the success of the Gestalt movement in America, where "the victory of phenomenology, made easier by Titchener's death, was no great triumph, for other strong forces were operating to swing American psychology toward behavioristics."[57] Boring was also troubled by the Gestalt assault on Wundtian psychology and asked, "Is Gestalt a protest against Wundt and his influence? What about Wundt's *Aktualitätstheorie*, his creative synthesis and the law of psychic resultants? Was Wundt nearly so atomistic as his critics would have him be, or did he too have a vision similar to that of James, and Ehrenfels, and Wertheimer?"[58]

Another follower of structuralism, Paul Chatham Squires, decried the approach of the "Configurationists" who

> portray structuralism in such a fashion as to set it up to unreserved ridicule. The advocates of Gestalt let slip no opportunity to caricature the teachings of structuralism. Such caricaturing would seem to have become almost an obsession with certain exponents of Gestalt-Theorie.... One thoroughly unfortunate result of this wholesale and destructive attack upon structuralism takes the form of a dulling of the critical sense of students.... In [Koffka's *Growth of the Mind*] a devastating onslaught is made upon structuralism. The young student, after a reading of the book, is apt to make up his mind that no good whatsoever is to be found in structuralism, and that Gestalt psychology either has solved or is well advanced on the high road toward the solution of all problems.[59]

Squires even intimated that the ill-defined aspects of Gestalt theory were reminiscent of the work of nineteenth-century phrenologists, who examined the structure of the skull to determine mental faculties: "More than a century ago Wundt wrote confidently that the faculty psychology had received its deathblow.... Occasionally, one might be willing to venture the appellation Neo-Faculty Psychology in respect to configurationism. Its manipulation of entities called Gestalten has frequently all the appearances of faculty psychology on masquerade."[60]

A significant portion of criticism was generated by representatives of other schools. Margaret Floy Washburn was troubled that the Gestalt psychologists failed to assign any importance to the motor response.[61] She had outlined her motor system, suggesting that thinking is based on "tentative movements," in a 1914 article and expanded upon it in her major 1916 book *Movement and Mental Imagery*. According to Scarborough, "She agreed with the Gestalt psychologists on subject matter but believed that hers was a far more adequate explanation for the phenomena."[62] One of Washburn's disciples suspected that the Gestalt psychologists might come to appreciate motor theory: "It is only fair to say that in Köhler's most recent writings [*Gestalt Psychology*] there are more signs than in the earlier that he is moving toward a motor theory of consciousness, though he seems yet to have a long way to go."[63]

Not surprisingly, the behaviorists attacked Gestalt theory for its emphasis on phenomenology, its mentalism, and its seeming lack of experimental rigor. John B. Watson confessed to E. G. Boring that he "struggle[d] with Köhler's presentation of Gestalt-psychologie [but] failed to get a kick out of it."[64] Clark Hull, the leading neobehaviorist at Yale University, was troubled by both Köhler and Koffka. After an unsuccessful attempt to study with Koffka in Germany, Hull managed to bring the Gestalt psychologist to the University of Wisconsin for the 1926-1927 academic year. According to Hull,

This move, while very expensive, was successful. When Koffka finally arrived, his personal charm captured everyone. However, his expository approach was strikingly negative.... Instead of converting me to *Gestalttheorie*, the result was a belated conversion to a kind of neo-behaviorism.[65]

In a 1941 letter to his colleague and former student Kenneth Spence, Hull described a heated exchange between himself and Köhler. After a meeting of the psychological section of the Philosophical Society in Philadelphia, Hull managed to converse with Köhler at a "beer joint." Hull tried to convince Köhler: "It would be better for the prestige of psychology if we did less fighting and cleared up, so far as possible at least, the pseudo-differences which stand between us." According to Hull, Köhler immediately countered: "The behaviorists had been the ones doing the attacking." Hull reports that Köhler then bluntly stated, "I have heard it said that a professor in one of the prominent eastern universities is accustomed, whenever he refers to the Gestalt psychologists, to call them, 'those goddamned Gestalters.'" Hull confessed to Spence

> that my face was pretty red. The whole crowd gave me a good horse laugh, and of course I had it coming to me. There again my uptake was so slow that it didn't occur to me to tell them that I always smile when I use that expression, which, it seems to me, does make a difference.... [Köhler] said that he was willing to discuss most things in a logical and scientific manner, but when people try to make [the human being] out to be a kind of slot machine, then he would fight. And when he said the word "fight," he brought his fist down on the table with a resounding smack, and he did not smile when he said it, either.[66]

Under the direction of neobehaviorist Walter Hunter at Clark University, two Harvard graduate students, B.F. Skinner and Dwight Chapman, tested squirrels in problem-solving tasks designed to refute Köhler's findings on insight; although the results did appear inconsistent with the assumption that squirrels can display insight, Skinner decided not to publish because their work was still "leaving too much to the supposed mental processes of the squirrels."[67] Following the 1940 American Psychological Association convention at Pennsylvania State University, Skinner wrote his colleague Fred Keller that a meeting with Köhler and Kurt Lewin produced "a hell of a violent argument. I don't know what they were trying to do—convert me, I guess."[68] Occasionally, Skinner spoofed Köhler's research on insight, as in the following parody:

> A "scientist" in a white lab coat is seen pointing to...a basket hanging from a high branch of a tree on a long rope, some boxes to be piled by the ape to reach the basket, and a banana.... The scientist picks up the banana, climbs a ladder against the tree, and reaches for the basket. He slips, grasps the basket, and finds himself swinging from the rope. He begs the ape to pile some boxes under

him so he can get down, but the ape refuses until the scientist throws him the banana.[69]

Despite the seeming incompatibility of the two approaches, early suggestions were even made about a possible theoretical synthesis of behaviorism and Gestalt psychology.[70]

Perhaps because of concerns about the partly phenomenological foundation of the theory, Gestalt psychology was at times attacked as having little or no experimental basis, or questions were raised about some specific experimental findings that it had generated. Gestalt research on perception and insight received both support and criticism from American psychologists. In particular, Wertheimer's publication on apparent movement received a substantial response from European and American psychologists; the 1912 paper inspired over 100 papers on apparent motion during the three decades following its publication.[71] But Wertheimer's short-circuit explanation was challenged in America. Titchener, for example, supervised a graduate student, Forrest Lee Dimmick, on a test of Wertheimer's phi phenomenon, which led Dimmick to reject the short-circuit theory.[72] Wertheimer's cortical explanation of apparent motion was also challenged by G. D. Higginson.[73] But one historical analysis of apparent movement concluded:

> Much of the controversy which followed was on matters of detail, some of it indeed no more than polemical hairsplitting. For instance Dimmick's contention…was an attack more on the specific contention of Wertheimer … than on the general proposition that here we had an experience not only independent of a stimulus correlate but a whole-quality in the absence of any part-quality.[74]

In addition to the many replications of the phi phenomenon, there were critical examinations of various claims of Koffka, Gottschaldt, Wertheimer, and Köhler about findings on spontaneous perception of figures, spatial configurations, brightness contrast, and transposition.[75]

Further, the Gestalt literature inspired many American psychologists during the 1920s and early 1930s to study such perceptual phenomena as the configurational properties of musical melodies, perception of tactual stimuli, comprehension of Chinese characters, and the role of attention in the perception of figure and ground.[76] Other psychologists applied Gestalt theory to problems in education and even sport psychology.[77] There were also attempts to update American psychologists on Gestalt research conducted in Germany on perception, as well as on action and "affection" (that is, how one thing affects others).[78] One of Koffka's most promising students at Smith College, Molly Harrower, reported to American psychologists on Köhler's response to an attack on Gestalt theory by Eugenio Rignano at the University of Pavia.[79] Köhler's research on insight and related studies became the focus of research in learning and comparative psychology.[80] In a 1933 review of the literature on human learning, McGeoch listed research inspired by Gestalt psychologists in the areas of insight, the influence of meaningful organization, and the whole-part problem.[81]

Advocates for Gestalt Theory in the United States

By no means were all commentators on the theory hostile to it. A number of prestigious psychologists, including Gordon Allport, Mary Whiton Calkins, J. R. Kantor, Walter B. Pillsbury, Charles Spearman (in England), and Robert Sessions Woodworth, were at least sympathetic to some aspects of the work of the Gestalt school, even if they were critical of other portions of the theory or research.[82] H. H. Hsiao, for example, outlined the principal themes and contributions of the school in two 1928 review articles, but included criticisms of several aspects of Gestalt theory.[83] George Wilfried Hartmann of Pennsylvania State College published a book in 1935 titled *Gestalt Psychology: A Survey of Facts and Principles*.[84] Hartmann had studied as a Social Science Research Council Fellow at the University of Berlin during the 1930-1931 academic year, and following his return to the United States, published his research on insight and syllogisms.[85] Offering "a sympathetic picture of the Gestalt system from the standpoint of a non-configurationist," Hartmann remarked that "an examination of the evidence has left me more favorably disposed toward the theory than I had originally anticipated."[86] But he apparently could not resist adding his version of a commonly-expressed concern about Gestalt theory: "German scientific writing is proverbially famous for its obscurity and there is much in the sheer phraseology of Gestalt which repels one by its vagueness. Precise definitions are conspicuous by their absence."[87]

While there was a plethora of both lukewarm and scalding critiques of Gestalt psychology, several American psychologists published books and articles with strongly favorable accounts of the school. Robert Morris Ogden was one of these. He served an important role in informing American psychologists about Gestalt theory in a manner different from that of the others. He earned his doctoral degree at the University of Würzburg from Oswald Külpe in 1903, one year before Wertheimer, and met Koffka in 1909.[88] While he was at Cornell University, Ogden translated Koffka's 1921 book *Grundlagen der Psychischen Entwicklung* into the 1924 English version *Growth of the Mind*, and actively collaborated with Koffka in producing a second edition of the book in 1928. In 1926 Ogden's own book *Psychology and Education* was published.[89] According to one commentator, Frank S. Freeman, it was "the first book by an American psychologist written from the viewpoint of Gestalt theory and principles."[90] Ogden analyzed the relationship of Gestalt theory to behaviorism and referred to it briefly in his

1938 book *The Psychology of Art*.[91] Ogden was also instrumental in arranging appointments for Koffka, Köhler, and Lewin as visiting professors at Cornell University.

Harry Helson's 1925 and 1926 articles in the *American Journal of Psychology* were among the earliest major efforts to inform American psychologists about Gestalt psychology.[92] Helson heard about Gestalt psychology from E. G. Boring, who directed Helson's dissertation on the topic.[93] He earned his Ph.D. from Harvard in 1924, and his dissertation became the basis for his four *American Journal of Psychology* articles— which spanned over 130 journal pages and summarized the content of 240 articles, the majority of which had been written in German. At the time Helson's articles were submitted to it, Edward Bradford Titchener, then the editor of the journal, provided a commentary on the manuscript.[94] In 1924 Helson lectured for a year at Cornell, where Ogden had just completed his translation of Koffka's *Growth of the Mind*. Later, when he was teaching at Bryn Mawr College, Helson wrote a glowing review of Köhler's *Gestalt Psychology*, ranking it as second only to "Köhler's *magnum opus* on Physical Gestalten."[95] In 1933, he published a paper outlining 114 properties of and general principles applying to "configurations."[96]

Willis Davis Ellis was another faithful early American proponent of Gestalt psychology. At the suggestion of E. C. Tolman, Ellis attended lectures by Wertheimer, Köhler, Koffka, Lewin, and Metzger in Germany, and then returned to the United States with the hope of spreading the message of the new psychology. In 1930 he published a book on *Gestalt Psychology and Meaning*.[97] The book was intended for the uninitiated reader, as evidenced by appendices on the terminology used in Gestalt theory. The book also contains discussions of the Gestalt position on a number of theoretical issues such as monism and the mind-body problem. While he was in Germany, in April 1931, Ellis attended the Twelfth Congress of German Psychologists and reported back to American readers that "the principle of wholeness and rejection of a summative elemental standpoint is dominant throughout modern psychology in Germany."[98] After returning from Europe during the spring of 1933, Ellis contacted Koffka about plans for an anthology in English of excerpts from the Gestalt literature. At the time, Koffka was busy writing his *Principles of Gestalt Psychology* and recognized the value of English translations of significant Gestalt works for the dissemination of the theory in the United States. In the autumn, Ellis went to Amherst to work on his anthology with the consultation of Koffka. Ellis devoted two years to the project; he condensed and translated 35 selections of major writings from the Gestalt corpus on perception, thinking, memory, animal research, psychopathology, and general theory published between 1915 and 1929. Included were several selections from Wertheimer's work, including excerpts from his 1912 essay on "Numbers and Numerical

Structures in Aboriginal Peoples," his 1924 address on "Gestalt Theory" to the Kant Society, his 1922 paper on "The General Theoretical Situation," his 1923 article on "Laws of Organization in Perceptual Forms," and his 1925 report on "The Syllogism and Productive Thinking." Koffka carefully supervised Ellis's work, particularly his translations of Wertheimer's intricate prose; for example, Koffka wrote in a 1933 letter to Molly Harrower: "I read the summary Ellis had written of Wertheimer's lecture and found, I'm sorry to say, a great many mistakes. We discussed these mistakes at length, he taking my criticisms in the best of spirits."[99] In 1938, while he was an assistant professor at the University of Arizona at Tucson, Ellis's condensed translations finally appeared with an introduction by Koffka, under the title *A Source Book of Gestalt Psychology.*[100]

In addition to Ogden, Helson, and Ellis, Edward Chace Tolman and Raymond Holder Wheeler actively supported the Gestalt cause in the United States, but their interpretations of the theory were sometimes at odds with Gestalt theory as envisioned by Wertheimer, Köhler, and Koffka.

At the conclusion of his first year of graduate study at Harvard in 1913, E. C. Tolman traveled to Germany to prepare for the Ph.D. examination in German. At the suggestion of Herbert Langfeld, he visited Koffka's laboratory at the University of Giessen, where he was formally introduced to Gestalt theory during a month-long stay. He was so impressed that he returned to Giessen again in the fall of 1923.[101] In time, the Gestalt perspective became for him more meaningful for understanding the psychology of learning than Thorndike's approach: "I was already becoming influenced by Gestalt psychology and conceived that a rat in running a maze must be learning a lay-out or pattern and not just having connections between atom-like stimuli and atom-like responses 'stamped in' or 'stamped out,' whether by exercise *or* by effect."[102] His appreciation of the Gestalt approach was evident in a 1928 review of the literature on habit formation in animals, in which he cited compelling evidence that many organisms display a "Gestalting" of the perceptual field in learning tasks.[103]

In 1932, Tolman published his influential book, *Purposive Behavior in Animals and Men,* and while he clearly admired Gestalt psychology, his "purposive behaviorism" proceeded in directions different from those of the Gestalt school. When Koffka reviewed Tolman's book for the *Psychological Bulletin*, he lamented that "even if we interpret his theory as a form of [G]estalt theory, it has a distinguishing feature, viz., what I could call its oversimplification."[104] For Koffka, Tolman's use of such concepts as "sign-[G]estalts" was, at best, "a very weak [G]estalt, containing very little of the main [G]estalt characteristics."[105] Walter Varvel at the University of Kansas also commented on purposive behaviorism from the standpoint of Gestalt theory and argued that Tolman's approach was closer to von Ehrenfels's *Gestaltqualität* position than to "modern" Gestalt theory.[106]

The work of Raymond Wheeler at the University of Kansas also played a part in the presentation of Gestalt theory to American psychology. Both Ogden and Helson had held appointments at the University of Kansas, and under Wheeler's direction as chair, the department was one of the earliest to make systematic efforts to educate students about Gestalt theory. Wheeler was also the person who suggested to Edwin B. Newman that he travel to Frankfurt to study with Wertheimer. In a 1928 article on "Persistent Problems in Systematic Psychology," Wheeler did express concern that Gestalt psychologists were overly critical of structuralism, but he explicitly used the theory in his research with a student, Theodore Perkins, on discrimination and "Configurational Learning in Goldfish."[107] Wheeler soon assumed the role of an apologist for the Gestalt school. In four articles published in the *Psychological Review*, Wheeler and his students defended Gestalt psychology against what they called "confused" criticisms of it[108] and of its unique development in the history of the science (as distinct from such antecedents as Jamesian psychology),[109] against criticisms based on Thorndike's system,[110] and against criticisms from Woodworth, Spearman and McDougall.[111] In an address at the convention of the Western Psychological Association in the mid-1930s, Wheeler traced the roots of Gestalt psychology back to previous cycles of "whole-mindedness" beginning as early as 300 B.C.[112] Despite his explicit efforts to defend Gestalt psychology, Wheeler also did not hesitate to modify the theory. Wheeler attempted to assimilate Gestalt theory with the holistic organismic movement in biology, as a challenge to atomism and mechanism in science and education.[113]

Wertheimer's Professional Relationships with American Psychologists

Wertheimer did not receive the same recognition in the United States that his younger colleagues Koffka and especially Köhler did, but perhaps he also had a less ambivalent impact on American psychology. In assessing Wertheimer's role in America, historian Michael Sokal wrote, "Max Wertheimer, the leader of the Gestalt school, did not cross the Atlantic during [the 1920s] and, because he published much less than his colleagues, especially Koffka and Köhler, remained in the background as far as Americans were concerned. To many in this country, he was the 'mysterious figure.'"[114] Wertheimer's influence was apparently due more to his ideas, his lectures, his discussions with colleagues, and his personality than to his sparse published writings. Köhler noted that Wertheimer

> could be a cheerful fighter. But it was his despair that the fighting had to be done in words in which the preconceptions of his opponents were firmly embodied. When he tried to use these treacherous tools and yet at the same time not betray his best convictions he often suffered bitter frustration. For this

reason what we…have from him in print can give no adequate impression of his extraordinary mind. It was only in lectures and in discussions that he forgot to worry about the pitfalls of language. Then skeptics and friends alike would be swept along by his thought as though by a torrent.[115]

Shortly after arriving in America, Wertheimer established professional contacts with a number of distinguished philosophers and psychologists. For example, Wertheimer and his wife were invited to the home of John Dewey, at the time in his eighties, to explain Gestalt theory to the renowned philosopher.[116] Although still struggling with his English, Wertheimer held forth on Gestalt theory in front of Dewey's fireplace until two in the morning. The last train back to the Wertheimer home had already left an hour earlier, and the Wertheimers had to take a taxi. Wertheimer also had some contact with the American philosopher Charles Hartshorne at the University of Chicago, who had a strong interest in the psychology of sensation.[117]

Wertheimer's membership in several professional organizations also led to a number of significant contacts. He was invited in 1934 to join the American Psychological Association.[118] Wertheimer was also invited to join the exclusive Society of Experimental Psychologists in 1936,[119] the same year in which Köhler too was invited to join.[120] Wertheimer attended several meetings of the Society, including ones held in 1937 and 1941.[121] These societies enabled Wertheimer to enhance his personal and professional ties to American psychology and, according to most accounts, Wertheimer's reception in America was not as ambivalent as Köhler's. To be sure, Wertheimer was far from immune to hostility from the American psychological community, but he did engage in lively and productive exchanges with a number of colleagues, including the unlikely prominent figures E. G. Boring and Clark L. Hull (see Chapter 11).

Wertheimer's Lectures throughout the United States

In addition to engaging in extensive correspondence with such influential psychologists as Boring and Hull, Wertheimer lectured on Gestalt theory widely throughout America. During his decade in the United States, he presented talks at more than twenty colleges and universities, including in the northeast Columbia, Princeton, Swarthmore, New York University, Yale, Brown, Brooklyn College, Pennsylvania, Bucknell, Rutgers, and Bryn Mawr; in the midwest Indiana, Wisconsin, Michigan, Iowa, and Minnesota; and in the west Oregon State, Oregon, Washington, Berkeley, and Utah. He spoke on a broad range of topics, from the Gestalt psychology of music and art to logic, social psychology, learning, perception, and thinking.

His invitations to present talks were not restricted to academia; in 1933 he addressed the third annual Herald Tribune Conference on Current Problems and the following year testified on personal injustice in Germany before a

U.S. Commission on Law and the State of Civil Liberties in Germany. Wertheimer was also in demand from faculty members at high schools; he spoke to the faculty of the Seward Park High School in Manhattan, and of the Boys High School in Brooklyn, to the Mental Hygiene Committee of the High School Teachers Association, to the Teaching Institute of Los Angeles, and to teachers in Pasadena and San Francisco.[122] He participated with John Dewey and other scholars in a panel discussion on education and anarchy for radio station WEVD's University of the Air in 1935. Wertheimer also attended several conventions of the Eastern Psychological Association as well as meetings of the American Psychological Association and of the Society of Experimental Psychologists. Thus, though he did not publish abundantly, and was not as prominent on the scene of American psychology as his colleagues Köhler and Koffka, and later Kurt Lewin, Wertheimer did engage in many activities that might eventually have contributed to changing his image from that of a "mysterious figure" in the "background" of American psychology, as Michael Sokal has described him.

Notes

1. Margaret Floy Washburn (1926). Gestalt psychology and motor psychology. *American Journal of Psychology*, 37, p. 516.
2. Michael M. Sokal (1984). The Gestalt psychologists in behaviorist America. *American Historical Review*, 89, p. 1250.
3. Wolfgang Köhler (1929). *Gestalt psychology*. New York: Liveright.
4. W. A. Koelsch (1990). The 'Magic Decade' revisited: Clark psychology in the twenties and thirties. *Journal of the History of the Behavioral Sciences*, 26, 151-175.
5. Mary Henle (1986), An American adventure. In M. Henle, *1879 and all that: Essays in the theory and history of psychology*. New York: Columbia University Press, pp. 238-240.
6. Wolfgang Köhler (1925). *The mentality of apes*. (Ella Winter, trans.). New York: Harcourt, Brace. (Original work published 1917)
7. Carl Murchison, "Introduction," *Psychologies of 1925*. Worcester, MA: Clark University Press, 1926, p. 1.
8. Kurt Koffka, Mental development. In Carl Murchison (ed.) (1926). *Psychologies of 1925*, pp. 129-143. Wolfgang Köhler, "Intelligence of apes," ibid, pp. 145-161. Köhler, "An aspect of Gestalt psychology," ibid, pp. 163-195. Together with Friedrich Sander from the University of Giessen, Köhler and Koffka also contributed to Murchison's *Psychologies of 1930*. See Carl Murchison (ed.) (1930). *Psychologies of 1930*. Worcester, MA: Clark University Press, pp. 143-204.
9. Koelsch, p. 160.
10. Ibid, p. 169. Duncker published his thesis in 1926 in the *Pedagogical Seminary*: A qualitative experimental and theoretical study of productive thinking (Solving of comprehensible problems), 33, pp. 642-708.

11. Koelsch, p. 160.
12. Karl Duncker (1927). Der Behaviorismus—die amerikanische Psychologie [Behaviorism—the American psychology], *Pädagogisches Zentralblatt*, 7, 690-702.
13. Karl Duncker (1932). Behaviorismus und Gestalt-psychologie. Kritische Bemerkungen zu Carnap's *Psychologie in physikalischer Sprache* [Behaviorism and Gestalt psychology. Critical remarks on Carnap's *Psychology in physical language*], *Erkenntnis*, 3, 162-176.
14. Despite his negative feelings about American psychology, Duncker, together with Donald Beates Watt, did prepare two books on the reading and translation of German and English scientific text. Karl Duncker and Donald B. Watt (1929). *Exercises for the rapid reading of scientific German psychological text (with interlinear translation of difficult words).* Ann Arbor, MI: Edwards Brothers. Karl Duncker and Donald B. Watt (1930). *A German-English dictionary of psychological terms.* Ann Arbor, MI: Edwards Brothers. Doubtless part of the motivation for these projects was the thought that if American psychologists were to learn to read German, they would have access to the original Gestalt literature in that language.
15. Wolfgang Köhler to Max Wertheimer, August 4, 1929, MW-CU.
16. Herbert S. Langfeld to Max Wertheimer, March, 11, 1929, MW-CU. Max Wertheimer to Herbert S. Langfeld, n.d., MW-CU.
17. The First International Congress was held in Paris in 1889 and, beginning in 1892, plans were made to have the International Congress convene in the United States. Following a series of setbacks, including the advent of the First World War, the Congress at Groningen successfully arranged to have the Ninth International Congress meet on American soil for the first time in New Haven. See Rand B. Evans and Frederick J. Down Scott (1978). The 1913 International Congress of Psychology: The American congress that wasn't. *American Psychologist*, 33, 711-724; Herbert S. Langfeld (1929, 18 October). The Ninth International Congress of Psychology. *Science*, 70, 364-368.
18. Michael M. Sokal (1984). James McKeen Cattell and American psychology in the 1920s. In Josef Brožek (ed.), *Explorations in the history of psychology in the United States.* Lewisburg, PA: Bucknell University Press, p. 296.
19. Carl P. Duncan (1980). A note on the 1929 International Congress of Psychology. *Journal of the History of the Behavioral Sciences*, 16, p. 3.
20. Sokal, James McKeen Cattell and American psychology in the 1920s, p. 297.
21. Katherine Adams Williams (1930). Psychology in 1929 at the International Congress. *Psychological Bulletin*, 27, 660.
22. Gordon W. Allport (1923). The Leipzig Congress of Psychology. *American Journal of Psychology*, 34, 614-615.
23. Karl S. Lashley (1930). Basic neural mechanisms in behavior. *Psychological Review* 37, 1-24.
24. In later years, Lashley became very critical of Gestalt psychology. See, for example, Karl Lashley (1942). An examination of the 'continuity theory' as applied to discriminative learning. *Journal of General Psychology*, 26, 241-265.
25. Kurt Koffka to Max Wertheimer, October 9, 1929, MW-CU.
26. Kurt Lewin to Max Wertheimer, October 26, 1929, MW-CU.

27. Quoted in Duncan, p. 3.
28. Langfeld, p. 366.
29. Ivan P. Pavlov (1955). In J. Gibbons (ed.), *I. P. Pavlov: Selected works* (S. Beisky, Trans.) Moscow: Foreign Languages Publishing House, p. 606.
30. George Windholtz (1984). Pavlov vs. Köhler: Pavlov's little-known primate research. *Pavlovian Journal of Biological Science*, 19, 23-31.
31. Walter B. Pillsbury (1929). *History of psychology*. New York: Norton, p. 304.
32. Gardner Murphy (1930). *An historical introduction to modern psychology*. New York: Harcourt, Brace.
33. Robert S. Woodworth (1931). *Contemporary schools of psychology*. New York: Ronald.
34. Edna Heidbreder (1933). *Seven psychologies*. New York: Appleton-Century-Crofts.
35. John Carl Flugel (1933). *A hundred years of psychology: 1833-1933*. New York: Macmillan.
36. Edwin R. Guthrie (1933). On the nature of psychological explanations. *Psychological Review*, 40, p. 124.
37. John A. McGeoch (1933). The formal criteria of a systematic psychology. *Psychological Review*, 40, p. 1.
38. John A. McGeoch (1933). Johannes Lindworsky, *Theoretical Psychology*. *Psychological Bulletin*, 30, p. 455.
39. J. H. Elder (1977). Gestalt psychology. *American Psychologist*, 32, pp. 1117-1118.
40. J. B. Maller (1934). Forty years of psychology: A statistical analysis of American and European publications, 1894-1933. *Psychological Bulletin*, 31, p. 537.
41. Although the majority of articles on Gestalt psychology during this period were in English, several appeared in German, with a few others in journals from other countries, including China, Italy, Poland, and the Soviet Union.
42. Most articles on Gestalt psychology were published in scientific journals, but several prominent psychologists published manuscripts about the school in American cultural magazines (for example, Edward S. Robinson (1929). A little German band: The solemnities of Gestalt psychology. *New Republic*, 16, Nov. 27, pp. 10-14).
43. George Wilfried Hartmann (1935). *Gestalt psychology: A survey of facts and principles*. New York: Ronald, p. v.
44. Ibid, p. v.
45. Grace A. De Laguna (1930). Dualism and Gestalt psychology. *Psychological Review*, 37, 187-213.
46. Walter B. Pillsbury (1933). The units of experience—meaning or Gestalt. *Psychological Review*, 40, p. 485.
47. F. M. Gregg (1932). Materializing the ghost of Köhler's Gestalt psychology. *Psychological Review*, 39, p. 258.
48. Frederick H. Lund (1929). The phantom of the Gestalt. *Journal of General Psychology*, 2, p. 320.
49. H. G. Wyatt (1928). The Gestalt enigma. *Psychological Review*, 35, 298-310.
50. Edward S. Robinson (1929). A little German band: The solemnities of Gestalt psychology. *New Republic*, 16, Nov. 27, 10-14, p. 11.

51. Wolfgang Köhler (1971). Gestalt psychology. In M. Henle (ed.), *The selected papers of Wolfgang Köhler*. New York: Liveright, pp. 108-122, p. 117. (Original work published 1967)

52. E. G. Boring (1928). The problem of originality in science. *American Journal of Psychology*, 39, p. 88.

53. E. G. Boring (1930). The *Gestalt* psychology and the *Gestalt* movement. *American Journal of Psychology*, 42, p. 308.

54. Ibid, p. 310.

55. Quoted in Henry L. Minton (1988). *Lewis M. Terman: Pioneer in psychological testing*. New York: New York University Press, p. 136.

56. W. D. Commins (1932). Some early holistic psychologists. *Journal of Philosophy*, 29, 208-217. W. Line (1931). Gestalt psychology in relation to other psychological systems. *Psychological Review*, 38, 375-391. O. A. Oeser (1930). Gestalt and the Gestalt hypothesis. *British Journal of Psychology*, 21, 73-94. One writer even suggested that the Gestalt principles of visual perception had been clearly stated in a 1909 book by American painter Abbot Henderson Thayer. See A. M. Keen (1932). Protective coloration in the light of Gestalt psychology. *Journal of General Psychology*, 6, 200-203.

57. E. G. Boring (1961). *Psychologist at large*. New York: Basic Books, p. 225.

58. E. G. Boring (1928). The problem of originality in science. *American Journal of Psychology*, 39, p. 88.

59. Paul Chatham Squires (1930). A criticism of the configurationist's interpretation of 'structuralism.' *American Journal of Psychology*, 42, 135-136.

60. Squires, p. 139.

61. Margaret Floy Washburn (1928). Gestalt psychology and motor psychology. *American Journal of Psychology*, 37, 516-520.

62. Elizabeth Scarborough (1990). Margaret Floy Washburn (1871-1939). In Agnes N. O'Connell and Nancy Felipe Russo (eds.), *Women in psychology: A bio-bibliographic sourcebook*. New York: Greenwood Press, p. 345.

63. Gregg, Materializing the ghost of Köhler's Gestalt psychology, p. 269.

64. John B. Watson to E. G. Boring. Quoted in Sokal, The Gestalt psychologists in behaviorist America, p. 1245.

65. Clark L. Hull (1952). Clark L. Hull. In E. G. Boring, H. S. Langfeld, H. Werner, and R. M. Yerkes (eds.), *A history of psychology in autobiography*, Vol. 4. Worcester, MA: Clark University Press, p. 154.

66. Clark L. Hull to Kenneth Spence, May 20, 1941. Quoted in A. Amsel and M. E. Rashotte (eds.) (1984). *Mechanisms of adaptive behavior: Clark L. Hull's theoretical papers with commentary*. New York: Columbia University Press, pp. 22-23.

67. B. F. Skinner (1979). *The shaping of a behaviorist*. New York: Knopf, p. 35.

68. B. F. Skinner to Fred S. Keller, 1940. Harvard University Archives.

69. Skinner, *The shaping of a behaviorist*, p. 31. Whatever his earlier feelings about Köhler may have been, Skinner did write in 1989, in commenting on a book suggesting that Köhler was a German spy while on Tenerife, that the "reputation of a great man like Köhler needs to be carefully protected." Letter from B. F. Skinner to Michael Wertheimer, August 2, 1989.

70. O. L. Reiser (1928). Behaviorism and Gestalt-psychology. *Psyche*, 8, 60-62.

71. E. G. Boring (1942). *Sensation and perception in the history of experimental psychology*. New York: Appleton-Century.

72. Forrest Lee Dimmick (1920). An experimental study of visual movement and the phi phenomenon. *American Journal of Psychology*, 31, 317-332.

73. G. D. Higginson (1926). Apparent visual movement and the Gestalt. I. Nine observations which stand against Wertheimer's cortical theory. II. The effect upon visual movement of colored stimulus objects. *Journal of Experimental Psychology*, 9, 228-252.

74. W. M. O'Neil and A. A. Landauer (1966). The phi-phenomenon: Turning point or rallying point. *Journal of the History of the Behavioral Sciences*, 2, p. 339.

75. W. H. Mikesell and Madison Bentley (1930). Configuration and brightness contrast. *Journal of Experimental Psychology*, 13, 1-23. M. G. Moore (1930). Gestalt vs. experience. *American Journal of Psychology*, 42, 453-455. H. Taylor (1932). The method of Gestalt psychology. *American Journal of Psychology*, 44, 356-361. H. Taylor (1932). A study of configuration learning. *Journal of Comparative Psychology*, 13, 19-26.

76. J. P. Guilford and Ruth A. Hilton (1933). Some configurational properties of musical melodies. *Journal of Experimental Psychology*, 16, 32-54. B. L. Rosenbloom (1929). Configurational perception of tactual stimuli. *American Journal of Psychology*, 41, 87-90. Siegen K. Chou (1930). Gestalt in reading Chinese characters. *Psychological Review*, 37, 54-70. E. G. Weaver (1928). Attention and clearness in the perception of figure and ground. *American Journal of Psychology*, 40, 51-74.

77. M. E. Grant (1929). 'Mysterious' tropisms: An illustration of the Gestalt law of precision. *Journal of Educational Psychology*, 20, 125-127. H. E. Jones and D. Dunn (1932). The configurational factor in children's learning. *Journal of Genetic Psychology*, 41, 3-15. R. R. Scott (1930). Some suggestions on learning from the point of view of Gestalt psychology. *Journal of Educational Psychology*, 21, 361-366. H. G. Hartgenbusch (1926). *Gestalt* psychology in sport. *Psyche*, 27, 41-52. In an address to the Ninth International Congress of Psychology, American industrial psychologist Morris S. Viteles argued that Gestalt psychology held promise for applied psychology. See Morris Viteles (1930). Die 'Gestalt'-Betrachtungsweise in der angewandten Psychologie [The Gestalt viewpoint in applied psychology]. *Zeitschrift für angewandte Psychologie*, 36, 525-531.

78. John G. Jenkins (1933). Dr. Metzger on '*Gestalt und Kontrast.*' *Journal of Experimental Psychology*, 16, 175-176. J. F. Brown (1929). The methods of Kurt Lewin in the psychology of action and affection. *Psychological Review*, 36, 200-221.

79. Molly R. Harrower (1928). *Gestalt* versus associationism. *Psyche*, 8, 55-71.

80. H. G. Wyatt (1926). Intelligence in man and ape. *Psychological Review*, 33, 375-384. M. B. Drury (1931). Can Gestalt theory save instinct? *Journal of General Psychology*, 5, 88-94. English sociologist Leonard T. Hobhouse revised his 1901 book *Mind in evolution* to include an appendix on Gestalt theory in the third edition. L. T. Hobhouse (1926). *Mind in evolution*. New York: Macmillan.

81. John A. McGeoch (1933). The psychology of human learning: A bibliography. *Psychological Bulletin*, 30, 1-62.

82. Gordon Allport (1924). The standpoint of Gestalt psychology. *Psyche*, 4, 354-361. Mary Whiton Calkins (1926). Critical comments on the 'Gestalt-theorie.' *Psychological Review*, 33, 135-158. J. R. Kantor (1925). The significance of the Gestalt conception of psychology. *Journal of Philosophy*, 22, 234-231. J. R. Kantor (1933). In defense of stimulus-response psychology. *Psychological Review*, 40, 324-336. W. B. Pillsbury (1926). *Gestalt* versus concept as a principle of explanation in psychology. *Journal of Abnormal and Social Psychology*, 21, 14-18. Charles Spearman (1925). The new psychology of shape. *British Journal of Psychology*, 15, 211-225. Charles Spearman (1929). Formalism or associationism. *British Journal of Psychology*, 19, 328-331. Robert Sessions Woodworth (1927). Gestalt psychology and the concept of reaction stages. *American Journal of Psychology*, 39, 62-69.

83. H. H. Hsiao (1928). A suggestive review of Gestalt theory. *Psychological Review*, 35, 280-297. H. H. Hsiao (1928). Some contributions of Gestalt theory from 1926 to 1927. *Psychological Bulletin*, 25, 613-620.

84. George Wilfried Hartmann (1935). *Gestalt psychology: A survey of facts and principles*. New York: Ronald.

85. George W. Hartmann (1931). The concept and criteria of insight. *Psychological Review*, 38, 242-253. George W. Hartmann (1931). Insight vs. trial-and-error in the solution of problems. *American Journal of Psychology*, 45, 663-677.

86. Hartmann, *Gestalt psychology: A survey of facts and principles*, p. v.

87. Ibid, p. v.

88. For a through analysis of Ogden's role in promoting Gestalt theory in America, see Mary Henle (1984). Robert M. Ogden and Gestalt psychology in America. *Journal of the History of the Behavioral Sciences*, 20, 9-19.

89. Robert Morris Ogden (1926). *Psychology and education*. New York: Harcourt, Brace.

90. Frank S. Freeman (1977). On the introduction of Gestalt psychology into America. *American Psychologist*, 32, p. 384. In another article, Freeman declared that Ogden "was the first and principal proponent and representative of Gestalt psychology in the United States." Frank S. Freeman (1977). The beginnings of Gestalt psychology in the United States. *Journal of the History of the Behavioral Sciences*, 13, p. 352.

91. Robert M. Ogden (1933). Gestalt psychology and behaviorism. *American Journal of Psychology*, 45, 151-155. Robert M. Ogden (1928). The *Gestalt* hypothesis. *Psychological Review*, 35, 136-141. Robert M. Ogden (1938). *The psychology of art*. New York: Scribner. The latter was inspired by Külpe and, although Köhler is briefly mentioned in it, the works of Koffka, Wertheimer, and Arnheim are hardly discussed in it at all.

92. Harry Helson (1925). Psychology of Gestalt. *American Journal of Psychology*, 36, 342-370, 494-526. Harry Helson (1926). Psychology of Gestalt. *American Journal of Psychology*, 37, 25-62, 189-223.

93. Harry Helson (1965). Harry Helson. In E. G. Boring and G. Lindzey (eds.), *A history of psychology in autobiography*, Vol. 5. New York: Appleton-Century-Crofts, pp. 195-230.

94. Helson, "Psychology of Gestalt," p. 342.

95. Harry Helson (1930). *Gestalt Psychology* by Wolfgang Köhler. *American Journal of Psychology*, 41, p. 661.
96. Harry Helson (1933). The fundamental propositions of Gestalt psychology. *Psychological Review*, 40,13-32.
97. W. D. Ellis (1930). *Gestalt psychology and meaning.* Berkeley, CA: Sather Gate.
98. Willis D. Ellis (1930). The Twelfth Congress of German psychologists. *Psychological Bulletin*, 28, 634-639.
99. Kurt Koffka to Molly Harrower, February 13, 1933. Quoted in Molly Harrower (1983). *Kurt Koffka: An unwitting self-portrait.* Gainesville, FL: University of Florida, p. 24.
100. Willis D. Ellis (1938). *A source book of Gestalt psychology.* New York: Humanities Press.
101. Edward Chace Tolman (1952/1968). Edward Chace Tolman. In E. G. Boring, Herbert S. Langfeld, Heinz Werner, and Robert M. Yerkes (eds.), *A history of psychology in autobiography*, vol. 4. New York: Russell and Russell, p. 327.
102. Ibid, p. 329.
103. Edward Chace Tolman (1928). Habit formation and higher mental processes in animals. *Psychological Bulletin*, 25, 24-53.
104. Kurt Koffka (1933). Edward Chace Tolman, *Purposive behavior in animals and men. Psychological Bulletin*, 30, p. 448.
105. Ibid, p. 449.
106. Walter A. Varvel (1934). A Gestalt critique of purposive behaviorism. *Psychological Review*, 41, p. 399.
107. Raymond Holder Wheeler and F. Theodore Perkins (1928). Persistent problems in systematic psychology. IV. Structural versus functional analysis. *Journal of General Psychology*, 1, 91-107. Raymond Holder Wheeler (1930). Configurational learning in goldfish. *Comparative Psychology Monographs*, 7, No. 31, pp. 1-50. Perkins followed up this research with a study of transposition of absolute light intensities by goldfish and determined that insight provided a better explanation of the results than trial and error. F. Theodore Perkins (1931). A further study of configurational learning in goldfish. *Journal of Experimental Psychology*, 14, 508-538.
108. Raymond Holder Wheeler, F. Theodore Perkins and S. Howard Bartley (1931). Errors in recent critiques of Gestalt psychology I. Sources of confusion. *Psychological Review*, 38. 109-136.
109. Raymond Holder Wheeler, F. Theodore Perkins and S. Howard Bartley (1933). Errors in the critiques of Gestalt psychology II. Confused interpretations of the historical approach. *Psychological Review*, 40, 221-245.
110. Raymond Holder Wheeler, F. Theodore Perkins and S. Howard Bartley (1933). Errors in the critiques of Gestalt psychology III. Inconsistencies in Thorndike's system. *Psychological Review*, 40, 303-323.
111. Raymond Holder Wheeler, F. Theodore Perkins and S. Howard Bartley (1933). Errors in the critiques of Gestalt psychology IV. Inconsistencies in Woodworth, Spearman and McDougall, *Psychological Review*, 40, 412-433.
112. Raymond Holder Wheeler (1935). Gestalt psychology in the light of history. *Psychological Review*, 42, p. 548.

113. Raymond Holder Wheeler (1932). *The laws of human nature: A general view of Gestalt psychology.* New York: Appleton. Raymond Holder Wheeler and F. Theodore Perkins (1932). *Principles of mental development: A textbook in educational psychology.* New York: Crowell. Wheeler was not the first to make his assumptions; W. E. Ritter also interpreted Gestalt theory as consistent with holistic organismic theories of biology, cytology, genetics, physiology, and endocrinology. See W. E. Ritter (1919). *The unity of the organism.* Boston: R. G. Badger.

114. Sokal, The Gestalt psychologists in behaviorist America, p. 1247.

115. Wolfgang Köhler (1944). Max Wertheimer: 1880-1943. *Psychological Review*, 51, p. 146.

116. Interview with Anni Hornbostel, November 30, 1968.

117. For a through overview of Hartshorne's theory of sensation and its fate during the behaviorist era, see Wayne Viney (1991). Charles Hartshorne's philosophy and psychology of sensation. In Lewis Edwin Hahn (ed.), *The philosophy of Charles Hartshorne.* The Library of Living Philosophers, Vol. 20. La Salle, IL: Open Court, pp. 91-112.

118. S. W. Fernberger to Max Wertheimer, October 18, 1934, MW-CU. Max Wertheimer to S. W. Fernberger, November 20, 1934, MW-CU.

119. Max Wertheimer to S. W. Fernberger, March 4, 1936, MW-CU. The Society of Experimental Psychologists had been founded in 1904 by Edward Bradford Titchener. At the time, it was "a small, closed group largely composed of his own students; he wanted to call it 'the Fechner club,' but the charter members would not go along with that, and it never had a regular name until Titchener's death [in 1927]. People referred to it as 'the Experimentalists' or even 'Titchener's Experimentalists.' Named the Society of Experimental Psychologists in 1928, it has been a self-conscious, select and exclusive club and continues to flourish as of the present writing. Meeting annually, its membership has been by invitation only and was until recently limited to 50; only the most prominent experimental psychologists have been included among its members." (Michael Wertheimer (2000). *A brief history of psychology*, fourth ed. Fort Worth: Harcourt College Publishers, p. 104.) Membership in the Society continues to be a high honor.

120. E. G. Boring (1938). The Society of Experimental Psychologists, 1904-1938. *American Journal of Psychology*, 51, 410-423.

121. Karl M. Dallenbach (1937). The Northampton meeting of the Society of Experimental Psychologists. *American Journal of Psychology*, 49, p. 487. Karl M. Dallenbach (1941). The New Brunswick meeting of the Society of Experimental Psychologists. *American Journal of Psychology*, 54, p. 295.

122. A. S. Luchins and E. H. Luchins (1988). Max Wertheimer in America: 1933-1943, Part II. *Gestalt Theory*, 10, 134-160; extensive correspondence in MW-CU.

11

Wertheimer's Correspondence with Three Psychologists: Boring, Hull, and Luria

> *You have rendered me very real assistance.... As so often happens, the persons who do not entirely agree with us are the very ones who really help us most.*
> —Clark L. Hull to Max Wertheimer (1936)

Wertheimer had extensive interactions with two of the more visible American psychologists of the 1930s, Edwin Garrigues Boring and Clark L. Hull. They represented two very different prominent viewpoints of the time, both of which were vehemently criticized by the Gestalt psychologists. Boring was a student of Edward Bradford Titchener, and was still attempting to defend a version of the "structuralism" of his mentor—and while that school's influence was declining, Boring's prestigious position as a professor at Harvard University did give him considerable credibility. Hull, at Yale University, was the major post-Watsonian proponent of behaviorism. There was also a brief interchange of correspondence with prominent Soviet psychologist Alexander Romanovich Luria that concerned a memorial volume for Lev Semonovich Vygotskii and that had some interesting and somewhat mysterious features.

The excerpts in this chapter from the previously unpublished Boring-Wertheimer and Hull-Wertheimer correspondence are fairly lengthy and detailed. The reason for their inclusion here is that they provide an unusual perspective on Wertheimer's pattern of personal interaction with two significant American psychologists for whom he had respect despite apparently insurmountable theoretical and epistemological differences. They also provide some information about Wertheimer's (and Boring's) personality and habits of social and professional interaction.

The Boring-Wertheimer Exchange

Edwin Garrigues Boring was born in 1886 to a Quaker family in Philadelphia. As an undergraduate and graduate student at Cornell

University, Boring switched from engineering to psychology and received his Ph.D. under E. B. Titchener in 1911. In a December 14, 1922, letter to Madison Bentley, Boring mentioned his ambivalence about German psychology's preoccupation with Gestalt psychology.[1] Yet Boring did try to bring a Gestalt psychologist to the faculty of Harvard University, and had heard positive reports about Wertheimer from several notable American psychologists, including Robert M. Ogden and Herbert Langfeld of Princeton University.[2] Langfeld wrote Boring a lengthy description of Wertheimer in a March 12, 1927, letter:

> When I think of Wertheimer, I am reminded of an Oriental ascetic or mystic. He has black hair, which he generally wears rather long, a sallow complexion, and a certain dreaminess of countenance. He is in disposition very kind and considerate, and almost soft and effeminate. Yet he is one of the most dynamic men I know, even more than Köhler. When he talks, his eyes flash and he holds his audience spell-bound, even though he says things at times that the uninitiated must certainly consider rank nonsense. I might even liken him to a religious leader. He is unusual, one does not often meet his type in our country in academic circles, but his is a pleasant and interesting queerness. His students are devoted to him, and I imagine he has more influence than anyone else in the laboratory. He has not the conventional social graces. He is shy, and I think prefers not to meet people unless he can talk to them on scientific subjects. From what I have written, it is evident that he is not of the physically aggressive type. Intellectually, however, he is apt to be very dogmatic and insistent, but seldom if ever to the extent of rudeness. One feels that he is entirely sincere, that he never talks for effect, and that his sole aim in life is to seek the truth.... I never appreciated Wertheimer in the old days. I thought him too vague and erratic, but I changed my mind at Groningen. I had a long talk with him, and was greatly impressed by the flood of original...ideas, and by his grasp of experimental methods and technique.[3]

By the time that Wertheimer arrived in America, Boring had become established as one of the most influential American psychologists. For many years, Boring had been an active leader in the American Psychological Association; he was its president in 1928. He was also a major figure in the elite Society of Experimental Psychologists, founded by E. B. Titchener in 1904.[4] On occasion, even though the Society was dominated by structural psychologists, visiting psychologists were invited as guests to Society meetings, including Koffka and Köhler in 1925.[5] Following Titchener's death in 1927, the Society of Experimental Psychologists was reorganized to include a broader representation of experimental psychologists in addition to adherents of structuralism.[6] The board of the Society made a conscious effort to seek prominent Gestalt psychologists for membership.

Koffka was elected to membership in the Society in 1929. On December 12, 1933, Boring wrote Wertheimer, inviting him to attend the April 1934 meeting of the Society.[7] Wertheimer had been in America for only a short time, but he wrote back that he would be pleased to attend.[8] Kurt Lewin joined Wertheimer as a guest at the meeting.[9] The first personal encounter between Boring and Wertheimer must have been positive, because several months later Boring wrote that "I still remember with great pleasure your visit to Cambridge in the spring, and I hope there will be many more."[10]

A small part of the extensive correspondence between Boring and Wertheimer concerned Boring's review of Koffka's 1935 book *Principles of Gestalt Psychology*. Boring had already published a fairly positive review of Köhler's *Gestalt Psychology* in 1930 and had written Wertheimer that the book will "make quite an impression."[11] But he was much more critical of Koffka's 1935 book. Among several objections, Boring was disappointed with Koffka's treatment of isomorphism.[12] Hoping to develop a better understanding of this concept, Boring turned to Wertheimer.[13] Boring engaged in a lengthy, warm, and respectful correspondence with Wertheimer that was aimed specifically at an effort to clarify the Gestalt concept of isomorphism.

On September 12, 1935, Boring wrote that he was "bothered about isomorphism. I do not believe that it is right, and I have now read Koffka's account, his argument for it, and I am even more doubtful. There is much more to be said, and someone must sometime say it effectively. It would be rather nice if *you* were that person. You would present it as a development of a concept which you have fathered, of course."[14] During the course of the letter, Boring argued that isomorphism is a version of the "constancy hypothesis" because it assumes that the relationship between a local stimulus and a percept is constant. But Wertheimer viewed this argument as untenable; the constancy hypothesis, that is, that there is a constant relationship between local parts of a stimulus and corresponding local parts of the resulting percept, Wertheimer and his colleagues argued, is disproved by many Gestalt phenomena, including perceptual contrast and the perceptual constancies such as size constancy, brightness constancy, and shape constancy. The constancy hypothesis has, for the Gestalt theorists, nothing to do with isomorphism. Wertheimer answered Boring seven days later:

> My dear Boring, Thank you very much for your letter and the interesting offprint. I shall add only a few words about isomorphism. Gestalt isomorphism does not claim any "isomorphic correlation between any two points in the physical system" and therefore your argument does not hit our isomorphism directly. I suppose you turn it against our isomorphism by your theory of consciousness or direct experience, which you developed in an earlier paper. If that is so, then the issue between us is not isomorphism but direct experience. For you might be willing to admit that our theory of the latter is compatible with isomorphism.[15]

This letter suggests that the crux of the issue between Boring and the Gestalt approach was the nature of direct experience rather than the theory of isomorphism. Wertheimer must have been frustrated, and unclear about how to respond further in a productive way to Boring's perspectives. Perhaps they might have made more progress if they had focused further on what each meant by "direct experience." At any rate, Wertheimer was concerned by Boring's insistence that direct experience consists of a one-to-one relationship between psychophysical stimulus dimensions and sensory attributes, a view which the Gestalt psychologists believed they had successfully disproven in many experimental studies. Wertheimer clearly voiced such concerns in another letter a few days later to Boring:

> I had been under the impression that on this theoretical point we—you and we—were now agreed. Now, we had never asserted isomorphism in the sense, defined by you, of a "one-one correlation." What, I asked myself, leads you to the conclusion that here should lie grounds for making isomorphism in general suspect? Now, it seems that by isomorphism you here understand and contest something quite different from what the isomorphism thesis of the [G]estalt theory is.[16]

Wertheimer pointed out in this letter that two patterns can be similar or isomorphic in the Gestalt sense regardless of numerical differences or lack of one-to-one correspondence, and provided the compelling example of a circle made up of twenty versus one composed of twenty-two dots: both circles are equally circular, and hence isomorphic. Isomorphism refers to molar (that is, large-scale), not molecular, processes. Wertheimer ended this letter with the hope that it "may help toward the removal of misunderstandings."

At the time that Wertheimer's letter arrived, Boring was "soaking in Koffka's book," which he was reviewing for the *Psychological Bulletin,* and mentioned that "Now I have gone over your letter and I have come to the conclusion that I do not understand the concept as you intend it. I want, therefore, to get hold of Pratt, Beebe-Center and Stevens and have a talk about it at this end, and then write you when I shall have given the thing serious enough consideration so as not to be too completely stupid."[17] Boring did discuss isomorphism with Carrol Pratt, a professor at Harvard from 1923 to 1937, John Gilbert Beebe-Center who was interested in psychophysics and the psychology of feeling and sensation, and who spent his entire career at Harvard, and S. Smith Stevens, a former student of Boring's, who was on the Harvard faculty and who was also skeptical of isomorphism. Together with Boring, they were all members of the Society of Experimental Psychologists.

On October 24, 1935, Boring reported that "Pratt and Beebe-Center and Stevens and I had our little dinner on isomorphism last Monday and now I want to write you. Of course I do not attempt to speak for the group, but I speak for myself in the light of that conversation and your letter. There seem to me to be several things that I should like to put before you for consideration."[18] Boring distinguished four primary issues of concern: isomorphism in general, the kinds of isomorphism, psychoneural isomorphism, and insightful isomorphism. Despite Wertheimer's hope that he could get Boring to understand isomorphism from the Gestalt perspective, it was evident that Boring continued to define the Gestalt position in physical, concrete, one-to-one terms incompatible with the Gestalt view.

Wertheimer, perhaps exasperated by Boring's continuing misunderstanding, did not respond to Boring's letter. More than a month later, Boring confessed to being bothersome:

> Dear Wertheimer: The greatest nuisances in the world are the people who insist on talking or writing to you at length about matters in which you are not at the present moment interested, and who then want you to do something about them! I am certainly not going to keep plaguing you about isomorphism. I got to thinking about it and wanted to get clear, and the final result was that long letter to you, which was almost too long to merit an answer.[19]

Boring still found the Gestalt concept of isomorphism inherently muddled, but he welcomed further opportunities to exchange ideas with Wertheimer:

> I wanted to mention to you...that Langfeld—I was talking about isomorphism to him—really suggested that the *Psychological Review* would like to have a symposium on the topic. I said that I did not know who there would be to contribute. If I wrote my article, then either you or Koffka might wish to write (I think Köhler avoids discussion of this sort). But Koffka has just quite sensibly preferred not to bother to comment on my review of his book, and you probably feel the same way about my letter. Thus I told Langfeld that I did not believe he would get a symposium although I should be very glad to see it happen. Perhaps Langfeld will ask you if I do my article finally, but that is between you and him.[20]

In a postscript, Boring asked "If I write my article, would you like to see it in manuscript, or would you rather not be bothered?"

Five days later, Wertheimer wrote back:

> Dear Boring, My best thanks for your letter of Dec. 5. "Bothering me?" No, no; I welcome the opportunity for real mutual understanding between us. ... I, too, have been thinking seriously on how these misunderstandings came about and perhaps one of the reasons may be that possibly you consider in your letter only some of general formulations in English books of Gestalt psychology and not the very concrete problems in the basic special investigations—otherwise I can hardly understand some statements in your letter. I think it would be very much easier to clear up the matter in a verbal personal discussion—perhaps you are coming sometime soon to New York or through New York, then I would like to see you.... The idea of Langfeld about a symposium is very nice and I would like very much if it can be accomplished.[21]

Wertheimer's interest in meeting with Boring in person was consistent with Boring's belief that the accounts of isomorphism in English were too general and Wertheimer's conviction that the experiments published in

German articles were very concrete. An informal meeting might permit Wertheimer to describe some of these studies, and might help overcome linguistic barriers that could be limiting the degree of understanding between Boring and himself. In response to Wertheimer's letter, Boring wrote "This is jolly! But New York is an awful place to get anything done, because there is so much to do that everything that is not absolutely essential goes by the way. But we shall see." By early 1936, Wertheimer had agreed to give a lecture at Harvard University. Boring invited Max and Anni to stay at his house.[22] Boring was still eager to have Wertheimer publish a reply to his manuscript on isomorphism:

> As you know, I have hoped that I could pique you into writing an article, perhaps in reply to this one of mine, setting forth some of the fundamental principles of Gestalt psychology as they appear in the isomorphic relation. I know that it is very difficult to get you to write papers, but I am still hoping that I might succeed.[23]

Wertheimer did not commit to writing an article on isomorphism but did mention to Boring that "I am looking forward with great pleasure to seeing you and the other friends very soon at Harvard."[24]

Boring did meet with Wertheimer during the latter's 1936 lecture trip to Harvard and concluded that their

> discussion was very good fun and we agreed on most points when either accepted the other's premises. But we did not agree on all, and perhaps the widest divergences lay in our opinion about the importance of publishing that paper. You advised me not to publish, but to hitch the idea onto an experimental result. On the other hand, our conference convinced me that the paper ought to be published.... I believe that all psychologists in theorizing believe that they are close to experimental fact, and that the persons who do not like their theorizing believe that they are remote from experimental fact and indulging in mere verbal play. Take Koffka's book. At least a third of that seems to me too remote from experimental fact to be important, but you can not expect Koffka to believe that. And so conversely about me and isomorphism. You see? The only independent judgments that I have are the (favorably prejudiced) persons here have wanted the discussion of this and that point added to the paper (that is why the paper has grown so long), and Langfeld urges me, after my discussion of its thesis with him, to send it to the *Psychological Review*. Actually, I should not be wasting valuable space with it; it must be as good as much which the *Psychological Review* prints.[25]

After outlining his reasons for wanting to publish the manuscript, Boring wrote,

> I told you that I should not publish without writing you, so here I am writing you. I have probably bored you, because I think this problem does not seem to you as important as it does to me. You must let me publish, because I want to. I

still wish that I could pique you into published discussion of the issue, but it is as unfair for me to try to argue you into publishing as it would be for you to try to argue me out of it.... Still, I shall not send my paper off to Langfeld right away. I shall wait for some early, if brief, reply from you.... I am still angry with the fate that let me see so little of you when you were here. It was not reasonable. And we should have had time to talk about other things where we agree better than we do concerning the usefulness of the concept isomorphism.[26]

Wertheimer answered less than a week later:

Dear Boring: Your letter involves again a lot of problems. Now, at first, certainly I do not want to say anything against publication! By all means publish the article. My only wish was that the article should deal with the concrete problem (and in a productive way). I had the feeling very strongly in our discussion that we reached a real understanding about the concrete problem.... I also was sorry that we had not a longer time for discussion. My best greetings and wishes and please tell my regards to Mrs. Boring and to the colleagues.[27]

Boring and Wertheimer obviously did not reach a full understanding even during their personal exchange at Harvard. This outcome may in part have been due to language problems, but more likely it was the result of the totally different set of implicit assumptions of the two because of their radically different orientations to psychology and psychological research. Wertheimer's insistence that Boring tie his discussion to concrete experimental results rather than talk in philosophical generalities seems, perhaps surprisingly, to have had little effect on Boring. The correspondence also suggests that it seemed to be important to Boring to appear open and affable, and to avoid personal confrontation if possible. He may have tried to minimize points of disagreement during their discussion, which may have given Wertheimer the impression that they had reached more of an understanding than they actually had. Clearly they were still far apart in their thinking. The two men met again in September 1936 and Boring wrote soon thereafter that:

With the Conference terminating today, I have no hesitation in saying that you were the most interesting person I met this week. I think it will go some way toward clearing up misunderstanding if I say that I think that some difference of view between Koffka and me, and perhaps between you and me, has been caused by different notions of the concept of immediate experience or whatever coordinate term is used for phenomenal data.... My notion of immediate experience was implanted firmly in Titchener's laboratory. To have experience is to be aware of having it.... Just one other point. I think of the crucial instance in this discussion as being Koffka's example of the book on the table: you see the table as continuous and not as interrupted by the book; you see two things in the same place; the table behind the book may have no color, but no matter, since the phi-phenomenon has no color either. Koffka's behavioral object, the continuous table, is to me a meaning, just as Koffka wants it to be. For me the perception of continuity in the table is a matter of knowledge and not of immediate experience, but I think now that this difference may lie in the time limits which can be set up for the given. In other words, you never can catch the immediate but only photograph it as just past, unless you define immediacy loosely in the way that we define the present. Then the looser you get, the more generous you are to the data, the wider the present, why then the more knowledge is brought in under the concept of the given.[28]

Although Boring hoped that he "might be clearing up a difference between us" with this letter, his adherence to the classic structuralist doctrine of sensation and meaning was probably an insurmountable obstacle to his ever being able to take on the Gestalt perspective. The difference between "the content of immediate experience" and "the phenomenologically given" could hardly be expressed more simply than in this example of the perception of a book on a table. Boring's and Wertheimer's basic epistemological convictions were incompatible.

Although associated with radically different systematic positions, Boring and Wertheimer displayed tolerance for each other's ideas. While Boring went through alternating periods of appreciation and disdain for Köhler (not to mention Koffka), the letters suggest that he may have been genuinely fond of Wertheimer. In his characteristically blunt fashion, Boring later wrote that Wertheimer published the least of the three principal Gestaltists, but that "it is interesting to observe that the originality of these three men varied inversely with their productivity."[29] As for Wertheimer, he clearly respected Boring's scholarly work and his position in American psychology, if not his views on psychology. In a September 1925 letter to his father, years before the correspondence on isomorphism, Wertheimer mentioned that he had just read Helson's articles on Gestalt theory, and described the author as "the student of the most significant living American psychologist."[30] One can only speculate whether Wertheimer altered his opinion after interacting in person with Boring in America.

Boring did publish his article in the *Psychological Review*. Although Wertheimer's 1912 paper was accorded passing reference in the 1936 article, Boring did not acknowledge the extensive exchange of correspondence. Boring's structuralist interpretation of the dynamic Gestalt conception of isomorphism permeates the entire article. Wertheimer did not accept the invitation to publish a rejoinder, but perhaps from his perspective Boring's article was so riddled with misconceptions and misunderstandings that he had no idea how to organize or even begin a rebuttal.[31]

Some American psychologists concurred with Boring's evaluation of isomorphism. Walter S. Neff of Cornell University, another representative of the Titchenerian perspective, was critical of Wertheimer's brand of isomorphism:

In Wertheimer's [short-circuit theory of isomorphism] we see the prototype of the physiological theories made so much of by the configurationists.... It merely represents another more or less plausible guess as to what goes on in the central nervous system as the physiological correlate of psychological function. Attempted criticism of it would be pointless and an arbitrary denial of its truth would be dogmatic.[32]

Neff further concluded that "those familiar with Titchener's systematic position can readily understand that certain of Wertheimer's statements would be very repugnant to him."[33] But Titchenerian (including Boring's) views of Wertheimer's ideas about isomorphism may have been equally problematic for Wertheimer.

Following the exchange with Boring, Wertheimer of course continued to discuss isomorphism, although he had not published on the concept since 1912. He frequently referred to isomorphism in his classes; and a letter from a Japanese psychologist, Katsumi Nakamura, formerly a graduate student at the New School, wrote Wertheimer in 1935 that he had recently published an article on isomorphism in a mathematical logic journal.[34]

The Hull-Wertheimer Exchange

As was true for the structuralist Boring, it would at first seem unlikely that Clark Leonard Hull would have solicited scholarly advice from Max Wertheimer since Hull was closely identified with the behaviorist camp. According to a 1988 article in the *Journal of the History of the Behavioral Sciences*, Hull felt a need to "distance and differentiate himself from the Gestalt school."[35] Yet he was clearly interested in the work of the Gestalt psychologists, and indeed praised the school and its contributions extensively in print. For example, in the 1937 edition of *The World Book Encyclopedia*, Clark Hull wrote a four-page item on "Modern Movements in Psychology" that contained discussions of animism, structuralism, Gestalt psychology, behaviorism, and psychoanalysis. Hull devoted approximately one-third of the article to a favorable review of Gestalt theory, and two of the three illustrations accompanying the article were derived from Gestalt literature.[36] In his friendly (if not entirely accurate) discussion, Hull wrote,

[The Gestalt] movement was originated by M. Wertheimer and his followers, notably W. Köhler and Kurt Koffka.... They...reject sensations as elements from which experiences are made. They use introspection to a considerable extent, however, though rejecting it as an instrument of analysis. They have a strong interest in the purposive aspect of human nature, agreeing with the animists and vitalists that purposes can never conceivably be accounted for by mechanism.... While the most noteworthy work of the Gestalt psychologists has been in the field of seen groupings of figures and visual illusions of movement, they have carried out ingenious experiments in many other fields.[37]

In January 1934, Hull turned personally to Wertheimer to solicit suggestions from him concerning a manuscript entitled "The Conflicting Psychologies of Learning"; the manuscript had implications for Gestalt theory, and Hull made his reason for consulting Wertheimer explicit: "I turn to you who are recognized by all as the original fountainhead of Gestalt theory."[38] Specifically, Hull requested quantitative experimental evidence from Wertheimer or other Gestalt theorists that would support "rigorous deductions" regarding their conviction that wholes are more primary and fundamental than parts. During the course of the letter, he implied that Gestalt theory is not based on a rigorous logical foundation, and challenged Wertheimer to produce some empirical findings that lend validity to the assumptions of Gestalt theory. Hull's challenge ended, however, with a polite and cordial note: "I assure you that I shall be deeply grateful for any remarks which you may care to make regarding the matters contained in my manuscript. I recall with pleasure the conversation I had with you at the dinner last spring of the New York Branch of the American Psychological Association in New York City."

As in his interactions with Boring, Wertheimer preferred to meet with Hull in person rather than write a formal review of the manuscript; indeed it was proposed that Wertheimer debate Hull in public in the presence of students. Hull wrote to Wertheimer:

> The only drawback which I can see in this plan is that when auditors are present even very philosophical persons sometimes become advocates rather than scientists in such a discussion. I frankly confess that I am personally a victim to such circumstances, however much I deplore such actions. It seems to me that the attitude of scientists meeting as we are to meet should be a mutual giving of aid in the search for truth.[39]

Encouraged by Hull's letter, Wertheimer assured Hull that

> I believe that we will find a great many points on which we are in complete agreement. I am looking forward with great pleasure to this discussion with you, (I agree with you in your sentence that scientific discussions have to be a mutual giving of aid in the search for truth.)... I may add in short that Gestalt Psychology is not founded on dogmatic metaphysical presuppositions.[40]

Wertheimer and Hull did meet in January 1935 and were joined by several students, including Edwin B. Newman. Two days later, Hull thanked Wertheimer for his "valuable criticism of my manuscript."[41] But Hull wrote the same day to Newman:

> I recall the repeated assertion made by Wertheimer and, possibly, by yourself, that at various times the Gestalt psychologists have put forward rigorous deductions of psychological phenomena based on their system of postulates. In this connection I am particularly anxious to secure some of this work produced

by one of their best-known leaders, such as Koffka, Köhler, Lewin or Wertheimer himself. The reason I am asking for this is that I frankly doubt whether the Gestalt people have really ever produced anything in the field of learning which satisfies what we all agree must be the characteristics of a genuine scientific theory as distinguished from metaphysics.... What I am doing is asking for the evidence.[42]

In a March 1, 1935 letter, Newman answered Hull:

> I felt that in your letter you had shifted the ground of the argument a little from what we had understood that evening at Jackson's.... Wertheimer's point was to deny your charge that there had never been any rigorous deductions and predictions which could be compared with the procedures of physics. It would be a little extravagant to maintain that no one had ever been logical or scientific who hadn't constructed a system of postulates.... [W]e agree that such a formulation as yours for learning was eminently helpful and desirable. It seems to me, however, just a bit dangerous to characterize anything else than a system of formal postulates metaphysics. I have never seen a system of formal postulates. I doubt very much if you could find them in the work of such men as Einstein, Bohr, Planck, or Heisenberg.[43]

Despite Hull's continuing concerns about the scientific integrity of Gestalt psychology and misgivings about the "metaphysical aspects" of the theory, his respect for Wertheimer's judgment was unmistakable. In 1935, Wertheimer lectured at Yale University and attended a dinner in honor of Yale's president, James R. Angell, who was also a prominent figure in the functionalist school of psychology. While Wertheimer was in New Haven, he and Hull engaged in an extensive debate about Gestalt theory and Hull's model of a formal hypothetico-deductive system of adaptive behavior. Hull was sufficiently impressed with Wertheimer that he asked Wertheimer to review a draft of his proposed American Psychological Association presidential address of 1936 on "Mind, Mechanism and Adaptive Behavior." Wertheimer studied the address and offered twelve suggestions to Hull.

In an October 1936 letter to Wertheimer, Hull asserted that approximately one-half of Wertheimer's comments, especially suggestions about the "direction of clarification and emphasis," were incorporated into Hull's new draft. In appreciation of Wertheimer's "very thoughtful letter," Hull graciously wrote

> I wish to thank you for your kindness in writing me the detailed criticism of my Presidential Address. Your letter came in time for me to use it effectively in my final revision.... You have rendered me very real assistance, despite my failure to agree with you wholly in your views. As so often happens, the persons who do not entirely agree with us are the very ones who really help us most.[44]

Hull's presidential address, presented at the forty-fourth annual convention of the American Psychological Association in Hanover, New

Hampshire in 1936 and published in the *Psychological Review* the following year, is an early version of the hypothetico-deductive model that would play such a fundamental part in his later learning theory.[45] Modest though the change in Hull's thought brought about by Wertheimer's suggestions may have been, Hull acknowledged Wertheimer's contribution in a footnote to the paper.[46]

Wertheimer's unpublished correspondence with Boring and Hull is striking in that it appears to contain no trace of the animosity and tension that characterized Köhler's exchanges with both men. The Boring-Wertheimer and Hull-Wertheimer correspondence is also noteworthy in its demonstration of the mutual respect and collegiality of these individuals, despite radically different perspectives on psychology.

Mystery of a Missing Manuscript:
Wertheimer's Correspondence with Alexander Luria

During 1936, Wertheimer also corresponded with a prominent Russian psychologist, Alexander Luria, who was trying to prepare a memorial volume for another illustrious Russian psychologist, Lev S. Vygotskii, who died in 1934. Four letters went from Luria to Wertheimer, and two from Wertheimer to Luria; all are in German, though Luria was in the Soviet Union and Wertheimer in the United States at the time. Two of the letters happen to be part of the Max Wertheimer collection at the New York Public Library (MW-NY) and four part of the collection at the University of Colorado (MW-CU). Their content, and the outcome of the exchange, are revealing about Wertheimer's working style—and also about the political situation in the Soviet Union at that time.

Vygotskii was born in Russia in 1896 and was an outstanding student at Moscow University, where he earned a joint degree in law and "philological studies" (literature and cultural history). He published his first articles of literary criticism in 1915 and earned his doctorate in 1925, although his dissertation was not published until 40 years later in the posthumous book *The Psychology of Art*. Vygotskii's interests were exceptionally broad; in addition to literary criticism, he published works on thinking, language, psychopathology, and developmental psychology. Vygotskii conducted some of the earliest studies of concept formation in schoolchildren with a test of abstract and concrete thinking, a test which is still widely used throughout the world today. He was severely critical of Ivan Pavlov and other Russian physiologists and reflexologists who sought to reduce consciousness to material causality. His more than 180 publications were generated in a remarkably brief period; in 1934, at the early age of 37, Vygotskii succumbed to tuberculosis while residing in Moscow.

Luria was born in Kazan in 1902 and revered Vygotskii as his mentor, although he was only a scant six years Vygotskii's junior. After an early interest in psychoanalysis, Luria began publishing with Vygotskii in 1924, and by the 1930s was an established Soviet neuropsychologist who had developed widely-discussed developmental and cognitive theories with a holistic bent, and who had spent some time studying in Germany with Wolfgang Köhler and his colleagues. He became a consulting editor for the *Journal of Genetic Psychology*, in which, not coincidentally, several of his articles on Vygotskii appeared, helping to generate international renown for Vygotskii's work on developmental cognitive psychology and psychophysiology. Luria's 1935 obituary on Vygotskii too was published in the *Journal of Genetic Psychology*. Luria worked on brain organization and speech function, and in later years did ground-breaking research on the cognitive deficits induced by brain injuries, and on the thought processes of expert chess players and of a famous mnemonist; in all, Luria published more than 300 scientific articles during his lifetime. And, as noted, early in his career Luria was sufficiently interested in the Gestalt school of psychology to have visited Berlin to study with the Gestalt psychologists there.

Luria's letters in the series are all handwritten clearly and legibly in ink. The sheets on which Luria wrote his missives are printed with a variety of different letterheads, which in three of the four documents are crossed out at least in part, with a new address added in ink. The two letters from Wertheimer to Luria are carbon copies of documents produced on a Monarch typewriter that has a simple, distinctive font, a typewriter that Wertheimer acquired soon after he arrived in the United States in September 1933.

The first letter in the series, on a sheet with letterhead printed all in capitals (Prof. Alexander R. Luria, 13 Frunse Street, Moscow, USSR), was redundantly dated Febr. 20.II.36. After the formal and polite listing of the name of the addressee and salutation that were standard at the time (Mr. Prof. Dr. Max Wertheimer, Most honored Herr Professor), the text of the letter, in its entirety, is as follows.

> Permit me to invite you to participate in a memorial volume for Prof. Vygotskii, the Russian psychologist who died too early. The deceased, whom we already lost two years ago, was the most prominent Russian psychologist. He devoted his life to the study of the development of human consciousness and its specific attributes; the theory of the development of word meaning was one of his especially valuable contributions.
>
> Many of our disciplinary colleagues knew him personally and loved him deeply; many of them—[Kurt] Koffka, [Kurt] Lewin, [Karl] Lashley, [Jean] Piaget, and also [Adhémar] Gelb, [Arnold] Gesell, [Karl] Bühler, etc. will contribute to the memorial volume.
>
> If I ask for your contribution to this volume—which will bear the title "Psychological Development and Decline"—it is because the deceased especially valued your work and because he was so fond of your studies of the Gestalt psychology of perception and especially of logic.

It would give us great joy if you would be willing to send us a work from your own pen for this volume within the next few months.

Luria ended by writing "With many greetings," and used the standard closing formula, "Your most obliged Al. Luria."

It turns out that Kurt Lewin encouraged Wertheimer to accept Luria's invitation to prepare a manuscript for the Vygotskii memorial volume. A letter to Wertheimer from Lewin dated March 10, 1936, in English, begins, "I just received the letter from Luria. I write in English to avoid some delay. I have known Viegotzky (sic) personally and I think it would be nice if you could contribute something. He certainly was a first rate man and scientist."[47] The letter goes on to mention some other matters not related to the Luria-Vygotskii theme (such as Lewin's contemplating a possible move from the State University of Iowa to Palestine).

It is not clear what Lewin meant by "the letter from Luria." It is unlikely that it was the same letter of invitation to contribute to the Vygotskii memorial volume that Luria had sent to Wertheimer during the preceding month, since Luria explicitly mentioned in his February letter to Wertheimer that Lewin was one of the psychologists who had already agreed to contribute. Perhaps Luria had written to Lewin, knowing that Wertheimer had not been prolific in his writings, and may even have asked Lewin whether he might be willing to add his recommendation that Wertheimer take the trouble to prepare an essay for the volume. At any rate, Lewin was clearly aware that Luria had asked Wertheimer to do so, and did add his own encouragement.

An earlier communication in German from Lewin to Wertheimer in October 1929 (MW-NY) reported at some length on Lewin's impressions of the International Congress of Psychology in New Haven, Connecticut, held during the preceding month, September, and explicitly mentioned Luria. He preceded his report on the congress with a query about a manuscript of Luria's handed at the 1929 congress to Lewin by Luria for possible publication in *Psychologische Forschung*, the chief journal of the Gestalt psychologists. The manuscript had a clearly Gestalt theme, showing that the task of making a single response to a single stimulus can be performed by a child only at a much later developmental stage than much more complex tasks. At any rate, the 1929 letter establishes that Lewin knew both Vygotskii and Luria personally, and Lewin's 1936 letter explicitly encouraged Wertheimer to contribute to the memorial volume.

Wertheimer's answer to Luria is dated almost two months after Luria's initial invitation: April 18, 1936. It is not known whether Luria's letter may have been delivered late, or whether Wertheimer—as he did on other occasions with mail that made requests of him—delayed answering the letter until he had a chance to think extensively about his response. The typed carbon of Wertheimer's April 18 letter gives the return address of Wertheimer's home, 12 The Circle, New Rochelle, NY, and begins:

> Dear Prof. Luria,
>   Many thanks for your letter; I was pleased to hear from you again." This sentence makes clear that there must have been earlier correspondence between Luria and Wertheimer, but that correspondence has not yet been located. A later letter from Luria suggests that Luria's visit to Berlin in 1929 may have occurred just after Wertheimer had moved from Berlin to the University of Frankfurt, so it is unlikely that the two ever met in person, unless such a meeting occurred at a convention that both attended. At any rate, no documents in the Max Wertheimer archives in either Boulder or New York suggest that the two met, nor is there any correspondence between the two in either depository aside from the 1936 interchanges summarized here.

Wertheimer continues,

> I would like very much to comply with your request to send a contribution to a memorial volume for Prof. Vygotski: I hope to be able to find some time soon and send you a brief manuscript. Your comment that Prof. Vygotski was especially interested in my logic studies was pleasing to me—I plan to send a small work in the field of logic (or the psychology of thinking); (I must confess that I don't know how something like that might fit with the title of the book that you mentioned).
>   I hope to find some time for it quickly; I would like very much to do it.
>   —Every now and then I hear of you and your studies through friends and of course I haven't had a letter from you in a long time; I would love to know how things are going for you and how your studies are progressing.

After this additional reference to earlier correspondence, Wertheimer echoes Luria's earlier friendly closing by writing, "With many greetings, your." The carbon of that letter contains, not surprisingly, no signature, so it is not known whether he simply wrote "Wertheimer" or "Max Wertheimer" or still something else.

The delay between Wertheimer's April 18 letter to Luria and Luria's response on May 9 was shorter than the delay between Luria's initial letter and Wertheimer's answer. Luria's May 9, 1936, handwritten letter to Wertheimer (MW-NY) is on a sheet with printed letterhead in English that reads: "I.N. Fedorow, M.D., Director"; "I.P. Rosenkow, M.D., Scientific Director"; "Union of Soviet Socialist Republics, The Council of People's Commissars"; "All-Union Institute of Experimental Medicine, Moscow, Voronzovo Polje 14." The last street address is crossed out in ink, and Luria wrote instead "Frunse Str. 13, W. 29.," presumably his home address in Moscow, and "9.V.1936." The salutation of the letter, to "Herrn Prof. Dr. M. Wertheimer, New York," is this time somewhat less formal: "Most honored Herr Wertheimer." The letter is a thoughtful reply to Wertheimer's request for information about what Luria and his students were doing. It begins,

With great joy I received your letter; it is a great honor for us to receive a manuscript of yours; we will eagerly await your sending of it; a work in the field of logic or the psychology of thinking will fit the volume superbly.

Thus Luria did not share Wertheimer's concern about whether Wertheimer's essay would be appropriate for a book the theme of which was "psychological development and decline." Luria next says,

It is true that I haven't written to you in a long time; when I was in Berlin in 1929 I was unable to meet you; I am therefore extraordinarily pleased that you are expressing an interest in all we are doing.

Once again, there is acknowledgment of earlier correspondence. Luria continues,

At the moment I am occupied experimentally with two questions; one concerns the general laws of psychological development; we are interested primarily in how during psychological development the meaningful representation of the world (which we see in the meaning of action and language) evolves, how in the course of the learning process there occurs a reorganization of the world of meaning and of psychological functions, and how learning can lead to a reorganization of the interrelation of the psychological functions. We have succeeded, with artificial intervention in identical twins, in obtaining very interesting displacements of psychological structures.

The second [issue] in which I am primarily engaged is the destruction of the world of meaning and of the construction of psychological functions with brain damage. Here too we succeeded in finding methods of analysis of the meaning of a word, of the living semantic syntax of language, which have become a good indicator of the decline of brain capability and which show a lawful deterioration with brain injuries. The pathological semantics, syntax, and functional structures of the psyche constitute the second part of the problem field with which we are very concerned here.

I would be most pleased to send you our studies—when they are published.

I now permit myself to greet you especially heartily and once again to express my thanks to you.

Luria closes with "Your most obliged Al. Luria."

Wertheimer apparently did not reply to this informative communication. After almost two months elapsed, and more than two months since Wertheimer's acknowledgment that he would try to prepare a manuscript for the memorial volume, Luria still had not heard anything further from Wertheimer. On July 5, 1936, Luria wrote an anxious, brief reminder. The letterhead is the same formal one, printed in English, that Luria used for his May 9 letter, again with the street address crossed out in ink, and the address "Frunse Str. 13, 1, 29." written in instead. The opening is the same as before: "Herrn Prof. Dr. M. Wertheimer, New York. Most honored Herr Wertheimer." The first of the three sentences composing the entire letter politely but insistently asserts, "It was extraordinarily pleasant for me to learn from your letter that a work from your pen for the memorial volume will arrive." The next sentence is succinct: "But no manuscript has yet arrived." The last sentence was a plea: "Since the material is already almost complete, —I would very much like to ask you to send your work to us—if possible—within this month." The letter again closes with "Your most obliged Al. Luria."

Given the rapidity with which Luria responded to Wertheimer's earlier communication, Luria's July 5 letter may have been received by Wertheimer before Wertheimer composed his next missive, dated July 16. Indeed, possibly it was the final goad needed to make Wertheimer fulfill his promise. A carbon copy of the July 16, 1936 typewritten letter from Wertheimer to Luria (MW-NY) is distinctly apologetic in tone. Wertheimer writes,

> Dear Herr Luria,
>
> Enclosed I am sending you my little manuscript for the memorial volume. Unfortunately I was unable to do so sooner. If it is too late, I would be very sorry. If it is not too late, I would ask you please to send me reprints after it is printed, if that would be possible. (I would of course be grateful if—by any chance—you could send me a copy of the book.)
>
> In case you need an institutional affiliation for me for the publication, it is as follows: I am a professor in the Graduate Faculty at the New School for Social Research, New York.
>
> Many greetings, and I would be delighted to receive a letter from you soon again.

There the letter ends, and without any closing salutation or greeting. No manuscript or carbon of a manuscript was with the carbon of this letter in the New York Public Library archives, and the letter itself contains no information about the title, the length, or the content of the manuscript, other than that Wertheimer himself considered it "little."

This time Luria took his time in responding. His letter, the last in this series, is dated just over two months later than the cover letter Wertheimer sent with his manuscript: September 19, 1936. Once again Luria used printed letterhead stationery; this time, again in English, the letterhead reads "Department of Psychology, Stoenna 16, Kharkow, U.S.S.R." As before, Luria crossed part of it out, and inserted instead, "13 Frunse Str. Moscow." But he also added a further return address in ink, "Gelehrtenheim [literally, "scholars' home"], Teberda, Caucasus." The letter contains a total of five sentences. "Most honored Herr Wertheimer" is the salutation, and the first paragraph reports that Luria had received the manuscript: "Please accept my heartiest thanks for your letter and manuscript. It arrived on time and it is a great honor and joy for us to be permitted to include it in the memorial volume." Luria adds, in response to Wertheimer's request, "Of course I will take care of reprints for you." But no such reprints have been located either in the collection of Max Wertheimer papers at the New York Public Library or in the collection in Boulder.

The rest of Luria's letter reads, "Now I send you my heartiest greetings from the beautiful Caucasus Mountains, where I am spending my summer vacation. Once more I thank you very much for the manuscript and send my heartiest greetings." The missive ends with "Your devoted Al. Luria."

The letter provides no information about the manuscript, other than that Luria received it. And that is all the material that appears to be extant about the mysterious manuscript. But further research has uncovered some relevant external history, provided a few additional parts that fit into the puzzle, and raised some additional questions.

The most innocent hypothesis about the missing manuscript is that it was actually published, but that insufficient efforts have been made to locate a record of its publication. Several reference librarians made a systematic attempt to find a bibliographic record of the Vygotskii memorial volume by searching both computerized and printed national and international databases. This attempt yielded no further sign of the volume. Granted, not every Russian or Soviet publication made it into western bibliographic records, but it would seem that a publication of this potential significance, to which a number of highly visible western psychologists contributed, would be recorded in the west somewhere. Published bibliographies of all of the other psychologists who Luria had said contributed to the volume (Bühler, Gelb, Gesell, Koffka, Lashley, Lewin, and Piaget) were also examined, and no reference was found in any of them to the Vygotskii memorial volume or to an essay any of them had written for such a volume. Correspondence was also initiated with several major libraries in Russia, asking if they could help in the effort to locate the book, but no responses were received from any of them.

The failure to locate any bibliographic record of any kind raises the question of whether the work was ever published after all. In fact, the year of its preparation, 1936, generates serious doubts about whether it could ever have been published. This was a time when countless numbers of people in the Soviet Union, including Communist Party members as well as a variety of professional people such as prominent scientists, engineers, and writers, were being arrested, imprisoned, sent to concentration camps—or executed, almost always on bogus charges or for almost no apparent reason at all.

A visiting scholar from Russia, at the time at Metropolitan State College in Denver, who also happens to be an expert on Vygotskii, Dr. Elena Bodrova, was consulted in March, 1994. She volunteered her opinion, or, more accurately, her conviction, that the book could not have been published.[48] She mentioned that a decree was issued in the Soviet Union in 1936 which declared "pedology" a "bourgeois science" and banned it as a scholarly field. Pedology is the science of childhood development, intended to serve as the basis for pedagogy and educational psychology. Vygotskii was prominently identified with this field at the time. Vygotskii's reputation was severely damaged by the decree, and thereafter in all articles about Vygotskii all references to Western psychologists (with the exception of Piaget) were summarily expurgated. Dr. Bodrova recommended two recent biographies of Vygotskii for further information: *Vygotsky's Psychology: A Biography of Ideas,* by Alex Kozulin, published by Harvard University Press in 1990, and *Understanding Vygotsky: A Quest for Synthesis* by René van der Veer and Joan Valsiner, published by Blackwell in 1991.[49] These volumes made clear that both Luria and Vygotskii had begun running into problems with Communist Party authorities in the early thirties with regard to their research and publications; their work was accused of being incompatible with Marxist dogma. At the same time, such Western schools of thought in psychology as behaviorism, Gestalt psychology, and William Stern's personalism were coming under explicit attack for ideological reasons.

Vygotskii's and Luria's political problems are summarized in the van der Veer and Valsiner book. For instance: "In 1933 the position of Vygotsky and his associates apparently grew worse. It seems possible to infer from a letter from Vygotsky to Luria (dated March 29, 1933) that some commission was investigating (the ideological content of?) his work, but that Vygotsky believed there would be a chance to continue his work. In another letter Vygotsky mentions that he had been summoned by the leading ideologist, Mitin, who suggested they work together: 'Maybe we will find support from this side. I have no more news. When I get to know something, I'll let you know. I am endlessly being interrogated and pulled about.' (Vygotsky in a letter to Luria, dated November 21, 1933). Obviously, no help was offered by Mitin and Vygotsky's position does not seem to have improved."[50] There is extensive material in the two works to establish that all was not well politically with either Luria or Vygotskii in the early thirties. But there is no hint of these problems in the correspondence between Luria and Wertheimer concerning Wertheimer's contribution to the Vygotskii memorial volume. The subject would, of course, have been too dangerous to mention, or even hint at, in a letter. One can only surmise that Wertheimer, and probably the other contributors as well, were ignorant—or at least not fully cognizant—of the situation in the Soviet Union.

The two books also document that several people who were important to Vygotskii died due to political repression: the prominent poets Nikolai S. Gumilyev and Osip Mandelshtam, and a cousin, David Vigodsky, who was a linguist and philologist. Gumilyev was executed by a firing squad in 1921 for having been a member of an "anti-Soviet conspiracy." Mandelshtam, Vygotskii's favorite poet, with whom Vygotskii was personally acquainted, was arrested on May 14, 1934, less than a month before Vygotskii's death on

June 11, for having written derogatory words about Stalin in a poem; he later died in a concentration camp. David Vigodsky was arrested in 1936 on "unknown charges" after having served in the Spanish Civil War as an intermediary between the Soviets and the Anti-Franco movement; prominent literary friends tried unsuccessfully to save him, and he too later perished in a concentration camp. This kind of information may explain why Luria had crossed out his professional affiliation address and had written in his home address in all his correspondence with Wertheimer, as well as why his letters were handwritten. These were most likely cautionary measures. Luria must have known that he was engaging in politically dangerous activities in corresponding with Wertheimer.

One critical issue was the date of the decree that condemned pedology. Van der Veer and Valsiner wrote: "Apparently, it was only with the Paedology Decree in 1936 that reference to Vygotsky's writings became definitely impossible."[51] The specific date of this decree could shed light on the mystery. A footnote in the Kozulin volume refers to Raymond A. Bauer's book, *The New Man in Soviet Psychology*, published in 1952. This volume contains both the substance of the decree and its date, July 4, 1936 (and the van der Veer and Valsinger volume corroborates the date), exactly one day prior to Luria's letter to Wertheimer in which, as noted, he says: "It was extraordinarily pleasant for me to learn from your letter that a work from your pen for the memorial volume will arrive. But no manuscript has yet arrived. Since the material is already almost complete, - I would very much like to ask you to send your work to us - if possible - within this month." Luria's urgency is obvious. This letter and its date raise several questions. Was Luria aware of the decree? Did he suspect that the decree might be impending and therefore hope to get the book published before that would happen? Did Luria really believe he could get the book produced, considering that everything published at that time in the Soviet Union was issued by state publishing houses and had to undergo scrutiny for ideological content by government censors before publication? Was he aware of the possible danger to himself for even attempting to publish a work with contributions from Western psychologists, who were known to be in disfavor in the Soviet Union? Such questions make Luria's letter to Wertheimer on Sept. 19, 1936 all the more intriguing; in it he thanked Wertheimer for his manuscript and wrote that it has "arrived on time."…"Of course I will take care of reprints for you."

Also: was Luria's two-month delay in acknowledging Wertheimer's manuscript a reflection of his uncertainty about how to handle the whole matter? What may have been in Luria's mind when he wrote that Sept. 19 letter? Did he still believe it really would be possible to publish the memorial volume? Did his devotion to Vygotskii outweigh his fear of the Communist authorities, and was he indeed still hoping it might be possible to have the work published? Perhaps he knew that it would not be possible, and was merely being polite by his assurance to Wertheimer that his manuscript arrived on time, knowing that it would be too perilous to reveal the real situation.

Clearly many questions remain unanswered. One relevant sidelight concerns Luria's publication record and career trajectory. Luria obtained his Ph.D. degree in 1936, the same year in which the correspondence occurred. He had in fact already been publishing prolifically for more than half a decade, but his publications stopped abruptly in 1936. There was only a trickle, mostly in American outlets, during the 1940s and 1950s, but he resumed his earlier record of prolific publications from the late 1960s until his death in 1977. Luria obtained a medical degree in 1943, and most of his later publications were on the effects of brain injury, an ideologically more neutral area than the politically sensitive field of individual differences among children in cognitive competence to which he had, like Vygotskii, devoted much of his early energies. Was Luria's switch to medicine and the study of brain injury at least in part politically motivated? One of his letters to Wertheimer in 1936 indicates that he was already working on brain injury at that time, but the political climate may have been a contributing factor.

The initial hope was to locate Wertheimer's contribution to the Vygotskii memorial volume, among other reasons, because Wertheimer published so little, and any additional publication by Wertheimer could have been inherently interesting. But it now looks as though it may be impossible ever to locate that manuscript—unless, as is possible, it is one of dozens of unidentified fragments and drafts that are in the collections of Wertheimer papers; but if it is, it may be difficult or impossible to identify the manuscript unequivocally.

No systematic attempt has been made to locate a depository of Luria papers or archives—if one exists. But the chance that the manuscript for the Vygotskii memorial volume would exist in such an archive is very poor, given the political situation at the time that Luria was putting it together. Prudence may have persuaded Luria to hide the entire collection of manuscripts for the volume, and all of the correspondence related to its creation, or to give it to a trusted confidant for safekeeping or, perhaps most likely, to destroy the manuscript and all of the potentially incriminating documents associated with it.

Notes

1.   E. G. Boring to Madison Bentley, December 14, 1922. Quoted in J. M. O'Donnell (1979). The crisis of experimentalism in the 1920s: E. G. Boring and his uses of history. *American Psychologist*, 34, 289-295.
2.   Herbert Sydney Langfeld taught at Harvard and Princeton and was a co-author with Boring of an influential psychology textbook.

3.   Herbert Langfeld to E. G. Boring, March 12, 1927, Harvard University Archives.
4.   E. G. Boring (1967). Titchener's Experimentalists. *Journal of the History of the Behavioral Sciences*, 3, 315-325.
5.   E. G. Boring (1938). The Society of Experimental Psychologists, 1904-1938. *American Journal of Psychology*, 51, 410-423.
6.   Boring, The Society of Experimental Psychologists, 1904-1938.
7.   E. G. Boring to Max Wertheimer, December 12, 1933, MW-CU.
8.   Max Wertheimer to E. G. Boring, December 20, 1933, MW-CU.
9.   S. W. Fernberger (1934). The Cambridge meeting of the Society of Experimental Psychologists. *American Journal of Psychology*, 46, 511.
10. E. G. Boring to Max Wertheimer, 1934, MW-CU.
11. E. G. Boring to Max Wertheimer, April 25, 1929, MW-CU.
12. E. G. Boring to Max Wertheimer, October 15, 1935, MW-CU. In Gestalt theory, isomorphism is the principle that the dynamic structure of the pattern of activation in the brain corresponds with the dynamic structure of that which is perceived.
13. Boring's difficulty in coming to grips with the idea of isomorphism is not uncommon; indeed, Henle has stated: "I know of no concept in psychology that has been more misunderstood, indeed more distorted, than isomorphism." Mary Henle (1984). Isomorphism: Setting the record straight. *Psychological Research*, 46, 317.
14. E. G. Boring to Max Wertheimer, September 12, 1935, MW-CU. Boring enclosed with this letter a reprint of a discussion of sensory attributes that had been presented at the meeting of the Society of Experimental Psychologists in Cambridge in the spring of 1934, which had been published in *Philosophy of Science*. E. G. Boring (1935). The relation of the attributes of sensation to the dimensions of the stimulus. *Philosophy of Science*, 2, 236-245.
15. Max Wertheimer to E. G. Boring, September 19, 1935, MW-CU.
16. Max Wertheimer to E. G. Boring, September 29, 1935, MW-CU.
17. E. G. Boring to Max Wertheimer, October 15, 1935, MW-CU.
18. E. G. Boring to Max Wertheimer, October 24, 1935, MW-CU.
19. E. G. Boring to Max Wertheimer, December 5, 1935, MW-CU.
20. Ibid. Langfeld was the editor of the *Psychological Review* at the time of this letter.
21. Max Wertheimer to E. G. Boring, December 10, 1935, MW-CU.
22. E. G. Boring to Max Wertheimer, February 16, 1936, MW-CU. Boring added that "it would be nice to know somewhat early about whether Mrs. Wertheimer thinks that she can come since it would make a difference in the dinner as to whether wives are to be invited or as to whether it is to be all men." Sexism was clearly still rampant in Cambridge, even though Margaret Floy Washburn had been elected a member of the Society of Experimental Psychologists by that time.
23. Ibid.
24. Max Wertheimer to E. G. Boring, February 24, 1936, MW-CU.
25. E. G. Boring to Max Wertheimer, March 29, 1936, MW-CU.
26. Ibid.
27. Max Wertheimer to E. G. Boring, April 4, 1936, MW-CU.

28. E. G. Boring to Max Wertheimer, September 11, 1936, MW-CU.

29. Boring, *A history of experimental psychology*, p. 594.

30. Max Wertheimer to Wilhelm Wertheimer, September 13, 1925, MW-CU.

31. Boring continued to expound similar beliefs about isomorphism in his later historical books and in his autobiography. Indeed, nearly 30 years after his exchange with Wertheimer, Boring was still describing the Gestalt version of isomorphism in the language of structuralism. As late as in a 1965 anthology, Herrnstein and Boring prefaced an excerpt from Wertheimer's 1912 paper on apparent movement with a structuralist interpretation of isomorphism that does not do justice to the Gestalt version of the concept: "The Gestalt psychologists have argued that there must be a one-to-one topological correspondence between the relations (spatial, temporal, qualitative) of the perceptual pattern and the corresponding relations of the underlying excitatory pattern in the cerebral cortex." R. J. Herrnstein and E. G. Boring, (eds.) (1965). *A source book in the history of psychology*. Cambridge, MA: Harvard University Press, p. 253.

32. Walter S. Neff (1936). A critical investigation of the visual apprehension of movement. *American Journal of Psychology*, 48, p. 13.

33. Ibid, p. 29.

34. Katsumi Nakamura to Max Wertheimer, December 25, 1935, MW-CU.

35. J. A. Mills (1988). The genesis of Hull's *Principles of Behavior*. *Journal of the History of the Behavioral Sciences*, 24, p. 392.

36. C. L. Hull (1937). Modern movements in psychology. *The World Book Encyclopedia*, Vol. 13. Chicago, IL: Quarrie, pp. 586-589. The three illustrations for the article include a figure for demonstrating Wertheimer's law of proximity, a photograph of the chimpanzees Grande and Sultan from Köhler's *The mentality of apes*, and a drawing of a dog in Pavlov's experimental apparatus.

37. Ibid, pp. 586-587.

38. Clark L. Hull to Max Wertheimer, January 8, 1934, MW-CU. Robert M. Ogden had apparently encouraged Hull to contact Wertheimer during a symposium on the psychologies of learning at the Pittsburgh meeting of the American Academy for the Advancement of Science.

39. Clark L. Hull to Max Wertheimer, January 15, 1934, MW-CU.

40. Max Wertheimer to Clark L. Hull, January 17, 1935, MW-CU.

41. Clark L. Hull to Max Wertheimer, January 26, 1935, MW-CU.

42. Clark L. Hull to Edwin B. Newman, January 26, 1935, MW-CU.

43. Edwin B. Newman to Clark L. Hull, March 1, 1935, MW-CU.

44. Clark L. Hull to Max Wertheimer, October 28, 1936, Clark L. Hull Archives, Yale University, New Haven, CT. Luchins and Luchins report that Hull did ask Wertheimer to review and comment on a draft of his presidential address but claim: "Although Hull acknowledged Wertheimer's comments in a footnote to the paper...apparently he was not influenced to revise the report." Luchins and Luchins (1987). Max Wertheimer in America 1933-1943, Part I, p. 91. This comment does not appear to do full justice to their interaction.

45. For a discussion of Hull's presidential address and its role in his later work, see E. R. Hilgard (1978). *American psychology in historical perspective: Addresses of the presidents of the American Psychological Association, 1892-1977*. Washington, DC: American Psychological Association, pp. 309 - 336.

46. C. L. Hull (1937). Mind, mechanism, and adaptive behavior. *Psychological Review*, 44, 1-32. Years later, Wertheimer described Hull's paper as "the basic character of the modern form of association theory in a nutshell." Max Wertheimer, *Productive thinking*, p. 11.

47. Letter from Kurt Lewin to Max Wertheimer, March 10, 1936 (MW-CU).

48. Personal communications to Michael Wertheimer from Dr. Elena Bodrova, Denver, CO, March, 1994.

49 Alex Kozulin (1990). *Vygotsky's psychology: A biography of ideas*. Cambridge, MA: Harvard University Press; René van der Veer and Joan Valsiner (1991). *Understanding Vygotsky: A quest for synthesis*. Oxford, England: Blackwell. On reading a draft of this chapter, Professor Lothar Sprung of Berlin recommended three further sources that discuss some of the issues raised in the Luria-Wertheimer correspondence; the authors are grateful for his suggestions. Michael Cole and Sheila Cole (eds.) (1979). *The making of a mind: A personal account of Soviet psychologist A. R. Luria*. Cambridge, MA: Harvard University Press. Kurek, N. S. (1995). Geschichte und Ursachen des Verbots der Psychotechnik und der Paedologie in der ehemaligen UdSSR [History and origins of the prohibition of psychotechnology and pedology in the former Soviet Union]. In S. Jaeger, I. Staeuble, L. Sprung and H.-P. Brauns (eds.), *Psychologie im soziokulturellen Wandel: Kontinuitäten und Diskontinuitäten* [*Psychology in sociocultural change: Continuities and discontinuities*]. Frankfurt am Main: Lang, pp. 194-199. G. L. Vygodskaya and T. M. Lifanova (2000). *Lev Semjonovic Vigotskij: Leben, Tätigkeit, Persoenlichkeit* [*Lev Semjonovic Vigotskij: Life, work, personality*]. (Translated and edited by J. Lompscher and G. Rueckriem). Hamburg: Kovac.

50. Van der Veer and Valsiner, 1991, p. 381.

51. Van der Veer and Valsiner, 1991, p. 384.

12

The Social Conscience of a Humble Empiric

Freedom is a Gestalt quality of attitude, of behavior, of a [person']s thinking, of [a person's] actions.
—Max Wertheimer,
"A Story of Three Days" (1940)

Max Wertheimer was always deeply interested in the news of the day, and expressed strong personal reactions to social and political events in the world around him. Intellectual and emotional realms were for him inextricably interwoven; separating them would be artificial and inappropriate. He was as passionate in his opinions about the political and social domain as he was about the philosophical and psychological. When in 1940 he wrote, "I shall report what happened in the course of three days to a good man who, facing the world situation, longed for a clarification of the fundamentals of freedom," the introductory sentence for his essay "A Story of Three Days,"[1] about the personal quest of a "humble empiric" for the meaning of freedom, he was finally committing to paper thoughts that had doubtless been in his mind for many years. While he had long wrestled with the dynamics of cognition and perception, and had for years been thinking and lecturing about broad philosophical and social issues, he had never before written extensively on the more global aspects of society in a form intended for publication. His exile to the United States may have further aroused his social conscience, inducing him to try to turn his long-standing, strongly-held views about crucial social issues into publishable manuscripts. He was to generate, during his decade in America, brief but powerful publications on the Gestalt perspective on truth, ethics, and the concept of democracy as well as on freedom.

Wertheimer's concern about the events in Europe must have contributed to his determination not only to lecture, but also to publish, on salient social issues. Part of Wertheimer's faith in Gestalt theory was a deep respect for the rationality of human nature. While, for example, his distaste for orthodox psychoanalytic theory was partly based on his disdain for associationism, it was probably even more thoroughly rooted in his abhorrence of the Freudian insistence on the irrational aspects of humanity. The success of the right-wing political developments in the Soviet Union and Germany, movements that in his view flew in the face of human dignity and reason, also troubled him.

Fascism, Communism, and Psychology

The ominous specter of totalitarian regimes also soon specifically impacted psychologists' lives and work, as for example in the Soviet government's pressure on two Russian admirers of Gestalt theory, Lev S. Vygotskii and Alexander R. Luria.[2] Luria's efforts to publish a memorial volume celebrating Vygotskii's accomplishments could not have come at a more disastrous time for Soviet academicians. After Lenin's death in 1924, Joseph Stalin eliminated opposing Communist leaders—Leon Trotsky, Grigory Zinovyev, Lev Kamenev, Nikolay Bukharin, and others—and established himself as virtual dictator. Following his "Five-Year Plan" to revitalize Russian industry and agriculture, Stalin launched his purges of the Communist party and of the Russian army in 1934. During the time of Luria's correspondence with Wertheimer, countless numbers of professionals in the Soviet Union were being persecuted or murdered.

Even though he may not have been fully informed about the Soviet government's crippling authority, Wertheimer harbored no illusions about Hitler's debilitating influence on German science. Through newspaper accounts, he closely monitored such events as the efforts of the National Socialist Party publicly to denounce Einstein's theory of relativity. In 1936, an editorial in the *Voelkischer Beobachter* [*National Observer*], an official Nazi newspaper, launched an aggressive attack on Einstein's relativity theory as unsound, and demanded that a truly "German" or "Aryan" physics take the place of Einstein's "Jewish physics."[3] Wertheimer saved a clipping of a *New York Times* editorial that reported the efforts of "Nordic" scientists who challenged the work of Einstein, Max Planck, Werner Heisenberg, and Max von Laue and called for an Aryan approach to the disciplines of physics, mathematics, and chemistry.[4]

Wertheimer was of course fully cognizant of the struggle of Köhler and other psychologists to maintain scientific progress in Germany. Köhler had become a courageous defender of beleaguered scientists as well as a champion of academic freedom in the face of fascism. More than five months after his defiant 1933 "Conversations in Germany" response to the Nazi civil service law, Köhler walked into his Berlin classroom on the evening of November 3, the first day of the fall semester, and openly protested a mandate requiring that all university classes begin with a salute to Hitler. The audience of more than two hundred people listened as he warned against the contaminating influence of political regulation on scientific discovery. An

American student, Clarke Crannell, witnessed the valiant actions of the man he and other assistants called "Der Chef." He reported that Köhler's "voice was calm and steady, but he kept his hands together and clenched them until his knuckles and fingers appeared bloodless. Of course, he was confronted with the likely consequences of violence, pain, torture, and death. Yet he had to speak his mind." Despite the formidable presence of more than a dozen brownshirted Nazi loyalists in the lecture hall, the audience broke into "thunderous applause" in support of Köhler's words.[5]

In December, activists of the National Socialist Students' League stormed the facilities of the Psychological Institute during Köhler's colloquium, ostensibly to investigate evidence of subversive activity by Karl Duncker and Otto von Lauenstein.[6] Köhler protested the unannounced raids and appeared to win the assurance of the new rector, Eugen Fischer, that he would be informed of any future raids on the Institute. But a little later, on April 12, 1934, during Fischer's absence, the Dean of the Philosophical Faculty, Ludwig Bierbach, authorized a search of the Psychological Institute. Köhler angrily insisted that such activity seriously threatened his authority as director of the Institute and turned in his resignation. While he was away on lecture tours in Scotland and the United States, Köhler was still hoping that university officials would ultimately respect his authority and yield to his demands for privacy.[7] But such requests were hardly of any value since the German constitution, from its inception, provided little in the way of privacy rights or protection from search and seizure laws, and also because of the ease with which Nazi officials could influence German magistrates to authorize entry. By mid-1935 Köhler seriously considered an offer from Swarthmore College's president, Frank Aydelotte, who tempted Köhler with postdoctoral fellows and laboratory facilities in the new Edward Martin Biological Laboratory.[8] By August he turned in his final resignation to the University of Berlin, bringing an end to his productive tenure as Director of the Psychological Institute.[9] In Köhler's absence, Wolfgang Metzger and Kurt Gottschaldt did maintain some degree of identification of Berlin with Gestalt theory during the Nazi period, when German psychology did not perish but instead became increasingly focused on practical and applied issues, largely in service of the military efforts.[10]

A Ruined Estate—and Citizenship

Although he had been granted temporary leave to lecture in the United States, Wertheimer received official word of his forced retirement in September 1933. In December, he was informed that he would not be granted pension benefits because he had not served as a full-time civil servant for at least a decade prior to his dismissal.[11] Although Wertheimer probably had not counted on receiving that income, this was hardly good news. He was earning a salary of about $6,000 from the New School, but in purchasing power that was much less than he had been earning in Frankfurt. His professional income was no longer supplemented by funds from his father's estate as it had been for most of his career in Europe. That estate had disappeared.

In Germany, Max had supervised the finances of his father's holdings but, after deciding to emigrate to America, believed that it would be more prudent to have someone in Europe assume responsibility for the estate. Wertheimer named as executor Julius Klein, the man with whom he had attended law school and who had co-authored his earliest paper, on the psychological diagnosis of guilt. Klein had completed his legal studies and had established a modest practice in Prague. Klein was apparently easily manipulated by a dominant and overpowering wife. According to one report, Klein's wife persuaded him to allocate funds from the Wertheimer estate to finance a tour by a theater troupe (in which Mrs. Klein was a member) as well as other personal projects.[12] In time, under Klein's inept management, Max's substantial inheritance (which he shared with his niece, Walti), was gone.

Wertheimer had always been frugal and modest, with little interest in luxurious clothing or accommodations, but he must have been distressed that Wilhelm's wish to provide for his children and grandchildren could not be realized. As the National Socialist government confiscated personal property from German and Czech citizens, it became clear that, even aside from Klein's incompetence and the consequent disappearance of the estate, it was not possible to retrieve whatever remained of the inheritance.

Although Max actively managed the finances of his father's estate in Germany, he became less involved in the family's day-to-day financial affairs as Anni increasingly took over responsibility for the family's budget. Richard Courant, the prominent professor of mathematics at New York University and a fellow resident of New Rochelle, put the family in touch with Benno Elkan, a philanthropist who had previously offered financial support to emigrating European scholars. The Elkan family agreed to provide the Wertheimers $100 each month for living expenses. One indulgence that the family maintained from their past was a maid; shortly after arriving in America, the Wertheimers hired a young German refugee named Anna to help Anni with the children and with household chores. On one occasion, Mrs. Elkan visited the house in New Rochelle and was surprised to learn that the Wertheimers had hired outside help. Considering such a luxury unacceptable, the Elkans stopped further funding shortly thereafter.

The political events in Germany and his forced retirement made clear to Wertheimer that the United States would become his permanent home, and he applied for U.S. citizenship. After the required waiting period and passing a perfunctory citizenship test, Max and Anni Wertheimer became United States citizens in a White Plains, New York, court on April 14, 1939, one day before Max's fifty-ninth birthday. He had been told to prepare for the citizenship hearing because he would be tested on the contents of the Constitution of the United States. Wertheimer's oldest son, Val, who later became a lawyer, said that his father

> studied the American Constitution as fully as I ever studied it when I went to law school many years later, making notations, annotations, and really becoming a Constitutional lawyer, almost. When he went to take his examination…he was given a paragraph to read, something to the effect that every morning the milkman delivers milk to Mrs. Cook's home. Question: Who delivers milk every morning on the steps of Mrs. Cook's home? What does the milkman deliver every morning on the steps of Mrs. Cook's home? Etc., etc…. But he remembered until his dying day the exact essence of the Constitution.[13]

Benno Elkan and Clara Mayer served as witnesses for the citizenship hearings. Val, Michael, and Lise were registered with their parents as citizens on the same day.

The Wertheimers were among nearly 100 candidates for citizenship at that hearing. In a May 1939 issue, the children's *Wertheimer Times* described the citizenship proceedings under the headline "WERTHEIMERS ARE CITIZENS." When Max and Anni returned from their citizenship hearings, they were greeted by a sign suspended between two American flags with red, white and blue letters that read "Welcome home, American citizens!"[14]

Wertheimer's early hopes for the demise of the Nazi regime might have paralleled those of the neo-Kantian philosopher Ernst Cassirer, who once remarked that "Hitler is an error of history; he does not belong in German history at all. And therefore he will perish."[15] But by the end of the 1930s, Wertheimer probably never expected to return to Germany. He had to a large extent managed to adjust to life in the United States. Unlike some European professors who had a difficult time accommodating to the United States, Wertheimer admired the American lifestyle and became a dedicated, devoted American citizen. He became impatient with some of his European colleagues who viewed American life and society with smug disdain.[16] Like several European refugees, Wertheimer did not alter his appearance to conform to an American dress code and "thought nothing of walking around New York wearing a loden coat and carrying a rucksack instead of a briefcase."[17] But he appreciated the vitality, independence, and individuality of Americans at work and play; for example, he admired the spirit of cooperation as well as the skill that permeates the American sport of basketball. Indeed, Wertheimer enjoyed a good game; when he taught chess to his children, he insisted that any stupid moves be taken back, so that the game itself would be as "good" as possible.[18] Wertheimer also adapted quite well to his work environment at the New School for Social Research which, like the Institute for Social Research at Frankfurt, became widely known as a center of ambitious and radical political, social and artistic activism.

Political and Interdisciplinary Activities at the New School

The political climate and activities of the New School fit in well with Wertheimer's interest in social issues. A center of activism from the beginning, the New School reflected Alvin Johnson's liberal leanings. Throughout his academic career, Johnson was a populist who worried about such issues as the impoverished lives of farmers and at the same time was disturbed by the faltering civil rights of women and African-Americans.[19] He was an outspoken opponent of anti-Semitism and was sometimes accused of constructing the New School as a "Communist outfit."[20] And although President Franklin D. Roosevelt and First Lady Eleanor Roosevelt publicly supported granting visas to foreign scholars, some officials at the State Department believed that Johnson was recruiting a surplus of Jews and socialists.[21]

In the founding year of the New School's Graduate Faculty of Political and Social Science, Johnson helped launch the General Seminar, an interdisciplinary meeting devoted each semester to a different shared topic of social and political interest. From 1933 to 1937 twelve scholars from the Graduate Faculty attended the weekly General Seminar, and from 1938 on between eighteen and twenty-five scholars were regular participants.[22] Graduate students and faculty from other institutions joined the Graduate Faculty in seminars devoted to such topics as "America and Europe," "Political and Economic Democracy," and "Power in the United States." Consistent with the liberal, interdisciplinary spirit that closely resembled that of the general seminar at Frankfurt, Wertheimer helped establish, and then oversaw, the New School seminar that met from 1933 to 1943. He participated over the years with a diverse group of social scientists, including Karen Horney, Albert Salomon, Arnold Brecht, and Adolph Lowe, in the exploration of such themes as "The Problem of Value," "Current Problems of the Social Sciences," and "Methodology of the Social Sciences." As leader of the seminar, Wertheimer "consciously sought to relate the political concerns of the General Seminar to more fundamental philosophical issues of epistemology and value."[23] In addition to his work in the seminar, he regularly taught such courses as "Basic Problems in Psychology," "The Psychology of Music and Art," "Gestalt Psychology of Teaching and Learning," "Logic and Scientific Method," and "On Better Thinking."

To strengthen further the impact of the Graduate Faculty's scholarship beyond the walls of the New School, Johnson spearheaded the founding of *Social Research*, a journal that published contributions from members of the General Seminar. Emil Lederer, dean of the University in Exile and later of the Graduate Faculty, joined sociologist Hans Speier in editing the new journal. Johnson declared in the inaugural volume that the Graduate Faculty at the New School, "the largest organic grouping of continental scholars abroad," had designed *Social Research* as a journal in which

The subject matter will be drawn from interests that transcend the boundaries of a single country. It will include theory, political, social and economic; problems of social and political organization that are world wide in their general character though national in specific characteristics, such as class differentiation, militarism, the labor movement; problems involving the interdependence of nations, like the phenomena of prosperity and depression, prices and currency, movements of international trade and investment.[24]

Wertheimer joined Ascoli, Johnson, Kallen, Lederer, Speier, Wunderlich, and other members of the Graduate Faculty as members of *Social Research*'s first editorial board, and the journal has been published quarterly in February, May, August, and November ever since its inception in 1934.

Wertheimer's participation in the New School seminars and affiliation with *Social Research* forged interdisciplinary ties and new avenues of understanding and communication with colleagues that otherwise might not have occurred. This was evident in Wertheimer's collegial alliance with an unlikely colleague, the neo-Freudian psychoanalyst Karen Horney, during a New School seminar on the relationship of sociology to psychology. Steeped in orthodox psychoanalysis, Horney emigrated to the United States in 1932 and began teaching at the New School at the invitation of Clara Mayer.[25] Like Sandor Ferenczi and Erich Fromm, Karen Horney incorporated psychoanalytic themes into her sociocultural lectures at the New School.

Although Hans Speyer and Kurt Riezler also participated in the seminar, the explosive exchanges between Wertheimer and Horney became a salient feature of the meetings. Speyer remembered that the seminar was "quite an event. People came from as far away as Boston, very distinguished people" including some visitors who attended "because they thought there would be fireworks"; such spectators were not disappointed by Horney and Wertheimer who "did clash in a friendly way."[26] It is doubtful that Wertheimer had read any of Horney's already substantial writings before the seminar; indeed, he may well have seen her as an emissary of Freudian psychodynamic theory. Wertheimer objected to the psychoanalytic emphasis on reductionism, irrationalism, associationism, and the sexual motive and would doubtless have empathized with Einstein's outrage at Freud's assertion that psychoanalysis "is a part of science and can adhere to the scientific *Weltanschauung*."[27] But Horney herself had become a major critic of Freudian views in her 1923 address "On the Genesis of the Castration Complex in Women" to the International Psycho-Analytic Congress in Berlin.[28] In a series of papers in the 1920s and 1930s, she sharply challenged Freud's libido theory, especially his controversial assumption that "anatomy is destiny," and commented that "Psychoanalysis is the creation of a male genius, and almost all of those who have developed the ideas have been men."[29] Far more than Freud, Horney proposed an interactive approach that emphasizes the mutual influence of individual and culture in the development of personality—and of neurosis.

Wertheimer may have been gratified by Horney's rejection of orthodox Freudian theory, but he was not convinced that her approach was much superior to it or even more scientific—at least not in comparison with Gestalt theory. Wertheimer attacked Horney's interpretations on several occasions during the course of the seminar. Despite such intimidation, Speyer reported that Horney "held her own against Wertheimer, which wasn't easy," given his "intellectually aggressive" style.[30] Horney drew upon her clinical and personal experiences in dealing with Wertheimer and diplomatically chose to "consider what he said and translate it into her language. To what extent is it true in view of what I have experienced with my patients? That seemed to be her approach." With his jaundiced view of psychoanalysis, Wertheimer probably was not convinced by Horney's clinical data. Nonetheless, in personal notes to him she complimented him on a "fascinating and *very* challenging" presentation and referred him to some of her own psychodynamic work and to the writings of the neoanalytic "individual psychologist" Alfred Adler.[31]

Barbara Burks and the APA Committee on Displaced Scholars

By 1938, approximately 1400 university professors and researchers had been displaced from German institutions and an additional 400 scholars had been dismissed from Austrian universities since 1933.[32] Among all of these, 520 found permanent security, 290 were temporarily placed, and over forty percent were "unplaced." Among psychologists, 27 were temporarily placed and 51 unplaced by 1939. At least two psychologists were known to be in concentration camps.

Alvin Johnson's efforts to invite European psychologists to the New School were joined by the labors of academicians at other American institutions in the early 1930s. An Emergency Committee in Aid of Displaced German Scholars, formed in 1933 and consisting of celebrated members including internationally renowned journalist Edward R. Murrow, engaged in extensive rescue efforts, but many large agencies and professional societies were somewhat slower to provide assistance to refugee scholars.[33]

The American Psychological Association established several committees to deal with a wide range of war-related issues, including classification of military personnel, selection and training of aircraft pilots, relocation of military psychologists, national morale, social aspects of the war, war services to children, and the role of applied psychology in the war. The APA's activities were sufficiently abundant and diverse that the *Psychological Bulletin* began publishing a regular section entitled "Psychology and the War" beginning with the March 1942 issue.[34] During the September 1938 meeting of the American Psychological Association, the Council of Directors instructed the then-incoming president, Gordon Allport, also to appoint a Committee on the Assistance of Employment of Refugee Psychologists.[35] As a relatively young professor at Harvard University, Allport had a stellar reputation in the study of personality and became a prominent spokesperson among psychologists in a campaign of peace at war's end.[36] Allport appointed Barbara Stoddard Burks to serve first in 1938 as secretary and later as chair of the APA Committee. Allport created the Committee at the request of the APA leadership, but Burks became the tireless force that made it function effectively.

As an undergraduate student at the University of California at Berkeley, Barbara Burks worked as a research assistant to the renowned learning theorist Edward Chace Tolman. At the end of her junior year in 1923, she transferred from Berkeley to Stanford University to study with Lewis M. Terman, a leading authority on gifted children. In the three years between 1926 and 1929, Burks published a dozen research articles, most of them dealing with the role of genetic factors in children's intellectual development. She was awarded a fellowship in 1934 that allowed her to travel to Europe, including seven months in Geneva, Switzerland, working with Jean Piaget on child egocentrism at the Rousseau Institute.[37] In a letter to Terman, Burks used some language from Gestalt psychology to describe Piaget and his work method:

> I will always be glad of this opportunity for close association with Piaget—for techniques acquired, and for an appreciation of his imaginative orientation toward problems, and for an insight into the Piaget man-of-science Gestalt. It is not a perfect Gestalt, his methods sometimes seem slipshod, and there is even a certain rigidity—an unwillingness on his part to consider his own techniques and his own conclusions in their relations to significant associated problems. But he approaches his work with such zest, his imagination is so fresh, and his ideas themselves so big, that one can forgive faults that would seem serious in most psychologists.[38]

Upon her return from Europe, Burks became a research associate at the Carnegie Institute in Cold Spring Harbor, Long Island, New York, continuing her work on physical and mental traits, and had already received recognition as a leader in the relatively new field of behavioral genetics. During her brief but stellar career, she generated over eighty publications. Her journal articles, book chapters, reviews, and monographs concerned general heredity and the genetics of behavioral traits, innovations in statistics and research methodology, and themes in developmental, personality, social, and educational psychology. Burks was also fascinated by the study of eugenics. From 1941 on, she served on the board of directors of the American Eugenics Society and was a vigorous advocate of the society's activities. Her affiliation did not mean, however, that she condoned racial extermination or related abuses of eugenics. According to her fiancé, Robert Cook,

The concept of eugenics which envisions it as a sterilization committee to "dispose of misfits" and a score card to "help the chosen" pick out their proper mates struck [Burks] as being essentially pathetic.... One whose work with foster children had brought her into close and sympathetic contact with the terror and tragedy of the world knew that eugenics must be infinitely more than that if it is ever to have a message for humankind.[39]

Burks's interest in social issues was also evident in her charter membership in the Society for the Psychological Study of Social Issues (SPSSI), an organization that has been called the "most activist group in mainstream psychology."[40] In 1941 she began a two-year editorship of the SPSSI *Bulletin,* published in the *Journal of Social Psychology.* In numerous editorials she urged the active participation of psychologists in the war effort, believing that science could be an effective agent in social action; in particular, she called on social psychologists to study such war-time issues as civilian morale and attitudes relating to gasoline rationing.[41] Her reaction to the events that led to the Second World War and her sense of obligation to eugenics made Burks, with her strong interest in humanitarian and social concerns, an appropriate choice to chair the APA Committee.

Despite her impressive publication record and her outstanding efforts to find jobs for foreign scholars, Barbara Burks had a difficult time herself finding employment in academia. Her situation was not uncommon in the separate labor markets for men and women in psychology during the Second World War:

Male Ph.D.s tended to hold high-status jobs in university and college departments, concentrating on teaching and experimental research. Female Ph.D.s, on the other hand, were usually tracked into service-oriented positions in hospitals, clinics, courts, and schools. Discouraged and frequently prevented from pursuing academic careers, women filled the ranks of applied psychology's low-paid, low-status workers. The few women who did gain academic employment were mostly relegated to women's colleges, and to university clinics and child welfare institutes linked to departments of psychology and education.[42]

Burks would have preferred a position in an academic research institution, but was instead forced to work in more applied settings. And although the Carnegie Institute offered the opportunity to conduct research, her position there lacked the salary and prestige of a university setting.

While in New York, Burks regularly attended Wertheimer's seminars at the New School, and almost extravagantly wrote to Terman that she would leave

always with the feeling that I have received a personal message from a genuinely great mind. He is as brilliant and as informing when discussing a philosophical or a purely experimental problem.[43]

Wertheimer and Burks became friends; at one point, Burks proposed a collaborative effort to test some of Piaget's theories of cognitive development, but this proposal did not come to fruition. On several occasions, Wertheimer wrote letters of recommendation supporting Burks's applications to universities and for research fellowships. Their warm relationship may have helped Burks persuade Wertheimer to participate on the newly-formed APA Committee. Although it was uncharacteristic for him to serve on committees, this was one that had a charge that doubtless was close to his heart.

Wertheimer may have been gratified by the stature of the people whom Burks and Allport had managed to assemble to work on the Committee. Over the years, many illustrious psychologists served as members, including Donald B. Klein, a specialist in clinical psychology at the University of Texas; Gardner Murphy, then of Columbia University, well known in personality, social psychology, the history of psychology, and parapsychology; Albert T. Poffenberger, an experimental and industrial psychologist also at Columbia University; Saul Rosenzweig of Clark University, a psychologist interested in personality and projective techniques; and E. C. Tolman, Burks's mentor at the University of California at Berkeley.

By October 1939, the now renamed Committee on Displaced Foreign Psychologists had begun a survey of the problems faced by foreign psychologists who had lost their positions, some of whom indeed were in grave danger. The Committee proposed for itself several aims: to provide regional representation and safety to refugee scholars in the U.S. and Canada, to ascertain the status and qualifications of displaced foreign psychologists, and to investigate placement opportunities for these scholars at American universities as well as other institutions. To this end, the Committee assumed the substantial task of collecting and filing curricula vitae and other relevant information concerning every psychologist who was an actual or potential refugee, and who could be contacted by the Committee.[44] Accomplishing this task was no small feat, but Burks and the Committee met it diligently and energetically. Allport later reported that

> At one time [Burks] had, I think, 200 names of displaced psychologists, most but not all in America…. For every placement, or instance of successful help, I estimate that she wrote twenty letters and made many personal calls. The reward was meagre and discouraging…. Her service stemmed from a deep generosity in her nature, and a willingness to take up dreary and thankless work which other people gladly escaped. Although she encountered discouragements and occasional hostility, she persevered without complaint.[45]

By the end of the first year, curricula vitae had been collected for some 220 displaced psychologists and scholars in related fields. For the remainder of the Committee's existence, a central repository of curricula vitae was maintained, from which information was available upon request.

Since other scholarly organizations were slow to address the problem, the APA Committee accepted applications from prominent scholars in other disciplines as well. By 1939, twenty physicians, a dozen philosophers, and several scholars from other fields related to psychology, the majority of whom were still unplaced, had been referred to the Committee.[46] Under Burks's direction, the Committee investigated placement opportunities for these scholars in American institutions, a difficult task that was exacerbated by the serious unemployment situation in the United States during the Depression era.

Like other members of the Committee, Wertheimer was flooded with letters detailing the heart-wrenching and occasionally critical circumstances of many refugee psychologists, and engaged in painstaking correspondence in an effort to find placement for these scholars. For example, Wertheimer received a letter dated April 28, 1938, that detailed the dire circumstances of Rudolf Ekstein, a young psychologist intending to become a teacher, who could no longer work in his native Austria. He wrote to Wertheimer in hope of securing work in America, preferably in a profession befitting his education, but indicated that he was willing to settle for "any kind of work." The last paragraph of Ekstein's letter reveals his slightly awkward English and his desperate plea for help:

> I know that I am asking much of you, as I am a perfect stranger to you. For all that I venture to write you, because I know, that you are keen on favouring the scientific intentions of young people. Excuse, please, my liberty. I am sure to prove worthy of your interest and help.[47]

Wertheimer supported one of Europe's most distinguished psychologists, Karl Bühler, who had been dismissed from the University of Vienna and thrown into a concentration camp. Fortunately, Bühler was released after several months and managed to come to the United States as a "visitor," but his visiting status was due to expire June 10, 1939. In May, Wertheimer received a letter from a New York attorney, Henry Abelson, who requested information on Bühler's standing and character.[48] Abelson was anxious to do whatever was necessary to keep Bühler in the country; he could remain at the College of St. Scholastica in Duluth, Minnesota, which offered Bühler an "engagement" if he was legally admitted to the United States. In response, Wertheimer composed a letter to the Department of Labor, praising Bühler's accomplishments.[49] Bühler was granted an extension and in 1940 joined the faculty at St. Thomas College in St. Paul.[50] His excellent professional reputation doubtless facilitated a quick placement; many of the lesser-known psychologists were not as fortunate.

In trying to deal with its formidable task, the Committee encouraged the consideration of foreign scholars for "noncompetitive" openings in schools, social agencies, and industries (including new positions created by local academic committees, positions in regions where psychologists were underrepresented, and positions in domains where the contributions of psychologists were just beginning to occur).[51] This strategy was intended to reduce the possible hostile perception that there might be partiality toward refugees in the fierce competition for more "mainstream" jobs.

By June 1940, the Committee had contacted many displaced scholars in psychology, philosophy, and medicine. That year the American Philosophical Association founded a Committee on Exiled Scholars and significantly decreased the number of philosophers that applied for help to the APA Committee. During the 1941-1942 academic year relatively few refugee psychologists arrived in the United States, and the activities of the Committee were therefore less intense. Correspondence with many of the displaced psychologists still abroad ended abruptly after the attack on Pearl Harbor, and many letters sent in the autumn of 1941 were returned the following summer, stamped "Return to sender, service suspended."[52]

The Committee participated in trying to solve the refugee problem on several levels, and its success must be measured relative to the conditions and restrictions within which it had to work. In light of its modest financial resources and of the nationwide Depression, the Committee appears to have functioned fairly well. By September 1939, of the approximately 220 displaced scholars and psychologists in the Committee's files, thirty had been placed, some in temporary internships and most in temporary research or teaching positions. The 1940 report of the Committee delivered comparable results. By then in touch with 269 displaced scholars, 148 of whom were psychologists, the Committee had managed to facilitate placements for sixteen during the previous year.

The Committee's success can also be assessed through the eyes of its members. They were all aware of the magnitude and difficulty of its undertaking. Even though they were far from able to help every displaced scholar with whom they came into contact, the members would have been justified in viewing the placement of even a few as a success; and the majority of the placements were made without competition between the refugees and American psychologists. The Committee saw its mission as central to the position of scientific psychology at the time of this international crisis; in 1940 the Committee's report asserted that "Virtually the only way now open to us to fight for our professional integrity is to strengthen our efforts in behalf of psychologists who have managed to take refuge here from tyranny abroad."[53]

By 1942, the Committee's workload was much lighter than that during the previous three years, due largely to the increasing inability of displaced psychologists to escape and partly to escalating transportation costs that became prohibitive even for those who could manage it politically. At the fiftieth annual meeting of the APA, the Council of Directors requested that the Committee turn over its functions to the Office of Psychological Personnel, particularly those functions concerning emigrés who had been in the United States for several years. During the 1943 APA annual meeting, the Council of Directors thanked the members of the Committee for their "effective services during a trying period for European Psychologists" and officially dissolved the Committee.[54]

The Committee on Displaced Foreign Psychologists did manage to help a few refugee psychologists to resume their careers in the United States. But the Committee not only pursued placement opportunities for the immigrants; it also contributed to their cultural and professional assimilation by providing information to them about American institutions and practices. During its five years of existence, the Committee played a humane role in the preservation and distribution of talent, scholarship, and indeed of life, and left a model of dedicated and focused humanitarian concern—and action.

A Quest for Ethics, Truth, and Democracy

The momentous events of these troubled years must have helped encourage Wertheimer to prepare several philosophical essays he wrote after migrating to the United States. Over the course of six years, he published four essays that explicate how Gestalt theory can help in developing an understanding of the serious social and political issues that were facing the world. These essays are abstracted in an appendix to this chapter. Like other members of the Graduate Faculty, Wertheimer was asked to contribute to *Social Research*. Shortly after arriving in the United States, he had tentatively agreed to write an article on "A Psychological Approach to Scientific Method," but by late January, 1934 he instead promised a manuscript on "Truth and Science" based on his contributions to the General Seminar. With the abbreviated title "On Truth," this essay appeared as the lead article in the May 1934 issue of *Social Research*.[55] It was clearly a product rooted in his relentless pursuit of truth, an uncompromising quality that many people found attractive in Wertheimer. Truth, Wertheimer insisted, is not a piecemeal attribute of an assertion, but a Gestalt property that depends upon the assertion's place, role, and function[56] within the context in which it occurs.

In a second essay, published a year after the paper on truth, again in the pages of *Social Research*, Wertheimer addressed "Some Problems in the Theory of Ethics." [57] From the beginning, Gestalt psychology severely criticized the implicit assumptions of the then current psychology about the need for reduction and about the rejection of such human dynamics as value. Köhler dealt squarely with the latter topic in his William James lectures at Harvard University, later published as the 1938 book *The Place of Value in a World of Facts*, as well as in other publications.[58] Koffka too gave a series of lectures at the New School, in September 1938, that stressed the importance of "value experience" in human nature and had already briefly dealt with values in his monumental 1935 work *Principles of Gestalt Psychology* as well as in one of his other 1935 publications.[59] For Wertheimer, values and ethics were a crucial component of his entire epistemology, not to be separated from natural science—and not to be dealt with superficially, as he believed they were in the cultural and ethical relativism prevalent at that time. An ethical decision is not a piecemeal, absolute conclusion based on a concatenation of individual, isolated facts or properties of a problematic situation but, he argued, a thoughtful decision that does full justice to all relevant features of a problem situation and its context.

As for the concept of democracy,[60] Wertheimer saw it as fundamentally a Gestalt quality of a political system that does not run roughshod over the rights of any minority—or individual—that is part of that political system. Franklin Delano Roosevelt's "New Deal" politics at that time was an exemplar of how a true democracy deals with massive social problems by finding solutions to them that benefit those in need without damaging any other sector of society. Institutions can be established or transformed in ways that do justice to the needs, rights, and responsibilities of all members of the society.[61]

Wertheimer's fourth essay, "A Story of Three Days," is an allegorical story of one man's hypothetical but fervent quest to understand the true meaning of freedom.[62] The protagonist of this parable, described as "a humble empiric, open-minded, thirsting for information," has set out to reach some real clarification of the questions "What at bottom is freedom? What does it require? Why is it so dear to me?" On the first day of his intellectual journey, he consults a sociologist, who tells his visitor about the power of societal influence in shaping human behavior, especially emphasizing the cultural relativism that Wertheimer had protested against in his essay on ethics. Unsatisfied, the man asked the sociologist: "Is that all?... Are our ideas of freedom merely the historical standards of a certain time, now perhaps outworn? Are there no fundamental standards; are the requirements of freedom a fairy tale?" Wertheimer's "everyman" walked home from the sociologist's office disturbed by what he had heard. He looked in several books that he had obtained for his investigation. He read passages in two books, one by a famous novelist, the other by a prominent psychoanalyst, but both left him as bewildered about human freedom as when he had left the sociologist.

In planning the second day of his search, Wertheimer's protagonist said to himself, "I must see a philosopher!" But the philosopher whom he consulted was not able to offer his guest any easy—or profound—philosophical truths about freedom and instead argued for a tough-minded determinism. Clearly, the second day was as disturbing as the first.

On the final day of his search, the man sat down to consider what he had learned in the previous days:

1. There is no freedom because all is determined, is the consequence of causes. Or,
2. Freedom is absence of external restraints, of compulsion, freedom to pursue whatever wish may come to one's mind. Or,
3. Because such wishes may be due to whatever standards may have been internalized on the basis of compulsion, freedom means to be able to follow those internal impulses without inhibitions.[63]

None of this was satisfactory. It missed what is crucial about freedom, missed its radix. In time, the man began to realize that freedom must be understood as a property of a whole system—freedom concerns the interrelation of various conditions and is a Gestalt quality. Appearing a year before America's entry into the Second World War, "A Story of Three Days" may be seen as part of Wertheimer's effort to come to terms with the crises in social issues of the world around him.[64] Albert Einstein valued this essay because it demonstrated that "superficiality and one-sided interpretation do occur not only in journalism but also in scientific work."[65] In preparation for this essay, Wertheimer consulted in the New School library several of Sigmund Freud's principal writings, including *An Introduction to Psychoanalysis, Civilization and its Discontents, Future of an Illusion*, and *The Ego and the Id*.[66] Wertheimer made reference in his essay only to "a famous psychoanalyst," but it was clear that Freud's views on culture were as repugnant to Wertheimer as Freud's associationist theory of the unconscious and Freud's theory of psychosexual development.

Wertheimer's essays, demonstrating his deep compassion for the human condition and his passionate dedication to the highest human ideals, finally made available in print what he had been discussing for decades in his lectures: how Gestalt theory can provide insight into such fundamental issues as truth, democracy, ethics, and freedom. A decade after the publication of "A Story of Three Days," Einstein wrote that Wertheimer's essays

> concern democracy, ethics, freedom, truth, with the intent of substituting for superficial observations an analysis which does justice to the total situation. Behind these essays lies above all a methodological need which derives from the [G]estalt-psychological point of view: beware of trying to understand a whole by arbitrary isolation of the separate components or by hazy or forced abstractions!... Rarely will one find honesty, striving for simplicity, and independence united in such purity.[67]

The essays were a new departure in Wertheimer's sparse writings. It is true that some of his earliest writings, on the music and the quantitative reasoning of aboriginal people, had a certain humanitarian flavor, but he had not directly addressed in print the implications of Gestalt theory for such broad social issues in his earlier publications in Germany.[68]

A Model of Self-Actualization

At the New School, Wertheimer continued to attract into his classrooms students who were fascinated by his passion for Gestalt theory. Some came to hear the fiery, vivacious lecturer, some to learn about Gestalt theory, and some for both reasons. As in Germany, his students tended to be polarized into two groups, one of which followed his discourses with an almost reverent zeal and the other of which remained hopelessly lost in trying to comprehend his applications of Gestalt theory. Among Wertheimer's students was a tall, shy man from Brooklyn, Abraham H. Maslow, who had only recently received his Ph.D. in psychology from the University of Wisconsin at Madison with Harry F. Harlow. As an undergraduate at Cornell University, Maslow had attended lectures in general psychology by Edward Bradford Titchener—and found the great structuralist's psychology to be "bloodless." Maslow had agreed to conduct research on dominance in the social and sexual behavior of primates in Harlow's laboratory, and was planning further work with Edward L. Thorndike when he first attended Wertheimer's lectures. Maslow had not adopted any one system, but his association with Wertheimer came at a time when he was questioning the basic tenets of behaviorism:

> When my baby was born that was the thunderclap that settled things. I looked at this tiny, mysterious thing and felt so stupid. I was stunned by the mystery and by the sense of not really being in control. I felt small and weak and feeble before all this. I'd say that anyone who had a baby couldn't be a behaviorist.[69]

In the challenging style and content of Wertheimer's lectures, Maslow discovered a refreshing alternative to the rigid molecular and mechanistic assumptions that he found implicit in both behaviorism and psychoanalysis. Maslow felt privileged to be part of an "historical accident of being in New York City when the very cream of European intellect was migrating away from Hitler." The presence of emigré psychologists made New York for Maslow into "the center of the psychological universe," and Maslow believed that "[t]here has been nothing like it since Athens."[70] In contrast with what he had experienced in his earlier education, Maslow encountered in Wertheimer's lectures a broad treatment of Western psychology and its relation to history, philosophy and the arts—as well as exposure to Eastern thought and reference to qualities of human experience such as playfulness, wonder, awe, and esthetic enjoyment.[71] In a 1962 discussion with New School students, Maslow remarked that his interest in a broader, more humanistic psychology

> began when I came from the Midwest, as an experimental psychologist, to the seminars of Max Wertheimer, who all alone [at the New School] formed the

best psychology department in the world. It was in a lecture that he called "Being and Doing," on Taoism, Lao-tze, and Zen Buddhism. I'd never even heard the words before. And this is what started me off, and a lot of other people as well.[72]

Maslow was surprised that his peers and colleagues would not attend Wertheimer's lectures; he wrote in his diary that "Wertheimer was probably the only first-rate psychologist in the whole city and the [idiots] couldn't be coaxed to come."[73]

Wertheimer helped Maslow rethink the methodology of his comparative psychology research and promoted his interest in the role of values in human experience, as well as convincing him of the desirability of studying healthy individuals. Frustrated by Wertheimer's lack of publications on philosophical, social, and epistemological topics, Maslow often referred to his mentor's unpublished New School lectures in articles during the 1930s and 1940s.[74] In one article in 1943, Maslow described the motivational drives of intelligent people as the "basic desire to know, to be aware of reality, to get the facts, to satisfy curiosity, or as Wertheimer phrases it, to see rather than to be blind."[75]

Maslow called Ruth Fulton Benedict, an eminent cultural anthropologist at Columbia University, whom he viewed as sharing some notable characteristics with Wertheimer, another "angel" in his life. Like Wertheimer, and to some extent also the Berkeley anthropologist Alfred Kroeber, Benedict was a passionate champion of holism and opponent of reductionism.[76]

After studying at the New School for Social Research, Ruth Benedict entered the graduate program in anthropology at Columbia University, where she earned her doctorate in 1923 from Franz Boas, then the "preeminent anthropologist in America."[77] Influenced by the evolutionary approach of G. Stanley Hall and the sociocultural psychology of Wilhelm Wundt, Boas made significant advances in anthropology, ethnology, and linguistics in his more than six hundred papers. In 1924, Benedict's friend and colleague, Margaret Mead, happened upon Kurt Koffka's *Growth of the Mind* and recommended it to their mutual friend, the prominent ethnolinguist Edward Sapir. Sapir was impressed by Gestalt psychology and wrote Benedict that Koffka's work was "the real book for background for a philosophy of culture, at least your/my philosophy," and described it as an "echo telling me what my intuition never quite had the courage to say out loud."[78] Benedict had also read Köhler and realized that the themes of Gestalt psychology were congruent with the orientation which she was developing of a "configurational" (or Gestalt) approach to cultural anthropology.

In 1932, Benedict's article on "Configuration of Culture in North America" appeared, followed two years later by her most famous work,

Patterns of Culture, in which she vigorously argued against piecemeal efforts to catalogue customs and cultural traits to the neglect of patterns and cultural influences.[79] As a corrective to reductionism, she looked to the psychology of Wertheimer, as well as to that of William Stern, for a holistic perspective that could be incorporated into anthropology: "The importance of the study of the whole configuration as over against the continued analysis of its parts is stressed in field after field of modern science."[80] She believed that the "*Gestalt* (configuration) psychology has done some of the most striking work in justifying the importance of this point of departure from the whole rather than from its parts."[81] Although aware that much of the work in Gestalt psychology had been on perception and thinking, Benedict believed that the basic premise and findings of the theory could inform cultural anthropologists: "The work in *Gestalt* psychology has been chiefly in those fields where evidence can be experimentally arrived at in the laboratory, but its implications reach far beyond the simple demonstrations which are associated with its work."[82] Benedict used broad holistic approaches in her configurational analyses of the Zuñi, Dobu, and Kwakiutl societies, writing that a "culture, like an individual, is a more or less consistent pattern of thought and action. Within each culture, there come into being characteristic purposes not necessarily shared by other types of societies," but where the culture as a whole "is not merely the sum of all its parts, but the results of an unique arrangement and interrelation of the parts that has brought about a new entity."[83] With her configurational orientation, she warned anthropologists about ignoring the fact that cultures "are more than the sum of their traits. We may know all about the distribution of a tribe's form of marriage, ritual dances, and puberty initiations, and yet understand nothing of the culture as a whole which has used these elements to its own purpose."[84] Over time, Benedict remained respectful of Gestalt psychology, but also became interested in other very different approaches, including the work of her friend Karen Horney as well as other New York intellectuals.[85]

While early she had been disturbed by the amount of time and effort that Boas spent on "good works" rather than on research, Benedict became increasingly dedicated, like Wertheimer, to issues of democracy and humanity as the Nazi crisis grew in Europe.[86] She wrote on racial issues in culture and worked during the war for the Bureau of Overseas Intelligence, Office of War Information, in an extensive analysis of Japanese culture, resulting in the publication of her influential 1946 book, *The Chrysanthemum and the Sword: Patterns of Japanese Culture*.[87]

Like Wertheimer, Benedict influenced Maslow's approach to the study of personality.[88] Both Benedict and Wertheimer not only offered Maslow promising new perspectives for studying human nature, but also offered a glimpse into what he considered a unique form of personality development. Maslow deeply appreciated Wertheimer as an instructor, especially his passion for truth—but he was also fascinated by his mentor's bold and unusual character. And he observed that Benedict's unusual personality had some basic similarities with his impression of Wertheimer's personality.

Secretly, Maslow began to watch Benedict and Wertheimer closely, trying to figure out what made them seem so special to him. These investigations, he freely admitted,

> started out as the effort of a young intellectual to try to understand two of his teachers whom he loved, adored, and admired and who were very, very wonderful people. It was a kind of high-IQ devotion. I could not be content simply to adore, but sought to understand why these two people were so different from the run-of-the-mill people in the world.... [T]hey were most remarkable human beings.[89]

Maslow was frustrated that his

> training in psychology equipped me not at all for understanding them. It was as if they were not quite people but something more than people. My own investigation began as prescientific or nonscientific activity. I made descriptions and notes on Max Wertheimer, and I made notes on Ruth Benedict.[90]

Maslow held a party at his home and was delighted when both Wertheimer and Benedict accepted his invitation to attend it.[91] Following this warm and stimulating evening at his home, Maslow mused about their traits and motivating features and tried to find a common theme:

> When I tried to understand them, think about them, and write about them in my journal and my notes, I realized in one wonderful moment that their two patterns could be generalized. I was talking about a kind of person, not about two noncomparable individuals.... I tried to see whether this pattern could be found elsewhere, and I did find it elsewhere, in one person after another. [92]

Although crude and informal at first, Maslow's project gradually evolved into a more disciplined undertaking as he tried to identify basic themes and patterns that he had seen in the lives, thoughts and personalities of Wertheimer and Benedict. Maslow soon began taking more systematic, although still spontaneous, notes in a "GHB" ("Good Human Being") notebook, from 1945 through 1949.[93] Many brief observations, such as Wertheimer's statement from an earlier year that many of the finest people that he had met in his life were not intellectuals, found their way into Maslow's notebook.[94]

Captivated by the personalities and motivations of Wertheimer and Benedict, Maslow began reading biographies and autobiographies of historically eminent women and men, searching for common characteristics of what he was by then calling "healthy-minded" people. One source of inspiration for Maslow, incidentally, might have been Wertheimer's thoughts—and essays—on ethics and freedom. Maslow's biographer wrote that Wertheimer's article on ethics

> briefly described the existence of what Maslow twenty-five years later would call peak experiences. Wertheimer observed that there are moments in our lives when we feel awakened and suddenly become aware of our finest and most worthy qualities, as if they had been long forgotten or missing. He also voiced an optimism, shared by Maslow, that behind the exterior of most people lie decent, moral qualities that are often rarely expressed.[95]

One passage in Wertheimer's "A Story of Three Days" is particularly compatible with some aspects of Maslow's later theories: "Are there not tendencies in [adults] and in children to be kind, to deal sincerely [and] justly with the other fellow? Are these nothing but internalized rules on the basis of compulsion and fear?"[96]

Maslow also studied with Kurt Goldstein, the German emigré who had joined Wertheimer and others in founding *Psychologische Forschung* (*Psychological Research*) in the 1920s. Goldstein was loosely associated with the Gestalt psychologists and had incorporated holistic themes into his work in neuroscience.[97] After rejecting terms like "good human being," "saintly person," "self-fulfilling person" or the awkward "almost ideally healthy human being," Maslow adopted Goldstein's concept of "self-actualization" as the most apt descriptor for his category of "Good Human Beings." In his 1943 paper, "A Theory of Human Motivation," Maslow referred to "self-actualized people," but did not publish a formal paper devoted to the concept until his 1950 article, "Self-Actualization: A Study of Psychological Health"; when he reprinted this article in his 1954 book *Motivation and Personality*, he indicated that it had been written around 1943 but that he had held up publication until 1950, when he finally "summoned up enough courage to print it."[98] Maslow claimed that his theory was "in the functionalist tradition of James and Dewey, and… fused with the holism of Wertheimer, Goldstein, and Gestalt psychology, and with the dynamicism of Freud and Adler."[99]

In developing his criteria for "healthy" people, Maslow was "fairly sure" that he had discovered nine people who seemed to be "self-actualizing" individuals. Thomas Jefferson and Abraham Lincoln joined Benedict and Wertheimer on Maslow's list, which also included several anonymous acquaintances of Maslow's.[100] Maslow also proposed a grouping of seven "highly probable" figures: Jane Addams, Albert Einstein, Aldous Huxley, William James, Eleanor Roosevelt, Albert Schweitzer, and Baruch Spinoza. There was also a group of thirty-seven "potential cases" of self-actualized people, among whom Maslow named Martin Buber, Ralph Waldo Emerson, Johann Wolfgang Goethe, Adlai Stevenson, George Washington, and Walt Whitman.

Maslow concluded that a number of favorable characteristics could be identified in self-actualized people, such as a realistic and problem-centered perception of the world, a refreshing sense of spontaneity and simplicity, and a genuine acceptance of one's self as well as of others. He observed that such "good specimens" have a mature, unhostile sense of humor together with a quality of detachment and a fierce need for privacy and autonomy, resulting in deep interpersonal relations with only a few friends. Quite early, some four months after beginning his "Good Human Being" journal, Maslow had written that

> I learned long ago that the older GHBs had an awfully strong sense of privacy, as Ruth Benedict tried to explain to me long ago. She as a matter of fact spoke more freely than any of them about personal things. There was no difficulty about impersonal things, and they would go on at length about their ideas or theories. I don't even dare approach Köhler. Same for Wertheimer.... They all seemed uneasy when I told them what I thought of them and what I wanted of them.[101]

Maslow believed that the self-actualized person exhibits a great need to identify with humanity, a tendency roughly analogous to Alfred Adler's concept of *Gemeinschaftsgefühl*, a kind of "fellow-feeling" or a strong sense of community or social interest. They also have a strong ethical sense and a deep commitment to democratic values that fosters resistance to the stifling effects of enculturation and obedience. Their need for creative expression and continued freshness of appreciation for and wonder about the world tends to manifest itself in periodic mystical or "peak" experiences. Maslow observed many of these traits in Wertheimer as, for example, when he would play on the floor with his children or leap onto a desk for emphasis during a lecture.[102]

Maslow cautioned that "there are no perfect people," adding five traits that may be perceived less favorably than the first set by other people who encounter a self-actualized individual. In their quest for truth, such individuals may exhibit unexpected ruthlessness and "surgical coldness"; Maslow and his fellow students were frequent witnesses to Wertheimer's intense and almost brutal attacks on "blind" psychologists who failed to understand or appreciate Gestalt theory. Maslow also identified traits of periodic absentmindedness, overkindliness and non-neurotic guilt and anxiety in the profiles of self-actualized people. Maslow eventually contemplated possible controlled empirical studies of the social and perceptual judgments of self-actualized individuals, but physical illness soon brought this line of work to an end.[103]

As for Wertheimer, had he had an opportunity to be consulted on this work, he doubtless would have preferred that his theory and not his personality serve as a focus of inquiry.

Appendix
Max Wertheimer's Four American Essays

This appendix presents somewhat fuller summaries of Wertheimer's essays on truth, ethics, democracy, and freedom than are included in the text of Chapter 12. None of these abstracts, though, does full justice to the content of the essays; this is especially true for the essay on freedom ("A story of three days"). The interested reader is strongly urged to consult the original essays, reprinted in Mary Henle's *Documents of Gestalt psychology* (Berkeley, CA: University of California Press, 1961), pp. 19-64.

On Truth

From *Social Research*, Vol. 1, No. 2, May, 1934, pp. 135-146.

"Science is rooted in the will to truth. With the will to truth it stands or falls. Lower the standard even slightly and science becomes diseased at the core. Not only science but [humans]. The will to truth, pure and unadulterated, is among the essential conditions of [human] existence; if the standard is compromised [humans easily become] a kind of tragic caricature of [themselves]."

"The...situation with reference to the theory of truth is complicated at present.... What follows has to do with things that...natural [humans feel] as self-evident."

The classical view: truth concerns whether propositions are true or false. A proposition is true if it corresponds with its object, and false if it does not.

But: "a man hires another to steal something out of a desk; the theft is discovered;...the second man was seen near the house; the judge, who does not know their connection, asks the first man whether he took the article from the desk; the first man answers, 'No,' gives his alibi, and is discharged. He did not take the article from the desk. His statement that he did not is true according to the definition. Nevertheless, he lied."

Old solutions to this problem don't fully solve it. The investigator's question "is not an isolated fact in a vacuum. It is an integral part of a...situation in which the investigator, the suspect, and the theft form a characteristic whole." The assertion "'I did not take it from the desk' corresponds...with a piecemeal reality, torn from its context.... A thing may be true in the piecemeal sense [but false]...as a part in its whole." Call piecemeal truth and falsity t and f, "real truth" T and F "in which the statement and its object are considered as parts in their related wholes." The present example is then tF.

If the world were "nothing more than the sum of isolated facts,...then the old definition of truth, t and f, would be adequate." But if facts exist "not in isolation but as parts of a whole, determined by their function in this whole, then it leads to blind and false conclusions." Traditional logic deals "with piecemeal content in a summation relation. And for this it is adequate."

There obviously are tT and fF cases; are there also fT ones? Yes, for example, caricatures.

In order really to "find out what is true and what is false, we must direct our attention to the role of any particular item in the whole of which it is a part." But that can be difficult. "The basic problem here is the function of a part as a part of its whole." Facts can occur in isolation or as parts of wholes, "and a part may figure in two or more different wholes."

Pointing to problems of definition or abstraction does not help.

"The question of establishing the boundaries of a Gestalt, as of a practical situation, is not a matter of choice but is subject to examination on grounds of being correct or incorrect, logical or illogical"; for example, does bringing up another "fact" change the Gestalt? If not, then that "fact" isn't part of the Gestalt.

Music can provide examples of how the same two notes, for instance, have entirely different roles in two different melodies; so can isolated members in a mathematical series. Or a line can appear straight but be the asymptote of a hyperbola.

Then there is the case of t(?). An answer to "Tell me the truth about this" could be "many facts that are individually valid [but] can leave the questioner entirely ignorant." One can know everything as a sum, but not grasp "the inner connections of the whole...if the individual data are not present as parts, transparent, determined as parts."

Limiting truth or falsehood to being mere qualities of propositions limits "the meaning of truth and falsehood artificially." Truth really applies not only to statements but primarily to what people do, in the will to do justice to the situations they are in; and this is "the inner connection between truth and justice."

Some Problems in the Theory of Ethics

From *Social Research*, Vol. 2, No. 3, August, 1935, pp. 353-367.

There is an old conception of humanity that views as central to homo sapiens "the ability and tendency to understand, to gain insight; a feeling for truth, for justice, for good and evil, for sincerity." Human dignity is an inner goal of people. But the development of these faculties is sometimes hampered or concealed.

But now there is a thesis of relativism: there is no absolute ethic. "All values are fundamentally relative, changing with place and time." Many consider "the relativity of ethics...self-evident." Recent findings in ethnology, etc., have documented "very different moral concepts and evaluations" and therefore "the old idea of unity [universality of ethical principles] is an empty fiction." There are different systems of ethical axioms, and there is no way to find out whether one is better or "more right" than another. You can get equally sensible systems of ethics by reversing evaluation signs for the axioms, substituting + for - and - for +. But surely that "is not true." There are common conditions in human societies. Facts of evaluation are embedded in their cultural contexts.

Consider the behavior of an individual in a crowd—participants later wonder how they could have acted so blindly. But that doesn't mean there were different sets of ethical axioms at work; rather, it is possible that "different conditions have led to different behavior and to different evaluations, although the principles of evaluation are identical." A given item can receive different evaluations in different situations.

In different whole situations, a given component "changes necessarily as part, in its role, in its function [and]...transcends the purely summative constellations." If one views different evaluations of what appears superficially to be similar in different social settings in their inner relation to relevant facts in these different settings, "then the facts seem to tend...in the direction of fundamental identities."

Historically, European concepts were first considered universal and self-evident in ethnology. Then differences were described and ascribed to "different ethical systems." Now we realize that sociological, religious, etc. context must be taken into account; "the apparent differences are not direct evidence for differences in the [ethical] axioms. Rather, the facts suggest 'fundamental identity' rather than 'contradictory norms.'"

The usual scheme is to assume that there is simply an arbitrary additive relation between an object and its evaluation. For example, a food is good because it tastes good to me, or is in fashion, or because others call it good; this may be true for me but not for someone else.

But: consider examples such as a judge convicting "an obviously innocent person because the guilty person has bribed" the judge, or of "an adolescent rowdy" who grabs a piece of bread from a poor hungry child and uses it as a football. If these situations are viewed "in terms of the arbitrary addition of a subjective evaluation to an object, then there is a lack of clarity, something does not jibe." One needs to clarify "the relation between the situation and the action." The behavior may be blind to the situation, or may do violence to the situation, or may "be appropriate to the structure of the situation, to accomplish what the situation requires." These are objective qualities to which my subjective evaluation is irrelevant.

If I add 7 + 7 and get 15, because I like the number 15 or like to have sums divisible by 5, that process violates the structure of the situation; the 15 is factually wrong, does not fill the gap, violates what is structurally required in this place; it is capricious. There is an "inner necessity" here as in many instances in mathematical curves.

The bribed judge's conviction may be preferred subjectively by the judge but is nevertheless unjust. Comparably blind is: I have a piece of bread in one hand and a brick in the other, and give the brick to a hungry child and the bread to a man who needs one more brick to finish the house he is building. And a larger system may be involved: "If a gangster needs a revolver...in order to carry out a particular task, then the gangster with his need is logically a part of the larger system of human society, in which he with his wishes is to be considered a functional part." It is not arbitrary; there is no "infinite regress."

Another example: a passionately prejudiced person, prejudiced because of vicious propaganda. This is not a case of ethical relativism.

Are "requirements," the "qualities" of justice and injustice, psychological realities? Often yes. Egocentrism is not necessarily always the case, in perception or in thinking. Often there are realizations, awakenings, reorganizations. The pessimistic thesis about human nature may well be false.

One can go "beyond a hasty, superficial relativism" concerning ethical problems, or sheer "factual evaluations," and focus on "their structural roles, their inner causation, their inner determination."

On the Concept of Democracy

From Max Ascoli & Fritz Lehmann (Eds.), *Political and economic democracy*. New York: Norton, 1937, pp. 271-283

The question of the meaning of democracy entails "certain logical-methodological problems."

There is the method of enumerating similarities and differences relative to other forms of government, but that ("exact") method may yield an and-sum that is blind to the hierarchical logical structure. An alternative, more difficult, is "to investigate the structural function of the items and the hierarchical structure of the whole idea."

One can begin the analysis with the people voting, and majority rule; various other things must be taken into account, for example, that the vote is free, not by threat or intimidation; this "is not an accidental addition but is logically determining in the structure." Comparably, voters must have access to full and true information, "and there must be free and open discussion."

Free voting means preserving one's rights, not one's private interests; voters are envisaged as responsible for a decision that is right for the community, not just for the voters themselves. Majority rule in a democracy also means preserving the rights of minorities. And if the minority is convinced the majority is wrong, it must try "to clear the matter up, to find better arguments," etc. And members of the majority "will not feel very happy if the proper aims of a minority are brutally overridden by majority vote." There must be respect for the minority, which must be given an opportunity to be heard. There must be freedom of speech, and freedom of the press (but this freedom is not "restricted to consequences for the individual and individual rights. It also has the social function of providing the [voting] public with better information"); "information is indispensable to voting in the true sense." This is "different from the meaning determined only by…freedom of business enterprise combined with freedom of expression."

The logical-methodological issue is the "difference between taking a single item as an item in itself or in one-sided determination, and trying to understand it in its function in the whole structure." It is viewing democracy as an and-sum or as "a hierarchical structure in which the items are conceived as parts in their relational place, in their function in this whole." "Is there an 'and-sum' or a structure?"

What is the structural center of the concept of democracy? *Not* "opposition to the kingdom, to the king as king, but opposition to injustice," to capricious rule; "the wish to create and assure a more just procedure," to have decisions not be arbitrary but be ruled "by reason and justice." "The principle of justice and reason as opposed to arbitrary dealing" is "structurally primary, central in this hypothesis." Items "like government by the people, voting, majority rule, etc." are secondary, "determined by the center." Alternatively, one might view the autonomy of the individual as the center; this generates a slightly different overall perspective and structure.

"There appears to be a logical structure of democracy with a hierarchy of parts…[T]he different points in the picture get their meaning in their place, in their role, in their function as parts in the picture along with the ethical and educational aims of democracy, the will to truth, to open-mindedness, to fair play, to honesty, etc. Viewed in this way the real essence of democracy seems to be not a form of government, a sum of institutions, etc., but a certain real attitude in life, behavior of a certain kind, not only in state matters but generally in relations between [people]. This attitude has some characteristic similarities to the role of the judge or the juror, rather than to the fighting of interests. The state is viewed not as a governing body, but as the guarantor of justice and reason which has not to create law but to fulfill it, to realize it by making the rules."

"The main point…[is] the difference between an item seen in itself…and an item envisaged as part of the hierarchical structure, democracy." But political democracy must also be viewed in the larger context, the overall "social field." This social field was different during the frontier period (when democracy had to deal with fewer challenges) than during industrialization, with the "development of big capitalistic forms,…masses of workers, depression, masses of unemployed, etc. Strains and stresses are born. The system democracy has to face new problems. Disequilibrium, strain, stresses in one part of the field, e.g., the economic, are not simply irrelevant for the 'part-system' democracy. Problems of the whole—dynamics of the whole system—arise."

A Story of Three Days

From Ruth Nanda Anshen (Ed.), *Freedom, its meaning*. New York: Harcourt, Brace, 1940, pp. 555-569.

A man "longed for a clarification of the fundamentals of freedom.... What at bottom is freedom? What does it require? Why is it so dear to me?"

A sociologist gives him information about the evolution of ideas of freedom historically in several societies, etc. The man inquires, but why is freedom so precious to me; "what is freedom essentially?" Answer: An individual's standards, evaluations, and goals are shaped by the social group of which that individual is a part. "Different periods in history, different societies, different nations, have different views. Ethical standards are relative."

The man is bewildered. Are our ideas merely historical accidents of a particular time? Are there no fundamental standards? Answer: they are "developed in and characteristic for certain historical, cultural, and social settings." But is there nothing more, "no features that are basic in people with regard to questions of freedom, no requirements for [people], as [people] should be...[; no] features that are desirable, required in human society?" Answer: "the fight for freedom was always a fight against certain concrete restraints or compulsions and meant, necessarily, different things in different times.... There are no axioms which would allow [one] to speak of fundamental standards.

"But if you ask for a definition of freedom, not in terms of the full reality of a specific society,...then [the] answer would have to be: absence of restraints, of compulsions, of external hindrances from doing what one desires to do."

The man goes home "sad, puzzled, bewildered," and starts reading a 1936 novel. In that novel a character muses that "all modern history is a History of the Idea of Freedom from Institutions. It is also the History of the Fact of Slavery to Institutions.... [T]he fact of freedom exists only for a very small number of individuals." That strikes the man as "utterly false and wrong." Next he reads a 1928 book by a psychoanalyst that expresses "basic assumptions which led straight to those bewildering passages he had encountered in the novel," for example, "every culture must be built up on coercion and instinctual renunciation"; "instinctual wishes are those of incest, of cannibalism, and of murder"; if "one could choose any woman who took one's fancy as one's sexual object, one could kill without hesitation one's rival or whoever interfered with one in any other way, and one could seize what one wanted of another man's goods without asking his leave: how splendid, what a succession of delights life would be!...[But] only one single person can be made unrestrictedly happy by abolishing thus the restrictions of culture, and that is a tyrant or dictator who has monopolized all the means of power." The man asks himself, is this really what people, society, freedom are about? "Is freedom lack of restraint of 'instinctual impulsions,' external or internal?"

Next the man consults a philosopher, and asks for the philosophical definition of freedom. The concept of free will, free choice played an important role in various religions and philosophies in the past, but that is wishful thinking. Science has shown that there are no free acts; every event and act is caused, is determined. Even criminal acts are not the result of free will, but are determined by causal forces within the criminal: desires, instincts, acquired habits. Even if one does not know of the forces that compel a particular act or decision, thus giving the illusion of free will, that does not mean that the act or decision was not determined. Doesn't this lead to fatalism, to renouncing responsibility? No, because people believe they have free will. But, the man points out, the determinism-free will issue is not really relevant: even if everything *were* determined, "all real concrete problems" of freedom would "remain just the same." The philosopher counters that one should "not mix up...practical problems with the philosophical issue." And the poor man is "more bewildered than before."

He summarizes what he has learned:

1. There is no freedom because all is determined, is the consequence of causes. Or,
2. Freedom is absence of external restraints, of compulsion, freedom to pursue whatever wish may come to one's mind. Or,
3. Because such wishes may be due to whatever standards may have been internalized on the basis of compulsion, freedom means to be able to follow those instinctual impulsions without inhibitions.

But all this appears "utterly strange, narrow, inadequate; superficial, oversimplified, wrongly directed, blind to all the real problems of freedom, appropriate neither to the nature of [humanity nor] society, out of focus on both." There are "strong and indeed very characteristic cases of [adults], of children, who [are] free, who [are] unfree." What are the essentials here?

Free people appear "frank, open-minded, sincerely going ahead, facing the situation freely, looking for the right thing to do and so finding where to go." Unfree people look "inhibited, pushed, or driven, acting by command or intimidation, one-track-minded, chained to certain ways of acting and of thinking...[,] like sorry products of external influences or like slaves of any desire that might have come to their minds...[;] like robots, somehow crippled, robbed of essential abilities, narrow-minded, stiff, rigid, mechanical...." Sometimes they appear "brutal and overproud." Occasionally such people transform from unfreedom to freedom; this is "similar indeed to regaining health after a long illness." One can restructure the problem into "what conditions, what institutions, make for the free? What for the unfree?"

The piecemeal view deals only negatively with freedom, and is like considering beauty only absence of ugliness, good thinking absence of mistakes, kindliness or friendship absence of hostility, or justice any legal rule imposed arbitrarily.

In history, people who "honestly fought for freedom...fought against the arbitrary...acts of their governments,...for fair and honest dealing."

It is piecemeal "to say 'restraint is restraint,' if a kidnapper restrains, imprisons, a child in order to extort ransom, and if another restrains the gangster from doing it in order to help the child."

The basic issues are not the three theses, but that "human beings are exposed to injustice,...to brutality; robbed of any hope of being treated with fairness, with kindness; that institutions are destroyed which had slowly developed, guaranteeing some justice, some fair dealing." And that people "are forced to keep silent in the face of acts of injustice,...forced even to help in performing those acts against their will and better knowledge." Also that people "by willfully distorted information become narrowed down, poisoned in their very souls, robbed of the preconditions of free judgment through being blinded, robbed of what in [people] and society is humane."

"Freedom is...a condition in the social field" and must be viewed "in its role, in its function, in its interactions, in its consequences for [people] and for society." It is also a "Gestalt quality of attitude, of behavior, of a [person's] thinking, of [a person's] actions." But freedom as condition and as Gestalt quality "must be viewed not as two pieces, but in their intimate interrelation."

Notes

1. Max Wertheimer (1940). A story of three days. In Ruth N. Anshen (ed.), *Freedom: Its meaning*, pp. 271-283. New York: Harcourt, Brace.
2. Wertheimer's correspondence with Luria about a planned memorial volume for Vygotskii is presented in detail in Chapter 11.
3. O. D. Tolischus (1936). Nazis would junk theoretical physics. *New York Times* (March 9), p. 19.
4. German science goose-steps. *New York Times* (1936, March 12), p. 20.
5. Crannell, "Wolfgang Köhler," p. 268.
6. Ash, *Holism and the quest for objectivity*, p. 484.
7. In an April 1935 letter to Karl Lashley, Köhler still expressed some hope that his problems at the university could be resolved. See Ash, *Holism and the quest for objectivity*, pp. 492-493.

8. Frances Blanshard (1970). *Frank Aydelotte of Swarthmore*. Middletown, CT: Wesleyan University Press, p. 281.

9. For a thorough account of Köhler's turbulent relations during the Nazi regime, see Henle, One man against the Nazis, and Ash, *Holism and the quest for objectivity* (especially Chapter 19).

10. See Ash, *Holism and the quest for objectivity*, and Ulfried Geuter (Richard J. Holmes, Trans.) (1992). *The professionalization of psychology in Nazi Germany*. Cambridge: Cambridge University Press.

11. Ash, *Holism and the quest for objectivity*, p. 478.

12. Interview with Anni Hornbostel (AH).

13. Valentin Wertheimer, quoted in Luchins and Luchins (1987), p. 75.

14. Wertheimers are citizens. *Wertheimer Times*, 1 (May 1939), pp. 1-2. (MW-CU)

15. Quoted in Lewis A. Coser (1984). *Refugee scholars in America: Their impact and their experiences*. New Haven, CT: Yale University Press, p. 11.

16. Interview with Anni Hornbostel. Several of Wertheimer's American colleagues at the New School also expressed disapproval of such provincial professors. Rutkoff and Scott, *New School: A history of the New School for Social Research*, p. 106.

17. Krohn, *Intellectuals in exile: Refugee scholars and the New School for Social Research*, p. 182.

18. Wertheimer's method of teaching and playing chess may have played a role in Val becoming an expert at the game; Val became the "first board" on Columbia University's chess team when he was an undergraduate student there in the 1940s.

19. Rutkoff and Scott, *New School: A history of the New School for Social Research*, p. 31.

20. Rutkoff and Scott, *New School: A history of the New School for Social Research*, p. 135.

21. Krohn, *Intellectuals in exile: Refugee scholars and the New School for Social Research*, pp. 86-91.

22. Rutkoff and Scott, *New School: A history of the New School for Social Research*, p. 104.

23. Rutkoff and Scott, *New School: A history of the New School for Social Research*, p. 105.

24. Alvin Johnson (1934). Foreword. *Social Research*, 1, 1-2.

25. Susan Quinn (1987). *A mind of her own: The life of Karen Horney*. New York: Summit, p. 282.

26. Hans Speyer. Quoted in Quinn, *A mind of her own: The life of Karen Horney*, pp. 282-283.

27. Sigmund Freud (1982). The question of a *Weltanschauung*. In James Strachey (ed.), *The standard edition of the complete psychological works of Sigmund Freud*, Vol. 22, pp. 158-182. London: Hogarth, p. 181. Einstein refused to support Freud's candidacy for a Nobel prize in 1928 although he later admitted that he admired "the beauty and clarity" of Freud's writings but vacillated between "belief and unbelief." See Peter Gay (1988). *Freud: A life for our time*. New York: Norton, pp. 456ff, 575.

28. Karen Horney (1967). On the genesis of the castration complex in women. In Harold Kelman (ed.), *Feminine psychology*, pp. 37-53. New York: Norton.

29. Karen Horney (1967). The flight from womanhood. In Harold Kelman (ed.), *Feminine psychology*, pp. 54-70. New York: Norton, p. 54.

30. Hans Speyer. Quoted in Quinn, *A mind of her own: The life of Karen Horney*, p. 283.

31. Karen Horney to Max Wertheimer, November 20 [n. d.], MW-UC. Karen Horney to Max Wertheimer, June 25, 1940, MW-UC.

32. Barbara S. Burks (1939). Progress report of the Committee on Displaced Foreign Psychologists. *Psychological Bulletin*, 36, p. 189.

33. S. Duggan and B. Drury (1948). *The rescue of science and learning*. New York: Macmillan.

34. John A. McGeoch (1942). Psychology and the war. *Psychological Bulletin*, 39, 179-181.

35. American Psychological Association (1938). Proceedings of Forty-Sixth annual meeting. *Psychological Bulletin*, 35, 579-725.

36. For example, Allport outlined what he believed to be the basic principles for planning peace in a 1945 statement printed in the *Psychological Bulletin*. The statement, entitled "Human nature and the peace," was signed by 2,038 American psychologists. Gordon W. Allport (1945). Human nature and the peace. *Psychological Bulletin*, 42, 376-378.

37. Gardner Murphy and Robert Cook (1943). Barbara Stoddard Burks. *American Journal of Psychology*, 56, 610-612.

38. Barbara S. Burks to Lewis M. Terman, March 17, 1936. Lewis M. Terman Archives, Stanford University.

39. Robert Cook (1943). Barbara Stoddard Burks, 1902-1943. *Eugenical News*, 28, p. 4.

40. J. H. Capshew and A. C. Laszlo (1986). 'We would not take no for an answer': Women psychologists and gender politics during World War II. *Journal of Social Issues*, 42, 157-180.

41. Barbara S. Burks (1942). A social psychology background for civilian morale. *Journal of Social Psychology: SPSSI Bulletin*, 16, 150-153.

42. Capshew and Laszlo, 'We would not take no for an answer': Women psychologists and gender politics during World War II, p. 160.

43. Barbara S. Burks to Lewis M. Terman, November 15, 1938. Lewis M. Terman Archives, Stanford University.

44. Burks, Progress report of the Committee on Displaced Foreign Psychologists, p. 188.

45. Gordon W. Allport (1944). Quoted in Lewis M. Terman, Barbara Stoddard Burks, 1902-1943, *Psychological Review*, 51, 136-141.

46. Burks, Progress report of the Committee on Displaced Foreign Psychologists, pp. 189-190.

47. Rudolf Ekstein to Max Wertheimer, April 28, 1938. MW-UC. Ekstein's efforts to emigrate to the United States were successful. Several years later, Ekstein, like Wertheimer, felt compelled to address the issue of freedom from the standpoint of a psychologist. See Rudolf Ekstein (1947). Psychological laws and human freedom. *Journal of Social Psychology*, 25, 181-191.

48. Henry Abelson to Max Wertheimer, May 20, 1939. MW-UC.

49. MW to Department of Labor, 1939 (Draft). MW-UC.

50. After immigrating to the United States Karl Bühler and his wife Charlotte did not receive the recognition that they had earned in European psychology, prompting

Coser to name them "casualties of exile." See Coser, *Refugee scholars in America: Their impact and their experiences*, pp. 37-41.

51. Burks, Progress report of the Committee on Displaced Foreign Psychologists, p. 190.
52. American Psychological Association Committee on Displaced Foreign Psychologists (1942). Report of the Committee on Displaced Foreign Psychologists. *Psychological Bulletin*, 39, p. 733.
53. American Psychological Association Committee on Displaced Foreign Psychologists (1940). Report of the Committee on Displaced Foreign Psychologists. *Psychological Bulletin*, 37, p. 718.
54. American Psychological Association (1943. Proceedings of the Fifty-First annual meeting. *Psychological Bulletin*, 40, p. 660.
55. Max Wertheimer (1934). On truth. *Social Research*, 1, 135-146.
56. *Place* is its position relative to other relevant assertions. *Role* is the specific task it performs in the whole situation. *Function* is its consequences or effects on the whole.
57. Max Wertheimer (1935). Some problems in the theory of ethics. *Social Research*, 2, 353-367.
58. Wolfgang Köhler (1938). *The place of value in a world of facts*. New York: Liveright. Mary Henle (1983). Man's place in nature in the thinking of Wolfgang Köhler. *Journal of the History of the Behavioral Sciences*, 29, 3-7.
59. Hoffman, *The right to be human: A biography of Abraham Maslow*, p. 95. Kurt Koffka (1935). *Principles of Gestalt psychology*. New York: Harcourt, Brace. Kurt Koffka (1935). The ontological status of value. In Horace Kallen and Sidney Hook (eds.), *American philosophy today and tomorrow*, pp. 275-309. New York: Furman.
60. Max Wertheimer (1937). On the concept of democracy. In M. Ascoli and F. Lehmann (eds.), *Political and economic democracy*, pp. 271-283. New York: Norton.
61. George W. Hartmann (1946). The Gestalt view on the process of institutional transformation. *Psychological Review*, 53, 282-289.
62. Max Wertheimer (1940). A story of three days. In Ruth N. Anshen (ed.), *Freedom: Its meaning*, pp. 555-569. New York: Harcourt, Brace.
63. Wertheimer, A story of three days, p. 563.
64. Mary Henle wrote a warm tribute to Wertheimer's essay, enlarging the theme to show how his approach followed from his perspective on productive thinking; confronting the same frustrations as Wertheimer's protagonist, she concludes that "Max Wertheimer's problems are still with us." Mary Henle (1986). A tribute to Max Wertheimer: Three stories of three days. In Mary Henle, *1879 and all that: Essays in the theory and history of psychology*, pp. 241-253. New York: Columbia University Press, p. 253.
65. Michael Wertheimer (1965). Relativity and Gestalt: A note on Albert Einstein and Max Wertheimer. *Journal of the History of the Behavioral Sciences*, 1, p. 87.
66. A note from the New School librarian mentions that he was also examining John Dewey's book on *Freedom and culture* as well as Plato's *Dialogues*. M. Hall to Max Wertheimer, February 6, 1940, MW-CU. In March 1931, Wertheimer had purchased Adolf Hitler's 1924 book *Mein Kampf*, which he also may have consulted in writing this essay.

67. Michael Wertheimer, "Relativity and Gestalt," p. 88.

68. In 1991, Hans-Jürgen Walter published Wertheimer's essays in German translation: Hans-Jürgen Walter (ed.) (1991). *Max Wertheimer: Zur Gestaltpsychologie menschlicher Werte* [*Max Wertheimer: On the Gestalt psychology of human values*]. Opladen, Germany: Westdeutscher Verlag.

69. Abraham H. Maslow. Quoted in M. H. Hall (1977). A conversation with Abraham Maslow. In Robert E. Schell (ed.), *Readings in developmental psychology today*. New York: CRM Books.

70. Abraham H. Maslow. Quoted in Edward Hoffman (1988). *The right to be human: A biography of Abraham Maslow*. Los Angeles, CA: Tarcher, p. 87.

71. Hoffman, *The right to be human: A biography of Abraham Maslow*, p. 93.

72. Abraham H. Maslow. Quoted in Mildred Hardeman (1986). Dialogue with Abraham Maslow. In Tom Greening (ed.), *Politics and innocence: A humanistic debate*. Dallas, TX: Saybrook, p. 75.

73. Abraham H. Maslow. Quoted in Hoffman, *The right to be human: A biography of Abraham Maslow*, p. 96.

74. According to Hoffman, "In Maslow's estimation, Wertheimer's stature as a discoverer of the human mind might have equaled Freud's had he been as forceful and productive an exponent of his own ideas." Hoffman, *The right to be human: A biography of Abraham Maslow*, p. 93.

75. Abraham H. Maslow (1943). A theory of human motivation. *Psychological Review*, 50, p. 385.

76. Alfred Louis Kroeber (1948). *Anthropology*. New York: Harcourt, Brace & World, p. 293.

77. Margaret M. Caffrey (1989). *Ruth Benedict: Stranger in this land*. Austin, TX: University of Texas Press, p. 96.

78. Edward Sapir. Quoted in Margaret M. Caffrey, *Ruth Benedict: Stranger in this land*, p. 154.

79. Ruth Fulton Benedict (1932). Configuration of culture in North America. *American Anthropologist*, 34, 1-27. Ruth Fulton Benedict (1934). *Patterns of culture*. Boston, MA: Houghton-Mifflin.

80. Ruth Benedict, *Patterns of culture*, p. 50.

81. Ruth Benedict, *Patterns of culture*, p. 51.

82. Ruth Benedict, *Patterns of culture*, p. 52.

83. Ruth Benedict, *Patterns of culture*, pp. 46-47.

84. Ruth Benedict, *Patterns of culture*, p. 47.

85. Margaret M. Caffrey, *Ruth Benedict: Stranger in this land*, pp. 249-251. Caffrey notes that Benedict's diary shows, for instance, that she scheduled a "lecture to Gestalt Psych" for the afternoon of December 30, 1936. Ibid, p. 286. Coser also mentions that Benedict and Margaret Mead joined Allport, Tolman, and another scholar in attending Kurt Lewin's "Topology Group" during this period. Coser, *Refugee scholars in America: Their impact and their experiences*, p. 24.

86. Margaret Mead (1974). *Ruth Benedict*. New York: Columbia University Press, p. 49.

87. Ruth Fulton Benedict and Gene Weltfish (1943). *The races of mankind*. New York: Public Affairs Committee. Ruth Fulton Benedict (1942). *Race and racism*.

London: Routledge. Ruth Fulton Benedict (1946). *The chrysanthemum and the sword: Patterns of Japanese culture.* Boston, MA: Houghton Mifflin.

88. Abraham H. Maslow and John J. Honigmann (1970). Synergy: Some notes of Ruth Benedict. *American Anthropologist*, 72, 320-333.

89. Abraham H. Maslow (1971). *The farther reaches of human nature.* New York: Viking, p. 41.

90. Maslow, *The farther reaches of human nature*, p. 42.

91. Hoffman, *The right to be human: A biography of Abraham Maslow*, p. 152.

92. Maslow, *The farther reaches of human nature*, p. 42.

93. Richard J. Lowry (1973). *A. H. Maslow: An intellectual portrait.* Monterey, CA: Brooks/Cole, p. 33.

94. Lowry, *A. H. Maslow: An intellectual portrait*, p. 95.

95. Hoffman, *The right to be human: A biography of Abraham Maslow*, p. 94.

96. Wertheimer, "A story of three days," p. 565. The influence of Wertheimer's essays is also evident in an article by Maslow that encouraged movement toward a more holistic "growth politics" that emphasizes human values and needs. See Abraham H. Maslow (1986). Politics 3. In Tom Greening (ed.), *Politics and innocence: A humanistic debate*, pp. 80-95. Dallas, TX: Saybrook.

97. Despite their long affiliation, Wertheimer was cool toward Goldstein's approach and criticized Maslow after he presented a paper at a New School seminar in which Maslow characterized Goldstein's work as "an application of Gestalt psychology to the study of personality." Maslow was

> puzzled about why [Wertheimer] was so antagonistic, and only later found out there was a personal antagonism between him and Kurt Goldstein. I questioned both Wertheimer and Goldstein about their relations with each other. The answers I got from Goldstein were more satisfactory to me. My impression was that Wertheimer was unreasonable and not big about it, although I don't remember the details. This was the only time in all the years that I knew Wertheimer of which I could say this, that he behaved in a somewhat childish fashion. Goldstein indicated that he was hurt by the separation, didn't quite understand it, and saw no necessity for it. Neither did I. Perhaps it was a characterological choice of the same kind which showed itself in the choice of topics to research with. Wertheimer gave me to understand that he thought my work with dominance, with motivation, sex, with needs was somehow unpleasant.... I found this to be true generally with the Gestalters, not only with Wertheimer, but also Koffka and Köhler, i.e., they preferred the cool subjects, perception, cognition, logic, thinking, rather than the warm subjects that Goldstein and I were interested in. Kurt Lewin was sort of in between.

Abraham Maslow. Quoted in Luchins and Luchins, "Max Wertheimer in America: 1933-1943," p. 137.

98. Abraham H. Maslow (1954). *Motivation and personality.* New York: Harper & Brothers, p. xiii.

99. Abraham H. Maslow (1943). A theory of human motivation. *Psychological Review*, 50, 370-396, p. 371.

100. Maslow, *Motivation and personality*, p. 152.

101. Abraham H. Maslow, September 8, 1945. Quoted in Lowry, *A. H. Maslow: An intellectual portrait*, p. 94.

102. Hoffman, *The right to be human: A biography of Abraham Maslow*, p. 92.

103. Hoffman, *The right to be human: A biography of Abraham Maslow*, p. 175.

13

Personal Challenges; Productive Students

*I have been able to use Wertheimer's basic
concepts in my research, especially those
concerning the nature and the role of sensible
processes in contrast to senseless processes and
those concerning the role of structure in
understanding, and I want to express here my
deeply felt thanks to Professor Wertheimer.*
—George Katona (1940)

By the time of the United States' involvement in the Second World War, Wertheimer had been in America for more than eight years but had not changed his lifestyle appreciably. His disposition, teaching style, writing habits, and daily activities remained largely unaltered after his immigration. But according to her own account, Anni was gradually developing a stronger sense of her own identity during her time in America. Before arriving in the United States, she had already become less involved in helping Max draft his ideas about Gestalt psychology and, by 1941, she stopped attending his lectures. Their relationship, while continuing to be warm and deeply valued by both, as Anni reported, was no longer a functioning marriage. Max's heart attack and his constant devotion to Gestalt theory were part of the problem. Anni also spent much time with Johannes von Hornbostel, the son of Max's friend and co-worker Erich von Hornbostel. Johannes (nicknamed "Schani") had earned his doctorate in physics at the University of Berlin and had early expressed an interest in Gestalt theory. Indeed, during Schani's youth he and Max had had a number of discussions about developing a Gestalt theory of physics, but their ideas never progressed beyond interested conversation. Wertheimer had also encouraged Einstein to write a letter of recommendation for the younger Hornbostel. Unlike Max, Schani was about the same age as Anni, and seemed to her to be more attentive to her and her interests than was Wertheimer. Schani left a minor position in the Physics Department at the University of Berlin and immigrated with his parents, Erich and Susanne ("Susi") von Hornbostel, to the United States a short time later than the Wertheimers. Erich had originally intended to lecture at the New School, but instead he and Susi moved to London, where he died after a long illness late in 1935.

Schani, when he came to America, anglicized his name to John Hornbostel, and obtained a job as an electrical engineer at Thomas A. Edison, Inc. in West Orange, New Jersey, a position that did not really satisfy his interest in theoretical physics—but considering the extremely tight job market in the United States at the time, he was fortunate to have found a job that fit reasonably well with his abilities and education.[1] Schani's and Anni's relationship continued to develop after their immigration to the United States.

In 1936, Anni gave birth to a healthy baby boy, Peter Anthony, who became a dynamic and cherished part of the Wertheimer family. Five years after Peter's birth, Anni and Max formally separated. On December 13, 1941, Max and Anni, with the help of an attorney, drafted a legal agreement outlining details of property rights and child custody. Anni went to Reno, Nevada, for a little over a month to establish residence there for the purpose of obtaining a divorce. Alone and ill from a thyroid disorder, she wrote to Max and the children almost daily from late December 1941 to early February 1942. Their divorce became final on February 2; Max was granted custody of Valentin, Michael, and Lise while Anni was given custody of Peter. As part of the settlement, Max agreed to pay $20 a month in alimony to support Anni and Peter.

On February 10, 1942, Anni and John Hornbostel were married in Montclair, New Jersey. Peter stayed with Max and the other children in New Rochelle until early March, 1942, when he moved to the Hornbostel home in New Jersey. Peter always enjoyed returning to New Rochelle to visit Max and the other children, but such trips could not be frequent because they had to be done by car and had to be restricted due to the rationing of gasoline during this time.[2]

As he had done with the Stern children long before, Max continued to captivate his children with varied demonstrations or "experiments." For instance, he mounted a mask backwards in a cardboard box, and asked his children to look at it with one eye closed while moving their heads back and forth a bit, resulting in the eerie impression that the mask was spontaneously turning its head in the opposite direction. The children delighted in brain-teasers and creative puzzles he would design for them, helping them achieve an insightful solution.

Others besides the family resided in the Wertheimer home for various lengths of time. Shortly after arriving in the country the family had hired a young German refugee, Anna, to help Anni with various jobs around the house. She only stayed for a short period, and, soon thereafter, the family hired Lillian, who helped with the laundry and general cleaning, and Rosa Mae Dixon, a vibrant woman in her forties who looked after the Wertheimers and whose primary responsibility was in the kitchen. While living in the family's house, Rosa met a young handyman named Albert Anderson whom Wertheimer had hired for occasional odd jobs around the house. Rosa and Albert married, and so Albert too moved in with the Wertheimers. Albert only survived a few more years; he soon became ill and died at a young age.

In late March of 1942, Hornbostel initiated formal proceedings to adopt Peter. Wertheimer was contacted by a New Jersey attorney, Philip Barbash, who requested Max's signature on a consent form in the adoption papers. Wertheimer was slow to respond to Barbash's request; as mentioned in a draft of a letter, he claimed that he was "overburdened with work" and that he had been informed "that the matter is not so urgent."[3] After several further letters from Barbash, Wertheimer finally signed the consent forms near the end of 1942, and Peter Wertheimer legally became Peter Anthony Hornbostel.

Many friends of the Wertheimer family were shocked to learn about the divorce. After a visit to New Rochelle, Barbara Burks included a poem in a letter to Wertheimer, doubtless in an attempt to console Wertheimer and to express her empathy for his situation, and added that "To practically no one else would I send this poem, but it is so terrifically relevant to the problem of *children*, and what it does to them to face the problems of their family life honestly."[4] The poem read as follows:

> Out of night comes a timid knock,
> The rooster crows at dawn;
> The wind is blowing through the rock,
> And window shades are gone.
> You see the blood-stained battle field,
> And wild and tearing beasts
> Are gnawing at the wall of sealed
> And solitary feasts.
> You hear a cry, and then the door
> Of mainly outer grief
> Is swung to show a bier—a poor
> And miserable thief.
> It's he who steals your happiness,
> It's Lot who took a wife,
> It's man who lives in thirsty press
> And captures Thetis' life.

Although Burks claimed that she "had really nothing to do with its composition," she did not cite an author and noted that in "all modesty I think it is a good poem." The words of Burks's poem might well have summed up some of the despair in her own short life. During the time of Anni's breakup with Wertheimer, he lost three valued and trusted colleagues: Karl Duncker, Kurt Koffka and Barbara Burks.

By the time of Wertheimer's immigration, Duncker's life and career had taken an ominous turn. In June 1934, he learned that his habilitation at the

University of Berlin would be prevented because of his suspect political character. During the same summer, he was committed to a Nazi ideological camp (*Dozentenlager*) for university instructors and professors.[5] These incidents, along with his family's political activity and prominence, prompted Duncker to leave Germany and emigrate to England; in February 1936, Köhler wrote Wertheimer that Duncker had accepted a position as research assistant to the illustrious Cambridge psychologist Frederic C. Bartlett.[6] Bartlett was the director of the Cambridge psychology laboratory, the University of Cambridge's first professor of experimental psychology, and editor of the *British Journal of Psychology* at the time of Duncker's arrival. While in England, Duncker conducted and published research on the psychology of pain and on the social modification of children's food preferences, using British school children as participants in his experiments.[7] But Köhler wrote Wertheimer in December 1936 that Duncker was having some difficulty: "I think he is still concerned that it isn't going to work in America. I think he considers England too much outside the world."[8] In a later letter, Köhler mentioned that David Katz was called to a chair at Stockholm and expressed the wish that Duncker would also get a position.[9] At the same time, Wertheimer tried to get Duncker a position in Turkey, but this effort failed because Duncker had not completed his habilitation thesis.[10]

By the late summer of 1937, Duncker was struggling with recurring bouts of depression. In an effort to rectify the problem, Duncker left England for Switzerland for treatment by the prominent psychiatrist Ludwig Binswanger.[11] A mutual friend, Lene Frank, arranged Duncker's stay with Binswanger and wrote to Wertheimer that Duncker had already been in an institution in London where the treatment had been rather expensive.[12] Indeed, for some time there was discussion about sending him, for his own protection, to a locked institution. Frank cautioned that Duncker should not be returned to Germany because of the stringent laws requiring sterilization of patients with psychopathology.[13]

During the two months that Duncker stayed with Binswanger in Switzerland, Wertheimer and Köhler struggled to find a position in America for him. In an August, 1937 letter to Wertheimer, Köhler mentioned the possibility of a position for Duncker in Kentucky which would require him to lecture for 12 to 14 hours per week.[14] Köhler was understandably worried about the strain that such a heavy teaching load would place on Duncker. Wertheimer also wrote Köhler about the possibility of an assistant professorship for Duncker at the New School for Social Research, but the prospects were not promising.[15]

Binswanger predicted a successful treatment and on October 10, 1937, Duncker wrote Köhler that he had been released from Binswanger's clinic.[16] Yet Köhler informed Wertheimer that he was troubled by a letter to Köhler from Duncker: "I am not happy with the letter—there is an artificiality and correctness. Duncker would like to come to America right away but may not leave until December."[17] Since his arrival in 1936, Köhler had been trying unsuccessfully to bring Duncker to Swarthmore College;[18] he finally did manage to arrange for Duncker's appointment as instructor for the Fall 1938 semester. In December 1937, Köhler wrote Wertheimer that Duncker would arrive by ship in New York City.[19] Although Duncker seemed to be functioning reasonably well, Köhler remained apprehensive. In May, 1938 he wrote Wertheimer, "I'm not sure whether Duncker is in order or well. This sharply thinking man occasionally makes errors in his discussion of things but remains effective in his investigations.... I doubt that a major production can be expected soon."[20] Duncker's research continued to be of superior quality, although he was not working at his earlier prolific rate

The move to America did not alleviate Duncker's depression, and he finally succumbed to it altogether. In a February 25, 1940 letter to Wertheimer, Köhler wrote of Duncker:

> I have sad news—he is dead.... I had hoped to have him come live with us to get through this difficult time.... [I]n Baltimore he bought himself a weapon and was found Friday morning [February 23, 1940] dead in his car. If he had stayed here I believe we could have rescued him. What would his future have been like then? He was a superb person and a moving child.[21]

Duncker committed suicide less than a month after his thirty-seventh birthday. Twelve years before Duncker's death, his wife, Gerda Duncker-Naef, had already written to Wertheimer with a prophetic question: "Would you condemn a person who is unemployed and is in a hopeless business situation and who therefore takes his own life?"[22]

Like Wertheimer and Köhler, Koffka too was shocked by the news. In a letter to his friend and former student Molly Harrower he wrote:

> There is one truly sad piece of news: I heard yesterday that Duncker had committed suicide. I knew that he had another nervous breakdown, the Köhlers had taken him into their house, and the crisis seemed to have passed when the catastrophe happened. I was badly shaken, an unusually gifted man, whose tragedy was perhaps that he was a German, and, as such could not find the connection between reality and the ideal. Psychology has suffered a great loss, of that I am certain.[23]

Just over one year later, psychology would also suffer the loss of Kurt Koffka.

Koffka was one of Wertheimer's most valued colleagues. In 1935, Koffka's magnum opus, his monumental work *Principles of Gestalt Psychology*, appeared in print; it was dedicated to "Wolfgang Köhler and

Max Wertheimer in gratitude for their friendship and inspiration."[24] In a volume of more than 700 printed pages, Koffka performed the enormous task of summarizing and integrating most of the published literature on Gestalt theory. According to Harrower, Koffka was disappointed that Wertheimer and Köhler were both late in acknowledging receipt of their gift copies after the publication of the book.[25]

Koffka suffered a heart attack in late 1936, and his health continued to decline thereafter. In 1939, he studied patients with brain lesions at the Nuffield Institute in Oxford and offered a series of lectures on "Gestalt Psychology and Neurology" before returning to the United States the following year. Koffka had managed to survive several further heart attacks while in England, but was unable to recover from a final series that began in the summer months of 1941. Although his heart problems forced him to cut back on his active schedule of research and teaching, Koffka remained optimistic about his health. In a letter to Harrower dated November 14, 1941, he wrote:

> For a while I went to the Lab to teach and typed my article but on Wednesday evening I had an attack of angina which I reported to Nathan [Koffka's physician] who forbade me to hold any class either in the Lab or at home. He came the following morning and forbade me to leave the house till Christmas. So I am spending most of my time in bed *but I want to get well!*[26]

A few days later, on November 22, 1941, Kurt Koffka, only in his mid fifties, died in Northampton, Massachusetts.

As was true of Duncker, Barbara Burks's productive career was cut short by an untimely self-inflicted death. In 1927, Burks had married Herman Ramsperger, a promising young chemist with an appointment at Stanford University and later at the California Institute of Technology. Lewis Terman described the marriage of Burks and Ramsperger as "an ideally happy one"; Ramsperger "took great pride in his wife's attainments and gave her every encouragement to continue her professional career."[27] But the marriage lasted only five years; Ramsperger died in 1932 of lung cancer. His death left her devastated. In a 1933 letter to the National Research Council, Terman wrote that Burks had "gone through a serious emotional upheaval as a result of losing her husband by death."[28]

As a research associate at Columbia University, Burks had continued her research on human heredity with a study, financed by the Carnegie Corporation, on the role of the foster-home environment in the adult adjustment of foster children of alcoholic and psychotic parents. Burks did not finish the study; she died at the age of 40 on May 25, 1943 when, according to the *New York Times* the next day, she "fell or jumped from the George Washington Bridge" to the street some 200 feet below.[29] After

Burks's death, the Carnegie study was completed by Anne Roe of Yale University and published in 1945. Only a month before her death, Burks had been awarded a prestigious Guggenheim Fellowship for the 1943-1944 year for research on identical twins reared in separate environments. And she had recently become engaged to be married to Robert Cook, a prominent geneticist.

As a tribute to her work, the Barbara Burks Memorial Fund was established, mainly through the work of Ruth Tolman (the wife of prominent psychologist Edward C. Tolman), a personal friend, as a "loan fund in aid of refugee psychologists or geneticists engaged in study or research in this country."[30] Wertheimer joined the Burks memorial committee together with other prominent psychologists who respected Burks's work, such as Gordon Allport, Kurt Lewin, Theodore Newcomb, Lewis M. Terman and Robert Sessions Woodworth.

The deaths of Duncker, Koffka, and Burks, his divorce from Anni, and his health problems, all burdened Wertheimer in the early 1940s. Nevertheless, Gestalt theory continued to consume his time and interest. In this period, he tried to devise a meaningful structural mnemonic based on Gestalt principles for learning the Morse code. He informed his student Erwin Levy that he had formulated a Gestalt theory of hypnosis but declined to share any details about it until it was finished.[31] He devoted extensive attention to the implications of Gestalt theory for social psychology. Wertheimer also directed the research of several graduate students at the New School and elsewhere. A Chinese student, Gwan-Yuen Li, conducted research under Wertheimer's supervision for her doctoral thesis on the Chinese concepts of *Wei* and *Wu-wei* (doing something actively or just "going with the flow" instead). Wertheimer was on the doctoral committees of other students— Edwin B. Newman, Abraham S. Luchins, Eric Goldmeier, Marian Hubbell, Jesse Orlansky and Herman Witkin. But more than these other scholarly activities, Wertheimer's preoccupation with productive thinking and Gestalt logic took up most of his time.

Constructing a Gestalt Approach to Problem Solving and Education: The Work of Wertheimer's Students

Wertheimer's principal scholarly focus in his last years, as it had been throughout most of his career, remained the psychology of thinking. Köhler noted that Wertheimer saw with disappointment that in the United States his name was connected with details of perception rather than with his contributions to the psychology of thinking. Yet Wertheimer's enthusiasm for the study of productive thinking deeply influenced the work of several of his students.

One of the first students to make extensive use of Wertheimer's approach to thinking was Karl Duncker. In 1926 Duncker's thesis, "A Qualitative Experimental and Theoretical Study of Productive Thinking (Solving of Comprehensible Problems)," appeared in the *Pedagogical Seminary*. Duncker noted in it that he "was most indebted" to a 1925 paper by Wertheimer, "Über Schlussprozesse im produktiven Denken" ["On Reasoning Processes in Productive Thinking"], and to "W. Köhler's study about intelligent behavior of apes."[32] Duncker's 66-page article clearly shows the direct influence of Wertheimer's work on thinking. According to Wertheimer, Duncker's interest in thinking was long-standing, dating back to 1924 when he and another student, Karl Zener, conducted "an investigation of the blinding effects of mechanical repetition in sequences of assigned tasks" at the Berlin Institute.[33]

In his thesis, Duncker studied five Clark University students who worked through a series of twenty tasks. Duncker challenged the participants in his study with a variety of problems, the most famous being the "radiation problem" in which he asked how a ray beam could be used to destroy only a stomach tumor without damaging the healthy tissue surrounding the diseased area. Duncker made extensive use of what is now called verbal protocols, encouraging participants to "Try to think aloud. I guess you often do so when you are alone and working on a problem. And draw as much as possible."[34] Despite his creative ideas in this paper, this work is often neglected in favor of his later and larger work on thinking.

In 1935, Duncker published his classic book on problem solving, *Zur Psychologie des produktiven Denkens* (*Psychology of Productive Thought*). It was dedicated jointly to Köhler and Wertheimer.[35] Under the guidance of his mentors, Duncker conducted an extensive series of studies on a variety of mathematical and practical problems, using again the methods set forth in his 1926 paper. Even more than Duncker's thesis, this work is now considered a landmark in the history of the study of problem solving and cognition.[36]

Following Wertheimer's theoretical orientation, Duncker distinguished between two types of problem solving: "organic" ("analysis from above") and "mechanical" ("analysis from below"). People who merely search their memory for a "solution of that such-and-such problem" may remain just as blind to the inner nature of the problem situation before them as people who, instead of thinking themselves, consult an intelligent acquaintance or an encyclopedia. Truly, these methods are not to be derided, for they have a certain heuristic value, and one can arrive at solutions in that fashion. But such problem solving has little to do with thinking.[37]

Duncker divided his book into three main content areas: the structure and dynamics of problem-solving processes; insight, learning, and simple finding; and the fixedness of thought material. While the first two parts of the monograph have been influential as well, the third section on "functional fixedness" received the most extensive attention from psychologists. Allen Newell remarked that

> This is the smallest part of the monograph—twenty-six pages vs. forty-five and thirty-four, respectively, for the first two parts. Yet it had by far the largest impact. Functional fixity generated one of the major streams of research in problem solving until the shift in the mid-1950s to information processing.[38]

In the preface to the English translation of Duncker's monograph on problem solving, Köhler wrote,

> This is not an easy book. The author did not write it when the hard labors of research lay far behind him so that he could serenely look upon his findings from a distance. Rather, every page seems to show him in the midst of his untiring struggle for clearness.[39]

Nearly a year after Duncker's death, Köhler wrote Wertheimer that he was "occupied for 2½ weeks to make Duncker's book readable for Americans. The book won't be read here, it is too different and American psychologists are so conservative, they ignore things."[40] Duncker's 1935 book on productive thinking finally did appear in English in 1945 in the *Psychological Monographs* series under the title "On Problem Solving," and fortunately Köhler was inaccurate in his prediction about the American reception of the publication.[41]

Forty years after its publication, Newell claimed that the 1945 "monograph reports essentially the only research Duncker did on problem-solving, his other work being mostly in perception. This may be because he died early."[42] But aside from his master's thesis, Duncker published two other papers on thinking which have been neglected by contemporary psychologists. In 1935, he published a somewhat abstract article in German on "Learning and insight in the service of goal-attainment" that has some similarities with Wertheimer's Gestalt logic, particularly Wertheimer's paper written in 1918 for the Carl Stumpf *Festschrift* and published in 1920. Duncker also co-authored an article in English with David Krech (né Krechevsky) in 1939 on solution-achievement in the *Psychological Review*.[43] This theoretical paper represents an attempt, based on both authors' previous research, to analyze the differences and similarities between learning and thinking. Drawing upon Krech's research with Tolman on learning and Duncker's work with Köhler and Wertheimer on thinking, the authors concluded that some unifying themes exist in both approaches, even if they used different technical vocabulary:

> Where Krechevsky and Tolman speak of means-end-readiness at its most generalized level, Duncker speaks of range; where in the formal analysis, the

term hypothesis is used, Duncker has the somewhat corresponding concept of specific solution. Both analyses describe the process of solution-achievement as involving an hierarchical succession of reductions or specifications.... Finally, both analyses consider the phenomenon of fixation and its inhibiting influence on problem-solving.[44]

Aside from the attempt to synthesize learning and thinking, the Duncker and Krech paper also discusses the theoretical bridge between Tolman's research and Gestalt psychology.

Overall, Duncker's work on thinking is an amalgam of Wertheimer's theory of productive thinking and Gestalt logic and of Köhler's and Wertheimer's work on insight. Duncker's work on problem solving was a major venture into the psychology of thinking during an era when studies of cognition were not as much in vogue as they are now. After Duncker's death, other students also undertook work based on Wertheimer's and Köhler's analyses of thinking.

Abraham S. Luchins, then a graduate student at New York University, attended Wertheimer's seminar on "Methodology for Social Research" at the New School and was encouraged by Wertheimer to study problem solving with a now-famous series of water-jar experiments.[45] Beginning in 1936, Luchins conducted research on the *"Einstellung* effect," a mental set used to solve problems; in 1939, he was awarded his doctorate from New York University for his dissertation on this area. Like Duncker, Luchins examined the rigidity of set or *Einstellung* in solving a problem. Luchins completed his work in 1940 and Wertheimer suggested that the research be published in the *Psychological Monographs* series.[46] Luchins continued to elaborate on the Einstellung effect in later years together with his wife and collaborator Edith H. Luchins.[47]

The phenomenon of "Einstellung" or "set" is evident, for instance, in a popular children's spelling trick. The procedure is to ask a participant to pronounce words presented as sets of letters, such as M-A-C-G-R-E-G-O-R. The participant duly says "MacGregor." Next might be M-A-C-I-N-T-Y-R-E. The answer is "MacIntyre." Then: M-A-C-D-O-N-A-L-D; answer: "MacDonald." After one or two more, such as M-A-C-G-U-I-R-E or M-A-C-P-H-E-R-S-O-N, the next group of letters is M-A-C-H-I-N-E, and the participant who is unfamiliar with the demonstration and who has been "set" to respond in a certain way by all the preceding examples may unwittingly say "MacHine," not recognizing that this time the sequence of letters is not a Scottish name but the common word "machine."

Under Wertheimer's supervision, Abraham S. Luchins undertook an elaborate set of experiments to study set or *Einstellung* in a series of numerical problems. He induced a particular procedure for solving arithmetic problems which, it turned out, was followed mechanically even if a much simpler strategy was available for solving later problems in the series. The task was to yield a particular number of units of water when the participant is given several jars that hold specified numbers of units. Thus the first task was to yield 20 units of water, when two jars are provided, one that holds 29 units and one that holds three. The solution: fill the large jar, then pour out three times from it into the smaller jar, discarding the water from the smaller jar each time: 29 minus three times three leaves exactly 20 units in the larger jar. Next problem: you are given three jars; A holds 21, B 127, and C 3 units respectively, and you are to end up with 100 units. The solution: fill jar B (127 units); pour off from it once into jar A (106 units left in jar B) and twice into jar C (100 units now left in jar B). For all of the next few problems, the same formula works: B-A-2C. The three jars hold 14, 163, and 25 units, and the task is to end with 99 units; they hold 18, 43, and 10 units, and the end result should be 5 units; 9, 42, and 6, to yield 21 units; 20, 59, and 4, yielding 31 units.

The next problem calls for jars holding 23, 49, and 3 units, with the goal of yielding 20 units; the one after that uses jars that hold 15, 39, and 3 units and asks for 18 units. As before, B-A-2C works fine. Now comes a problem with jars holding 28, 76, and 3 units, with the goal being 25 units; now B-A-2C no longer works. Participants may be stumped for a short time, until they realize that there is a simple solution: A-C! And simple solutions work for the two preceding problems as well: A-C and A+C respectively. Few participants who have been exposed to problems 2 through 6 spontaneously discover the simpler solutions to problems 7 and 8, while virtually all control participants who go directly from problem 1 to problems 7 and 8, who have not been "blinded" to the simpler solutions by the set induced by problems 2 through 6, come up with the A-C and A+C solutions immediately (none use B-A-2C). One minor variation on the procedure, warning participants "Don't be blind!" after solving problem 6 and before presenting problem 7, had almost no effect; apparently the set induced by problems 2 through 6 is so strong that participants continue to use the unnecessarily elaborate procedure for solving the two problems for which a simpler, more elegant, solution is possible. The "blinding" effect of set, which may initially be useful in solving problems, may be so mechanical and persistent as to interfere with effective problem solving.

Although the issue was not explicitly addressed in the work of Duncker and Luchins, the Gestalt approach has major implications for education and teaching. Wertheimer had long realized the relationship between his theoretical work and pedagogy. Indeed, during the fall of 1934, Wertheimer was preparing to offer a seminar on "Consequences of the Gestalt Theory of Psychology for Education and Teaching." The course was announced in a pamphlet issued by the New School preserved in the family's archives (MW-CU).

The handout reads:

GESTALT PSYCHOLOGY FOR TEACHERS
BY
MAX WERTHEIMER

This is the first time that the consequences of the Gestalt psychology will be presented here with specific reference to teaching. Dr. Wertheimer will consider the psychology of children: the preschool child, the primary school child, the child in the higher grades; psychological factors in good and bad instruction; the psychology of the teacher and of teaching. The course will be conducted throughout with experiments and with special attention to practical problems.

The lectures cover a period of fifteen weeks, one session weekly, from 5:10 to 7 P.M. on Wednesdays, beginning February 6... .

FEE FOR THE COURSE: $20. SPECIAL RATE TO TEACHERS: $15

In a foreword to his colleague George Katona's Gestalt-inspired book *Organizing and Memorizing*, which appeared in 1940, Wertheimer deplored "tired, arbitrary, piecemeal" methods of teaching:

> Every good teacher enjoys teaching and learning when really sensible learning takes place: when eyes are opened, when real grasping, real understanding occurs, when the transition takes place from blindness or ineptness to orientation, understanding, mastery; and when, in the course of such happenings, mind develops.
>
> Experimental psychological investigations of learning have for the most part taken a direction foreign to these issues. Repetition, drill, has become the focus of investigations; the very concept of learning—the idea of what learning is— seems now for many psychologists to be centered essentially in the feature of repetition, of memorizing. Teachers are often seriously puzzled when they realize that memorizing series of nonsense syllables is taken, broadly, as the appropriate materials for establishing *the* laws of learning.[48]

Wertheimer lists characteristics of the then-prevalent psychology of learning that still were typical of much of the work in this field later in the twentieth century.

> Historically various factors have brought this about. I mention some. First: Drill is used in school teaching. Although the range of its use has changed through the centuries, it is emphasized that after all we have to learn such things as the alphabet, have to memorize not-understood or not-understandable aggregations, so-called "memory stuff." Second: In certain developments of philosophy and psychology the assumption has been made that forming connections of this kind (connections between arbitrary aggregated items or data) is the essential

issue for learning; there is the belief—or the hope—that learning of sensible material is nothing but a complication of such connections. Third: Another important factor developed with the aim to make psychology scientific in terms of quantitative, exact investigations in experiments in which all the elements were controllable. To this end the use of nonsense syllables, mazes, and similar material, that is, of arbitrary aggregates of items, seems technically in contrast to the much more difficult problems involved in other kinds of learning. The possibility of reaching clear-cut, exact, quantitative laws in a comparatively easy way, added weight to the general assumption.[49]

Wertheimer emphasized the efficacy of Gestalt theory in countering—and correcting—the traditional reliance on sheer repetition and drill that were the result of applying what he considered to be the misguided educational psychology of the time:

> The very first idea of [G]estalt psychology involved the confrontation of sensible structures with senseless aggregations. Scientifically, by studying structural features, it put the problem whether or not it is appropriate to view sensible structures as sheer products of and-summative aggregations. Contrasting the senseless and the sensible, [G]estalt psychology envisaged senseless aggregations as a special rather than the general case—the case in which inner-correlatedness, sensible structural whole-qualities, approach zero (and which, psychologically, may be not nearly so simple as supposed).
>
> Methods were developed, tools of scientific approach, which opened the way to structural features, features other than and-summation and repetition. They led to a reunderstanding of what grasping is, what understanding is, and what it requires—in perception, in learning, in other fields of psychology.[50]

Wertheimer's critique of education was consistent with a prevalent sentiment that had emerged in the nineteenth century concerning the failure of the educational system in the United States.[51] Spearheaded by the work of John Dewey, a progressive school reform movement in education had gained popularity in the country. Advocates of the progressive movement called for sweeping reform in educational practices, vocational preparation, and teacher training as well as in the social order.[52] Like Wertheimer, many critics deplored the formal recitation method of drill and memorization and called for greater cooperation and "discovery learning" in the classroom. In 1930, William Bagley, a professor at Teachers College, Columbia University, conducted a survey of teaching methods with educators in over thirty states and concluded that "the work of the typical American classroom, whether on the elementary or secondary level, has been and still is, characterized by a lifeless and perfunctory...recitation of assigned textbook materials."[53] But scholars who challenged formal recitation methods did see at least a few modest changes in classroom demeanor by the 1940s:

> Verbal exchanges between teacher and students still pivoted on questions asked by the teacher and could either slip into a quasi-conversation or shift back

toward the formal recitation. Students standing at their desks reciting, a familiar image in classrooms for decades, had become by the 1940s a custom outmoded in urban classrooms. It was replaced by the now-familiar image of arm-waving pupils vying for the teacher's attention.[54]

Educators and reformers were basing their practices and proposals on the educational psychologies of John Dewey, G. Stanley Hall, and Edward L. Thorndike; Thorndike's associative "connectionist" model in particular was sharply at odds with the approach of the Gestalt school. But a few progressive educators explicitly turned to Gestalt psychology for improved ideas and solutions.[55] Both Kurt Koffka, in *The Growth of the Mind*, and Robert Ogden, in *Psychology and Education*, described the ameliorative role that Gestalt theory could play in education. In a 1930 article, Ogden argued against the mechanistic image of education based on association and encouraged educators to adopt the Gestalt approach to instruction.[56] But one critic as early as 1926 declared that the proposed Gestalt solution to pedagogical problems was only general and theoretical, and did not provide specific, practical solutions to problems in education.[57] George Humphrey, and Raymond Wheeler and F. Theodore Perkins, briefly discussed the advantages of a Gestalt approach to educational psychology,[58] but a review by John McGeoch of Wheeler and Perkins's approach was very critical of it.[59] Other Gestalt-oriented efforts made suggestions for teaching practice that combined Tolman and Gestalt theory,[60] and proposed various educational tasks involving perceptual and other Gestalt phenomena.[61] Kurt Lewin's Gestalt-related explorations of group dynamics also had implications for education.[62] But the works of George Katona and Catherine Stern probably came closest to Wertheimer's vision of a Gestalt theory of education.

Born in 1901 in Budapest, George Katona earned his doctoral degree with G. E. Müller from the University of Göttingen.[63] Thereafter Katona worked with Wertheimer at Berlin and at Frankfurt and, after immigrating to the United States in 1933, at the New School, where Wertheimer was instrumental in arranging for a grant from the Carnegie Corporation of New York for Katona.[64] Katona also taught at the New School from 1938 to 1942. Despite his earlier association with Müller, Katona was thoroughly identified with the Gestalt school for the ideas in his work on organizing and memorizing:

> Because of extraneous circumstances, Professor M. Wertheimer's psychological lectures and his researches on "productive thinking" have not yet been brought before the public.... I have been able to use Wertheimer's basic concepts in my research, especially those concerning the nature and the role of sensible processes in contrast to senseless processes and those concerning the role of structure in understanding, and I want to express here my deeply felt thanks to Professor Wertheimer.[65]

Katona's 1940 book on learning and education, titled *Organizing and Memorizing*, like Duncker's work on problem-solving, was firmly grounded in Wertheimer's approach to productive thinking, and showed how it can be applied to specific issues and problems in educational psychology. Near the end of his book, Katona considered the tenability of three assertions about learning: "1. memorizing is the prototype of learning; 2. understanding is the prototype of learning; and 3. memorizing and understanding are distinct and independent learning processes."[66] In the tradition of Gestalt theory, he concluded that the second and third assertions are correct and that the first is invalid.

In a series of studies, Katona demonstrated that "meaningful learning," which involves the understanding of information based on insightful grouping, yields superior results to "senseless learning," artificial learning without real structural understanding.[67] Whereas meaningful learning is the product of meaningful organization and genuine understanding of a principle, senseless learning is the outcome of rote memorization and drill exercises. The results of his research led Katona to conclude that memorization yields much faster rates of forgetting than understanding and is also less likely to transfer to the learning of new tasks and the solution of new but related problems. In the final chapter, devoted explicitly to the educational implications of his research, Katona admonished that "Pupils should learn to learn—that is the best that the school can do for them. They should not merely learn to memorize—they should learn to learn by understanding."[68]

After the publication of *Organizing and Memorizing*, Katona conducted several further studies of pedagogical procedures for teaching meaningful learning.[69] Later in his career, Katona turned primarily to the study of behavioral economics, successfully applying field theory to economic enterprises in numerous books and articles. In 1946, Katona joined the faculty at the University of Michigan at Ann Arbor, where he served as professor of economics and psychology until 1972. He was a pioneer in establishing the new field of the synthesis of psychology and economics, which began to thrive by the middle of the century.[70]

In addition to Katona, Catherine Stern was another scholar whose work with Wertheimer helped show the promise of applying Gestalt theory to educational settings. Stern was a research assistant for Wertheimer from 1940 to 1943, with funding from the New York Foundation and the Oberlaender Trust. In her work, she explicitly applied Wertheimer's ideas about "structural understanding" to teaching school children the basics of mathematics. Stern developed what she called "Structural Arithmetic," an education program based largely on Wertheimer's ideas about productive thinking. Rather than using drill and associative learning, Stern constructed situations in which genuine discovery plays an essential role in the learning of arithmetic. She argued that arithmetic should be taught so that the structural characteristics of the number system are understood, not just memorized, by children. For example, she gave students blocks of different unit lengths and encouraged them to measure instead of count, so that, for instance, it became obvious to a child that a block of 10 units long is the same length as the sum of a 6-block and a 4-block. These methods were intended to enhance the probability of students discovering the number relationships that are the basis of arithmetic. "In many years of study with children," Wertheimer remarked, "Dr. Catherine Stern has developed tools and methods for the teaching of arithmetic in which genuine discovery in tasks of a structural nature plays an essential role. The results in learning—and in happiness—seem extraordinarily good as compared with the usual teaching by drill which focuses on forming associative bonds, etc."[71] Stern indeed found that the participants in her studies reported greater satisfaction with this procedure than with traditional drill methods. She presented her findings at the 1941 convention of the Eastern Psychological Association.

In 1944, she co-founded (with her daughter, Toni S. Gould, and another colleague) the Castle School, an experimental institution in New York City based on her system of learning. As director of the school, Stern designed many pedagogical techniques for the improvement of mathematical learning, including numerical symbols which need not be learned by rote memorization and drill; several teachers at other public and private New York state schools also implemented her programs.[72] In 1949, she published *Children Discover Arithmetic: An Introduction to Structural Arithmetic*, a book which she dedicated to Wertheimer.[73]

In later years, Stern continued to explore other facets of educational practice and experience based on the learning methods of discovery and insight.[74] In particular, she argued that the teaching of alphabetic characters, like the teaching of arithmetic, was, but need not be, based on memorization and drill (or the "sight method"). In collaboration with her daughter, she concluded that the methods of teaching reading skills to students should start with the analysis of the familiar word as it is built up by sounds. Based on this assumption, and in some ways parallel to her structural arithmetic, Stern developed a program of "Structural Reading" which teaches children to grasp structural characteristics common to whole groups of words, and to grasp sentence structure in such a way that henceforth they can read a great many words and sentences with comprehension. Promising though her ideas and proposals were, Stern did not have strong and effective ties with the educational establishment, so despite her insightful ideas, Stern's proposals for how to teach reading had little impact on educational practice.[75] Nonetheless, Stern's work directly and explicitly applied Wertheimer's ideas about thinking to specific issues in the realm of education.

The publications of these four students bear the unmistakable stamp of Max Wertheimer. He strongly encouraged Duncker and Luchins in their application of his theoretical analysis of productive thinking to specific studies of problem solving, as well as Katona and Stern in their efforts to apply it to concrete issues in educational psychology, and contributed extensive amounts of time to consulting with all four of them on their projects. With his encouragement, Wertheimer's students were generating publications based on his theory of thinking long before there was a formal published statement of the theory by Wertheimer.

Notes

1. John Hornbostel became a United States citizen on September 17, 1939, just a few months after the Wertheimers became citizens.
2. Anni Hornbostel to Max Wertheimer, February 1, 1943, MW-CU.
3. Max Wertheimer to Philip Barbash, June 7, 1942, MW-CU.
4. Barbara S. Burks to Max Wertheimer (no date), MW-CU.
5. Ash, *Holism and the quest for objectivity*, p. 495.
6. Wolfgang Köhler to Max Wertheimer, February 19, 1936, MW-CU.
7. Karl Duncker (1937). Some preliminary experiments on the mutual influence of pain. *Psychologische Forschung*, 21, 311-326. Karl Duncker (1938). Experimental modification of children's food preferences through social suggestion. *Journal of Abnormal and Social Psychology*, 33, 489-507.
8. Wolfgang Köhler to Max Wertheimer, August 1, 1936, MW-CU.
9. Wolfgang Köhler to Max Wertheimer, December 24, 1936, MW-CU.
10. Max Wertheimer to Alexander Rüstow, September 13, 1936, MW-CU. Alexander Rüstow to Max Wertheimer, November 30, 1936, MW-CU.
11. Karl Duncker to Max Wertheimer, August 20, 1937, MW-CU.
12. Lene Frank to Max Wertheimer, August 27, 1937, MW-CU.
13. A variety of etiologies have been proposed for Duncker's depression. Mandler and Mandler suggest that Duncker was "depressed by the outbreak of the war." But Köhler wrote Wertheimer that the physicians believed that Duncker's disorder was endogenous depression, a diagnosis supported by Binswanger. Duncker described his depression to Wertheimer as a "veil of unreality over everything, especially the future" and added that "I'm a poor manager of my own things, that's part of my illness." The correspondence between Binswanger and Wertheimer suggests that Duncker's divorce, the recent developments in Germany, and an unhappy stay in England were all contributing factors. Wertheimer and Binswanger had corresponded since the early 1930s, and upon Duncker's arrival in Binswanger's clinic, Wertheimer wrote Binswanger that "It was a consolation to me that he came to you and I hope that he will soon recover.... I am convinced that being with you is a blessing." In a later undated letter to Köhler, Wertheimer appeared to be satisfied with Binswanger's treatment of Duncker. See J. M. Mandler and G. Mandler (1969). The diaspora of experimental psychology: The Gestaltists and others. In D. Fleming and B. Bailyn (eds.), *The intellectual migration: Europe and America, 1930-1960*, pp. 371-419. Cambridge, MA: Harvard University Press, p. 393. Wolfgang Köhler to Max Wertheimer, August 6, 1937, MW-CU. Ludwig Binswanger to Max

Wertheimer, November 10, 1932, MW-CU. Karl Duncker to Max Wertheimer, August 20, 1937, MW-CU. Ludwig Binswanger to Max Wertheimer, September 27, 1937, MW-CU. Max Wertheimer to Ludwig Binswanger, September 1, 1937, MW-CU.

14. Wolfgang Köhler to Max Wertheimer, August 6, 1937, MW-CU.
15. Max Wertheimer to Wolfgang Köhler, no date, MW-CU.
16. Ludwig Binswanger to Max Wertheimer, September 27, 1937, MW-CU. Wolfgang Köhler to Max Wertheimer, October 27, 1937, MW-CU.
17. Wolfgang Köhler to Max Wertheimer, October 27, 1937, MW-CU.
18. Wolfgang Köhler to Max Wertheimer, January 17, 1936, MW-CU.
19. Wolfgang Köhler to Max Wertheimer, December 11, 1937, MW-CU.
20. Wolfgang Köhler to Max Wertheimer, May 8, 1938, MW-CU.
21. Wolfgang Köhler to Max Wertheimer, February 25, 1940, MW-CU.
22. Gerda Duncker-Naef to Max Wertheimer, July 14, 1928, MW-CU.
23. Kurt Koffka, March 10, 1940. Quoted in Harrower, *Kurt Koffka: An unwitting self-portrait*, p. 243.
24. Kurt Koffka (1935). *Principles of Gestalt psychology*. New York: Harcourt, Brace.
25. Molly Harrower, *Kurt Koffka: An unwitting self-portrait*, p. 25.
26. Kurt Koffka, November 14, 1941. Quoted in Molly Harrower, *Kurt Koffka: An unwitting self-portrait*, p. 73.
27. Lewis M. Terman (1944). Barbara Stoddard Burks, 1902-1943. *Psychological Review*, 51, p. 139.
28. Lewis M. Terman to William J. Robbins, February 21,1933, Lewis M. Terman Archives, Stanford University.
29. Woman Dies in Plunge: Body of Ex-Research Worker Lands Under Hudson Bridge. *New York Times*, May 26, 1943, p. 44.
30. Ruth S. Tolman to Lewis M. Terman, October 27, 1943, Lewis M. Terman Archives, Stanford University.
31. Abraham S. Luchins and Edith H. Luchins (1988). Max Wertheimer in America: 1933-1943. Part II. Wertheimer never did publish his Gestalt theory of hypnosis.
32. Karl Duncker (1926). A qualitative experimental and theoretical study of productive thinking (Solving of comprehensible problems). *Pedagogical Seminary*, 33, p. 645.
33. Max Wertheimer, *Productive thinking*, p. 131.
34. Duncker, A qualitative experimental and theoretical study of productive thinking (Solving of comprehensible problems), p. 664.
35. Karl Duncker (1935). *Zur Psychologie des produktiven Denkens* [*Psychology of productive thought*]. Berlin: Springer, 1935.
36. Allen Newell (1985). Duncker on thinking: An inquiry into progress in cognition. In Sigmund Koch & David Leary (eds.), *A century of psychology as science*. New York: McGraw-Hill, pp. 392-419.
37. Duncker, *Zur Psychologie des produktiven Denkens*, p. 20.
38. Newell, Duncker on thinking: An inquiry into progress in cognition, p. 413.
39. Wolfgang Köhler (1945), in Duncker, On problem solving. *Psychological Monographs*, 58, Whole No. 270, p. iv.
40. Wolfgang Köhler to Max Wertheimer, February 25, 1940, MW-CU.

41. Karl Duncker (1945) (L. S. Lees, Trans.). On problem solving. *Psychological Monographs*, 58 (1945, Whole No. 270). One of Duncker's former students, Lynne Lees, translated Duncker's book. Duncker is primarily remembered for this monograph, although less than half of his publications were devoted to problem solving, the rest focusing on such diverse psychological and philosophical topics as the psychological experience of pain, a productive series of experiments on the perception of induced motion, studies of the modification of children's food preferences through social suggestion, the phenomenology and epistemology of consciousness, ethics, experimental work on the influence of past experience upon perceptual properties, and an analysis of pleasure, emotion, and striving, as well as a German-English dictionary of psychological terms. See D. Brett King, Michaela Cox, and Michael Wertheimer (1998). Karl Duncker. In Gregory A. Kimble and Michael Wertheimer (eds.), *Portraits of pioneers in psychology, Vol. III*, pp. 163-178. Mahwah, NJ: Erlbaum and Washington, DC: American Psychological Association.

42. Newell, Duncker on thinking: An inquiry into progress in cognition, p. 393.

43. Karl Duncker (1935). Lernen und Einsicht im Dienst der Zielerreichung [Learning and insight in the service of goal attainment]. *Acta Psychologica, Hague*, 1, 77-82. Karl Duncker and I. Krechevsky (1939). On solution-achievement. *Psychological Review*, 46, 176-185. Duncker and Krechevsky collaborated while the former was an instructor and the latter a research associate for Köhler at Swarthmore from 1938 to 1939. While preparing his article with Krech for publication, Duncker wrote Wertheimer that he was also working on the larger issue of problem solving and hedonism. Karl Duncker to Max Wertheimer, March 22, 1938, MW-CU.

44. Karl Duncker and I. Krechevsky (1939). On solution-achievement. *Psychological Review*, 46, p. 182.

45. Abraham S. Luchins and Edith H. Luchins (1994). The water jar experiments and Einstellung effects. Part I: Early history and surveys of textbook citations. *Gestalt Theory*, 16, 101-121.

46. Abraham S. Luchins (1942). Mechanization in problem solving: The effect of Einstellung. *Psychological Monographs*, 54, 6, Whole No. 248. Luchins completed the manuscript in 1940, but could not afford to pay for its publication until 1942.

47. Abraham S. Luchins and Edith H. Luchins (1959). *Rigidity of behavior: A variational approach to the effect of Einstellung.* Eugene, OR: University of Oregon Books.

48. Max Wertheimer (1940). Foreword. In George Katona, *Organizing and memorizing: Studies in the psychology of learning and teaching.* New York: Hafner, p. v.

49. Wertheimer, Foreword, pp. v-vi.

50. Wertheimer, Foreword, p. vi.

51. Larry Cuban (1993). *How teachers taught: Constancy and change in American classrooms, 1890-1990.* New York: Teachers College Press, Columbia University, p. 133.

52. John S. Brubacher (1966). *A history of the problems of education.* New York: Mc-Graw-Hill. H. Warren Button and Eugene F. Provenzo, Jr. (1989). *History of education and culture in America.* Englewood Cliffs, NJ: Prentice Hall.

53. Quoted in Cuban, *How teachers taught: Constancy and change in American classrooms, 1890-1990*, p. 137.

54. Cuban, *How teachers taught: Constancy and change in American classrooms, 1890-1990*, p. 134.

55. See John D. Pullman (1987). *History of education in America*. Columbus, OH: Merrill, p. 178.

56. Robert M. Ogden (1930). The Gestalt psychology of learning. *Journal of Genetic Psychology*, 38, 280-287.

57. A. I. Gates (1926). The Gestalt theory in education. *Journal of Educational Psychology*, 17, 631-637.

58. George Humphrey (1924). The psychology of the Gestalt. *Journal of Educational Psychology*, 7, 401-412. Raymond Holder Wheeler and F. Theodore Perkins (1932). *Principles of mental development: A textbook in educational psychology*. New York: Crowell.

59. John A. McGeoch (1933). The configurational psychology of learning as represented by R. H. Wheeler and F. T. Perkins, *Principles of mental development*. *Journal of Applied Psychology*, 17, 83-96.

60. R. R. Scott (1930). Some suggestions on learning from the point of view of Gestalt psychology. *Journal of Educational Psychology*, 21, 361-366.

61. H. E. Jones and D. Dunn (1932). The configural factor in children's learning. *Journal of Genetic Psychology*, 41, 3-15. M. E. Grant (1929). 'Mysterious' tropisms: An illustration of the Gestalt law of precision. *Journal of Educational Psychology*, 20, 125-127. R. F. Street (1931). A Gestalt Completion Test. Teachers College Contributions to Education, No. 481, 1-65.

62. See, e.g., Kurt Lewin (1948). *Resolving social conflicts*. New York: Harper and Row.

63. Wertheimer was not one of Müller's admirers; indeed he called him a "master of associationism," hardly a compliment in the Gestalt language. Max Wertheimer (1940). Foreword. In George Katona, *Organizing and memorizing: Studies in the psychology of learning and teaching*. New York: Hafner, p. vi.

64. Katona expressed a sense of appreciation and affection for his adopted country in the preface to his book:

    In these times I cannot lay down my pen without expressing my gratitude to the country in which this work was done and in which scientific research flourishes in the atmosphere of freedom and democracy. The development that is this book is due not least to the spiritual stimulation I have encountered here.

    George Katona (1940). *Organizing and memorizing: Studies in the psychology of learning and teaching*. New York: Hafner, p. ix.

65. Katona, *Organizing and memorizing*, p. ix.

66. Katona, *Organizing and memorizing*, p. 246.

67. In reviewing *Organizing and memorizing*, Arthur W. Melton, a respected verbal learning theorist, questioned the validity and reliability of Katona's results. See Melton (1941). *Memorizing and organizing* by George Katona. *American Journal of Psychology*, 54, 455-457. Melton appears inadvertently to have reversed the order of the words "Organizing" and "Memorizing" in his version of the title of the book he undertook to review.

68. Katona, *Organizing and memorizing*, p. 260.

69. George Katona (1942). On different forms of learning by reading. *Journal of Educational Psychology*, 33, 335-355. George Katona (1942). The role of order of presentation in learning. *American Journal of Psychology*, 55, 328-353.

70. While Katona helped establish economic psychology or the psychology of economics in the middle of the twentieth century, Margaret Floy Washburn had already been referring to an Economic Psychology Association as early as 1917. See her article (1917). Some thoughts on the last quarter century in psychology. *Philosophical Review*, 26, 46-55. The authors are grateful to Professor Wayne Viney of Colorado State University for bringing this information to their attention.

71. Max Wertheimer, *Productive thinking*, p. 127.

72. In a review of Stern's work, Miles A. Tinker wrote, "Since it represents a radical change from the traditional drill methods, there will be resistance to adopting it...[, but] the technique may turn out to be a very important contribution to the teaching of arithmetic." See Tinker (1951). Catherine Stern. *Children discover arithmetic: An introduction to structural arithmetic. Journal of Educational Psychology*, 42, p. 250.

73. Catherine Stern (1949). *Children discover arithmetic: An introduction to structural arithmetic*. New York: Harper.

74. Catherine Stern and Toni S. Gould (1955). *The early years of childhood: Education through insight*. New York: Harper.

75. Michael A. Wallach and Lise Wallach (1976). *Teaching all children to read*. Chicago, IL: University of Chicago Press, p. 68.

14

The Dynamics and Logic
of Productive Thinking:
The Crystallization of a Life Study

*What occurs when, now and then, thinking really
works productively? What happens when, now
and then, thinking forges ahead? What is really
going on in such a process?*
—Max Wertheimer, *Productive Thinking* (1945)

In late September 1935, Critchell Rimington, an executive with the Dodge Publishing Company, expressed interest in a book based on Wertheimer's lectures: "I have just seen a recent catalogue of The New School and it occurs to me that you might be interested in doing a book based on your course, *On Better Thinking*."[1] Wertheimer had doubtless considered elaborating on his 1920 paper on the syllogism and productive thinking ("Über Schlussprozesse im produktiven Denken")—indeed he had been lecturing on such topics for years—but may not seriously have contemplated addressing it to a popular audience or expanding it into a book until Rimington suggested it.

Early in 1936, Wertheimer met personally with Max Lincoln Schuster, the publisher and co-founder in 1924 of the publishing firm of Simon and Schuster, about the preparation of a manuscript on Gestalt theory in general and productive thinking in particular. Schuster was enthusiastic about the project and encouraged one of his editors, Quincy Howe, to discuss the project with Wertheimer and attend one of his New School lectures.[2] For decades, Wertheimer had been making notes to himself about problem solving and thinking, including many examples that he had developed in his classroom and at home with his children. In response to the inquiries, he drafted several versions of the possible content and scope of the book, but progress was slow and, despite continued encouragement from Howe over the next few years, Wertheimer did not make significant progress on the manuscript. In a brief response to Howe's repeated queries about how the manuscript was coming, Wertheimer admitted that "I have delayed my answer to your letter in the hope that the preliminary work which I was doing for my book might result very soon in a completion of one or two chapters. Unfortunately other work has interfered in the execution of my plans. I thank you for your letter and I hope that some day I may be able to show you some part of my manuscript."[3] Perhaps Howe's encouragement helped Wertheimer decide in the fall semester of 1938 to take a formal leave of absence, to work on the manuscript for a book with the tentative title *Productive Thinking*.

During his leave, Kurt Koffka assumed responsibility for Wertheimer's weekly evening graduate seminar at the New School. Maslow attended Koffka's class and "learned from it and enjoyed it and liked Koffka, but was not inspired by it or thrilled in the way that I was with Wertheimer. ...He was a cool English gentleman, the last one I ever saw with a wing collar, quite pleasant, but in a polite way rather than in an intimate way.... I didn't get the sense of a powerful mind from him that I did from Köhler or Wertheimer."[4] Wertheimer still came to the New School on occasion and would sit in on Koffka's lectures. He found it difficult to contain his ideas about the evening's topic and would often interrupt Koffka and dominate the discussion. Luchins and Luchins report that

> Students particularly enjoyed the sessions that Wertheimer attended, especially when he and Koffka disagreed. Koffka would attempt to placate Wertheimer by saying "I agree with you, I agree with you," and would try to proceed, but Wertheimer would point out new difficulties. One result of these exchanges was that the students realized that the founders of Gestalt psychology were not like-minded, but had different points of view on important issues.[5]

Despite their similarity of thought and respect for each other, the three principal early Gestalt psychologists did have disputes. In November 1935, Koffka described "a long discussion on [memory] traces, in which Köhler and I explained and defended our views which were identical to a point, to Wertheimer, who now, I believe, accepts them."[6] The following January, he wrote Harrower: "It was nice at Wertheimer's. I also reported on Ego psychologist Erik Homburger Erikson's paper. You would have liked my defense of him and his theory against Wertheimer's first emotional reactions."[7]

In 1939, Wertheimer spent some time working on his manuscript while staying at the Sharon Springs, New York, summer home of Clara Mayer, by then Dean of the School of Philosophy and Liberal Arts at the New School. He later recalled her encouragement: "But for her untiring effort the manuscript would not have reached its final form; she was intensely interested in its subject matter and deeply devoted to its aims. That she never failed to find time for it notwithstanding her full time activities at the School, was a source of inspiration."[8]

During writing sessions, Wertheimer would pace around his study, desperately trying to do justice to the turbulent thoughts in his mind. Occasionally he would dictate to Anni or Val, who would try to help him formulate his ideas into words that might meet his uncompromising standards.

In the early 1940s, Rudolf Arnheim visited Wertheimer's house in New Rochelle and offered assistance:

> Our meetings had two main purposes. I consulted him on my studies in which I applied the [G]estalt principles of perception to the psychology of the visual arts. In addition I tried to give him a hand with the preparation of his manuscript on productive thinking, on which he had been working for so long. I offered to take dictation, which would help him to give final shape to the boundless material scribbled in shorthand on the thousands of sheets of notepaper stacked high in his study.[9]

But the person who provided the greatest assistance in helping Wertheimer bring his manuscript to fruition was Solomon Eliot Asch. Born in Warsaw, Poland in 1907, Asch migrated with his family to New York in 1920. After earning a Bachelor of Science degree at the City College of New York in 1928, he began graduate studies at Columbia University, where he attended seminars by Ruth Benedict and Franz Boas and worked on his master's thesis under the direction of Robert Sessions Woodworth. He earned his doctoral degree in psychology in 1932 from Columbia University. The next year he read a *New York Times* report of Wertheimer's appointment at the New School. Although Asch had completed his formal graduate work, he nevertheless, like Katona and Maslow, faithfully attended several of Wertheimer's seminars at the New School. Asch was fascinated both by Gestalt theory and by Wertheimer's

> inner qualities, the way he looked at psychological questions. They were for him more than simply technical questions that we had to study. He had a truly esthetic approach. When he spoke of certain ways of thinking as "ugly," he meant it. He represented to me a kind of ideal of what a psychologist should be. For the first time I was meeting a man whose range of interest and whose concern with human questions was what psychology needed. It was exactly the dimension I had not encountered in anyone before, or, I might add, since.[10]

Captivated by Wertheimer's work on thinking, Asch conducted research related to Gestalt theory and presented a paper based on it at the 1940 convention of the Eastern Psychological Association, on "Some Effects of Speed on the Development of a Mechanical Attitude in Problem Solving."[11] Wertheimer, incidentally, was instrumental in arranging Guggenheim Foundation fellowships for both Asch and Arnheim. Asch was teaching at Brooklyn College when he first began helping Wertheimer with his manuscript on productive thinking during the later 1930s.

Asch's dedication to Wertheimer and the book was heroic. Although largely unpaid for his services, he spent innumerable hours helping Wertheimer draft the manuscript. It was not uncommon for him to stay the night at 12 The Circle working with Wertheimer, even though he had a wife and a young son at home in Brooklyn. Asch was one of Wertheimer's most loyal colleagues, but was repeatedly forced to bear the brunt of the frustrations Wertheimer encountered in trying to bring the manuscript up to his exacting standards. Anni marveled at Asch's self-control and reserve, asserting that he possessed the "patience of an angel," and sympathized with his typically exhausted appearance after enduring a day of Wertheimer's passionate shouting and frustrated excitement.[12] Asch patiently took dictation, provided stylistic and substantive suggestions about the manuscript, and persisted in helping Wertheimer render his drafts into better English.[13]

Asch became functionally a part of the Wertheimer family, and often continued working on the manuscript while Wertheimer indulged in his habitual afternoon nap. He tried out unpublished portions of the manuscript in his course on the psychology of thinking at Brooklyn College. In 1943, Solomon and Florence Asch and their son Peter moved into the Wertheimer household for a short time as the book began to approach completion. After years of labor, the manuscript was finally taking shape and Wertheimer was sufficiently satisfied with its style and content to begin a formal search for a publisher.

Wertheimer's Attempt to Publish *Productive Thinking*

In a draft of a prospectus for publishers, Wertheimer declared that "the emphasis is on ~~straight and~~ productive thinking (as against bad thinking, unproductive thinking, no thinking at all)" and mentioned that he had conducted "investigations and lectures on the topics involved through the last 25 years."[14] The words "straight and" were crossed out in the draft. Wertheimer added (again with the words "as it was often done" crossed out in the draft itself):

> The problems will be discussed not ~~as it was often done~~ in "generalities" and in lifeless, unimportant examples but in concrete, important, dramatic processes (discussion of some of the finest achievements of human thought and of lively processes in daily life). The book shall give an introduction in a *new dynamic theory of thinking (Gestalt theory of thinking)*.[15]

Wertheimer wrote that the book was "long due" as promised "in lectures at Harvard, Ann Arbor and Chicago," and mentioned the impact of his ideas on the earlier works of Duncker, Katona, Stern, Luchins, and others:

> The writing of the book is long expected (students of mine have used my theories in a number of special publications referring to my lectures etc, but

dealing always only with small parts, there is in the literature again and again referring to this my still unpublished book).[16]

In considering the potential audience, Wertheimer wrote that the book was "addressed not only to scientists[,] not only to teachers[,] but to the broad public"—in some ways the same diverse cross-section of people who attended his lectures at the New School. He was optimistic about the applied and educational value of a book on meaningful thinking:

> The book is due; but I feel the demand is not only out of the *scientific* situation; I feel there is a real need for it with regard to the actual *situation in life*, in political life, in education. The book will imply the problem: *how to improve thinking* (which is very much needed) with concrete consequences and proposals.... (I shall report...also on investigations made in the last years in New York schools of students and friends of mine under my advice, which brought some surprising results about "thinking" in the schools.) Beside that I am working on various topics on some of which I hope to report soon in articles, especially with regard to problems in Social Psychology.[17]

The awkward prose in this draft of a prospectus, incidentally, shows how difficult it still was for Wertheimer to express himself precisely and idiomatically in English. His command of the language was, and remained, shaky.

During the summer of 1942, Wertheimer wrote to Quincy Howe at Simon and Schuster, some six years after the company had first expressed interest in his manuscript. After apologizing for the long delay, he assured Howe that "the manuscript is nearly in shape (A friend [Asch] helped me in revising the English.)" In a rough draft of this letter, Wertheimer addressed the principal themes of the manuscript in a more succinct and direct manner than in his earlier draft proposal:

> The book brings, as you will remember, the Gestalt-approach of Thinking, but in a very concrete way: the main chapters deal, very concretely, with fine examples of productive thinking, starting with cases in children, leading in the end to how Einstein has made his discovery (here, for the first time, the actual development of the dramatic thought process is described, and in a way which is, I think, understandable for the common reader.)—As you will also remember, the book was planned for the common reader no less than for the psychologists, philosophers, teachers.[18]

After receiving a positive note from Howe, Wertheimer worked over the manuscript for more than a month before shipping it to Simon and Schuster. He was disturbed that the "general appearance does not look better" and added that the manuscript was still far from complete:

> I had again to make quite a number of pencil corrections in the text; in some parts the english is still not fully corrected (a friend is working on this); the

figures will have to be redrawn, the quotations in the footnotes substituted by brief references to a list of literature on the end of the book; the chapter on Einstein which I read to him in a first draft I want to show him again before I really consider it finished. The numbering of the pages is done sofar only within the chapters; the mscpt as typed here has 314 pages; some less important parts are here still lacking and so several appendices which I plan to add.[19]

On August 13, Howe wrote to Wertheimer with appreciation for the "high intellectual level" of the manuscript but also with the company's decision not to publish it:

The books we have done in this field—Abbe Dimnet's ART OF THINKING and STRAIGHT AND CROOKED THINKING by Robert Thouless—were either more practical in purpose or more concrete in style. You have written a fine, general analysis of productive thinking, but I am afraid it does not seem to us the kind of book that we could publish most effectively at the moment.[20]

A week later, Wertheimer responded to Howe with "regret that you find the manuscript not fitting for your publishing house, but I understand that it is not the book you had been looking forward [to]. Best thanks for your advice."[21] While he must have been disappointed by Howe's decision, he had already been in touch with other possible companies about the book's publication before receiving the rejection notice from Simon and Schuster.

In his search for a publisher, Wertheimer consulted several American colleagues, mostly during meetings of the Society for Experimental Psychology and during his guest lectures across the country. One of his more valued correspondents was Robert Sessions Woodworth at Columbia University, who personally sent a copy of his freshly published book *Experimental Psychology* to Wertheimer in 1938. Wertheimer expressed his pleasure at receiving it and wrote Woodworth that the book would be helpful to him in drafting his manuscript on thinking.[22] On August 10, 1942, he solicited advice from Woodworth about publication and included an outline of the "finished" manuscript.[23] Woodworth quickly responded with praise for Wertheimer's "stimulating" outline and intention to publish: "I congratulate you and congratulate all of us, on the completion of your book on productive thinking."[24] Woodworth did not think the manuscript could be marketed as a textbook and suggested several publishers of psychology series as well as Columbia University Press which, as Woodworth pointed out, had published Katona's book, *Organizing and Memorizing.*

Several days after Woodworth's letter, Gardner Murphy, then a member of the psychology department at the College of the City of New York, responded to a query from Wertheimer with words of caution about the effect of the war on American collegiate publishing:

I believe that the more enterprising publishers are continuing to do basic books, but that the more conservative ones are using the war as an excuse for doing nothing that is not commercially perfectly safe. I have gradually grown rather bitter, I am sorry to say, towards my conservative publishing friends who simply cannot get to a temperature more than 20C. about any book which is not a clear-cut popular or commercial venture. For this reason, I can only counsel you as a friend to keep away from the great "established," reputable houses, if you care anything about active promotion (advertising, circularizing, and above all, pushing of the book with the retailers).[25]

Several of Wertheimer's correspondents took the liberty of forwarding his outline directly to publishers. Herbert S. Langfeld at Princeton responded positively to Wertheimer's "unusual and interesting" outline and, as advisor to John Wiley and Sons Publishers, forwarded the proposal to Wiley's president E. P. Hamilton, who in turn asked Wertheimer for a copy of the manuscript.[26] Wertheimer waited almost two months before apologetically writing to Hamilton that "he had been waiting all the time to get back from a friend the one good copy of my manuscript" and informed him that another copy was being typed.[27] The "friend" in Wertheimer's letter was Alvin Johnson, who had sent the manuscript to Macmillan publishers.[28] Although a vice president found the "material [to be] superior to so much that is offered in this field," Macmillan declined to publish Wertheimer's book because "there just isn't in our sales department the enthusiasm for it which there should be if a work of this kind is to be successfully issued. I am finding more and more and this is particularly true in these days, that a requirement for successful publication is a genuine belief in the book editorially and commercially."[29] In the spring months of 1943, Wertheimer sent a copy of the manuscript to Oxford University Press under the title "Studies and Materials in the Psychology of Thinking."[30] None of these efforts met with success, and the manuscript remained unpublished until after his death. After all the encouragement Wertheimer had received for the preparation of his book, his failure to find a willing publisher must have been disappointing. The rejection of the manuscript by several prominent publishing houses may in part have been due to the growing "conservatism" of publishers that Murphy ascribed to the war, and in part due to the still unfinished status of the manuscript. If the awkward use of the English language typical of Wertheimer's correspondence about the book also still characterized the manuscript to some degree, that too may have played a role in publishers' unwillingness to commit themselves to the project.

The Style and Content of Productive Thinking

The informal style of Wertheimer's prose in *Productive Thinking* is a significant departure from that of his earlier writings and was perhaps closer to the style of his lectures than was true of any of his other publications. He offers an invitation to explore productive thinking, sharing with the reader his personal experiences in the study of thinking:

I do not know whether you will enjoy as much as I did some of the experiences of which I am going to tell you here. I think you will, if you will travel with me on this exploratory journey on which problems arose and difficulties had to be faced for which I had to find tools and methods in order to clarify the psychological problems involved."[31]

Wertheimer invites discovery in relaxed, conversational words: "Think it over yourself, reader…. Try to do justice to the points I am going to mention" or "Try to [solve the problem] before reading what I report in this chapter. You may enjoy what follows more." He also continues to indulge in the polemics of his lectures in his description of unenlightened associationist procedures as "ugly" and "blind." As one prominent reviewer would later observe, "Though [*Productive Thinking*] treats of technical matters, it exhibits Professor Wertheimer's informal manner, his contagious enthusiasm, and his charm."[32]

But one of Wertheimer's close colleagues objected to the style and tone of the manuscript. A little over a year before his death, Kurt Koffka, who had been given the opportunity to read a draft of a chapter for the book, wrote to his close friend Molly Harrower that Wertheimer's

book seems to be almost finished, and I really believe now it will be printed. I read the greater part of one chapter. It is fascinating and interesting. But whether this mode of presentation, his general style, his mixture of the scientist, the prophet and the reformer will have the effect he wants to produce I don't know. I can take it because I know him but if I came across such a book, by an author unknown to me, I might resent it. I gave a few hints but the matter is far more general."[33]

Wertheimer does not allow the informal style to compromise the integrity of Gestalt psychology. He augments the otherwise informal style with the more technical ideas and language of his theory, explaining the process of thinking with such Gestalt terms as "function in the whole" and "change with regard to part-items."[34]

In his introduction, Wertheimer does not formally define productive thinking. Rather, he describes it as thinking that "really forges ahead," that "really grasps an issue." It is the "transition from a blind attitude to understanding in a productive process." Meaningful comprehension occurs only when details are seen in their appropriate interrelation. Although he acknowledges that other psychologists, logicians, and educators have studied thinking, he concludes that their work seems not to "touch the core of the problem at all" but rather to "show a dead picture stripped of all that is alive." The major cause of this deficiency, he argues, lies in the traditions of deductive logic and associationism in philosophy, sociology, education, and psychology. Wertheimer's text is intended to correct the "blindness" of these traditions:

This book has been written because the traditional views have ignored important characteristics of thought processes, because in many other books those views are taken for granted without real investigation, because in such books the discussion of thinking runs largely in mere generalities, and because, for the most part, the [G]estalt view is only superficially known.[35]

Wertheimer provides an agenda for the book through a series of questions addressed to the reader:

What happens if one really thinks, and thinks productively? What may be the decisive features and the steps? How do they come about? Whence the flash, the spark? What are the conditions, the attitudes, favorable or unfavorable to such remarkable events? What is the real difference between good and bad thinking? And in connection with all these questions: how improve thinking? your thinking? thinking itself? Suppose we were to make an inventory of basic operations in thinking—how would it look? What, basically, is at hand? Could the basic operations themselves be enlarged and improved, and thus be made more productive?[36]

As one commentator later observed, "Wertheimer does not introduce his examples of problem solving with the accompaniment of classification.... I consider this an attempt on Wertheimer's part to confront the given facts as free as possible from any prior conceptualization or theorizing."[37] Yet Wertheimer does distinguish among three different types of thinking processes. Productive thinking is characterized by the pattern of "Type α" thinking, which involves looking for gaps, closure of gaps, centering, grouping, and a transition from poor structures to good structures. By contrast, "Type γ" thinking is characterized by blind, premature conclusions with no real sense of direction. Less important in his discourse than Type α and Type γ is a "Type β" that "seems to be a hybrid set of operations and processes that are quasi-structural and quasi-blind."[38] Wertheimer does not provide a detailed definition or an extensive elaboration of Type β, other than that it lies somewhere between the other two types.

For Wertheimer, the "structural dynamics of the situation" are fundamental in understanding productive thinking:

Generally speaking, there is first a situation
    S_1, the situation in which the actual thought process starts, and then, after a number of steps,
    S_2, in which the process ends, the problem is solved.[39]

As the instigator of productive thinking, the S_1 state is structurally incomplete and contains stresses, strains, "a gap or structural trouble." The goal state of S_2 is "structurally better, the gap is filled adequately, the structural trouble has disappeared. It is sensibly complete as against S_1."[40] The cognitive steps involved in the transition from S_1 to S_2 may include grouping, envisaging, and centering, and a transition from a subjectively-centered view to a perspective with an objective grasp of the structural and functional requirements of the whole situation. He acknowledges that some problems are characterized by a structural clarity in which the particular requirements of the problem are clear and straightforward while other problems have a hiddenness that appears to obscure an obvious solution.

Productive thinking as a process is consistent with Wertheimer's devotion to the rational aspects of human nature and to people's "thirst for true orientation."[41] He asserts that

> To live in a fog, in an unsurveyable manifold of factors and forces that prevent a clear decision as to action, as to the main lines of the situation, is for many people an unbearable state of affairs.... Here lie great tasks for democracy. Critical attitudes, skepticism, do not suffice. What is needed is structural clearness.[42]

Wertheimer observes that people's problem-solving orientation is accompanied by other particular patterns of attitudes. He documents, for example, different reactions by adults and children when confronted with the problem of finding the area of a parallelogram. One type of participants provides him with no reaction other than indignation, frustration or simple dismissal of the problem with "Whew! Mathematics! I don't like mathematics." A second type "search their memories intensively, some even frantically, to see if they can recall anything that may be of help. They search blindly for some scraps of knowledge that might apply."[43] This orientation might inspire people to try to find the solution in a geometry book, an approach that Wertheimer admits is "certainly one way of solving problems." Such a strategy, however, fails the criterion of productive thought. Another type "start making speeches. They talk around the problem, telling of analogous situations. Or they classify it in some way, apply general terms, perform some subsumptions, or engage in aimless trials."

Clearly critical of what he considers the narrow approaches of these three types, Wertheimer is impressed by a fourth type of person who demonstrates an orientation of what he calls "real thinking." By drawing on paper or discussing the details of the problem, these individuals approach the parallelogram problem in a qualitatively different manner: "Something has to be done. I have to change something, change it in a way that would lead me to see the area clearly. Something is wrong." He reports, with some pride, "cases in which the thinking went straight ahead. Some children reached the solution with little or no help in a genuine, sensible, direct way. Sometimes, after strained concentration, a face brightened at the critical moment. It is wonderful to observe the beautiful transformation from blindness to seeing the point!"[44]

Wertheimer insists that the mechanical drill methods of a traditional classroom do not foster productive thinking and that

> the dangers to the development of such fine processes are mainly blind recall, blind application of something learned, a piecemeal painstaking attitude, a failure to view the whole situation on its merits, in its structure and in its structural requirements. It seems to me, although I do not have sufficient quantitative data on this point, that the ability to produce such fine, genuine processes often decreases considerably in school children when they become accustomed to drill.[45]

In his critique of formal training, he chastises instructors who demand "instantaneous response." Although not meaningful, mechanical procedures may become so familiar to them that students may develop "blind, piecemeal habits—tendencies to perform slavishly instead of thinking, instead of facing a problem freely." After citing his own and Katona's work, Wertheimer concludes:

> Type γ corresponds to learning by drill, by external association, by external conditioning, by memorizing, by blind trial and error. Type α focuses on developing structural insight, structural mastery, and meaningful learning in the real sense of the word. There is a widespread assumption that sensible learning, that learning of sensible material, is at bottom nothing but a complication of what is found in the rote learning of syllable series, etc., as though this latter provided *the* laws of learning. It does not seem possible that the characteristics of α are reducible to factors and operations of this kind.[46]

Wertheimer's book treats a varied array of examples of dynamic thinking, beginning with children in a classroom and ending with Albert Einstein's insights in physics. He addresses instances of thinking of his own children and of friends and colleagues, as well as notable intellectual achievements by such prominent scientists as Galileo Galilei, Karl Friedrich Gauss, Dmitry Mendeleyev, and Albert Einstein. As one commentator noted, Wertheimer "assumes that any of his examples can without undue distortion be taken as instances of one basic process."[47] He uses his formulations as readily to describe meaningful thinking in young children and in scientific discovery as in generating solutions to social problems.

Seven chapters are devoted to a series of concrete problems ranging from the construction of proofs for mathematical theorems to the readjustment of personal attitudes and perspectives in ordinary life situations. Asking specific focused questions, Wertheimer investigates basic issues in learning arithmetic and examines how school children struggle with elementary problems of geometry such as finding the area of a parallelogram, calculating the square of a binomial and proving the equality of vertical angles formed by two intersecting straight lines. He addresses the principle of organization used in discovering an elegant Gaussian theorem for the sum of a series. In a chapter on "Finding the Sum of the Angles of a Polygon," Wertheimer traces the evolution of his own insight into how the sum of the angles of a closed polygon must include a full rotation, or 360°.

A chapter that differs from the mathematical sections explores two social problems. In the first, Wertheimer describes two boys playing badminton. One is much better at the game than the other, so the first one eagerly wants to play while the other becomes progressively more reluctant to do so. A solution that both can embrace enthusiastically restructures the game from a competitive to a cooperative one: how many times can they hit the shuttlecock back and forth across the net without it touching the ground? The second problem involves the efforts of a young woman to describe her relationships with her co-workers in an office environment. Her ego tendencies distort or confuse the structure of the office hierarchy, centering it inappropriately on herself; a dispassionate description provides a much simpler and more realistic structure of the office hierarchy. In these two examples, restructuring changes the way problems are viewed and gives rise to solutions in the areas of work and play.

Wertheimer also uses instances from the history of science that illustrate productive thinking in major intellectual discoveries. In one chapter, he reconstructs Galileo's formulation of the law of falling bodies by detailing Galileo's observations of the motion of a pendulum and of freely falling balls in the study of acceleration and deceleration. Galileo's insights helped set the stage for the later development of Newtonian physics. But the most ambitious chapter is one devoted to "Einstein: The Thinking That Led to the Theory of Relativity." Wertheimer summarizes the "drama" of Einstein's discovery of relativity in ten "acts." In Wertheimer's analysis, Einstein's thinking involved a restructuring of assumptions in theoretical physics about the velocity of light.

Wertheimer was not alone in his attempt to analyze Einstein's thought processes. A book on *The Psychology of Invention in the Mathematical Field* by the eminent French mathematician Jacques Salomon Hadamard, for example, appeared in English in the same year as Wertheimer's book.[48] Acknowledging that he had little knowledge of psychology, Hadamard tended to use anecdotal rather than experimental evidence to buttress his ideas, and argued for the role of the unconscious mind in creative mathematical thinking. He discussed mathematical work by people from Jules-Henri Poincaré to Einstein as well as his own contributions to functional analysis.[49] In an earlier book, *Our New Ways of Thinking*, in 1930, George Boas had briefly described Einstein's analysis of special relativity and had used it as an illustration of a "most beautiful example" of thinking.[50]

One way in which Wertheimer's treatment differs from other accounts of Einstein's thinking was that he repeatedly discussed the matter with Einstein himself. "Those were wonderful days," Wertheimer recalls, beginning in 1916, when for hours and hours I was fortunate enough to sit with Einstein, alone in his study, and hear from him the story of the dramatic developments which culminated in the theory of relativity. During those long discussions I questioned Einstein in great detail about the concrete events in his thought. He described them to me, not in generalities, but in a discussion of the genesis of each question.[51]

Wertheimer's relationship with Einstein was consistent with the other Gestalt psychologists' personal relations with physicists and their appreciation of physics; Köhler studied with Mach and Koffka corresponded with British physicist Sir Arthur Eddington. Even observers from outside the school commented on the close relationship between Gestalt theory and field theory in physics.[52]

Wertheimer's book ends with a general discussion of the "Dynamics and Logic of Productive Thinking." In addition to outlining the properties of S_1 and S_2 situations and the characteristics of Type α, Type γ and Type β thinking, he elaborates on what he views as the deficiencies of formal logic, associationism, and trial-and-error learning in explaining dynamic thinking. Although acknowledging that a wholly adequate account of thinking does not yet exist, Wertheimer summarizes the advantages of Gestalt theory in correcting the "errors" of associationism and logic. First, Gestalt theory focuses on examples of "genuine, fine, clean, direct, productive processes— better than some might have expected." Second, several cognitive operations are crucial in productive processes: reorganization, centering, and grouping, which are "alien to the gist of the traditional approaches and to the operations they consider."[53] Third, the features of productive operations are not piecemeal but are intimately related to the specific properties of a dynamic and structured whole. Fourth, even the mechanisms of thinking described in the theories of formal logic and associationism, when properly understood, "function in relation to whole-characteristics." Fifth, thought processes demonstrate a consistent development that cannot be accounted for by "and-summative aggregation" or "piecemeal, chance happenings." Finally, thinking can "often lead to sensible expectations," and calls for verification of "structural truth" rather than arbitrary, piecemeal truth.

Wertheimer had many ideas, examples, and conclusions about productive thinking that did not find their way into this book. The manuscript, he admits in the preface to the book, is only a beginning, a preview of more ambitious works still to come:

I had limited this book mostly to subject matters which contain summative features as, e.g., the size of an area, the sum of a series, in order to focus the reader on just the [G]estalt in the thinking process itself; I have discussed only some formally elementary cases of [G]estalt features in the subject matter. In a second book I will have to deal also with the subject matters that are themselves real [G]estalten. Whereas methods and tools for piecemeal or structure-blind operations are highly developed, this by comparison is not the case for problems in [G]estalten, problems characteristic for the development of [G]estalt theory.

Two books must follow: one on the broader aspects of the psychology of thinking, the other on the problem of [G]estalt logic in which the traditional issues appear as the Euclidean special case. Here also the features of productive [G]estalt heuristics will have to be treated.[54]

There is no record to indicate that either of these books was ever even outlined. Their contents disappeared with Wertheimer's death, although hints of what he might have written in them had been included in his lectures for decades. The still-extant voluminous pages of notes he wrote to himself about such matters, mostly in his idiosyncratic shorthand, are so condensed and cryptic that, at least so far, no one has tried to generate a coherent account from them.

In his acknowledgments for the book, written on September 23, 1943, Wertheimer thanks, among others, Clara Mayer, Solomon Asch, Alvin Johnson, and his colleagues on the faculty at the New School. He adds:

To the [participants in] my experiments, the adults and the children, I am thankful for having learned so much. And I am very grateful to the distinguished men of science—Einstein above all—who made it possible for me to study intimately, in many conversations, how some of their great achievements in thinking developed.[55]

He ends his preface with the diffident assertion, "In spite of its limitations I hope [the book] may be of use." After years of tortured labor and countless alternate drafts of many chapters, the manuscript for *Productive Thinking* had been brought to reasonably satisfactory closure.

Early in the fall of 1943, the New School faculty and student body attended a special convocation to celebrate the completion of Wertheimer's manuscript.[56] Wertheimer publicly thanked the people mentioned in his acknowledgments, and also expressed his gratitude for the support of his research assistants. Given Wertheimer's well-known difficulty in completing even short articles for publication, many colleagues might have thought that he would be unlikely to produce a book, even a small one. Arnheim observed, "It took, I believe, the premonition of his death to make him finally overcome his hesitation and complete, with a supreme effort, the writing of the book that was to remain his only one."[57]

Wertheimer's health declined seriously during the summer of 1942. His legs gave him discomfort and he experienced some problems in walking. As early as November 1941, Wertheimer wrote to Einstein, "my difficulties in walking (disturbance of the circulation in the legs) do not bother me too much—our kind of people does not exactly work essentially with our legs—

and I hope that it will improve sometime."[58] By August 1943, he informed Einstein that "Personally I am not particularly well (the difficulties in walking which are connected with the blood circulation are a big hindrance) but the work goes well."[59] He took frequent hot baths and prescription medication, which provided only temporary relief. During his last months, he occasionally immersed his lower legs and feet in buckets of very warm water in which Epsom salts had been dissolved, in an effort to improve the circulation in his lower extremities. His weakened condition was doubtless further aggravated by his life-long habit of chain smoking; in the United States he continued it with strong unfiltered cigarettes.

Anni phoned the Wertheimer residence in New Rochelle on the afternoon of October 12, 1943, to congratulate Lise on her fifteenth birthday. Later that day, Wertheimer was getting ready to lecture at the New School when he suddenly slumped over, suffering from a massive coronary embolism. Minutes later he was dead.

Wertheimer was buried in New Rochelle's Beechwood Cemetery. Many friends, colleagues, students, and neighbors gathered to pay their final respects, including Wolfgang Köhler and Richard Courant. Several weeks later a memorial service was held at the New School; on that occasion, Albert Einstein joined many others who filled the New School auditorium to celebrate Wertheimer's life and work.

A number of further tributes to Wertheimer occurred in later years. Among many others were several symposia celebrating the centenary of Wertheimer's birth at the 1980 American Psychological Association convention, a memorial symposium at the New School in New York in 1988, a major memorial exhibit displayed in several different institutions, a special issue of a journal, a lecture series at Frankfurt University named for Wertheimer, and the posthumous award in 1988 by the German Psychological Society of its highest honor to Wertheimer.

Two symposia commemorating the centenary of his birth were presented at the 1980 convention of the American Psychological Association in Montreal, Canada. Participants in these symposia included Molly Harrower speaking on Kurt Koffka and his relation to Wertheimer, Solomon E. Asch commenting on Wertheimer's social psychology and his style of thinking, Irvin Rock detailing the impact of Gestalt theory on the field of perception, Miriam Lewin talking about her father Kurt Lewin and his relation to Gestalt psychology, Hans Wallach and John Ceraso concentrating on Gestalt psychology and the field of research on memory, and other presentations by Abraham S. Luchins and Edith Luchins, Ulric Neisser, and Mary Henle.

Another memorial symposium was held at the New School for Social Research in New York in 1988, to commemorate Wertheimer's work and to examine the continuing contributions of Gestalt theory to modern psychology. The symposium was related to a Max Wertheimer exhibit organized by Viktor Sarris, the incumbent of the same professorship at the University of Frankfurt that Wertheimer held between 1929 and 1933. The exhibit was first shown at the University of Frankfurt, traveled to New York, and was mounted in other places as well, including the University of Würzburg. Papers presented at the New School symposium, together with a few additional articles, were published in a special Max Wertheimer Memorial Issue, edited by Viktor Sarris, as the second issue of Volume 51, for 1989, of *Psychological Research*, the successor to the journal *Psychologische Forschung*, of which Wertheimer had been a co-founding editor in 1921.

In 1994, at the instigation of Viktor Sarris, the University of Frankfurt established a Max Wertheimer Lecture Series, consisting of two lectures each year. Most of the lecturers in the series have been from outside the Johann Wolfgang Goethe University of Frankfurt am Main itself, indeed from outside Germany. The fourth lecture in the series, on October 26, 1995, was given by Max Wertheimer's son, Michael, on the topic "A contemporary perspective on the psychology of productive thinking." The talk was held in the same lecture hall, Hörsaal H in the university's main building, in which Max Wertheimer regularly lectured while he was a professor in Frankfurt between 1929 and 1933.

On October 3, 1988, the Deutsche Gesellschaft für Psychologie (the German Society for Psychology) presented its highest honor, the Wilhelm Wundt Medallion, posthumously to Wertheimer at its convention in Berlin. Wertheimer's son, Michael, was invited to the convention to accept the medallion in his father's stead. The citation for the award (which has only been made to about a dozen individuals in the Society's history), signed by its 1988 President, Klaus Foppa, indicated that it was presented "in recognition of his exceptional services toward the founding of psychology on a Gestalt-psychological basis and his path-breaking experimental investigations which opened new avenues for research; in acknowledgment of the humanitarian conduct to which he remained true despite emigration and personal humiliation during his life."

After Wertheimer's death, Köhler took leave from Swarthmore College to assume responsibility for Wertheimer's classes at the New School. Asch also taught classes at the New School now that Wertheimer was gone, and eventually became chair of the department before accepting a position at Swarthmore in 1947.[60] Asch and Köhler joined Clara Mayer in editing Wertheimer's draft into a final manuscript and, in the course of their work,

> found that certain linguistic revisions were necessary. Mere difficulties of expression, it seemed to us, should not be allowed to obscure the meaning which Wertheimer clearly had in mind. The reader may be assured, however, that changes have been made only where the purpose of clarity could not

otherwise have been attained. The content and the form of the discussion have not been altered in any place.[61]

An appendix based on Wertheimer's notes about the sum of a series was added to the text. In 1945, Harper and Brothers published *Productive Thinking*, a book of 224 small-format pages, for $3.00.[62]

Critical Reception of *Productive Thinking* in the United States

Following its publication, Wertheimer's book was reviewed in some fifteen American newspapers, literary magazines, and scientific, philosophical, and educational journals.[63] The critical reaction was largely positive. After reading *Productive Thinking*, Walter B. Pillsbury declared that "Psychology is the richer for it.... The study of Einstein's processes alone would make the book a remarkable contribution."[64]

One reviewer called Wertheimer the "guiding genius" of the Gestalt school but noted that he

> did not find it easy to write books: this one has long been awaited by those who were aware of its gestation. It is probably the best exposition to date of the Gestaltist theory of "insight" learning, and one may fancy that its simplicity and clarity result in part from the author's residence in this country and from his consequent response to the pressure upon him by his American colleagues to eliminate the "mysticism" which bothered them in his earlier statements of his views.[65]

Poet Genevieve Taggard told readers of the *New Republic* that Wertheimer's book is "not for jargonists. It might be called the crystallization of a life's study."[66] "For what Professor Wertheimer is demonstrating in talking simply of '[G]estalts,'" wrote Taggard,

> is the inner experience of all artists and of all workers—their ability to think deeply and solve specific problems. One has been amazed by such solutions on the part of farmers and fishermen who rig devices to cope with their problems, or of women who handle people in tangled situations, of the anonymous tinkerer; and to these Wertheimer has added Gauss, Galileo and Einstein. It is the savvy of picking up the real world. One finds it in diverse places, and nearly always today, disregarded.[67]

Wertheimer's book also appealed to another poet, a prominent one. W. H. Auden wrote one of the more enthusiastic and light-hearted reviews of *Productive Thinking*:

> Your reviewer's immediate reaction to this book is one of incredulous astonishment. Something impossible has occurred; he has finished a book concerned largely with mathematics, and has not only been fascinated but has

actually (at least he hopes so) understood it. How different life might have become, he reflects, if Professor Wertheimer had only been the math master at his private school, for then he might now be an educated person.... How does Professor Wertheimer do it? First and foremost by assuming that the truth is one.... Secondly, Professor Wertheimer (like Virginia Woolf) never lets us forget that thinking is as much and as exciting a form of action as fighting. He inspires us to emulation by giving us historical examples of heroic thinking.... It is typical of Professor Wertheimer that he should have the honesty and courage to use the word "joyful" [to describe the elation of solving a polygon problem], just as he uses the word "ugly" to describe solutions which are formally correct but blind to structural relations.... Meanwhile, the final impression left by the book is a profound regret that Professor Wertheimer is no longer with us to bring his charm, his wisdom, his patience to our "world" classroom, which, I must say, looks very dreary indeed right now.[68]

Not surprisingly, Robert M. Ogden offered a positive review of the book as well. In particular, he was

struck by the significance of Wertheimer's analysis of a few simple problems: problems with which we are all confronted, yet seldom pursue to the point of an intelligible solution. It is futile to ask for more than Wertheimer has given in his primer-like presentation of the genius of insight and understanding.... The wider "view" which inspired Wertheimer in his patient survey of what actually takes place when a meaning is revealed should inspire others to reconsider and re-write the elementary texts that guide our courses of instruction in number, word, design, manipulation, and even music, for the purpose of making obvious the essential steps whereby we operate and gain knowledge of what we are and what we do.[69]

Another psychologist described *Productive Thinking* as "a brilliant contribution to contemporary psychology.... Its style is vigorous and enthusiastic," but the reviewer, Nathan Israeli, found the author's viewpoint to be "one-sided."[70]

Koffka's concern about the style of the manuscript was not reflected in the reviews of the book. Harold Guetzkow of the University of Michigan found "a sparkle and warmth about this book that is captivating. Rarely does the psychologist actually use the principles he extols in the very construction of his book. Wertheimer does.... Perhaps the quality which preserves the book's freshness from beginning to end is Wertheimer's attitude that he has highly satisfying and enjoyable insights to share with the reader."[71] Guetzkow, clearly unaware of the relationship between the two works, wondered why Wertheimer "never once refers to Duncker's *Zur Psychologie des produktiven Denkens* (1935), which bears such a close resemblance to his book."[72]

As Wertheimer might have hoped, several reviewers recommended the book to educators. One reviewer noted that the "problems are approached with fresh outlooks which make the work a 'must' for the teacher who would get out of the traditional groove and bring to…students something of the joy that attends intellectual discovery."[73] Another observed that "At a time when American education is subjecting itself to a major shake-up, it should be grateful for this treatment of the focal phase in the education process," and adds that "every one who tries to teach or execute creative thinking can benefit from it."[74]

It was also argued that Wertheimer's ideas can be productively applied in social work. Arthur L. Swift, Jr. of the Department of Church and Community at Union Theological Seminary recommended the book to social workers and groupwork executives, suggesting that Wertheimer could be viewed as "a leader in whose presence the group becomes alive with new ideas and the enthusiasm to fulfill them."[75] Although Wertheimer did not directly deal with social psychology in his book, Swift extolled the implications of productive thinking in social relations:

> The caseworker, trained in older psychological theory, can ill afford to miss this daring application of Gestalt psychology to the practice of productive thinking. And the community organizer, perhaps more than the rest, must struggle to possess this gift of seeing details in their true perspective, the part in relation to the whole, and this power to move creatively and to carry others with him [or her] as co-workers in building a city patterned to unity and order and growth.[76]

Still other reviewers proposed applying the ideas of productive thinking to sociometrics and political systems[77] and to personnel counseling.[78]

The most prevalent criticism of Wertheimer's book concerned the alleged vagueness of the theory. Some, such as Rice, urged that the theory be combined with other perspectives: the

> Gestaltist perspective still seems more valuable as a description of the broadest features of insight learning than as an explanation or analysis of its details and its specific varieties. We must continue to hope for a synthesis which will embrace the partial emphases of Gestalt, formal logic, associationism, and probably several other perspectives including those of psychoanalysis, semantics, and anthropology.[79]

Accusations of vagueness were central in a review by Virgil C. Aldrich, who wrote that Wertheimer gave

> the impression that something important is being said, something that needs to get said as a corrective for the old associationist and rationalist psychologies; but precisely *what* is being said remains a mystery. The reviewer, for one, wishes that as great a psychologist as Wertheimer had written at least one whole chapter of *Gestalt* theory of learning without once using the semi-metaphorical term "inner." Doubtless there are "inner meanings" to be

apprehended, but a theory of these should contain some literal analysis of the term, to provide means to identify and manipulate them in an objective way. Else we have simply a picturesque and intriguing formulation parading as a theory.[80]

Wertheimer, in a way, had already recognized such problems by admitting that "My terms should not give the impression that the problems are settled; they themselves are loaded with—I think—productive problems."[81]

Although he found Wertheimer's discussions "valuable to teachers and educators, for he shows persuasively the limitations of routine drill," the prominent philosopher Ernest Nagel protested the author's attack on "blind" systems, especially those derived from traditional logic:

> Professor Wertheimer is at his best in his positive delineations of the operations of successful thinking, and least plausible in his general formulations and in his criticism of points of view to which he feels himself hostile.... It is also curious to find a writer as well-informed as Professor Wertheimer accusing traditional logic (even in its modern mathematical form) of not being conducive to productive thinking, of introducing assumptions which do not "generally fit real thinking," and of being blind to structures—as if the professed task of formal logic were the descriptive study of thought processes, and as if the notion that logic is the general science of abstract order were not integral to one phase of formal studies.[82]

One reviewer, C. West Churchman at the University of Pennsylvania, was concerned more about the lack of experimental rigor than the theoretical vagueness of Wertheimer's book and found it

> unfortunate indeed that he has left certain basic concepts in such a vague state. What is an "adequate" structure?... Without making explicit how the contentious scientist would check for "adequacy," "understanding," and so forth, Wertheimer tries to make his point clear by numerous examples; but the reader is left, on the whole, with a decided feeling of dissatisfaction.... If a ray of hope is to be found in all this, it is that there is a growing realization of a real problem for psychology in the properties of the creative act, and the "gloom" lies in ignoring the experimental aspects of the problem.[83]

Wertheimer was also criticized for his "sketchy" treatment of attitudes and emotions in the thinking process:

> Wertheimer saw the emotions as a dynamic set of factors favorable to Type α thought processes. He did not consider the relation between the effects of the tendencies and emotions and the effects of structural or functional requirements of situations. There are many questions here which can be put to [G]estalt theory and which would probably require experimentation for answer.[84]

Productive Thinking, one might conclude, is an introduction to further systematic contributions that Wertheimer never fully worked out, at least not in printed form. Although described as a prolegomenon to two other books that he intended to write, this book instead became Wertheimer's *magnum opus*. Max Wertheimer did not live to see the publication of *Productive Thinking*, nor could he experience the quiet but persistent impact that the book has managed to exert on psychology during more than half a century after his death. One reviewer of *Productive Thinking* expressed the opinion that

> The main value of Wertheimer's book will rest in its live challenge to psychologists to work in the field of creative thought, stressing the dynamic aspects. He wants contemporary psychologists to "look at the situation freely, open-mindedly,...to penetrate, to realize and trace out the inner" relationships of the thought process. The crucial test of the power of Wertheimer's invitation will be found in the number and quality of research workers who accept his challenge. Let us hope there will be many, for our world needs "clean" thinking. Wertheimer has done a remarkable job of blazing the trail; the way is no longer uncharted.[85]

A number of psychologists have accepted Wertheimer's "invitation," although not always in a deliberate or explicit way. While, according to such critics as Mary Henle, a few contemporary representations of Wertheimer's work are superficial or distort it in its essential character, Wertheimer's work and the spirit of Gestalt theory have continued to inform much of the psychology that has evolved since his death. Its traces are still evident in modern cognitive psychology, cognitive neuroscience, and other major fields of late twentieth-century and early twenty-first-century behavioral and brain science.

Notes

1. Critchell Rimington to Max Wertheimer, September 27, 1935, MW-CU.
2. Quincy Howe to Max Wertheimer, February 7, 1936, MW-NY. Quincy Howe to Max Wertheimer, March 24, 1936, MW-CU.
3. Max Wertheimer to Quincy Howe, no date, MW-CU.
4. Abraham H. Maslow (1969). Unpublished memoirs. Comments on J. & G. Mandler (1968) 'The diaspora of experimental psychology: The Gestaltists and others.' *Perspectives in American History*, 2, 371-419, p. 391.
5. Abraham S. Luchins and Edith H. Luchins, "Max Wertheimer in America: 1933-1943. Part II," p. 145.
6. Molly Harrower, *Kurt Koffka: An unwitting self-portrait*, pp. 20-21.
7. Molly Harrower, *Kurt Koffka: An unwitting self-portrait*, p. 129.
8. Max Wertheimer, *Productive thinking*, p. xi.

9. Rudolf Arnheim (1984). Remembering Max Wertheimer. *History of Psychology Newsletter*, 16, p. 8.

10. Solomon E. Asch. Quoted in John Ceraso, Irvin Rock, and Howard Gruber (1990). On Solomon Asch. In Irvin Rock (ed.), *The legacy of Solomon Asch: Essays in cognition and social psychology*, pp. 3-19. Hillsdale, NJ: Lawrence Erlbaum Associates, p. 7.

11. Max Wertheimer, *Productive thinking*, p. 131.

12. Interview with Anni Hornbostel (AH), November 30, 1968.

13. In his acknowledgments, Wertheimer thanked only one person for help with manuscript preparation: "I am very grateful to Dr. S. E. Asch for his fine help in preparing the manuscript." Max Wertheimer, *Productive thinking*, p. xi. Possibly Asch's earlier struggle with the English language might have played a role in his becoming such a proficient and patient assistant to Wertheimer. According to his wife, Asch struggled in the sixth grade of a public school after he immigrated to the United States; "his most vivid memory of that early period was a complete inability to comprehend what was said." He learned to speak English by reading the works of Charles Dickens until he "slowly began to catch on," and within a couple of years, "he found himself in Townsend Harris High School." Florence Asch. Quoted in Ceraso, Rock, and Gruber, "On Solomon Asch," p. 4.

14. Max Wertheimer, Draft of a proposal for *Productive thinking*, no date, MW-CU. Wertheimer's mention of his "investigations and lectures on the topics involved through the last 25 years," incidentally, extends his work in this field almost back to his 1912 publication on the numerical thinking of aboriginal peoples.

15. Ibid.

16. Ibid.

17. Ibid.

18. Max Wertheimer to Quincy Howe, June 1, 1942 (draft), MW-CU.

19. Max Wertheimer to Quincy Howe, July 8, 1942 (draft), MW-CU.

20. Quincy Howe to Max Wertheimer, August 13, 1942, MW-CU.

21. Max Wertheimer to Quincy Howe, August 20, 1942, MW-CU.

22. Max Wertheimer to Robert Sessions Woodworth, 1938, MW-NY. Woodworth was enthusiastic in his treatment of Gestalt theory in his book *Experimental psychology* and cited in it Wertheimer's work on guilt detection, sound localization, form and motion perception, and productive thinking.

23. Max Wertheimer to Robert Sessions Woodworth, August 10, 1942, MW-NY.

24. Robert Sessions Woodworth to Max Wertheimer, August 21, 1942, MW-CU.

25. Gardner Murphy to Max Wertheimer, August 25, 1942, MW-CU. Wertheimer was already aware of the impact of the war on publishing houses; in his June 1, 1942 letter to Quincy Howe, Wertheimer had written, "I do not know whether you are still interested in the book as the war situation may have changed your plans." Max Wertheimer to Quincy Howe, June, 1, 1942, MW-CU.

26. Herbert S. Langfeld to Max Wertheimer, August 28, 1942, MW-CU. E. P. Hamilton to Max Wertheimer, September 2, 1942, MW-CU.

27. Max Wertheimer to E. P. Hamilton, October 31, 1942, MW-CU.

28. Alvin Johnson to Max Wertheimer, November 16, 1942, MW-CU.

29. H. S. Latham to Alvin Johnson, November 13, 1942, MW-CU.

30. Wertheimer mentioned in an August 1943 letter to Einstein that the "Oxford Press, which is interested in the book, would like to have the whole manuscript in a few weeks." Max Wertheimer, August 9, 1943. Quoted in Edith H. Luchins and Abraham S. Luchins (1979). Introduction to the Einstein-Wertheimer correspondence. *Methodology and Science*, 12, p. 199.

31. Max Wertheimer, *Productive thinking*, p. 13.

32. Ernest Nagel (1947). *Productive thinking* by Max Wertheimer. *Journal of Philosophy*, 44, p. 22.

33. Kurt Koffka, August 29, 1940. Quoted in Molly Harrower, *Kurt Koffka: An unwitting self-portrait*, p. 28.

34. Max Wertheimer, *Productive thinking*, p. 53.

35. Max Wertheimer, *Productive thinking*, p. 3.

36. Max Wertheimer, *Productive thinking*, p. 2.

37. Gayne Nerney (1979). The Gestalt of problem-solving: An interpretation of Max Wertheimer's *Productive thinking*. *Journal of Phenomenological Psychology*, 10, p. 58.

38. Nathan Israeli (1947). Wertheimer, Max, *Productive thinking*. *Journal of General Psychology*, 37, p. 100.

39. Max Wertheimer, *Productive thinking*, p. 238.

40. Max Wertheimer, *Productive thinking*, p. 238.

41. Max Wertheimer, *Productive thinking*, p. 244.

42. Max Wertheimer, *Productive thinking*, pp. 244-245.

43. Max Wertheimer, *Productive thinking*, p. 45.

44. Max Wertheimer, *Productive thinking*, p. 47.

45. Max Wertheimer, *Productive thinking*, p. 52.

46. Max Wertheimer, *Productive thinking*, pp. 246-247.

47. Gayne Nerney (1979). The Gestalt of problem-solving: An interpretation of Max Wertheimer's *Productive thinking*. *Journal of Phenomenological Psychology*, 10, p. 58.

48. Jacques Salomon Hadamard (1945). *The psychology of invention in the mathematical field*. Princeton, NJ.: Princeton University Press.

49. Since the books were published in the same year, they were reviewed jointly; Edward S. Jones concluded that "Max Wertheimer's contribution seems to be of greater merit from the psychologist's viewpoint in getting at the heart of the same problem of creative thinking." See Edward S. Jones (1947). *Productive thinking* by Max Wertheimer. *Philosophy and Phenomenological Research*, 8, 298-301.

50. George Boas (1930). *Our new ways of thinking*. New York: Harper, p. 186.

51. Max Wertheimer, *Productive thinking*, p. 213.

52. See, e.g., George Humphrey (1924). The theory of Einstein and the *Gestalt-Psychologie*: A parallel. *American Journal of Psychology*, 35, 353-359. O. L. Reiser (1930). Gestalt psychology and the philosophy of nature. *Philosophical Review*, 39, 556-572. P. C. Squires (1930). A new psychology after the manner of Einstein. *Scientific Monthly*, 30, 156-163. Squires even referred to Gestalt theory as "psychological relativity."

53. Max Wertheimer, *Productive thinking*, p. 234.

54. Max Wertheimer, *Productive thinking*, pp. xv-xvi.

55. Max Wertheimer, *Productive thinking*, p. xi.

56. Abraham S. Luchins and Edith H. Luchins, "Max Wertheimer in America: 1933-1943. Part II," p. 144.

57. Rudolf Arnheim (1984). Remembering Max Wertheimer. *History of Psychology Newsletter*, 16, p. 8.

58. Max Wertheimer to Einstein, November 28, 1941. Quoted in Edith H. Luchins and Abraham S. Luchins (1979). Introduction to the Einstein-Wertheimer correspondence. *Methodology and Science*, 12, p. 197.

59. Max Wertheimer to Einstein, August 9, 1943. Quoted in Edith H. Luchins and Abraham S. Luchins (1979). Introduction to the Einstein-Wertheimer correspondence. *Methodology and Science*, 12, p. 199.

60. The tradition of Gestalt psychology was kept alive at the New School following Wertheimer's death. Mary Henle left her position at Bryn Mawr to replace Asch after he moved to Swarthmore. Several Gestalt psychologists on the Swarthmore faculty lectured at the New School, including Asch, Köhler, and Hans Wallach.

61. Max Wertheimer, *Productive thinking*, p. xvii.

62. An enlarged edition of *Productive thinking*, edited by Michael Wertheimer, appeared in 1959. This edition added materials that Max Wertheimer had drafted during one stage of writing the book but which had not been in the original edition. The 1959 volume was based on an expanded table of contents found among Wertheimer's papers, and included chapters on "The bridge problem," "Plus three, minus three," and "The square of a binomial; learning arithmetic" that had not been part of the original edition. An English translation of Wertheimer's 1933 essay "On the problem of the distinction between arbitrary component and necessary part" joined four new appendices on additional problems in productive thinking that had been found among Wertheimer's papers. A complete bibliography of Wertheimer's publications concluded this volume. In 1982, the enlarged edition was reprinted by the University of Chicago Press with a new preface by Anders Ericsson, Peter G. Polson, and Michael Wertheimer that considered the impact of *Productive thinking* on cognitive psychology and emphasized its continuing relevance.

63. Harold A. Larrabee (1945-1946). *Productive thinking* by Max Wertheimer. *Ethics*, 56, p. 323. Wertheimer's book was also briefly noted in *School and Society* and *Current History*. *Productive thinking* by Max Wertheimer. *Current History*, 10 (March 1946), p. 257. Wertheimer, Max. *Productive thinking*. *School and Society*, 63 (January 5, 1946), p. 15.

64. W. B. Pillsbury (1946). *Productive thinking* by Max Wertheimer. *American Journal of Psychology*, 59, 490-492. Pillsbury's positive reaction to the book was all the more striking since he was an adherent of a rival school of psychology, and was by no means generally an advocate of Gestalt theory.

65. Philip B. Rice (1946). *Productive thinking* by Max Wertheimer. *Kenyon Review*, 8, p. 343.

66. Genevieve Taggard (1946). Thought in action: *Productive thinking* by Max Wertheimer. *New Republic*, 115, July 29, p. 109.

67. Taggard, p. 109.

68. W. H. Auden (1947). Old formulae in a new light: *Productive thinking* by Max Wertheimer. *New York Times*, March 30, pp. 34-35.

69. Robert M. Ogden (1946). *Productive thinking* by Max Wertheimer. *Philosophical Review*, 55, p. 300.

70. Nathan Israeli (1947). Wertheimer, Max, *Productive thinking. Journal of General Psychology*, 37, p. 99.

71. Harold Guetzkow (1946). Wertheimer, M. *Productive thinking. Psychological Bulletin*, 43, p. 377.

72. Harold Guetzkow (1946). Wertheimer, M. *Productive thinking. Psychological Bulletin*, 43, p. 377.

73. Ralph T. Flewelling (1948). *Productive thinking* by Max Wertheimer. *Personalist*, 29, p. 303.

74. Philip B. Rice (1946). *Productive thinking* by Max Wertheimer. *Kenyon Review*, 8, p. 343.

75. Arthur L. Swift, Jr. (1946). *Productive thinking*, by Max Wertheimer. *Survey*, 82 (November), p. 304.

76. Swift, p. 304.

77. Nathan Israeli (1947). Wertheimer, Max, *Productive thinking. Journal of General Psychology*, 37, 102-103.

78. Edward S. Jones (1947). *Productive thinking* by Max Wertheimer. *Philosophy and Phenomenological Research*, 8, 300-301.

79. Philip B. Rice (1946). *Productive thinking* by Max Wertheimer. *Kenyon Review*, 8, p. 344.

80. Virgil C. Aldrich (1946). Learning by insights: *Productive thinking* by Max Wertheimer. *Christian Century*, 63, December 4, p. 1471.

81. Max Wertheimer (1945). *Productive thinking.* New York: Harper, p. 4.

82. Ernest Nagel (1947). *Productive thinking* by Max Wertheimer. *Journal of Philosophy*, 44, 22-23.

83. C. West Churchman (1947). Wertheimer, Max. *Productive thinking. Annals of the American Academy of Political and Social Science*, 250, p. 173.

84. Nathan Israeli (1947). Wertheimer, Max, *Productive thinking. Journal of General Psychology*, 37, 104.

85. Harold Guetzkow (1946). Wertheimer, M. *Productive thinking. Psychological Bulletin*, 43, p. 377.

15

The Legacy of Max Wertheimer
and Gestalt Psychology

*Wherever the understanding of [humanity] will
take a step forward, there people will honor the
name of Max Wertheimer and turn back to his
thought with a sense of gratitude and affection.*
—Solomon E. Asch (1946)

More than half a century ago, Solomon Asch wrote that the "thinking of
Max Wertheimer has penetrated into nearly every region of psychological
inquiry and has left a permanent impress on the minds of psychologists and
on their daily work. The consequences have been far-reaching in the work of
the last three decades, and are likely to expand in the future."[1] Asch's article,
"Max Wertheimer's Contributions to Modern Psychology," appeared in
Social Research in part as a tribute, and in part as a response to a challenge
by Alvin Johnson, the president of the New School for Social Research, to
study "the work of Max Wertheimer and its meaning for social science."[2]
Asch's extravagant prophecy was fairly accurate; Max Wertheimer's legacy
has been substantial.

Wertheimer, reacting to the "blind atomism" that prevailed in the
psychology of his day, developed Gestalt theory while he was in Frankfurt
and then explored in detail its implications for a wide array of problems and
issues while he was in Berlin, Frankfurt again, and New York. He was
convinced that the scientific method offered the best hope for exploring and
demonstrating his holistic ideas. For Wertheimer, Gestalt theory was not
merely a theory of perception or of thinking, or a theory of psychology; it
was, rather, a *Weltanschauung*, almost an all-encompassing religion. The core
of it is a faith that much in the world is a comprehensible coherent whole, that
reality is organized into meaningful parts, and that natural units have their
own inherent structure. Although no human mind might be able fully to
fathom all of creation, it is nevertheless possible for humans to discover these

structures, and a faithful description of any phenomenon can—and must—do justice to the internal rules and principles of the phenomenon itself.[3]

Wertheimer argued vehemently against the narrow application of an arbitrarily analytical, "and-summative," mechanical mode of thought in scientific work—indeed in any area. Viewing wholes as the mere sum of their component parts, he insisted, does violence to the true nature of these wholes; parts must be seen in terms of their place, role, and function in the whole of which they are parts. While a few wholes in nature in some sense are just the sums of their parts (perhaps a pile of pebbles or a handful of coins), such instances are rare cases of an extreme of inertness. In the great majority of cases, the whole does not equal the sum of the parts, nor is it merely more than the sum of the parts—the typical whole is so different from a sum of its parts that thinking in any such summative terms yields only a distorted, impoverished caricature of genuine reality. One of his favorite examples of a Gestalt was a soap bubble. Its "component parts" are not indifferent to each other. A tiny alteration such as a pinprick in one minute part produces a dramatic change in the whole.

Wertheimer, together with his colleagues Kurt Koffka and Wolfgang Köhler and their students, established Gestalt psychology as a major international movement in psychology by the 1920s. Although he published little, several of his publications are widely regarded as classics in psychology. A foreshadowing of later Gestalt thought was evident in his 1910 paper on the structure and Gestalt characteristics of the music of the Veddas, and his article in 1912 on the quantitative thinking of aboriginal people was the first clear and detailed application of the Gestalt mode to cognition. Shortly thereafter, his analysis of the perception of apparent movement was published in the *Zeitschrift für Psychologie*; this article is still commonly viewed as the founding document of Gestalt psychology. Among his most widely recognized and cited works is the 1923 article in *Psychologische Forschung*, bearing the modest title "Untersuchungen zur Lehre von der Gestalt: II." ("Investigations in Gestalt Theory: II.")[4], in which Wertheimer demonstrated in detail how human perception is inherently organized into meaningful *Gestalten* on the basis of natural relationships within the stimulus pattern; form perception is not driven by associative factors but by a dynamic process of organization. Rich natural stimuli—and even assemblages of lines and dots—are not perceived as unrelated, piecemeal units or as a chaotic mass, but are instead grouped into meaningful configurations based on their similarity, proximity, closure, and continuity. This process is governed by the dynamic principle of *Prägnanz*, a tendency toward simple, coherent *Gestalten*.

Several of Wertheimer's early publications focused on perception, but throughout his entire career he was primarily interested in the psychology of thinking. This concern with cognition continued to be his principal obsession during his last years. It consumed him from before the time of the preparation of his 1912 work, "Über das Denken der Naturvölker" ("On the thinking of aboriginal peoples"), dominated his lectures from the earliest years of his professional career in Germany, and continued in his teaching in the United States, where he taught many courses on the topic, such as his course "On Better Thinking" at the New School. The Gestalt analysis of thinking was his primary interest from the beginning, and remained his main focus throughout his professional career.

By 1935, Wertheimer had seriously begun work on the book-length manuscript for his *Productive Thinking*. It presented in detail many concrete examples of productive thought, many of which he had used in lectures for decades and some of which had been discussed in a paper finished in 1918 and published in 1920.[5] He argued that meaningful comprehension is achieved only when parts and details are seen in their appropriate interrelatedness. He analyzed the thought processes of adults and children when confronted with geometrical and mathematical problems as well as with social conflicts. One of the later chapters, on Albert Einstein, was a chronological account of how the famous physicist evolved his theory of relativity. The manuscript was finished only during the last months of his life. Although Max Wertheimer died in 1943, his ideas continued to have a vital impact on psychology in the latter part of the twentieth century and into the twenty-first.

The Fate of Gestalt Psychology After Wertheimer's Death

Max Wertheimer's friend and colleague Wolfgang Köhler kept Gestalt theory in the limelight with his research and writing until his own death in 1967, but by mid-century Gestalt psychology had already been characterized by some as an antiquated and largely moribund school of psychology. In 1950, Edwin G. Boring expressed the opinion that "Gestalt psychology has been successful.... The movement has produced much new important research, but... Gestalt psychology has already passed its peak and is now dying of its success by being absorbed into what is Psychology."[6] These somewhat ambiguous words, initially written during the heyday of the reductionist school of behaviorism, may have been fairly accurate at the time. Other scholars have echoed Boring's pronouncement as well, prompting Mary Henle to observe:

> Ever since that time we have been invited to funerals of Gestalt psychology.... Even Mark Twain would have been dismayed by so many exaggerated reports. One cannot escape the thought that a movement that has required so many funerals must have extraordinary vitality. I believe that we still have important things to learn from Gestalt psychology.[7]

In recent years, a growing number of psychologists appear to agree with Henle, and there is a renewed recognition of the value of Gestalt theory.

Following Wertheimer's death, Gestalt theory was actively pursued by scholars in many countries. Even an incomplete list is lengthy: the countries include not only the United States and Germany (see p. 373) but also China, Egypt, Great Britain, France, India, Italy, Japan, Poland, Romania, Spain, and the former Soviet Union, and the internationally illustrious scholars who have supported the Gestalt cause include Agostino Gemelli, Gaetano Kanizsa, Alexander R. Luria, Albert Michotte, Eugenio Rignano, Jean Piaget, and Lev Vygotskii. In Wertheimer's adopted countries of Germany and the United States the spirit of Gestalt theory continued to be viable in the work of many prominent psychologists, including, among others, Rudolf Arnheim, Solomon E. Asch, Leon Festinger, James J. Gibson, Kurt Gottschaldt, Fritz Heider, Mary Henle, Friedhart Klix, Kurt Lewin, Abraham H. Maslow, Wolfgang Metzger, Ulric Neisser, Theodore Newcomb, Edgar Rubin, Viktor Sarris, Muzafer Sherif, Herbert A. Simon, Lothar Spillmann, Edward Chace Tolman, Hans Wallach, Hans-Jürgen Walter, and Herman Witkin. Outside of psychology itself, Gestalt theory has also been explicitly applied to many different problems in a wide range of disciplines, including anthropology, art, biology, chemistry, the cinema, economics, education, industry, mathematics, music, philosophy, physics, and sociology.[8]

Psychology of Art and Music

Wertheimer's fascination with the Gestalt structure of music and art was shared by several prominent artists. During the 1920s and 1930s, artists Paul Klee, Vasily Kandinsky, and Josef Albers explicitly drew upon Gestalt theory for inspiration in their writings, paintings, and lectures at the German Bauhaus school.[9] The Dutch graphic artist M. C. Escher was also demonstrably influenced by some of the work on figure-ground relationships in the Gestalt literature on perception.[10] Wertheimer's interest in this area continued after he immigrated to America, as shown by his course on "The Psychology of Music and Art" at the New School. Koffka too was interested in the area and devoted several publications to the contributions of Gestalt theory to the analysis of art.[11]

It was Rudolf Arnheim (who took over the New School course on the psychology of art when Wertheimer died) who developed in greatest detail the implications of Gestalt theory for the understanding of architecture, music, painting, poetry, sculpture, radio, cinema, and theater. His books have been used extensively in courses on art history, art appreciation, the performance arts, and communication.[12] A successful artist organizes sensory facts according to such fundamental Gestalt principles as unity, balance, *Prägnanz*, and segregation. Like Wertheimer, Arnheim saw the principles of Gestalt theory as ubiquitously evident in the natural world and the domain of the arts, not only in the rigorous constraints of the laboratory.[13] Mandler and

Mandler have expressed the widely-shared judgment that Arnheim's work "has been central and seminal and is certainly one of the milestones in the contribution of Gestalt psychology to American culture."[14]

Although not as systematic, exhaustive, or visible as Arnheim, other scholars too have examined the psychology of art and music from a Gestalt perspective. Gestalt theory was used by critic Max Kobbert to interpret and analyze modern informal art, in particular the work of Jackson Pollock.[15] One scholar analyzed Gestalt patterns in classical art as well as in wallpaper in trying to understand the "unconscious appeal" of much modern art.[16] A book by H. E. Rees employed the Gestalt principles of *Prägnanz*, integration, adjustment, and purposive differentiation in describing the creative processes various artists have used in architecture, dance, literature, music, painting, and sculpture.[17] Others such as Adelbert Ames at Dartmouth College and Hoyt Sherman at Ohio State University argued that the Gestalt principles of perceptual organization can be used constructively for art education,[18] and Gestalt theory has been advocated as an effective tool in music instruction as well.[19] Raymond Holder Wheeler at the University of Kansas and a colleague even analyzed the epochs in the history of music by contrasting what they called cold, atomistic periods (for example, program music and lyrics) with warm, Gestalt periods in music (for example, serious operas, tragedies, and institutionalized music).[20] Gestalt principles have also been used in the literary analysis of poetry, and specifically in efforts to understand how people comprehend metaphors.[21]

Personality and Psychotherapy

Although Wertheimer published little that was explicitly devoted to problems of personality or psychotherapy, Gestalt ideas have also occasionally been applied in these areas. Kurt Lewin's field theory, while only somewhat loosely an outgrowth of Gestalt psychology, was highly influential in the study of personality dynamics. The neuroscientist Kurt Goldstein, an early associate of Wertheimer's but not, strictly speaking, a Gestalt theorist, constructed an organismic theory that assumed a holistic, biological view of personality.[22] Goldstein borrowed explicitly from the Gestalt school in describing the interaction between the whole organism and the environment. Andras Angyal also provided an organismic orientation in his concept of "biospheres," holistic systems that include individuals and their environments.[23] As was true of Goldstein, Angyal's work used language related to Gestalt theory even if most of his concepts were not.

An early attempt at a Gestalt-theoretical approach to personality was made by one of Wertheimer's students, Werner Wolff, who used Gestalt ideas in his analysis of the expression of personality as manifest in gestures, stride, and posture.[24] One of Wolff's colleagues, Abraham Maslow, used

Goldstein's concept of "self-actualization" in his efforts to understand "optimal" personality development; Maslow's later "humanistic psychology" preserved the holistic flavor of Gestalt theory although it was by no means consistent with Wertheimer's emphasis on rigor in content and method.

Gestalt psychology was utilized in studies of the self and also of humor.[25] Although Wertheimer dismissed Freud's work as excessively associationistic and unscientific, several theorists have tried to link psychoanalysis and Gestalt theory in such areas as the study of archetypes, subliminal perception, and the unconscious.[26] It has even been suggested that there is some affinity between certain ideas of Freud and those of Gestalt theory, especially ideas in Lewin's field theory.[27]

Some efforts to use Gestalt theory in the study of personality, psychotherapy, and psychopathology have been in name only, and not at all in substance. As a prime example, the "Gestalt therapy" of Fritz Perls was popular for some time within the clinical community, but Mary Henle (1978) demonstrated (without addressing the efficacy of the therapy) that Perls's approach bears literally no intellectual resemblance to the Gestalt theory of Wertheimer, Köhler, and Koffka.[28] Arnheim voiced a similar conclusion about the relationship between Gestalt therapy and Gestalt theory, noting, "I can see Max Wertheimer fly into one of his magnificent rages, had he lived to see one of the more influential tracts of the therapeutic group in question dedicated to him as though he were the father of it all."[29]

A number of clinicians outside of the Perls camp recognized the value of a holistic perspective long before Fritz Perls inappropriately named his neo-Freudian version of psychotherapy. Wertheimer had several students who pursued the clinical implications of Gestalt theory. As early as 1923, Heinrich Schulte published an article based on his work with Wertheimer on a Gestalt theory of paranoia that differed radically from the traditional Freudian interpretation.[30] (This paper, as mentioned in Chapter 7, was apparently at least as much Wertheimer's own work as it was Schulte's.[31]) Wertheimer's student, the psychiatrist Erwin Levy, published a number of Gestalt-inspired papers on psychopathology, including one on schizophrenia.[32] Molly Harrower, one of Koffka's most promising students, studied the effect of brain damage on the perception of figure and ground.[33]

From the 1930s through the early 1960s, a number of articles appearing in the German and American literature developed in some detail the contributions of Gestalt theory to a variety of specific—and general—problems in psychiatry, neurology, and clinical psychology.[34] Gestalt theory was also applied in child pathology, speech disability, shock therapy, and the analysis of criminal behavior during this same period.[35] In the early 1930s, psychiatrist Lauretta Bender was working on a test that required subjects to reproduce simple line figures, using Gestalt principles to analyze the distorted reproductions made by brain-injured patients.[36] The Bender-Gestalt Test for the diagnosis of brain injury enjoyed widespread popularity (even though Wertheimer expressed some reservations about it), and several other psychometric tests were developed based on Gestalt principles.[37] The Gestalt concept of *Prägnanz* and other Gestalt principles of organization were also, not surprisingly, reported as offering some of the best theoretical bases for understanding the Rorschach psychodiagnostic inkblot test.[38] And during the last quarter century, serious efforts have been made by two scholars closely involved with the Society for Gestalt Theory and its Applications (who are also co-editors of its journal, *Gestalt Theory*), Gerhard Stemberger and especially Hans-Jürgen P. Walter, and their colleagues, to apply classical Gestalt theory to psychotherapy. The Society, of which Walter was a co-founder in 1978, continues to hold biennial conventions in German-speaking Europe. Its foci, and those of its quarterly international and interdisciplinary journal, include not only clinical issues, but many others as well, from general psychology through history, philosophy, art, perception, and cognitive neuroscience to personality and social psychology.

Education

Gestalt theory, as repeatedly emphasized in Wertheimer's *Productive Thinking*, has important implications for education and teaching. In the fall of 1934, Wertheimer explicitly dealt with these implications in a seminar at the New School on "Consequences of the Gestalt Theory of Psychology for Education and Teaching." One commentator asserted that the Gestalt perspective parallels closely the functionalist ideology of progressive education as opposed to the more structuralist orientation of traditional education.[39] Another remarked that the holistic goals of progressive education are closely linked to Gestalt theory:

> When the subject memorizes by studying the whole selection, the details are organized into a total configuration, each element in its proper relationship; the subject who uses the part method learns a jumble of details which have no organization.[40]

A number of scholars over the years have proposed educational programs based on Gestalt psychology, especially for the teaching of reading.[41] But Wertheimer's vision of a Gestalt theory of education came to fruition most in the work of several of his students, such as Karl Duncker and Abraham Luchins, and especially George Katona and Catherine Stern, as discussed in some detail in Chapter 13.

Social Psychology

Three chapters in William Sahakian's book, *History and Systems of Social Psychology*, are devoted to the role of Gestalt theory in the development of social psychology. Sahakian even wrote that "[G]estalt psychology, predicated on wholes and grouping, is itself basically a social psychology, not only of human groups but of nonhuman grouping as well. Grouping principles are [also] quite pertinent in the investigation of social perception."[42] While Wertheimer might have been uncomfortable with Sahakian's somewhat awkward phrasing, clearly Sahakian believed that Gestalt theory has much to contribute to social psychology.

Soon after Wertheimer's arrival in America, several prominent scholars were promoting the value of Gestalt theory in sociological and anthropological investigations.[43] At the New School, Wertheimer taught a number of courses specifically on social psychology, and he addressed the contributions of Gestalt theory to broad social issues in his essays on truth, ethics, freedom, and democracy (discussed in Chapter 12 and its appendix). Following his lead, several of his students and colleagues further extended Gestalt theory into the domain of social psychology.

Drawing upon basic Gestalt themes, Kurt Lewin's field theory profoundly impacted social psychology in general and the study of group dynamics and of leadership in particular. In estimating the enormous impact that Lewin had on social psychology, Lewis Coser observed that, in less than a decade at the University of Iowa, Lewin "raised a whole generation of social psychologists who were to dominate the field for several decades."[44] Wertheimer's indefatigable assistant and successor at the New School, Solomon Asch, used the Gestalt perspective in his widely-cited research on group pressure.[45] Usually considered a study of conformity, these experiments of Asch's focused more on the coordination of the individual's perspective with the perspective of the group and on the disturbing feeling that arises when those perspectives are incongruent. Asch also developed a full-scale Gestalt theory of social psychology, which he published in an influential book in 1952. Among Asch's admonitions is that the social psychologist must consider the individual in relation to the larger social context:

> To understand [people] we must see [them] in [their] setting, in the context of [their] situation and the problems [they are] facing. If we wish to understand a given quality in a person we must not isolate it; we must see it in relation to [that person's] other qualities. For this reason, also, the "same" quality in two persons is often not the same psychologically.... When the phenomena being observed have order and structure, it is dangerous to concentrate on the parts and to lose sight of their relations.[46]

Asch's close identification with the Gestalt position emerges clearly in this passage. He also used the same orientation in a number of far-reaching investigations of perception, learning, memory, and personality.[47] Indeed, Solomon Asch became the premier, the pre-eminent, Gestalt social psychologist.

In addition to the contributions of Lewin and Asch, the work of other notable social psychologists was also informed by Gestalt psychology. Fritz Heider's extensive use of Wertheimer's perspectives is evident in his seminal work on attribution and in his cognitive theory of interpersonal relations, and is explicitly acknowledged in Heider's autobiography.[48] Muzafer Sherif's ground-breaking research on the autokinetic effect and intergroup conflict and cooperation contains substantial Gestalt themes.[49] Another important figure at the New School, Leon Festinger, was influenced by Wertheimer via Lewin in the development of his theory of cognitive dissonance and in the many experimental studies that it generated.[50] Sahakian declares that Gestalt theory provided the foundation for several other influential social psychology theories, such as Newcomb's theory of communicative acts, Cartwright and Harary's theory of structural balance, Abelson and Rosenberg's balance model, and the congruity principle of Osgood and Tannenbaum.[51] In considering more recent developments, Carl Graumann concluded that although not explicitly part of mainstream social psychology in 1989,

> Gestalt theory, in various modifications and fusions, is a very dynamic undercurrent of social psychology's mainstream.... Even some of the more specific Gestalt principles and theorems that are no longer cited or quoted have retained their dynamic part, functioning, however, as hidden or implicit assumptions.... If I am correct in proposing that Gestalt theory has been incorporated in social psychology as a fundamental implicit theory and has finally become a frame of reference for further theorizing, then the Gestalt heritage in social psychology has a much better and a more enduring place than many of the fleeting theories and theorettes of the present.[52]

Perception and Neuroscience

An area in which Wertheimer's work and Gestalt psychology in general have maintained a vital and explicit impact is human and animal perception; a review article on perception in the *Annual Review of Psychology* in 1991 reported that among researchers in this field are "descendants of the Gestalt tradition, which constitute modern perceptual psychology. Although the Gestalt descendants are diverse, their lineage influences both their similarities and their disagreements."[53] Gestalt properties and the Gestalt laws of grouping continued to be a productive research heuristic in research in perception during the 1990s.[54] Modern perceptual psychologists have continued to undertake fruitful investigations of such Gestalt topics as perceptual organization, figure-ground segregation, and perceptual combination of attributes.[55] The literature on perceptual organization and on the role of motion of the perceiver in perception of the environment also still bears a distinct Gestalt stamp.[56] But Mary Henle has argued that not all modern perceptual psychologists—even the ones who explicitly identify themselves with the Gestalt tradition—are in complete agreement with or have a full understanding of Gestalt theory.[57]

Gestalt psychology assumes a kind of functional and structural comparability of phenomenal experiences and of their underlying physiological events. Perceptual experience is directly and dynamically related with the isomorphic pattern of neural functioning in the brain. This view has much in common with a number of recent trends in cognitive neuroscience.[58] The field of cognitive neuroscience is now examining relations between cognitive functions and neural processes in a manner that is clearly consistent with the classic Gestalt concept of isomorphism.[59] The recent neuroscience of perception has also continued to concentrate on, and is beginning to shed new light on, traditional Gestalt problems and ideas.[60]

Contemporary research on the neurological foundation of visual perception has returned to the Gestalt orientation and findings for two major reasons. First, the single-neuron approach, the successor to theory and research more than a century ago by Santiago Ramón y Cajal and Charles Scott Sherrington, was unable to provide a fully satisfactory account of complex visual phenomena. Many twentieth-century investigations of visual perception were undertaken in the context of this theory, but the single-neuron doctrine proved too simplistic to explain many complex visual perceptual phenomena studied by Gestalt theorists, such as figure-ground relations, grouping, and context-dependent percepts. Second, research on vision in the past few decades has identified interactive neural mechanisms that can begin to explain perceptual events described much earlier by Gestalt psychologists. As a result, the past few decades have produced a shift from research on individual cell functions to the integration of neural functions into organized wholes. Findings about receptive fields, neuronal networks, and the interaction between "magnocellular" and "parvocellular streams" have provided promising new possible explanations of how simple stimuli are synthesized into a meaningful whole by the brain.

As a consequence, neuroscientists are again examining perceptual phenomena and neural events described in early Gestalt literature. For example, coherent motion of parts of a stimulus display is believed to play a key role in figure-ground separation, in a process described by neurophysiologists as "binding" but earlier discussed by Gestalt psychologists as "common fate." Gestalt researchers also proposed long ago that perceived concavity and convexity are determined by the illumination gradient, while today's researchers use the terms "shape-" and "depth-from-shading" to describe the same phenomenon. As yet another example, the Gestalt principle of closure is prominent in recent experiments on stereokinetic effects.[61]

A sophisticated understanding is developing of the workings of individual neurons interacting with one another in complex networks within the visual system. Gestalt theory and experiments made clear the inadequacy of the single-neuron model in explaining how visual stimuli are coalesced into coherent meaningful wholes by the brain, and thoroughly documented the rich, organized nature of complicated visual percepts. According to neuropsychologists Lothar Spillmann and Walter Ehrenstein, "The search for distributed processing and global cooperation in neural networks testifies to the resurgent interest in such holistic approaches."[62] With extensive and technologically highly sophisticated research on visual systems, neurophysiologists are reexamining questions that earlier Gestalt research identified, and are beginning to develop tentative answers that the Gestalt psychologists could not achieve with their much cruder apparatus.

Friedhart Klix, a distinguished psychologist in Germany, argued that Gestalt psychologists raised issues in the field of perception and its neurophysiological underpinnings that "for decades affected and strongly influenced the substance of psychology. But [Gestalt theory] will most probably continue to affect the field for a long time into the next century." [63] The theory's heyday, in Klix's opinion, is long since past; research has shifted into new directions. But "Does this new development spell the demise of classical Gestalt psychology? I believe not; and this is the most astonishing feature of this entire development over its almost one hundred years. In an almost personal conversation…Köhler asked me why nobody really seems to be concerned about Gestalt psychology any more. More than 30 years ago I answered him, basically: 'No movement in German psychology around the turn of the century withstood the wear and tear of time as strongly as Gestalt psychology.' 'Why so?,' he asked me in response. My answer: 'Because the phenomena of human perception were studied and specified with a degree of precision that had rarely been practiced before. Whoever engages in the psychology of perceptual phenomena must be able to explain what you (Köhler) and your collaborators have found. Because your facts are incontestable.'"[64]

Earlier in his essay, Klix wrote, "The original Gestalt psychologist, the ponderer of the phenomena, the one who thought about the regularities in them, who saw what was new, that was Max Wertheimer. The compiler of the phenomena, the man who brought them together, compared them, tested them for inner consistency, was Kurt Koffka…. But the theorist who joined it all together into a coherent view that was oriented to natural science, that was Wolfgang Köhler. He accomplished the transition from Wertheimer's Gestalt phenomenology to the strictly natural-science-oriented Gestalt theory."[65]

Referring to other fields in which Gestalt theorists worked, including social psychology and the psychology of emotion, Klix offered a summary evaluation of the overall achievements of Gestalt theory. "The phenomenology of perception, the thermodynamic explanation of the phenomena and their identification with phenomena of human social life as well as the origins of anger, of striving for goals, of satiation in activities; this kind of unification of heterogeneous phenomena did not exist before in psychology. Nor has it since existed again down to today. Psychology lost this high degree of integration in 1933 and has not since (yet?) ever achieved it again."[66]

More specifically limited to visual neuroscience was a 1999 article by Gerald Westheimer of the Division of Neurobiology at the University of California, Berkeley.[67] The abstract of this paper indicated a somewhat critical evaluation of the contributions of Gestalt theory, as well as an appreciation of its value: "In the 1920s Max Wertheimer enunciated a credo of Gestalt theory: the properties of any of the parts are governed by the structural laws of the whole. Intense efforts at the time to discover these laws had only very limited success. Psychology was in the grips of the Fechnerian [psychophysical] tradition to seek exact relationships between the material and the mental and, because the Gestalt movement could not deliver these, it never attained a major standing among students of perception. However, as neurophysiological research into cortical processing of visual stimuli progresses[,] the need for organizing principles is increasingly making itself felt. Concepts like contour salience and figure segregation, once the province of Gestalt psychology, are now taking on renewed significance as investigators combine neural modeling and psychophysical approaches with electrophysiological ones to characterize neural mechanisms of cognition. But it would be perilous not to take heed of some of the lessons that the history of the Gestalt movement teaches."[68]

Westheimer begins his paper (which was his Max Wertheimer Lecture, delivered at the University of Frankfurt am Main in May 1998) with an historical overview. "In perhaps the most concentrated expression of the credo of the Gestalt movement," he writes,[69] "Max Wertheimer, widely credited with being its guiding spirit, went even further [than Christian von Ehrenfels, who had argued that the whole is more than the sum of its parts: its parts plus a Gestalt quality of the whole]. Not only is there more to the whole than merely the sum of its parts, but the properties of the parts are conditioned by those of the whole: 'There are entities where the behavior of the whole cannot be derived from its individual elements nor from the way these elements fit together; rather the opposite is true: the properties of any of the parts are determined by the intrinsic structural laws of the whole.'" Westheimer next briefly summarizes Wertheimer's 1912 experiments on the perception of apparent motion, the phi phenomenon studies, and writes, "In his assessment of Wertheimer's monograph, Sekuler (1996) has admirably shown how seminal [Wertheimer's] ideas proved to be in subsequent research.

"Phi motion was, however, only the beginning of Gestalt psychology. When Wertheimer made his pronouncements of the early 1920s that the properties of the parts are determined by the laws of structure of the whole, he was well aware that this is not a viable research program unless the laws were actually discovered. During the decade of the 1920s there were many attempts to do just that. The single best example is Wertheimer's 1923 contribution." This contribution was the principles of perceptual organization, such as proximity, similarity, common fate, and closure. Westheimer writes that Köhler tried to explain these principles in terms of hypothetical isomorphic processes in the central nervous system, but "Köhler's original formulation, using brain analogues of electromagnetic and thermodynamic theories (field theories), obviously was premature given the state of knowledge about cortical anatomy and physiology of those days, but the idea of isomorphism, albeit in much more sophisticated form, lives on."[70] Westheimer points to recent research using single-cell recordings and computational models in studying how "neural connections might lead to contour salience," and in attempts to explain how "a figure becomes conspicuous in the field owing to the arraying or arrangement of elements which by themselves are not individually salient. This is surely the same problem posed by Wertheimer in his 1923 study."[71] Further, Westheimer points out that the orientation-selective neurons discovered by Hubel and Wiesel, and their activation depending upon whether or not they are "flanked in the right manner by other elements, suitably positioned and oriented"[72] fit with the earlier Gestalt speculations. "We have here a fulfillment of Köhler's premonition of isomorphism between perception and brain state." Westheimer acknowledges that "now we are more aware that we need information about neuronal populations and circuits even more than about single cells. In particular, the pertinent question at the present state of knowledge is the extent to which any change in firing of single neurons early on in the stream of visual processing in the brain is an expression of influences on those neurons of higher neural centers feeding back signals to the earlier ones—top-down influences, as they are called.... Is there a better example of Wertheimer's vision of a whole determining the behavior of its constituent parts than an experimental verification of the fact that what a visual cortical neuron responds to best depends more on the properties of the overall configuration in the visual field than on the parameters of the stimulus in its receptive field?"[73] Westheimer concludes that "in conformity with the vision of the early Gestalt theorists, the very idea of dynamic, top-down and context-driven brain states invites the consideration of a global structure that, in turn, conditions the properties of its parts rather than the reverse.... It seems we have difficulty escaping a dilemma so well articulated by Wertheimer when he pointed to the many kinds of stimulus layouts, in which some pattern components segregate themselves into perceptual wholes or figures whereas others appear separate, and then asked: 'Are there principles for the kinds of resulting arrangements? What are they?'"[74]

Westheimer asserts that in his "search for laws of structure of 'wholes,'" Wertheimer anticipated "theories and experiments of the 1990s," although the Gestalt theorists, in the absence of late twentieth-century technology, could not specify the particular brain mechanisms involved.[75] "Modest starts yield modest successes," Westheimer writes. "We are comfortable with matches between retinal photochemistry and dark adaptation, between the eye's optics and cone spacing and visual acuity, between cone pigments and color matching and mixing. Spectacular progress in the neural apparatus as the visual stream enters the brain now makes us wish to match that knowledge of neurobiology with the recognition of spatial forms and the assignment of position, depth, and movement attributes of simple visual features. For knowledge of the latter we find the Fechnerian psychophysics limiting and hence naturally turn to what Gestalt theorists kept dwelling on in the 1920s."[76]

Perhaps the most detailed effort to relate recent and current research in cognitive and visual neuroscience to the work of the Gestalt theorists during the first half of the twentieth century has been made by Lothar Spillmann, a prominent psychophysicist and neuroscientist at the University of Freiburg, Germany. He published two major articles on "Brain and Gestalt" (Gehirn und Gestalt) in 1999 and 2001 based on his contributions to a conference held in June 1999 in Delmenhorst near Bremen on the occasion of the centenary of the birth of Wolfgang Metzger. Since the papers provide much concrete information about the relationship between recent work in visual neuroscience and the classical Gestalt work, the following pages present translations of extensive parts of Spillmann's two papers. The first of the two papers is specifically focused on Metzger's work, especially his book *Laws of Seeing* (*Gesetze des Sehens*), and the second deals with neuronal mechanisms.

Spillmann begins his first paper[77] with a brief eulogy of Metzger and a general introduction. He writes that the psychology of the primary Gestalt theorists still has "something to say to us today." Spillmann provides his estimation of the chief contributions of the main figures as follows: "While Wertheimer, the primary founder of Gestalt psychology, was esteemed as profound, almost mystical (like an Old Testament prophet) and Köhler was described as sagacious and brilliant, Metzger (in addition to Koffka) was the great systematizer of Gestalt psychology, who compiled and organized in his books everything that was known in the field of perceptual research."[78] Clearly, different writers (for example, Klix, cited earlier) draw slightly different conclusions about the roles of the different Gestalt theorists.

Spillmann develops his analysis of Metzger's book on seeing by stating early in his essay that "anyone, like Metzger, who occupies himself with the psychology of perception will sooner or later make three astonishing observations. The first is that one sometimes sees something that actually is not there.... The second observation is that one does not see certain things even though they actually are there.... The third observation, finally, is that we do perceive some things, but not in the way in which they really are." He provides such examples as apparent contours, camouflage, and various illusions. "Concern about these deviations of immediate perception from the physical stimulus was a central theme of the Gestalt psychologists.... Perceptual illusions—as well as veridical perceptions—cannot be denied. They possess a special reality...."[79] One can convince oneself over and over that they falsely mirror the objective world, yet one nevertheless always falls right into them again.

"In fact under certain circumstances we see our environment 'correctly' only because of active visual processes which reorganize and complete the perception of a stimulus so that it agrees with the external world. The principles expressed in these processes are responsible for why a particular order prevails over all others: that is why they have been designated as *laws of seeing*.

"The laws of seeing determine what, in a potentially ambiguous stimulus complex, becomes *figure* and what *ground*, how the *internal structure* of the figure is constituted, and what the relation is of the figure to the environment or to the ground. In no way are we free to organize what we wish to see as we please. Rather in perception there are *natural* rules according to which everything that is seen organizes *itself* into wholes and parts, groups and members." Spillmann observes that all principles of perceptual organization find expression in camouflage in the animal world, and in the perception of complete wholes in our environment, even though most actual objects are partially occluded by objects between them and the viewer; furthermore, the so-called size, form, and color constancy of seen objects occurs in animals as well as in humans and is largely innate. "Without such invariances, we could not survive."[80]

Spillmann summarizes the classic distinctions between figure and ground as these were taken over by the Gestalt psychologists from Edgar Rubin, and emphasizes that current perceptual research is again focused on these functional distinctions as well as on the effect of shadows on the perception of a figure as convex or concave.[81]

Spillmann points out that the concept opposite to the Gestalt concept is the and-sum, the aggregate, the pile.[82] "While in a Gestalt the parts interact, with each part influencing the others and therefore achieving a certain local value (a role, a meaning) in the whole, in an and-sum, like the little stones in a mosaic that is randomly thrown together, the elements are not related to one another." He briefly characterizes Wertheimer's work on apparent movement, and writes that "Koffka saw in Wertheimer's apparent motion a phenomenon which permitted investigation of psychological events and physiological mechanisms from the point of view of *psychological facts and not of physiological hypotheses.*"[83]

"As did Wertheimer, Köhler, and Koffka before, Metzger always reemphasizes that one and the same stimulus, depending upon its embeddedness in a larger total context, can result in different percepts and that conversely different stimuli can result in the same or similar percepts." Köhler used "this so-called stimulus indeterminacy of psychophysical processes as a basis for his hypothesis that our perception is not founded upon rigid wirings, but is founded on dynamic self-organization," on field processes. Spillmann cites recent work that comparably bases Gestalt formation on coherence and global interaction,[84] and relates it as well to Wertheimer's principle of *Prägnanz*, namely the tendency of our perception to form a good Gestalt. Spillmann summarizes the classical Gestalt principles of perceptual organization, arguing that they are still highly relevant today, and show that our perception is not exclusively stimulus bound but also "brain bound."[85] He writes, "all these Gestalt laws are responsible for our perceiving a multiply ambiguous (in a physical sense) stimulus array not as we wish or at random, but always corresponding in the same pregnant [prägnant] way with the autonomous rules and tendencies of the perceptual apparatus. The organization does not require a creative synthesis in the sense of Wundt (1887), but occurs spontaneously and without our adding anything. It is immediate, and naturally given."[86]

Spillmann ties the discussion into recent work[87] which shows that retention of a percept over time normally requires contours, structures, textures, and gradients as well as eye movements, and into research on perception of the motion of elements and groups. He also relates it to the now classical work of Gunnar Johansson on *"biological movement,* in which dot figures defined by weak lights can be recognized as Gestalten (for example, dancers) without any trouble, on the basis of their movement trajectories in the dark"[88] and to *"kinetic depth effects."*[89] "The contribution of Wertheimer, Koffka, Köhler, and the other Gestalt psychologists was primarily the demonstration of *field-dependent* perceptual phenomena, i.e., their struggle against associationism and the *constancy hypothesis*, according to which the same stimuli must always lead to the same percepts and different ones to different percepts."[90] Today there is increasing attention to the Gestalt theorists' insight that "perception is a matter of *relational* events which are codetermined by earlier processes and simultaneously by processes occurring in other brain areas."[91] Meanwhile, "the *figural aftereffects* which Köhler and Wallach interpreted as evidence for a change in electrical resistance ('satiation') in the [brain] field still have not yet been explained."[92] And "top-down" processes are now recognized as equally important as "bottom-up" processes.[93] Spillmann specifically refers to the work of Stephen E. Palmer

(1999)[94] as attempting to provide a broad overview of visual perception, including the current efforts to come to grips with the issues raised long ago by the Gestalt theorists.

Spillmann also cites recent work on the classic Gestalt observations concerning completion phenomena across gaps in the visual field produced by lesions (scotomata).[95] Such perceptual completions and closures apparently follow the principles of perceptual organization first identified by Wertheimer in 1923.

The final section of Spillmann's paper on the laws of seeing, entitled "Gestalt-correlates in the neuron?," concerns recent efforts to identify neurophysiological and computer mechanisms that could help explain the Gestalt phenomena described early in the twentieth century. Spillmann writes[96] that "a major problem for the Gestalt psychologists was that they could only define their concepts *descriptively*, since they lacked both the neurophysiological and the neuroinformatic bases for formalizing the relationships they were investigating. As a consequence, their explanations were necessarily *post hoc*, and their predictions only qualitative, hence not quantifiable. This is a reason why soon after its greatest successes Gestalt psychology came to a temporary standstill. Further, during the sixties the Gestalt psychologists neglected to connect phenomenal analysis with quantitative psychophysics and the emerging neurophysiology.

"But now, Gestalt-psychological research is enjoying a renaissance.... There are three reasons for this: First, one can create complex perceptual phenomena better on a computer screen than was possible with the earlier methods. It is therefore also easier to quantify the investigated effects. Second, the results can be correlated with single-cell recordings in the monkey and the cat.... In the human, the stimulus processing can be investigated in addition with imaging procedures, thus gaining information about the nature and locus of the underlying brain mechanisms. Third, in the context of neuroinformatic model building, one can model the psychophysical observations and explain them hypothetically with appropriate algorithms.

"The newly awakened interest in Gestalt phenomena within cognitive neuroscience (including neuroinformatics) is so great, that one would wish that Metzger's 1953 book *Laws of Seeing* would be translated into English. Questions such as the neuronal bases of the Gestalt laws, the relation between the whole and the parts, the genesis of order (and of reorganization) according to the principle of *Prägnanz* are once again in the foreground. It also raises the question concerning the *psychophysical level*...at which the correlation between brain process and perception (the isomorphism problem) occurs.

"The first neuronal correlates exist for the regularities that the Gestalt psychologists derived from perception. Quite early, neurons were already found that selectively responded to stimulus parameters such as light density, wave length, orientation, angular nature, and movement, and were therefore able to code a stimulus in terms of its dependence on its physical characteristics.... Subjective phenomena (illusions) too became accessible to explanation." It became possible to demonstrate that "movement neurons in the frog could not discriminate between stroboscopic apparent motion (Wertheimer's phi phenomenon) and actual motion. Further possible neuronal correlates concern the *laws of continuity* and *of common fate....*

"Significant is the recent finding...that neurons in the monkey respond to contrast in orientation: a dashed rectangle generates a lively response when, on the basis of its orthogonal orientation, it contrasts itself as figure from the ground, but is responded to only relatively feebly if it is embedded in a background with the same orientation and therefore loses its figural characteristics. Investigations of cells that selectively respond to faces...as well as cells that respond in a relatively invariant manner despite changes in distance, form, and position...also lead neurophysiology increasingly to the complex perceptual phenomena described by the Gestalt psychologists. All these achievements are naturally not the result of processing in a single neuron; rather, they require a multitude of cells that function in unison with one another and thereby result in our visual achievements. The concept of the 'perceptive field' as a psychophysical correlate of the receptive field of a single neuron...includes this kind of interaction.

"An important question to which so far there is no proper answer is how it can happen that we do not see any contour framing ('null channels')...but bounded surfaces of a certain brightness and color. In other words, how does the visual brain manage to contribute light, color, and shadow tones to a line sketch which depicts reality without surfaces...? Proposed solutions to these questions are emerging from neuroinformatics...[but] a proof of the mechanisms postulated here does not yet exist via neurophysiology.

"The Gestalt psychologists set out at the beginning of the [twentieth] century to explain why we see the world in the way we do. They did not completely answer this question, but they brought us a long way toward the answer. Now it is up to us to take the next step, to call the unresolved problems into consciousness and promote our understanding of the *Laws of Seeing* through interdisciplinary research."

Spillmann begins his second article[97] with the comment, "The central theme of perceptual psychology is the articulation of the perceptual field into figure and ground. Wertheimer (1923, p. 301), at the outset of his work, *Untersuchungen zur Lehre von der Gestalt*, writes, 'I stand at the window and see a house, trees, sky. Theoretically I might say there were 327 brightnesses and nuances of color. Do I *have* "327"? No. I have sky, house, and trees.'

"What occupied the Gestalt psychologists more than eighty years ago is now once again highly germane, but the emphasis now is less on the description of the phenomena and far more on their possible explanation.... Important questions to which psychologists, neurophysiologists, and neuroinformaticists in visual research are now trying to find answers are (1) How does a figure that is organized and coherent and is segregated from the ground arise from a myriad of individual stimuli? (2) How does the grouping of individual stimuli occur? (3) What are the factors according to which a continuum (surface) and a discontinuity (border) arise in perception? (4) Whereby are form, size, location, and inner structure, as well as the interactive relation of figure and ground and to other figures in the field, determined?...

"Aside from these questions concerning the principles of organization of perception, the goal of the Gestalt psychologists was to find out whether the form of an object is composed of the *combination* of its parts or is *articulated* out of the whole. In other words: Does perception go from the parts to the whole, or does it grasp the whole before its parts?

"The *atomistic orientation* in early perceptual theory (Locke, Berkeley, Hume, Helmholtz) emphasized an ordering of stimuli on the basis of their spatiotemporal proximity: Accordingly frequent conjoint and contemporaneous occurrence (repetition) of elements causes lasting connections and combines them into more complex structures (forms). The Gestalt psychologists...(Wertheimer, Köhler, Koffka) attacked this associationistic psychological conception of perception as 'hook-up theory'...and proposed their own opposing perspective, which claimed that perceptual structures are always *autochthonous* (primary), i.e., more than a mere sum of elements. Wertheimer (1912) speaks in this connection of the *parts being determined by the whole*."

Spillmann's article continues with consideration of the microgenesis [*Aktualgenese*] or development of perception, the role of contours or edges, and the emphasis on contour in art, then briefly considers the pre-eminence of line and border in neurophysiology. A major portion of his article, devoted to figure-ground segregation, contains discussions of how figure and ground arise, the role of contour detectors in figure-ground articulation, and presumed brain processes in this articulation. A second major section on "from contour to surface" asks how extended surfaces are coded neuronally, and considers the perception of extended surfaces over time, active "filling in" versus after-images, and possible brain mechanisms that may be responsible for such perceptual phenomena. A third major section concerns perception of motion in the visual field, and a fourth discusses eye movements and attention. All four of these sections include extensive references to recent work in cognitive neuroscience, visual neuroscience, psychophysics, and neuroinformatics.

In the last part of Spillmann's 2001 paper on brain and Gestalt, entitled "Concluding remarks," he writes,[98] "If one examines research progress during the last 50 years in the field of visual perception, it is striking that, after the initially predominant investigation of the coding achievements of individual cells (detection of attributes), increasing attention has been paid to more complex working processes.... Combined with this is a change in stimuli from simple dot and line elements to patterns which lead to spatial (apparent figures, texture contrast) and temporal (relative motion, tunnel effect) Gestalten.... Characteristic of this change is the question: 'Where do visual signals become a perception?' Neurophysiologists today investigate not only genuine perceptual phenomena such as the dependence of the observed direction of motion on the orientation of boundary lines, the so-called *aperture problem*...or the depth layering of superimposed fields of motion..., but also central psychological problems such as the role of attention and the influence of eye movements.

"Perceptual phenomena that were brought into the discussion by the Gestalt psychologists more than eighty years ago are reaching more and more into the sphere of neurophysiological explanation. In addition to the receptive field and its psychophysical correlate, the perceptive field..., there has long been recognized the expanded response field..., which draws in stimulus information from the broader environment. Many such overlapping fields could—understood as a *microgestalt*—form the foundation for the context-dependent phenomena of the Gestalt psychologists....

"In the neuronal analysis of this *field dependency* one must distinguish between sensory-perceptive and perceptual-cognitive phenomena. The first kind mediates between neighboring stimuli in the close range of a receptive field ('beyond the classical receptive field'). This kind of interaction concerns primarily colinearly arranged interrupted contours...as well as stimuli that are distinguished from one another by their orientation and texture (pattern contrast). The second kind has hardly been investigated so far, and renders possible an interaction between areas in the visual field that are far apart from one another. Examples of this are relational perceptions...between test and reference stimuli within an ordered system, such as transposition (in the sense of Wertheimer and Köhler) of size and form, brightness and color, and also orientation and speed. Both kinds require global, symmetrically distributed attention (a holistic Einstellung...).

"Fundamental questions remain for the future, such as the neural processing of the abundance of forms in our environment. Question: How does the *coordination* of the pattern of neuronal stimulation result in recognition of the inducing stimuli (object recognition)? Furthermore: Where does the *synthesis* of the visual information (brightness, color, orientation, form, and movement) that is separately analyzed in the early levels of processing result in an object...? How do we connect and complete a sequence of partially given impressions into a whole ('biological movement')...?

"The neurophysiological investigation of these and other perceptual achievements and their modeling in neuroinformatics has barely begun. New methods such as functional MRI in conjunction with transcranial magnet stimulation promise a detailed brain topography of visual functions, including the modulating effects of attention, imagination, memory, motivation, and consciousness in the near future.

"In view of this knowledge one may ask, how much of our perception is 'bottom-up' and how much 'top-down'? Modern neurophysiology has for a long time viewed the visual system as a rising ('feed-forward') cascade of levels of processing, in which the sensory information delivered by the eye is evaluated step by step. This approach...has led to pioneering knowledge. Today it appears that this assumption is too simple. In the visual pathway there are numerous descending fibers ('re-entry connections') which suggest a dynamic interaction ('feedback') from higher to lower levels of processing.... Furthermore, as mentioned above, many intracortical cross connections are known, which connect areas that are far apart with one another via long horizontal axons...." Here Spillmann adds a footnote: "Investigations of the monkey visual system have revealed that visual perception is based upon high-grade parallel neuronal information processing, in which numerous cortical and subcortical centers are involved.... Thus a myriad of areas have been identified in the visual cortex that are specialized for the analysis of optical stimulus attributes...and which can be divided into a dorsal ('where') and a ventral ('what') pathway.... These two pathways obtain their signals primarily from the previously tuned magnocellular or parvocellular levels of processing.... Between these specialized areas there nevertheless exist numerous cross and back connections." Returning to the main text, Spillmann quotes the article by Westheimer summarized above.

"In a noteworthy article Westheimer (1999)... asks, 'Is there a better example of Wertheimer's vision of a whole determining the behavior of its constituent parts than an experimental verification of the fact that what a visual cortical neuron responds to depends more on the properties of the overall configuration in the visual field than on the parameters of the stimulus in its receptive field?' And he continues,...'the very idea of dynamic, top-down and context-driven brain states invites the consideration of a global structure that, in turn, conditions the properties of its parts rather than the reverse.' In a similar manner Sekuler (1996) describes how Wertheimer's ideas are still fertilizing, down to today, the research in the area of the perception of motion.

"The ultimate goal of experimental neurophysiology at the threshold of the new millennium is the answer to the question, how do perceptual constancies or invariants occur in humans and animals...? Thus at higher levels of the visual system, cells have been found that signal one and the same stimulus relatively independently of its illumination, distance, and the location of the observer.... Such cells even respond with partial obstruction of the stimulus.... It is our task to understand how a visual object retains its apparent identity despite constantly changing size, position, and location (perceptual constancy), and how, conversely, one and the same stimulus can generate different percepts depending upon its embeddedness in a larger context (context dependency).

"This weighty problem is dealt with today in visual computer science, for example, under the concept of representative direction of gaze ('canonical view'), in the context of the independence of the angle of regard and the source of illumination.... It is only one among a growing number of examples that show how phenomenological description, psychophysical measurement, neurophysiological derivation, and neuroinformatic modeling in research on visual perception can complement one another and lead to deeper insights."

Cognitive Psychology

A number of prominent cognitive psychologists explicitly acknowledge the relevance of Gestalt theory to contemporary issues in their field. Cognitive science led to the demise of behaviorism, and investigators returned to the study of a broad range of mental processes. Wertheimer's work on productive thinking and other cognitive processes is widely cited in the literature on problem solving and insight. Gestalt themes have also been resurrected in studies of learning and memory, especially in studies of the role of organization in learning.[99] It has also been proposed that Gestalt theory can be useful for the current connectionist conception of brain functioning that focuses on parallel distributed processing.[100] But the Gestalt legacy is perhaps most evident in recent cognitive work on problem solving and thinking.[101]

Prominent in accounts of cognition is Wertheimer's first student to make extensive use of his work on thinking and problem solving, Karl Duncker. Duncker's 1935 book on problem solving, *Zur Psychologie des produktiven Denkens* (*Psychology of Productive Thought*),[102] is now widely viewed as a classic in the history of cognitive psychology. Drawing on Wertheimer's thought, Duncker distinguished between "organic" and "mechanical" problem solving, and argued, like Wertheimer, that productive thinking depends on reorganization and on a structural understanding of the problem situation.

Almost as frequently cited as Duncker are Luchins's water-jar experiments on the effects of set or *Einstellung* in solving a problem.[103] The difficulty in reorganizing a conception of a familiar problem domain in such a way that a new but similar problem becomes soluble remains a major focus of research.

Cognitive psychologists have been studying the structural processes of thinking, reasoning, and problem solving very much along the line of the Gestalt tradition of Wertheimer, Duncker, and Luchins. Consistent with the Gestalt approach, cognitive psychologists have concentrated on complex abstract knowledge structures such as schemas, scripts, and frames.[104] Wertheimer's conception of the nature of insight and understanding in thinking continued to be viewed as raising important questions for computer simulations of cognition.[105] The widely popular information-processing model of such influential scholars as Allen Newell and Herbert Simon views problem solving as a goal-directed search among possible solutions within a specific problem space.[106] Their pioneering work on the General Problem Solver, an artificial-intelligence program that solves cryptoarithmetical problems by breaking down a given problem into a variety of subgoals, is, as Newell himself has written, directly related to Duncker's earlier work.[107] More recently, at least one computer program based on Gestalt assumptions has been created that attempts to simulate insightful problem solving and functional fixedness.[108] But despite these developments, computer simulations of cognition still appear unable to account fully for the role of insight in problem solving.[109] As Ericsson, et al. have noted, "Many of the examples so lucidly described by Wertheimer remain only partially understood and continue to represent significant challenges to cognitive scientists who wish to advance [the] understanding of the psychological mechanisms that underlie humanity's highest intellectual accomplishments."[110]

The "cognitive challenges" of Wertheimer's book *Productive Thinking* were the focus of an article early in 1997 in *Psychology Teacher Network*, an ephemeral publication for psychology teachers sponsored by the American Psychological Association. Entitled "A contemporary perspective on the psychology of productive thinking," it asserted that the Gestalt approach to productive thinking developed in Wertheimer's book is still fresh and relevant today. It begins with a few illustrations of "reorganization" or "restructuring" (different from those used by Max Wertheimer in his book), summarizes Wertheimer's main points, and ends with reference to some of the recent literature in cognitive psychology that bears on, or was affected by, Max Wertheimer's *Productive Thinking*. The remainder of this chapter is a slightly modified version of that article.[111]

The book *Productive Thinking*[112], published over a half century ago (two years after the author's death), has been translated into several foreign languages and has been reissued repeatedly in English; it continues to be cited frequently in the Social Science Citation Index. It was also described and summarized in a book in German in 2000 as one of 36 "classics in psychology."[113] Why are people still reading it, still citing it?

Wertheimer introduced his book by asking, "What occurs when, now and then, thinking really works productively? What happens when, now and then, thinking forges ahead? What is really going on in such a process?"

He answered that what characterizes productive thought is its fit with the situation to which it is applied. Productive thinking involves going from a state of confusion about some issue that is blind to the core structural features and properties of that issue, to a new state in which everything about the issue is clear, makes sense, and fits together. At the core of the process is a kind of reorganization or restructuring, going from a state that makes no sense to one that displays insight, is crystal clear.

In his lectures on thinking, and in his book, Wertheimer used numerous concrete examples to illustrate his principles. They may help clarify his approach. Consider first a perceptual illustration of what he meant by "reorganization," "restructuring," "insight," "understanding."

What does the following mean?: "Pas de l'y a Rhône que nous." This example comes from the American philosopher-psychologist William James.[114] The French might be translated roughly as "Not of there is Rhône [a river] than we," which makes no sense at all. Try saying it out loud. Does that help? Try reading it with an American accent: "Pah de'l ya rown ke-new"— or "Paddle your own canoe." The reorganization achieves a transition from meaninglessness to a new structure, in which the sequence of sounds symbolized by the letters now makes some sense.

A rebus almost cries out for reorganization. What does this
stood
well   mean?
view
"Well" is under "stood," and both are over "view"—which, slightly reorganized, becomes "well" under "stood" over "view," or well-understood overview. That is what you need to generate about any problem, to think about it productively.

Such "catching on" characterizes productive thinking and problem solving as well, whether in physics, geometry, or any other field, and Wertheimer analyzed dozens of concrete examples. Here is one instance: why is any sequence of three repeated digits (abc,abc or, say, 276,276 or 341,341, etc.) divisible without remainder by 13? The solution requires realizing that the factors of the number abc,abc are abc—and 1001 (1001 times abc equals abc,abc), and that 1001 is divisible by 13 without remainder. Think it through!

A striking example of reorganization is an extension of a popular puzzle. A hunter sees a bear one mile due south of where the hunter is standing. The hunter aims a gun at the bear, shoots, and misses. The hunter next walks the one mile due south to where the bear was when the shot was fired, then walks one mile due east, then one mile due north—and ends up standing at exactly the same place from which the gun was shot. The usual version next asks,

"What color was the bear?" For someone who has never heard this story, the question is astonishing. How could the information provided have anything to do with the color of the bear? To solve the problem, the query has to be reformulated into, "Where on the surface of the earth might it be possible to go successively one mile due south, then one mile due east, then one mile due north, and end up standing at the same place one started from?" Most readers will already know that the spot is the north pole. From there, you go one mile due south, then turn left 90 degrees and walk exactly one mile due east, then turn left again and go exactly one mile due north—and end up standing on the north pole again. The spherical triangle you have traversed looks a bit different from a planar triangle (all three sides are curved and the sum of its interior angles is 3 times 90 or 270 rather than 180 degrees), but the north pole clearly satisfies the specified constraints. What can you conclude about the color of the bear? Of course: any bear in the Arctic is apt to be a polar bear, so the color of the bear must be white.

But that is where the extension of this problem starts. Where *else* on the earth's surface, other than at the north pole, can one go one mile due south, then one mile due east, then one mile due north, and end up standing at the same place one started from? Perhaps the reader should stop here and ponder the puzzle for a while.

Such examples may help convey what Max Wertheimer meant by "reorganizing" or "restructuring." He argued that productive thinking requires an insightful revision of one's representation of the problem domain, to use more modern terminology.

In summary, he proposed three broad generalizations about productive problem solving, all of which can be viewed as challenges to modern cognitive psychology, and all of which have been addressed by contemporary writers. First, productive thought involves transforming the representation of a problem from a vague, fuzzy, incomplete, and confused one that is "blind" to essential structural features of the problem to one that is clear, has no gaps in it, makes sense, and views each part of the problem in terms of its place, role, and function within the problem as a whole.

Second, such transformations are (a) hampered by blind search, "functional fixedness," empty associations, "and-sums," conditioning, school drill, bias, and so on, and are (b) aided by open-minded exploration of the problem, searching for its essential, crucial features, and its "rho relations." By "functional fixedness" Wertheimer (like his student Karl Duncker) meant that if an object is seen as fulfilling a particular useful function in one context, this makes it less likely that one will recognize that it could perform a different function as well in another context. An "and-sum" is a mere conglomeration of items that are arbitrarily connected, without regard to the attributes of those items or their meaningful relations to one another. The term "rho relation" was used by Wertheimer to indicate a feature that is crucial to the essence of a problem. For example, if you are to build a toy bridge of wooden blocks, there is a rho relation between the distance separating the two uprights and the length of the horizontal member (it cannot be shorter than the distance between the two uprights), as well as a rho relation between the heights of the two vertical blocks—they must be at least roughly comparable if the bridge is to stand. But the color of the blocks bears no rho relation to whether the bridge will stand or not. (This example comes from the enlarged 1959 edition of *Productive Thinking*.)

Third, this perspective on productive problem solving generates several potentially heuristic areas for research: (a) laws governing segregation, grouping, centering, and structural transposability, (b) how relations between parts and their wholes govern the possible operations on parts that take into account the part's place, role, and function within its whole, and (c) the nature of "outstanding wholes," "good Gestalten," indeed of "rho relations" themselves.

Wertheimer illustrated these observations with numerous examples, ranging from finding the area of a parallelogram to how Albert Einstein formulated the theory of relativity. To paraphrase Ericsson and his colleagues in their preface to the 1982 edition of *Productive Thinking*,[115] the examples set a challenge for the modern cognitive psychologist—indeed for any thoughtful human being. They contrast pure memory, or reproductive thinking, which can be accounted for reasonably well by the associationist paradigm that prevailed half a century ago (and by its modern counterpart, much of the connectionist approach to computer modeling) with *productive* thinking, or insight-based reasoning, which is not so easily handled by an associationist or connectionist strategy. Examples of productive problem solving and thinking compel consideration of complex mental structures and processes, typically ones that are idiosyncratic to a particular problem and do not generalize from one problem domain to another.

The advent of the computer a few decades ago generated what is now called the "cognitive revolution." The computer became the model for the human mind. Newell, Shaw and Simon,[116] Newell and Simon,[117] and Simon[118] formalized what has become the prototype of the kinds of paradigms that have been taken for granted by cognitive psychologists ever since. Problem solving is conceived as a goal-directed search among perceived possible solutions within a specified domain called the "problem space." Such a conception works well in simulations of the problem-solving efforts of novices who have little experience with attempting to solve novel problems, but cannot readily account for how experts like chess masters, physicists, or designers, who have a thorough knowledge and an organized understanding of a domain, go about solving difficult problems in the area of their expertise. One consequence of this failure was the postulation by Walter Kintsch[119] and others of complex abstract knowledge structures such as schemas, scripts, or frames to account for text comprehension and other complex cognitive processes. From this perspective, as Greeno[120] put it, "insight" involves the discovery of the applicability of an existing general schema to a novel situation. But what processes generate genuinely productive thinking, that is, yield representations that can in fact be used successfully to solve a novel problem, remained—and remains—elusive. Blind schema-generalization cannot work; the restructuring and insight emphasized by Wertheimer are still missing in computer models of cognitive processes. Ericsson and his co-authors in 1982[121] concluded that while modern cognitive science has made some modest progress on several issues raised in the book *Productive Thinking*, "it has by no means solved all of them. All of Wertheimer's examples raise serious problems for an associationistic paradigm of mental processes. Today, the information-processing psychologist considers the solution of the issues raised by Wertheimer central to progress in [the] understanding of problem solving and productive thinking."

It has been proposed[122] that the inherently blind connections that make up a computer and a computer program can never achieve insight: understanding and meaning may in principle be outside the capacity of any computer or computer program; to the extent that a program might be able to mimic or simulate productive thinking, the insight or understanding is not in the program or computer itself, but in the *programmer*.

Many recent publications are clearly relevant to the issues raised in Wertheimer's book. People are still thinking about, writing about, and doing empirical work on these matters. Consider a brief sample of these publications. The question about all these items, it could be argued, should be whether recent developments demonstrate real progress on the central problem that Max Wertheimer addressed in his analyses of productive thinking: the crucial role of reorganization, of restructuring, of insight. Ward Edwards of southern California, a long-time systems analyst, mentioned in another context[123] that he believes that one should let computers do what they do well, the "intellectual" processes of evaluation, inference, and decision—and let people do what they are good at, which is the tasks required to structure the problem in the first place and to provide inputs to those three processes. This viewpoint reinforces the thought that computers and an information-processing model, because they are inherently blind, excruciatingly literal, and incapable of processing meaning, may be unable in principle to simulate the most critical property of productive thinking, restructuring.

Holyoak and Spellman's chapter on thinking for the 1993 *Annual Review of Psychology* contrasts what they call the production-systems approach of Simon and his colleagues, which handles "well-defined" problems that have clear goals, a clear starting state, and obvious operators reasonably well, with the approach to less well-defined problems on which Gestalt psychologists like Max Wertheimer worked, that typically require "restructuring" of the problem representation if solution is to be achieved. They wrote,[124] "It is unlikely...that connectionism will undermine the traditional view that human thinking requires a symbol system," and gave credit to Tweney[125] for indicating that the complex interrelatedness of hypotheses provides a major challenge for computational theories of scientific reasoning.

Holyoak and Spellman pointed out, "A crucial question for theories of thinking concerns relevance," another term for what Wertheimer meant by rho relations. As Holyoak and Spellman put it[126]: "a crucial aspect of the general characterization of a representational system is that it involves specifying which aspects of the represented world are relevant." How do you program a computer so it can recognize the difference between rho relations and trivial, superficial attributes of a problem? Yet another issue[127] is transfer, the transfer of knowledge learned in one context to other related situations: "Essentially by definition, transfer is based on the perception that prior knowledge is relevant to the current context." Again: how can a computer be programmed to make such metaphorical and analogical jumps?

Sternberg and Davidson's 1995 book, *The Nature of Insight*,[128] is full of references to Wertheimer's *Productive Thinking*, and David Murray published a book in 1995 entitled *Gestalt Psychology and the Cognitive Revolution*.[129] Murray states, and documents in detail, that "the Gestalt psychologists...foreshadowed the cognitive revolution";[130] he "emphasizes the value of the insights of Gestalt psychology for our understanding of cognitive psychology, and argues that we need to re-evaluate many of Gestalt psychology's ignored insights."[131]

A paper by Newell[132] extolled the virtues of the concept of a problem space, arguing that people construct and improve such spaces as they gain experience in a problem domain, and that the problem-space idea "has strong implications for the transfer of skill.... If a [person] maps a task into an existing problem space, then the transfer of this knowledge to the new task is implied."[133] But Newell does not address the critical issue of rho relations: how does one know into which (already-familiar) particular problem space to transfer a new problem?

Studies by Metcalfe[134] and her colleagues provide an empirical, functional distinction between the processing of memory tasks and of problem-solving tasks, the same distinction that Wertheimer made between "*reproductive*" and "*productive*" thinking. While people are generally able to predict their future performance on reproductive memory tasks, they cannot predict future performance on productive problems that require transformation of the problem representation for their solution. Kounios and Smith[135] provide comparable findings, using a sophisticated method to study the time-course of partial information accumulation during the processing of anagram tasks, which require some degree of reorganization or insight. Both of these lines of research imply that it may be inherently impossible for the current continuity models of information processing to account for the all-or-none or discontinuity features of problem solving that requires a changed representation.

Winston, Chaffin, and Herrmann,[136] in a taxonomy of part-whole relations, recognize that such relations are not limited to logical inclusion or class membership. Indeed, there are many kinds of part-whole relationships, some relatively empty and some relatively rich and pregnant. Rho relations in a new guise? The authors do not mention them, nor do they refer to an appendix in the later editions of *Productive Thinking* in which Wertheimer distinguished at length between "arbitrary components" and "necessary parts."

Kaplan and Simon's 1990 paper, "In search of insight,"[137] refers extensively to the Gestalt literature and then reports empirical work on a classic mathematical puzzle, the mutilated-checkerboard problem. Attaining "insight," they wrote, requires discovering an effective problem representation, and the likelihood that such a representation will be discovered is related to the search for invariants, what they call the "notice invariants heuristic." Yet it is unlikely that such a heuristic could be generalized to other problems, since it is specific to this particular problem—and it also remains unclear how one should go about generating a good problem representation in the first place. What commands could one give a computer that would have this desired effect? Nobody knows yet how to program a computer so that it can be sensitive to rho relations.

Most of the chapters in Sternberg and Davidson's 1995 book on insight are directly relevant. Mayer's opening chapter, for instance, is on "The Search for Insight: Grappling with Gestalt Psychology's Unanswered Questions."[138] Dominowski and Dallob, in "Insight and Problem Solving," deal with characteristics of problem solving, the difference between reproductive and productive thinking, and the nature of insight, understanding, functional fixedness, and restructuring. Schooler, Fallshore, and Fiore's "epilogue," entitled "Putting Insight into Perspective,"[139] touches on the definition of insight, the causes of impasses during the process of solving a problem, how impasses are overcome, coherence, and other crucial issues.

Two things remain. First, will the modern computer-based information-processing paradigm that is dominating cognitive psychology be able to deal adequately with the central issue of productive thinking? There is no need to belabor the answer to that question. In any event, people today are still reading and pondering Max Wertheimer's book, *Productive Thinking*. Its striking descriptions and analyses of insights are as fresh today as they were more than a half century ago, and pose a serious challenge to any blind or mechanical models of human thinking. No theory of cognition can afford to ignore the fact that productive thought is often insightful, indeed sometimes exhilarating.

The other final item concerns those spherical triangles. Where on the surface of the earth, other than at the north pole, can one go one mile south, then one mile east, then one mile north, and end up at the spot one started from? The solution requires a major reorganization of the concept of a triangle. Start anywhere one mile north of a circle just north of and surrounding the south pole, that is exactly one mile in circumference. One goes a mile south to that circle, goes east around the circle, and then heads north for one mile, *exactly retracing, in the opposite direction, the route one had taken south.* This perfectly acceptable spherical triangle, of course, does not look anything like a planar triangle. Further: the locus of points from which one could start is a circle, but *that* circle is not the only solution. The critical circle on which one goes east need not be exactly one mile in circumference; any *perfect fraction* of a mile would work just as well. If it were, say, one third of a mile in circumference, one could walk one mile due south to the circle, then go east around it three times, then head back north for one mile, exactly retracing the route one had gone south. It is a fascinating problem; the reader might enjoy thinking about it some more.

*   *   *

More than half a century after Max Wertheimer died, his ideas, and the Gestalt perspective, continue to influence psychology—and many related fields as well. This chapter has been expanded in several drafts over the years, and no doubt should be expanded again in order to give attention and credit to the most recent work in the lodes that he helped to open. As Solomon E. Asch wrote in an appreciation of Wertheimer, he

> has handed on to us a problem of permanent significance and the sharp tools he forged in tireless labor.... We cannot speak with assurance about the future of our science. But this much we can say with confidence: wherever the understanding of [humanity] will take a step forward, there people will honor the name of Max Wertheimer and turn back to his thought with a sense of gratitude and affection.[140]

Notes

1. Solomon E. Asch (1946). Max Wertheimer's contributions to modern psychology. *Social Research*, 13, 81-102, p. 81.
2. Alvin Johnson (1943). Max Wertheimer 1880-1943. *Social Research*, 10, 397-398, p. 398.
3. This paragraph and the next are largely paraphrased from Michael Wertheimer (1980), Max Wertheimer, Gestalt prophet. *Gestalt Theory*, 2, 3-17.

4. Max Wertheimer (1910). Musik der Wedda [Music of the Vedda]. *Sammelbände der internationalen Musikgesellschaft*, 11, 300-309; Max Wertheimer (1912). Experimentelle Studien über das Sehen von Bewegung [Experimental studies of the seeing of motion]. *Zeitschrift für Psychologie*, 61, 161-265; Max Wertheimer (1923). Untersuchungen zur Lehre von der Gestalt: II [Investigations in Gestalt theory: II]. *Psychologische Forschung*, 4, 301-350.

5. See Appendix to Chapter 6.

6. Edwin G. Boring (1950). *A history of experimental psychology*, 2nd Ed. Englewood Cliffs, NJ: Prentice Hall, p. 600.

7. Mary Henle (1985). Rediscovering Gestalt psychology. In Sigmund Koch and David E. Leary, eds., *A century of psychology as science*. New York: McGraw-Hill, p. 100.

8. The concluding chapter of Mitchell G. Ash's thorough and rich book, *Gestalt psychology in German culture 1890-1967: Holism and the quest for objectivity* (Cambridge, England: Cambridge University Press, 1995), pp. 405-412, presents a sophisticated and nuanced account of the fate of Gestalt psychology in the latter half of the twentieth century both in Europe and elsewhere. Among other astute observations, he argues (p. 411), "Gestalt theory has been a worthy participant in two intellectual trends of our time: the revolt against dualism in twentieth-century thought; and the ongoing struggle between science as technological manipulation and control, and science as an attempt to understand and appreciate order in nature."

9. Marianne L. Teuber (1973). New aspects of Paul Klee's Bauhaus style. In *Paul Klee: Paintings and watercolors from the Bauhaus years*, 1921-1931. Des Moines, IA: Des Moines Art Center; Marianne L. Teuber (1976). *Blue Night* by Paul Klee. In Mary Henle, ed., *Vision and artifact: Essays in honor of Rudolf Arnheim*. New York: Springer, pp. 131-151.

10. Marianne L. Teuber (1974). Sources of ambiguity in the prints of Maurits C. Escher. *Scientific American*, 231, 90-104.

11. Kurt Koffka (1940). Problems in the psychology of art. *Bryn Mawr Notes and Monographs*, 9, 179-273; Kurt Koffka (1942). The art of the actor as a psychological problem. *American Scholar*, 11, 315-326.

12. e.g., Rudolf Arnheim (1966). *Toward a psychology of art*. Berkeley, CA: University of California Press; Rudolf Arnheim (1974). *Art and visual perception: A psychology of the creative eye*. Berkeley, CA: University of California Press; Rudolf Arnheim (1986). *New essays on the psychology of art*. Berkeley, CA: University of California Press.

13. Rudolf Arnheim (1943). Gestalt and art. *Journal of Aesthetics*, 2, 71-75.

14. J. M. Mandler and G. Mandler (1969). The diaspora of experimental psychology: The Gestaltists and others. In D. Fleming and B. Bailyn, eds., *The intellectual migration: Europe and America, 1930-1960*. Cambridge, MA: Harvard University Press, p. 394.

15. Max Kobbert (1989). Annäherung an 'informelle Kunst' mit Mitteln der Gestaltpsychologie: Aufgezeigt an Jackson Pollock's Nr. 32 von 1950 [Approach to 'informal art' with Gestalt psychology methods: Demonstrated with Jackson Pollock's No. 32 from 1950], *Gestalt Theory*, 11, 205-218.

16. Anton Ehrenzweig (1948). Unconscious form-creation in art. *British Journal of Medical Psychology*, 21, 185-214.

17. H. E. Rees (1942). *A psychology of artistic creation as evidenced in autobiographical statements of artists.* New York: Teacher's College.

18. Harold J. McWhinnie (1992). Gestalt psychology and art education: Adelbert Ames and Hoyt Sherman. *Perceptual and Motor Skills*, 75, 1233-1234.

19. H. Steinitz (1953/1954). Hapsihologia Hatavnitit v'-horaat Hamusika [Gestalt psychology and teaching of music]. *Hahinuh*, 26, 45-53.

20. R. H. Wheeler and T. Gaston (1941). The history of music in relation to climatic and cultural fluctuations. *Proceedings of the Music Teachers' National Association*, 432-438.

21. Reuven Tsur, Joseph Glicksohn, and Chanita Goodblatt (1991). Gestalt qualities in poetry and the reader's absorption style. *Journal of Pragmatics*, 16, 487-500. Goodblatt and Glicksohn developed a "Gestalt-Interaction Theory of Metaphor" based upon Richards's "Interaction Theory of Metaphor." See, e.g., Joseph Glicksohn (1994). Putting interaction theory to the empirical test: Some promising results. *Pragmatics and Cognition*, 2, 223-235; Glicksohn, J., and Chanita Goodblatt (1993). Metaphor and Gestalt: Interaction theory revisited. *Poetics Today*, 14, 83-97; Goodblatt, C. (1991). Semantic fields and metaphor: A case study. *Journal of Literary Semantics*, 20, 173-187; Goodblatt, C. (1996). Semantic fields and metaphor: Going beyond theory. *Empirical Studies of the Arts*, 14, 65-78; Goodblatt, C. (2001). Adding an empirical dimension to the study of poetic metaphor. *Journal of Literary Semantics*, 30, 167-180; Goodblatt, C. and Glicksohn, J. (2002). Metaphor comprehension as problem solving: An online study of the reading process. *Style*, 36, 428-445; Goodblatt, C., and Glicksohn, J. (2003). From *Practical Criticism* to the practice of literary criticism. *Poetics Today*, 24, 207-236; I. A. Richards (1923/24). Psychology in the reading of poetry. *Psyche*, 4, 6-23; Richards, I. A. (1926). *Principles of literary criticism.* London: Routledge & Kegan Paul; Richards, I. A. (1929). *Practical criticism: A study of literary judgment.* New York: Harcourt, Brace & World; Richards, I. A. (1936). *The philosophy of rhetoric.* New York: Oxford University Press.

22. Kurt Goldstein (1939). *The organism.* New York: American Book Co.

23. Andras Angyal (1939). The structure of wholes. *Philosophy and Science*, 6, 25-37; Andras Angyal (1941). *Foundations for a science of personality.* New York: Commonwealth Fund.

24. Werner Wolff (1943). *The expression of personality.* New York: Harper.

25. C. C. Josey (1935). The self in the light of Gestalt psychology. *Journal of Abnormal and Social Psychology*, 30, 47-56; N. R. F. Maier (1932). A Gestalt theory of humour. *British Journal of Psychology*, 23, 69-74; P. Schiller (1938). A configural theory of puzzles and jokes. *Journal of General Psychology*, 18, 217-234.

26. K. W. Bash (1946). Gestalt, Symbol und Archetypus; über einige Beziehungen zwischen Gestalt und Tiefenpsychologie [Gestalt, symbol, and archetype; Some relations between Gestalt and depth psychology] *Schweizerische Zeitschrift für Psychologie*, 5, 127-138; Charles Fisher and I. H. Paul (1959). The effect of subliminal visual stimulation on images and dreams: A validation study. *Journal*

of the American Psychoanalytic Association, 7, 35-83; K. Prasd (1932). A Gestalt approach to the concept of the unconscious. *Philosophical Quarterly,* 8, 227-241.

27. S. Bernfeld (1934). Die Gestalttheorie [Gestalt theory]. *Imago,* 20, 32-77; see, e.g., Kurt Lewin (1951). *Field theory in social science: Selected theoretical papers,* ed. by Dorwin Cartwright. New York: Harper.

28. Mary Henle (1978). Gestalt psychology and Gestalt therapy. *Journal of the History of the Behavioral Sciences,* 14, 23-32.

29. Rudolf Arnheim (1974). 'Gestalt' misapplied. *Contemporary Psychology,* 19, 570.

30. Heinrich Schulte (1923). Versuch einer Theorie der paranoischen Eigenbeziehung und Wahnbildung [Attempt at a theory of paranoid ideas of reference and delusion development]. *Psychologische Forschung,* 5, 1-23. See also Gerhard Stemberger (1999). Gestalttheoretische Beiträge zur Psychopathologie. Lecture presented at the 11th annual convention of the Society for Gestalt Theory and its Applications in Graz, Austria, March 11-14. [Gestalt-theoretical contributions to psychopathology], *Gestalt Theory,* 2000, 22, 27-46.

31. E. Levy, *Gestalt Theory,* 230.

32. Erwin Levy (1943). Some aspects of the schizophrenic formal disturbance of thought. *Psychiatry,* 6, 55-69.

33. Molly R. Harrower (1939). Changes in figure-ground perception in patients with cortical lesions. *British Journal of Psychology,* 30, 47-51.

34. e.g., G. Clauser (1960). Die Gestaltungstherapie [Gestalt therapy]. *Praxis der Psychotherapie und Psychosomatik,* 5, 268-275; Alfred Katzenstein (1956). Gestalt und klinische Psychologie [Gestalt and clinical psychology]. *Psychiatrie, Neurologie, und Medizinische Psychologie,* Leipzig, 8, 211-217; G. W. Kisker and G. W. Knox (1942). Gestalt dynamics and psychopathology. *Journal of Nervous and Mental Disease,* 95, 474-478; A. O. Prakash (1958). Dynamics of behavior. *Educational Psychology,* 5, 171-188; G. Y. Rusk (1935). Gestalt psychiatry. *Journal of Abnormal and Social Psychology,* 29, 376-384; H. Syz (1936). The concept of the organism-as-a-whole and its application to clinical situations. *Humanistic Biology,* 8, 489-507; H. Werner and A. A. Strauss (1940). Pathology of the figure-background relation in the child. *Psychological Bulletin,* 37, 440.

35. e.g., G. W. Kisker and G. W. Knox (1943). Pharmacological shock therapy as a psychobiological problem. *Journal of General Psychology,* 28, 163-179; Aldo Semerari, Augusto Balloni, and Antonio Castellani (1966). L'importanza nella criminogenesi dei disturbi del campo percettivo dello schizophrenico [The importance of the schizophrenic's perceptive field disturbances in criminality]. *Annali di Neurologia e Psichiatria,* 60, 223-242; C. H. Voelker (1942). A new therapy for spasmophemia on Gestalt principles. *Archives de Pediatrie,* 59, 657-662.

36. Lauretta Bender (1938). A visual motor Gestalt test and its clinical use. *Research Monographs of the American Orthopsychiatric Association,* No. 3, 1-176.

37. e.g., C. M. Mooney and G. A. Ferguson (1951). A new closure test. *Canadian Journal of Psychology,* 5, 129-133; R. F. Street (1934). The Gestalt completion test and mental disorder. *Journal of Abnormal and Social Psychology,* 29, 141-

142; L. L. Thurstone (1944). *A factorial study of perception* (Psychometric Monographs, No. 4). Chicago: University of Chicago Press.

38. H. W. Brosin and E. Fromm (1942). Some principles of Gestalt psychology in the Rorschach experiment. *Rorschach Research Exchange*, 6. 1-15; Michael Wertheimer (1957). Perception and the Rorschach. *Journal of Projective Techniques*, 21, 209-216.

39. W. D. Commins (1937). What may we expect of Gestalt psychology? *Catholic Educational Review*, 35, 135-143.

40. John W. Carr, Jr. (1934). The relationships between the theories of Gestalt psychology and those of a progressive education. *Journal of Educational Psychology*, 1, 192-202, pp. 199-200.

41. e.g., G. L. Bond and E. Bond (1943). *Teaching the child to read.* New York: Macmillan; Edward R. Fagan (1969). An insight on reading comprehension. *Reading Improvement*, 6, 43-46; Diack Hunter (1960). *Reading and the psychology of perception.* New York: Philosophical Library; R. H. Wheeler (1933). The crisis in education. *School and Society*, 38, 756-759.

42. William Sahakian (1982). *History and systems of social psychology*, 2nd ed. Washington, D.C.: Hemisphere, p. 296. For another treatment of Gestalt theory's influence on social psychology see Arthur Aron and Elaine N. Aron (1986). *The heart of social psychology.* Lexington, MA: Lexington.

43. e.g., Ruth Fulton Benedict (1934). *Patterns of culture.* Boston, MA: Houghton-Mifflin; J. Gillin (1936). The configuration problem in culture. *American Sociological Review*, 1, 373-386; Robert M. Ogden (1934). Sociology and Gestalt psychology. *American Journal of Psychology*, 46, 651-655.

44. Lewis A. Coser (1984). *Refugee scholars in America: Their impact and their experiences.* New Haven, CT: Yale University Press, p. 25.

45. Solomon E. Asch (1951). Effects of group pressure upon the modification and distortion of judgments. In H. Guetzkow (ed.), *Groups, leadership, and men.* Pittsburgh, PA: Carnegie, pp. 177-190.

46. Solomon E. Asch (1952). *Social psychology.* Englewood Cliffs, NJ: Prentice Hall, p. 60.

47. Irvin Rock, ed. (1990). *The legacy of Solomon Asch: Essays in cognition and social psychology.* Hillsdale, NJ: Erlbaum.

48. Fritz Heider (1958). *The psychology of interpersonal relations.* New York: Wiley; Fritz Heider (1983). *The life of a psychologist: An autobiography.* Lawrence, KS: University Press of Kansas.

49. Muzafer Sherif and Carolyn W. Sherif (1969). *Social psychology.* New York: Harper and Row.

50. Leon Festinger (1957). *A theory of cognitive dissonance.* Stanford, CA: Stanford University Press.

51. Sahakian, *History and systems of social psychology*, p. 296.

52. Carl F. Graumann (1989). Gestalt in social psychology. *Psychological Research*, 51, 75-80, p. 79.

53. William P. Banks and David Krajicek (1991). Perception. *Annual Review of Psychology*, 42, 305-331, p. 306.

54. e.g., Paul C. Quinn, Sherry Burke and Amy Ruch (1992). Part-whole perception in early infancy: Evidence for perceptual grouping produced by lightness

similarity. *Infant Behavior and Development*, 16,19-42; Irvin Rock, Romi Nijhawan, Stephen Palmer and Leslie Tudor (1992). Grouping based on phenomenal similarity of achromatic color. *Perception*, 21, 779-789; Pertti Saariluoma (1992). Do visual images have Gestalt properties? *Quarterly Journal of Experimental Psychology*, 45, 399-420.

55. Banks and Krajicek, Perception, p. 314.

56. M. Kubovy and J. R. Pomerantz (1981). *Perceptual organization*. Hillsdale, NJ: Erlbaum; Robert E. Remez, Phillip E. Rubin, Stefanie M. Berns, Jennifer S. Pardo and Jessica M. Lang (1994). On the perceptual organization of speech. *Psychological Review*, 101, 129-156; Hans Wallach (1987). Perceiving a stable environment when one moves. *Annual Review of Psychology*, 38, 1-27.

57. Mary Henle (1989). Some new Gestalt psychologies. *Psychological Research*, 51, 81-85.

58. William Epstein and Gary Hatfield (1994). Gestalt psychology and the philosophy of mind. *Philosophical Psychology*, 7, 163-181.

59. Eckart Scheerer (1994). Psychoneural isomorphism: Historical background and current relevance. *Philosophical Psychology*, 7, 183-210.

60. Lothar Spillmann and John S. Werner (1990). *Visual perception: The neurophysiological foundations*. San Diego, CA: Academic Press.

61. Lothar Spillmann and Walter H. Ehrenstein (1996). From neuron to Gestalt: Mechanisms of visual perception. In R. Greger and U. Windhorst (eds.), *Comprehensive human psychology*, Vol.1, pp. 861-893. Heidelberg: Springer. See also Walter M. Ehrenstein, Lothar Spillmann, and Viktor Sarris (2003). Gestalt issues in modern neuroscience. *Axiomathes*, 13, 433-458.

62. Spillmann and Ehrenstein (1996), p. 862.

63. Friedhart Klix (2001). Über Gestaltpsychologie [About Gestalt psychology]. *Zeitschrift für Psychologie*, 209, 1-16, p. 15.

64. Klix, p. 14.

65. Klix, p. 7.

66. Klix, p. 7.

67. Gerald Westheimer (1999). Gestalt theory reconfigured: Max Wertheimer's anticipation of recent developments in visual neuroscience. *Perception*, 28, 5-15.

68. Westheimer, p. 5.

69. Westheimer, p. 6.

70. Westheimer, p. 7.

71. Westheimer, p. 9.

72. Westheimer, p. 10.

73. Westheimer, p. 11.

74. Westheimer, p. 12.

75. Westheimer, p. 13.

76. Westheimer, p. 14.

77. Lothar Spillmann (1999). Gehirn und Gestalt [Brain and Gestalt]. *Psychologische Beiträge*, 41, 458-493. The present condensed translation of this well-documented article omits the more than 150 references that Spillmann cites.

78. Spillmann (1999), p. 460.

79. Spillmann (1999), p. 462.

80. Spillmann (1999), p. 463.

81. Spillmann (1999), p. 465.

82. Spillmann (1999), p. 466.
83. Spillmann (1999), p. 467.
84. Spillmann (1999), p. 467.
85. Spillmann (1999), p. 469.
86. Spillmann (1999), p. 469.
87. Spillmann (1999), p. 472.
88. Spillmann (1999), p. 472.
89. Spillmann (1999), p. 473.
90. Spillmann (1999), p. 473.
91. Spillmann (1999), p. 474.
92. Spillmann (1999), p. 474.
93. Spillmann (1999), p. 478.
94. Spillmann (1999), p. 478.
95. Spillmann (1999), p. 479.
96. Spillmann (1999), p. 482-489.
97. Lothar Spillmann (2001). Gehirn und Gestalt: II. Neuronale Mechanismen [Brain and Gestalt: Neuronal mechanisms]. *Kognitionswissenschaft*, 9, 122-143. This article, like the first in the series, is well documented, with over 250 references, more than half of them published since 1990. Once again, almost all the references are omitted in the condensed translation presented here.
98. Spillmann (2001), p. 137ff.
99. e.g., Alan Baddeley (1990). *Human memory: Theory and practice.* Boston, MA: Allyn & Bacon; Richard E. Mayer (1997). *Thinking and problem solving: An introduction to human cognition and learning.* Glenview, IL: Scott, Foresman; Michael Wertheimer (1980). Gestalt theory of learning. In G. M. Gazda and R. J. Corsini (eds.), *Theories of learning: A comparative approach.* Itasca, IL: Peacock, pp. 208-251.
100. e.g., William Epstein (1988). Has the time come to rehabilitate Gestalt theory? *Psychological Research*, 50, 2-6; Cees van Leeuwen (1989). PDP and Gestalt. An integration? *Psychological Research*, 50, 199-201.
101. e.g., Frank S. Kessel and William Bevan (1985). Notes toward a history of cognitive psychology. In Claude E. Buxton (ed.), *Points of view in the modern history of psychology.* Orlando, FL: Academic Press, pp. 281-284; Henry Montgomery (1988). Mental models and problem solving: Three challenges to a theory of restructuring and insight. *Scandinavian Journal of Psychology*, 29, 85-94.
102. Karl Duncker (1935). *Zur Psychologie des produktiven Denkens [Psychology of productive thought].* Berlin: Springer.
103. Abraham S. Luchins (1942). Mechanization in problem solving: The effect of Einstellung. *Psychological Monographs*, 54, 6, Whole No. 248.
104. K. Anders Ericsson, Peter G. Polson, and Michael Wertheimer (1982). Preface to the Phoenix edition. In Max Wertheimer, *Productive thinking.* Chicago: University of Chicago Press, pp. xi-xvi.
105. Herbert A. Simon (1979). Information processing models of cognition. *Annual Review of Psychology*, 30, 363-396.
106. Allen Newell and Herbert A. Simon (1972). *Human problem solving.* Englewood Cliffs, NJ: Prentice-Hall.

107. Allen Newell (1985). Duncker on thinking: An inquiry into progress in cognition. In S. Koch and D. Leary (eds.), *A century of psychology as science*, pp. 392-419. New York: McGraw-Hill.

108. Mark Keane (1989). Modelling problem solving in Gestalt 'insight' problems. *Irish Journal of Psychology*, 10, 201-215.

109. Henle, Rediscovering Gestalt psychology. Michael Wertheimer (1985). A Gestalt perspective on computer simulations of cognitive processes. *Computers in Human Behavior*, 1, 19-33.

110. Ericsson, Polson, and Wertheimer, Preface to the Phoenix edition, p. xvi.

111. Michael Wertheimer (1997). Briefing: A contemporary perspective on the psychology of productive thinking. *Psychology Teacher Network*, January-February, pp. 2, 3, 6, 8, 13.

112. Wertheimer, Max (1945). *Productive thinking*. New York: Harper. Translations: Japanese (1952), Italian (1965), German (1957, 1964); enlarged editions (1959, 1971 and 1982).

113. Michael Wertheimer and Viktor Sarris (2000). Max Wertheimer: *Productive Thinking* (1945). In Helmut E. Lück, Rudolf Miller and Gabi Sewz-Vosshenrich (eds.), *Klassiker der Psychologie* [*Classics of psychology*]. Berlin: Kohlhammer, pp. 183-187.

114. James, W. (1890). *Principles of psychology*. 2 vols. New York: Holt.

115. Ericsson, A., Polson, P.G., & Wertheimer, Michael (1982). Preface to the Phoenix edition. In Wertheimer, M., *Productive thinking*, enlarged edition, pp. xi-xvii. Chicago: University of Chicago Press.

116. Newell, A., Shaw, J.C., & Simon, H.A. (1958). Elements of a theory of human problem solving. *Psychological Review*, 65, 151-166; Newell, A., Shaw, J.C., & Simon, H.A. (1962). The process of creative thinking. In H.E. Gruber, G. Terrell, & Michael Wertheimer (eds.), *Contemporary approaches to creative thinking*. New York: Atherton, pp. 63-119.

117. Newell, A., & Simon, H.A. (1972). *Human problem solving*. Englewood Cliffs, NJ: Prentice-Hall.

118. Herbert A. Simon (1978). Information-processing theory of human problem solving. In W.K. Estes (ed.), *Handbook of learning and cognitive processes*, Vol. 5: *Human information processing*. Hillsdale, NJ: Erlbaum, pp. 271-295.

119. E.g., Kintsch, W., & van Dijk, T.A. (1978). Toward a model of text comprehension and production. *Psychological Review*, 85, 363-394.

120. Greeno, J.G. (1977). Process of understanding in problem solving. In N.J. Castellan, D.B. Pisoni, & G.R. Potts (eds.), *Cognitive theory* (vol. 2), pp 43-83. Hillsdale, NJ: Erlbaum.

121. Ericsson, Polson, & Wertheimer, pp. xv-xvi.

122. Wertheimer, Michael (1985). A Gestalt perspective on computer simulations of cognitive processes. *Computers in Human Behavior*, 1, 19-33.

123. Personal communication to Michael Wertheimer.

124. Holyoak, K.J., & Spellman, A. (1993). Thinking. In Porter, L.W. & Rosenzweig, M.R. (eds.), *Annual Review of Psychology*, 44, 265-314, p. 269.

125. Holyoak & Spellman (1993), p. 273; Tweney, R.D. (1990). Five questions for computationalists. In J. Shrager & P. Langley (eds.), *Computational models of*

scientific discovery and theory formation, pp. 471-484. San Mateo, CA: Morgan Kaufmann.

126. Holyoak and Spellman, p. 302.

127. Holyoak and Spellman, p. 297.

128. Sternberg, R.J., & Davidson, J.E. (eds.) (1995). *The nature of insight.* Cambridge, MA: Bradford/MIT Press.

129. Murray, D.J. (1995). *Gestalt psychology and the cognitive revolution.* London: Harvester Wheatsheaf (a division of Simon & Schuster International).

130. Murray, p. xi.

131. Murray, back cover.

132. Newell, A. (1980). Reasoning, problem solving, and decision processes: The problem space as a fundamental category. In R. Nickerson (ed.), *Attention and performance*, Vol. 7 (pp. 693-718). Hillsdale, NJ: Erlbaum.

133. Newell, p. 715.

134. E.g., Metcalfe, J. (1986). Feeling of knowing in memory and problem solving. *Journal of Experimental Psychology: Learning, Memory, and Cognition*, 12, 288-294.

135. Kounios, J., & Smith, R.W. (1995). Speed-accuracy decomposition yields a sudden insight into all-or-none information processing. *Acta Psychologica*, 90, 229-241.

136. Winston, M.E., Chaffin, R., & Herrmann, D. (1987). A taxonomy of part-whole relations. *Cognitive Science*, 11, 417-444.

137. Kaplan, C.A., & Simon, H.A. (1990). In search of insight. *Cognitive Psychology*, 22, 374-419.

138. Mayer, R.E. (1995). The search for insight: Grappling with Gestalt psychology's unanswered questions. In R.J. Sternberg & J.E. Davidson (eds.), *The nature of insight*, pp. 3-32. Cambridge, MA: Bradford/MIT Press.

139. Schooler, J.W., Fallshore, M., & Fiore, S.M. (1995). Epilogue: Putting insight into perspective. In R.J. Sternberg & J.E. Davidson (eds.), *The nature of insight*, pp. 559-587. Cambridge, MA: Bradford/MIT Press.

140. Asch, Max Wertheimer's contributions, p. 102.

Index